Building the Knowledge Society on the Internet:
Sharing and Exchanging Knowledge in Networked Environments

Ettore Bolisani
University of Padua, Italy

INFORMATION SCIENCE REFERENCE

Hershey · New York

Acquisitions Editor:	Kristin Klinger
Development Editor:	Kristin Roth
Senior Managing Editor:	Jennifer Neidig
Managing Editor:	Jamie Snavely
Assistant Managing Editor:	Carole Coulson
Copy Editor:	Angela Thor
Typesetter:	Chris Hrobak
Cover Design:	Lisa Tosheff
Printed at:	Yurchak Printing Inc.

Published in the United States of America by
Information Science Reference (an imprint of IGI Global)
701 E. Chocolate Avenue, Suite 200
Hershey PA 17033
Tel: 717-533-8845
Fax: 717-533-8661
E-mail: cust@igi-global.com
Web site: http://www.igi-global.com

and in the United Kingdom by
Information Science Reference (an imprint of IGI Global)
3 Henrietta Street
Covent Garden
London WC2E 8LU
Tel: 44 20 7240 0856
Fax: 44 20 7379 0609
Web site: http://www.eurospanbookstore.com

Library of Congress Cataloging-in-Publication Data

Building the knowledge society on the Internet : sharing and exchanging knowledge in networked environments / Ettore Bolisani, editor.

     p. cm.

  Summary: "In today's networked societies, a key factor of the social and economic success is the capability to exchange, transfer, and share knowledge. This book provides research on the topic providing a foundation of an emerging and multidisciplinary field"--Provided by publisher.

  Includes bibliographical references and index.

  ISBN 978-1-59904-816-1 (hbk.) -- ISBN 978-1-59904-818-5 (ebook)

  1. Knowledge management. 2. Computer networks. 3. Information networks. I. Bolisani, Ettore, 1963-

  HD30.2.B853 2008

  303.48'33--dc22

                              2008017470

British Cataloguing in Publication Data
A Cataloguing in Publication record for this book is available from the British Library.

List of Reviewers

Chandra S. Amaravadi
Western Illinois University, USA

Derek Asoh
Southern Illinois University, USA

Antonio Badia
University of Louisville, USA

Marco Bettoni
Swiss Distance University of Applied Sciences, Switzerland

Patrice Braun
University of Ballarat, Australia

Ricardo Chalmeta
University Jaume I of Castellón, Spain

Satyadhyan Chickerur
M.S. Ramaiah Institute of Technology, India

Alton Chua
Nanyang Technological University, Singapore

Chris Crawford
Fort Hays State University, USA

Massimo Gastaldon
University of Padua, Italy

Mohand-Said Hacid
University Lyon I, France

Matthew Hall
Aston University, UK

Deogratias Harorimana
Southampton Solent University, UK

Donald Hislop
Loughborough University, UK

Tracy A. Hurley
Texas A&M University-Kingsville, USA

Barbara Igel
Asian Institute of Technology, Thailand

Ashok Jashapara
Royal Holloway University of London, UK

Krzysztof Juszczyszyn
Wroclaw University of Technology, Poland

Andrew Kok
University of Johannesburg, South Africa

Josephine C. Lang
Nanyang Technological University, Singapore

Sandra Moffett
University of Ulster, UK

Theresia Olsson Neve
Skanska Sweden AB, Sweden

Craig Parker
Deakin University, Australia

Jon Pemberton
Northumbria University, UK

Table of Contents

Section I
Models

Chapter I
Knowledge Sharing: Interactive Processes Between Organizational
Knowledge-Sharing Initiative and Individuals' Sharing Practice 1
  Shuhua Liu, University of Washington, USA

Chapter II
The Centrality of Team Leaders in Knowledge-Sharing Activities:
Their Dual Role as Knowledge Processors...24
  Evangelia Siachou, Athens University of Economics and Business, Greece
  Anthony Ioannidis, Athens University of Economics and Business, Greece

Chapter III
Knowledge Sharing in Virtual and Networked Organisations in Different
Organisational and National Cultures 45
  Kerstin Siakas, Alexander Technological Educational Institution of Thessaloniki, Greece
  Elli Georgiadou, University of Middlesex, UK

Chapter IV
Towards an Implicit and Collaborative Evolution of Terminological Ontologies 65
  Axel-Cyrille Ngonga Ngomo, University of Leipzig, Germany

Chapter V
Computer-Mediated Knowledge Sharing 89
  Kimiz Dalkir, McGill University, Canada

Section II
Applications

Detailed Table of Contents

Section I
Models

Chapter I

Knowledge Sharing: Interactive Processes Between Organizational

Shuhua Liu, University of Washington, USA

Based on a review of established theories in sociology, management science, and organisational behaviour, the chapter explores the interactions between organizational context and individuals' sense-making processes. Elements of a new model, which explains how the organisational settings influence the way individuals share knowledge, are developed. Essential implications for knowledge management and ICT design are also discussed.

Chapter II

The Centrality of Team Leaders in Knowledge-Sharing Activities:

Evangelia Siachou, Athens University of Economics and Business, Greece

Anthony Ioannidis, Athens University of Economics and Business, Greece

The chapter analyses the role of team leaders as sources and recipients of net-based knowledge. The particular case of action teams that deal with unpredictable situations and need to make instant use of accurate knowledge is mainly considered. Reflections are made on leaders' active role in knowledge sharing considering the multifaceted nature of knowledge exchange, the time boundaries, and the costs of knowledge search and sharing. The analysis also provides insights into the complex relationship between the way organisations are structured and the effective processes of knowledge transfer among their members.

Chapter III
    Kerstin Siakas, Alexander Technological Educational Institution of Thessaloniki, Greece
    Elli Georgiadou, University of Middlesex, UK

The chapter discusses the issue of knowledge sharing in culturally diverse networked organisations and virtual teams. By examining the different cultural values and perceptions related to knowledge exchange, the human and cultural dynamics that influence the success of knowledge sharing are discussed. The study analyses the potential conflicts in culturally diverse team members and the crucial issue of trust building. It also provides indications for fruitful knowledge sharing in global networked environments.

Chapter IV
    Axel-Cyrille Ngonga Ngomo, University of Leipzig, Germany

The problem of capturing the tacit components of knowledge in a way that can be handled automatically is a challenging issue for both Knowledge Management researchers and computer programmers. This chapter analyses the use of terminological ontologies for representing personal knowledge. It is argued that each individual needs a personal knowledge model to represent her/his knowledge. Subsequently, the chapter presents a method for implicitly and collaboratively evolving such personal knowledge models, with the purpose to improve the efficacy of knowledge transfer over the Internet.

Chapter V
    Kimiz Dalkir, McGill University, Canada

Internet-based knowledge-sharing channels differ in their effectiveness when used for exchanging knowledge. It is therefore necessary to define key knowledge and channel attributes in order to understand how knowledge can be effectively shared using computers. This chapter examines the computer-mediated knowledge-sharing mechanisms, and proposes a typology based on media richness and social presence characteristics that can serve as a preliminary conceptual basis to select the most appropriate Internet-based channel for the specific purpose.

Chapter VI
    Ettore Bolisani, University of Padua, Italy

To systematise the conceptual backgrounds of Knowledge Management as a branch of management, a more direct connection with the models and approaches of the economic disciplines is necessary. The chapter examines the contribution that the current studies of the emerging field of the Knowledge

Economy can give to the clearer understanding of Knowledge Management and, particularly, of the processes of knowledge transfer. The open research questions that may result from such an "economics-based" approach to Knowledge Management are also analysed.

Chapter VII

  Jengchung V. Chen, National Cheng Kung University, Taiwan
  J. Michael Tarn, Western Michigan University, USA
  Muhammad A. Razi, Western Michigan University, USA

This chapter explores the motivation of virtual community members to share knowledge, and the underlying factors of such sharing behaviors. A conceptual model illustrating the relationship between transaction cost, expectancy value, and knowledge-sharing behaviour is illustrated. The notions of knowledge transaction and knowledge market are also further examined, since knowledge sharing can be seen as a form of knowledge transaction, and a knowledge market provides an essential platform for this.

Section II
Applications

Chapter VIII

  Margarita Echeverri, University of Maryland, USA & Tulane University, USA
  Eileen G. Abels, Drexel University, USA

The access to scientific knowledge is considered essential to foster research and development, improve quality of education, and advance professional practices. Although the Web was conceived to encourage knowledge sharing, restrictions still reduce access to knowledge, especially to those in developing countries. This chapter presents a conceptual framework of the knowledge transfer cycle and examines key factors affecting the dissemination of scientific knowledge. Current challenges facing the open-access initiative of making scientific knowledge free and available worldwide are also discussed.

Chapter IX

  Molly McLure Wasko, Florida State University, USA
  Samer Faraj, McGill Unversity, Canada

This study examines knowledge exchange in a worldwide, extra-organizational, Usenet-based electronic network, where participation is voluntary, globally distributed, and where participants generally do not have personal or organizational ties. The purpose was to investigate two questions: first, what type of knowledge is being transferred in these networks, and second, how is knowledge transferred across participants. To address these questions, messages posted to "comp.lang.C++" were observed for a period of 7 weeks. The study illuminates how people use computer-mediated communication to support knowledge transfer, the types of knowledge transferred, as well as how knowledge flows in this kind of networks.

This chapter explores the emergence of social structures in Internet-based systems over time. Based on results of an empirical investigation of an Internet-based knowledge sharing system, the study shows the change of roles, expectations, and activities in online communities. Finally, the author sketches some essential criteria for developing online communities, which are extended part of organizations (e.g., companies and institutions), are characterized by a large size, and supplement the formal organization.

The aim of this chapter is to provide an introduction to technologies, practices, and open problems for knowledge management in disaster and crisis situations. New technologies and Knowledge Management practices, particularly with the Internet and Web 2.0, are creating opportunities for individuals, responders, and trainers to share knowledge. However, the use of networked technologies diffuses with very little cohesion among researchers and practitioners. It is argued that although the Internet is already in extensive use in disaster management, its integration with Knowledge Management practices will only be effected if top-down and bottoms-up approaches to information gathering, organisation, and dissemination are implemented.

This chapter introduces a theoretical framework to study how Internet technologies enable organizations to handle various forms of communication and decision-making complexities. It investigates how specific use-based combinations of Internet technologies emerge within operational contexts. Illustrations are drawn from the U.S. military uses of Tactical Internet during recent operations in Afghanistan and Iraq.

The conditions for which combined uses generate additional value for organizations are discussed, and the essential role of final users in exploiting the benefits of Internet applications are illustrated.

This chapter examines the role of knowledge gatekeepers as channels by which knowledge is created and transferred among distinct firms. The obstacles that inhibit knowledge transfer are first examined, and it is argued that leading firms can create a shared sociocultural context that enables the codivision of tacit meanings and the codification of knowledge. Leading firms can thus act as knowledge gatekeepers through the creation of shared (virtual) platforms. This role can be played by large multinationals, connecting several clients and suppliers, but even by focal firms in industrial districts.

The chapter discusses the role of online knowledge mediators in knowledge exchanges between a source and a receiver. Their task is to assist and facilitate the transfer process when performed through Internet-based technologies. In the rapidly evolving world of Internet, many types of virtual knowledge mediators come out with different features and functions, but little effort has been devoted to examine their practices. The study also develops an analytical framework to classify the role of knowledge mediators based on two complementary conceptual views of knowledge transfer: the cognitive and the economic view.

The new global business environment requires loose and flexible business schemes shaped in the form of Virtual Enterprises, but this transformation would never have been successful without the support of Information Technologies, and particularly the Web. Building upon the current state of the art, this chapter discusses the issue of Knowledge Management support for Virtual Enterprises, and aims to identify the major knowledge requirements in such organisations, in an effort to provide a roadmap towards a holistic framework to understand and handle the huge and complex knowledge needs of Virtual Enterprises at the interorganizational level.

The Internet offers new opportunities to use knowledge assets, defines new types of knowledge assets, and readily spreads knowledge beyond the borders of the organization. This potential is tempered, however, by new threats to the security of proprietary knowledge. The Internet also makes knowledge assets more vulnerable to competitive intelligence efforts. The chapter proposes a model that integrates three dimensions of knowledge (tacitness, complexity, appropriability), and relates these with its vulnerability in a KM Internet-based environment. This discussion provides interesting insights into the issue, and new proposals for practice and research.

This chapter integrates three linguistic methods to analyse a company's Web site, namely a) elements from a community of practice theory (CoP), b) concepts from the communication theory, such as modality and transitivity, and c) elements from discourse analysis. The investigation demonstrates how the use of a Web site can promote a work attitude that can be considered as an endorsement of a particular organizational behaviour. The Web pages display the organizational identity, which will be a magnet for some parties and deject others. Thus, a Web site represents a window to the world that needs to be handled with care, since it can be interpreted as a projection of the company's identity.

Foreword

The book, edited by Ettore Bolisani, has the special merit to explore the sense of what is going on in the interplay between information technology and knowledge management. The contributions focus on the role played by the Internet in knowledge development and exploitation. The answer is not trivial, as the question involves a deep reconsideration of many different issues, which are usually taken for granted: epistemological issues about the nature of knowledge, engineering issues about functionalities and reliability of technologies, and management issues about proper rules and methods to gain advantages from available technologies.

Surprisingly, after about two decades of debate on the role of knowledge and learning within and between organizations, only few things appear to be widely accepted by the community of scientists and practitioners. First, that knowledge is the principal asset of any organization. Second, that the incessant development of ICT technologies continuously reframes the issue of knowledge exploration and exploitation. Several couples of concepts have problematic relationships: objective vs. subjective knowledge, tacit vs. explicit knowledge, declarative vs. procedural knowledge, engineering view vs. sociological view of knowledge, knowledge vs. knowing, and last but not least, knowledge vs. information.

An evident cue that a research community is undergoing a cultural revolution is that taken-for-granted concepts and habits become more and more enigmatic. This is the case with knowledge. Creating and diffusing knowledge is becoming a relevant business, with global and local players. Companies producing ICTs provide organizations with different solutions, which have significant impact on organizational processes. Diversity is the major feature of an emerging market, as it was for the car market in the first decades of 1900's. Of the 2500 motor vehicles counted for 1899, 1681 were steam propelled, 1575 electric and 936 gasoline. In 1920, a single vehicle dominated the US market—Ford's Model T. The process of exploration, selection, and convergence toward a dominant design is a typical trend of any new market.

It is not easy to forecast when convergence to dominant design will happen. Many trade-offs contribute to delay the convergence process:

- Trade-off between organizational and local KM levels. Organizational complexity is not only related to company size and articulated external relationships, but also to the complexity KM different levels: individual, group, business units, functions, departments, the whole company. At each level KM issues present different and contrasting needs;
- Trade-off between standardization and diversity. Knowledge and learning are aimed to fostering internal diversity, which is one of the major sources of competitive advantage. Any technological standardization in knowledge management and learning process, while improving efficiency, is a menace to the company's ability to promote diversity;
- Trade-off between technological innovation pace and organizational exploitation of technology potentialities. The fast-pace and unpredictable directions of ICTs innovations move away from any

attempt to converge and redefine the range of possible KM solutions. Between the 1978 double loop model by Argyris and Shon and today's collective intelligence model there is an amazing flow of radical ICTs innovations, which dramatically reframed the problem setting in KM. This flow doesn't seem to decrease. Thus, it is likely that the range of possible solutions will widen in the near future.

We are expected to face a high-grade of uncertainty in KM until a dominant design will emerge. Nevertheless, reading this book will help the reader to define main topics that will shape the research agenda of following years. In particular, I would like to focus on three major issues.

Knowledge codification. The simplest approach to knowing is the classical scheme of knowledge transfer. A knowledge object is passed by a knowledge source to a receiver, who makes some use of it. But this is a very naïve view. A more sophisticated view distinguishes among three concepts organized into a hierarchy: data, information and knowledge. Data are collections of raw measures of some event. Information comes as an elementary structure built on data, and knowledge is a more complex structure built on information, in order to link what is coming from the experience to existing knowledge and plans. At a first glance, this seems a very useful conceptualization. By using those three concepts we can easily recognize the number "8" as data, the message "It is eight o'clock" as information, and "I'm late to the meeting" as the knowledge extracted from the message. But, what can we can say about the sentence "It was now the hour that turns back the desire of those who sail the seas and melts their heart" (from "The Divine Comedy" by Dante Alighieri, the Carlyle-Wikstreed Translation)? Eventually, I can extract from the Dante's verses, more or less, the same information about the daytime, and then decide if I'm late at the meeting. But in Dante's sentence there is much more. I can make many possible connections with my future plans and my past experience. And, as knowing is foremost the act of connecting, I can develop more knowledge from Dante verses than from the sentence "It is eight o'clock". This richness of the message is built in its form, and we cannot mechanically separate the message content from its form. The codification/decodification process is very complex. The cognitive, emotional, and situational context plays a major role both in the codification of raw data and experiences and in the decodification process. On the contrary, ICTs, as any technology, tend to support processes which are context-free. As this goal is impossible to attain, ICT engineers choose another strategy—they define a given context of codification and decodification and derive a list of requisites for the design of effective information and communication formats. It is easy to preview that the research agenda in next years will give more attention to the efficiency and effectiveness of information formats in given organizational contexts. Many theoretical issues are involved in this research area, such as relationships between tacit and explicit knowledge, information and knowledge, and much more.

The sense-making frame. A key point of knowledge management is that a knowledge asset is useful inasmuch that it is continuously redefined by individual and collective learning. If the organization is not able to actively reconstruct its knowledge assets, knowledge disappears. Thus, any organization based on knowledge assets must be a learning organization, able to produce knowledge from knowledge. We know that the learning activity is a linking activity that makes connections between different pieces of information and a sense-making activity that constructs meaning for linked items. ICTs play a major role in supporting the connecting activity, while their role in supporting the sense-making is extremely poor. Probably we need a better understanding of time dimensions involved in developing new knowledge by cognitive actors (individuals and groups). The cognitive actor, while considering new pieces of information, constructs hypotheses, conjectures, inferences, images within three temporal coordinates. The first coordinate is the actual flow of messages coming from context. The second coordinate is that of intentions, desires, goals, plans, and the imagined future being sought. The third coordinate is that of the past experiences and previous knowledge. These three temporal coordinates define the structure of sense-making. Up to now, the research agenda on ICTs has been mainly focused on spatial dimensions of knowledge management and the efficiency of spatially dispersed knowledge resources and communities. Nevertheless, previous years have found researchers devoting more attention to time issues involved in knowledge management, and to the impact of ICTs on duration and rhythms of individual and group tasks. In the future, it is expected that the research on how IT can support sense-making will receive more attention.

Learning society. The most important claim of researchers and practitioners in the field of KM is that information is widely dispersed in society. Individuals have pieces of information from which others can benefit, but groups often fail to access to the information that the individuals have. In this respect, ICT is expected to produce a dramatic impact in helping people to elicit, transfer and aggregate relevant and dispersed information. The prerequisite is that individuals, groups and institutions are able to create a digital world, where most of knowledge circulating in the human society is encoded in digital artifacts. This digital layer of packaged information is inherently chaotic, as it is built bottom-up without a general design. Moreover, each day new information, new databases, and links modify this world. Thus, it is hard to have stable patterns in this chaotic world. Consequently, patterns could emerge only through the continuous work of knowledge mediators, learning agents of sorts, which patrol the chaotic digital world and construct coherent patterns of links between knowledge committers and knowledge suppliers (Google is an example of such a mediator). A knowledge mediator is one of the players that are necessary to build an effective socio-digital learning society. The task of mediators is to construct a coherent pattern of relationships between knowledge committers and knowledge suppliers. It is easy to forecast that huge research efforts in next years will be dedicated to design and build mediation technologies for the socio-digital learning society. The integration of several mediation technologies, such as wikis, blogs and other collaborative platforms is already bringing about effective exploitation of the collective intelligence of large mass of knowledgeable users. More sophisticated tools, capable to enable easy access to huge bodies of knowledge, are expected to come.

This book, carefully edited by Ettore Bolisani, will provide a wide audience of readers with a general view on research questions and recent advancements on the impact of Internet on knowledge management.

Giuseppe Zollo,
University of Naples "Federico II"
September, 2007

Preface

KNOWLEDGE MANAGEMENT FOR THE KNOWLEDGE SOCIETY

Even in the scientific context, sometimes the words can become *buzzwords,* after they are used for some time. This is the case of "Knowledge Society". An impressive number of studies in many disciplines deals with, mentions, or has something to do with this term (more than 17.000 documents that include this keyword can be retrieved with a simple look-up in "Google Scholar"). Indeed, the knowledge is increasingly recognised as the pivotal element of our activity, our economy, and, thus, our society. Today, much of the work of scientists and practitioners, in several fields, is centred on how this "asset" can be produced, handled, exchanged, stored, and more generally used to generate value for individuals and organisations.

But what does "knowledge society" exactly mean, and how will the term be interpreted in this book? Here, it is not a matter of definitions (which we will happily leave to philosophers and luminaries) but, rather, of more basic questions: what is exactly the difference between "knowledge society" and just "society"? Does this mean that we witness some sort of change, the birth of something that did not exist before? Does it mean that only today we are aware that something (the "knowledge") can assume unprecedented forms, or is finding fresh ways to be processed, which justifies our new (or renewed) attention?

It would be easy to say that the key of this change has to be found in the impressive advancements of ICT and Internet technologies. Indeed, it appears even obvious to associate the development of the knowledge society with the progress and widespread use of ICT applications. Unfortunately, this is not an answer but, rather, raises additional questions. The revolutionary potential of these technologies has been fully recognised only decades after their invention. Computers were invented about 70 years ago, an almost biblical time, considering the speed of our current lives. The Internet was ideated in the 1950s, and its technical feasibility was demonstrated a few years later.

The experts of innovation studies would probably say that this is common because the processes through which an invention becomes and innovation, spreads and finally, impacts the world significantly, depend on complicated dynamics, and are affected by the interactions of several factors, which takes a much longer time than often predicted. All this is true, but still does not explain the nature of today's change. Why just a few years ago we used to talk of "information society" and "information paradigm," and now we have turned to the "knowledge society"? What is the difference? What did it change, and how? And does this mean that, in the next future, we must expect to deal with "another kind of society"?

Actually, this is not a book of history, and we do not need to find the explanations of how we arrived somewhere, and why. Nor we are interested in making forecasts. Rather, focusing on the research on knowledge management, this book lives in the *present*, and intends the knowledge society not as a paradigm or a model that already exists and just needs to be explained, but something that we are *trying to build*, both conceptually and practically. It is the view of this book: a sort of *constructivist* perspective on the emerging knowledge society and, in this, of the role, knowledge management (KM).

KM, intended as the set of deliberate, coordinated, and systematic methods for the management of knowledge in organisations by means of appropriate organisational practices and ICT tools, is increasingly popular, but its development is relatively recent. It can be said that managing knowledge has always been one of the major concerns of humanity, but the origins of KM as a branch of management can be traced back to the early 1990s (Prusak, 2001), although KM scholars often cite antecedent works of eminent scholars (e.g., Drucker, 1967; Machlup, 1962; Polanyi, 1967). It is not the purpose here to go further into the definitions or history of KM (the reader can, however, find many references in the various chapters). What is clear is that the idea of KM is strictly intertwined with the idea of *building the knowledge society*, as it represents one of its *concrete bricks*.

If the building of a knowledge society relies on the development of KM, here we have both good and bad news. The good news is that there is an impressive effort of practice, research, and education in KM rises the expectation of a bright future for this field. The investments in KM programmes by companies are increasing, and regard not only the major multinationals but also smaller companies, in many industries and countries. Courses and even entire "universities" are devoted to KM. KM-related jobs are increasingly offered by companies, and there are professionals and consultants whose services specialise in KM. As regards the scientific research, there is a huge and increasing number of studies, books, and specialised conferences.

The bad news refers to a some persistent weaknesses of KM, seen as a scientific discipline. A first problem comes from the extreme heterogeneity of approaches, conceptual references, and application fields that can be found. KM initiatives are proposed in totally different environments: in business and in non-profit organisations; in multinationals and smaller companies; in very heterogeneous areas ranging from R&D to operations management, from healthcare management to ICT design. This witnesses the transversal interest in the issue, but at the same time, arises the question of *consistency* of approaches and methods. Although, sometimes, common viewpoints or approaches are proposed, even the conceptual backgrounds of researchers and practitioners are often heterogeneous. More generally, it is even difficult to draw the boundaries between KM and all the related areas (Information Systems and Computer Science, Sociology, Business Management, Economics, etc.).

Should we resign ourselves to develop distinct KM approaches for the different situations, or are there some "shared fundamentals" that we can try to build up? This is, indeed, what distinguishes a well-established discipline from just "a set of practices." As KM researchers, we need to proceed with the setting of these *fundamentals*. This work has been started by the KM community in recent years (see recent collections such as Holsapple, 2003; Schwartz, 2006), but it still requires efforts of analysis, systematisation, and formalisation. In relation to this, the book deals with this question by focusing particularly on a specific topic: the *processes of knowledge exchanges in networks* that, in the current context of research and practice of KM, appear to be particularly important.

KNOWLEDGE EXCHANGES IN NETWORKED ENVIRONMENTS

The problem of managing knowledge is, essentially, a problem of *knowledge exchange*. To be managed, the knowledge needs to be retrieved from some source, processed, and then distributed to other users (Garavelli, Gorgoglione, & Scozzi, 2002).

Thus, knowledge exchanges are the essential ingredients of KM. Although the topic of knowledge exchange seems well focalised, a rapid glance at the KM literature is enough to highlight that there are several problematic aspects that make this topic a challenging terrain for both the research and the practice. An essential problem results from the extreme variety of situations to which the issue of knowledge exchange can be related. It can be said that a myriad of knowledge exchanges continuously occurs in disparate contexts, even when they are not explicitly identified and recognised. An interpersonal communication is an exchange of knowledge, but also economic transactions between two trading firms can be seen as (or involve) a knowledge exchange. Even two computers exchanging messages are, somewhat, part of a kind of knowledge exchange. What's more, one can speak of knowledge exchange even when there is someone that communicates a message to a broad audience: a TV programme is a process of knowledge exchange, as is the publication of a book or a Web site.

Thus, there is a problem of definition. There is no clear consensus here, and distinct terms (such as knowledge sharing, transfer, exchange) are used (Boyd, Ragsdell, & Oppenheim, 2007; King, 2006), also with different shades of meaning (in this preface, we will just speak of knowledge exchanges, but we will more generally mean all the terms previously indicated).

In addition, the exchange of knowledge is a process that involves various elements (i.e., the knowledge objects exchanged, the sources and receivers, the carrier or medium, the mechanisms used, etc.). Thus, a researcher can decide to centre the analysis on one specific element, or to include different variables or factors, or to focus on the intertwined relationships among all these.

Due to these complications, the characterising aspect, the implications, and the practical questions of knowledge exchange are many. Here, we will explicit focus on the perspectives adopted by researchers whose main field is that of KM. The contributors to this book were asked to explain their viewpoints, research methods and interpretative models, and to debate the findings of their studies, with the purpose to clarify the state of our knowledge about this issue and discuss the prospective fields of study. In particular, they were invited to provide insights into some open questions that we will briefly recall in the following pages.

Processes

How do people and organisations exchange knowledge? An effort or modelisation of the mechanisms and rules that are employed is essential. Also, the nature of the "object" of exchange has to be specified. The classic distinction between tacit and explicit knowledge is fundamental, but needs further explanation.

Another open question is the difference between interpersonal and interorganisational exchange. Knowledge exchanges between organisations are, or involve, knowledge exchanges among individuals. The relationships among these two kinds of exchange need a conceptualisation that has not been achieved yet, and the literature often focuses on specific aspects or specific practical cases.

The human-machine knowledge exchange is a related issue. Technologies are the fundamental support of KM practices. The way knowledge embedded in an individual can be "extracted," codified, stored in a device, and then retrieved and delivered to other individuals for reuse, is one important field to explore. Also, the connection between the findings of technical research with the problems of interpersonal or interorganisational relationships still requires a conceptualisation.

Value

The *motivation* of exchanging knowledge with others, or in other terms, the value that the players ascribe to this activity, is another hot issue for KM, and a central theme of this book as well. The current practice shows that KM initiatives that do not account for the motivations of participants in knowledge exchanges are likely to fail (Brydon & Vining, 2006). There is, thus, the need to explain the factors that can facilitate and hinder the personal participation in a process of knowledge exchange. Motivation can be seen from different viewpoints, and based on various conceptual references. It can be related to distinct but intertwined concepts, such as the personal *utility* (i.e., knowledge is exchanged to solve a problem or accomplish a task), the economic *value* (knowledge is exchanged as a sort of *good*), or the *social motivation* (individuals exchange knowledge because they belong to a particular context). A systematisation of all these aspects is thus necessary. Again, the difference between personal or organisational value should be clarified.

Networks

Although knowledge exchange can be simply depicted as involving one source and one receiver, this process does not occur in a vacuum but, instead, in a complex configuration of relationships that involve several players. The structure and nature of the networks of interpersonal or interorganisational links, and the distinct roles performed by the various players, are thus an essential focus of analysis. The web of social relationships is one element that attracts the interest of researchers. Hot issues in the KM literature are, for example, the cultural distance between players and the trustworthy climate that facilitates the sharing of knowledge. Here, various models and references are often drawn from a multiplicity of disciplines and fields. An effort of systematisation is required.

The technological infrastructure of the network is another essential issue. There is a rich and significant literature on knowledge management systems and, more generally, on the use of ICT applications for supporting knowledge exchange between individuals and/or organisations. However, technology is not the panacea for any problem of knowledge exchange. The multidimensional and elusive nature of the notion of knowledge often challenges the efforts of ICT researchers and designers. The potential, but also the limitations of technology and the future prospects, and the way these are related to the other elements previously mentioned, are another area that still deserves an in-depth analysis.

AIMS OF THE BOOK AND AUDIENCE

As mentioned, the aims of the book are to illustrate, compare, and discuss models, perspectives, and approaches that can be helpful to understand the state-of-the-art of the current studies of the topic of knowledge exchange in networked environments seen from different viewpoints, and to depict the possible trajectories of the future developments both in the research and in the practice.

The collected chapters provide a rich panorama of the prospects of research on the topic, formulated by scholars working in independent areas. The reader will thus be given a good view of the variety of viewpoints and approaches and, at the same time, indications of the "shared elements" (language, terms, conceptual references) that can be intended as the foundations of an emerging and fascinating field of study.

In this sense, and in coherence with the constructivist view of the knowledge society, this book project should be intended more as a "laboratory of ideas" rather than an "encyclopedia." The comparison of contrasting viewpoints and the "remote debate" among scholars working on distinct but related fields, provides essential food for thought to the reader, and helps to build a "common interface" enabling the communication between different disciplines and areas. The assumption (and the hope) is that this "cross-fertilisation" can help to overcome the limitations of the single viewpoint, and that the systematic comparison and discussion of different but converging approaches can set the grounds for a shared language and an agreed conceptual framework, can favour the exchange of findings and ideas and builds the foundations of the future research.

Clearly, any multidisciplinary project is risky, since it involves different disciplines and academic traditions that can be distant (and, sometimes, idiosyncratic). However, the nature itself of the problem makes the effort valuable. In addition, the possible drawbacks have been minimised by organising the process of collection and revision of chapters in an appropriate way. Contributors were asked to submit chapters on specific topics, but aiming at explaining concepts, theories, approaches, and perspectives underpinning their current research (rather than illustrating the "last empirical findings"). Secondly, a double-stage reviewing process of chapters has been conducted, to ficilitate the understanding by readers specialising in other disciplines. Each chapter has been reviewed by both referees specialising in the same area of the author, who assessed the scientific quality of the chapter in that specific field, and referees specialising in a completely different field, who assessed the "readability" of the chapter and provided suggestions to simplify the language, clarify concepts, make bridges towards other disciplines, and so forth.

The principal audience of this book will consist of scholars and researchers in KM. The book is, in fact, firstly designed to provide "food for thought" for the future research. However, practitioners might find new ideas for a dynamic sector such as knowledge-based or Internet-based services. Graduate and postgraduate students might also find useful references for their work.

The sources of value can be various. As mentioned, the book can help to understand the broad picture of the state-of-the-art of the current research on the topic, and depict the possible trajectories of the future developments. Secondly, it can enable the building of a common set of concepts, terms, references, and approaches in disciplinary areas that are sometimes too distant. Another element of significance is the huge amount of references that is collected here. The contributors were asked to attach a special "additional reading" section that, added to the references directly quoted in their chapters, thus constitutes a comprehensive collection of the current literature on the topic of knowledge exchange, and a unique source of reference to the reader.

STRUCTURE OF THE BOOK AND CONTRIBUTIONS

Once the chapters were collected, the book was organised in two parts. The first section is entitled "Models," and gathers the contributions that focus on the conceptual modelisation of the context where knowledge exchanges occur, or deal with general key factors affecting these processes. Compared with the second section of the book, these first chapters have fewer links with specific application problems, although their analysis can provide elements that can be of use both to formulate research hypotheses or to inspire practical implementations of KM. These first chapters can be further classified in relation to their conceptual backgrounds and the main focus of analysis, or better, to their distinct *viewpoints* of the topic.

A first viewpoint refers to a *human-oriented approach* to KM, and highlights the social and personal issues affecting the exchange of knowledge. In her "Knowledge Sharing: Interactive Process Between Organizational Knowledge Sharing Initiative and Individuals' Sharing Practice," Shuhua Liu reflects on the relationships occurring between individuals' practices and organisational settings in knowledge exchange. As mentioned before, KM programmes have the aim to facilitate the exploitation of knowledge by organisation, but since organisations are made of individuals, the complex relationships between these different entities need a clarification. In particular, based on a review of established theories in sociology, management science, and organisational behaviour, the author attempts to develop elements of a new model that explains how the organisational settings influence the way individuals share knowledge. Knowledge is not something that can be "detached" from the individual, but rather it is built through a *sense-making process* occurring in a context of social interactions, and subjected to the institutional and organisational arrangements that regulate or influence these interactions. This view has interesting implications for KM. In particular, for a successful knowledge management initiative, both the formal and informal organisational factors that influence the individuals' behaviours and their knowledge-sharing practices need to be clearly identified. Also, this analysis sheds a new light on the role of ICTs in knowledge exchange that should be designed in relation to the social processes and the organisational activities.

The next chapter, "The Centrality of Team Leaders in Knowledge-Sharing Activities: Their Dual Role as Knowledge Processors" by Evangelia Siachou and Anthony Ioannidis, also investigates the relationships between individuals and organisations in knowledge exchange. The authors analyse the crucial role of team leaders as *knowledge processors* in favour of the other team members. In particular, they focus on *action* teams that deal with unpredictable situations and thus, need to obtain and make instant use of accurate knowledge, although their analysis might be applied to other virtual structures. The authors argue that team members cannot have access to critical knowledge directly, for lack of time or other constraints. Thus, the team leaders, being knowledge processors, act both as recipients of knowledge transferred from outside the team (from Internet repositories, external colleagues, or other sources) and as sources of knowledge for their team members. The capability to seek, filter, and deliver knowledge contents in the right way represents an essential skill. Well beyond the particular context considered here, the analysis of the role of leaders proposed by the authors provides useful insights into the complex relationship between the way organisational units are structured, and the effective processes of knowledge transfer that occur among their members.

The theme of the social context is also treated by Kerstin Siakas and Elli Georgiadou in their "Knowledge Sharing in Virtual and Networked Organisations in Different Organisational and National Cultures." The authors, however, have a wider focus, and discuss the factors that affect knowledge sharing processes in culturally diverse networked organisations. Indeed, considering that the most important KM programmes are implemented by large and dispersed multinationals, this issue becomes of particular interest. There is often the assumption that ICT applications, providing standard communication platforms, can "magically" solve all the problems of knowledge exchange in virtual organisations between physically remote members. As the authors argue effectively, this view neglects the issue of the cultural distance that can hinder the effective transfers of knowledge. Indeed, this is an emerging issue for the management of multicultural companies (see, for instance, the related studies of the so-called "diversity management"), but is relatively new in the field of KM, and often treated without the necessary theoretical background. Based on authoritative studies of the notion of culture, the contribution examines the impact of different cultural values and perception on knowledge sharing and, consequently, on the effectiveness of KM programmes.

The following two chapters treat much more directly the issue of technology for KM. Axel-Cyrille Ngonga Ngomo, in his "Towards an Implicit and Collaborative Evolution of Terminological Ontologies," opens a window to one of the more advanced fields of computer science applied to KM: the development and use of ontologies. This contribution has also the merit to provide a good example of technical literature in KM that has reached a considerable degree of formalisation. The problem of capturing the tacit components of knowledge in a way that can be handled and delivered automatically, can be seen as a particular process of knowledge exchange that challenges both KM researchers and computer programmers. The use of ontologies, which can be roughly defined as representations of knowledge in a form that can be interpreted by machines (and other persons), raises several issues that have not been resolved completely. Here, the author stresses some problematic questions: first, the connection between the representations of an individual's knowledge (i.e., personal ontologies) and a representation of knowledge that should be valid for a group of individuals (global knowledge); second, the problem of how ontologies can evolve along with time as the result of individual and organisational learning; and third, how personal ontologies can evolve autonomously by interacting with other personal ontologies. Although the chapter contains a high level of formalisation, even a non-specialist reader can have a good idea of the current problems that this field raises.

The chapter by Kimiz Dalkir, "Computer-Mediated Knowledge Sharing," offers a view of technology that leaves apart the idea of ICT applications as the panacea of any problem of KM. Instead, she highlights that not all Internet-based knowledge-sharing systems are created equal: they differ in their effectiveness when used for exchanging knowledge. Communication channels support different levels of social interaction and this has an impact on knowledge sharing. It is necessary to define key knowledge and channel attributes in order to understand how knowledge can be effectively shared using computers. Dalkir's chapter examines the computer-mediated knowledge sharing mechanisms, and proposes a typology based on media richness and social presence characteristics that can serve as a preliminary conceptual basis to select the most appropriate channel. Also, as the author notes, computer-mediated communication should not be thought of as a single communication channel, but rather a family of different technological applications. The proposed framework of knowledge and channel characteristics provides an alternative to the "one size fits all" approach to knowledge sharing on the Internet. Individuals wishing to communicate and collaborate using channel-mediated connections will be in a position to adopt a more systematic and deliberate approach to matching each type of knowledge with the best channel. As the computer-mediated communication technology evolves, and usage continues to intensify and diversify, being able to assess the best vehicle for knowledge sharing will provide a valuable means of ensuring both efficiency and effectiveness of the knowledge sharing. To this purpose, the modelisation proposed by Dalkir represents a valuable conceptual tool.

The last two chapters of the first section treat the issue of how knowledge exchange is perceived and valued by individuals and organisations, and the implications of this, especially in networked environments. Here, the KM literature still suffers a lack of formal modelisation for which a more direct relation with the economic models can be of use.

My chapter, "Understanding Knowledge Transfer on the Net: Useful Lessons from the Knowlewdge Economy," discusses the contribution to the development of KM that can come from an "economic reading" of KM practices and, particularly, from the recent studies in the so-called "knowledge economy." Indeed, KM is making its way among the other more established branches of business management, and a more direct link with the models and approaches of the economic disciplines would be useful to systematise the conceptual backgrounds and to improve the formal modelling. However, KM and Economics have often been distant areas, although recently, the attention to the economic models by KM researchers has increased and, on the other hand, eminent economists show interest in the study of knowledge as an explicit object of analysis. From these converging efforts, useful elements for the conceptual systematisation of KM can arise, and can give theoretical robustness to both the practice and the research. The chapter especially focuses on the process of knowledge transfer that can be seen as a sort of "market" between a source and receiver. This kind of modelisation provides novel interpretations of the value and motivation that individuals and organisations can have when exchanging knowledge with others. Additional issues (such as the cost and benefit of knowledge codification, and the mechanisms that can favour or hinder knowledge markets) are also analysed.

Similarly to the previous chapter, in their "Knowledge-Sharing Motivation in Virtual Communities," Jengchung V. Chen, J. Michael Tarn, and Muhammad A. Razi treat the issue of motivation in exchanging knowledge and in particular, they explore the motivation of members to exchange knowledge in virtual communities. They analyse the underlying factors of such sharing behaviours and, like the previous chapter, they found their analysis on elements drawn from economic theories. The authors present a novel conceptual model that illustrates the integrated relationship between transaction cost, expectancy value, and knowledge sharing in a context of virtual communities. The notion of knowledge market is also examined, since knowledge sharing is a form of knowledge transaction, and the concept of market provides an essential reference for understanding knowledge transactions and, thus, knowledge exchanges.

The second section of the book is entitled "Applications." Here, however, the reader will not necessarily find detailed descriptions of methods, techniques, or tools (this was not the aim of the book). Rather, these chapters are placed here because they focus more directly on particular issues of knowledge exchange in specific contexts, which represents a good linkage between the formulation of general models and the practical problems of their use. As the reader can notice, the chapters offer a good panorama of the extreme variety of issues and situations. However, as done in the first section, they are classified based on the similarity of applications or approaches. In particular, the first chapters are more focused on "non-profit networks" or, in other words, on open environments, where the exchange of knowledge appears a question of sharing rather than trading. The last chapters are, instead, more focused on business contexts.

Margarita Echeverri and Eileen G. Abels, in "Opportunities and Obstacles to Narrow the Digital Divide: Sharing Scientific Knowledge on the Internet," consider a problem that has become particularly important with the upsurge of the Internet: the digital divide. This chapter is a good demonstration of how the typical issues treated in the KM literature regard several heterogeneous fields. In particular, the authors reflect on the possibility to freely exchange scientific knowledge, (that is, one that, by its very nature, tends to be considered "public," being the essential ingredient of education and development). Here, the Internet has provided a new channel for disseminating scientific materials, for instance, in the form of electronic journals: the access through the Internet is currently the fastest and least expensive way to access this kind of knowledge. However, although the Web itself was conceived to encourage knowledge sharing, several limitations can restrict the freedom of access, especially to those users that, for various reasons, do not possess specific resources. In the literature of KM, there is little theoretical and empirical work that addresses knowledge transfer through the use of open electronic networks. The authors propose a conceptual framework of the knowledge transfer cycle, and examine the key factors affecting the dissemination of scientific knowledge on the Web. Also, they discuss the results of a vast survey that shows how having access to the Internet is not a guarantee of successful transfer of public scientific knowledge. In relation to this, the current challenges facing the open-access initiative, of making scientific information free and available worldwide, are also discussed.

The chapter "Knowledge Exchange in Electronic Networks of Practice: An Examination of Knowledge Types and Knowledge Flows," by Molly McLure Wasko and Samer Faraj, analyses an open environment for knowledge sharing, but is more delimited in focus and in boundaries, compared to the previous chapter. The study examines knowledge exchange in a global, interorganisational electronic network of practice based on the Usenet. Similarly to the previous chapter, this kind of network is based on a voluntary and globally distributed participation of members that do not have personal or organisational ties. This can thus be defined as an open community, although, as the reader can see, the members share a common interest in a particular topic, and the willingness to use a special infrastructure to transfer knowledge. The scientific literature (and the press as well) often emphasises the importance of these networks in supporting open knowledge exchanges, but there are few attempts to investigate in detail why and how these processes occur. The purpose of this study is twofold: on the one hand, the authors investigate what type of knowledge is being transferred in these networks, and second, how knowledge is transferred across individuals. The chapter analyses and classifies the contents exchanged in the messages (for this, the study also provides a good example of method applied to this kind of KM research), and illuminates how people use computer-mediated communication to support knowledge transfer, the types of knowledge transferred, the different roles of participants in the structure, as well as how knowledge flows in this network. The reader can find a number of stimulating results. For instance, the heterogeneity of individuals participating with varying motivations is an important element that raises the intensity of knowledge transfers and encourages knowledge flows. Additionally, these networks can succeed only if participants are intrinsically motivated to keep abreast of new ideas and innovations and to help others with their problems. Without individuals seeking answers and interested in building social ties with others, there would not be an audience for others interested in sharing their knowledge. Here, one can say that the electronic network reflects the characteristic of any other social group.

Isa Jahnke, in her "Knowledge Sharing Through Interactive Social Technologies: Development of Social Structures in Internet-Based Systems over Time," also analyses the exchange of "public" knowledge contents, but in a restricted environment represented by a campus university connection. The author illustrates the history and results of a vast campus project aimed to build a "common interface" for the exchange of "educational contents" among a network of students, tutors, and teachers. Indeed, as she argues, the developments towards the idea of a "Web 2.0" is based on new interactive Web-based tools, for example wikis and discussion boards, which enable the exchange of user-generated contents. The effect of existing social structures and roles in such a network, and the evolving nature of these, are analysed in her empirical research. In line with other contributions presented in this book, this research offers a good practical demonstration that the dynamics of social structures in online communities influence the effective processes of knowledge exchange. It is also important to notice that the way people communicate (i.e., face to face or online) does make a difference. The line of thought that "all people are the same" when they communicate online must be rejected, and unexpected behaviours may arise. The study demonstrates the change of roles, expectations, and activities in online communities. An interesting result for the reader is the conclusion about the complex relationships between intentional design efforts by the creators of the online communities, and the unpredicted emergence of social structures in Internet-based systems over time. This analysis has also a practical utility, since the author is able to sketch some essential criteria for designing online communities.

The next chapter, "Information Technology in Times of Crisis: Considering Knowledge Management for Disaster Management," by Kalpana Shankar, David J. Wild, Jaesoon An, Sam Shoulders, and Sheetal Narayanan, treats the issue of knowledge sharing in emergency situations, and has various reasons of interest. First, it analyses a context for knowledge sharing that has some similarities with the previous environments (e.g., non-profit context, and exchange of public knowledge in wide heterogeneous networks), but that has some peculiarities (e.g., the time of knowledge exchanges) that allow the reader to make useful comparisons. Also, this issue has been, so far, little studied in the KM literature. Indeed, crisis and disaster management requires the sharing of complex information among numerous entities and individuals. After examining the problematic issues of this context and the current practices and ICT applications typically used, the authors especially illustrate and discuss the potential and limitations of new technologies, such as the Internet and Web 2.0 applications, combined with new KM practices. They show how the use of networked technologies like the Internet is still in its infancy, and with very little cohesion. They argue that although the Internet is already in extensive use in disaster management, knowledge management will only be affected if top-down and bottoms-up approaches to information gathering, organisation, and dissemination are implemented. The aim of this chapter is to provide an introduction to some of the many technologies, practices and open problems for knowledge sharing in disaster situations, outline some persistent challenges, and suggest venues for exploration and practice.

The following chapter, "Managing Knowledge-Based Complexities Through Combined use of Internet Technologies" by Cécile Godé-Sanchez and Pierre Barbaroux, can also be seen, in connection to the previous chapters. This study introduces a theoretical framework to examine how Internet technologies provide organisations with additional capabilities to handle various forms of knowledge exchange and decision-making complexities. The authors refer their investigation to the specific field of tactical military operations that, due to the criticality and complexity of decision making, represent an excellent area for the experimentation and use of new technologies and practices. Also, the military contexts offer relevant illustrations of organisations that use Internet within complex decision environments for which short-term responsiveness and tactical adaptability are critical. The findings of the study can be well extended to other organisational contexts, ranging from emergency management to critical business environments. In particular, the authors investigate how specific combinations of Internet technologies can enable knowledge sharing processes to generate valuable supports for decisions. But they also argue that, although critical decision-making environments are generally designed following a top-down hierarchical structuring, the effective use of interactive technologies for knowledge sharing relates to the evolving social practices that fold together the planned and the unexpected, the tacit and the codified, into a complex combination of uses. Thus, an effective managerial solution for the implementation and use of these technologies requires the involvement of users in a bottom-up approach.

The last chapters deal more specifically with the business applications of knowledge exchange. Especially, they all focus on the emerging issue of interfirm cognitive relationships, which is a still an under-explored area of KM research. Deogratias Harorimana, in "Leading Firms as Knowledge Gatekeepers in a Networked Environment," examines how distant relationships can be a source of novel ideas and insights, which are useful for innovation processes. Firms can develop global channels and create platforms not only to exchange products or services, but also to benefit from outside knowledge inputs. The business success can be derived from the ability to identify and access external knowledge sources located far away, and to convert this knowledge into an explicit format that can be transferred and reused. However, all this is not easy, even with the use of advanced ICT applications. Here, the analysis of KM and KT processes becomes essential. In this tradition, the author analyses the critical activities of knowledge conversion that have to take place to make the interfirm knowledge exchange possible. The effectiveness of these processes is affected not only by the nature of the knowledge exchanged, but also by the social and cultural environment where these processes occur. To favour these, there is increasing attention on the role player by some firms in a network of connecting organisations. These firms are called "knowledge gatekeepers" since their role is to create a shared social and technological platform that can enable knowledge transfers among networking firms by means of the sharing of tacit meanings or the codification of knowledge. The notion of knowledge gatekeeper proposed here, whic extends concepts already developed in the organisational literature (from knowledge brokers to knowledge mediators), also sheds light into new interpretations of the role that is generally ascribed to leading, and builds a bridge toward the economic analysis of the transformations of industrial systems.

Enrico Scarso in "The Role of Knowledge Mediators in Virtual Environments" examines the functions of online knowledge mediators as well, but seen as independent businesses whose mission is explicitly targeted at facilitating the knowledge exchange among business partners. Such firms, of which the author provides examples, specialise in performing activities that are related to KM and KT. After illustrating the different models that are adopted in the literature to describe the nature and functioning of interorganisational knowledge transfer, the author raises the important issue that the role of knowledge mediators should be interpreted as a combination of strictly cognitive (or KM) functions with those typically performed by the classic economic mediators in business. He also suggests a two-dimensional framework based on these two complementary views that can provide interesting elements for the research and practice in the field.

The chapter by Stavros T. Ponis, George Vagenas, and Ilias P. Tatsiopoulos, "Knowledge Management in Virtual Enterprises: Supporting Frameworks and Enabling Web Technologies," deals the issue of interfirm cognitive relationships as well, but focuses on the particular context of virtual enterprises. This organisational structure, which emerges as a shift from traditional hierarchical organisations to more loose and flexible business relationships, strongly relies on the exchange of knowledge among partners supported by an intense use of ICTs. However, the practical implementation and management of virtual enterprises still needs research and practical development. In this sense, as the authors argue, although these organisational forms are strongly based on the management of interfirm knowledge exchanges, the literature on KM has so far showed little interest in this area. After characterising the peculiar problems of knowledge exchange in these complex contexts, the authors propose a good illustration of the current state-of-the-art of the most advanced ICT applications for networked infrastructures in virtual enterprises, from multiagents systems to Web services. They argue that the most critical issue that these technologies have to deal with is the high heterogeneity (seen at different levels) that characterises virtual enterprises. Finally, the authors attempt to combine the various elements discussed in the chapter with the purpose to illustrate a possible comprehensive framework for KM in virtual enterprises.

Scott Erickson and Helen Rothberg, in "Sharing and Protecting Knowledge: New Considerations for Digital Environments," propose a completely different perspective of interfirm knowledge exchanges. Indeed, as KM practice increasingly moves to the Internet, it is worth highlighting not only the new opportunities that are offered, but also the threats to the security of proprietary knowledge. The Internet, as a matter of fact, also makes knowledge assets more vulnerable to competitive intelligence efforts made by competitors. The authors analyse various aspects and elements of this problem, and illustrate possible threats that can come from the spread of KM practices in organisations that, by their nature, are designed to make knowledge more explicit and to facilitate their circulation and, at the same time, make such knowledge more difficult to protect. However, as they argue, both the potential and the vulnerability of knowledge on the Internet varies according to the nature of knowledge assets, and there is the need to examine all these factors in combination. The authors propose a model that integrates three dimension of knowledge (tacitness, complexity, appropriability), and relates these with its vulnerability in a KM Internet-based environment. This discussion provides interesting insights into the issue, and new proposals for further research. For instance, an interesting direction of study is exploring the balance and tension between how far to share knowledge and how far to protect it. The attempts to find appropriate models to answer this question can provide fresh lessons.

The last chapter, "Identifying Knowledge Values and Knowledge Sharing Through Linguistic Methods: Application to Company Web Pages," by June Tolsby, proposes an original viewpoint of the knowledge transfer process. The author analyses the way a company "communicates" knowledge about its organisational identity and values to the external environment by means of its Web pages. Indeed, with the increasing use of the Web as a communication tool, this becomes a sort of "open window" towards the inside of an organisation. It might thus be interesting to find useful methods of analysis that enable a better understanding of the contents that a company is (intentionally or not) communicating. Here, the author proposes a novel combination of approaches developed in the KM field (such as the building of identity in a community of practice) with elements of communication theories (i.e., the concepts of modality and transitivity in a text, and the discourse analysis). For an empirical test, she proposes the application of her method to the analysis of a company's Web site, illustrating how this approach can be of use to identify the firm's identity and the values that the organisation communicates. This experimental use of methods and approaches developed in completely different areas from KM interesting prospects of application.

CONCLUSION

Seeking a Shared Conceptual Space for Research and Practice

The contributions collected here provide a good sample of the variety of viewpoints, approaches, models, elements of analysis, and application fields that the KM-related literature proposes on the issue of knowledge exchange. The authors, specialising in different fields, offer a very stimulating picture of research prospects, and provide novel ideas and food for thought to the reader.

As mentioned before, the extreme heterogeneity of the KM literature can be an element of richness, but can also lead to idiosyncratic approaches, which can make the research and the practice difficult. As said, one purpose of the book was to investigate, by means of a collection of various contributions, about one essential question: is the KM field going towards a unification of some shared "foundational" elements that can make this discipline more robust at a scientific level? Or at least, can we persepctives, vocabulary that facilitates the sharing of models and perspective, and boosts the field? Or coversely, is the research evolving in direction to a fragmentation of viewpoints, approaches, and models?

With regard to these questions, and with particular reference to the processes of knowledge exchange that was the main object of the book, the contributions gathered represent an excellent survey of "hot issues," that are summarised in the points illustrated.

a. Definition of Knowledge

The notion of knowledge is, to some extent, difficult to capture. A fundamental acquisition of the KM literature is the distinction of knowledge from data and information. this distinction represents the foundations of the notion of knowledge that is widely used in KM research, and in many of the chapters of this book as well. But problems may emerge when this distinction is applied to the specific context of analysis. For instance, in some cases, the adopted notion of knowledge is not very far from the current idea of information, while in others, there is more emphasis on the difference. Also, sometimes the researchers focus on the "material" manifestations of knowledge (e.g., its representation) that can be somewhat modelled and handled, in others they underline its "intrinsically" intangible essence.

b. Knowledge Exchanges in Networks

The reader can note that there is no shared definition nor single use of some basic terms. As regards, for instance, knowledge exchange, knowledge sharing, and knowledge transfer, these terms are sometimes used as synonyms or, in others cases, different definitions of the same word are adopted. The same happens to notions such as electronic networks, virtual communities, online communities, and communities of practice. As in the case of of knowledge, it can be said that the various authors tend to adopt the definitions that better fit their particular viewpoint, or that are drawn from the reference literature they use. This is clearly very appropriate for the specific purpose of each piece of research, and, indeed, is probably necessary to facilitate the readability of the single work. But it also represents an element of divergence, and a limitation for a more effective communication in the KM scientific community.

c. Attributes of Knowledge

There are also elements that can now be considered shared across the entire KM scientific community. One of these is the well-known distinction between tacit and explicit forms of knowledge. Today, this classification can be considered a basic entry of a KM dictionary. As the reader can see, this element crosses the various approaches of analysis and application fields proposed by the various authors, transversally. Unfortunately, the definitions of tacit and explicit knowledge are somewhat elusive, which explains why there is less uniformity when we pass the application of this classification to the different situations of knowledge exchange that are considered by the various authors.

d. Application Fields and Research Methods

As mentioned, the heterogeneity of the application fields is an element of richness, but raises essential questions about the possibility to adopt common backgrounds and research methods. For instance, what is the fundamental unit of analysis? Is knowledge exchange a process involving individuals or organisations? If we need to treat both cases (which we probably cannot avoid doing), can we model this phenomenon in a single and uniform way? In addition, what does it mean when an individual exchanges knowledge with a system? What is really exchanged in these processes? What is the role played by the "context"where knowledge exchange occurs? How can we delineate the boundaries between the context and the players involved?

Indeed, the variability of situations often demands different approaches both to modelisation and to empirical research, and to the practice as well. In this sense, the contributions presented here offer a good example of that. As the reader can see, all the chapters deal with all the above-mentioned questions in some way, but the solutions they propose are not always compatible to one another. The scholars are increasingly aware that there is need to combine and integrate various viewpoints and methods in a common viewpoint, but this still requires an effort of systematisation and convergence. Even the references quoted by the contributors reflect this multifaceted challenge. On the one hand, there is a substantial part of references that is shared by the various chapters. but there are also specific backgrounds that correspond to the working discipline of the researcher or are related to the particular application.

e. Quantitative or Qualitative Models?

This is a crucial question in many disciplines, and has often represented a reason of contrast between the natural sciences (mostly based on mathematical models) and human or social sciences (that often deal with more elusive and ambiguous objects), with other fields in the middle (such as economics). In the case of KM, which indeed *is* a multidisciplinary field, this debate appears still at the beginning, and the scholars are more involved in defining the fundamental concepts or analysing the practical implications of KM solutions. As other areas of management, the mathematical modelisation is often relegated to the "hard" technological approaches, while the studies that treat the "soft" issues (i.e., social and relational aspects of knowledge exchange) are much based on qualitative models. An integration of quantitative and qualitative modelisation approaches would be desirable and useful (on this point, see also the following).

OPEN ISSUES AND FUTURE RESEARCH DIRECTIONS

Based on what was previously said, and on other ideas that emerge from the chapters, it is now possible to mention some promising areas for research. A first point for a future agenda is the general issue of modelisation. As mentioned before, the analysis of knowledge exchange becomes central in any study of KM. There is, thus, the need to build some basic models of these processes, in other words, a schematic view consisting of a few variables or elements. Once these fundamental models are defined, it will be possible to build the particularisation and the adaptations to the specific object of research or practice. As some of the chapters also show, there is an increasing effort of basic formalisation by researchers. In the various chapters, the reader will find an important source of ideas and references.

Another issue that deserves further analysis is the codification of knowledge within knowledge exchanges. Indeed, as the chapters collected here also show, two contrasting viewpoints have, for a long time, predominated and are frequently considered separately: one that sees knowledge exchange as a process that involves just coded knowledge, and the other that focuses on whether and how it is possible to exchange tacit knowledge. These are two faces of the same coin: any practical implementation of KM requires that both the aspects are considered together. An effort of integration of the mentioned perspectives would be of use: the recent literature (as the present contribution show clearly) stresses the concerns about how these two views can be combined with one another. For instance, an in-depth analysis of the benefits and problems of codification in to specific knowledge exchange processes would be of significance.

A similar dichotomy of approaches can be found with regard to technology. On the one hand, technologies are often treated as a world apart, an ideal and comfortable environment where knowledge can be treated as a detached and explicit object that has just to be carried from one place to another. This sometimes neglects the intangible and elusive nature of knowledge, and imposes simplifications that can be too drastic. On the other hand, those that privilege a social approach to KM often neglect that, without technologies, KM would simply not exist the way we know it. The richness of formality of the models implemented by technology experts can provide useful lessons for social approaches. A further point for a research agenda is how these two contrasting areas can be connected. Again, the chapters presented here shows a rich variety of positions and viewpoints on which to reflect.

Finally, another important point of a future research agenda is the connection with the models developed in the economic disciplines. An area of notable importance for KM is the analysis of costs and benefits of knowledge exchanges and, more generally, the issue of value. As our chapters clearly show, there are several ways to see the value of knowledge. The economic disciplines that place the notion of value at the centre of their research can provide useful lessons here, but the connection with the KM field still requires further study.

REFERENCES

Boyd, J., Ragsdell, G., & Oppenheim, C. (2007). *Knowledge transfer mechanisms: A case study from manufacturing*. Paper presented at the 8th European Conference on Knowldege Management, Barcelona.

Brydon M., & Vining A. R. (2006). Understanding the failure of internal knowledge markets: A framework for diagnosis and improvement. *Information & Management, 43,* 964–974.

Drucker P. (1967). *The effective executive*. New York: HarperCollins.

Drucker P. (1969). *The age of discontinuity; Guidelines to our changing society*. New York: Harper & Row.

Garavelli, A. C., Gorgoglione, M., & Scozzi, B. (2002). Managing knowledge transfer by knowledge technologies. *Technovation, 22,* 269-279.

Holsapple, C. W. (Ed.) (2003). *Handbook of knowledge management*. Berlin: Springer-Verlag.

King, W. R. (2006). Knowledge transfer. In D. G. Schwatz (Ed.), *Encyclopedia of knowledge management*. Hershey (PA): Idea Group.

Machlup F. (1962). *The production and distribution of knowledge in the United States*. Princeton: Priceton Univercity Press.

Polanyi M. (1967). *The tacit dimension.* Garden City, NY: Doubleday Anchor.

Prusak, L. (2001). Where did knowledge management come from? *IBM Systems Journal, 40*(4), 1002-1007.

Schwartz, D. (Ed.). (2006). *Encyclopedia of knowledge management*. Hershey, PA: Idea Group.

Acknowledgment

Coming to the end of a hard but exciting project, one becomes aware of the many people without whose support this job could not have been satisfactorily completed. It is a pleasure to acknowledge the help of all those that, with various roles, have been involved in this project.

First, my gratitude is due to all the authors that accepted to contribute to this book with their precious works. Many thanks for the patience and care with which they followed the various steps, and the comprehension with which they responded to my (sometimes insisting) requests as book editor.

Thanks go to all those that generously donated their time to referee the manuscripts submitted for potential inclusion, offering insights, positive critiques, and suggestions. Their names appear in the list included in this book. The efforts of these people contributed to the quality of this volume (although, of course, I bear the entire responsibility for the final acceptance of the chapters), and I also learnt much from their acute analysis.

My special thanks also to the publishing team at IGI Global, for the enthusiasm with which they accepted and supported this project throughout the whole process, from inception of the initial idea to final publication. I would especially like to mention Mehdi Khosrow-Pour (Senior Academics Editor), Jan Travers (Managing Director), Michelle Potter, (Acquisitions/Development Editor), and Nicole Dean (Assistant Marketing Manager).

And I am extremely grateful to Kristin Roth, Managing Development Editor, and Deborah Yahnke, Assistant Development Editor, who provided invaluable support, encouragement, and assistance during the long months it took to give birth to this book.

Let me finally dedicate this work to my family, without whom this work would have made little sense to me. To my wife Paola, for the sweetness of her love, and for the patience and constant support, especially in the final rushing moments of this project. And to my beloved daughters Federica and Margherita, *"pezzi di cuore"* ("pieces of hearts") as some Italians would say: maybe one day they will read the book (or at least the acknowledgements!) and will understand why their father spent a lot of time sitting in front of a computer.

Ettore Bolisani
Universiy of Padua, Italy
September 2007

Section I
Models

Chapter I
Knowledge Sharing:
Interactive Processes Between Organizational Knowledge-Sharing Initiative and Individuals' Sharing Practice

Shuhua Liu
University of Washington, USA

ABSTRACT

Knowledge is one of the most important competitive resources a business can have. However, the failure of knowledge management initiatives in the last decade, especially the failure of knowledge management (sharing) systems, directly points out the inadequacy of current approaches to knowledge sharing. This chapter, expanding on the current view of knowledge and knowledge management, offers an alternative approach to knowledge sharing. It is argued that to understand employee knowledge-sharing behavior, we have to understand the interactions between organizational context and individuals' sense-making processes before achieving success. Studies in knowledge sharing are reviewed before the missing organizational factors are pointed out. Established theories in sociology, management science, and organizational behavior are introduced where the influences of both formal and informal organizational factors on employee knowledge sharing are elaborated. Theoretical and practical implications of current study on knowledge-sharing research are discussed in the end.

INTRODUCTION

Knowledge is one of the most important competitive resources a business can have. This has been repetitively emphasized in the literature of knowledge management, strategic management, and organization science (Argote & Ingram, 2000; Davenport & Prusak, 1997; Ipe, 2003;). A constant finding is that in order to effectively maintain this advantage for long-term development and survival, an organization must rely on its employees, the real creators, and users, to effectively share knowledge and thereby enhance the collective innovative capability of the organization (Argote, McEvily, & Reagans, 2003; Bechky, 2003; Cabrera & Cabrera, 2002; Kelloway & Barling, 2000). However, the failure of knowledge-management initiatives in the last decade, especially the failure of knowledge management (sharing) systems (Storey & Barnett, 2000), not only directly points out the inadequacy of knowledge sharing via information technology, but brings the current epistemological approach toward knowledge sharing into question (Bechky, 2003; Cook & Brown, 1999; Hislop, 2002;). It is suggested in this chapter that there is one unresolved question fundamental to the discussions on knowledge transfer, knowledge-based companies, and knowledge sharing: Is knowledge the objective truth, a static entity that has a constant meaning or a dynamic creation of humans in constant social interaction? Different answers to this question lead to varying views of knowledge sharing in current research and varying success of sharing inside the organization, involving different roles that information technology can play.

Taking a process view, this chapter argues that knowledge sharing is an integral part of individuals' work behavior and is constantly guided by individuals' behavior rules (DiMaggio, 1997; Swidler, 1986). These behavioral rules are constantly being revised during an individual's social interactions with organizational contexts. At the same time, social reality is also being constructed by individuals' social interactions guided by their selective sense making (Weick, 1995) and internalization of certain behavioral rules (Burger & Luckman, 1966). Thus, the iterative interactions between social context and individual actions must be captured in the study of knowledge sharing.

Informed by theories from sociology, organizational sciences, and knowledge management, the chapter is structured as follows:

First, the definitions of knowledge sharing held in this chapter will be described; second, current approaches on knowledge sharing are detailed and examined for missing concepts that could be borrowed from other disciplines, such as organization sciences and sociology; following that, the fourth section discusses important organizational and institutional factors that influence organizational knowledge sharing; both theoretical and practical implications are offered in the fifth section; a brief summary of the contribution of this chapter to current studies of knowledge sharing is offered in the conclusion.

WHAT IS KNOWLEDGE SHARING?

What is meant by knowledge sharing in this chapter? As mentioned, different understandings of the origin of knowledge and its dimensionality make a unanimous definition of knowledge sharing almost impossible. Early system designers and researchers defined knowledge as an objective truth and thus, knowledge sharing as simply the physical transferring of knowledge via information systems or communication channels (books, documents, etc.) from knowledge owners to receivers (Scarbough et. al., 1999; Storey & Barnett, 2000). This definition has been widely criticized for its ignoring of subjective knowledge (Fernie, Green, Weller, & Newcombe, 2003). The view of knowledge as something subjectively held by individuals in their minds currently holds a higher popularity in a handful of recent publications from knowledge-sharing researchers (Cook & Brown, 1999). Thus, it is not surprising to see some researchers maintain the distinction between the tacit dimension and the explicit dimension, and deem the conversion between these two dimensions a core part of knowledge sharing (Nonaka & Takeuchi, 1995).

Looking closely at the latter definition, we can find an underlying epistemological approach, where knowledge is perceived as something that has a constant meaning and can be carried over in the conversion or externalization process (Hendriks, 1999; Herschel, Nemati, & Steiger, 2001; Roberts, 2000). Before advancing my argument against this way of defining knowledge sharing, the example of riding a bicycle, from Polanyi (1969), can usefully be reexamined to illustrate that knowledge is actually generated and immersed in the process of knowing and thus, can only be shared via the social process where it is generated. Pure conversion/externalization between dimensions, without taking account of knowing contexts and individuals' sensemaking process, may not be sufficient for knowledge to be fully shared (Lave & Wenger, 1991).

In Polanyi's example of riding a bicycle, even though it is hard for people to clearly articulate what exactly a person needs to do to ride a bicycle, they can still ride the bicycle with ease. Polanyi defined the inarticulable part of knowledge that people use to ride a bicycle as the "tacit dimension of knowledge" (Polanyi, 1966), while the clear articulation of how to ride a bicycle is perceived as the explicit dimension of knowledge (Nonaka & Takeuchi, 1995).

Based on this point of view, tacit knowledge and explicit knowledge are two distinct forms of knowledge, and neither is a variant of the other (Cook & Brown, 1999). Each works in a way that the other cannot achieve and one complements the other, so it is not possible to produce one by purely making it out of another. Cook and Brown's (1999) elaboration compellingly demonstrates the importance of committing to social process in knowledge sharing:

"To be able to ride a bicycle, one needs to have the (tacit) knowledge of how to stay upright. This is knowledge one possesses, it is not the activity of riding itself. Possessing this tacit knowledge makes it possible to keep upright, which is something that the explicit knowledge of which way to turn cannot do. We can't put a novice on a bicycle saying. 'ok, take off- and if you start to fall like so, turn this way' and expect the person to be able to ride successfully. The novice would have the explicit knowledge but not the necessary tacit knowledge. Whatever epistemic work that explicit bit of knowledge can make possible, it cannot do all of the work that is necessary for someone to know how to ride…the novice has to spend a certain amount time on a bicycle. (p. 384*)"*

As we can see from these arguments, when one is committed to a knowledge-sharing activity, in order to get the full knowledge of riding a bicycle, there has to be a sensemaking process for individuals to use both dimensions of knowledge (Weick, 1995). Thus, this chapter, informed by both social constructionist approach and social cognition research (Tsoukas & Chia, 2002), defines knowledge sharing as *"the process where individuals exchange their (tacit or explicit) knowledge and jointly create new knowledge in a knowing process within a social context that is also constructed out of these activities."* This definition not only emphasizes the importance of social interaction in creating common understandings among knowledge-sharing partners, but also points to individuals' sensemaking process, where one's personal interpretation of the shared understanding is created. This personal interpretation (the personal version of that shared understanding) is potentially what individuals use reflectively in their later sharing process, which feeds into the next cycle of organizational knowledge-sharing practices. The knowing process may occur in a classroom setting, in a work setting, and in daily life. The exact knowing activities people commit to, and the knowledge they exchange, generate, and internalize, largely depends on the context for that sharing. Within the organizational context, knowledge sharing is shaped by constant interaction with specific institutional environments and organizational contexts. Individual employees regularly refine their knowledge-sharing rules and working practices to decide what exact knowledge they want to share, who to share with, and through what channels (Morrison, 2002; Weick, 1995). Collectively, the individuals' knowledge-sharing practices have the potential to influence or even change the knowledge-sharing environment in the organization (Feldman & Pentland, 2003).

CURRENT APPROACHES TO KNOWLEDGE SHARING (KS)

Due to the varying definitions of knowledge, at least three approaches are evident in the current studies of knowledge sharing. The first approach perceives knowledge sharing as the act of transferring objective knowledge through communication channels (Nonaka, 1994; Shannon & Weaver, 1949); the second believes knowledge is composed of both tacit and explicit dimensions, where the tacit dimension can be readily converted into the explicit dimension without changing or losing meaning inherent in that tacit bit. Thus, knowledge sharing is perceived as the conversion/externalization of tacit knowledge into explicit knowledge, and activities involved in that conversion process (Berends, 2005; Fernie et. al., 2003; Herschel et al., 2001); the final group defines knowledge sharing as a social process involving individuals who interact and create a shared meaning (Cook & Brown, 1999; Hislop, 2002; Hooff & Ridder, 2004; Ipe, 2003; Kelloway & Barling, 2000). The following is the review of important studies and central concepts celebrated in each approach, followed by discussion of the alternative view offered by this chapter, expanding upon the current approaches.

APPROACH 1: OBJECTIVE KNOWLEDGE AND PHYSICAL TRANSFER VIA SYSTEMS

According to this approach, Knowledge is defined as "justified belief" (Moser & Nat, 1987; Winograd & Flores, 1986). Thus, its perception of knowledge sharing is largely influenced by the communication model created by Shannon and Weaver (1949), where knowledge sharing is the act of transferring the objective knowledge via any communication channels from the owners to the receivers. Figure 1 represents the knowledge-sharing process defined according to this view point. The proponents of this approach argue that the only mediator that can influence the quality of sharing is the quality of communication channels that users use to communicate knowledge or "communication noise" (Shannon & Weaver, 1949).

In focusing on means of reducing communication noise, the dominant view in this approach is the promotion of high quality tools, knowledge depositories (Pipek, Hinrichs, & Wulf, 2002), or expertise-sharing systems (Linton, 2003) for knowledge sharing in the organization (Ackerman, 1994). In her famous study of expertise-sharing system named "Answer Garden," Ackerman (1994) maintains that organizational memories can be stored in the system and may be accessed

Figure 1. Objective knowledge sharing

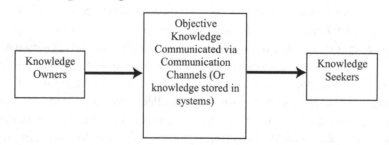

Figure 2. Knowledge conversion (sharing) process

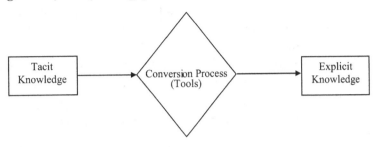

by anybody in the organization if authorized by experts. Things that are stored in the system are perceived as knowledge that is objectively certified by the experts in the organization. In other words, knowledge in the system is already justified as truth for further use.

According to this approach, the most prominent ICT tool for facilitating knowledge sharing is an intranet (Hendriks, 1999). Some author even equates promoting knowledge sharing with the challenges and pitfalls associated with the introduction and deployment of an intranet (Marshall, 1997).

The advantage of tools, like Answer Garden, for knowledge sharing is that it is available any time, and that knowledge so stored is perceived as more reliable. The knowledge expert has the option of directing (repetitive) questioners towards systematic answers readily available in the system, while still being able to focus on more interesting and complicated questions. However, these tools cannot take into account any special working contexts of stored information (Hislop, 2002). Thus, it manages what mostly can be called knowledge-related information; neither can individuals change arbitrary content available in the system. These disadvantages greatly constrain employees' active contribution to the collective knowledge retained in the organization.

APPROACH 2: THE DISTINCTION BETWEEN THE TACIT DIMENSION AND THE EXPLICIT DIMENSION: INDIVIDUALS' IMPORTANCE EMPHASIZED

The definitive work of Nonaka and Takeuchi (1995) recognizes the importance of individual employees in the process of knowledge creation and sharing. Their work argues that organizations cannot create knowledge without individuals, and unless individual knowledge is shared with other individuals and groups, the knowledge is likely to have limited impact on organizational effectiveness. An organization's ability to effectively leverage its knowledge then is highly contingent on the individuals who actually create, share, and use the knowledge.

According to this approach, knowing only occurs in an individuals' mind; thus, the focus of this approach is on the externalization of tacit knowledge held by individuals into explicit knowledge that can be shared with other members in the organization. Many conversion protocols (Herschel et. al., 2001) and knowledge taxonomies (Zhao & Reisman, 1992) have been created in order to facilitate the externalization/conversion processes. Figure 2 represents the knowledge conversion process defined according to this approach.

Citing speech act theory, Berends (2005) defines the exact moves (Description, Suggestions, Evaluation, Questions, Actions) that members in the organization need to take in order to externalize knowledge they hold privately. He argues that by providing an adequate representation of reality, these moves can secure the tacit knowledge held by knowledge owners for the knowledge seekers in the organization.

Herschel et al. (2001) go further to test the effectiveness of knowledge exchange protocols by evaluating the conversion precision of tacit knowledge in presentations and movies. Recording narratives participants later recall from watching movies and presentations after being trained with exchange protocol, Herschel and colleagues claim that if we can structure tacit knowledge into certain formats (protocols), the effort to share its structured replacement (explicit knowledge) should be the focus of knowledge sharing.

Zhao and Reisman's (1992) review of taxonomies used by different disciplines to facilitate technology transfer is another example of this externalization initiative. They argue that since researchers in each discipline seem to be able to understand the technology transferred, the tacit knowledge needed to use the technology has already been transferred to the recipients via an externalization artifact, in this case, the taxonomy.

Ironically, although Polanyi (1966, 1969) is often quoted as being the first to make the distinction between tacit knowledge and explicit knowledge, recent interpretations of his work by Pritchard (2000) reveal that Polanyi (1969) himself ultimately seems to reject the notion of explicit knowledge and therefore, the idea of externalization process:

"The ideal of a strictly explicit knowledge is indeed self contradictory. Deprived of tacit co-efficients, all spoken words, all formulae, all maps and graphs are strictly meaningless. (Polanyi, 1969, p. 195)"

Thus, according to Polanyi (1966), once devoid of its tacit counterpart and related social contexts, explicit knowledge could be meaningless. Our question here becomes: How can tacit knowledge be shared if not via the externalization process?

APPROACH 3: SOCIALLY GENERATED KNOWLEDGE AND SHARED UNDERSTANDING CREATED IN SOCIAL INTERACTIONS

Another theme that starts to emerge from the literature seems able to help answer this ques-

Figure 3. Knowledge sharing defined in social interactions

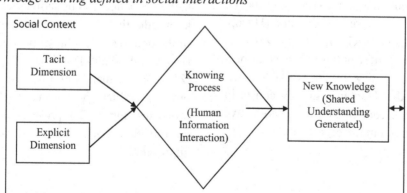

tion. This approach perceives knowledge as being embedded in social interactions involving knowledge owners, seekers, and sharers. It can also be embedded in an organization's rules, routines, cultures, structures, and technology use (McGrath & Argote, 2001; Walsh & Ungson, 1991). For organizational members, *knowledge and knowing lie in the use of knowledge as a tool of knowing within situated interaction between the actors and the social and physical world* (Gherardi, Nicolini, & Odella, 1998).

Cook and Brown (1999) contribute greatly by arguing for the importance of a knowing process for generation of new knowledge out of tacit and explicit knowledge. They argue that the central theme in knowledge sharing should be on the knowing process, where individual and group, tacit and explicit knowledge are connected. When knowledge is used as a tool in interaction with the world, it also gives shape and discipline to knowing. It is the reciprocal interplay between knowledge and knowing that bridges the gap between tacit knowledge held by knowledge owners and (tacit or explicit) knowledge acquired by recipients. This interplay of knowledge and knowing is demonstrated in Figure 3, where knowledge-sharing process is presented according to this approach.

While arguing for the intrinsic nature of change in organizations, Tsoukas and Chia (2002) suggest that individual members gain their insights and tacit knowledge about the organization through interactions in the socialization process. They suggest that although organizational routines are used by management as a way to structure individuals' behavior, they are also constructed in this process by individuals' operationalization of routines.

Hooff and de Ridder (2004) deliberate on the importance of the communication climate of an organization under which individuals communicate. Communication climate is defined as "the atmosphere in an organization regarding accepted communication behavior." They sug-

gest that a supportive communication climate is characterized by open exchange of information, accessibility of coworkers, confirming and cooperative interactions, and an overall culture of sharing knowledge. The results of their study demonstrate that a constructive communication climate can positively influence individuals' knowledge donating, knowledge collecting, and affective commitment to the organization.

Situated curriculum, a specific form of social order that instructs the socialization of novices within the context of ongoing work activities, for example, situated learning in organization is examined by Gherardi et al. (1998). Arguing that no skills can be considered in isolation, they suggest that learning in the workplace is to be understood both as a cognitive and as a social activity. For them, on-the-job learning is an ongoing social activity aimed at discovering what is to be done, when and how to do it according to specific routines, what specific artifacts to use, how to give a reasonable account of why it is done, and of what sort of person one must become in order to be a competent member of that community.

When studying knowledge-sharing behavior among engineers, technicians, and assemblers on a production floor, Bechky (2003) proposes that the difficulties of knowledge sharing among these communities actually lies in differences in their language, the locus of their practices, and their conceptualization of the product. She suggests that when sharing problems arise, if members of these communities provide solutions that invoke differences in work contexts and create a common ground among sharers, they can transform understandings of all members, and generate a newer and richer understanding of the product and the problems they face.

The Toyota case studied by Dyer and Nobeoka (2000) also echoes the importance of creating a shared understanding among suppliers towards collective benefits of the whole network. They argue that social networks initiated by Toyota, and activities inherent in the network, facilitate the creation of a shared understanding of common norms among suppliers.

The study of Hansen (2002) on production innovation teams also suggest that a common understanding of knowledge needs to be created before it is transferred between knowledge sources and knowledge seekers. One important point made by Hansen is that knowledge access available to individual members in social network directly determines what can be shared in the knowing process (Hansen, 2002).

WHAT IS MISSING FROM CURRENT RESEARCH IN KS?

While current research informs on the study of knowledge sharing as a process to a great extent (Baldwin & Rice, 1997; Leckie, Pettigrew, & Sylvain, 1996; Sonnenwald & Pierce, 2000), the eye is drawn to the gap where an important point is missing: If individuals need to go through a knowing process to share knowledge and create shared understanding, what organizational factors are the most important factors in determining their exact knowledge-sharing practices?

Although current knowledge-sharing research repeatedly claims the importance of the institu-

tional environment and organizational context, they have never been able to detail the exact processes individuals go through in order to achieve their social goals and task goals, neither did they offer a systematic way in identifying crucial organizational factors motivating active human information interaction, the core of knowledge sharing. For answers to these questions, we must turn to established theories in sociology, organization behavior, and management science for additional support and investigation tools.

We must acknowledge that definition of knowledge sharing presented here is slightly different from views currently popular in the knowledge-sharing area. It emphasizes the importance of individual members' constant sense making, and their interpretation process of shared understanding for later knowledge sharing. That is, while socially constructed reality sets the boundary for human behavior, individuals' sense making and interpretation determines what exact acts they will perform. The collective practice (and its variations) of that shared understanding serves as the basis for further knowledge-sharing processes. Thus, organizational factors influencing employees' sense-making under constraints of social reality are actually fundamental to un-

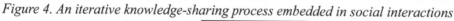

Figure 4. An iterative knowledge-sharing process embedded in social interactions

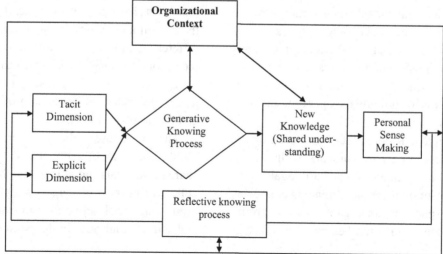

derstanding of employees' knowledge-sharing practices (Weick, 1995).

Elaborated by Figure 4, the importance of this perception of knowledge sharing will be fully displayed in the later discussion of organizational factors and their interaction with individuals' sharing behavior in daily work.

BRING IN THE ORGANIZATIONAL CONTEXT

Supported by established theories investigating individual actions and institutional environment (Barley, 1986; Barley & Tolbert, 1997), we first look at the relationships among the institutional environment, organization factors, and individual actions, where social contexts and individuals' sensemaking are related. Following is a detailed but still incomplete list of organizational factors that heavily influence knowledge sharing.

INSTITUTIONAL RULES, ORGANIZATION AND INDIVIDUAL ACTION

As argued by many researchers (Barley & Tolbert,1997; Van Maanen, 1973; Weick, 1995), human actions are constituted by ,and a constituent part of, underlying institutional rules and social organization, its explicit representation (precise or not). Therefore, social organization is actually patterned human action, interaction behavior, and cognitions that are suspended in a web of values, norms, rules, beliefs, and taken-for-granted assumptions, that are at least partially of individuals' own making (Barley, 1986). These cultural elements define the way that each role in the social web is, and how it should be played out. Therefore, social organization sets bounds on rationality by restricting opportunities and alternatives we perceive in our social roles and thereby, increases the probability of certain types of behavior (Simon, 1979).

Meanwhile, by making sense of (agreeing or disagreeing) the shared rules and typifications that identify categories of social actors and their appropriate activities or relationships (Burns & Flam, 1987; Weick, 1995), individuals dynamically define and revise their role

behavior scripts (Barley & Tolbert, 1997), tool-kit (Swidler, 1986), frame of reference (Skaalvik & Skaalvik, 2002), or behavior schema (DiMaggio, 1997). By interacting with other social actors, an individual attains his/her personal power while performing his/her role defined according to shared norms (Hamilton & Biggart, 1985). These social interactions emerge over time, become relatively stable, and take an institutionalized, although informal quality (Brass & Burkhardt, 1993).

Thus, due to the nature of knowledge as valuable resources (Argote & Ingram, 2000; Cabrera & Cabrera, 2002; Ciborra & Andreu, 2001; Hall, 2001), individuals' interactions with information is inevitably influenced by the interplay between individuals' attempts to achieve more personal power in role making, and the organizations' efforts to structure individual actions by role defining (Salancik & Preffer, 1977). This leads to the different functions played by formal and informal organizational factors on human information interactions.

FORMAL ORGANIZATIONAL FACTORS INFLUENCING KS

Formal Organizational Routines and Structure

Traditionally, managerial and organizational choice is perceived as emanating from routinized behavior (Cyert & March, 1963; Nelson & Winter, 1982). Organizations adopt elaborate structures and communication channels in order to cope with the complexity of their environments (Deutsch, 1952). Moreover, such structures embody the organization's predictions about the problems it will need to solve and members' behavior it wants to manipulate (Berger, 1979). Routines thus originated are defined as patterns that the organization might use in order to deal with problems and afford the stability that the organization needs to further develop (Feldman & Pentland, 2003; Pentland, 1995). Thus, routines set the boundaries and formal processes for individuals' role performing in organizations.

In their evolutionary work, Nelson and Winter (1982) point out the added importance of routines as organizational memory. They suggest that "the routinisation of activity in an organization constitutes the most important form of storage of the organization's specific operational knowledge (p. 99)" in the sense that they represent successful solutions to particular problems (Dosi, Winter, & Teece, 1992). What sets organizational routines as a different type of repository from other so-called knowledge warehouses, databases, and documents is its dynamic nature in storing tacit knowledge (Feldman & Pentland, 2003). In other words, routines capture the "individually- held-knowledge-applied in the firm" at its joints, particularly in its application. The powerful role played by organizational routines can be clearly observed when looking at how organizational knowledge is stored, applied, decayed, and changed in routinized business practices (Becker, 2004).

In addition, the duality of routines points to the importance of individual behavior on organizational operation when official routines are dysfunctional (Feldman & Pentland, 2003). Routines always involve people doing things, reflecting on what they are doing, and changing their behavior as a result of reflections on routines. With the accumulating changes in daily practice by individuals, routines-in-practice (Feldman & Pentland, 2003) actually change the way organizations are operating. By executing daily business routines, individuals share their understanding with colleagues and form common understandings among themselves about the "behavioral norms" (Weick,

1979). This common understanding may be the same as the previous routines so that some patterns of behavior can be maintained throughout the development of the organization. Major revisions may also be made so that the outdated patterns can be dropped. With the dynamic development of the organization, this shared behavioral norm underlies change and individuals' readjustment according to the new norms. In this way, organizational routines become a process of organizational learning executed by individuals. The effect of a functional and flexible organizational routine on human information interaction is thus, clearly demonstrated.

Formal Reward System and Motivational Factors

Knowledge work is a discretionary human behavior (Kelloway & Barling, 2000). Thus, the intensive involvement of individuals in human information (knowledge) interactions is a requirement for successful knowledge sharing (Cabrera & Cabrera, 2002).

One method that organizations may use to motivate individuals towards desirable sharing/transferring behavior is through formal reward systems, where both monetary rewards and social rewards are granted on the basis of evaluations of individuals' sharing efforts in daily work (Argote et. al., 2003). Although many studies demonstrate that the influence of a formal reward system is only somewhat effective in promoting knowledge sharing (Hooff & Ridder, 2004; Meyer & Allen, 1997), the absence of formal rewards for knowledge sharing or information transfer can send a negative message, thus, demotivating individuals from committing to such interactions (Herzberg, 1964). Therefore, studies suggest that the evaluation of knowledge-sharing efforts and active interaction of individuals should be included in the current performance evaluation system so that it can gain legitimacy among organization members (Tyler, 1997)

Cabrera and Cabrera (2002) describe another interesting type of reward system. In attempting to deal with the inefficiency of traditional formal reward mechanisms, they argue that instead of rewarding individuals for certain behavior, organizations should focus on increasing the value of collective gain, combining a knowledge exchange program with a gain-sharing or profit sharing plan (Lawler, 2000) in which every individual receives a bonus based on the success of the knowledge-sharing program. This motivating mechanism is clearly different from rewarding individuals with selective incentives (Davenport & Prusak, 1997). Since an individual is not rewarded directly for contributing to the shared databases, the motivation to contribute and get involved comes from the fact that employees receive a reward if knowledge-sharing program is successful (Cabrera & Cabrera, 2002). Thus, an individuals' commitment to the group, as well as motivations to be involved in sharing activities, is both heightened for the long term (Wiener, 1982).

Formal Communication Channel and Information Technology

As with formal reward systems, the information technology and communication channels provided by the organization are hygiene motivating factors (Herzberg, 1964) for knowledge sharing (Hendriks, 1999; Hislop, 2002; Hooff & Ridder, 2004; Roberts, 2000). In other word, although the availability of these communication channels does not motivate employees, the lack of organizational communication facilitated by information technology can demotivate individuals from participating in related activities.

In questioning the role that information technology and systems can play in knowledge sharing, Hislop (2002) discusses how certain factors can affect the dynamics of knowledge sharing and the role of information systems. The barriers he proposes for effective information and communication technology (ICT) use in knowledge sharing include: The tacitness of knowledge shared among partners; the degree of common language that exists between the parties involved in sharing; the trust that exists between relevant parties (Pan & Scarbrough, 1999; Roberts, 2000;). He concludes that the best scenario for the success of knowledge sharing through ICT is when all these barriers have been effectively removed.

Different from Hooff and Ridder (2004), who argue that information technology has no direct impact on knowledge sharing, Hendriks (1999) claims that by removing space and time difference, providing access to information, improving the process and locating knowledge carriers/seekers in the organizations, information and communication technology can affect the motivation for knowledge sharing both directly (as a hygiene factor) and indirectly (by influencing the motivation factors).

INFORMAL ORGANIZATIONAL FACTORS INFLUENCING KS

Informal Knowledge (Information) Sharing Networks and Knowledge Access

Recent studies of workplace practices indicate that the ways people actually work usually differ fundamentally from the ways organizations would describe that work in manuals, training programs, organizational charts, and job descriptions (Nelson & Winter, 1982). Hence, the embedded nature of knowledge in its social context mandates a look into the important role served by informal structure, the relationships, attitudes, and behaviors that are not fully specified in the formal scheme (Searing, 1991).

Informal organizations are important, since it would be impossible for organizations to operate (Selznick, 1943), or carry out knowledge-sharing initiatives without them. While formal organizational structures set the boundaries of informal structure, the latter, and its originated norms and values, are the main driving force of human behavior (Cobb, 1980). The informal structure bound to knowledge sharing is the informal knowledge-sharing networks in organizations (Wenger, 2000).

Most empirical studies have found that an employee's centrality in an intraorganizational network is related to the power individuals can enjoy in the organization (Krackhardt, 1990; Marsden, 1983; Tushman & Romanelli, 1983). Based on this argument, Brass and Burkhardt (1993) argued that people in central network positions might have greater access to, and potential control over, relevant resources such as information and knowledge. Therefore, positions in a knowledge-sharing network will have a direct impact on individuals' capability to access certain knowledge (Fidel & Green, 2004) and share it thereafter.

In his empirical study of 120 new product development projects, Hansen (2002) suggests that building different ties with different strengths in the organizational knowledge-sharing network under different contexts can contribute significantly to the project teams' success in securing useful knowledge for new product design. While the presence of a strong tie is essential for tacit knowledge transfer across units and new knowledge generation, a weak-tie network is more likely to be associated with non-redundant contacts and information resources. Thus, for a project team to fully explore the benefits of knowledge sharing via informal social networks, it needs to carefully decide what kind or combination of networks with different tie strengths to maintain between knowledge seekers and knowledge owners.

The benefits of different types of social networks were also investigated by Morrison (2002) in her study on the influence of informal social networks on newcomers' knowledge acquisition and sharing. Her results also suggest that different types of social networks (Informational network; friendship network) offer different benefits for the newcomers' learning of organizational knowledge, task mastery, and role clarity.

Organizational Climate and Informal Norms

The influence of organizational climate (culture) on employee behavior and motivation has been a popular topic (Denison, 1996; O'Reilly & Chatman, 1996). Defined by Tagiuri and Litwin (1968) as "the relatively enduring quality of the total [organizational] environment that (a) is experienced by the occupants, (b) influences their behavior and (c) can be described in terms of the values of a particular set of characteristics (or attributes) of the environment," nine climate dimensions are generally used to describe the organizational environment perceived by individual members: structure, responsibility, reward, risk, warmth, support, standard, conflict, and identity (Litwin & Stringer, 1968). Originating from climate, three types of organizational factors closely related to knowledge sharing are: Shared norms of individual members regarding knowledge sharing (Related to structure and responsibility) (Biggart & Hamilton, 1984; Cremer, 2002; Tyler, 1997;); Trust and reciprocity (related to reward and risk) (Dirks & Ferrin, 2001; Ostrom, 2003); and competition and promotional aspiration (related to warmth and organizational support) (Hooff & Ridder, 2003; Wiener, 1982).

As mentioned before, organizational norms underlying informal structure are the main constructing factor of individual behavior (Cremer, 2002). Scores of studies have confirmed the likelihood of conformity within small groups to their norms (Stein, 1982) and compliance to norms that persons attribute to others (Fishbein & Ajzen, 1975). Thus internalized norms shared by all members could bring positive knowledge-sharing behavior while instrumental norms could prevent group members from effectively sharing (O'Reilly, 1978; Read, 1962).

Zucker (1977) discusses the importance of shared norms in facilitating active human information interaction in organizations within and across generations. She argues that by institutionalizing the same knowledge-sharing norms and values across units and across generations, organizations can maintain uniformity of cultural understanding about knowledge sharing and information behavior, and thus maintain the tradition of knowledge-sharing related behavior.

These results have been confirmed by O'Reilly and Chatman (1996) in their study of shared norms as a social control system in organizations. From a psychological perspective, they demonstrate how a shared normative order can influence members' focus of attention, shape interpretations of events, and guide attitudes and behavior. Thus, a strong organizational climate, where knowledge sharing is highly valued, could lead to better outcomes for sharing.

When the situation strength (Mischel, 1977) of the organizational climate is not strong, that is to say, when norms in the organizational climate are insufficiently strong to provide guidance and incentives for individuals to behave in a particular way or construe particular events in a similar way (Mischel, 1977, p. 347), trust between members becomes the leading determinant factor for individuals to decide whether to actively participate in knowledge sharing (Dirks & Ferrin, 2001).

In writing about knowledge communities ("groups or organizations whose primary purpose is the development and promulgation of collective knowledge"), Kramer (1999) refers to trust as being a critical factor that influences the way knowledge is shared within these communities. According to Kramer, barriers to trust arise from perceptions that others are not contributing equally to the community or that others might exploit their own cooperative efforts. From this knowledge sharing, dilemmas emerge in the community where individuals are reluctant to share knowledge cooperatively and attempt to exploit sharing efforts made by others in the same community (Cabrera & Cabrera, 2002).

The importance of perceived trustworthiness in organizational knowledge sharing is also confirmed by Andrews and Delahaye (2000). They argue that trust plays a central role in deciding how knowledge is shared among organization members. Their study demonstrates that in the absence of trust, formal knowledge-sharing practices are insufficient to encourage individuals to share knowledge with others in the same community. Especially in a competitive working environment, members' decisions on whether to share knowledge are largely determined by the presence or absence of trust between the sharers (Read, 1962; Roberts, 2000).

Reciprocity, defined as "acts that individuals take to help others and share information without negotiation of terms and without knowledge of whether or when the other will reciprocate" (Molm, Takahashi, & Peterson, 2000), is another informal motivator for knowledge sharing that does not require the presence of a positive knowledge-sharing climate (Ipe, 2003).

Empirical evidence on the relationship between reciprocity and knowledge sharing indicates that receiving knowledge from others stimulates a reciprocal flow of knowledge in the direction of the sender both horizontally and vertically (Schulz, 2001). Support for the relationship between reciprocity and knowledge sharing is also found by Hall (2001) and Dyer and Nobeoka (2000). Similar to trust, a negative aspect of reciprocity is the fear of exploitation, which has been found to be a serious threat to knowledge sharing between individuals (Empson, 2001). Fear of exploitation can cause extreme anxiety in the knowledge-sharing community, particularly when individuals perceive that they are being asked to give away valuable knowledge without knowing what benefit they will receive in return (Ipe, 2003).

When compared to other factors with a positive influence on knowledge sharing outside a positive communication climate (Hooff & Ridder, 2004), the presence of competition and promotion aspiration revels itself as a potentially serious barrier to cooperative knowledge sharing and intraorganizational communication (Read, 1962).

In three field studies conducted in three major industrial organizations in the US, Read (1962) confirms that the stronger the mobility aspirations of subordinates, the more likely they are to communicate with supervisors in a way that maximizes positive and minimizes negative aspects. Thus, they would be likely to withhold, restrict, or distort information about the problems that they experience in their daily work. Only the positive and harmonious relationships among organizational members, particularly those who differ in formal authority, can mediate this tendency to withhold negative information.

Using two lab experiments and one field study, O'Reilly (1978) investigates the influence of competition among peers on their lateral information transfer. The results show that competition among peers can easily result in the distortion of information transmitted. This study also confirms that the mobility aspiration of subordinates can distort negative information and the free flow of accurate information among peers.

Opportunities for Effective Socialization

The last but not the least critical organizational factor we will discuss in human information interactions is the opportunity for effective socialization. While the informal organization and norms offer the possibility of knowledge generation and information communication necessity (Ipe, 2003), the socialization process is where these information and knowledge are communicated efficiently among organizational members and carried over through generations (Zucker, 1977).

According to Van Maanen and Schein (1979), what people learn about their work roles and organizational environment is often a direct result of how they learn it. Organizational socialization

is such a process whereby an individual acquires both social and task-related knowledge and the skills necessary to assume an organizational role (Blankenship, 1980). As suggested by Shibutani (1962), the perspective individuals gain through the socialization process provides an ordered view of the work life that will run ahead of and guide experiences, order and shape personal relationships in the work setting, and provide the ground rules under which everyday conduct will be managed. This perception might or might not fit with management's expectations, but it will determine the individuals' behavior (Weick, 1995) in knowledge sharing.

At the same time, individuals can change the backbone of organizational survival: the current organizational value and norm structure (Wiener, 1982). By socializing personal values and norms via watercooler chat or hallway encounters (Davernport & Prusak, 1997), individuals can share their knowledge and opinions with colleagues (Blankenship, 1980). It is also in this socialization process that new knowledge is generated and shared. Thus Van Maanen and Schein (1979) conclude that because of the ubiquity and persistence of socialization processes, management must pay close attention to the design of socialization tactics that direct individuals' behavior towards desirable directions.

By putting these organizational factors into the knowledge-sharing process model offered earlier by this chapter, we can get a model of organizational knowledge sharing. Of course, there may be more organizational factors that need to be taken into account when studying specific organizational knowledge-sharing phenomenon. However, organizational factors presented here enjoy a more salient role in shaping knowledge sharing. Systematic categorization of formal and informal organizational factors also offers a more flexible analyzing tool in accommodating additional organizational factors.

IMPLICATIONS

Theoretical Implications on KS

When organizational contexts are combined with the iterative process view of knowledge sharing, two major theoretical implications emerge to affect future studies of knowledge sharing:

1. The detailed presentation of formal and informal organizational structures, motivating factors, and communication channels used in the knowing process offers a systematic model for investigating knowledge sharing in an organizational context. Although the importance of institutional environment, organizational factors and informal organization have been stressed in previous research, this chapter is among the first attempts to systematically detail organizational factors that influence human information behavior and knowledge-sharing activity, where Organizational initiatives (formal and informal)--- Communication channels (formal and informal)--- and Motivating factors (formal and informal) for individuals' commitment are related in investigating individuals' sharing behavior. While formal organizational structure and reward systems aim to motivate employees into participating in active human information interaction, it will not occur until a knowledge-sharing-friendly organizational climate is present among organizational members. Neither will it occur if the organization lacks an informal socialization process (with or without the presence of formal tools). Thus, the presence of these six types of organizational factors is imperative for active knowledge sharing.

2. The complex nature of organizational knowledge also requires the creation of a more complex categorization of knowledge, where organizational context and knowledge shared under that context can be related.

When talking about the importance of learning and social assimilation for newcomers, Saks and Ashforth (1997) mention the importance of acquiring and integrating a wide range of new information. They point out that in order for newcomers to pursue long-term development in the organization, they must master at least four types of knowledge: (a) Organizational knowledge (knowing about the larger organizational context); (b) Task mastery (knowing how to perform the job); (c) Role clarity (knowing the responsibilities and constraints associated with one's position); and (d) Social assimilation (establishment of successful and satisfying work relationships) (Morrision, 2002).

While these four categories are all part of either the tacit dimension of knowledge or its explicit counterpart, they provide a more powerful analytic tool for integrating the organizational context of human-knowledge-related behavior.

PRACTICAL IMPLICATIONS

Knowledge Management System Design

With the introduction of this new approach towards knowledge sharing, the role played by modern information technology in knowledge management in organizations is brought to our attention again.

On one hand, the dimensionality of knowledge points to the central role of human motivation in the success of knowledge sharing; on the other, as part of the daily business practice (social context), individuals employ information systems to store information (information accumulation), exchange work-knowledge-related information (Pipek et al., 2003) and locate experts (Ackerman, 1994). Thus, when designing and implementing a knowledge management system, designers, system implementers, and managers have to pay attention to the following issues:

1. With the generation of various types of knowledge repositories, knowledge databases, and knowledge archives in organizations, managers need to make a clear distinction between information that can be stored in the system and knowledge that is accumulated in individuals' mind. Thus, the central focus of design should be on motivating human knowledge sharing and information interaction instead of trying to use the technology to transfer and share knowledge directly.

2. When designing an information system, designers, and system analysts should make sure that the operation of the system reflects how employees actually conduct their daily business. In other words, the system operation should be reflecting daily business processes. Thus, less discrepancy will be generated during installation, acceptance, and use of the new system. The buy-in of experienced workers and experts play a central role in this regard.

3. To ease the cognitive load of employees in using information stored in the system for daily work, designers, and managers should pay attention to the tradeoff between information sufficiency and specificity. In other words, while ensuring that employees can find sufficient information, managers, and designers also have to make sure that information stored in the system can be easily tailored towards the requirements of a specific knowledge-intensive task.

4. The tradeoff between system flexibility and information accessibility is something that has been discussed for a long time in IS literature. On one hand, managers, system designers, and implementers want employees to contribute what they know to the system and organizational memory, so that valuable knowledge can be accumulated for the benefit of sustainability. On the other hand, the system designers and management have to maintain the quality of information that is shared and constantly updated. How to design and install a system that can iteratively incorporate knowledge-related information contributed by individual employees while still maintaining the quality criteria for daily business practice is a constant challenge that an organization faces when initiating knowledge management in organizations.

The Balance Between Organizations Learning and Exploitation

In addition to emphasizing the central role played by motivating systems, this chapter argues that a learning environment where knowledge sharing is highly valued can greatly improve both individuals' learning efficiency (Szulanski, 1996) and the organizations' collective benefits. Thus, it suggests that the focus for management of knowledge workers should actually be switched from "knowledge" back to "workers." In other words, fundamentally, the knowledge-sharing problem is closely related to the existence of friendly organizational learning environment and individualized motivating mechanisms. Once management can solve these problems, the barriers to individuals' knowledge sharing can be expected to fall down easily.

CONCLUSION

Borrowing a process view from human information behavior research, this chapter expands on the current view of a socially constructed reality of knowledge and its sharing in the organizational context. An iterative view where the close relationship among individuals' sensemaking of organizational rules, organizational members' collective knowledge-sharing practice, and organizational initiatives embedded in a knowing process is emphasized. Thus, an alternative approach to knowledge sharing is created, and can be defined as *"The process where individuals exchange their (tacit or explicit) knowledge and jointly created new knowledge in a knowing process under certain social contexts that are also constructed out of these activities."*

In conclusion, this chapter suggests that knowledge sharing in organizations is a complex process that is value laden and driven by power equations within the organization. Knowledge in organizations is dynamic in nature, and is dependent on social relationships between individuals for its creation, sharing, and use. Thus, to launch a successful knowledge management initiative, both researchers and practitioners need to clearly identify formal and informal organizational factors that have a significant influence on individual knowledge-sharing practices, which holds the key to a successful knowledge-sharing initiative. Different from what is maintained by some research, this chapter emphasizes that we cannot afford to ignore the role that can be played by information technology with its widespread use in the organizational setting. Thus, while it is important for management to recognize the facilitating role played by information technology, they also need to clearly define the role of IT in knowledge sharing. A clear role definition of IT will surely help management face the challenge of characteristics of knowledge, generated, transferred, and shared in embedded social processes underlying organizational activities. .

FUTURE RESEARCH DIRECTIONS

While this new way of defining knowledge sharing offers us a new and comprehensive lens in studying knowledge sharing, it is very important in the future research to empirically study this process in real work practices, where interactions between individuals' sensemaking and organizational factors influence knowledge sharing can be empirically understood. Specific attention must be paid to the following questions:

- How does each factor exert its influence on individuals' information/knowledge behavior? Do they function by exerting their influence directly on individuals' knowing behavior or do they need to first go through individuals' sensemaking process?
- How do these organizational factors interact in influencing human information interaction?
- Do informal factors have stronger influence on human information behavior than formal organizational factors? How?

REFERENCES

Ackerman, M. S. (1994). Augmenting the organizational memory: A field study of Answer Garden. In R. Furuta & C. Neuwirth (Eds.), *Proceedings of CSCW'94* (pp. 243–252). Chapel Hill, NC: ACM.

Andrews, K. M., & Delahaye, B. L. (2000). Influences on knowledge processes. In Organizational learning: The psychosocial filter. *Journal of Management Studies, 37*(6), 797-810.

Argote, L., & Ingram, P. (2000). Knowledge transfer: A basis for competitive advantage in firms. *Organizational Behavior and Human Decision Processes, 82*(1), 150-169.

Argote, L., McEvily, B., & Reagans, R. (2003). Managing knowledge in organizations: An integrative framework and review of emerging themes. *Management Science, 49(4)*, 571-582.

Baldwin, N. S., & Rice, R. E. (1997). Information-seeking behavior of securities analysts: Individual and institutional influences, information sources and channels and outcomes. *Journal of the American Society for Information Science, 48*(8), 674-693.

Barley, S. R. (1986). Technology as an occasion for structuring: Evidence from observations of

CT scanners and the social order of radiology departments. *Administrative Science Quarterly, 31*, 78-108.

Barley, S. R., & Tolbert, P. S. (1997). Institution and structuration: Studying the links between action and institution. *Organization Studies, 18*(1), 93-117.

Bechky, B. (2003). Sharing meaning across occupational communities: The transformation of understanding on a production floor. *Organization science. 14*(3), 312-330

Becker, M. C. (2004). Organizational routines: A review of the literature. *Industrial Corporate Change, 13*(4), 643-677.

Berends, H. (2005). Explore knowledge sharing: Moves, problem solving and justification. *Knowledge Management Research & Practice, 3*, 97-105.

Berger, C. J. (1979). Organizational structure, attitude and behavior. *Research in Organizational Behavior, 1*, 169-208.

Biggart, N. W., & Hamilton, G. (1984). The power of obedience. *Administrative Science Quarterly, 29*, 540-549.

Blankenship, R. L. (1980). *Colleagues in organization.* Huntington, NY: Robert E. Krieger Publishing Company.

Brass, D. J., & Burkhardt, M. (1993). Potential power and power use: An investigation of structure and behavior. *Academy of Management Journal, 36*(3), 441-460.

Burger, P. L., & Luckman, T. (1966). *The social construction of reality.* Garden City, NY: Doubleday & Company.

Burns, T., & Flam, H. (1987). *The shaping of social organization.* London: Sage.

Cabrera, A. & Cabrera, E. F. (2002). Knowledge-sharing dilemma. *Organization Studies, 23*(5), 687-710.

Ciborra, C. U., & Andreu, R. (2001). Sharing knowledge across boundaries. *Journal of Information Technology, 16*(2), 73-81.

Cobb, A. T. (1980) Informal influence in the formal organization: Perceived sources of power among work unit peers. *Academy of Management Journal, 23*, 155-161.

Cook, S. N., & Brown, J. S. (1999). Bridging epistemologies: The generative dance between organizational knowledge and organizational knowing. *Organization Science, 10*(4), 381-400.

Cremer, D. D. (2002). Respect and cooperation in social dilemmas: The importance of feeling included. *Personality and Social Psychology, 28*(10), 1335-1341.

Cyert, R. M., & March, J. G. (1963). *A behavioral theory of the firm.* Englewood cliffs, NJ: Prentice-Hall.

Davenport, T. H., & Prusak, L. (1997). *Working knowledge.* Boston, MA: Harvard Business School Press.

Denison, D. R. (1996). What is the difference between organizational culture and organizational climate? A native's point of view on a decade of paradigm wars. *Academy of Management Review, 21*, 619-654.

Deutsch, A. (1952). *The mentally ill in America* (2nd ed.). New York: Columbia University Press.

DiMaggio, P. (1997). Culture and cognition. *Annual Review of Sociology, 23*, 263-287.

Dirks, T. K., & Ferrin, D. (2001). The role of trust in organizational settings. *Organization Science, 12*(4), 450-467.

Dosi, G., Winter, S. G., & Teece, D. J. (1992). Towards a theory of corporate coherence. In G. Dosi, R. Giannetti, & P. A. Toninelli (Eds.), *Technology and enterprise in a historical perspective.* Oxford, UK: Clarendon Press

Dyer, J. H., & Nobeoka, K. (2000). Creating and managing a high-performance knowledge-sharing network: The Toyota case. *Strategic Management Journal, 21,* 345-367

Empson, L. (2001). Fear of exploitation and fear of contamination: Impediments to knowledge transfer in mergers between professional service firms. *Human Relations, 54*(7), 839-862

Feldman, M. S., & Pentland, B. T. (2003). Reconceptualizing organizational routines as a source of flexibility and change. *Administrative Science Quarterly, 48*(1), 94-113.

Fernie, S., Green, S. D., Weller, S. T., & Newcombe, R. (2003). Knowledge-sharing context confusion and controversy. *International Journal of Project Management, 21,* 177-187

Fidel, R., & Green, M. (2004). The many faces of accessibility: Engineers' perception of information sources. *Information Processing and Management, 40,* 563-581.

Fishbein, M., & Ajzen, I. (1975). *Belief, attitude interaction and behavior: An introduction to theory and research.* Reading, MA: Addison-Wesley.

Gherardi, S., Nicolini D., & Odella, F. (1998). Towards a social understanding of how people learn in the organization. *Management learning, 29*(3), 273-297.

Hall, H. (2001). *Social exchange for knowledge exchange.* Paper presented at Managing knowledge: Conversations and critiques, University of Leicester Management Center, 10-11 April 2001.

Hamilton, G., & Biggart, N. W. (1985). Why people obey: Theoretical observations of power and obedience in complex organizations. *Sociological Perspectives, 28*(1), 3-28.

Hansen, T. M. (2002). Knowledge networks: Explaining effective knowledge sharing in multiunit companies. *Organization Science, 13*(3). 232-248.

Hendriks, P. (1999). Why share knowledge? The influence of ICT on the motivation for knowledge sharing. *Knowledge and Process Management, 6*(2), 91-100.

Herschel, R. T., Nemati, H., & Steiger, D. (2001). Tacit to explicit knowledge conversion: Knowledge exchange protocols. *Journal of Knowledge Management, 5*(1), 107-116.

Herzberg, F. (1964). The Motivation-Hygiene Concept and the problems of manpower. *Personnel Administration, 27,* 3-7.

Hislop, D. (2002). Mission impossible? Communicating and sharing knowledge via information technology. *Journal of Information Technology, 17,* 165-177.

Hooff, B., & de Ridder, J. A. (2004). Knowledge sharing in context: The influence of organizational commitment. Communication climate and CMC use on knowledge sharing. *Journal of Knowledge Management, 8*(6), 117-130.

Ipe, M. (2003). Knowledge sharing in organizations: A conceptual framework. *Human Resource Development Review, 2*(4), 337-359.

Kelloway, E. K., & Barling, J. (2000). Knowledge work as organizational behavior. *International Journal of Management Review, 2*(3), 287-304.

Krackhardt, D. (1990). Assessing the political landscape: Structure, cognition and power in organizations. *Administrative Science Quarterly, 35,* 342-369.

Kramer, R. M. (1999). Trust and distrust in organizations: Emerging perspectives, enduring questions. *Annual Review of Psychology, 50,* 569-598

Lave, J., & Wenger, E. (1991). *Situated learning. Legitimate peripheral participation,* Cambridge: University of Cambridge Press.

Lawler, E. E. III (2000). *Rewarding excellence.* San Francisco, CA: Jossey-Bass.

Leckie, G. J., Pettigrew, K. E., & Sylvain, C., (1996). Modeling the information seeking of professionals: A general model derived from research on engineers, health care professionals, and lawyers. *Library Quarterly, 66*(2), 161–193.

Linton, (2003). OWL: A system for the automated sharing of expertise. In M. Ackerman., V. Pipek, & V. Wulf (Eds.), *Sharing expertise.* Cambridge MA: MIT-Press.

Litwin, G., & Stringer, R. (1968). *Motivation and organizational climate.* Boston: HUP

Marsden, P. V. (1983). Restricted access in networks and models of power. *American Journal of Sociology, 88*(4), 686-717

Marshall, L. (1997). Facilitating knowledge management and knowledge sharing: New opportunities for information processionals. *Online, 21*(5), 92-98.

McGrath, J. E., & Argote, L. (2001). Group processes in organizational contexts. In M. A. Hogg & R. S. Tindale (Eds), *Blackwell handbook of social psychology, vol. 3* (pp. 603–627). Group Processes. Oxford, UK: Blackwell,.

Meyer, J. P., & Allen, N. J. (1997). *Commitment in the workplace: Theory, research, and application.* Thousand Oaks, CA: Sage Publications.

Mischel, W. (1977). The interaction of person and situation. In D. Maggusson, & N. S. Endler (Eds.), *Personality at the crossroads: Current issues in interactional psychology.* Hillsdale, NJ: Earlbaum.

Molm, L. D., Takahashi, N., & Peterson, G. (2000). Risk and trust in social exchange: An experimental test of a classical proposition. *American Journal of Sociology, 105*, 1396-1426.

Morrison, E. W. (2002). Newcomers' relationships: The role of social network ties during socialization. *Academy of Management Journal, 45*(6), 1149-1160.

Moser, P. K., & Nat, A. V. (1987). *Human knowledge.* Oxford: Oxford University Press.

Nelson, R. R., & Winter, S. G. (1982). *An evolutionary theory of economic change.* Cambridge, MA: Harvard University Press.

Nonanka, I. (1994). A dynamic theory of organizational knowledge creation. *Organization Science, 5*(1), 14-37.

Nonaka, I., & Takeuchi, H. (1995). *The knowledge creating company: How Japanese companies create the dynamics of innovation.* Oxford: Oxford University Press

O'Reilly, C. (1978). The intentional distortion of information in organizational communication: A laboratory and field investigation. *Human Relations, 31*,173-193.

O'Reilly, C. A., & Chatman, J. A. (1996). Culture as social control: Corporations, cults and commitment. *Research in Organizational Behavior, 18*, 157-200.

Ostrom, E. (2003). Toward a behavioral theory linking trust, reciprocity and reputation. In E. Ostrom & J. Walker (Eds.), *Trust and reciprocity: Interdisciplinary lessons from experimental research* (pp. 19-79). New York: Sage.

Pan, S. L., & Scarbrough, H. (1999). Knowledge management in practice: An exploratory case study. *Technology Analysis & Strategic Management, 11*(3), 359 - 374.

Pentland, B. T. (1995). Grammatical models of organizational processes. *Organization Science, 6*(5), 541-556.

Pipek, V., Hinrichs, J., & Wulf, V. (2002). Sharing expertise: Challenges for technical support. In M. Ackerman, V. Pipek, & V. Wulf (Eds), *Beyond knowledge management: Sharing expertise,* Cambridge MA: MIT-Press.

Polanyi, M. (1966). *The tacit dimension.* New York: Doubleday & Company Inc.

Polanyi, M. (1969). *Knowing and being.* London: Routledge and Kegan Paul.

Pritchard, C. (2000). Know, learn and share! The knowledge phenomena and the construction of a consumptive-communicative body. In C. Pritchard, R. Hull, M. Chumer, & H. Willmott (Eds.), *Managing knowledge: Critical investigations of work and learning.* London: MacMillan Press.

Read, W. H. (1962). Upward communication in industrial hierarchies. *Human Relations, 15*(1), 3-15

Roberts, J. (2000). From know how to show how: Questioning the role of information and communication technology in knowledge transfer. *Technology Analysis & Strategic Management, 12*(4), 429-443.

Saks, A. M., & Ashforth, B. E. (1997). Organizational socialization: Making sense of the past and pre sent as a prologue for the future. *Journal of Vocation al Behavior, 51*, 234-279.

Salancik, G. R., & Pfeffer J. (1977). Who gets power and how they hold on to it: A strategic contingency model of power. *Organizational Dynamics, 5*, 3-21.

Scarbough, H., Swan, J., & Preston, J. (1999). *Knowledge management: A literature review.* London: Institute of Personnel and Development.

Schulz, M. (2001). The uncertain relevance of newness: Organizational learning and knowledge flows. *Academy of Management Journal, 44*, 661-681.

Searing, D. D. (1991). Roles, rules and rationality in the new institutionalism. *The American Political Science Review, 85*(4), 1239-1260.

Selznick, P. (1943). An approach to a theory of bureaucracy. *American Sociological Review, 8*, 47-54.

Shannon, C., & Weaver, W. (1949). *The mathematical theory of communication.* Urbana, IL: University of Illinois Press.

Shibutani, T. (1962). Reference groups and social control. In *Human Behavior and Social Processes* (pp. 128-147). Boston, MA: Houghton Mifflin.

Simon, H. A. (1979). *Models of thought.* New Haven, CT: Yale University Press.

Skaalvik, E. M., & Skaalvik, S. (2002). Internal and external frames of reference for academic self-concept. *Educational Psychologist, 37*(4), 233-244.

Sonnenwald, D. H., & Pierce, L. (2000). Information behavior in dynamic group work contexts: Interwoven situational awareness, dense social networks and contested collaboration in command and control. *Information Processing and Management, 36*(3), 461-479.

Stein, R. T. (1982). High status group members as exemplars: A summary of field research on the relationship of status to congruence conformity. *Small Group Behavior, 13*, 3-21.

Storey, J., & Barnett, E. (2000). Knowledge management initiatives: Learning from failure. *Journal of Knowledge Management, 4*(2), 145-156.

Swidler A. (1986). Culture in action: Symbols and strategies. *American sociological Review, 51*, 273-286

Szulanski, G. (1996). Exploring internal stickiness: Impedients to the transfer of best practice. *Strategic Management Journal, 17,* 27-43.

Tagiuri, R., & Litwin, G. (1968). *Organizational climate.* Boston: Division of Research, Harvard Graduate School of Business

Tsoukas, C. & Chia, R. (2002). On organizational becoming: Rethinking organizational change. *Organization Science, 13*(5), 567-582.

Tushman, M. L., & Romanelli, E. (1983). Uncertainty, social location and influence in decision making: A sociometric analysis. *Management Science, 29*(1), 12-23.

Tyler, R. T. (1997). The psychology of legitimacy: A relational perspective on voluntary deference to authorities. *Personality and Social Psychology Review, 1*(4), 323-345.

Van Maanen, J., & Schein, E. H. (1979). Toward a theory of organizational socialization. *Research in Organizational Behavior, 1*, 209-264.

Walsh, J. P., & Ungson, G. R. (1991). Organizational memory. *Academy of Management Review, 16*, 57–91.

Weick, K. E. (1979) *The social psychology of organizing*. Reading, MA: Addison-Wesley.

Weick, K. E. (1995). *Sensemaking in organizations*. Thousand Oaks, CA: Sage Publications, Inc.

Wenger, E. (2000). Communities of practice and social learning systems. *Organization, 7*(2), 225-246

Wiener, Y. (1982). Commitment in organizations: A normative view. *Academy of Management Review, 7*(3), 418-428.

Winograd, T., & Flores, F. (1986). *Understanding computers and cognition*. Reading, MA: Addison-Wesley.

Zhao, L., & Reisman, A. (1992). Toward metaresearch on technology transfer. *IEEE Transactions on Engineering Management, 39*(1), 13-21.

Zucker, L. G. (1977). The role of institutionalization in cultural persistence. *American Sociological Review, 42*, 726-743.

ADDITIONAL READING

Bosworth, S. L., & Kreps, G. A. (1986). Structure as process: Organization and role. *American Sociological Review, 51*(5), 699-716.

Brown, J. S., & Duguid, P. (1991). Organizational learning and communities of practice: Toward a unified view of working, learning and innovation. *Organization Science, 2*(1), 40-57.

Drucker, P. F. (1999). Knowledge-worker productivity: The biggest challenge. *California Management review, 41*, 79-94.

Feldman, M. S. (2000). Organizational routines as a source of continuous change. *Organization Science, 11*(6), 611-629

Grant, R. M. (1996). Prospering in dynamically-competitive environments: Organizational capability as knowledge integration. *Organization Science, 7*(4), 375-387.

Hansen, M. T. (1999). The search-transfer problem: The role of weak tie in sharing knowledge across organization subunits. *Administrative Science Quarterly, 44*(1), 82-111.

Kim, W. C., & Mauborgne, R. A. (1998). Procedural justice, strategic decision making and the knowledge economy. *Strategic Management Journal, 19*, 323-338.

Lam, (2000). Tacit knowledge, organizational learning and societal institutions: An integrated framework. *Organization Studies, 2*(3), 487-513.

Lawler, E. E. III, Hall, D. T., & Oldham, G. R. (1974). Organizational climate: Relationship to organizational structure, process and performance. *Organizational Behavior and Human Performance, 11*, 139-155.

Levinthal, D. A., & March, J. G. (1993). The myopia of learning. *Strategic Management Jour-*

nal, 14 (Special Issue: Organizations, decision making), 95-112.

Manning, P. (1980). Talking and becoming: A view of organizational socialization. In R.L. Blankenship (Ed.), *Colleagues in Organization*. Huntington, NY: Robert E. Krieger Publishing Company.

McDermott, R., & O'Dell, C. (2001). Overcoming structural barrier to sharing knowledge. *Journal of Knowledge Management, 5*(1), 76-85.

Meyer, J. P., & Allen, N. J. (1997). *Commitment in the workplace: Theory, research, and application*. Thousand Oaks, CA: Sage Publications.

Nonaka, I. (1994). A dynamic theory of organizational knowledge creation. *Organization Science, 5*(1), 14-37.

Pentland, B. T., & Rueter, H. H. (1994). Organizational routines as grammars of action. *Administrative Science Quarterly, 39*(3), 484-510.

Selamat, M. H., & Jyoti, C. (2004). The diffusion of tacit knowledge and its implications on informa- tion systems: The role of meta-abilities. *Journal of Knowledge Management, 8*(2), 128-139.

Silverman, D. (1971). *The theory of organizations*. New York: Basic Books.

Starbuck, W. H. (1992). Learning by knowledge- intensive firms. *Journal of Management Study, 29*(7), 13–738.

Tsoukas, H. (1996). The firm as a distributed knowledge system: A constructionist approach. *Strategic Management Journal, 17(Special Issue: Knowledge and the firm)*, 11-25.

Tyler, R.T. (1999). Why people cooperate with organizations: An identity-based perspective. *Research in Organizational Behavior, 21*, 201-246.

Van Maanen, J. (1973). Observations on the making of policemen. *Human Organizations, 32*, 407-418.

Weick, K. E. (1993). Collapse of sensemaking in organizations: The Mann Gulch Disaster. *Administrative Science Quarterly, 38*, 628-652.

Chapter II
The Centrality of Team Leaders in Knowledge–Sharing Activities:
Their Dual Role as Knowledge Processors

Evangelia Siachou
Athens University of Economics and Business, Greece

Anthony Ioannidis
Athens University of Economics and Business, Greece

ABSTRACT

This chapter focuses on the extraction of accurate knowledge embedded in various Internet repositories, liable to frequent updates of content, and the effective sharing within organizational teams; an area that has not been extensively researched. We will address this issue by exploring the central and dual role of team leaders in their capacity as knowledge processors, functioning both as "sources" and "recipients" of net-based knowledge. The case of action teams that have to deal with unpredictable situations and thus, need to obtain and make instant use of accurate knowledge, is also considered. Further suggestions are made regarding team leaders' active participation in particular knowledge-sharing channels, the multifaceted nature of the knowledge exchange, the essentiality of time boundaries, as well as knowledge-search and knowledge-sharing costs. Besides making concrete suggestions, and far from exhausting the various issues in the literature of knowledge sharing, this study offers a potentially new scope for the team leader's role in the knowledge society on the Internet.

INTRODUCTION

Seeking information through Web sites has become one of the principal activities for the majority of employees working, within various organizations, who are in great need of obtaining and using new knowledge to productively carry out their daily work-related tasks (Voorbij, 1999).

The extensive implication of the World Wide Web concerns, among other issues, the easy utilization, convenience of downloaded material, retrieval speed, and numerous tools available to users that facilitate their navigation through the Web. Accordingly, both individuals and teams, within or among organizations, have vast amounts of information at their disposal (ranging from general to very specific) accessed through the knowledge embedded in various Internet repositories, which is increasing at an unprecedented rate. The Internet provides storage devices of valuable knowledge whose effective utilization assists each individual and/or work team within an organization in successfully completing assigned tasks. However, decisions concerning the extraction and use of the appropriate knowledge embedded in various Web sites are still difficult to make, especially since this body of knowledge is enormous and comes from a multitude of sources. Moreover, knowledge obtained through the Internet is liable to frequent updates of content and thus, reusing it unquestioningly is not always recommended in similar situations in the future. Such issues may not allow the members of organizational work teams to promptly and effectively utilize net-based knowledge.

More specifically, looking into the case of action teams, which operate as "knowledge communities" within an organization and which are comprised of members with special skills who have to deal with unpredictable situations, such limitations may impair their performance outcomes. That is to say, in order for members of action teams to effectively overcome difficult situations, they increasingly need to obtain, and instantly use, accurate and specific knowledge, which they do not always possess, at a faster rate (Edmondson, 2003). If this is the case, the new, incoming knowledge derived from Internet repositories (large, accessible and valuable information storage devices) may enable action teams to complete their tasks successfully.

Furthermore, in order for such a transfer of knowledge to be effective and enable action teams to make valuable use of the new knowledge acquired from outside the team, the whole process should take place within strict time constraints, in a coordinated sequence of actions (Davenport & Glaser, 2002). It should also be noted that the quality of the incoming knowledge, together with the immediate transfer to the team members, determines the effectiveness of the sharing of knowledge accessed through various Web pages. Consequently, there is a great need for a team leader to play the dual role of knowledge processor, behaving both as a knowledge "recipient" and as a "source" in the analysis, acceptance/ rejection, assimilation, sharing, and effective utilization of incoming knowledge from Internet repositories.

Taking into account the complexity of knowledge-sharing activities (Argote, McEvily, & Reegans, 2003; Darr, Argote, & Epple, 1995; Epple, Argote, & Devadas, 1991), it is expected that knowledge processors support and promote the sharing of knowledge within action teams, exhibiting a number of characteristics that could affect the efficiency of the exchange of net-based knowledge. Building on Szulanski's (1996) proposed characteristics of "sources" and "recipients" of knowledge in his prior work, team leaders, when playing the dual role of knowledge processors, need to recognize the value of incoming knowledge, make the necessary modifications in order for the newly obtained knowledge to be implemented successfully where necessary, or, similarly, to institutionalize the utilization of the incoming knowledge. The implication here is that the characteristics that knowledge processors have to manifest, in their roles as knowledge sources or knowledge recipients, affect the value of the transfer and the use of the incoming knowledge within the team and thus, could be barriers or enablers when a knowledge exchange occurs.

In addition, team leaders can share knowledge obtained from outside the team in two ways:

through "personal formal" or "personal informal" communication channels. The former is taken to mean scheduled communication activities while the latter refers to similar, though unscheduled, communication activities (Alavi & Leidner, 2001; Nelson & Cooprider, 1996). Furthermore, the level of the team leader's active or non-active participation in the aforementioned communication channels, where knowledge-sharing activities occur, affects the performance outcomes of the action teams. In particular, it is considered that the team leader's active participation in communication channels (formal or informal) will enable the members of the team to make valuable use of the incoming knowledge acquired from outside the team (i.e., accessed from Internet repositories), thus, allowing them to complete their tasks successfully, yielding beneficial performance outcomes.

THE SIGNIFICANCE OF THIS STUDY

The significance of knowledge processors examined in this chapter lies in it constituting a conceptual study aiming to approach issues concerning the valuable sharing of knowledge embedded in Internet repositories. These issues can be seen from the viewpoint of the wider field of Knowledge Management, focusing particular attention on the case of action teams. It can be said that the relationships that the proposed framework recognizes do provide some support for suggestions concerning the role of the team leaders in the effective knowledge-sharing channels, as they are part of internal core organizational activities. At the same time, scope is left for further empirical study to provide a more accurate assessment of the potential effect of team leaders' dual role in coping with the demands of the profitable exploitation of Internet-based knowledge.

In this chapter, we review the management literature on knowledge sharing, and provide a comprehensive overview of different perspectives of organizational knowledge sharing, evaluating subject-related studies by various well-known researchers in this field. This review contributes to the exemplification of the multifaceted nature of the sharing of knowledge within organizations. The subsequent section comprehensively addresses the fundamental role of knowledge processors in knowledge-sharing activities by using the case of action teams (which operate as knowledge communities) as the content of this analysis. A different perspective of knowledge sharing is provided by discussing significant issues, concepts, and ideas related to the complexity of knowledge-exchange activities. Then, an insight into the value of knowledge exchange in the performance outcomes of knowledge communities is also given. The final section compares and contrasts the fundamental role of the human factor in the knowledge transfer process and presents the general conclusions of this work. Scope is left for further study to provide a more extensive assessment of the potential ability of knowledge processors to cope with the demands of the exchange of knowledge derived from the Internet, while parallel suggestions for future research are made.

LITERATURE REVIEW

The sharing of knowledge can be generally described as a knowledge management activity that takes place within organizations when one party gains access to new knowledge through personal experience and the experiences of another party. These two parties, in turn, exchange considerations, elaborations, and modifications to the original knowledge, that broaden and add considerable value to the ongoing growth of knowledge (Cabrera & Cabrera, 2002; Hansen, Mors, & Lovas, 2005). Knowledge sharing can occur on various levels: among individuals, within teams, or among teams in an organization

(Alavi & Leidner, 2001; Argote & Ingram, 2000; Rulke, Zaheer, & Anderson, 2000). On each of these levels, there is a relationship of knowledge exchange, between a source (or sources) and a recipient (or recipients), that depends on the characteristics of everyone involved; that is to say, on the willingness or unwillingness of the source to share knowledge, and/or the recipient's absorptive capacity or lack of this capacity (Jarvenpaa & Staples, 2001; Szulanski, 1996).

Scholars in the field of knowledge management have approached knowledge sharing, from different viewpoints, by drawing a distinction between the knowledge shared within (Allen, 1977; Dahlin, Weingart, & Hinds, 2005; Hackman, 1990; Katz, 1982; Nelson & Cooprider, 1996) and outside (Ancona & Caldwell, 1992; Brown & Utterback, 1985; Cummings, 2004; Hackman, 1987) organizational subunits. In particular, a distinction has been made between the intraorganizational (Brown & Duguid, 1991; Szulanski, 1996) and interorganizational sharing of knowledge (Hardy, Philips, & Lawrence, 2003). On the intraorganizational level, the sharing of knowledge occurs among different individuals or groups within an organization comprising a network, whilst on the interorganizational level, knowledge is shared among the same subunits of the organization (e.g., group, department, or division) (Tsai, 2001). However, it is evident that in both of the aforementioned cases, the sharing of knowledge embedded in various organizational sources is positively linked with organizational effectiveness (Argote & Ingram, 2000; Argote et al., 2003) and superior performance outcome.

Moreover, other subject-related studies have focused on the nature of knowledge to be shared that can be tacit (i.e., knowledge originating from beliefs, experience and view points, and hardly codified) vs. explicit (i.e., knowledge expressed, impressed, and communicated in symbolic form and easily codified) (Polanyi, 1966), codified (i.e., knowledge embedded in a firm's electronic systems format in the form of written documents)

vs. personal (i.e., knowledge held by a firm's (talented) employees in the form of expertise) (Haas & Hansen, 2005; Hansen, Nohria, & Tierney, 1999; Nonaka & Takeuchi, 1994, 1995; Zander & Kogut, 1995), or rooted in various organizational sources vs. gained from sources outside the organization (Dushnitsky & Lenox, 2005; Inkpen & Dinur, 1998; Simonin, 1999). Knowledge can also signify the specification (know-how, crafts, skills applied in a specific context) or provide access to unique information about a product, service, or practice, that is, the knowledge in products, processes, and practices, including organizational routines, offered by organizations (Cummings, 2004; Hansen, 1999). Organizational knowledge to be shared can also vary in terms of its contribution (know-why), relatedness (know-with), context conditional (know-when) (Zack, 1998, as cited in Alavi & Leidner, 2001), and/or the usefulness of its implementation in areas of the organization where it is needed, yielding beneficial outcome.

Researchers have also approached the sharing of knowledge by analyzing informal and/or formal relations among individuals, and within teams or among teams in an organization (Ancona & Caldwell, 1992; Gupta & Govindarajan, 2000; Levin & Cross, 2004). The members of an organization (either individually or on a teamwork level) are connected to each other through developing both formal (e.g., scheduled face-to-face and/or departmental meetings, speak-up groups, conferences relevant to the tasks undertaken) and informal (e.g., unscheduled face-to-face and/or departmental meetings, coffee-break conversations) communication channels. Such (communication) channels are also dependent on the hierarchical structure dominant in the organization that they are employed (Lu, Leung, & Koch, 2006). Furthermore, such formal and/or informal structures and systems could effectively promote the sharing of knowledge within an organization (Argote & Ingram, 2000; Darr et al., 1995; Rulke et al., 2000). The relevant literature has isolated several mechanisms that could facilitate the sharing of knowledge, given the appropriate conditions: personnel movement, ongoing training, the development of formal and/or informal communication channels, patents, replications of routines, interactions with suppliers and customers, as well as different forms of organizational corporations (e.g., mergers or acquisitions, and alliances such as international joint ventures, investments in corporate venture capitals, etc.) (Argote & Ingram, 2000; Dushnitsky & Lenox, 2005; Gupta & Govindarajan, 2000; Inkpen & Dinur, 1998; Simonin, 1999).

Additionally, other scholars (Nelson & Cooprider, 1996) have used an organizational behavior perspective to propose factors that could affect the transfer of knowledge among functional groups in an organization. They have found, specifically, that mutual trust and influence increase the levels of shared knowledge between the functional groups, leading to further beneficial organizational performance outcomes. In the same vein, the role of weak ties in distributing knowledge across organizational subunits in a multiunit organization is discussed by Hansen (1999), who found that the effective exchange of complex knowledge requires strong ties among the parties involved in a knowledge-exchange activity. The same author expanded his previous work, which addressed similar issues, by developing a multiple network viewpoint and explaining the outcome of knowledge sharing that occurs in different subsets of social networks (Hansen et al., 2005). Using this perspective, other authors have focused on the specific roles (e.g., problem-solving or decision-making actors) that various parties can undertake during their participation in a knowledge-sharing process (Choo, 1996; Nohria & Ghoshal, 1997; Schulz, 2003).

The sharing of knowledge has further been conceptualized within multinational corporations as a function of several elements (e.g., the motivational tendency of the source to share its knowledge with others). Additional examined concepts within the formulation of multinational corporations include the types of embedded knowledge to be shared (organization specific, industry specific, know-how, partnering, and resource-integration knowledge), the collaborative experience, the size of the firm, and the life span of various kinds of corporations (e.g., strategic alliances, joint ventures, corporate venture capitals, mergers and acquisitions) (Simonin, 1999). In other words, organizations are viewed as repositories of knowledge and, what is more, they are also in possession of a range of different types of organizational knowledge and carriers to share it. Additionally, the ability of these organizations to share their knowledge across the corporations they have created is also examined (Inkpen & Dinur, 1998).

The notion of organizational knowledge-sharing, residing in the several different theoretical perspectives discussed, offers a broad view of the organizational context in which the sharing of knowledge takes place. Namely, the presence of an appropriate organizational context within an organization to support the sharing of knowledge is almost a prerequisite for such a process to occur. In other words, organizations have to first create the appropriate organizational culture that respects knowledge sharing and second, to establish a suitable knowledge infrastructure (i.e., the appropriate communication channels) that enhances and facilitates the exchange of knowledge among or within its constituent functional parties. Thus, the aspects of an organizational context can be summarized into the organizational culture, structure, knowledge management systems, and the relationships developed among the members of an organization, either individually or on a teamwork level (Argote & Ingram, 2000; Lu et al., 2006; Rulke et al., 2000).

Although it is very difficult to pinpoint the proper organizational context to support the sharing of organizational knowledge, it is believed that formal and informal structures and systems (i.e., formal and informal communication channels), sources and coordination of expertise, familiarity with knowledge-oriented technologies, and the behavior-framing characteristics of knowledge sharing could effectively promote the knowledge exchange within an organization. In the present work, the focus is on following specific aspects of the organizational context. Firstly, the organizational context impels employees, either individually or within their work teams, to share the specific knowledge required in order to complete their tasks effectively (appropriate organizational culture). Secondly, the structure of the organization in which they are employed facilitates the implementation of knowledge-sharing mechanisms, and also supports certain employees' actions aimed at sharing specific knowledge extracted mainly from Internet repositories (appropriate structure). Thirdly, team leaders function as knowledge processors, and their actions may increase the effectiveness of knowledge sharing (appropriate team leadership).

THEORETICAL FOUNDATIONS

The teams to be analyzed in this framework are defined as action teams, owing to the unpredictable situations that their members frequently face. In other words, the tasks undertaken by the members of such teams cannot be characterized as well-defined and static tasks. In contrast, action teams have to complete complicated tasks that are often inadequately supported by the task design, the composition of their team, and the organizational activity. These tasks can sometimes only be performed through additional access to specific and accurate knowledge derived from Internet repositories. What needs to be stressed in this situation is that this knowledge must be extracted and used within specific time constraints in a coordinated sequence of actions (Edmondson, 2003; Kanter, 1982; Masrick, 1994; Senge, 1990).

This is the main difference between action and non-action teams. More specifically, the

members of non-action teams that often deal with routine work tasks do not feel such time pressure. In case they have to assimilate knowledge from outside their team, they have time at their disposal to search for, scan, analyze, and elaborate the majority of the accessed Internet repositories in order to extract and apply the most appropriate knowledge (where it is/as it is) required. Thus, they manifest an increased participation in net-based knowledge-searching activities, in comparison with the members of action teams. Members of non-action teams are also grouped together to complete specific tasks, and are in great need of team leader's supervision, who often takes on the dual role of the knowledge processor. Owing to the fact that the routine work tasks can normally be performed without the assimilation of new knowledge, the development and the establishment of a knowledge-sharing culture depends mainly on the team leader's active participation in such activities. As opposed to routine tasks, the nature of the tasks that have been undertaken by the members of action teams presupposes a greater sense of knowledge-sharing culture and close collaboration.

From this perspective, action teams are also considered "knowledge communities." According to the organizational school's point of view, knowledge communities consist of people, with common interests, experiences, and problems, that have been formally created in order to carry out a specific task (Brown & Duguid, 1991; Earl, 2001; Ferran-Urdaneta, 1999; Lindkvist, 2005; Shanei, Sena, & Stebbins, 2000). The members of knowledge communities are bound by formal relationships, and they have to share their specific knowledge and expertise in order to complete their tasks successfully. The key features of knowledge communities, defined for the purposes of this work, are that they are supported by technology and, by the same token, operate in a behavioral framework that supports the knowledge sharing and exchange among their members, who interact with each other frequently on a routine basis. It is important to distinguish these communities from the so-called communities-of-practice, which consist of knowledge possessors bound by informal relationships that share similar roles and a common context (Lesser & Prusak, 1999). It is also important to mention here that well-known companies, like Xerox, Shell, and BP, make extensive use of knowledge communities by bringing together experts who possess large amounts of unique knowledge in order to achieve high levels of productivity by completing demanding tasks and dealing with unpredictable situations (Earl, 2001).

Another dominant issue in question is the knowledge embedded in different Internet repositories (the total of various Web sites that include subject specific archives). This knowledge is subject related to action teams' assigned tasks, and can greatly increase their productivity. From an information-technology perspective, explicit knowledge (whose latent value is revealed through its communication) (Grant, 1996, as cited in Hislop, 2002) can be codified and shared electronically; hence, it supports the information exchange through the Internet infrastructure (Swan et al., 1999, as cited in Hislop, 2002). In contrast, tacit knowledge that, according to Nonaka and Takeuchi (1994), represents the knowledge that people possess, (and is thus "highly personal"), is hard to codify in documentation and, therefore, hard to communicate, since it consists of both physical skills and a cognitive framework, which are difficult to find within particular repositories. Consequently, tacit knowledge is difficult to share electronically.

In the context of this approach to action teams within the structure of knowledge communities, the team leader's participation in knowledge-sharing activities inside that team may affect the value of the organizational net-based knowledge. Team leaders are considered to be knowledge processors, playing a fundamental role in filtering through enormous volumes of data found in numerous Internet sites, in order to pinpoint the most relevant knowledge at that point in time. In this way, they can reshape and transform such data into accessible information, which is then used by the members of the action teams to successfully complete their tasks. Therefore, it is expected of team leaders to set up the conditions required to obviate the inherent difficulties in the process of sharing knowledge. This process is, by nature, a complex series of actions that afford maximum benefit when many different components are heeded simultaneously (Davenport & Prusak, 1998; Rulke et al., 2000).

Figure 1.

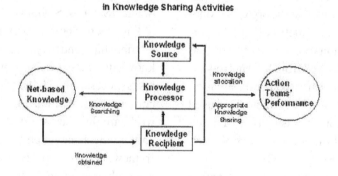

The Centrality Of Knowledge Processors
In Knowledge Sharing Activities

Figure 1 depicts the sharing of net-based knowledge within action teams. Team leaders, in their role of knowledge processors, share the net-based knowledge that has already been obtained from Internet repositories and, after the necessary elaborations made, this knowledge has been allocated for immediate implementation (as discussed in detail later on in this chapter). In turn, the knowledge processor shares the specific knowledge required with the members of the action team using either formal or informal communication channels. Finally, the members of action teams implant the incoming knowledge, making valuable use of it in order to perform their assigned tasks successfully.

THE CENTRALITY OF KNOWLEDGE PROCESSORS IN KNOWLEDGE-SHARING ACTIVITIES

Although the ability to share and assimilate Internet-derived knowledge within organizations often promises organizational success (as it has been found to improve organizational performance), effective knowledge sharing remains a problem for many organizations (Argote & Ingram, 2000; Becker, 2001; Cabrera & Cabrera, 2002; Hansen, 1999, 2002; Szulanski, 1996). A plausible explanation could be the tendency within some organizations to unquestioningly accept the unidimensional nature of intraorganizational knowledge sharing, combined with the failure to subject incoming information to sufficiently rigorous analysis (Becker, 2001). In addition, the nature of employment relations often does not ensure efficient knowledge exchange (Scarbrough, 1999), owing to lack of familiarity among employees in an organization, lack of direct relationships due to status and/or cultural differences, physical distance or, even the unwillingness on the part of the knowledge owners to distribute it to different parties in an organization (Okhuysen & Eisenhardt, 2002, see also Bechky, 1999; Hansen, 1999, 2002; Szulanski, 1996). Closely related to these knowledge-sharing obstacles is the trend followed by many organizations to employ extensive and highly advanced information technology (Knowledge Management Systems) that supports the process of knowledge sharing (Voelpel, Dous, & Davenport, 2005). Information technology alone, however, is not always adequate enough to distribute accurate and specific knowledge to the parties of the organizations where it is needed and can be used effectively (Cross & Baird, 2000; McDermott, 1999; Newell, Scarbrough, Swan, & Hislop, 1999; Newell, Scarbrough, & Swan, 2000).

Figure 2.

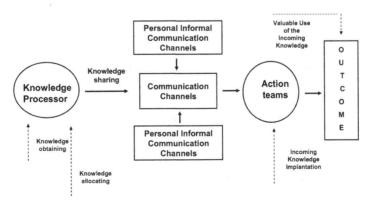

The Centrality Of Knowledge Processors

In Knowledge Sharing Activities

These elements sum up the complexity of knowledge-sharing activities by also indicating that their effectiveness is the outcome of different organizational elements. This discussion focuses on the fundamental role of team leaders in a knowledge-exchange procedure, by playing the dual role of knowledge processors, that is, by functioning both as the "source" and the "recipient" of knowledge derived from the Internet. The nature of the explicit knowledge found in various Web sites creates the need for a processor to extract the vast amount of information, and then isolate and allocate the exact knowledge that will allow the team to effectively deal with unpredictable situations. The processor must subsequently make the appropriate judgments that will, in turn, help him/her make the right decisions concerning which knowledge must be distributed among the members of the action team. These decisions are probably the most important, given the time constraints that usually accompany assigned tasks (Hult, Ketchen, Jr. & Slater, 2004; Vandenbosch & Huff, 1997).

The dual role of knowledge processors is depicted in Figure 2. The arrows indicate the activities that team leaders have to adequately perform in their dual role as knowledge processors. Specifically, knowledge processors have, first, to look for the specific knowledge required by accessing various Internet repositories. As "recipients" of net-based knowledge, team leaders have to obtain the subject-related knowledge assigned to action team tasks. As "sources" of knowledge, team leaders have to scan and allocate the appropriate amounts of knowledge needed for the instant/immediate implantation by the members of the action team. In turn, team leaders have to participate extensively in knowledge-sharing activities in order to transfer the knowledge to their team. The effectiveness of the knowledge-sharing activities is associated with the performance outcome of action teams.

In other words, the issue being analyzed is the effect that the team leader's participation in knowledge-sharing activities within the action team may have on the value of the organizational knowledge that can be found on the Internet. It is generally expected of team leaders to set up the conditions required to forestall the inherent difficulties involved in the knowledge exchange within an action team in an organization (Davenport & Prusak, 1998; Rulke et al., 2000). However, some leaders' actions may impair the effectiveness of knowledge sharing, as such leaders lack the ability to motivate team members to accept and assimilate knowledge from outside the team or are unable to exploit, or indeed efficiently search for available knowledge outside the organization.

In the present discussion, team leaders' active participation in knowledge sharing is examined in terms of their participation either in formal or informal communication channels. Specifically, personal formal communication channels refer to scheduled communication activities. Personal informal communication channels, on the other hand, refer to similar unscheduled communication activities. Furthermore, formal or informal communication tools refer to scheduled or unscheduled e-mail exchanges and phone calls, respectively (Eppler & Sukowski, 2000; Huysman & Wit, 2004).

The implication here is that the level of team leaders' participation in communication activities positively affects the knowledge-sharing procedure within their teams. When team leaders collect knowledge from outside the team through participating extensively either in formal or informal communication activities, they enable the members of action teams to obtain, within time constraints, the specific new knowledge required to successfully deal with unpredictable situations, which are a common part of action teams' daily work. Thus, team leaders take on the role of processor, as earlier described. Team leaders are also viewed by the action team as "sources" of the necessary knowledge in order to increase their performance outcome. As a result, effective knowledge-sharing procedures contribute so that the members of action teams are aptly informed on the rapid and ongoing changes occurring in their work environment and affecting their daily performance. Also, as the level of team leaders' participation in knowledge exchange increases, the uncertainty that the members of action teams may feel about the immediate gathering and allocation of the required knowledge from outside the team decreases.

Another basic element closely related to the high levels of team leaders' participation in either formal or informal communication activities is the frequency with which communication occurs. Prior research (Allen, 1977; Ancona & Caldwell, 1992; Nilakanta & Scamell, 1990; Uzzi & Gillespie, 2002) supports that well-constructed communication channels together with adequately frequent communication are good predictors of effective knowledge-exchange activities. In other words, it is suggested that teams that demonstrate a high frequency of communication are positively affected by the value of the incoming knowledge extracted from the Internet, thus, achieving a higher performance rate as opposed to those teams whose members rarely communicate.

An additional benefit of team leaders' active participation in the knowledge-sharing process is that team members do not have to be involved in knowledge-search activities. That is to say, the members of action teams do not devote time to searching the Internet repositories, and can thus concentrate fully on their tasks. What needs to be stressed here is that when team members have to discuss and evaluate information from the Internet, in order to complete their tasks productively, they often fail to perform at capacity. Indeed, there is also the likelihood of action-team members avoiding to deal with a situation that requires them to assimilate knowledge from outside the team.

We can look, for instance, at the case of consulting teams that need to obtain knowledge related to their projects, in an ongoing, updated format, by downloading archives from various Internet repositories. The consultants have, in turn, to work with such knowledge in order to offer the appropriate advice to their clients. The central-ity of a team leader (playing the dual role of the knowledge processor) in this process can keep the consultants away from the time-consuming information gathering, scanning, and analyzing. Thus, they have more time at their disposal to provide superior customer service on time, also being of major significance for the organization's performance (outcome) as well.

Knowledge-sharing activities, even when coordinated, are, by nature, time consuming, and likely to impair the expected performance outcomes, when the conditions appropriate for obviating the inherent difficulty of knowledge transfer are not established (Haas & Hansen, 2005). In the case of the action teams mentioned previously, transfer costs could be determinative factors in the team's performance outcomes. Members of action teams that have to deal with unprecedented situations, and have to complete their tasks within time limits, are more likely to be affected by search and transfer costs. More specifically, search and transfer costs include the considerable amount of time spent searching in order to identify the appropriate new knowledge required, as well as the effort to effectively distribute this knowledge within the action teams.

Through a coordinated sequence of procedures (Davenport & Glaser, 2002; Hansen, 1999), the action teams that are in greater need of obtaining and using accurate and specific knowledge instantaneously are affected by knowledge-searching and knowledge-sharing activities only when they last for a short time; time-consuming activities of that kind may impair the action teams' performance, since the members of the teams will not be able to meet the estimated task completion time (i.e., to overcome the unpredictable situations on schedule).

A number of organizations that promote knowledge-management activities often emphasize the great need to motivate employees to exploit several online sources of information in order to obtain the necessary knowledge for their tasks to be completed successfully (Haas & Hansen, 2005). The rationale behind these incentive practices is that they may increase the willingness of employees to learn how to assimilate new knowledge, while simultaneously increasing the stock of already existing organizational knowledge (Gupta & Govindarajan, 2000). However, the establishment of incentive practices, which may come to dominate organizations and urge team members to search, discuss, and evaluate all knowledge derived from the Internet, does not yield the desired task performance outcomes; rather, it increases the risk of a poor organizational outcome. In addition, the nature of the tasks that action teams have to perform is a significant factor that determines the role of a team leader in the exchange of organizational knowledge within the team. Action teams comprised of members with special skills, who have to deal with unpredictable situations, are in greater need of obtaining and using accurate and specific knowledge from outside the team within time constraints, in a coordinated sequence of actions (Edmondson, 2003). Consequently, increased pressure on action teams to obtain and use knowledge from the Internet decreases the chances of their members completing tasks on time, and obtaining and using the appropriate knowledge in order to perform these tasks successfully. This implies that the absence of appropriate active participation of team leaders in the sharing of knowledge prevents the desired team's, and thus the organization's, performance outcomes from being achieved.

Hence, it is expected of team leaders, functioning both as the "source" and the "recipient" in knowledge exchange, to support and promote the desired culture for effective knowledge sharing among the members of the action teams they lead. In so doing, knowledge processors have to manifest a number of characteristics [notably an absorptive and/or retentive capacity, (Szulanski, 1996)], which could be conceptualized as constraint variables (in their absence) or enabling variables (when they exist) in knowledge-sharing activities. More specifically, Szulanksi (1996) tested motivational and knowledge-related fac-

tors, such as the recipient's lack of absorptive capacity and/or retentive capacity, concluding that specific characterizations of the source or recipient of knowledge could be barriers or enablers in a knowledge exchange.

Taking into account these distinct characteristics, it is further assumed that the leaders of action teams, when playing the role of the "recipients" of knowledge obtained through a range of net-based sources, have to exhibit high levels of absorptive capacity, meaning that they should be able to appreciate the latent value of knowledge, making any necessary modifications so that the incoming knowledge can be implemented effectively where necessary (Szulanski, 1996, see also Cohen & Levinthal, 1990; Dushnitsky & Lenox, 2005). Additionally, the recipients of knowledge have to be capable of detecting the dysfunctions that the assimilation of incoming knowledge may cause within the action teams, and to promote the valuable utilization of the new knowledge acquired from net-based storage devices. Furthermore, from the point of view of "sources" of knowledge, team leaders have to manifest high levels of retentive capacity, meaning that they have to be able to institutionalize the utilization of that incoming knowledge. Moreover, as "sources" of new knowledge, the team leaders also have to develop the appropriate competences (e.g., technical skills) so as to update the stock of knowledge that they possess on an ongoing basis. This also requires thorough familiarity with the changes occurring in the work environment; a comprehensive awareness concerning the increasing and frequently changing demands on the part of the team.

KNOWLEDGE PROCESSORS VS. TECHNOLOGIES

Trends in organizations currently view organizational knowledge as invaluable information that can be used practically, and whose effective utilization is often assessed by measuring task performance outcomes (Haas & Hansen, 2005). Although organizations are increasingly making efforts to control the amounts of ever-increasing knowledge, and to acquire and distribute it among the organizational action teams that need new knowledge from outside their team boundaries, knowledge processing still does not easily meet the demanding objectives of those teams. Therefore, new models and frameworks should be developed.

In the case of the action teams discussed previously, most of the knowledge needed in order for the members of these teams to perform their day-to-day activities productively can be found online. Not only does the knowledge in question have to be extracted, but its value and accuracy also have to be legitimated at the same time. Team leaders, who play the dual role of knowledge processors by participating in net-based knowledge-sharing activities, obviate their inherent difficulties and therefore, achieve better performance for the team and for the organization as a whole. The proposed framework defines new roles for team leaders who have to enrich and transform their roles from that of mediators, who merely handle awareness and manage stocks of organizational knowledge, into facilitators, who conceive and develop mechanisms in order to isolate the appropriate net-based knowledge and communicate it effectively to their teams.

The role of the knowledge processor, as discussed in detail earlier in this chapter, determines the primary responsibility of team leaders to manage the vast amounts of information from a multitude of net-based sources and then share it effectively among the members of action teams. The key factor here is that the knowledge distribution is valuable to action teams by enhancing their performance if knowledge, in its most updated and appropriate version, is instantly used when it is needed (Davenport & Glaser, 2002). Thus, the focus of knowledge-sharing initiatives has to be more on the person responsible for collecting and managing the knowledge to be processed. In

their dual role as recipients of knowledge derived from the Internet, and as sources of net-based knowledge, knowledge processors enhance the practical value of the information found in Internet repositories.

The significance of the dual role of knowledge processors stresses the human role in knowledge-sharing activities, which cannot be effectively replaced with technologies. In particular, the team leader of an action team is responsible for a spectrum of specific actions: (i) decisions concerning the extraction and use of the accurate knowledge embedded in various Web sites, (ii) tracking the frequent updates of knowledge content provided on the Internet, and (iii) the provision of the appropriate knowledge to members of the action teams on time. Arguably, some organizations make extensive use of knowledge technologies, namely repositories of structured knowledge; explicit knowledge often in document form in order to search and retrieve the knowledge appropriate for each work application. Some examples of these are various specific software programs like Lotus Notes, processes for managing project documents like Intranet Webs, databases like Online Thesaurus, and yellow page type systems like Expert Locator, and Knowledge-Based Systems. The last are also known as Expert Systems like Knowledge Domains, Constraint-Based Systems, and Case-Based Reasoning. It is also considered that technologies of this kind facilitate the sharing of organizational knowledge. In practice, "tech-knowledgy"[1] facilitates the knowledge-sharing services; however, its effectiveness is dependent on the human factor who properly uses these technologies.

Another tech-case is "ontologies," which operates as libraries of reusable knowledge components (Easterby-Smith, Snell, & Gherardi, 1998). It is commonly believed that knowledge libraries of this kind enable the sharing of organizational knowledge by giving everyone the opportunity to gain access to these online repositories to extract the knowledge needed. Nevertheless, the dual role of team leaders examined in this chapter is not limited to the effective exchange and communication of knowledge. It decreases the time for searching and accumulating the appropriate knowledge required that is crucial for action teams that increasingly need to quickly obtain and instantly use accurate knowledge for their daily work tasks. Another considerable point is that the software of "ontologies" that contains reusable knowledge is quite difficult to update regularly, thus, the chances of missing relevant up-to-date information increase.

Consequently, the knowledge technologies applied extensively by many organizations aiming at effective knowledge-sharing activities facilitate the exchange and the communication of net-knowledge along with the contribution of the human factor. The specific range of actions performed by team leaders cannot be replaced by knowledge technologies. The significance of technology is that "smart" sources of general knowledge are created and are accessible to everyone involved in specific work tasks. Nevertheless, the addition of more specific knowledge applicable to specific work cases cannot be offered to members of teams, and especially to action teams, within strict time constraints, where meeting the deadline is crucial for their performance.

CONCLUSION

We have found that the most important condition for the analysis of knowledge sharing is the focus on the complexity and multifaceted nature of this activity and thus, on how knowledge can be shared effectively. This chapter has focused on knowledge derived from the Internet, and has highlighted the dual role of the team leader as a "source" of the knowledge required for action teams to complete assigned tasks successfully, as well as a "recipient" of knowledge obtained from outside the team. In particular, the characteristics of knowledge embedded in various Internet re-

positories do not allow for the instant utilization of this knowledge by the members of action teams. Moreover, what needs to be pointed out here is the difference between net-based knowledge and organizational knowledge, such as documents or texts (i.e., knowledge in its codified type), or knowledge possessed by employees in an organization (i.e., knowledge in its personal type). The former consists of previously unexploited information extracted from various Web sites, whilst the latter is found to be the stock of knowledge that organizations have gained through dealing with a variety of problematic situations earlier on (Olivera, 2000). Thus, net-based knowledge cannot be put into valuable use for an organization if it is not implemented within the right context. For this to take place, knowledge processors have to make the right judgments.

It is suggested that knowledge processors play a central role in the effectiveness of knowledge processing within their teams. Nonetheless, many organizational factors, such as the appropriate organizational and technological infrastructure (e.g., information services), corporate vision, and mission statements that support a culture promoting knowledge sharing (Javidan, Stahl, Brodbeck, & Wilderom, 2005; Voelpel et al., 2005) may also determine the value of the net-based knowledge exchange. The focus of this analysis has been on the level of team leaders' active participation in knowledge-sharing activities regardless of the quality and the quantity of the knowledge derived from the Internet. Indeed, high levels of team leaders' active participation reflect the effectiveness of knowledge-sharing activities and thus, lead to a better performance for the team and for the organization as a whole. Moreover, the characteristics that team leaders manifest in playing the dual role of knowledge processors are found to function as enablers (if they exist) when a knowledge exchange occurs within the action teams of an organization.

The current focus is not only on the quantity and the quality of knowledge that can be found on the Internet, but also on the factors that prevent employees from using such knowledge resources ineffectively. Internet repositories do provide knowledge of significant importance, the implementation of which is often necessary for action teams to overcome the unpredictable problems that they face in their day-to-day activities. Nevertheless, the value-added benefits of net-based knowledge do not originate from the mere extensive use of popular Web sites. In this case, employees are likely to be overwhelmed and thus, incapacitated by the sheer bulk of the available knowledge rather than energized and motivated to make valuable use of the comprehensive implementation of this knowledge (Wildavsky, 1983). The framework discussed in this chapter identifies the fundamental role of knowledge processors and numerous factors related to action teams that can add value to net-based knowledge-sharing activities. It is further supported that the amounts of knowledge provided on various Internet repositories can be turned into core organizational and intangible assets when they are placed in the appropriate context (Gold, Malhotra, & Segars, 2001). In particular, the fundamental role of knowledge processors, as discussed in this chapter, determines this context.

The final purpose of this study is to facilitate organizations in making valuable use of knowledge embedded in Internet repositories and thus, gain benefits and achieve further development by focusing mainly on the fundamental role of knowledge processors in the sharing of this knowledge. In addition, scope is left for further investigation of additional features, as indicated earlier, that will also enable an organization to cope with the demands of the sharing of knowledge derived from the Internet successfully.

FUTURE RESEARCH DIRECTIONS

In order for knowledge processors to perform their dual role efficiently, they should manifest a number of characteristics such as absorptive or retentive capacity, as mentioned in the main part of the chapter. What is proposed here is that these characteristics should be interpreted as constraint variables in the absence of knowledge processors, or enabling variables where they exist. Future research should also concentrate on the conceptualization of these characteristics, again as constraint or enabling variables that have to be manifested not only by knowledge processors, but also by the members who make up action teams. Prior research (Dahlin et al., 2005; Haas & Hansen, 2005; Hackman, 1990; Katz, 1982) has identified several variables, such as team size (the maximum number of individuals involved in the team), team skills diversity (the educational background of the members involved in the team), team cognition (familiarity with knowledge related to the assigned tasks), and team turnover homogeneity (the time team members spend working together), that have an impact on the effectiveness of knowledge-sharing activities within organizational teams. Other characteristics, such as technical competences, clear division of roles and responsibilities within the team, familiarity with the work environment, or adaptability to situations not experienced before, however, may be factors that have not been considered in this chapter, but that may influence the broader content of the sharing of net-based knowledge.

This work has also shown great interest in action teams that work as "knowledge communities." The key feature of these knowledge communities is that they are created to carry out a specific task (Earl, 2001). This leads to further research on the issue of how to retain the knowledge that the members of action teams possess. In other words, after the specific task has been carried out, knowledge communities are usually disbanded. Thus, the amounts of knowledge derived from the Internet and effectively used by the members of knowledge communities, is now obviously in the possession of both the team leader and the members of the communities. Therefore, the way to store this net-based knowledge so as to be reused in its updated form (Hoopes & Postrel, 1999; Olivera, 2000) is another element of major importance that needs further consideration. Prior research has indicated that communities which may have facilitated "knowledge flows" internally among their members, may still limit knowledge flows across communities and in this way, place barriers to sharing knowledge throughout different organizational parties (Dennis, 1996; Gupta & Govindarajan, 2000). Accordingly, the factors to be analyzed are those that facilitate the net-based knowledge flows among organizational knowledge communities in situations where either knowledge communities exist simultaneously within the same organization, or one knowledge community is created after the disbanding of another for similar business purposes.

REFERENCES

Alavi, M., & Leidner, D. (2001). Knowledge management and knowledge management systems: Conceptual foundations and research issues. *MIS Quarterly, 25*(1), 107-136.

Allen, T. (1977). *Managing the flow of technology.* Cambridge, MA: MIT Press.

Ancona, D., & Caldwell, D. (1992). Bridging the boundary: External activity and performance in organization teams. *Administrative Science Quarterly, 37*(4), 634-665.

Argote, L., & Ingram, P. (2000). Knowledge transfer: A basis for competitive advantage in firms. *Organizational Behavior and Human Decision Processes, 82*(1), 150-169.

Argote, L., McEvily, R., & Reegans, R. (2003). Managing knowledge in organizations: An integrative framework and review of emerging themes. *Management Science, 49*(4), 571-582.

Becker, M. (2001). Managing dispersed knowledge: Organizational problems, managerial strategies, and their effectiveness. *Journal of Management Studies, 38*(7), 1037-1051.

Bechky, B. (1999). *Creating shared meaning across occupational communities: An ethnographic study of a production floor.* Paper presented at the annual meeting of the Academy of Management, Chicago, IL.

Becker, M. (2001). Managing dispersed knowledge: Organizational problems, managerial strategies, and their effectiveness. *Journal of Management Studies, 38*(7), 1037-1051.

Brown, J. W., & Utterback, J. (1985). Uncertainty and technical communication patterns. *Management Science, 31*(3), 301-311.

Brown, J. S., & Duguid, P. (1991). Organizational learning and communities-of-practice: Toward a unified view of working, learning, and innovation. *Organization Science, 2*(1), 40-57.

Brown, J. W., & Utterback, J. (1985). Uncertainty and technical communication patterns. *Management Science, 31*(3), 301-311.

Cabrera, A., & Cabrera, E. (2002). Knowledge-sharing dilemmas. *Organization Studies, 23*(5), 687-710.

Cohen, W., & Levinthal, D. (1990). Absorptive capacity: A new perspective on learning and innovation. *Administrative Science Quarterly, 35*(1), 128-152.

Choo, C. (1996). The knowing organization: How organizations use information to construct meaning, create knowledge, and make decisions. *International Journal of Information Management, 16*(5), 329-340.

Cohen, W., & Levinthal, D. (1990). Absorptive capacity: A new perspective on learning and innovation. *Administrative Science Quarterly, 35*(1), 128-152.

Cross, R., & Baird, L. (2000). Technology is not enough: Improving performance by building organizational memory. *Sloan Management Review, 41*(3), 69-78.

Cummings, J. (2004). Work groups, structural diversity, and knowledge sharing in a global organization. *Management Science, 50*(3), 352-364.

Dahlin, K., Weingart, L., & Hinds, P. (2005). Team diversity and information use. *Academy of Management Journal, 48*(6), 1107-1123.

Darr, E., Argote, L., & Epple, D. (1995). The acquisition, transfer, and depreciation of knowledge in service organizations: Productivity in franchises. *Management Science, 41*(11), 1750-1762.

Davenport, T., & Prusak, L. (1998). *Working knowledge: How organizations manage what they know.* Boston, MA: Harvard Business School Press.

Davenport, T., & Glaser, J. (2002). Just-in-time delivery comes to Knowledge Management. *Harvard Business Review, 80*(7), 107-111.

Davenport, T., & Prusak, L. (1998). *Working knowledge: How organizations manage what they know.* Boston, MA: Harvard Business School Press.

Dennis, A. (1996). Information exchange and use in group decision making: You can lead a group to information, but you can't make it think. *MIS Quarterly, 20*(4), 433-457.

Dushnitsky, G., & Lenox, M. (2005). When do incumbents learn from entrepreneurial ventures? Corporate venture capital and investing firm innovation rates. *Research Policy, 34*(5), 615-639.

Earl, M. (2001). Knowledge management strategies: Toward a taxonomy. *Journal of Management Information Systems 18*(1), 215-233.

Easterby-Smith, M, Snell, R., & Gherardi, S. (1998). Organizational learning: Diverging communities of practice? *Management Learning, 29*(3), 259-272.

Edmondson, A. (2003). Speaking up in the operating room: How team leaders promote learning in interdisciplinary action teams. *Journal of Management Studies, 40*(6), 1419-1452.

Epple, D., Argote, L., & Devadas, R. (1991). Organizational learning curves: A method for investigating intraplant transfer of knowledge acquired through learning by doing. *Organization Science, 2*(1), 58-70.

Eppler, M., & Sukowski, O. (2000). Managing team knowledge: Core processes, tools and enabling factors. *European Management Journal, 18*(3), 334-341.

Ferran-Urdaneta, C. (1999). Teams or communities? Organizational structures for knowledge management. In ACM SIGCPR (Ed.), *Conference on Computer Personnel Research* (pp. 128-134). New York, NY: ACM Press.

Gold, A., Malhotra, A., & Segars, A. (2001). Knowledge management: An organizational capabilities perspective. *Journal of Management Information Systems, 18*(1), 185-214.

Grant, R. (1996). Toward a knowledge-based theory of the firm. *Strategic Management Journal, 17*(*Winter Special Issue*), 109-122.

Gupta, A., & Govindarajan, V. (2000). Knowledge flows within multinational corporations. *Strategic Management Journal, 21*(4), 473-496.

Haas, M., & Hansen, M. (2005). When using knowledge can hurt performance: The value of organizational capabilities in a management consulting company. *Strategic Management Journal, 26*(1), 1-24.

Hackman, J. (1987). The design of work teams. In J. Lorsh (Ed.), *Handbook of organizational behavior* (pp. 315-342). Englewood Cliffs, NJ: Prentice Hall.

Hackman, R. (Ed.). (1990). *Groups that work and those that don't: Creating conditions for effective teamwork.* San Francisco: Jossey-Bass.

Haas, M., & Hansen, M. (2005). When using knowledge can hurt performance: The value of organizational capabilities in a management consulting company. *Strategic Management Journal, 26*(1), 1-24.

Hansen, M., Nohria, N., & Tierney, T. (1999). What's your strategy for managing knowledge? *Harvard Business Review, 77*(2), 106-116.

Hansen, M. (1999). The search-transfer problem: The role of weak ties in sharing knowledge across organization subunits. *Administrative Science Quarterly, 44*(1), 82-111.

Hansen, M. (2002). Knowledge networks: Explaining effective knowledge sharing in multi-unit companies, *Organization Science, 13*(3), 232-248.

Hansen, M., Mors, M., & Lovas, B. (2005). Knowledge sharing in organizations: Multiple networks, multiple phases. *Academy of Management Journal, 48*(5), 776-793.

Hansen, M., Nohria, N., & Tierney, T. (1999). What's your strategy for managing knowledge? *Harvard Business Review, 77*(2), 106-116.

Hardy, C., Philips, N., & Lawrence, T. (2003). Resources, knowledge and influence: The organizational effectiveness of interorganizational collaboration. *Journal of Management Studies, 40*(2), 321-347.

Hislop, D. (2002). Mission impossible? Communicating and sharing knowledge via information technology. *Journal of Information Technology, 17*(3), 165-177.

Hoopes, D., & Postrel, S. (1999). Shared knowledge, "glitches," and product development performance. *Strategic Management Journal, 20*(9), 837-865.

Huysman, M., & de Wit, D. (2004). Practices of managing knowledge sharing: Towards a second wave of knowledge management. *Knowledge and Process Management, 11*(2), 81-92.

Hult, T., Ketchen, Jr. D., & Slater, S. (2004). Information processing, knowledge development, and strategic supply chain performance. *Academy of Management Journal, 47*(2), 241-253.

Huysman, M., & de Wit, D. (2004). Practices of managing knowledge sharing: Towards a second wave of knowledge management. *Knowledge and Process Management, 11*(2), 81-92.

Inkpen, A., & Dinur, A. (1998). Knowledge management processes and international joint ventures. *Organization Science, 9*(4), 454-468.

Jarvenpaa, S., & Staples, S. (2001). Exploring perceptions of organizational ownership of information and expertise. *Journal of Management Information Systems, 18*(1), 151-183.

Javidan, M., Stahl, G., Brodbeck, F., & Wilderom, C. (2005). Cross-border transfer of knowledge: Cultural lessons from project GLOBE. *Academy of Management Executive, 19*(2), 59-76.

Kanter, R. M. (1982). Dilemmas of managing participation. *Organizational Dynamics, 11*(1), 5-27.

Katz, R. (1982). The effects of group longevity on project communication and performance. *Administrative Science Quarterly, 27*(1), 81-104.

Levin, D., & Cross, R. (2004). The strength of weak ties you can trust: The mediating role of trust in effective knowledge transfer. *Management Science, 50*(11), 1477-1490.

Lesser, E., & Prusak, L. (1999). Communities of practice, social capital and organizational knowledge. In E. Lesser, M. Fontaine, & J. Slusher (Eds), *Knowledge and communities.* Woburn, MA: Butterworth-Heinemann.

Lindkvist, L. (2005). Knowledge communities and knowledge collectivities: A typology of knowledge work in groups. *Journal of Management Studies, 42*(6), 1189-1210.

Lu, L. Leung, K., & Koch, P. (2006). Managerial knowledge sharing: The role of individual, interpersonal and organizational factors. *Management and Organization Review, 2*(1), 15-41.

Masrick, V. J. (1994). Trends in managerial reinvention: creating a learning map. *Managerial Learning, 25*(1), 11-34.

McDermott, R. (1999). Why information technology inspired but cannot deliver knowledge management. *California Management Review, 41*(4), 103-117.

Nelson, K., & Cooprider, J. (1996). The contribution of shared knowledge to IS group performance. *MIS Quarterly, 20*(4), 409-432.

Newell, S., Scarbrough, H., Swan, J., & Hislop, D. (1999). Intranets and knowledge management: Complex processes and ironic outcomes. In IEEE Computer Society (Ed.), *32nd Annual Hawaii International Conference on System Sciences: Vol. 1. HICSS-32* (pp.10-27). Los Alamitos, CA: IEEE Computer Society.

Newell, S., Scarbrough, F., & Swan, J. (2000). Intranets and knowledge management: De-centred technologies and the limits of technological discourse. In C. Prichard, R. Hull, M. Chumer, & H. Willmott (Eds.), *Managing knowledge: Critical investigations of work and learning* (pp. 88-106). London, UK: Macmillan Business.

Newell, S., Scarbrough, H., Swan, J., & Hislop, D. (1999). Intranets and knowledge management: Complex processes and ironic outcomes. In IEEE Computer Society (Ed.), *32nd Annual Hawaii International Conference on System Sciences: Vol. 1. HICSS-32* (pp.10-27). Los Alamitos, CA: IEEE Computer Society.

Nilakanta, S., & Scamell, R. (1990). The effect of information sources and communication channels on the diffusion of innovation in a data base development environment. *Management Science, 36*(1), 24-40.

Nonaka, I., & Takeuchi, H. (1995). *The knowledge-creating company: How Japanese companies create the dynamics of innovation.* Oxford, UK: Oxford University Press.

Nonaka, I., & Takeuchi, H. (1994). A dynamic theory of organizational knowledge creation. *Organization Science, 5*(1), 14-37.

Nohria, N., & Ghoshal, S. (1997). *The differentiated network: Organizing multinational corporations for value creation.* San Francisco: Jossey-Bass.

Nonaka, I., & Takeuchi, H. (1994). A dynamic theory of organizational knowledge creation. *Organization Science, 5*(1), 14-37.

Nonaka, I., & Takeuchi, H. (1995). *The knowledge-creating company: How Japanese companies create the dynamics of innovation.* Oxford, UK: Oxford University Press.

Okhuysen, G., & Eisenhardt, K. (2002). Integrating knowledge in groups: How formal interventions enable flexibility. *Organization Science, 13*(4), 370-386.

Olivera, F. (2000). Memory systems in organizations: An empirical investigation of mechanisms for knowledge collection, storage and access. *Journal of Management Studies, 37*(6), 811-832.

Polanyi, M. (1966). *The tacit dimension.* London, UK: Routledge & Kegan Ltd.

Rulke, D., Zaheer, S., & Anderson, M. (2000). Sources of managers' knowledge of organizational capabilities. *Organizational Behavior and Human Decision Processes, 82*(1), 134-149.

Scarbrough, H. (1999). Knowledge as work: Conflicts in the management of knowledge workers.

Technology Analysis and Strategic Management, 11(1), 5-16.

Schulz, M. (2003). Pathways of relevance: Exploring inflows of knowledge into subunits of multinational corporations. *Organization Science, 14*(4), 440-459.

Senge, P. (1990). *The fifth discipline: The art and practice of the learning organization.* London, UK: Random House.

Shanei, A., Sena, J., & Stebbins, M. (2000). Knowledge work teams and groupware technology: Learning from Seagate's experience. *Journal of Knowledge Management, 4*(2):111-124.

Simonin, B. (1999). Transfer of marketing know-how in international strategic alliances: An empirical investigation of the role and antecedents of knowledge ambiguity. *Journal of International Business Studies, 30*(3), 463-490.

Swan, J., Newell, S., Scarbrough, H., & Hislop, D. (1999). Knowledge management and innovation: Networks and networking. *Journal of Knowledge Management, 17*(2), 109-122.

Szulanski, G. (1996). Exploring internal stickiness: Impediments to the transfer of best practice within the firm. *Strategic Management Journal, 17*(Winter Special Issue), 27-43.

Tsai, W. (2001). Knowledge transfer in intraorganizational networks: Effects of network position and absorptive capacity on business unit innovation and performance. *Academy of Management Journal, 44*(5), 996-1004.

Uzzi, B., & Gillespie, J. (2002). Knowledge spillover in corporate financing networks: Embeddedness and the firm's debt performance. *Strategic Management Journal, 23*(7), 595-618.

Vandenbosch, B., & Huff, S. (1997). Searching and scanning: How executives obtain information from executive information systems. *MIS Quarterly, 21*(1), 81-107.

Voelpel, S., Dous, M., & Davenport, T. (2005). Five steps to creating a global knowledge-sharing system: Siemens' ShareNet. *Academy of Management Executive, 19*(2), 9-23.

Voorbij, H. J. (1999). Searching scientific information on the Internet: A Dutch academic user survey. *Journal of American Society for Information Science, 50*(2), 598-615.

Wildavsky, A. (1983). Information as an organizational problem. *Journal of Management Studies, 20*(1), 29-40.

Zack, M. (1998). An architecture for managing explicated knowledge. *Sloan Management Review, 39*(4), 45-58.

Zander, U., & Kogut, B. (1995). Knowledge and the speed of the transfer and imitation of organizational capabilities: An empirical test. *Organization Science, 6*(1), 76-92.

ADDITIONAL READING

Boisot, M., & Griffiths, D. (1999). Possession is nine tenths of the law: Managing a firm's knowledge base in a regime of weak appropriability. *International Journal of Technology Management, 17*(6), 662-676.

Boland, R., & Tenkasi, R. (1995). Perspective making and perspective taking in communities of knowing. *Organization Science, 6*(4), 350-372.

Bolisani, E., & Scarso, E. (1999). Information technology management: A knowledge-based perspective. *Technovation, 19*(4), 209-217.

Collis, D. J. (1994). Research note: How valuable are organizational capabilities? *Strategic Management Journal, 15*(Winter Special Issue), 143-152.

Davenport, T., De Long, D. W., & Beers, M. C. (1997). Building successful knowledge management projects. In T. Davenport, J. Gilbert, B. Probst, & P. VonHeinrich (Eds.), *Managing the Knowledge of the Organization*, Ernst & Young LLP.

Davenport, T., Gilbert, J., Probst, B., & VonHeinrich, P. (eds.) (2002). (2nd Ed.). *Knowledge Management case book: Siemens best practices.* Germany: Willey – VCH.

Davies, J., Fensel, D., & Van Harmelen, F. (Eds.). (2002). *Towards the semantic Web: Ontology-driven knowledge management.* England: Willey.

Drucker, P. F., Garvin, D., Leonard, D., Straus, S., & Brown, J. S. (Eds.). (1998). *Harvard business review on knowledge management.* Boston, MA: Harvard Business School Press.

Feher, P. (Ed.). (2006). *Proceedings of the 7th European Conference on Knowledge Management* (September 4-5, Carvinus University of Budapest, Hungary). Reading: Academic Conference Limited.

Gulati, R. (2007). *Managing network resources: Alliances, affiliations, and other relational assets.*: Oxford University Press.

Hislop, D., Newell, S., Scarbrough, H., & Swan, J. (2000). Networks, knowledge and power: Decision making, politics and the process of innovation. *Technology Analysis & Strategic Management, 12*(3), 399-411.

Hislop, D. (Ed.). (2005). *Knowledge management in organizations: A critical introduction.*: Oxford University Press.

Hislop, D., Newell, S., Scarbrough, H., & Swan, J. (2000). Networks, knowledge and power: Decision making, politics and the process of innovation. *Technology Analysis & Strategic Management, 12*(3), 399-411.

Holsapple, C. W., & Joshi, K. D. (2001). Organizational knowledge resources. *Decision Support Systems, 31*(1), 39-54. Retrieved May 10, 2007, from http://www.portal.acm.org

Jack, S. (2005). The role, use and activation of strong and weak network ties: A qualitative analysis. *Journal of Management Studies, 42*(6), 1233-1259.

Kogut, B., & Zander, U. (1992). Knowledge of the firm, combinative capabilities, and the replication of technology. *Organization Science, 3*(3), 383-397.

Ivon Krogh, G., Ichijo, K., & Nonaka, I. (2000). *Enabling knowledge creation: How to unlock the mystery of tacit knowledge and release the power of innovation.*: Oxford University Press.

Levin, D. Z. (2000), Organizational learning and the transfer of knowledge: An investigation of quality improvement. *Organization Science, 11*(6), 630-647.

O'Leary, D. E. (1998). Using AI in knowledge management: Knowledge bases and ontologies. *IEEE Intelligent Systems, 13*(3), 34-39.

Pan, S. L., & Scarbrough, H. (1999). Knowledge management in practice: An exploratory case study. *Technology Analysis and Strategic Management, 11*(3), 359-374.

Reagans, R., & McEvily, B. (2003). Network structure and knowledge transfer: The effects of cohesion and range. *Administrative Science Quarterly, 48*(2), 240-267.

Roberts, J. (2000). From know-how to show-how? Questioning the role of information and communication technologies in knowledge transfer. *Technology Analysis and Strategic Management, 12*(4), 429-443.

Scarbrough, H., Swan, J., & Preston, J. (Ed.). (1999). *Knowledge management: A literature review.* Woodstock: Beekman Publishers.

Szulanski, G. (2000). The process of knowledge transfer: A diachronic analysis of stickiness.

Organizational Behavior and Human Decision Processes, 82(1), 9-27.

Styhre, A. (Ed.). (2003). *Understanding knowledge management: Critical and postmodern perspectives*. Malmö, Sweden: Copenhagen Business School Press.

Swan, J., & Scarbrough, H. (2001). Editorial. *Journal of Information Technology, 16*(2), 49-55.

Szulanski, G. (2000). The process of knowledge transfer: A diachronic analysis of stickiness. *Organizational Behavior and Human Decision Processes*, *82*(1), 9-27.

Wenger, E. (1999). *Communities of practice: Learning, meaning and identity.*: Cambridge University Press.

Wiig, K. M. (1994). *Knowledge management foundations: Thinking about thinking – how people and organizations represent, create, and use knowledge*. Schema Press, Limited.

ENDNOTE

[1]   Term used by Davenport & Prusak (1998) to call the technologies for Knowledge Management implemented by the organizations (i.e., Knowledge Management Systems).

Chapter III
Knowledge Sharing in Virtual and Networked Organisations in Different Organisational and National Cultures

Kerstin Siakas
Alexander Technological Educational Institution of Thessaloniki, Greece

Elli Georgiadou
University of Middlesex, UK

ABSTRACT

In today's competitive business environment, increasingly large numbers of organisations use virtual distributed teams in their operations. This chapter provides a basis for discussion and analysis of knowledge sharing in culturally diverse networked organisations. Examining the different cultural values and perceptions related to knowledge sharing, we aim at making the human and cultural dynamics that bear on knowledge sharing and knowledge management success more explicit. The objectives are to foster an effective knowledge-sharing culture within virtual distributed teams. The chapter provides mechanisms for understanding the potential for conflict, for knowledge sharing, and building of trust among culturally diverse team members. Guidelines for successful knowledge sharing in the global environment are developed providing indications of the expected benefits for the organisation and the individuals involved. An outline of future trends and further work complete the chapter.

INTRODUCTION

"Knowledge becomes wisdom only after it has been put to practical use." Anonymous

Knowledge is one of the most valuable strategic assets of businesses and an important competitive factor. Organisations in the new knowledge-based global economy place great importance on creation, use, and distribution of information and knowledge by focusing on maintaining and enhancing their knowledge capital. The ability of organisations to learn, adapt, and change has become a core competency for their survival. Successful organisations are those that create new knowledge, disseminate it throughout the organisation, and swiftly embody it into new products and services.

Information and Communication Technologies (ICTs) and the Internet have provided new opportunities for sharing the explicit knowledge, not only within one single organisation, but also between actors of global partnerships and knowledge networks. However, many organisations are still struggling to comprehend the Knowledge Management (KM) concept and do not perform any KM activity (Holsapple & Joshi, 2002). In a global context, the problem is exacerbated because of the increased complexity of global organisations and their dependency on people with different underlying norms, values, and beliefs. On one hand, ICTs favour globalisation and knowledge sharing of explicit ICT transferable knowledge and on the other hand, they hinder knowledge sharing of content with implicit attributes enabled by face-to-face interaction. The gap between implicit and explicit knowledge becomes more visible, and organisations that can exploit the value-creation opportunities generated by global presence and meet these challenges will gain competitive advantage. If knowledge is seen as a resource critical to an organisation's survival and success in the global market, then the knowledge assets and the knowledge flows demand good management.

This chapter aims to make the human and cultural dynamics that influence knowledge sharing within virtual teams, which hardly ever meet, more explicit. Particular emphasis is put on national cultures and their impact on globally networked organisations. Scholars have recently started to pay attention to global and cultural dynamics influencing the KM process (Ai-Alawi, Al-Marzooqi, & Mohammed, 2007; Ang & Massingham, 2007; Bhagat, Kedia, Harveston, & Triandis, 2002, Holden, 2001; Siakas & Georgiadou, 2006). Although the field is under researched, there are clear indications that organisations that demonstrate cultural sensitivity and take advantage of cultural differences gain added business value and competitive advantage. However, the complexity and multidisciplinarity of the field call for particular caution.

KM today is emerging as a distinct academic discipline of research and practice with roots in a many disciplines, such as management sciences, social sciences, economics, computing science, psychology, and philosophy. A multitude of KM models with a broad range of approaches are evident in the literature. However, two distinctions seem to be prevailing, namely analytical or technology-oriented models and actor or people-oriented models (Herder, Veeneman, Buitenhuis, & Schaller, 2003; Moffett, McAdam, & Parkinson, 2003). Technology-oriented models emphasise the importance of explicit knowledge, the technological infrastructure, and the codification of knowledge into ICT systems. People-oriented models, on the contrary, emphasise the importance of tacit knowledge, the social infrastructure, and the business performance.

Our approach is people-oriented by concentrating on the importance of culture in knowledge sharing in virtual and networked organisations. We recognise the importance of the technology-oriented models, but consider, by using the iceberg metaphor (Siakas & Georgiadou, 1999), that the tacit knowledge-sharing challenges hide under water and end up being the greater part of the iceberg. If these challenges are acted properly upon, they can help to create an effective knowledge-sharing environment and if neglected, they hinder successful knowledge sharing. Our research method is an interdisciplinary behavioural approach involving three main disciplines, namely psychology (the study of human behaviour, focusing on the individual as a whole), sociology (study of relationships among groups focusing on the social system), and anthropology (study of human behaviour as a whole focusing on the cultural system, beliefs, customs, ideas, and values within a society, and comparison of behaviour among different cultures (Siakas, 2002). Our arguments are derived from recent literature reviews and reports on the state-of-the-art in KM and cross-cultural research. Our results of field studies related to knowledge sharing between members of virtual teams carried out in both academia and industry in several countries are reported. We also reflect on our own experience from different European countries with different academic and work values.

Throughout this chapter, we examine the KM paradigm outlined as follows: The chapter firstly considers knowledge-sharing concepts and the role of ICTs, followed by a discussion of virtual teams and networked organisations influencing global knowledge sharing, where all stakeholders are open, flexible, and prepared to take responsibility.

Subsequently, an extended analysis of culture (both organisational and national) is presented in order to raise understanding and awareness of the importance of taking culture into consideration. We explore the significance of developing a deeper understanding of cultural norms of other team members in order to avoid pitfalls in knowledge sharing between members of virtual and networked organisation. Cultural factors influencing successful KM and national cultures with knowledge sharing potential are demonstrated, with reference to Hofstede's work-related national value dimensions.

We encapsulate the interrelationships of cultural norms, attitudes, beliefs, experience, decisions, and actions. We emphasise the need for continuous review and improvement based on empowerment and participation of all stakeholders in diagrammatic form, and generate semiformal guidelines for successful knowledge sharing among culturally diverse virtual teams.

The chapter concludes with an outline of future trends and indications of future research.

KNOWLEDGE MANAGEMENT CONCEPTS AND THE ROLE OF INFORMATION AND COMMUNICATION TECHNOLOGIES

KM can be viewed as the process of turning data into information (data in context) and, further on, to knowledge (use of information) (Kanter, 1999; Spiegler, 2000), or as the organisationally specified systematic process for acquiring, organising, and communicating both tacit and explicit knowledge of employees so that other employees may make use of it (knowledge sharing) in order to be more effective and productive (Alavi & Leidner, 2001). KM is a business philosophy. It is an emerging set of principles, processes, organisational structures, and technology applications that help people share and leverage their knowledge to meet their business objectives (Gurteen, 1999). This focuses the individual and places responsibility on the individual, the knowledge worker. At the same time, KM programmes in organisations emphasise the holistic nature of creating, sharing, and managing knowledge. Organisations formally capture, manage, and explicitly store knowledge with the help of computer-based systems, such as Management Information Systems (MIS), Decision Support Systems (DSS), and Expert Systems (ES), which today are becoming ubiquitous in organisations (Davenport & Prusak, 1998). However, technology by itself often does not solve an organisation's inherent problems relating to intellectual capital, knowledge and information management. Information and Communication Technologies (ICTs) seem to enhance the KM capabilities of organisations (Alavi & Leidner, 2001; Tanriverdi, 2005). Davis et al. (Davis, Subrahmanian, & Westerberg, 2005) argue that KM is based 30% on implemented systems and the rest on people. The fact is that the view of knowledge is changing and today, it is seen as human capital that "walks out the door at the end of the day" (Spiegler, 2000).

Organisations are facing a new challenging environment, characterised by globalisation, dynamism, and increasing levels of complexity due to rapid changes in technology and its connected intricate knowledge. Internet-based virtual tools have created new opportunities for rapid access to business information worldwide. Identifying potential business partners and developing business links with organisations in other countries has become easier for organisations that are experienced in monitoring Web-based information sources, and are able to combine tacit knowledge with new knowledge sources that are enabled by ICTs, such as Internet, intranet, groupware, and Computer Supported Cooperated Work (CSCW) systems. Explicit knowledge is transferable through formal and systematic languages. Tacit or implicit knowledge is context-specific, personal, and subjective, including cognitive elements and thus, difficult to formalize and communicate (Davis et. al 2005, Siakas & Georgiadou, 2006). Knowledge sharing (transfer) is the process where individuals mutually exchange both tacit and explicit knowledge, and jointly create new knowledge. This process is essential in transferring individual knowledge into organisational knowledge. The capability of an organisation to create, recognise, widely disseminate, and embody knowledge in new products and technologies is critical when faced with turbulent markets, high competition, and financial instability (Nonaka, 1991). Continuous knowledge creation requires

voluntary actions including openness, scrutiny, trust, and tolerance towards different views and interpretations. Organisations expect employees to keep professionally up-to-date by continuously obtaining internal and external information relating to their profession. Knowledge evolves continuously as the individual and the organisation adapt to influences from the external and the internal environment. Elron and Vigoda-Gadot (2006) found that when ICTs are used as the main communication channel between team members, the limitations of the communication increase, as technology cannot provide the same richness as face-to-face interactions, and potentially hinder the effectiveness of knowledge sharing. They also found that influence tactics and political processes in virtual teams are more restrained and milder than in face-to-face teams. This seems to indicate that however effective ICTs may be, they cannot replace personal contact.

Views on Knowledge Management (KM) and ICTs are wide ranging between two poles, one considering the relationships between KM and ICTs incidental, the other considering ICTs being the core of KM (Holsapple, 2005). This chapter considers KM being a social and human phenomenon that, by using ICTs as a tool, can improve the efficiency of knowledge creation, visualisation, transfer, evolution, and preservation. ICTs facilitate the amplification, augmentation, and leverage of innate human-knowledge handling capabilities. The advances in ICTs provide organizations with increased flexibility and responsiveness, permitting them to rapidly form dispersed and disparate experts into a virtual team that can work on an urgent project. ICTs support faster, cheaper, and more reliable knowledge work of large scale, and the existence of efficient ICTs is inevitably an imperative requirement for the existence of virtual collaboration. However, the emphasis in this chapter is to unfold the human and cultural challenges that can create added competitive value for global and networked organisations.

VIRTUAL TEAMS AND NETWORKED ORGANISATIONS

In today's highly competitive and rapidly changing global environment, more and more organisations strive to form virtual teams comprised of experts situated in different locations, organisations, countries, and time zones. The increased complexity of international organisations and worldwide business relationships has become a dynamic business reality with intensified competition. Virtual teams are teams of people who primarily interact electronically, and who may meet face-to-face occasionally and in some projects not at all. In a virtual team, the members work interdependently towards a shared goal using Webs of ICTs across time and space, and often across organisational boundaries (Handy, 2000; Lipnack & Stamps, 1997; Mansour-Cole, 2001). According to Bal and Teo (2000), virtual teams consist of goal-oriented team members/knowledge workers who are dispersed geographically, and work supported by ICTS more apart than in same location. They solve problems and make decisions jointly; they are involved in a coordinated undertaking of inter-related activities, and are mutually accountable for team results. Virtual teams have usually a finite duration (few teams are permanent). Virtual teams, by their very nature, imply the presence of a group of geographically dispersed individuals, often from different cultural, educational, and professional backgrounds. They work on a joint project or common task, and communicate mainly by using e-mail for the duration of a specific project (Järvenpää & Leidner, 1999). A potential conflict arises when the team members belong to different organisational and cultural units, because the teammates do not know where to place their loyalty (Balstrup, 2004). In a virtual environment, this is exacerbated because informal communication is reduced, due to the fact that members rarely meet face-to-face. A successful leader of a virtual team must excel in applying the right choice of ICTs to enable effective communication and knowledge sharing. Communica-

tion, and thus, also knowledge sharing, in virtual teams in a global context is considerably much more difficult due to language, culture, time issues, and distance. Knowledge sharing with bad communication is a big challenge and a difficult issue to achieve. Teams lacking communication and knowledge sharing will turn into detached groups of uninvolved strangers out of leadership and cooperation. The individual members of the virtual team and the leader must build a unified team committed to the common goal, and through interdependent interaction, generate group identity and create the feeling of belonging to a group (Balstrup, 2004).

Despite the many technologies that support collaboration among distributed work groups, organisations still face difficulties building online work environments. What is lacking in most virtual workplaces is a proven methodology, or at least guidelines, for identifying and converting individual expertise, skills, and experience into organisational knowledge, knowledge transfer, and learning investment with organisational value outcome. By sharing information across the organisation, virtual teams naturally build their own knowledge bases that are consistent with the rest of the company. The ideal environment and working practices will be to change the mindset and behaviour of team members so that instead of perceiving knowledge sharing as an extra task for the team members, isolated from the knowledge of other team members, it (knowledge sharing) becomes the natural way of working for everyone. The result will be a well-integrated, highly responsive organisation whose employees can quickly take action regardless of location.

In today's competitive environment, increasingly large numbers of organisations, such as Information Technology (IT) companies, use virtual teams in their international operations, which can constitute subsidiaries, outsourcing relationships, or global partnerships (Siakas & Balstrup, 2006).

The organisation's responsibility is to provide the necessary structure, and to create systematic ways to identify and convert individual expertise, skills, and experience into organisational knowledge, and to strategically align organisational knowledge transfer and learning investment with organisational value outcome, taking into account both current and future organisational tasks. Harorimana (2006) argues that it is impossible to transfer knowledge that is not embedded in local cultural practices and settings, because reciprocity norms dominate successful knowledge transfer. We believe that this is a challenge we can face by raising cultural diversity awareness. The main contribution of this chapter is the analysis of the cultural dynamics influencing knowledge sharing in different cultural settings, and the development of guidelines for avoiding conflict and changing potential failure to competitive advantage. In distributed ICT environments enhanced with a shift in mindsets, the individuals learn and contribute their knowledge to the group, the group learns and contributes to the organisation, and the organisation facilitates/sponsors the processes in a perpetual cycle of exchange of information, sharing of knowledge and maximises process improvement.

CULTURAL DYNAMICS AND KNOWLEDGE MANAGEMENT

Culture has been identified as the biggest impediment to knowledge transfer (Ruggles, 1998) and an utmost complex and simultaneously important factor affecting knowledge transfer at all levels, especially at the transnational level (Duan, Xu, & Fu, 2006). Culture influences and moulds beliefs about the value of knowledge for the individual, the team, and the organisation. De Long and Fahey (2000) identified four issues influenced by culture central to knowledge creation, sharing, and use, namely:

1. Culture shapes assumptions about what knowledge is and which knowledge is worth managing;

2. Culture defines the relationship between individual and organisational knowledge, determining who can utilise it, share it, control it, and how it can be used in a certain situation;
3. Culture creates the context for social interaction;
4. Culture shapes the processes by which new knowledge is created, legitimated, and distributed.

Recent research on knowledge creation, capture, storage, and distribution, as well as on organisational learning, indicates that communication, knowledge sharing, and learning in organisations are profoundly influenced by cultural values of individual stakeholders (Hambrick, Davison, Snell, & Snow, 1998; Hofstede, 2001; Hutchings & Michailova, 2004; Pfeffer & Sutton, 2000; Siakas & Georgiadou, 2003; 2006). Many scholars and practitioners also claim that a supportive organisational culture can enable the successful implementation of KM (Ardichvili, Mauner, Li, Wenting, & Stuedemann 2006; De Long & Fahey, 2000; Lopez, Peon, M., Ordas, 2004; Park, Ribiere, & Schulte, 2004; Siakas & Georgiadou, 2006). Since culture seems to be an issue of utmost importance, but also a multifaceted issue involving many different research disciplines and views, we consider that a deeper presentation, drawn from the literature, is needed for a better comprehension of cultures and their importance in KM. In particular, the impact of national culture on KM has been neglected in the literature.

CULTURAL DIVERSITY AND ITS IMPACT ON ORGANISATIONS

In 1952, Kroeger and Kluckholm (1952) found 164 different definitions, with different meanings for the concept of culture. Culture has different layers or levels often overlapping. The lack of clarity on definitions and meanings of different terms commonly used in a cultural context could be attributed to the fact that, regarding cultural studies, many different academic disciplines are involved, where the same terms have different meanings; different terms are also used for the same concept.

However, there are similarities in the different approaches to identifying and defining culture. Researchers (Inkeles & Levison, 1969; Kluckhohn, 1951; Kluckhohn & Strodtbeck, 1961; Kroeger & Kluckhoh, 1952) relate differences between cultures to different approaches to solving common human problems. More recent research (Hofstede, 2001; Schein, 1985) seems to have adopted this approach. There are cultures of, for example, a family, a tribe, a region, a national minority, or a nation. Hofstede recognises that there is cultural variation within and among cultures, and there are different levels and forms of cultures.

ICTs provide the bedrock of globalisation. Increasing numbers of organisations operate on a global scale using culturally diverse teams working across different languages, time zones, and locations. Hofstede et al. (Hofstede, Neuijen, Ohayv, & Sanders, 1990) provided strong evidence that national cultural differences shape organisational behaviour at a local level, and that differences in national and regional cultures affect work values. He argued that culture is a collection of characteristics possessed by people who have been conditioned by similar socialisation practices, educational procedures, and life experiences. The cultural orientation of the members of a network reflects the complex interaction of values, attitudes, and behaviours displayed. They are all part of the cultural learning, and give rise to misunderstandings and misinterpretation of intent.

Hofstede (2001) stated that everyone belongs to a number of different groups and categories of people at the same time. He calls this mental programming within people, corresponding to different levels of culture, for example, at a national, professional, and organisational level.

Hofstede (1994, 2001) distinguished five elements, or dimensions, of culture as described next.

- *Power distance* (PD), which describes the extent to which hierarchies and unequal distribution of power is accepted;
- *Uncertainty avoidance* (UA), which indicates the extent to which a society feels threatened by ambiguous situations and tries to avoid them by providing rules, believing in absolute truths, and refusing to tolerate deviance;
- *Masculinity vs. Femininity* (Mas/Fem), which describes the relationship between the masculine assertiveness, competitiveness, and materialism opposed to the feminine concern for quality of relationships, nurturing, and social well being;
- *Individualism vs. Collectivism* (Ind/Col), which describes the relationship between the individual independence and the collective interdependence of a group;
- *Long-term vs. Short-term Orientation* (influenced by Confucius and introduced later) describes the relationship between persistence and thrift opposed to personal stability and respect for tradition. This dimension has not been well received because it appears confusing both to western readers and to Chinese minds (Fang, 2003).

All these dimensions are a continuum between two extremes (0 and 100), and only very few national cultures, if any, are wholly at one or the other extreme.

In the current literature, the main focus seems to be on organisational culture (Hatch, 1993) and the organisational cultural changes imposed by globalisation, networks trying to create added value, and the unprecedented development of ICTs. Changes in strategy with subsequent changes in structure and operations create new organisational cultures with different team settings (Brannen

& Salk, 2000; Sackmann & Phillips, 2004). The ultimate objective of a value-creating network is to create superior customer value (Kothandaraman & Wilson, 2001). The degree of value creation is influenced by core capabilities of the members of the network, as well as by the nature of the relationships that the stakeholders in the network have with each other. The cultural orientation of the members of a network reflects the complex interaction of values, attitudes, and behaviours displayed. They are all part of the cultural learning, and give rise to misunderstandings and misinterpretation of intent.

According to Redding (1994), research in organisational cultural issues and comparative organisational theory suffer from theoretical poverty and lack of clear direction in general. In order to provide adequate perspectives in the multiple and complex field, inputs from other disciplines are required. These inputs improve understanding not only of facts, but also of the underlying meaning. Hofstede's work contains references to various theoretical approaches, especially to psychology, and can, according to Cray and Mallory (1998), be considered more theoretically sophisticated than the majority of the comparative work in the field.

The rapidly changing environment and increasing international activity has created new demands on organisations, and on those who participate in cross-cultural activities. The emergence of cross-cultural organisations has also created a new awareness of the importance of understanding other cultures. Comparative cross-national studies provide not only substantial information, but also perspectives on that information, and have reflected the increased complexity of international organisations (Redding, 1994). National culture is a major barrier to making global business effective. Different nationalities have different expectations as to how employers and employees should act. The need for understanding the effects of the intercultural complexity in the era of globalisation has emerged.

Harris and Morgan (1991) suggest that when global organisations are aware of cultural strengths and biases in terms of national and organisational characteristics, they can build upon such foundations. International managers can take advantage of both differences and similarities, such as commonalities, through mutual cross-cultural synergy, for growth and development.

CULTURAL FACTORS INFLUENCING KNOWLEDGE SHARING

The basic assertion in cross-cultural studies is that national culture, expressed in terms of values and beliefs, has a direct impact on organisational culture and individual behaviour (Hofstede 1994, 2001; Schein, 1985). The economical, political, and legal environment imposed by governmental rules, the technical environment, such as communication networks, and the sociocultural environment in which the organisation exists, directly affect organisational culture and functioning of organisations.

Organisational culture, in turn, directly affects individual behaviour by imposing guidelines on, and expectations from, the members of the organisation. Values of other stakeholders, like employees, also create impact on the organisational culture. One of the key issues for managers in globally networked organisations is collaboration and shared commitment. Collaboration presupposes trust, which is a fundamental requirement of every economic activity (Clarke, 2002). Business activities, in the normal sense, are very complex, and require a great deal of trust in order to be fully and successfully carried out. This trust requirement becomes even more challenging and complex when the type of business is operating globally. One major contributory factor to this heightened state of trust requirement is the fact that this type of collaboration, for example, e-commerce, is characterised by the "invisibility" factor (IDA, 2000), and is conducted in the virtual realm that, in most cases, does not offer face-to-face contact among the participants (Ojukwu & Georgiadou, 2007).

The organisational structures can formally indicate and facilitate connections and communications between individuals, as well as they may place limitations on communications, or create intentional or unintentional obstacles both within and across organisational boundaries. Structural elements of organisations influence the collaboration and sharing of knowledge within organisations (O'Dell & Grayson, 1998), as well as hinder these activities (Gold, Malhotra, & Segars, 2001). Similarly, Goh (2002) stresses that a cooperative and collaborative organisational culture can lead individuals or groups to have higher propensity to share knowledge.

A knowledge-oriented organisational culture is clearly one of the most influential factors for successful KM and knowledge transfer (Davenport & Prusak, 1998), because a culture that promotes

change and innovative behaviour encourages active exchange of ideas and increased knowledge sharing. An orientation, promoting information transfer and information flows, is reflected in a general atmosphere of inventiveness, creativity, and willingness to make changes (Menon & Varadarajan, 1992).

A company's ability to use knowledge depends on how enthusiastic people are about sharing it. Leveraging knowledge is possible only when people value building on each other's ideas and sharing their own insights. Much of this is shaped by the culture of the organisation (Siakas, 2002).

Clarke (1994) argued that the essence of sustainable change is to understand the culture of the organisation. He stressed that if planned changes contradict cultural traditions and biases, resistance to the change and difficulties in its implementing are likely to occur. This entails global organisations to recognise the importance of national culture when planning a radical change, such as initiating networked collaboration. The

Table 1. Trust and knowledge sharing potential in different cultural settings (Siakas & Georgiadou, 2006)

Dimension	Characteristic relating to KM	Trust	Knowledge Sharing
High Power Distance	Authoritative leadership, Centralised decision structures, Inequality between higher ups and lower downs	Low	If instruction so requires
Low Power Distance	Participative leadership, Decentralised decision structures	High	A natural process
High Uncertainty Avoidance	Suspiciousness to innovations and new knowledge, Uncertainty for ambiguous situations	Low	Has to be enforced by regulations and instructions
Low Uncertainty Avoidance	Problem-solving tasks preferred	High	Expected
Masculinity	Assertiveness, Sympathy for strong	Low	Hiding of knowledge for competition reasons
Femininity	Cooperation important Sympathy for weak	High	A basic value
Individualism	"I" consciousness	Low	If personal advantage can be identified
Collectivism	In-groups	High	Trust has to be established before any knowledge sharing can take place between in- and out- groups
	Out-groups	High	Can be enhanced by intrinsic motives (e.g., higher reputation and status)

more committed the members of an organisation are to the current frame, the more resistance is likely to occur when introducing a new system, particularly if this is likely to bring a major cultural change. People who have been steeped in the traditions and values of an organisation will experience considerable uncertainty, anxiety, and pain in the process of change. The difficulties are exacerbated when introducing new ICTs to inexperienced team members who, in addition, may need to collaborate in a foreign language with people having different underlying norms, values, and beliefs.

In the above sections, we demonstrated that culture may hinder or facilitate the knowledge-sharing process. As a result of studies, we derived the principal relationships between Hofstede's dimensions of work-related values to KM, trust, and knowledge sharing (Siakas & Georgiadou, 2006) presented in Table 1, which shows that in low Power Distance (PD) countries, low Uncertainty Avoidance countries (UA), and Feminine countries, trust is high and knowledge sharing is an expected natural process, one of the basic values of the culture. In individualistic cultures, voluntary knowledge sharing is relatively hard to achieve, and other supplementary activities, such as incentive systems, are recommended. In collectivistic cultures, knowledge sharing can be enhanced if knowledge sharing is rewarded and made prominent with higher reputation and status (Handzic & Lagumdzija, 2006).

Evidence from a 2-month field study and observations in a global Danish organisation, with subsidiaries in the USA and Germany, confirm the correctness of the theoretical judgement derived from the literature review. In total, 56 interviews with employees in software development on different levels was conducted in Denmark, USA, and Germany (Siakas, 2002). The field study was the validation stage of a larger survey study encompassing 306 questionnaire respondents from other countries as well.

Hofstede's values for the three countries in the field-study are outlined together with the conclusive remarks in the final report (Siakas, 2002) to the Danish global organisation regarding the cultural differences observed in the interviews.

Denmark: PD – 18 (low), UA – 23 (low), Mas/Fem – 16 (Fem), Ind/Col – 74 (Ind)

"The Danes seem to be very easygoing and taking their roles seriously (due to Femininity).... They are proud of working for the organisation and they are committed to what they are doing. There is no competition and everybody seems to willingly both ask for help if needed and also proud of being able to give help if asked for [Knowledge sharing]. They work well in teams and they are empowered to take delegated decisions."

USA: PD – 40 (low), UA – 46 (low), Mas/Fem – 62 (Mas), Ind/Col – 91 (Ind)

"The Americans were very keen on stressing that they are ambitious, hard working and that they like to be productive (due to Masculinity). The structure is more hierarchical and competitive. They feel they do not have enough information from the mother organisation about what is going on and about the future. They would also like to play a more active role in the change process and in decision making... They think that the Danes are somehow conservative, not willing to take risks and not very innovative. They are very individualistic, but they also want to feel like a team. Trust, seems to be an important thing for collaboration. They would like more focus on target market issues and on being at the leading edge. They want things to happen faster.... They also want acknowledgement for their efforts and respect from colleagues .... They think management in Denmark is not aware of their professional level and of how ambitious and good professionals they are."

Germany: PD – 35 (low), UA – 65 (high), Mas/Fem – 66 (Mas), Ind/Col – 67 (Ind)

"The organisational structure in Germany is higher than in Denmark. They are competitive, task-oriented and in general committed to the organisation philosophy. They feel they need more instructions or direct rules about how to work (due to high UA) They also feel that they do not have enough information from the mother organisation in general and that there is a need for training especially in quality issues (Not enough knowledge sharing). They have a good team spirit and they seem to accept things they don't like more easily than the Americans do. They want to be acknowledged for their achievements and they want to be respected as equals by the Danes."

The evidence shows that a knowledge sharing culture is almost occurring naturally in an environment with low Power Distance and low Uncertainty Avoidance values, whilst in cultures with a higher Power Distance and Uncertainty Avoidance, a more serious cultural change will be needed for embracing knowledge sharing as a natural process.

GUIDELINES FOR SUCCESSFUL KNOWLEDGE SHARING AMONG CULTURALLY DIVERSE TEAMS AND ORGANISATIONS

Global organisations and virtual teams, by definition, are required to operate in a multicultural setting where technology plays a central role. Trust now involves additional technology aspects, including compatibility, reliability, privacy, maintenance contracts, data management, and ownership. Uncertainties on any of these aspects result in poor communication and performance.

The influence of culture (organisational and national) is instrumental in the setting of objectives, decisions, and actions. Experience itself generates and modifies knowledge. For successful knowledge sharing, empowerment of all involved and regular review at all points are necessary.

Figure 1 (an adaptation of a model developed by Georgiadou (2001)) represents a model for KM initiatives encapsulating the interactions and influences of values, beliefs, and experiences on decisions and actions. The

Figure 1. Technology-enabled knowledge sharing approach

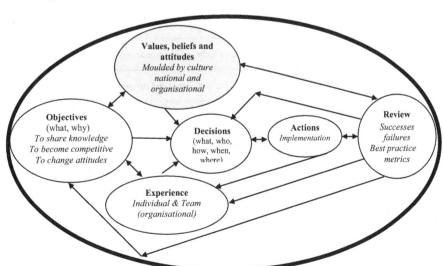

emphasis here is on continuous review and feedback for improvement.

The outer ellipse signifies a world of ICTs acting as a reflective dome/dish through which the exchange and sharing of information and knowledge are affected. In a virtual team, each individual member needs to understand and accept that a shared purpose will guide the sharing of knowledge, sharing of the work load, providing mutual support, engaging in negotiation and compromise where necessary, trusting the other members to do the same for the benefit of the project/organisation, but without compromising the individual. The success of the team, the project, and the organisation at large must be viewed as an enriching and rewarding experience for the individual who will gain experience, ad-

ditional perspectives, and learn to listen to others. Empowering all the stakeholders to engage in externalising and sharing data, information, and knowledge, results in a learning organisation. Progressing from data to information answers the fundamental questions of "who," "what," "where," and "when." Going from information to knowledge, we need to be able to answer the "how" question, whilst understanding requires an appreciation of the "why."

The creation of a knowledge-sharing culture is an essential part of KM initiatives. Changing deep-rooted attitudes and values is, however, one of the most difficult undertakings. In the case of virtual organisations, differences in attitudes are even more difficult to identify and address. Effective Knowledge Sharing presupposes a change

Table 2. Guidelines for successful knowledge sharing among culturally diverse virtual teams

Step	Description	Expected Benefits
1.	Agree collaboration strategies, objectives, and outcomes	Ensure that stakeholders have the same understanding of the knowledge value statement and how it relates to business strategies, objectives, and outcomes, together with their interrelationships
2.	Assess fit of individual, organisational, and national culture by using the DivA (Diversity Assessment) automated tool (Siakas & Hyvärinen, 2006) developed from the SQM-CODE model (Siakas, 2002)	Indication of possible contradictions or conformity of values. Depending on the results action needs to follow to avoid conflict and instead, view diversity as an enriching opportunity
3.	Design and deliver appropriate training programme for cross-cultural awareness	Improvement of cultural awareness as a basis of mutual respect and trust
4.	Design and deliver appropriate training programme for technical aspects	Improvement of technical skills ensuring seamless ICT use
5.	Design and deliver appropriate training programme for knowledge sharing	Awareness of the importance and opportunities offered by knowledge sharing
6.	Develop a motivational strategy (benefits for the individual, team and organisation)	Sustainability combining top-down strategy by individual commitment. Individuals learn and contribute to the group, the group learns and contributes to the organisation, and the organisation facilitates/sponsors the processes in a perpetual cycle of exchange of information, sharing of knowledge, and process improvement
7.	Identify current practice, complimentary experience, and knowledge	The use of common systems and common processes, such as shared communication processes, task allocation, ownership, and responsibility help team members increase their understanding of both the project and the view of the partners
8.	Apply best practice and knowledge to pilot project or Reflect on success/failure of earlier project(s)	Validation of process Leadership identification and development
9.	Review reasons for success/failure	Continuous improvement through the understanding of cause-effect analysis Formalise processes in view of insights gained through application and review

of attitude, a move from the belief "Knowedge is Power" to Knowledge Sharing is Power," from compromise to accommodation and consensus, from conflict to collaboration. Different cultures have different attitudes to scrutinity and criticism. They also have different levels of acceptance, openness, and trust, as well as varying levels of tolerance towards different views and interpretations. Political, religious, and social prejudices soon become barriers to trust and openness to sharing. It is important for a team/project leader to be sensitised to potential conflict arising from such differences.

Commonalities in all cultures include striving for success (at organisational and personal level), seeking individual recognition for successful contribution, respect for knowledge. Successful teams and projects in virtual environments require that the team members must become familiar/comfortable with the use of the technologies, develop awareness of cultural norms of other team members, be open and flexible, and take responsibility.

We provide a semiformal set of guidelines for effective knowledge in virtual environments outlining the main benefits that are likely to derive from the use of these guidelines. It is assumed that participating individuals, teams, and/or organisations have the intention, in principle, to share knowledge and to become competitive.

CONCLUSION

The ability of organisations to learn, adapt, and change has become a core competency for their survival. Successful organisations are those that create new knowledge, disseminate it throughout the organisation, and swiftly embody it into new products and services.

Information and Communication Technologies (ICTs) and the Internet have provided new opportunities for sharing the explicit knowledge, not only within one single organisation, but also between actors of global partnerships and knowledge networks.

The main contribution of this chapter was the analysis of the human and cultural dynamics that bear on knowledge sharing and KM success. These dynamics were unfolded by extensively analysing cultural issues (national and organisational) on knowledge sharing and networked organisations in order to promote an effective knowledge-sharing culture within virtual teams existing in a global context. Cultural characteristics, revealed from the literature and validated in a field study conducted in a Danish-based global organisation, with subsidiaries in the USA and Germany, were mapped to Hofstede's dimensions and conclusions regarding trust and knowledge sharing, were presented (Table 1).

Commonalities in all cultures include striving for success (at organisational and personal level), seeking individual recognition for successful contribution, and respect for knowledge. Successful teams and projects in virtual environments require that the team members must become familiar/comfortable with the use of the technologies, develop awareness of cultural norms of other team members, be open and flexible, and take responsibility.

A diagrammatic representation of a technology-enabled knowledge sharing approach (Figure1) was proposed, encapsulating the interrelationships of cultural norms, attitudes, beliefs, experience, decisions, and actions. This approach places emphasis on continuous review and improvement, based on empowerment and participation of all stakeholders.

Finally, a set of semiformal guidelines for Successful Knowledge Sharing among culturally diverse virtual teams was developed and presented (Table 2).

We conclude that in today's interconnected world, more attention should be paid to studying the cultural dimension in order to develop awareness and sensitivity to cultural diversities. Deeper awareness of what divides people from different cultures is likely to avoid conflicts and engender harmony that, in turn, builds trust.

FUTURE RESEARCH DIRECTIONS

In future, the successful organisation will become a learning organisation, where all employees perceive themselves as knowledge workers. ICTs will continue to develop and play a central role in the Information Society. The widespread use of ICTs has generated new cultural groupings and ways of working, ranging from social computing and Communities of Practice (CoP) (Wenger & Snyder, 2000), both emerging phenomena influencing global knowledge sharing.

In June 2005, the European Union launched a new strategic framework "i2010 - European Information Society 2010" (COM 229, 2005), aiming to foster economic growth, and to create jobs in the information society and media industries by deploying and modernising EU policy instruments that encourage development of the digital economy. The i2010 initiative emphasises ICTs as a driver of inclusion and quality of life, and convergence as a main factor for change for the ICT sector and the society at-large (i2010 HLG, 2006). To achieve the objectives of the i2010 strategy, the challenges appearing from the continuous changes of the technological issues need to be carefully analysed and acted upon.

The future European core vision (shared across both industries and governments) allows every user to be able to connect everywhere, anytime, with access to adapted and high quality content and communication services, in a safe and accessible environment. The reality of convergence is developing rapidly (i2010 HLG, 2006). However, the digital divide between administrations in EU member states that have implemented electronic government platforms and those with limited projects or plans is obvious. Differences in economic performances between industrialised countries are determined by the level of ICT investment, research, and use, and by the competitiveness of information society and media industries (COM 229, 2005). Deep-rooted cultural and social patterns are likely to influence the differences in performance.

Tsatsou (2005) articulates a major critique on the current EU policy process regarding the failure of the EU to recognize and adjust its policy to the existing cultural particularities of its Member States. She poses the question of whether digital divides constitute "cultural divides" having an impact on the policy, regulation, and future evolution of the EU Information Society. She addresses the need of an EU policy that takes into account the sociocultural particularities of each EU Member State without losing its broad scope and common aim throughout the EU. The importance of taking cultural differences into consideration was also recognised in a large scale European project (Segalla, 2001) aimed at studying cultural differences in interrelations between clients, shareholders, and company employees, with the view of contributing the process of the integration of European companies and the European economy as a whole.

Future work will involve the use of the DivA tool, together with the guidelines to plan, introduce, and monitor KM programmes in selected organisations in different countries spanning cultural diversity in order to collect further qualitative and quantitative empirical data. The data will subsequently be analysed, the guidelines revised, and customised versions for different cultures produced.

Organisations, groups, and individuals benefit from relevant and timely knowledge that is delivered/reached in a cost-effective manner. In future, we also aim to explore the principles and methods for converting knowledge to wisdom, and go some way towards answering the questions posed by T. S. Eliot (1934):

Where is the wisdom we have lost in knowledge?
Where is the knowledge we have lost in information? [T.S. Eliot (1888-1965)]

ACKNOWLEDGMENT

The authors would like to thank the reviewers, and particularly, Prof. Ettore Bolisani for his incisive comments and constructive criticism.

REFERENCES

Ai-Alawi, A. I., Al-Marzooqi, N. Y., & Mohammed Y. F. (2007). Organizational culture and knowledge sharing: Critical success factors. *Journal of Knowledge Management, 11*(2), 22-42.

Alavi, M., & Leidner, D. E. (2001). Review: Knowledge management and knowledge management systems: Conceptual foundations and research issues. *MIS Quarterly, 25*(1), 107-136.

Ang, Z., & Massingham, P. (2007). National culture and standardization vs. adaption of knowledge management. *Journal of Knowledge Management, 11*(2), 5-21.

Ardichvili, A., Mauner M., Li, W., Wenting, T., & Stuedemann R. (2006). Cultural influences on knowledge sharing through online communities of practice. *Journal of Knowledge Management, 10*(1), 94-107.

Bal, J., & Teo, P. K. (2000). Implementing virtual teamworking. Part 1: A literature review of best practice. *Logistics Information Management, 13*(6), 346-352.

Balstrup, B. (2004). *Leading by detached involvement – Success factors enabling leadership of virtual teams.* MBA Dissertation, Henley Management College, UK.

Bhagat, R. S., Kedia, B. L., Harveston, P. D., & Triandis, H. C. (2002). Cultural variations in the cross-border transfer of organizational knowledge: An integrative framework. *The Academy of Management Review, 27*(2), 204-221.

Brannen, M.Y., & Salk, J. (2000). Partnering across borders. *Human Relations, 53*(4), 451–487.

Clarke, L. (1994). *The essence of change.* London, UK: Prentice-Hall.

Clarke, R. (2002). Trust in the context of e-business. *Internet Law Bulletin, 4*(5), 56-59.

COM 229. (2005). *i2010 – A European Information Society for growth and employment.* Communication from the commission to the council, the European parliament, the European economic and social committee and the committee of the regions, Brussels, 1.6.2005.

Cray, D., & Mallory, G. R. (1998). *Making sense of managing culture.* London, UK: International Thomson Business Press.

Davenport, T. H., & Prusak, L. (1998). *Working knowledge: How organisations manage what they know.* Boston: Harvard Business School Press.

Davis, J. G., Subrahmanian, E., & Westerberg, W. (2005). The "global" and the "local" in knowledge management. *Journal of Knowledge Management, (1),* 101-112.

De Long, D. W., & Fahey, L. (2000). Diagnosing cultural barriers to knowledge management. *Academy of Management Executive, 14*(4), 113-127

De Long, D. W., & Fahey, L. (2000). Diagnosing cultural barriers to knowledge management. *Academy of Management Executive, 14*(4), 113-127.

Dorfman, P. W., & Howell, J. P. (1988). Dimensions of national culture and effective leadership patterns: Hofstede revisited. *Advances in International Comparative Management, 3,* 127-50.

Duan, Y., Xu, X., & Fu, Z. (2006). Understanding transnational knowledge transfer. In P. Feher (Ed.), *Proceedings of 7th European Conference of Knowledge Management (ECKM06)* (pp. 126-135), 4-5 Sept., Public Academic Conferences Ltd. Reading, UK.

Eliot, T. S. (1934). *The rock.* MA: Harcourt, Braintree Book Rack.

Elron, E., & Vigoda-Gadot. E. (2006). Influence and political processes in cyberspace: The case of global virtual teams. *International Journal of Cross Cultural Management, 6*(3), 295–317.

Fang, T. (2003). A critique of Hofstede's Fifth National Culture Dimension. *International Journal of Cross Cultural Management, 3*(3), 347–368.

Georgiadou, E. (2001). *Software measurement for process and product improvement - controlled experiments and derivation of reengineering metrics.* School of Informatics and Multimedia Technology, Faculty of Science Computing and Engineering, University of North London, Transfer Report from Mphil to PhD.

Goh, S. C. (2002). Managing effective knowledge transfer: An integrative framework and some practice implications. *Journal of Knowledge Management, 6*(6), 23-30.

Gold, A. H., Malhotra A., & Segars A. H. (2001). Knowledge management: An organisational capabilities perspective. *Journal of Management Information Systems, 18*(1), 185-214.

Gurteen, D. (1999). Creating a knowledge sharing culture. *Knowledge Management Magazine, 2*(5). Retrieved from http://www.gurteen.com/gurteen/gurteen.nsf/0/FD35AF9606901C42802567C70068CBF5/

Hambrick, D., Davison, S., Snell, S., & Snow, C. (1998). When groups consist of multiple nationalities: Toward a new understanding of implications. *Organisation Studies, 12*(2), 181-205.

Handy, C. (2000). Trust and the virtual organisation (HBR OnPoint Enhanced Edition). *HBR On Point,* June 2000

Handzic, M., & Lagumdzija, A. (2006). Motivational influences on knowledge sharing. In P. Feher (Ed.), Proceedings of *7th European Conference of Knowledge Management (ECKM06)* (pp. 208 – 212), 4-5 Sept., Public Academic Conferences Ltd. Reading, UK.

Harorimana, D. (2006). Knowledge networks: A mechanism of creation and transfer of knowledge in organisations? In P. Feher (Ed.), *Proceedings of 7th European Conference of Knowledge Management (ECKM06)* (pp. 211-222), 4-5 Sept., Public Academic Conferences Ltd. Reading, UK.

Harris, P. R., & Morgan, R. T. (1991). *Managing cultural differences,* (3rd ed.). Houston, TX: Gulf Publishing Company.

Hatch, M. J. (1993). The dynamics of organisational culture. *Academy of Management Review, 18*(4), 657–693.

Herder, P. M., Veeneman, W. W., Buitenhuis, M. D. J., & Schaller, A. (2003). Follow the rainbow: A knowledge management framework for new product introduction. *Journal of Knowledge Management, 7*(3), 105-115.

Hofstede, G. (1994). *Cultures and organisations, intercultural cooperation and its importance for survival, software of the mind.* UK: McGraw-Hill.

Hofstede, G. (2001). *Culture's consequences: Comparing values, behaviours, institutions, and organisations.* Thousand Oaks, CA, London: Sage Publications.

Holden, N. (2001). Knowledge management: Raising the specter of the cross-cultural dimension. *Knowledge and Process Management, 8*(3), 155-63.

Holsapple, C. W., & Joshi, K. D. (2002). Knowledge management: A threefold framework. *The Information Society, 18,* 47-63.

Holsapple, C. W. (2005). The inseparability of modern knowledge management and computer-based technology, *Library Hi Tech News incorporating Online and CD Notes, Volume 9,*

Number 1, 2005 , pp. 42-52(11), Emerald Group Publishing Limited

Hunt, J. W. (1981). Applying American behavioural science: Some cross-cultural problems. *Orgnisational Dynamics, 10*(1), 55-62.

Hutchings, K., & Michailova, S. (2004). Facilitating knowledge sharing in Russian and Chinese subsidiaries: The role of personal networks and group membership. *Journal of Knowledge Management, 8*(2), 84-94.

i2010 HLG. (2006). *The challenges of convergence.* Information Space Innovation & Investment in R&D Inclusion, i2010 High Level Group, 12.12.2006.

IDA. (2000). *A proposed framework on building trust and confidence in electronic commerce: A consultation paper*, (September 2000). Retrieved 17/09/07, from http://unpan1.un.org/intradoc/groups/public/documents/APCITY/UNPAN004853.pdf

Inkeles, A., & Levinson, D. (1969). National character: The study of module personality and sociocultural systems. In G. Lindsay & E. Aronson (Eds.), *The handbook of social psychology, vol. 4.* Addison-Wesley.

Järvenpää, S. L., & Leidner, D. E. (1999). Communication and trust in global virtual teams. *Organization Science, 10*, 791 – 815.

Kanter, V. D. (1999). Knowledge management, practically speaking. *Information Systems Management, Fall*, 7-15.

Kluckhohn, F. (1951). Values and value-orientation in the theory of action: An exploration in definition and classification. In T. Parsons & E A. Shils (Eds.), *Towards a general theory of action.* Cambridge MA: Harvard University Press.

Kluckhohn, F., & Strodtbeck, F. (1961). *Variations on value orientations.* Evanstone, IL: Row, Peterson & Company.

Kothandaraman P. & Wilson D. T. (2001). The future of competition: Value creating networks. *Industrial Marketing Management, 30(4)*, 379-389.

Kroeger, A., & Kluckhohn, F. (1952). *Culture: A critical review of concepts and definitions.* Cambridge: Harvard Business Review.

Lipnack, J., & Stamps, J. (1997). *Virtual teams: Reaching across space, time and organisations with technology.* New York: Wiley.

Lopez, S. P., Peon, J. M. M., & Ordas, C. J. V. (2004). Managing knowledge: The link between culture and organisational learning. *Journal of Knowledge Management, 8*(6), 93-104.

Mansour-Cole, D. (2001). Team identity formation in virtual teams. In S. Beyerlein, M. Beyerlein, & D. Johnson (Eds.), *Virtual teams, Advances in interdisciplinary studies of work teams, vol. 8.* Oxford: Elsevier Science.

Menon, A., & Varadarajan, P. R. (1992). A model of marketing knowledge use within firms. *Journal of Marketing, 56*(4), 53 – 71.

Moffett, S., McAdam, R., & Parkinson, S. (2003). An empirical analysis of knowledge management applications. *Journal of Knowledge Management, 7*(3), 6-26.

Nonaka, I. (1991). The knowledge-creating company. *Harvard Business Review, 69*(6), 96-104.

O'Dell, I., & Grayson, C. J. (1998). If only we knew what we know: Identification and transfer of internal best practices. *California Management Review, 40*(3), 154 - 174.

Ojukwu, D., & Georgiadou, E.(2007). *Towards improving inter-organisational trust amongt SMEs – A case study from developing countries.* Paper presented at the 9th IFIP International Conference on the Social Implications of Computers in Developing Countries, May 2007, Sao Paolo, Brazil. Retrieved from http://www.ifipwg94.org.br/fullpapers/R0096-1.pdf

Park, H., Ribiere, V., & Schulte, W. D. (2004). Critical attributes of organisational culture that promote knowledge management technology implementation success. *Journal of Knowledge Management, 8*(3), 106-117.

Pfeffer, J., & Sutton, R. (2000). *The knowing doing gap: How smart companies turn knowledge into action.* Boston Ma: Harvard Business School Press.

Redding, S. G. (1994). Comparative management theory: Jungle, zoo or fossil bed? *Organisation Studies, 15*(3), 323-359.

Rodrigues, C. A., & Blumberg, H. (2000). Do feminine cultures really behave more feminine than masculine cultures? A comparison of 48 countries' femininity-masculinity ranking to their human development rankings. *Cross-Cultural Management - An International Journal, 7*(3), 25-34.

Ruggles, R. (1998). The state of notion: Knowledge management in practices. *California Management Review, 40*(3), 80-89.

Sackmann, S. A., & Phillips, M. E. (2004). One's many cultures: A multiple cultures perspective. In N. A. Boyacigiller (Ed.), *Crossing cultures: Insights from master teachers.*

Schein, E. H. (1985). How culture forms, develops and changes. In R. H. Kilmann, M. J. Saxton, & R. Serpa (Eds.), *Gaining control of the corporate culture.* San Francisco: Jossey Bass.

Segalla M. (2001). Overview: Understanding values and expectations of foreign employees creates a better company. *European Management Journal, 19*(1), 27-31.

Siakas K. V. & Hyvärinen J. (2006). On-line Assessment of the Fit between National and Organisational Culture; A new tool for Predicting Suitable Software Quality Management System. In R. Dawson, E. Georgiadou, P. Linecar, M.

Ross., & G. Staples (eds), *Perspectives in Software Quality: Proceeding of the 14th Software Quality Management Conference (SQM 2006)*, April, Southampton, UK, The British Computer Society, pp. 197-204

Siakas, K. V. (2002). *SQM-CODE: Software quality management – Cultural and organisational diversity evaluation.* PhD Thesis, London Metropolitan University, UK.

Siakas, K. V., & Balstrup, B. (2006). Software outsourcing quality achieved by global virtual collaboration, software process. *Improvement and Practice (SPIP) Journal, 11*(3), 319-328.

Siakas, K. V., & Georgiadou, E. (1999). Process improvement: The societal iceberg. In *European Software Process Improvement Conference, EuroSPI '99* (pp. 25-37), Pori, Finland, 25 - 27.10.

Siakas K. V., & Georgiadou E. (2003). Learning in a changing society and the importance of cultural awareness. In *IADIS 2003 (International Association for development of the Information Society)* (pp. 696-702), International Conference, Algarve, Portugal, 5-8 Nov. 2003, Vol. I.

Siakas, K. V., & Georgiadou, E. (2006). Knowledge sharing: Cultural dynamics. In P. Feher (Ed.), *Proceedings of 7th European Conference of Knowledge Management (ECKM06)* (pp. 505-513), 4-5 Sept., Public Academic Conferences Ltd. Reading, UK.

Siakas K. V., Georgiadou E.(2003). Learning in a Changing Society and the Importance of Cultural Awareness, Paper presentet at *IADIS 2003 (International Association for development of the Information Society)* International Conference, Algarve, Portugal, 5-8 Nov. 2003, Vol. I, 696-702

Siakas, K. V., & Georgiadou, E. (1999). Process Improvement: The Societal Iceberg. Paper presented at the *European Software Process*

Improvement Conference, EuroSPI '99, Pori, Finland, 25 - 27.10, pp. 25-37

Siakas K. V., & Hyvärinen J. (2006). On-line assessment of the fit between national and organisational culture; A new tool for predicting suitable software quality management system. In R. Dawson, E. Georgiadou, P. Linecar, M. Ross., & G. Staples (Eds), *Perspectives in software quality: Proceeding of the 14th Software Quality Management Conference (SQM 2006)* (pp. 197-204), April, Southampton, UK, The British Computer Society.

Sondergaard, M. (1994). Research note: Hofstede's consequences: A study of reviews, citations and replications. *Organisation Studies*, 15, 447-456.

Spiegler, I. (2000). Knowledge management: A new idea or a recycled concept? *Communications of the Association for Information Systems (AIS)*, June, 3(14), 1-23.

Tanriverdi, H. (2005). Information technology relatedness, knowledge management capability and performance of multi-business firms. *MIS Quarterly*, 29(2 - June), 311-334.

Tsatsou P. (2005). *Civil society in Greece: Shaping new digital divides? The digital divides as "cultural" divides.* Implications for closing divides, ESRC Seminar on "Bridging the Digital Divides," Oxford Internet Institute, UK, 4 March 2005. Retrieved from http://www.oii.ox.ac.uk/collaboration/seminars/20050304_Panayiota_Tsatsou_Paper.pdf

Wenger, E. (1999). *Communities of practice: Learning, meaning and identity.* Cambridge: University Press.

Wenger, E., & Snyder,B (2000). Communities of practice: The organisational frontier. *Harvard Business Review*, 78(1), 139–145.

ADDITIONAL READING

Ackoff, R. L. (1989). From data to wisdom. *Journal of Applied Systems Analysis*, 16, 3-9.

Barab, S. A., Kling, R., & Gray, J. H. (2004). *Designing for virtual communities in the service of learning.* Cambridge University Press, Cambridge, UK.

Bettoni, M., Andenmatten, S., & Mathieu R. (2006). Knowledge cooperation in online communities: A duality of participation and cultivation. In P. Feher (Ed.), *Proceedings of 7th European Conference of Knowledge Management (ECKM06)* (pp. 36-42), 4-5 Sept., Public Academic Conferences Ltd. Reading, UK. Brown, A. D. (1998). *Organisational culture.* London, UK: Financial Times Management, Pitman Publishing.

De Carolis, M., & Corvello, V. (2006). Multiple competences in distributed communities of practice: The case of a community of financial advisors. In P. Feher (Ed.), *Proceedings of 7th European Conference of Knowledge Management (ECKM06)* (pp. 116-125), 4-5 Sept., Public Academic Conferences Ltd. Reading, UK. Fang, T. (2006). From "onion" to "ocean," paradox and change in national cultures. *International Studies of Management & Organisation*, 35(4), 71–90.

Georgiadou, E., Siakas K. V., & Berki, E. (2006). Knowledge creation and sharing through student-lecturer collaborative group coursework. In P. Feher (Ed.), *Proceedings of 7th European Conference of Knowledge Management (ECKM06)* (pp. 678-689), 4-5 Sept., Public Academic Conferences Ltd. Reading, UK.

Goodstein, L. D. (1981). American business values and cultural imperialism. *Organisational Dynamics*, 10(1), 49-54.

Groeschl, S., & Doherty, L. (2000). Conceptualising culture. *Cross Cultural Management, An International Journal*, 7(4), 12-17.

Hofstede, G. (1985).The interaction between national and organisational value system. *Journal of Management Studies, 22*, 347-57.

Hofstede, G. (1995). Multilevel research of human systems: Flowers, bouquets and gardens. *Human System Management, 14*, 207-217.

Hofstede, G., & McCrae, R. R. (2004). Personality and culture revisited: Linking traits and dimensions of culture. *Cross-Cultural Research, 38*(1), 52-85.

Hofstede, G., Neuijen, B., Ohayv, D., & Sanders, G. (1990). Measuring organisational cultures, a qualitative study across twenty cases. *Administrative Science Quarterly, 35*, 286-316.

Jabri, M. M. (2005). Commentaries and critical articles : Text–context relationships and their implications for cross cultural management. *International Journal of Cross-Cultural Management, 5*(3), 349–360.

Joynt, P., & Warner, M. (1996). Introduction: Cross-cultural perspectives. In P. Joynt, & M. Warner (Eds.), *Managing across cultures: Issues and perspectives.* International Thomson Business Press

Kwai Fun IP, R., & Wagner C. (2007). Weblogging: A study of social computing and its impact on organizations. *ScienceDirect – Decision Support Systems*, 1-8.

Lave, J., & Wenger, E. (1991). *Situated learning: Legitimate peripheral participation.* Cambridge, New York: Cambridge University Press.

Leung, K., Bhagat, R. S., Buchan, N. R., Erez, M., & Gibson. C. B. (2005). Culture and international business: Recent advances and their implications for future research. *Journal of International Business Studies, 36*, 357–378.

Lofland, J., & Lofland, L. H. (1995). *Analytic social settings, A guide of qualitative observation and analysis.* Wadsworth Publishing Company.

McSweeney, B. (2002). Model of national cultural differences and their consequences: A triumph of faith—a failure of analysis. *Human Relations, 55*(1), 89–118.

Mullins, L. J. (1989). *Management and organisational Behaviour.* London: Pitman Publishing.

Neches, R, Fikes, R., Finin T., Patil, R., Senator, T., & Swartout, W. R. (1991). Enabling technology for knowledge sharing. *AI Magazine, 12*(3), 16-36.

Sahni, A. K., & Rastogi, A. K. (1995). Transforming corporate culture through total quality commitment. In *5th World Congress on Total Quality* (pp.42 – 45), New Delhi, Feb.

Schwen, T. M., & Hara, N. (2003). Community of practice. A metaphor for online design? *The Information Society, 19*, 257-270.

Siakas, K. V., & Siakas E. (2008). The need for trust relationships to enable successful virtual team collaboration and software outsourcing. *The International Journal of Technology, Policy and Management,* special issue on Human Aspects of Information Technology Development, Fall 2007.

Storck, J., & Hill P. (2000). Knowledge diffusion through "strategic communities." *Sloan Management Review, 41*(2), 63–74.

Tayeb, M. (1988). *Organisations and national culture: A comparative analysis.* London, UK: Sage Publishers.

Trompenaars, F., & Hampden-Turner, C. (1997). *Riding the waves of culture.* Nicholas Brealey.

Williamson, D. (2002). Forward from a critique of Hofstede's model of national culture. *Human Relations, 55*(11), 1373–1395.

Chapter IV
Towards an Implicit and Collaborative Evolution of Terminological Ontologies

Axel-Cyrille Ngonga Ngomo
University of Leipzig, Germany

ABSTRACT

This chapter is concerned with the evolution of terminological ontologies used for representing personal knowledge. It first argues that each member of the knowledge society will need a personal knowledge model representing his/her knowledge. Subsequently, it presents a method for implicitly and collaboratively evolving such personal knowledge models, improving by these means the knowledge transfer in the knowledge society over the Internet. The authors hope that an understanding of the importance of personal terminological ontologies, and especially of a low-bias approach to their implicit and collaborative evolution, will contribute to the transformation from the information to the knowledge society.

INTRODUCTION

In recent years, the significance of knowledge sharing and exchange over the Internet has been recognized by the scientific community to be crucial for the arising knowledge society, which will be based on the next generation of the Internet, that is, the semantic Web (see e.g., Abidi & Pang, 2004). The transfer and management of knowledge over the Internet demand the existence of several technologies, per se.

First, it demands techniques for representing knowledge in a way accessible to both machines and human users. Much work has been done in the areas of knowledge representation (KR) and artificial intelligence (AI). In the seventies, several approaches to KR methods, such as connectionist (Block, 1962; McCulloch & Pitts, 1943) and logic based (Tarski, 1956) were already developed. In the following decade, main KR projects such as Cyc (Lenat & Guha, 1989) arose. KR languages and formats such as CycL (Lenat & Guha, 1989), the knowledge interchange format (KIF) (Hayes & Menzel, 2001) and Loom (McGregor, 1990) were subsequently developed. These methods then made room for ontology representation languages. Meanwhile, they are the standard for representing machine-readable knowledge with RDF/OWL (resource description framework/Web Ontology Language) as W3C (World Wide Web Consortium) standards (W3C, 2006). Ontologies are considered to be the backbone of the future semantic Web and hence, of the knowledge representation in the knowledge society based on it. They are universally utilizable KR structures that have already been used in several contexts such as data description (Dwight, Harris, Dolinski, Ball, Binkley, Christie, et al., 2002), knowledge communication for software agents (Takeda, Iino, & Nishida, 1995), modeling of linguistic knowledge (Omelayenko, 2001), and Information Retrieval (Müller, Kenny, & Sternberg, 2004). A rapidly growing number of organizations have realized the need to make their knowledge accessible in such a way (Kingston, 2008).

Second, exchanging knowledge demands a knowledge transfer architecture, which can be based on shared knowledge bases, personal knowledge bases (linked using peer-to-peer technologies for example), or a combination of both (personalized knowledge bases). In knowledge-intensive organizations, techniques for KR will be potentially used not only to represent global knowledge shared by the members from a certain domain, but also the personal knowledge of each user, enabling intelligent agents to perform tasks demanding specific knowledge about the context, needs, and preferences of the user, for example, personalized semantic information retrieval, customized translation, automatic planning, and so forth. By these means, contextually relevant content and knowledge will be made accessible to the user, improving his/her effectiveness and therefore, the competitiveness of the whole organization. Improved innovation cycles, shorter time-to-market, and better reuse are only a few of the advantages that such an approach promises. In order to enable such personalized and customized operations and services, Knowledge Management (KM) systems will necessitate a representation

of the interests, knowledge, and requirements of each user. Yet modeling such knowledge manually would be a very costly process with regard to time and resources. Other operations, such as updating personal knowledge bases, would also demand a considerable amount of resources. Due to the fact that the knowledge of single individuals grows with time, productive KM systems will need to continuously capture the growth of personal knowledge, and include it in the personalized knowledge models. Thus, the need for approaches for the evolution of personal knowledge bases is undeniable. Yet, updating solely the personal ontologies of employees would not be of use to a company if the growth of knowledge of the employees is not reflected in the global ontology of the company. A method for subsuming personal ontologies to a global ontology is thus, also needed.

The goals of this chapter are twofold: first, chosen approaches to KR in the context of KM will be presented, and the use of ontologies for KR in KM will be discussed. The main goal of this chapter will yet be to introduce a user-centered collaborative evolution approach for personal knowledge bases. Several technical concepts necessary to implement concepts, such as the similarity of users within a community and of ontologies, will be introduced. Finally, a possible approach for collaborative and semiautomatic ontology evolution, based on natural language processing, will be presented.

This chapter is structured as follows: In the following section, background knowledge on KR and the use of KR mechanisms for IT-supported KM will be presented. Criteria for selecting an appropriate technique for KM will be defined and applied to state-of-the-art approaches. Furthermore, existing approaches for automatic extraction and evolution will be presented. The subsequent section will be concerned with a collaborative and user-centered ontology evolution, focusing on personal terminological ontologies. Finally, the conclusion will be concerned with presenting some pros and cons of these methods, and depicting some of the problems that arise and possible solutions.

BACKGROUND

According to Song, Nerur, and Teng (2007), Knowledge Management (KM) is concerned with the "creation, storage, access and dissemination of intellectual assets." It combines several disciplines, such as psychology, sociology, IT, and management, and aims at finding methods and techniques for capturing the explicated and tacit knowledge of employees, and diffusing it within the enterprise to enhance its performance. The area of IT-supported KM began with the arousal of techniques for knowledge storage and retrieval (Kautz & Mahnke, 2003). IT-supported KM is mainly concerned with the development of techniques to support the digitalization of knowledge into knowledge models, its externalization into content assets, and the retrieval and manipulation of assets to improve the knowledge transfer within companies. This chapter will be exclusively concerned with this aspect of KM, focusing especially on the use of ontologies for the description of content and the associated semantics.

In order to support the diffusion, creation, and reuse of knowledge, KM tools have to implement basic operations on knowledge models and content. These operations will play a central role when defining an evolution strategy, based on the assumption that they are implemented in all KM tools. Knowledge will be considered as contained implicitly in content assets, and explicitly stored in knowledge models. For this reason, software tools for KM must implement these operations on both content and knowledge models, enabling the users to manipulate the available knowledge implicitly or explicitly. In the following, several basic operations on content and knowledge will be presented. Then, criteria for selecting suitable KR techniques for KM will be depicted. These

criteria will be used for choosing appropriate KR techniques for KM. Subsequently, existing techniques for the evolution of knowledge represented using the chosen paradigm will be presented. This will then lead to the core of this chapter, a new approach to the evolution of the given KR model.

Operations on Content and Knowledge

In order to define necessary semantic operations on content, the interdependencies between information (i.e., content assets), knowledge (contained in the assets), and working process of the end users (i.e., the context in which they need the information/knowledge) has to be taken into consideration and applied to the standard content lifecycle. Haertwig and Boehm (2005) defined the coherency model displayed in Figure 1.

It displays the interdependencies existing between information, knowledge, and work activities with respect to information supply and thus, to the transfer of knowledge within organizations. The users, as knowledge holders, need to access relevant information (i.e., content) within a given

Figure 1. Coherency model for information, knowledge, and process (Haertwig & Boehm, 2005)

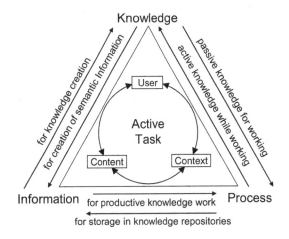

Figure 2. Content lifecycle (Dutta, 2000)

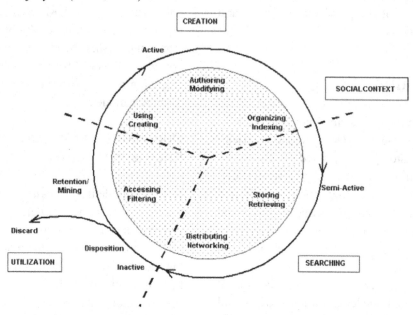

context set by the business process in which they are to complete a given task. To achieve that goal, different operations between the elements of the model can be used. Haertwig and Boehm (2005) argue that it is necessary to support both the externalization of knowledge during the work process (so called knowledge coproduction) and the internalization of semantically enriched information to knowledge. Since the knowledge of a company is not yielded by a single individual, but by the whole set of employees, the externalization and internalization of knowledge must be realized as a collaborative sharing process within the context of the company. Yet, since each single user has special needs with respect to relevant knowledge, the possibilities of personalized knowledge-based (i.e., semantic) operations are required as well.

Based on these considerations and on the content lifecycle as displayed in Figure 2, four basic operations must be implemented in and supported by KM systems: creation, consumption, curation and abstraction. The operations aggregate the functionality of the operations proposed by Dutta (2001) and extend them by taking knowledge and collaborative concepts into consideration.

Creation

This operation can be subdivided in two main parts: content and knowledge creation. Content creation consists of the explication of knowledge in the form of documents or other content assets, and in making these available to the rest of the employees. It usually involves a group of users (proofreaders, quality management, etc.), and is implemented as a collaborative process, per se. To improve the accessibility of created content, techniques, such as *content annotation,* need to be implemented. This concept is borrowed from free tagging, which is state-of-the-art in most collaborative tools. The drawback of free tags is their semantic independence. For example, it cannot be inferred that synonym tags characterize the same concept. Using the concepts yielded in knowledge models for tagging would enable linking content and knowledge directly. The other aspect of creation, that is, knowledge creation, refers to the manual or automatic generation of knowledge models and resources. Since every user needs to be able to perform this task, appropriate tool support is required. Knowledge created by a single user might be only valid for this given user and not globally. Once more, the need for personalized knowledge models is evident. Globally accepted knowledge can be considered as being generally valid for the organization, and can be integrated in a global knowledge model.

Consumption

Consuming knowledge can be realized on both content and knowledge models. From the point of view of content, it is the task of the KM system to provide the user with special tools for supporting information retrieval, since users do not usually know where relevant information is to be found. Techniques for the automatic provision of contextually relevant information must, thus, be implemented. Once again, personalized knowledge models are required to model the information needed by users in a given context. The main drawback of automated information supply, that is, the discrepancy between the granularities of available content assets and needed information, can be addressed by combining two operations: *content segmentation* for extracting contextually relevant information out of content assets and presenting these, and *agglomeration* for merging such content segments to larger content assets focused on a particular topic (Ngonga Ngomo & Schumacher, 2006).

Abstraction

Abstraction can be defined as the process of formulating general concepts based on common properties of available instances. Information abstraction is the externalization step from content assets (analyzed by human cognition) to knowledge. KM systems must provide the user with functionality for modeling out available knowledge using, for example, a KR kit. This operation models the knowledge explication per se. Since it is realized by a single user in a given context, it must be applied to the personal knowledge models

of the given user. In order to ensure a transfer of this knowledge to other users, means for selecting similar users and transferring updates between ontologies need to be implemented. This implicitly collaborative technique is of central importance, since it requires minimal supplementary effort from single users while enabling a continuous knowledge sharing over the whole company.

Curation

Data curation is a concept borrowed from the world of databases and consists of validating existing information; a document segment being regarded as valid when it contains reliable information. The validation process is a collaborative process on information segments, and consists of the alteration of content assets in order to ensure their validity and superior semantic quality. Through the internalization of the knowledge contained in existing documents, the curation of the knowledge bases can be carried out. Similar to "abstraction," this operation must be carried out on the personalized knowledge base of each user, and is an important component for the support of knowledge transfer with companies.

Criteria for Knowledge Representation Techniques

The operations presented bear several similarities. First, they are all of collaborative nature, enabling an extensive knowledge sharing between the knowledge stakeholders of the company. Second, they all allow users to integrate implicitly their specific knowledge in the global knowledge model used in the company in a fast and efficient way. Third, they demand the existence of a mapping between personalized ontologies and the knowledge model representing the global knowledge of the organization.

These analogies require a KR paradigm that supports the paradigm of *knowledge distribution*: In order to link the personal knowledge bases to the company-wide knowledge model, the KR technique used must support distributed storage and collaborative manipulation through the knowledge stakeholders themselves. This implies the need for *accurate support* with easy-to-use tools designed for non-specialists. Especially, methods based on formal description languages do not provide such support since they were primarily designed for specialists. A further criterion for the use of a KR technique in KM is related with the *representational power* of the language. Most formal languages used in KR have the representational power of first-order logics (FOL). On the other end of the spectrum are purely visual languages that do not permit the representation of semantics (Myers, 1990). Languages for KM do not primarily necessitate formal descriptions, since they are mostly used to describe terminological concepts. Yet they should be able to support the specification of formal relations in order to enable concepts, such as inference, when necessary.

Knowledge Representation

Techniques for KR can be differentiated according to different axes. From the point of view of the type of knowledge to model, one can differentiate two main classes of knowledge: procedural and declarative. According to Polanyi (1967), procedural knowledge is of tacit nature and thus, difficult to model. Therefore, we will address methods for modeling declarative knowledge. Declarative KR models are "a set of ontological statements" (Davis, Shrobe, & Szolovits, 1993), that is, they describe the way in which we do or should think about the world. The representation of factual knowledge can be carried out using several techniques that can belong to one or more of the following groups (Sowa, 2000):

- *Frame-based languages* specify the objects in the world of reference using so-called concepts, and describe the knowledge about the relations between these objects (Minsky,

1975). The description of the world generated by frame-based systems is of static nature. Therefore, frame-based systems are limited when dealing with procedural knowledge (Winograd, 1975), but are highly suitable for representing factual knowledge as necessary in KM.

- *Logic-based languages* represent knowledge using the concepts of first-order logic, and are thus suitable for the representation of factual knowledge (see e.g., McCarthy, 1968). Each object modeled using frame-based constructs can be described using an existential statement in first-order logic. Yet this representation is usually longer and thus, less easy to handle. Logic-based systems can represent sequences of actions and can thus be used to represent procedural knowledge.

- *Rule-based languages* represent knowledge through logical statements, called rules or production rules, that define possible actions when given premises are fulfilled. Based on factual knowledge stored in their working memory (the initial conditions), rule-based languages allow the inference of new knowledge (see e.g., Gallaire & Minker, 1978).

- Modern *ontological languages* combine the advantages of frame, logic- and rule-based languages. They allow statements about entities, the definition of global rules, and the usage of inference tools for the extraction of supplementary knowledge. Further, they permit different degrees of formalism ranging from no formal specification at all to FOL (see e.g., Pulido, Ruiz, Herrera, Cabello, Legrand, & Elliman, 2006).

With the emergence of the Web2.0, the effort invested in the development of ontological languages increased considerably. As stated, all declarative KR models are a set of ontological statements, that is, they describe either elements of the world or relationships between these. Ontological languages such as OWL (see http://www. w3.org/TR/owl-features/ for an exact description of OWL and its features), the current W3C standard for ontology description, have been developed exactly for this purpose. Being able to describe factual knowledge like frame-based and logic-based languages, they can also define global rules associated with the objects and their relations, and integrate different levels of formal description from none to full FOL.

The *distribution* of the knowledge to describe over several ontologies and locations is an integral part of the current standard OWL that allows the integration of classes from other ontologies into a given one. All other languages can potentially support such a distribution, although it is usually not explicitly desired, like in the case of ontologies.

Due to the rapid expansion of the semantic Web, *tools* for the graphical modeling, manipulation, and maintenance of ontologies through non-experts have been created. The tools necessary to manipulate the other languages are mostly difficult to understand and require a strong background in formal logics, making them not suitable for non-specialists.

The representational power of ontologies can be varied by selecting the dialect used. The languages OWL-Lite and OWL-DL are decidable and thus, less complex than FOL. OWL-Full, on the other hand, bears the same complexity as FOL, and can thus be used to represent the knowledge explicated using frame, logics, and rule-based languages. It is, therefore, obvious that ontologies are best suited for being used in KM.

Classification of Ontologies

Ontologies are defined as "specification of a conceptualization" (Gruber, 1993), that is, as description of entities that might exist in a certain domain and of the relations between them. There are at least two views on ontologies: structural and user-driven. From the point of view of structure,

one can distinguish three types of ontologies (Sowa, 2003):

- *Formal ontologies*, which include a fully axiomatized set of relationships between labeled concepts.
- *Prototype ontologies*, which describe concepts using a set of typical instances and are usually of hierarchical nature.
- *Terminological ontologies*, which describe semantic worlds using labeled concepts, and a set of usually not or partly axiomatized relationships, on which we shall focus in this chapter.

From the point of view of usage, ontologies can be categorized as global and personal ontologies:

- Global ontologies are ontologies in the commonly used sense. They describe agreements on global knowledge and are valid for a group of individuals. Numerically, global ontologies can be seen as the mean of the personal knowledge of each of the individuals in a group. All three structural categories of ontologies can be used to describe common knowledge. Usually formal ontologies are preferred, since they allow operations such as inference, which are very useful for software agents.
- Personal ontologies describe a domain from the point of view of a single individual in a machine-readable form, and are only valid for the given user. Although this concept is not completely new, this view of ontology has gained a broader interest within the scientific community only during the past few years (see e.g., Carmichael, Kay, & Kummerfeld, 2004; Chaffee & Gauch, 2000). It is known that different individuals have at least slightly different semantic worlds and thus, cannot mean exactly the same thing when they refer to the same concept (Korzybski, 1933). Since knowledge-based

services, such as personalized semantic information retrieval, are an integral part of the knowledge-sharing process over the Internet (knowledge pull and push), the representation of the exact semantics of each user will be needed to ensure a high level of quality when retrieving knowledge (knowledge pull), describing knowledge (knowledge push), and extracting the knowledge of organizations from the stakeholders themselves, that is, the users. As displayed in Figure 3, the organizational knowledge is the conjunction of the personal knowledge of the employees of the companies, which itself was acquired through world and personal experiences. This personal knowledge, which should be expressed in personal ontologies, might differ only slightly from one employee to the other. Since a description of fuzziness and therefore, a characterization of slight differences are not possible in formal ontologies, it is preferable to use the less formal ontology categories to describe personal knowledge.

Existing evolution methods were designed taking formal ontologies into consideration. Still, analyzing some of the existing ontology evolution techniques will be of help when considering the evolution of personal terminological ontologies.

Ontology Generation and Evolution

One of the main drawbacks of the semantic Web idea is linked to the high investments required for modeling ontologies manually (see Lopez, 1999 for a good overview of methods and principles for manually modeling ontologies). For this reason, methods for automatically extracting ontologies were created. Most of these methods use machine learning techniques, such as propositional learning (Maedche & Staab, 2000), Bayesian learning (Craven, DiPasquo, Freitag, McCallum, Mitchell, Nigam, & Slattery, 2000), clustering (Bisson, Nedellec, & Canamero, 2000) on a different set of features, such as distributional patterns as syntactic patterns (Hindle, 1990), or extraction patterns such as Hearst-patterns (Caraballo, 1999). Omelayenko (2001), Ding and Foo (2002), and

Figure 3. Conceptual relationships between personal and organizational ontologies (Bennett & Theodoulidis, 1998)

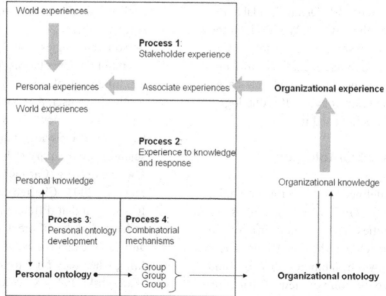

Biemann (2005) provide a good overview over such techniques. Most of the techniques for ontology extraction require a considerable amount of text to produce acceptable results. The extracted ontologies usually have to be corrected manually, which can also be a very expensive undertaking. The expenses involved in the semiautomatic generation of ontologies are yet, always below those necessary when modeling the ontology manually. Automatically generated ontologies do not reflect the semantics of the single users, but solely the semantics of the corpus they were extracted from. Therefore, the need is for methods for evolving terminological ontologies, which can transform an ontology into a correct model of each user's knowledge.

Evolution is defined by the Cambridge English Dictionary as "a gradual process of change and development." Ontology evolution can, therefore, be understood as the continuous process of modifying and expanding an ontology in such a way that it shapes up into a correct model of the user's semantics. Another definition was proposed by Stojanovic (2004, p.15), who defines ontology evolution as "the timely adaptation of an ontology to the arisen changes and the consistent propagation of these changes to dependent artifacts." This definition is coherent with the one proposed previously, with the sole nuance that the consistency of a change within the existing ontology can only be evaluated by the user for whom the ontology is intended.

Much work has been done on ontology modeling and extraction, but ontology evolution has yet not been deeply investigated, although the need for ontology evolution techniques is clearly existent (Flouris, 2006): Klein and Fensel (2001) discuss the decreasing flexibility of applications when the included knowledge models are not updated. Haase et al. (Haase, Ehrig, Hotho, & Schnizler, 2004) propose that ontologies can be highly dynamic and evolve drastically over time, using the example of a bibliographic peer-to-peer system. Since domain knowledge grows

with time, ontologies are unavoidably bound to change in order to keep on modeling a domain correctly. According to Stojanovic (2004), the ontology evolution process can be subdivided into six phases:

- **Requirements capturing:** The domain to model and the granularity of the model are defined in this phase. For automatic extraction, the choice of the domain is the steering factor for the choice of the corpus.
- **Change representation:** This phase is concerned with the modeling of the required changes according to their granularity, which can range from atomic (only one concept or relation has to be modified) to complex (subsumption of atomic changes).
- **Semantics of change:** This phase is concerned with the systematic resolution of inconsistencies that might occur when a change takes place. In the case of formal ontologies, this can be realized by defining key axioms that always have to hold, and cascading changes as long as the key axioms hold. Changes that lead to a negation of the key axioms are rolled back.
- **Change propagation:** The forwarding of changes to related ontologies and the securing of their consistency after these changes have been overtaken takes place in this phase.
- **Implementation:** This phase is concerned with informing the knowledge engineer requesting changes with the consequences of its requests, applying and logging the changes. In this phase, the ontology evolution, as such, takes place.
- **Validation:** This phase is concerned with checking the evolved ontology for correctness.

Although the area of ontology evolution is related to areas, such as ontology management and versioning in literature, we will focus on the purely evolutionary aspect of ontology evolution, that is, on the process of transforming ontologies into more accurate models.

Klein and Noy (2003) present a framework for ontology evolution, and underline some of the main restrictions when transforming ontologies, pointing out, especially, ontology update, verification, and approval restrictions, yet assuming that all users share a single common ontology. Since the views of different users might differ on certain points, it should be more accurate to have local ontologies for each user that are evolved using the user's knowledge. A merging of such local ontologies would be the equivalent to the global ontology for all users asserted by Klein and Noy.

Stojanovic et al. (Stojanovic, Maedche, Stojanovic, & Studer, 2003) consider ontology evolution to be a reaction to changes, and propose a configuration-design approach to tackle the evolution problem. The same approach is more widely described in Stojanovic (2004), who proposes that "ontology evolution is accommodated when an ontology management system facilitates the modification of an ontology by preserving its consistency." Changes that occur without consistency check are referred to as "ontology modification." As stated, the consistency check is realized by the user and not the system, in the case of terminological ontologies. Thus, terminological ontologies can also be evolved and not solely modified. Other approaches propose the use of formalisms such as ACL (Sindt, 2003) or an algebraic representation of DL-ontologies (Flouris, Plexousakis, & Antoniou, 2006) for ontology evolution.

All approaches to ontology evolution, cited previously, were based on manually modeled formal ontologies. As known to the author, the evolution of terminological ontologies has not yet been considered in literature. The following section is concerned with presenting a possible approach to such an evolution. The formal concepts, presented as formulae, are explained within the text.

EVOLUTION OF TERMINOLOGICAL ONTOLOGIES

The collaborative evolution of terminological ontologies follows the process depicted in Figure 4 (the different colors depict the evolution processes of different users).

First, an alteration of an existing ontology takes place. It is propagated by the ontologies of similar users and implemented in them. The validation step then consists in accepting or refusing the proposed alteration.

Figure 4. Steps of the collaborative evolution of terminological ontologies

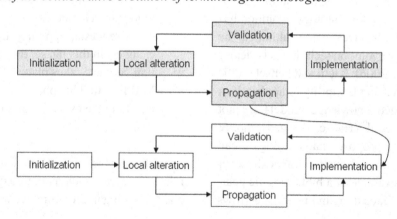

Preliminary Considerations

A theory for the evolution of terminological ontologies demands a precise comprehension of terminological ontologies; of techniques for measuring the similarity between ontologies and of the evolution paradigm. These will be described in this section.

Terminological Ontologies

Formally, a terminological ontology O is characterized by a set C of concepts, a set of relations R, a labeling function λ, and a set of labels L. The concepts depict elements of thought that characterize existing or fictional artifacts. These concepts are mapped to a name (called label), but are not equivalent to this name. For example, the concept labeled "car" is the abstract representation of all entities that belong to a certain degree to the family of cars, automobiles, vans, trucks, and so forth. Interestingly, the concept car is interpreted differently by different human beings. While "car" designates, especially, a personal car for some, it might much more designate a van for another. Concepts in ontologies are modeled through their relationships with each other. The labeling function λ maps each concept and relation to a label, that is, to a term that designates it. The set L is the set of all used concept and relation labels. Each label is used only once in an ontology in order to prevent the existence of polysemes, that is, concepts with more than one meaning.

Since terminological ontologies for describing personal ontologies would be too costly when created manually, they need to be extracted automatically from text corpora dependent on the user. This extraction can be realized using some of the techniques for automatic ontology extraction mentioned previously, and will be considered as given in the following. Common to most extraction algorithms is that they define a similarity function over a set of keywords K and use it to generate relations between objects. There are two

possibilities of doing so: either mapping single words with concepts, or mapping sets of terms to a single concept and using a label function to determine the label of the concept. Goodenough (1957) suggests that the use of the latter is more adequate in relation to human cognition. He proposes to break down the meaning of concepts into atomic sense units called "semantems." Each semantem can be identified with a single term from the domain corpus, and is a feature that a concept can have or not. By these means, concepts can be mapped to a crisp (i.e., non-fuzzy) subset of the set of terms. For example, the concept "car," as described previously, would be mapped to a set containing the terms car, automobile, van, and truck. Yet this crisp mapping is unable to capture concepts such as nuances in meaning and the fuzziness of semantics, which are both inherent in human language, as the existence of expressions such as "approximately" and "more or less" proves. Thus, an extension of the concept of semantems to the concept of fuzzy semantems is necessary. Each concept is, thus, mapped to a weighted set of terms, with the weights describing the degree to which a term characterizes a concept. A possible fuzzy description of car would then be car (0.7), automobile (0.3), van (0.3), and truck (0.1). With this description paradigm, the description of nuances and other fuzzy characteristics of natural languages are possible.

Three main steps are needed in order to extract semantem vectors (also called term vectors) from text. First, relevant terminology and the relation between the termini need to be extracted. For this purpose, a term similarity metric is required. Second, the extracted termini must be mapped to concepts by computing a fuzzy description of concepts in the term space. Here a concept-term mapping is needed. Third, the relations between the concepts need to be extracted. This can be achieved by a concept-similarity metric. In the case of fuzzy clustering-based approaches, for example, distributional patterns or collocations (Biemann, 2005) can be used to characterize semantems. A vector metric (such as the cosine or the Manhattan distance, see NIST, 2007) can then used as a term-similarity measure. A fuzzy clustering algorithm (e.g., CBC, Pantel & Lin, 2002) can subsequently be utilized for the extraction of clusters (term-concept mapping), which are subsequently labeled and used as concepts. The results of a relation-harvesting algorithm are finally combined with the concepts to create an initial ontology. The concept-similarity metric is based on the underlying fuzzy description. Since the number of relevant words in a corpus is finite, the term-similarity metric can be fully described using a term-term similarity matrix, which is equivalent to a weighted graph called term net. The goal of an approach for the automatic evolution of terminological ontologies is to modify this matrix according to the needs of the user and the subsequent propagation of these changes in the clustering, the labeling, and the relation harvesting. Figure 5 depicts this extraction process.

Measuring the Similarity of Terminological Ontologies

The description of ontological concepts using fuzzy semantems presents several advantages.

Most importantly, it results in a numerical comparability of ontologies. Several approaches for measuring the similarity of ontological structures have been developed over the years, of which a few follow: Bisson (1992) designed an approach for learning in FOL using a similarity measure based on the computation of the similarity of pairs of occurrences in expressions integrated in a Jacobi Matrix. Dieng and Hug (1998) represented ontologies as conceptual graphs, and developed a technique for comparing and merging such ontologies. Rahm and Bernstein (2001) present several approaches for measuring the similarity of schemata in the area of databases, which can partly be used in ontology evolution. They present a classification of schema matchers, and subdivide these in four main classes of matchers: schema-based, instance-based, hybrid, and composite matchers. More recently, Haase et al. (Haase, Hotho, Schmidt-Thieme, & Sure, 2005) designed an approach for collaborative and usage-driven evolution of formal personal ontologies.

The approaches presented in these papers presuppose the use of formal ontologies. Purely terminological ontologies are not considered. Using the proposed description for concepts, the comparison of terminological ontologies can

Figure 5. Exemplary ontology extraction process

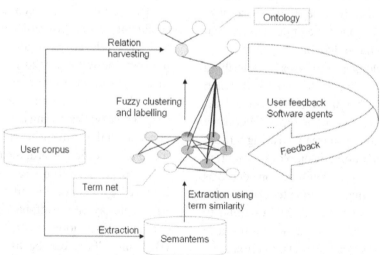

be reduced to the comparison of a set of vectors in a given vector space, in this case the space of semantems. Fuzzy semantem description of concepts and therefore, the similarity of terminological ontologies, can thus be easily compared using existing metrics on vector similarity. The NIST dictionary of algorithms and data structures (NIST, 2007) provides a good overview of prominent metrics. An advantage of the existence of a similarity metric for personal ontologies is that it allows the computation of the similarity of users by measuring the similarity of their ontologies. In the areas of peer-to-peer networks and information retrieval, several techniques for measuring the similarity of users have been developed (see e.g., Xiao, Zhang, Jia, & Li, 2001). In the rest of this chapter, the similarity of the personal ontologies of users will be used as value for the similarity of the users themselves. Based on these premises, an ontology evolution based on change propagation to similar users can be defined.

Ontology Evolution Process

The evolution of personal terminological ontologies does not demand an automation of every phase necessary to evolve formal ontologies. In particular, all consistency checks are realized by the user. Furthermore, the paradigm of collaborative evolution of terminological ontologies presupposes that personal ontologies are related to similar personal ontologies. This is necessary for changes in personal ontologies to be used to alter other ontologies of a community. We will first shortly present some considerations on the initialization of the evolution approach. Then, we will present formal considerations related to the evolution of single personal ontologies. Subsequently, the impact of these evolutionary steps on the other ontologies will be discussed. These considerations will lead to the third part of this section, that is, our vision of an ontology system that could underlie knowledge communities. Personal ontologies will be assumed to be

extracted and described as stated. In particular, each concept will be considered as being mapped to a fuzzy set of terms.

Initialization

The computation of the initial similarity between users requires the evaluation of the weights of each term in the description of the concepts included in each personal ontology. An important question for this initial ontology extraction step is the choice of a representative corpus for given users. Several solutions are possible: First, seed documents could be used in an iterative process to retrieve a representative subset of the organizational corpus. This method presents the advantage of demanding little effort from the user. Yet the choice of inappropriate seed documents could potentially lead to a non-representative corpus. Another possibility is the collection of typical user queries and the merging of their results to a data corpus, as used in the domain of personalized information retrieval. Here, the choice of the appropriate thresholds for a maximal coverage of the organizational data with a minimal loss of specificity is of great importance. More interactive approaches using hierarchical document clustering/classification, as in Information Retrieval, are another possibility for the determination of an initial user corpus. Baeza-Yates and Ribeiro-Neto (1999) give a good overview over modern IR techniques.

Independently from the method chosen for the selection of the initial user corpus and the extraction of an initial ontology, the key for the evolution of terminological ontologies are the typical functions required for the extraction of ontologies. Through the definition of a similarity function between terms and concepts (e.g., the cosine similarity, see Appendix A), the similarity of concepts and thus, of ontologies and users, can be determined. Given an initial similarity matrix for users, the propagation of local alterations can be implemented.

Local Alteration

The local alteration of ontologies can be carried out either implicitly through its usage in applications and the provision of feedback, or explicitly by modifying the ontology manually. The implicit alteration of personal knowledge bases is of great importance because it can be carried out not only by the user, but also by software agents representing the user. For example, a retrieval agent in charge of keeping the local repository of an employee up-to-date could modify his/her ontology implicitly by changing the underlying corpus and thus, the underlying match between concepts and their description as vectors of semantems. Furthermore, feedback collected from the owner of the ontology during his/her work, with/on results generated using the ontology, could be used for local alteration. The explicit modification of terminological ontologies is very similar to the modification of formal ontologies as described in literature. Therefore, it will not be further considered in this chapter. Stojanovic (2004) presents up-to-date approaches on this topic.

The implicit alteration of ontologies demands the collection of feedback from the user and its integration in the ontology. Feedback can be won in several ways: explicitly, by asking the user to rate results computed automatically using some knowledge included in the ontology, or implicitly,

by monitoring the interactions of the user with computation results, and cumulatively mapping these to a feedback value (see e.g., Ngonga Ngomo & Schumacher, 2006). The collection of feedback can be eased, using the KM operations described, since all KM tools must implement these. The resulting feedback can be used to alter either the concept description, that is, the term-concept mapping, or the term-similarity function, or both. If the term-concept mapping is chosen, the feedback can be propagated to the underlying term-term matrix using spreading activation techniques borrowed from the area of neural networks. Figure 6 displays an example of such a feedback propagation: The selection of a concept activates the underlying terms (second image from the left, activated concept, and terms are marked with double lines). The generation of positive feedback (third figure) strengthens the relation between concept and terms and in between terms (fourth figure, ticker lines mark a stronger relation). Ripley (1996) gives a good overview over existing techniques in this area.

Especially important during this process is the selection of the subnet used for the completion of the process leading to a given feedback. This ensures that only the knowledge used to produce the feedback is altered by the feedback. Positive feedback increases the similarity values between concepts and terms and in-between terms.

Figure 6. Exemplary propagation process

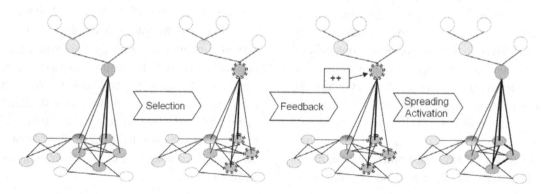

It is thus possible to suppose that every feedback results in an alteration of the term similarity matrix of the user, that is, of the semantem space. The ontology evolution then takes place by applying the initial ontology extraction algorithms on the new similarity values, and combining the resulting ontology with the current ontology of the user.

Propagation

A central aspect of collaborative ontology evolution is the propagation of changes from the ontology of single employees into the ontologies of similar employees. Again, the numerical description of concepts as vectors of semantem plays an important role. Users with similar term-similarity matrices will have similar semantic worlds, since the extracted ontologies will also be similar. Yet detecting similar users over the Internet/intranet can be a difficult task even within a company. One possible solution for this problem is to have users explicitly decide to participate in the knowledge interchange and thus, to register into a community designed for this purpose, and offering some value-added services based on these semantics. The registration would guarantee an accountability of the users, and allow the automatic detection of subdomains within the user community and thus, further refinements of the storage strategy (such as ontology clustering for better accessibility, for example) when necessary. Another possibility of ensuring a central storage of the personal ontologies of all users is the definition of administrative guidelines.

Supposing the existence of such a community, a network of similar users, can be defined over their term-similarity matrices. A well-known phenomenon that can then occur is the "small-world" phenomenon, which was initially proposed by Milgram (1967). He supposed that every two individuals in the world can be linked together by a chain of maximally six acquaintances. Further experiments showed that this phenomenon is common to many different areas of research (Newman, 2003). The principle of small worlds holds when trying to cluster users in generic communities, for example, in peer-to-peer networks (Iamnitchi, Ripeanu, & Foster, 2002). The number of small worlds is equal to the number of distinct domains represented in the whole community of users. Within each of those small worlds, changes in the ontology of a user A can be forwarded to the ontology of another user B in three steps:

- Converting the modification of the ontology into a modification of the term-similarity matrix using the spreading-activation principle, as used in neural networks and Information Retrieval (Preece, 1981), if necessary.
- Propagating the modifications in the term-similarity matrix of A into the term-similarity matrix of B using the similarity between the two matrices as weight. The result of this operation is a modified term-similarity matrix of B.
- Applying the ontology extraction process on the updated matrix and implementing the changes in the ontology of B, if they are accepted by B. The changes not accepted by B are simply rolled back in the term-similarity matrix.

Implementation and Validation

The implementation of this propagation strategy can be realized either by a sequential or a cumulative update of the term-similarity values. A sequential application of the possible updates bears the advantage that the user can revoke each atomic change. Yet since the number of atomic changes can be great, the user might spend more time updating his/her ontology than using it. The other alternative, the cumulative update, leads to the user having the possibility to revoke one complex update at a time. Yet this method may not permit the selection of acceptable parts of the ontology update. A solution might be a hybrid approach that would update the ontology of B using changes of a maximal, user-specific complexity. Either way, the validation of the alteration can be undertaken by the user only. The changes refused are rolled back in the term-similarity metric.

The five steps proposed in Figure 4 fully describe a technique for the evolution of ontologies, presupposing the existence of techniques for the automatic extraction out of text. The concrete implementation of the different steps is not explicitly stated, since several approaches are possible, as the proposed literature shows. Nevertheless, the method suggested is concrete enough to show that a collaborative evolution of personal terminological ontologies is possible.

Resulting Framework

The framework resulting from the considerations presented is displayed in Figure 7. Its life cycle can be subdivided into three main phases: ontology generation, personal-ontology evolution, and collaborative-ontology evolution.

During the ontology generation phase, the user chooses a basis corpus and uses a suitable ontology extraction algorithm to generate his/her initial ontology. Since users can have more than one domain of interest, the extracted ontology can be enriched using the global ontology of small worlds containing related concepts. Once his/her initial ontology is constructed, the user can manipulate the concepts in personal ontologies using a set of applications. Concepts can be manipulated explicitly by modifying the ontology using an ontology-modeling tool such as Protégé (Stanford, 2006). Implicit feedback can be collected when the user uses semantic services such as semantic retrieval engines and manipulates the information he accesses (Ngonga Ngomo & Schumacher, 2006), or when the user interacts indirectly with concepts using local software connected to his/her ontology. Every type of numeric user feedback can be used to evolve the ontology by updating the term-similarity matrix.

The collaborative ontology-evolution phase consists in forwarding the changes that occurred

Figure 7. Framework for collaborative ontology evolution

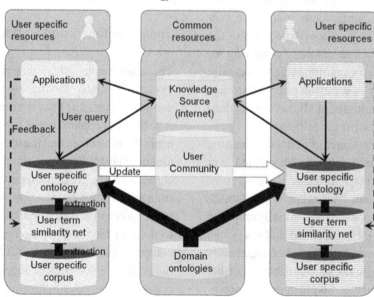

in an ontology to all other users sharing the same common global ontology, that is, in the same small world. These changes can be revoked by the single users or accepted. Especially interesting is the introduction of new concepts, which can lead to steadily growing ontologies, as is the case with the set of pages of Wikipedia. Furthermore, implicit knowledge sharing can lead to social phenomena such as the emergence of unexpected user networks, giving the administration of enterprises hints towards the creation or improvement of communication channels between the administrative roles included in the emerging small worlds.

The local ontologies can be aggregated to a domain ontology by periodically merging the personal ontologies of users in a given cluster (same or similar roles, tasks, small world cluster …). The necessary manual steps, especially the validation, would be carried out by knowledge engineers.

CONCLUSION

We presented an approach to collaborative ontology evolution especially designed for personal terminological ontologies, pointing out how a fuzzy version of Goodenough's compositional semantics could be used to define the semantics of concepts and for collaboratively evolving personal ontologies. The idea of practically each human being having his/her own ontology can seem unfeasible, yet the personalization of semantic services will be impossible without a transfer of the knowledge of users to the software agents implementing the services they need to access. Thus, there is an existing need for the representation of the evolving personal knowledge.

Collaborative ontology evolution requires that groups of similar users interchange knowledge. The small worlds in user communities are the basis on which we propose to generate such user groups automatically if other clustering patterns, such as their roles in the organization, are not clearly defined. Yet the probability distribution

for a user being a group might present some heavy-tail characteristics, leading to small worlds containing a very little number of users. Such users with atypical ontologies could not directly profit from collaborative ontology evolution. A possible solution for this problem would be to utilize a combination of fuzzy and hard clustering for user clustering. It would approximate atypical ontologies using a linear combination of typical ontologies.

From a global point of view, collaborative ontology-sharing communities could lead to an increase of the "opacity" (i.e., non-transparency) of users acting on the net. The users would have to log in in a platform and open their knowledge to agents with uncontrollable functionality (i.e., Internet search engines). Their personal knowledge could be used by the community service providers to serve their own profits, for example. Since a representative subset of the user's knowledge could be contained in such an ontology, illegal ontology transactions could lead to third-persons possessing a considerable amount of knowledge about individuals without the will nor the knowledge of the latter. Nevertheless, the trend towards the utilization of personal ontologies will develop with the integration of semantic Web technologies in our working environment. Their evolution would thus demand either the integration of technologies for explicit and implicit feedback in all working environments, or generic techniques able to monitor the user and compute feedback independently. Generating such feedback and using it during the ontology evolution process should be one of the research trends for the years to come.

Collaborative ontology evolution will be profitable for different parties: primarily, the users will gain new knowledge through the collaborative evolution of their ontology. Especially when using implicit techniques, the users will be able to update their and other ontologies with a low effort (the validation of changes). The low intrusiveness of such a technique is vital for its acceptance. Yet from a practical point of view, parameters, such as the update frequency of the underlying term-similarity matrix and the complexity of the changes to realize, at once, must be set manually.

Organizations would profit from this form of knowledge sharing as well. From their point of view, a proper handling of knowledge would mean a proper handling of the sources for innovation, improvement, and improved competitiveness, per se. Employees spend a considerable amount of time looking for information that either already exists or producing information that is never reused by any other employee, due to a lack of knowledge transfer. The use of collaborative techniques to propagate knowledge around the organization could be a remedy to the typical state of companies not being aware of their own potential. The implications for the organization are clearly a higher competitiveness through the reuse of existing knowledge and products, the improved efficiency of its employees through an improved knowledge supply, the internalization of the knowledge of current employees leading to a reduction of the loss of knowledge due to employees retiring from the organization, and the improvement of the interoperability of semantic applications through a more effective supply of required information, just to name a few. Possible side effects of collaborative ontology evolution are the emergence and dissociation of social networks. The emergence of new networks could be used to discover correlations between roles, and shorten the administrative paths between these to enhance their collaboration. On the other hand, the dissociation of networks could be a hint towards conflicts within user groups, an inaccurate tagging of users with roles, or a need for differentiation within user groups.

FUTURE RESEARCH DIRECTIONS

Ontologies have been used in several different settings, usually as a mean for sharing common agreements on some semantics or facts. The trend of service automation over the Web yet already demands a shift from this view of ontologies to a more user-centered approach. Personal ontologies will be used for customizing autonomic software agents that implement specific functionality, making the sharing of common agreements to be only one possibility of using ontologies. The evolution of these ontologies will demand the creation of more techniques for acquiring feedback from different sources, interpreting the collected data, and using it for ontology evolution.

The use of multiperspective ontologies (i.e., ontologies able to model data from different points of view and with variable granularities) will propagate from the area of research to applications, making mechanisms for their integration and evolution necessary. This might also demand approaches, such as automatic ontology extraction and relation harvesting, to be redesigned or modified.

Where non-crisp facts are necessary or exclusively available, the use of fuzzy ontologies to represent contextual dependences and further numerically expressible dependences will also play an important role in the upcoming knowledge society. Again, accurate techniques for their extraction and evolution will need to be developed. Furthermore, software agents implementing fuzzy logic will be more prominently used. Techniques for the representation of fuzzy ontologies seem very promising, yet are still at their beginning, and need to be studied carefully and supported by software tools more widely.

Ontologies will evolve from the knowledge representation technique for professionals that they are today, to a knowledge representation technique for every man. This demands the conception and implementation of ergonomic tools to facilitate the user-centered modeling/extraction, evolution, and tracking of ontologies, for example, through the implementation of exploration and feedback techniques with low intrusiveness. Such personal ontologies would state some beliefs that would enable agents to perform customized operations.

Another future research direction is the prediction of the evolution of knowledge through software agents. This would allow the agents to carry out personalized operations in a more efficient manner. Alternative representation of knowledge, such as multiperspective (Kingston, 2008) and multifaceted ontologies, could be used to improve the interoperability of knowledge-driven applications through their improved reusability.

REFERENCES

Abidi, S. S. R., & Pang, X. (2004). Knowledge sharing over P2P knowledge networks: A peer ontology and semantic overlay driven approach. *International Conference on Knowledge Management*, Singapore, 13-15.

Baeza-Yates, R., & Ribeiro-Neto, B. (1999). *Modern information retrieval*. Wokingham: Addison-Wesley.

Bennett, B. R., & Theodoulidis, B. (1998). *Towards a notion of personal ontology*. University of Manchester.

Biemann, C. (2005). Ontology learning from texts: A survey of methods. *LDV-Forum 20*(2), 75-93.

Bisson, G. (1992). Learning in FOL with a similarity measure. *AAAI*, 82–87.

Bisson, G., Nedellec, C., & Canamero, D. (2000). Designing clustering methods for ontology building - The Mo'K Workbench. In S. Staab, A. Maedche, C. Nedellec, & P. Wiemer-Hastings (Eds.), *Proceedings of the Workshop on Ontology Learning, 14th European Conference on Artificial Intelligence*, Berlin, Germany.

Block, H. D. (1962). The perceptron: A model for brain functioning. *Reviews of Modern Physics, 34*, 123-135.

Caraballo, S. A. (1999). Automatic construction of a hypernym-labeled noun hierarchy from text. *Proceedings of the 37th Annual Meeting of the Association for Computational Linguistics*, 120-126.

Carmichael, D. J., Kay, J., & Kummerfeld, B. (2004). Personal ontologies for feature selection in intelligent environment visualisations. In *Proceedings of the Workshop on Artificial Intelligence in Mobile Systems*.

Chaffee, J., & Gauch, S. (2000). Personal ontologies for Web navigation. *Proceedings of the Ninth international Conference on information and Knowledge Management*, 227-234.

Craven, M., DiPasquo, D., Freitag, D., McCallum, A., Mitchell, T., Nigam, K., & Slattery, S. (2000). Learning to construct knowledge bases from the World Wide Web. *Artificial Intelligence, 118*, 69-113.

Davis, R., Shrobe, H., & Szolovits, P. (1993). What is a KR? *AI Magazine, 14(1)*, 17-33.

Dieng, R., & Hug, S. (1998). Comparison of personal ontologies represented through conceptual graphs. *Proceedings of the 13th European Conference on Artificial Intelligence*, 341-345.

Ding, Y., & Foo, S. (2002). Ontology research and development. Part 1 - A review of Ontology Generation. *Journal of Information Science, Information Science, vol. 28, pp. 123-136, 2002.*

Dutta, S. (2001). NCLIS policy recommendation on linking the information life cycle concept with digital libraries. *A comprehensive assessment of public information dissemination*, 214.

Dwight, S. S., Harris, M. A., Dolinski, K., Ball, C. A., Binkley, G., Christie, K. R., Fisk, D. G., Issel-Tarver, L., Schroeder, M., Sherlock, G., Sethuraman, A., Weng, S., Botstein, D., & Cherry, J. M. (2002). Saccharomyces Genome Database provides secondary gene annotation using the Gene Ontology. *Nucleic Acids Research 30(1)*, 69-72.

Flouris, G. (2006). *On belief change and ontology evolution*. PhD. Thesis. University of Crete.

Flouris, G., Plexousakis, D., & Antoniou, G. (2006). Evolving ontology evolution. In *Proceedings of the Current Trends in Theory and Practice of Computer Science Conference*, 14-29.

Gallaire, H., & Minker, J. (Eds) (1978). *Logic and databases*. New York: Plenum Press.

Goodenough, W. (1957). Componential analysis and the study of meaning. *Language, 32*, 195–216.

Gruber, T. R. (1993). A translation approach to portable ontologies. *Knowledge Acquisition 5*(2), 199-220.

Haase, P., Ehrig, M., Hotho, A., & Schnizler, B. (2004). Personalized information access in a bibliographic peer-to-peer system. *Proceedings of the AAAI Workshop on Semantic Web Personalization*, 1-12.

Haase, P., Hotho, A., Schmidt-Thieme, L., & Sure, Y. (2005). Collaborative and usage-driven evolution of personal ontologies. *Proceedings of the European Semantic Web Conference*, 486-499.

Haertwig, J., & Boehm, K. (2005). A process framework for an interoperable semantic enterprise environment. In *Proceedings of the 6th European Conference on Knowledge Management*, 227-236.

Hayes, P., & Menzel, C. (2001). A semantics for the knowledge interchange format. In *Proceedings of IJCAI 2001 Workshop on the IEEE Standard Upper Ontology.*

Hindle, D. (1990). Noun classification from predicate-argument structures. *Meeting of the Association for Computational Linguistics*, 268-275.

Iamnitchi, A., Ripeanu, M., & Foster, I. T. (2002). Locating data in (Small-World?) peer-to-peer scientific collaborations. In P. Druschel, M. F.

Kaashoek, & A. I. Rowstron (Eds.), Revised Papers From the First international Workshop on Peer-To-Peer Systems. *Lecture Notes in Computer Science 2429* (pp. 232-241). London: Springer-Verlag.

Kautz, K., & Mahnke, V. (2003). Value creation through IT-supported KM? The utilisation of a KM system in a global consulting company. *Informing Science, (6)*, 75-88.

Kingston, J. (2008). Multiperspective ontologies: Resolving common ontology development problems. *Expert Systems With Applications 34*(1), 541-550.

Klein, M., & Fensel, D. (2001). Ontology versioning for the Semantic Web. *Proceedings of the 1st International Semantic Web Working Symposium*, 75-91.

Klein, M., & Noy, N. (2003). *A component-based framework for ontology evolution*. Technical Report IR-504, Vrije Universiteit Amsterdam.

Korzybski, A. (1993). Science and sanity - An introduction to non-aristotelean systems and general semantics. *Institute of General Semantics*, Lakeville, USA.

Lenat, D., & Guha, R. V. (1989). *Building large knowledge-Based systems: Representation and inference in the Cyc Project*. Addison-Wesley.

Lopez, F. (1999) Overview of methodologies for building ontologies. *Proceedings of the International Joint Conference on Artificial Intelligence workshop on Ontologies and Problem-Solving Methods.*

McGregor, R. (1990). *Loom users manual*. Working Paper ISI/WP 22, University of Southern California.

Maedche, A., & Staab, S. (2000). Semiautomatic engineering of ontologies from text. In *Proceedings of the Twelfth International Conference on Software Engineering and Knowledge Engineering.*

McCarthy, J. (1968). Programs with common sense. In M.Minsky (Ed.) *Semantic information processing* (pp. 75-91). Cambridge MA: MIT Press.

McCulloch, W. S., & Pitts, W. (1943). A logical calculus of the ideas immanent in nervous activity. *Bulletin of Mathematical Biophysics 5*, 115-133.

Milgram, S. (1967). The small world problem. *Psychology Today*, 60-67.

Minsky, M. (1975). A framework for representing knowledge. In P. Winston (Ed.), *The psychology vision*. McGraw-Hill.

Müller, H. M., Kenny, E. E., & Sternberg, P. W. (2004). Textpresso: An ontology-based information retrieval and extraction system for biological literature. *PLoS Biology 2*(11).

Myers, B. A. (1990). Taxonomies of visual programming and program visualization. *Journal of Visual Languages and Computing 1*(1), 97-123.

Newman, M. E. J. (2003). The structure and function of complex networks. *SIAM Review 45*(2), 167-256.

Ngonga Ngomo, A.-C., & Schumacher, F. (2006). Implicit knowledge sharing. In *Proceedings of the 7th European Conference on Knowledge Management* (pp. 736-747).

NIST. (2007). *Dictionary of algorithms and data structures*. Retrieved August 29, 2007 from http://www.nist.gov/dads/

Omelayenko, B. (2001). Learning of ontologies from the Web: The analysis of existing approaches. In *Proceedings of the International Workshop on Web Dynamics*.

Pantel, P., & Lin, D. (2002). Document clustering with committees. In *Proceedings of the 25th Annual international ACM SIGIR Conference on Research and Development in information Retrieval* (pp. 199-206).

Polanyi, M. (1967). *The tacit dimension*. London: Routledge and Kegan Paul.

Preece, S. E. (1981). *A spreading activation network model for information retrieval*. PhD thesis, Universtiy of Illinois at Urbana-Champaign.

Pulido, J. R., Ruiz, M. A., Herrera, R., Cabello, E., Legrand, S., & Elliman, D. (2006). Ontology languages for the semantic Web: A never completely updated review. *Knowledge-Based Systems 19*(7), 489-497.

Rahm, E., & Bernstein, P. (2001). A survey of approaches to automatic schema matching. *VLDB Journal 10*(4), 334–350.

Ripley, B. D. (1996). *Pattern recognition and neural networks*. Cambridge: Cambridge University Press.

Sindt, T. (2003). Formal operations for ontology evolution. In *Proceedings of the International Conference on Emerging Technologies*.

Song, S., Nerur, S., & Teng, J. T. (2007). An exploratory study on the roles of network structure and knowledge processing orientation in work unit knowledge management. *SIGMIS Database, 38*(2), 8-26.

Sowa, J. F. (2000). *KR: Logical, philosophical, and computational foundations*. Pacific Grove: Brooks Cole Publishing Co.

Sowa, J. F. (2003). *Ontology*. Retrieved January 10, 2007 from http://www.jfsowa.com/

Stanford. (2006). *The Protégé Ontology Editor and Knowledge Acquisition System*. Retrieved January 16, 2007 from http://protege.stanford.edu/

Stojanovic, L. (2004). *Methods and tools for ontology evolution*. PhD thesis, University of Karlsruhe.

Stojanovic, L,. Maedche, A., Stojanovic, N., & Studer, R. (2003). Ontology evolution as reconfiguration-design problem solving. In *Proceedings of the 2nd International Conference on Knowledge Capture* (pp. 162-171).

Takeda, H., Iino, K., & Nishida T. (1995). Ontology-supported agent communication. In *Proceedings of the American Association for Artificial Intelligence Symposium*.

Tarski, A. (1956). *Logic, semantics, and metamathematics*. Oxford: Oxford University Press.

W3C. (2006). *Web Ontology Language (OWL)*. Retrieved January 11, 2007 from http://www.w3.org/2004/OWL/

Winograd, T. (1975). Frame representations and the declarative/procedural controversy. *Readings in Knowledge Representation*, 185-210.

Xiao J., Zhang, Y., Jia, X., & Li, T. (2001). Measuring similarity of interests for clustering Web-users. In *Proceedings of the 12th Australasian Database Conference. ACM International Conference Proceeding Series*, 107-114.

ADDITIONAL READING

Bishop, C. (1995). *Neural networks for pattern recognition*. Oxford: University Press.

Brachman, R., & Levesque, H. J. (2004). *Knowledge representation and reasoning*. San Francisco: Morgan Kaufman.

Davies, J., Fensel, D., & van Harmelenhard, F. (2002). *Towards the semantic Web: Ontology-driven knowledge management*. UK: Wiley.

Fausett, L. (1994). *Fundamentals of neural networks*. New York: Prentice Hall.

Frakes, W. B., & Baeza-Yates, R. A. (1992). *Information retrieval: Data structures & algorithms*. Prentice-Hall.

Gómez-Pérez, A., Fernandez-Lopez, M., & Corcho, O. (2004). *Ontological engineering: With examples from the areas of knowledge management, e-commerce and the semantic Web (Advanced Information and Knowledge Processing)*. Berlin - Heidelberg - New York: Springer.

Han, J., & Kamber, M. (2001). *Data mining: Concepts and techniques*. San Francisco: Morgan Kaufmann Publishers.

Haykin, S. (1994). *Neural networks: A comprehensive foundation*. New York: Macmillan Publishing.

Kaufman, L., & Rousseeuw, P. (1990). *Finding groups in data: An introduction to cluster analysis*. UK: Wiley.

Kleinberg, J. (2000). The small-world phenomenon: An algorithm perspective. *Proceedings of the thirty-second annual ACM symposium on Theory of computing* (pp. 163-170).

Kleinberg, J. (2002). Small-world phenomena and the dynamics of information. *Advances in Neural Information Processing Systems (NIPS), 14*.

Levesque, H. J., & Lakemeyer, G. (2000). *The logic of knowledge bases*. Cambridge: MIT Press.

Nonaka, I. (1994). A dynamic theory of organizational knowledge creation. *Organisation Science, 5*(1), 14-37.

Nonaka, I., & Takeuchi, H. (1995). *The knowledge-creating company*. Oxford: Oxford University Press.

Patterson, D. (1996). *Artificial neural networks*. Singapore: Prentice Hall.

Salton, G., & McGill, M. J. (1983). *Introduction to modern information retrieval*. New York: McGraw-Hill.

Witten, I. H., & and Eibe, F. (2000). *Data mining: Practical machine learning tools and techniques with Java implementations*. San Francisco: Morgan Kaufmann Publishers.

APPENDIX: FORMAL CONSIDERATIONS

A terminological ontology O is given by:

$$O = (C, R, \lambda, L), \qquad (1)$$

where:

- C is the set of concepts,
- R is the set of relations with $C \cap R = \{\}$
- λ is the labeling function and
- L is the set of labels.

The relations r_i are elements of R and mappings from C in C:

$$r_i : C \to C \qquad (2)$$

λ is a bijective mapping:

$$\lambda : C \cup R \to L \text{ with } \forall\, x, x^1 \in C \cup R \mid (x) \neq (x^1) \,\&$$
$$\forall\, x \in C \; \exists!\, y \in L : y = (x) \qquad (3)$$

Goodenough (1957) defines a mapping between each concept from a set C of concepts to a subset of the power set of Θ, the set of terms. This crisp mapping does not allow describing the fuzziness of semantics and nuances in the understanding of concepts. We shall thus adopt a fuzzy mapping between concepts and semantems, matching each concept to a multiset of semantems, that is, of terms. Let M be the family of mappings between concepts and fuzzy subsets of Θ, where μ_i is the semantem membership function for the concept c_i and can adopt values between 0 and 1.

The estimation of the family of mappings M for a given ontology is the key for the correct description of the semantics of each user. Furthermore, it can be used to compute the similarity σ of two users A and B with mappings M^A and M^B respectively, using for example the cosine similarity see equation (4).

Let $O = \{o_1 \dots o_n\}$ be a family of ontologies, and $U = \{u_1 \dots u_n\}$ be the universe of users with some background in a given domain, o_i being the personal ontology of u_i. Furthermore, let each user u_i have a document collection d_i. Since the users are all from the same domain, documents can belong to more than one document collection. Using one of the available ontology extraction methods and tools (Biemann, 2005), a beginning ontology o_i can be generated for each user u_i. Each ontology extraction technique possesses

- A term similarity function t_{sim},
- A concept to term mapping t_c as explained above and depending on t_{sim}:
  $$t_c = f(t_{sim}, t_i, c_j) \; t_i \in \Theta, c_j \in C$$
- A concept similarity function c_{sim} depending on t_{sim}:
  $$c_{sim} = f(t_{sim}, t_c, c_i, c_j) \; t_c \in \Theta, c_i, c_j \in C.$$

Since there is a finite number of relevant words in a corpus, t_{sim} can be fully described using a similarity matrix Γ with $\gamma_{ij} = t_{sim}(t_i, t_j)$. The goal of an approach for the automatic evolution of terminological ontologies is to modify this matrix according to the needs of the user. Atomic changes in terminological ontologies can be reduced to an alteration of the mapping t_{sim}, reflected in the ontology by changes of c_{sim} and t_c. Complex changes can be reduced to a se-

Equation (4).

$$\sigma(A, B) = \sum_{\substack{\mu_i^A \in M^A \\ \mu_i^B \in M^B}} \cos(\mu_i^A, \mu_i^B) \text{ with } \cos(\mu_i^A, \mu_i^B) = \frac{\sum_{t \in \Theta} \mu_i^A(t) \mu_i^B(t)}{\sqrt{\sum_{t \in \Theta} \mu_i^A(t)^2 \sum_{t \in \Theta} \mu_i^B(t)^2}}$$

quence of atomic changes. Similarly, to manually modeling ontologies, demanding from the user to fill in the γ_{ij} values would imply demanding high investments with regard to time and costs. Using the operations on ontologies described in this chapter, hints on the quality of the similarity function can be won and utilized to update the ontology of each user. Propagating changes from a user to the other consists of building a weighted sum of the changes in the similarity matrix of A

$(\Delta\Gamma^A)$ and the similarity matrix of B (Γ^B). When assuming n users in a small world:

$$\Gamma_{new}^B = \left(1 - \sum_{i=1}^{n-1} \alpha_B^{A_i}\right)\Gamma_{old}^B + \sum_{i=1}^{n-1} \alpha_B^{A_i}\Delta\Gamma^{A_i} \qquad (8)$$

The value of the weights $\alpha_B^{A_i}$ is functionally related to the similarity of the users A and B (computed for example according to (4)).

Chapter V
Computer–Mediated Knowledge Sharing

Kimiz Dalkir
McGill University, Canada

ABSTRACT

Computer-mediated communication has become the foremost means of sharing knowledge in today's knowledge-based economy. However, not all Internet-based knowledge-sharing channels are created equal: they differ in their effectiveness when used for exchanging knowledge. A number of factors influence the efficacies of knowledge exchange, including: (1) characteristics of the knowledge being exchanged and, (2) characteristics of the channels used. It is therefore necessary to define key knowledge and channel attributes in order to understand how knowledge can be effectively shared using computers. This chapter examines the computer-mediated knowledge sharing mechanisms and proposes a typology based on media richness and social presence characteristics that can serve as a preliminary conceptual basis to select the most appropriate channel. The chapter concludes with a discussion of key issues and future research directions. While much of the research has been done in organizational settings, the chapter is applicable to all forms of computer-mediated communication.

INTRODUCTION

Computer-mediated communication may be defined as "communication that takes place between human beings via the instrumentality of computers" (Herring, 1996, p. 1). Computer-mediated knowledge sharing makes use of a number of computer-based channels, where a channel is defined as the specific technological application or tool used to communicate. The means of computer-mediated communication we have at our disposal today are much more diverse than just a decade or so ago. From the original e-mail and Usenet messages of the mid-1980s, communication channels have expanded to include, among others:

- E-mails, listservs, and mailing lists
- Newsgroups, bulletin boards, personal homepages, and blogs

- Internet relay chat and instant messaging
- Collaborative workspaces such as wikis
- Streaming media such as Web cams, Web casts, podcasts, or Youtube
- Business teleconferencing, videoconferencing
- Internet commerce, for example, iTunes to purchase and download music
- Voice over Internet such as Skype, and
- Collaborative or Web-based learning (e.g., Kreijns, Kirschner, & Jochems, 2003).

Knowledge sharing is no longer constrained by synchronous on-site face-to-face meetings. Furthermore, new tools continue to emerge such as synchronous broadcast messaging. Wiesz et al. (2006) describe the IBM Community Tools, a computer-mediated communications system used to broadcast instant messages within IBM. The most common form of broadcast is an invitation to a group chat (called a "FreeJam"). "Jamming" continues to be a popular and frequently used application, and the feature most valued by users, due to its immediacy. The speed with which questions can be answered, and problems can be solved, provided valuable boosts to productivity of all community members.

Boase et al. (Boase, Horrigan, Wellman, & Rainie, 2006) purport that computer-mediated communication, such as the Internet, is rapidly becoming seamlessly integrated with other knowledge-sharing channels such as the telephone and face-to-face exchanges. They report the phenomenon of "media multiplicity"; the more people see each other in person and talk on the phone, the more they use the Internet. This suggests interconnectedness and an embedding of new channels within existing channels. The Internet is contributing to this trend by moving society towards "networked individualism" by allowing people not only to socialize online, but also to link up with more knowledgeable peers and experts to make better decisions.

Computer-mediated communication has evolved into person-to-person connections (much like the cell phone transformed calling a physical place to calling a specific individual, regardless of their physical location). Computer-mediated knowledge sharing thus appears not only to help people find answers to questions and work together, but also to cultivate or maintain the online social networks that people have become a part of. The communication channels provide an easy means of reaching out to tap into this form of "social capital" in both professional and personal contexts (Field, 2004). Social capital is an important form of intellectual capital (or knowledge resource) that encompasses the value of networks and the value inherent in the movement or sharing of knowledge with others in the network.

It is therefore quite important to better understand the factors that affect computer-mediated knowledge sharing. Following a review of the literature from such diverse disciplines as educational technology, computer-mediated communication, human-computer interaction, library and information studies, and knowledge management, a number of critical factors that impact the effectiveness of knowledge sharing can be identified, namely:

- The type of channel (e.g., e-mail), the mode of communication it enables (e.g., text, audio, etc.) together with the degree of social presence possible (the perception of being in communication with another individual, for example, facial expressions, tone of voice etc.), and the degree of media richness (interactivity, immediacy, cues);
- The characteristics of knowledge (stickiness vs. leakiness);
- The characteristics of the participants (gender, age, number, one-to-one, many-to-many, degree of Internet literacy);
- The length and nature of the relationships (e.g., long-term, professional, personal);

- The context, topic, and purpose of the knowledge sharing (e.g., medical advice, scholarly collaboration);
- Synchronous vs. asynchronous interaction (real-time or delayed);
- Whether the knowledge-sharing activity is public or private (e.g., closed group, public Web site) and whether it is moderated or not.

Computer-mediated communication should therefore, not be thought of as a single communication channel, but rather a family of different technological applications. These applications are quite diverse but they all have one thing in common: they serve to facilitate interaction between users; social interaction niches where people can "meet" virtually. As Thurlow et al. (Thurlow, Engel, & Tomic, 2004) states, "there's more to technology than technology. It's human communication and what we do with technology that really counts…..it's all about the transformation of our patterns of social interaction." (p.2). Communication channels support different levels of social interaction that, therefore, have an impact on knowledge sharing. When examining computer-mediated knowledge sharing, there appears to be a consensus that two main factors, at a minimum, must be addressed: the characteristics of the knowledge to be shared, and the characteristics of channels available for sharing that knowledge.

CHARACTERISTICS OF COMPUTER-MEDIATED KNOWLEDGE-SHARING CHANNELS

The basic premise of this chapter is that the communication channel used by people will influence and be influenced by the knowledge they share, who they share this knowledge with, why they are sharing the knowledge, and how often they do so. By developing a deeper understanding of knowledge types and how the various types can be shared, organizations can improve their efforts to identify and share critical knowledge assets, for a vast range of sharing objectives and applications. This means that channels or "Electronic Communication systems (ElCom)" should be selected for different types of knowledge in order to ensure the "best fit" and to ensure that knowledge-sharing objectives are successfully met (Bolisani & Scarso, 2000).

Types of Channels

E-mail was one of the first computer-mediated communication channels to be widely embraced by both business and personal users.

A 2x2 matrix is commonly used to describe the major kinds of computer-mediated communication systems, as shown in Figure 1.

Figure 1. Channel type matrix

	Same Time	**Different Time**
Same Place	Synchronous colocated (e.g., face-to-face meeting, presentation, voting)	Asynchronous colocated (e.g., computer-supported collaborative work)
Different Place	Synchronous distant (e.g., instant messaging, tele- or videoconference, voice over Internet VOIP, Web cast, online course)	Asynchronous distant (e.g., e-mail, discussion group, wiki)

The types of knowledge-sharing channels range from

- Face-to-face, technologically unmediated (conversing with colleague at water cooler, storytelling): the key advantage here is that individuals can customize and clarify knowledge on demand. Disadvantages include the need for both parties to be present at the same place and time. Additionally, this type of knowledge sharing typically goes unrecorded, potentially leading to greater distortion and recall biases (Keong & Al-Hawamdeh, 2002).

- Face-to-face, technologically mediated (video conferencing, some online collaboration software): the key advantage here is that individuals do not have to be in the same location and yet, many of the advantages of face-to-face communication are maintained. While the ability to customize knowledge for the receiver continues to be possible, often this type of knowledge sharing continues to go unrecorded (Keong & Al-Hawamdeh, 2002).

- Technological, synchronous (telephone, instant messaging, some online collaboration software, chat rooms): these communication channels once again free individuals from needing to be in the same location to share knowledge. These channels can thus be very useful for distributed organizations. The disadvantage here, however, is that these channels have varying abilities to properly convey all the fine nuances of a message and can easily result in miscommunications. Additionally, not all of these channels permit immediate or accurate recording of the shared knowledge.

- Technological, asynchronous (e-mail, communities of practice, discussion groups, written documents): the ultimate advantage with these channels is that individuals are not only free from being in the same location,

but also from being available at the same time. Senders can transcribe knowledge that is immediately captured for storage and re-use, and receivers can access the knowledge entities when they are needed most. The disadvantages here are once again related to the absence of immediate clarification and often the context in which the original knowledge entity was recorded.

Tiwana and Ramesh (2001) enumerate a number of technologies that are well suited for sharing knowledge, such as project management systems, data warehouses, digital libraries, and organizational memory systems. The authors note that a knowledge server, in the form of a Web server, can act as a content aggregator, linking and organizing explicit knowledge from multiple sources with tacit knowledge pointers.

Recent trends in blogs and wikis may provide valuable knowledge-sharing channels for tacit knowledge. Blogging is defined as the writing of Web logs (Blood, 2002). Jorn Barger coined the term "Web log" in 1997 (http://www.jjg.net/infosift). Web logs (or blogs for short) are link-driven sites offering personal thoughts, commentary, and essays by individuals or groups (group blogs). Blogs are typically short, frequently updated postings arranged chronologically, much like an online version of a journal or diary. Web logs provide a valuable filtering function for their readers, providing only the more relevant and vetted content. Blogs are therefore useful tools for community members, and serve to further cement community cohesion as people feel more connected to other readers of the blog.

Similarly, wikis are also good ways of sharing knowledge. A wiki is a collaborative authoring environment that allows for bottom-up content development. A well-known example is that of wikipedia (http://www.wikipedia.com). Wikis may be public or limited to members, but each participant is, in effect, an author and can submit content. More specifically, a wiki is composed of Web pages where people input information and then create hyperlinks to another or new pages for more details about a particular topic. A wiki site grows and changes at the will of the participants. Wikis provide open content virtual spaces where community members can "store" shared stories, best practices, and other forms of valuable knowledge.

Given the plethora of choices, there needs to be some criteria used in selecting the most appropriate channel for various types of knowledge. In addition to identifying where knowledge falls on the tacit-explicit continuum, media richness and social presence are two additional criteria that can be used in selecting the most appropriate technology-mediated knowledge-sharing channel.

Media Richness and Social Presence Theory

In terms of distinguishing between the various communication channels that are used for knowledge sharing, the literature focuses on measuring the degree of social presence that is possible, and the richness of the media of the channel.

Social presence is defined as the degree to which individuals perceive that they are interacting with another human being when using an ElCom. For example, being able to see such cues as facial expression, or hear differences in tone of voice, increase the degree of social presence afforded by a knowledge-sharing channel. In text-only channels, such as e-mail, users often make use of emoticons to convey different emotions with their text. The Social Presence Model (Thurlow, 2004) ranks different channels and finds, for example, that "e-mail falls somewhere between business letters and the telephone in terms of its social presence....face-to-face communication comes out pretty high." (p. 49). A number of other researchers (Daft & Lengel, 1984; McGrath, 1990) identify a continuum whereby communication media can be classified according to their degree of social presence, and they place e-mail lowest,

followed by teleconferencing, desktop videoconferencing, and face-to-face meetings.

The media richness of various technologies is defined "by its capacity for immediate feedback, its ability to support natural language, the number of cues (non-verbal) it provides, and the extent to which the channel creates social presence for the receiver" (Chua, 2001). The Media Richness Model proposed by Daft and Lengel (1984) assessed richness using (1) feedback capability (speed), (2) communication modes used (visual, audio, etc.), (3) source (personal, impersonal), and (4) language (natural, numeric, etc.). The researchers found that people prefer to use richer channels to be able to more efficiently and more effectively understand one another. The more complex the knowledge-sharing task, the richer the channel that is needed. Vickery et al. (Vickery, Droge, Stank, Goldsby, & Markland, 2004) illustrate by stating, "rich media permit the transmittal of highly complex and/or tacit knowledge and support extensive versus routine problem solving" (p. 1107).

A number of researchers have studied channel media richness and social presence, and their findings are sometimes contradictory. Selected studies will be summarized in order to convey the complexity of the phenomena under study. Keong and Al-Hawamdeh (2002) and Chua (2001) analyzed various communication channels ranging from face-to-face unmediated communication, which has the highest media richness, to text only documents, which have the lowest media richness, and bandwidth, and found the same sort of spectrum Daft and Lengel reported in 1984 (in order of decreasing richness): face-to-face, telephone, e-mail, written personal letters, written formal documents, numeric, formal outputs (e.g., computer-generated).

Conversely, Panteli (2002) found that e-mail is a richer communication medium than is reflected on the scale of media richness theory. He studied e-mail communication over several months and found that the way in which e-mail is constructed may convey more social cues than was previously believed. Panteli's findings suggest that text-based e-mail is socially constructed by the context of the organization in which the e-mail is used. Messages were found to have characteristics of spoken communication with frequent use of diverse social cues (found in tone, emoticons, signatures, etc.).

Robert and Dennis (2005) refer to a "paradox of richness" (p. 1) as they found that high media richness and social presence resulted in greater motivation for users to process the message; however, at the same time, the ability to process the information is decreased. Media that is less rich and low in social presence improved processing ability but decreased motivation. Users appear to prefer to receive large amounts of content via channels with low social presence, and smaller amounts of content via richer media. Andres (2002) conducted empirical studies on virtual teams and found that social presence and media richness had a significant impact on team productivity, perceived interaction quality, and group process satisfaction. Channels characterized as high in media richness and social presence are found to create a greater sense of interaction quality. Thurlow et al. (2004) report that researchers found increased and decreased productivity, depending on contextual factors such as time-dependence of tasks, degree of task interdependence, and temporal and/or spatial constraints. There are, of course, exceptions to these generalizations; some seek very low social presence channels purposively in order to ensure anonymity, to overcome anxiety, to break "bad news" and so forth. Again, the purpose or context of the knowledge sharing will play a role in determining the best channel to use.

Burgoon et al. (Burgoon, Bonito, Ramierez Jr., Dunbar, Kam, & Fischer, 2002) found that selecting the channel type and level of media richness depended on the objectives of the knowledge sharing, which range from "higher involvement, greater mutuality, favorable social

judgments or task performance" (p. 271). For example, the authors found that audio-enabled channels led to increased trust (presumably due to speech cues). Decreased social presence was not found to decrease the quality of decisions, however, and in some cases actually improved quality (presumably due to a more narrow focus on factual information needed for the task at hand, making nonverbal cues less essential for task completion). Conversely, more ambiguous tasks, requiring judgment, collaboration, group trust, morale, may require channels with higher social presence and media richness. Task demands and knowledge-sharing goals must therefore play a large role in the selection of the appropriate knowledge-sharing channel.

Andres (2002) conducted empirical studies on virtual teams and found that social presence and media richness had a significant impact on team productivity, perceived interaction quality, and group process satisfaction. Channels characterized as high in media richness and social presence, are found to create a greater sense of interactivity. Other researchers found changes in productivity depending on contextual factors such as time-dependence of tasks, degree of task interdependence, and temporal and/or spatial constraints. There are also exceptions to these generalizations as some people seek very low social-presence channels purposively in order to ensure anonymity, to overcome anxiety, to break "bad news," and so forth. Again, the purpose or context of the knowledge sharing will play a role in determining the best channel to use (Thurlow, 2004).

Finally, Kock (2005) offers an alternative to the concept of media richness; that of media naturalness. The author postulates a link between the degrees to which the channel emulates our natural preferences for collocated, face-to-face, synchronous knowledge sharing with the degree of cognitive effort required. Channels that have high media naturalness will require less cognitive effort on the part of participants

The Limitations of Technology-Based Channels

Knowledge sharing represents a dynamic exchange of information; it is a bidirectional process. Technical challenges typically consist of interaction constraints, access difficulties, the continuous capture of newly generated content and retrieval of content for future use, and reuse by both the original participants in the exchange and by other groups of people. The participants in the knowledge-sharing exchange must be able to connect with one another and with content relevant to, and required for, their work; in other words, to hold a conversation that includes information resources as both by-products of the conversation (artifacts) and as objects of the conversation (e.g., e-mail attachments).

In 1998, O'Dell and Grayson discussed technology as a catalyst to support knowledge sharing initiatives, but warned against relying on it as a solution. They argue that while technology can play a facilitating role in knowledge sharing, it cannot be the driver of sharing knowledge because all the important information about a process is too complex and too experiential to be captured electronically. Additionally, they argue that incentives for, and barriers to, sharing are not really technical, therefore, technology cannot solve the whole problem.

Swan et al. (Swan, Newell, Scarbrough, & Hislop, 1999) highlighted the overwhelming emphasis on information and communication technologies (ICT) and the major gap this leaves in terms of the importance of people in knowledge sharing. By examining case studies of the use of ICT in network creation, they found that focusing on ICT could limit the potential for encouraging knowledge sharing across social communities. An ICT focus blinds many organizations to the importance of the social and cultural aspects that are critical in facilitating the development of a truly global, knowledge-sharing network. In Swan et al. (1999), the cases they studied showed how people-management practices are often more fundamental to knowledge sharing than the use of IT.

As the APQC (1999) also noted, ICT can act as an enabler of the knowledge-sharing process, but cannot act as the solution to it in and of itself. Allee (2000) also noticed that as knowledge complexity increased, the degree to which technology could be counted on to assist with the task of knowledge sharing was reduced. No database or technology system can fully capture and distribute all the knowledge that floats around a company; nor should it. Thus, the challenge for information technology (IT) developers is not to develop systems that aim to replace people as the primary source of expertise. Rather, as Swan et al. (1999) point out, the aim should be to develop systems that allow experts to engage in active knowledge sharing through environments that are sufficiently media-rich to support the transfer of knowledge.

McDermott (2000) focused on the importance of making ICT easy to use so that employees can easily contribute to, and access, organizational knowledge. From his perspective, ease of use had less to do with software functionality as much as with the degree to which the ICT channels are integrated into people's daily work. Additional effort and friction in the use of ICT can easily discourage employees from making use of the channels. Choo et al. (Choo, Detlor, & Turnbull, 2000) also discuss learning curve as a major limitation of most knowledge-sharing technologies. The lengthy learning period can prove to be a strong deterrent as people quickly become discouraged, frustrated, and only too willing to resort to more familiar tools. Dalkir and Wiseman (2006) noted a similar difficulty when studying a distributed community of practice that quickly abandoned a complex knowledge network in favor of a grassroots solution in the form of Skype (telephony over the Internet).

Sharing the Knowledge Context

Unlike other resources, information or knowledge resources are subject to different interpretations; they can be stored, presented, and understood in many different ways. Knowledge to be shared tends to be more subjective in nature than physical objects or even data. Knowledge is much too dependent on human perception and a shared context between participants in the knowledge exchange to lend it easily to purely technical solutions. It is critical that knowledge sharing includes sharing of the context.

Individuals or groups in different organizations will likely operate in different contexts (Bolisani & Scarso, 2000). This may be manifested as differences in technological systems used, software standards, Internet protocols, open networks, as well as differences in language itself (different language, different terms used for the same concept, etc.).

This difference in context may easily lead to differences in interpreting knowledge that has been received, as different groups will have a different set of values, procedures, perspectives, and so forth. It therefore becomes imperative to not only share knowledge, but to share knowledge "in situ," that is, together with its context. This is especially true for knowledge that is complex and more tacit in nature. This indicates that a certain minimum level of media richness is required when sharing knowledge as opposed to sharing data or information.

Hislop (2002) notes that in the social constructivist view of knowledge, the transmitter-receiver metaphor of knowledge sharing is inappropriate because the sharing of knowledge does not involve the simple transferal of a fixed entity (explicit knowledge) between two people. Instead, the sharing of knowledge involves two people actively inferring and constructing meaning from two different experiences." (p. 172) He goes on to note that the single most important factor influencing the knowledge-sharing process is the degree of tacitness of the knowledge to be shared. Related to this is the fact that the greater the degree of common knowledge that exists between the knowledge sharers, the easier it will be to share the tacit knowledge in context. The challenge lies in the potential of information technology, such as the Internet, to offer the required level of social presence, credibility, trust, and frequency of interaction required for knowledge sharing to occur. As is the case with communities of practice, it is likely that for truly effective knowledge sharing to take place, some level of face-to-face interaction will be required.

Added to the challenge is the fact that the sharing of tacit knowledge often requires the members in the exchange to have similar cultural experiences and backgrounds to enable them to properly decode and internalize the messages they are receiving. This fact means that as knowledge becomes more tacit in nature, it becomes more difficult to share through standard communication channels (Archer & Wang, 2002). Von Hippel (1994) refers to this as knowledge stickiness: the incremental cost of transferring a given piece of knowledge in a form that is usable by the recipient of that knowledge. Szulanski (2003) uses the term stickiness to refer to the attribute of knowledge that is particularly difficult to share, due to characteristics of the knowledge itself as well as characteristics of the channel used to transfer the knowledge. Some factors that may increase stickiness include ambiguous or unproven knowledge, lack of motivation on the part of the source or owner of the knowledge, lack of credibility of the source, lack of motivation and/or absorptive capacity of the recipient, and organizational context. Tacit knowledge, then, is a form of highly sticky and difficult to transfer knowledge.

Brown and Duguid (2002) use the complementary term "leakiness" to describe knowledge that is more easily and more widely shared. Computer-based networks and communication media can serve to increase knowledge leakiness by overcoming institutional, geographical, and temporal barriers. Knowledge is said to leak over networks and stick to organizational silos.

There are ways of decreasing the stickiness of tacit knowledge. For example, Roberts (2000) emphasizes the role of trust in the sharing of tacit knowledge. Foos et al. (Foos, Schum, & Rothenberg, 2006) note "technologically mediated transfer of tacit knowledge will be more successful when it is between agents who share common social, cultural and linguistic characteristics." (p. 8). Sarker (2005) also found that effective knowledge transfer resulted from frequent exchanges between individuals perceived to be credible and trustworthy. Finally, Mooradian (2005) notes that the tacit-to-tacit sharing appears to bypass explicit knowledge completely as it goes directly from one mind into another; "tacit knowledge flows over a separate channel." (p. 108). He goes on to note that transfer mechanisms are not well characterized, nor are they related to the tacit/explicit distinction. The author notes that the degree of tacitness is directly related to the degree of stickiness and is, thus, a strong predictor of how successful knowledge transfer will be.

Motivating People to Share Knowledge

Companies install e-mail or collaborative software and expect knowledge to flow freely through the electronic pipeline. When it doesn't happen, they are more likely to blame the software or inadequate training than to face a fact of life: people rarely give away valuable possessions (including knowledge) without expecting something in return. (Davenport & Prusak, 2000, p. 26)

There are a number of non-technological factors that influence the use (or lack of use) of computer-mediated channels for knowledge sharing. Light et al. (Light, Bell, & Halpern, 2001) describe the four pillars of collaboration as dependability, consistency, congruency, and mutuality of shared risks and rewards. The authors note that if any of these pillars are "broken" or damaged,

collaboration will not be able to take place. In fact, they define collaboration as "the process of working together toward a common purpose or goal in which the participants are committed and interdependent, with individual or collective accountability for the results of the collaboration, and each of the participants shares a common benefit" (p.1). In order for computer-mediated knowledge sharing to be effective, then, participants need to share a common objective, they need to feel they can rely on the other participants (mutual trust), that each is credible and will contribute to the achievement of the goal.

Riege (2005) provides a comprehensive list of barriers to knowledge sharing. The author divides these barriers into three categories: individual, organizational, and technological barriers. Some individual barriers are

- General lack of time to share knowledge, and time to identify colleagues in need of specific knowledge;
- Low awareness and realization of the value and benefit of possessed knowledge to others;
- Poor verbal/written communication and interpersonal skills;
- Lack of social network;
- Lack of trust in people because they misuse knowledge or take unjust credit for it;
- Lack of trust in the accuracy and credibility of knowledge due to the source;
- Differences in national culture or ethnic background, and values and beliefs associated with it (language is part of this).

Some organizational barriers are:

- Shortage of formal and informal spaces to share, reflect, and generate (new) knowledge;
- Lack of transparent rewards and recognition systems that would motivate people to share more of their knowledge;

- Communication and knowledge flows are restricted into certain directions (e.g., top-down);
- Physical work environment and layout of work areas restrict effective sharing practices;
- Internal competitiveness within business units, functional areas, and subsidiaries can be high;
- Lack of leadership and managerial direction in terms of clearly communicating the benefits and values of knowledge-sharing practices.

Some technological barriers to knowledge sharing are:

- Reluctance to use IT systems due to lack of familiarity and experience with them;
- Lack of training regarding employee familiarization of new IT systems and processes;
- Unrealistic expectations of employees as to what technology can do and cannot do;
- Lack of compatibility between diverse IT systems and processes;
- Mismatch between individuals' need requirements and integrated IT systems and processes restrict sharing practices;
- Lack of integration of IT systems and processes impedes on the way people do things.

RELATIONSHIP BETWEEN CHANNEL AND KNOWLEDGE CHARACTERISTICS

The research on media richness and social presence is quite diverse and sometimes reports conflicting findings. However, most authors concur that knowledge-sharing channels may be ranked with respect to how media rich they are and how much social presence they are able to foster during exchanges. Face-to-face knowledge sharing has the highest social presence and media richness, while text-only exchanges have the lowest. The attributes that make it easier or more difficult to share knowledge over Internet channels also appear to contribute to other factors such as level of cognitive processing required by recipients, the degree of trust and/or credibility that is established, and how group productivity. An important initial step in optimizing knowledge sharing over the Internet will therefore be to characterize the available knowledge-sharing channels with respect to their media richness and social presence. This will enable a better matching of channels to knowledge types in order to ensure that knowledge-sharing goals are met (e.g., sharing information, collaborating, attaining group performance objectives, etc.).

Table 1 summarizes the media richness and social presence characteristics of knowledge-sharing channels

As shown in Table 1, media richness and social presence are usually either both high or both low,

Table 1. Computer-mediated knowledge-sharing channels characterized with respect to their media richness and social presence.

Channel	Media richness	Social presence
E-mails, listservs, and mailing lists	Low	Low
Newsgroups, bulletin boards, personal homepages, and blogs	Low	Moderate
Internet relay chat and instant messaging	High	High
Collaborative workspaces such as wikis	Moderate	Moderate
Streaming media such as Web cams, Web casts, podcasts or Youtube	High	High
Business teleconferencing, videoconferencing	High	High
Internet commerce, for example, iTunes to purchase and download music	Low	Low
Voice over Internet such as Skype	High	High
Collaborative or Web-based learning	Moderate	Moderate

with some exceptions, such as a personal blog or Web page, which may have high social presence but little in the way of immediacy, feedback, and number of cues.

It has been argued that a misfit in the types of knowledge and the communication channels used to transfer it will result in poor knowledge-sharing performance. Scholars have proposed that there is a match between explicit knowledge and technology-based mechanisms, as well as between tacit knowledge and people-based mechanisms in terms of success of knowledge sharing. As such, there is a need to match sticky knowledge with rich communication media, such as face-to-face channels (people-based mechanisms), while leaky knowledge can be more reliably transferred through written media (technology-based mechanisms). For example, knowledge, such as belief and insight (which are more tacit in nature), can be shared more easily through a communication channel with high media richness (such as face-to-face conversation) than through that with low media richness (such as a text-only document).

Figure 2 summarizes the relationship between channel and knowledge characteristics.

A review of key research to date (e.g., Dyer & Singh, 1998; Kumar & van Dissel, 1996; Majchrzak, Rice, Malhotra, King, & Ba, 2001; May & Carter, 2001; Nomura, 2002; Tsui, 2003) ap-

pears to indicate that an ideal combination would be to share highly mobile knowledge over very media-rich channels. Knowledge sharing under these conditions will be more efficient and more effective, with little loss of meaning or lack of motivation on the part of participants. Media rich channels will typically offer multiple modes (e.g., audio and video) and high social presence in the form of immediacy of feedback. Knowledge that is more difficult to move ("sticky" knowledge) may still be shared to some degree if the media richness of the channel is high enough.

Face-to-face meetings continue to top the list of highest media richness and social presence. No computer-mediated knowledge-sharing channel can compete with such interactions. However, compromises have to be made as face-to-face meetings become increasingly difficult to schedule, given people's schedules, workload, and the fact that they may not be in the same place at the same time.

E-mail is the oldest, most basic and ubiquitous form of computer-mediated communication (Yarmosh, 2006). The use of emoticons and other forms of emphasis, such as capitalizing letters, represents a limited means of increasing social presence and media richness. E-mail also often serves as the means of accessing other channels such as newsgroups, listservs, discussion groups,

Figure 2. Relationship between knowledge characteristics and channel media richness

Channel Media Richness

	LOW	HIGH
HIGH	Knowledge may be easily shared for dissemination purposes (e.g. for your information (FYI) type emails, discussion groups)	Most effective computer-mediated knowledge sharing (e.g., online workspaces, wikis)
LOW	Computer-mediated knowledge sharing not recommended as the sole channel (e.g. instant messaging (IM) with other channels including face-to-face interactions).	More difficult barriers must be overcome before knowledge can be shared (e.g., building of trust, social ties, community identity with some face-to-face interactions in a community of practice)

and so on. Finally, e-mail provides at least two major advantages: there is persistence (i.e., e-mails can and often are saved, forwarded, archived, etc.), and there is the ability to attach documents. The most basic advantage likely lies in its almost universal adoption and lack of any appreciable learning curve. The major drawback is that it is often asynchronous, and it is not a particularly rich medium, usually not rich enough to provide sufficient context for the knowledge to be shared. There is also the mitigating problem of information overload; people receive too many e-mails and are spending too much time on e-mail management. The cognitive overload often outweighs the advantages offered by this channel. E-mail is probably best reserved for "broadcast" or FYI types of knowledge exchanges.

Instant messaging has higher immediacy and provides greater social presence. The knowledge-sharing interaction "feels" more like a conversation. IM also has the same advantages as e-mail; it is widely used and easy to learn to use. However, unlike e-mail, there is no persistence, no capture of the conversation. No artifacts are automatically generated. These are valuable tools, for maintaining social ties, that often work best when combined as a complement to other computer-mediated communication tools.

Online communication, conferencing, and collaboration workspaces appear to offer a more balanced approach to knowledge sharing. Participants can hold virtual meetings and generate content in a participatory fashion. Wikis, for example, allow all participants to contribute to the online "document" that may be related to a specific topic or a specific project. Online message and discussion boards are typically organized around topics, and conversations are organized as message threads for each topic. Participants read and post responses that remain on the system after they leave. These channels offer the advantage of unlimited time to read postings without the need to be available at a scheduled time. The content can be stored, which again provides a contribution to organizational memory. The disadvantage is that there is less social presence, as participants perceive they are interacting with content more than connecting with other people.

Online workspaces are collaborative work environments such as intranets or knowledge portals. Intranets are typically environments provided for all employees, whereas portals tend to be designed to meet the needs of specific groups. Both can offer all the advantages without the disadvantages of e-mail and IM: there is no messaging overload, it can be synchronous or asynchronous, and there is a cumulative preservation of the valuable content generated, forming the foundation for an organizational memory for that company or that community.

For example, at the U.S. Federal Aviation Administration (FAA), employees have found online workspaces to be vastly better than trying to get everyone together for a face-to-face meeting (Olsen, 2006). They were even able to "break their e-mail habit" by posting to the workspace rather than e-mailing all participants and sending e-mail attachments. The FAA has about 22,000 employees who are storing many of their documents in online libraries provided on workspaces. All content posted becomes simultaneously available to all employees. The organization found unexpected benefits from their move to online collaboration: in addition to providing greater efficiency in meeting group objectives, employees also noted that they felt less isolated, that they had a greater sense of belonging and group identify as a result of using the collaborative workspace.

Online workspaces are especially well suited to communities of practice. Wenger (2001) devised a categorization scheme of technology or channels that are best suited to different activities carried out by communities of practice. This approach can be adapted for computer-mediated knowledge sharing in general as it provides a good means of assessing the purpose of the interaction. Table 3 is an excerpt outlining some of these categories.

Table 3. Categories of community-oriented technologies (adapted from Etienne Wenger, 2001).

Community Purpose	Type of Technology
Conversation	Discussion group
Getting work done	Project online workspace
Learning (formal)	E-learning
Learning (informal)	Synchronous online communication

A potential disadvantage of collaborative workspaces are that they require familiarity with the technology or application, and that they often impose too artificial and rigorous a structure on participants, which in turn decreases their media richness and social presence (Anderson, Mullin, McEwan, Bal, Carletta, Grattan, & Brundell, 2005).

There are many different types of knowledge-sharing channels available, each with its pros and cons and each with varying degrees of media richness and social presence. The purpose of the knowledge sharing, the characteristics of the knowledge to be shared, and the specific features of each channel should be considered in a systematic manner in order to be able to provide the best possible support for online interactions. There is no one best solution, even within a single organization. Instead, the approach should be that of a toolbox, selecting those channels that together will provide the best-integrated knowledge-sharing environment for all participants.

CONCLUSION

This chapter presented an overview of channels used in computer-mediated knowledge sharing. The critical success factors were identified that influence how effective knowledge exchanges, with knowledge stickiness, and channel media richness and social presence as being three of the more influential factors. Typologies to characterize the type of knowledge to be shared and the media richness of channels were described. Together, these typologies can be used to select the best channel to use to share different types of knowledge.

The proposed framework of knowledge and channel characteristics provides an alternative to the "one size fits all" approach to knowledge sharing on the Internet. Individuals wishing to communicate and collaborate using channel-mediated connections will be in a position to adopt a more systematic and deliberate approach to matching each type of knowledge with the best channel to carry that knowledge, whether they be knowledge workers in organizations or the general public. As the computer-mediated communication technology evolves, and usage continues to intensify and diversify, being able to assess the best vehicle for knowledge sharing will provide a valuable means of ensuring both efficiency and effectiveness of the knowledge sharing.

Rosen (2007) uses the term "presence awareness" to denote an "...integrated videoconferencing, Web conferencing, phone systems, e-mail, calendar, directory programs and public IM systems to create a presence-enabled work environment that is as close to real time as you can get" (p. 1). This sort of multichannel, synchronous work environment is posed to become the de facto standard in today's fast-paced world. Decision making and collaboration are no longer tolerant of any time delays; participants are expected to be accessible at all times, and able to provide an almost instant turnaround with respect to joint work. Presence-enabled workspaces provide a high degree of social presence, and the integration of a multitude of different tools ensures a high degree of media richness.

FUTURE RESEARCH DIRECTIONS

Further research is needed to better characterize the diverse computer-mediated channels available for knowledge sharing, and to provide a more fine-grained typology of the type of knowledge to be shared. Past research has tended to highlight tacit and explicit knowledge as knowledge characteristics, where tacit knowledge is said to reside in people's heads, and explicit knowledge has been documented or captured in some tangible form. However, this dichotomy does not provide much help in selecting the appropriate channel to use to communicate or share knowledge. The dimensions of knowledge stickiness or leakiness better characterize how easy it will be to share that knowledge, but additional dimensions remain to be identified and better defined.

A number of researchers have researched participants' preferences such as whether they prefer using e-mail or a phone (e.g., Wagner, Eisenstadt, Hogan, & Pankaskie, 1998). However, additional empirical research is needed to better characterize the knowledge-sharing interaction and how it can best be mediated, taking into account as many critical variables as possible: channel characteristics, participant characteristics, objectives of the knowledge sharing, and characteristics of the knowledge to be shared.

In addition to collaborative teams, computer-mediated communication has facilitated the emergence of communities of practice (Wenger, 1998), networks of like-minded professionals who typically share knowledge to improve their professional practice. Brown and Duguid (2000) note, "people in such networks have practice and knowledge in common" (p. 141). One of the major benefits of such knowledge sharing is peer-to-peer mentoring and collective learning. The best-known example of such learning is the Eureka project at Xerox (Brown, 2000), which had the objective of trying to have photocopier repairmen learn from the experiences of their colleagues. There were many stories exchanged in an informal fashion amongst the repairmen, some "war stories" of extremely challenging problems that were solved. Eureka was an attempt to use a computer-mediated tool, a virtual workspace, to collect and share such stories:

To transform their opinions and experiences into 'warranted beliefs,' actionable, contributors had to submit their ideas for peer review, a process facilitated by the Web. The peers would quickly vet and refine the story, and connect it to others. In addition, the author attaches his or her name to the resulting story or tip, thus creating both intellectual and social capital, the latter because tech reps who create really great stories become local heroes and hence more central members of their community of practice. (p. 7)

More research is needed to help select knowledge-sharing channels for such communities to better create, preserve, and share their valuable knowledge and know-how.

Finally, to quote the old adage: "it is not what you know, it is who you know." Social network analysis, which is the mapping and measuring of how knowledge flows through online interactions, can be used to conduct empirical research on the effectiveness of knowledge sharing for different participants, different purposes, different knowledge content, and different channels.

Further research will result in a better understanding of the strengths and limitations of computer-mediated communication channels: those in use today, emerging channels that will be increasingly adopted in the short term as well as future channels that we cannot yet envisage.

REFERENCES

Allee, V. (2000). Knowledge networks and communities of practice. *OD Practitioners: Journal of the Organization Development Network, 32*(4). Retrieved May 25, 2007, from http://www.odnetwork.org/odponline/vol32n4/knowledgenets.html

Anderson, A., Mullin, J., McEwan, R., Bal, J., Carletta, J., Grattan, E., & Brundell, P. (2005). Exploring why virtual teamworking is effective in the lab but more difficult in the workplace. In R. Bromme, F. Hesse & H. Spada (Eds), *Barriers and biaes in computer-mediated knowledge communication. And how they may be overcome* (pp. 119-142). NY, NY: Springer-Verlag.

Andres, H. P. (2002). A comparison of face-to-face and virtual software development teams. *Team Performance Management, 8*(1/2), 39-48.

APQC: American, Productivity & Quality Center. (1999). Creating a knowledge-sharing culture: Consortium benchmarking study best-practice report. *APQC International Benchmarking Clearinghouse.*

Archer, N., & Wang, S. (2002). Knowledge management in network organizations. *Michael G. DeGroote School of Business,* working paper #456.

Blood, R. (2002). *We've got blog. How Web logs are changing our culture.* Cambridge, MA: Perseus Publishing.

Boase, J., Horrigan, J. B., Wellman, B., & Rainie, L. (2006). *The strength of Internet ties. The Internet and e-mail aid users in maintaining their social networks and provide pathways to help when people face big decisions.* PEW Internet and American Life Project Report, Report Number 202-419-4500. Retrieved May 25, 2007, from http://www.pewinternet/org

Bolisani, E., & Scarso, E. (2000). Electronic communication and knowledge transfer. *International Journal of Technology Management, 20*(1-2), 116-133.

Brown, J. (2000). Growing up digital, the Web and the new learning ecology. *Change, the Magazine of Higher Learning,* March/April, 11-22.

Brown, J., & Duguid, P. (2002). *The social life of information.* Boston, MA: Harvard Business School Press.

Burgoon, J. K., Bonito, J. A., Ramierez Jr., A. Dunbar, N. E., Kam, K., & Fischer, J. (2002). Testing the interactivity principle: Effects of mediation, propinquity, and verbal and nonverbal modalities in interpersonal interaction. *Journal of Communication, 52*(3), 657-678.

Choo, C., Detlor, B., & Turnbull, D. (2000). *Web work: Information seeking and knowledge work on the World Wide Web.* NY, NY: Springer.

Chua, A. (2001). Relationship between the types of knowledge shared and types of communication channels used. *Journal of Knowledge Management Practice* October, 2001. Retrieved May 25, 2007, from http://www.tlainc.com/articl26.htm

Dalkir, K., & Wiseman, E. (2006). Knowledge elicitation, organization and dissemination in a knowledge network: The role of knowledge brokers. In V. Guerrero-Bote (Ed.), *Current research in information sciences and technologies.*

Multidisciplinary approaches to global information systems.. University of Extremadura and the Open Institute of Knowledge.

Daft, R. L. & Lengel, R. H. (1984). Information richness: A new approach to managerial behaviour and organizational design. *Research in Organizational Behaviour, 6,* 191-233.

Davenport, T., & Prusak, L. (2000). *Working knowledge: How organizations manage what they know.* Boston, MA: Harvard Business School Press.

Dyer, J., & Singh, H. (1998). The relational view: cooperative strategy and sources of interorganizational competitive advantage. *Academy of Management Review, 23*(4), 660-79.

Field, J. (2004). *Social capital.* London, UK; New York, NY: Routledge.

Foos, T., Schum, G., & Rothenberg, S. (2006). Tacit knowledge transfer and the knowledge disconnect. *Journal of Knowledge Management,* *10*(1), 6-18.

Herring, S. (1996). *Computer-mediated communication: Linguistic, social and cross-cultural perspectives.* Amsterdam, The Netherlands: Benjamins.

Hislop, D. (2002). Mission impossible? Communicating and sharing knowledge via information technology. *Journal of Information Technology, 17,* 165-177.

Keong, L. C, & Al-Hawamdeh, S. (2002). Factors impacting knowledge sharing. *Journal of Information & Knowledge Management, 1*(1), 49-56.

Kock, N. (2005). Media richness or media naturalness? The evolution of our biological communication apparatus and its influence on our behaviour toward e-communication tools. *IEEE Transactions on Professional Communications, 48*(2), 117-130.

Kreijns, K., Kirschner, P., & Jochems, W. (2003). Identifying the pitfalls for social interaction in computer-supported collaborative learning environments: A review of the research. *Computers in Human Behaviour, 19,* 335-353.

Kumar. K., & van Dissel, H. (1996). Sustainable collaboration: Managing conflict and cooperation in interorganizational systems. *MIS Quarterly, 22*(2), 199-226.

Light, M., Bell, M., & Halpern, M. (2001). *What is collaboration? Virtual team success factors.* Gartner Research Note COM-14-4302. Gartner, Inc.

Majchrzak, A., Rice, R., Malhotra, A., King, N., & Ba, S. (2000). Technology adaptation: The case of a computer-supported inter-organizational virtual team. *MIS Quarterly, 24*(4), 569-600

May, A., & Carter, C. (2001). A case study of virtual team working in the European automo-

tive industry. *International Journal of Industrial Ergonomics, 27,* 171-86.

McDermott, R. (2000). Knowing in community: 10 critical success factors in building communities of practice. *IHRIM Journal.* Retrieved May 25, 2007, from http://www.co-i-l.com/coil/iknowledge

McGrath, J. (1990). Time matters in groups. In, J. Galegher, R. E.Kraut, & C. Egido

(Eds.), *Intellectual teamwork: Social and technical bases of collaborative work* (pp. 23-61). Hillsdale, NJ: Erlbaum..

Mooradian, N. (2005). Tacit knowledge:Pphilosophic roots and role in KM. *Journal of Knowledge Management, 9*(6), 104-113.

Nomura, T. (2002). Design of "Ba" for successful knowledge management – how engterprises should design the places of interaction to gain competitive advantage. *Journal of Network and Computer Applications, 25,* 263-78.

O'Dell, C., & Grayson, C. J. (1998). If only we knew what we know: Identification and transfer of internal best practices. *California Management Review, 40*(3), 154-174.

Olsen, F. (2006). *FAA: Knowledge sharing shouldn't be forced. Agency's use of online collaboration space has expanded to solve workgroup problems.* Retrieved May 25, 2007, from http://www.fcw.com

Panteli, N. *(2002).* Richness, power cues and e-mail text. *Information and Management, 40,* 75-86.

Riege, A. (2005). Three-dozen knowledge-sharing barriers managers must consider. *Journal of Knowledge Management, 9*(3), 18-35.

Robert, L., & Dennis, A. (2005). Paradox of richness: A cognitive model of media choice. *IEEE Transactions on Professional Communication, 48*(1), 10-21.

Roberts, J. (2000). From know-how to show-how? Questioning the role of information and communication technologies in knowledge transfer. *Technology Analysis and Strategic Management, 12*(4), 429-493.

Rosen, E. (2007). Real-time collaboration gets real. *Network World.* January 23, 2007. Retrieved May 25, 2007, from http://www.techworld.com

Sarker, S. (2005). Knowledge transfer and collaboration in distributed US-Thai teams. *Journal of Computer-Mediated Communication, 10*(4). Article 15. Retrieved May 25, 2007, from http://jcmc.indiana.edu/vol10/issue4/sarker.html

Swan, J., Newell, S., Scarbrough, H., & Hislop, D. (1999). Knowledge management and innovation: Networks and networking. *Journal of Knowledge Management, 3*(4), 262-275.

Szulanski, G. (2003). *Sticky knowledge. Barriers to knowing in the firm.* London, UK: Sage Publications.

Thurlow, C., Engel, L., & Tomic, A. (2004). *Computer-mediated communication: Social interaction and the Internet.* London, UK: Sage Publications.

Tiwana, A., & Ramesh, B. (2001). Integrating knowledge on the Web. *IEEE Internet Computing, 5*(3), 32-39.

Tsui, E. (2003). Tracking the role and evolution of commercial knowledge management software. In C. Holsapple (Ed.), *Handbook of Knowledge Management. Volume 2* (pp. 122-58). NY, NY: Springer-Verlap.

Vickery, S. K., Droge, C., Stank, T. P., Goldsby, T. J., & Markland, R. E. (2004). The performance implications of media richness in a business-to-business service environment: direct and indirect effects. *Management Science, 50*(8), 1106-1119.

Von Hippel, E. (1994). Sticky information and the locus of problem solving: Implications for innovation. *Management Science, 40,* 429-440.

Wagner, M., Eisenstadt, S., Hogan, W., & Pankaskie, M. (1998). Preferences of interns and residents for e-mail, paging, or traditional methods for the delivery of different types of clinical information. In *Proceedings of the AMIA 1998 Symposium,* Washington DC. Retrieved May 25, 2007, from http://www.amia.org

Wenger, E. (1998). *Communities of practice: Learning, meaning, and identity.* Cambridge, UK: Cambridge University Press.

Wenger, E. (2001). *Supporting communities of practice: A survey of community-orientedtechnologies.* Shareware Report. Retrieved May 25, 2007, from http://www.ewenger.com/tech/

Wiesz, J. D., Erickson, T., & Kellog, W. A. (2006). Synchronous broadcast messaging: The use of ICT. In *Proceedings, Computer-Mediated Communication, CHI2006,* 22-27 April, 2006. Montreal, Canada. ACM.

Yarmosh, K. (2006). Why Web 2.0 matters to your business – knowledge sharing. Posted April 25, 2006 to *Tech and Productivity.* Retrieved May 25, 2007, from http://www.technosight.com/why-web-20-matters-to-your-business-knowledge-sharing/

ADDITIONAL READING

Agrawal, A. (2006). Engaging the inventor: Exploring licensing strategies for university inventions and the role of latent knowledge. *Strategic Management Journal, 27,* 63-79.

Albino, V., Garavelli, A. C., & Schiuma, G. (2001). A metric for measuring knowledge codification in organisation learning. *Technovation, 21,* 413-422.

Argote, L., Ingram, P, Levine, L., & Moreland, R. (2000). Knowledge transfer in organizations: Learning from the experience of others.

Organizational Behavior and Human Decision Processes, 82, 1-8.

Athanassiou, N., & Nigh, D. (2000). Internationalization, tacit knowledge and the top management teams of MNCs. *Journal of International Business Studies, 31*(3), 471-487.

Barson, R., Foster, G., Struck, T., Ratchev, S., Pawar, K., Weber, F., & Wunrum, M. (2000). Inter- and intra-organisational barriers to sharing knowledge in the extended supply-chain. In B. Stanford-Smith &P. T. Kidd (Eds.), *E-business: Key Issues, Applications and Technologies.* Washington, DC: IOS Press.

Bhatt, G. (2000). Organizing knowledge in the knowledge development cycle. *Journal of Knowledge Management, 4*(1), 15-26.

Bloodgood, J., & Salisbury, W. (2001). Understanding the influence of organizational change strategies on information technology and knowledge management strategies. *Decision Support Systems, 31* 55-69.

Bock, G., & Kim, Y-G. (2002). Breaking the myths of rewards: An exploratory study of attitudes about knowledge sharing. *Information Resources Management Journal, 15*(2), 14-21.

Bontis, N., Fearon, M., & Hishon, M. (2003). The e-flow audit: An evaluation of knowledge flow within and outside a high-tech firm. *Journal of Knowledge Management, 7*(1), 6-19.

Boutelier, R., Gassman, O., Macho, H., & Roux, M. (1998). Management of dispersed product development teams: The role of information technologies. *R&D Management, 28*(1), 13-25.

Bromme, R., Hesse, F., & Spada, H. (Eds.) (2005). *Barriers and biases in computer mediated knowledge communication. And how they may be overcome.* NY, NY: Springer-Verlag.

Brown, S. A., Dennis, A. R., & Gant, D. B. (2006). Understanding the factors influencing the value of person-to-person knowledge sharing. In *Proceedings of the 39ᵗʰ Hawaii Conference on Systems Science.* 4-7 January 2006, Kauai, HI, USA. IEEE Computer Society.

Cavusgil, S., Calantone, R., & Zhao, Y., (2003). Tacit knowledge transfer and firm innovation capability. *Journal of Business and Industrial Marketing, 18*(1), 6-21.

Chi, L., & Holsapple, C. (2005). Understanding computer-mediated interorganizational collaboration: A model and framework. *Journal of Knowledge Management, 9*(1), 53-75.

Contractor, F., & Ra, W. (2002). How knowledge attributes influence alliance governance choices: A theory development note. *Journal of International Management, 8,* 11-27.

Davenport, T. H., & Prusak, L. (1998). *Working knowledge: How organizations manage what they know.* Boston, MA: Harvard Business School Press.

Dixon, N. (2000) *Common knowledge: How organizations thrive by sharing what they know.* Boston, MA: Harvard Business School Press.

Englehart C. S., & Simmons, P. R. (2002). Creating organizational space to for learning. *The Learning Organization, 9*(1), 39- 47.

Figallo, C., & Rhine, N. (2002). *Building the knowledge management network.* NY, NY: Wiley and Sons.

Galbraith, C. S. (1990). Transferring core manufacturing technologies in high tech firms. *California Management Review, 32*(4), 56-70.

Gallupe, B. (2001). Knowledge management systems: Surveying the landscape. *International Journal of Management Reviews, 3*(1), 61-77.

Gherardi, S., & Nicolini, D. (2000). The organizational learning of safety in communities of practice. *Journal of Management Inquiry, 9(*1), 7-18.

Goh, S. C. (2002). Managing effective knowledge transfer: An integrative framework and some practice implications. *Journal of Knowledge Management, 6*(1), 23-30.

Gorman, M. F. (2002). Types of knowledge and their roles in technology transfer. *Journal of Technology Transfer, 27,* 219-231.

Gupta, A., & Govindarajan, V. (2000). Knowledge flows within multinational corporations. *Strategic Management Journal, 21,* 473-496.

Hahn, J., & Subramani, M. (2000). A framework of knowledge management systems: Issues and challenges for theory and practice. In *Proceedings, 21st International Conference on Information Systems* (pp. 302-312). Brisbane, Queensland, Australia. Atlanta, GA: Association for Information Systems.

Hendricks, P. (1999). Why share knowledge? The influence of ICT on the motivation for sharing knowledge. *Knowledge and Process Management, 6*(2), 91-100.

Herschel, R. T., Nemati, H., & Steiger, D. (2001). Tacit to explicit knowledge conversion: Knowledge exchange protocols. *Journal of Knowledge Management, 5*(1), 107-116.

Holden, M., & Wedman, J. (1993). Future issues of computer-mediated communication: The results of a Delphi study. *Educational Technology, Research and Development, 41*(4), 5-24.

Husted, K., & Michailova, S. (2002). Diagnosing and fighting knowledge-sharing hostility. *Organizational Dynamics, 31*(1), 60-73.

Huysman, M., & de Wit, D. (2002). *Knowledge sharing in practice.* Dordrecht, The Netherlands: Kluwer Academic.

Iverson, J. O., & McPhee, R. D. (2002). Knowledge management in communities of practice. *Management Communication Quarterly, 16*(2), 259.

Jackson, P. (1999). Organizational change and virtual teams: Strategic and operational integration. *Info Systems Journal, 9,* 313-332.

Jones, S. (Ed.). (1998). *Cybersociety 2.0. Computer-mediated communication and community.* Thousand Oaks, CA: Sage NMC.

Karhu, K. (2002). Expertise cycle - an advanced method for sharing expertise. *Journal of Intellectual Capital, 3*(4), 430-446.

Koch, N. (1999). *Process improvement and organizational learning: The role of collaboration technologies.* Hershey, PA: Idea Group Publishing.

Kogut, B., & Zander, U. (2003). Knowledge of the firm and the evolutionary theory for the multinational corporation. *Journal of International Business Studies, 34,* 516-529.

Koskinen, K. (2003). Evaluation of tacit knowledge utilization in work units. *Journal of Knowledge Management, 7*(5), 67-81.

Ladd, A., & Ward, M. A. (2002). An investigation of environmental factors influencing knowledge transfer. *Journal of Knowledge Management Practice, 3.* Retireved May 25, 2007, from http://www.tlainc.com/articl38.htm

Lesser, E. L., & Storck, J. (2001). Communities of practice and organizational performance. *IBM Systems Journal, 40*(4), 831-41.

Levin, D., & Cross, R. (2004). The strength of weak ties you can trust: The mediating role of trust in effective knowledge transfer. *Management Science, 50*(11),1477-1490.

Maqsood, T., Finegan, A., & Walker, D. (2004). Biases and heuristics in judgment and decision making: The dark side of tacit knowledge. *Journal of Issues in Informing Science and Information Technology, 1,* 295-301.

Marquardt, M. J. (2002). *Building the learning organization: Mastering the 5 elements for cor-*

porate learning (2ⁿᵈ ed.). Palo Alto, CA: Davies-Black Publishers.

Matzat, U. (2004). Academic communication and Internet discussion groups: Transfer of information or creation of social contacts? *Social Networks, 26,* 221-255.

McDermott, R., & O'Dell, C. (2001). Overcoming cultural barriers to sharing knowledge. *Journal of Knowledge Management, 5*(1), 76-85.

McInerney, C. (2002). Knowledge management and the dynamic nature of knowledge. *Journal of the American Society for Information Science and Technology, 53*(12), 1009 -18.

Nardi, B. (2005). Beyond bandwidth: Dimensions of connection in interpersonal communication. *Computer Supported Coop Work, 14,* 91-130.

Nickols, F. W. (2000). The knowledge in knowledge management. In J. W. Cortada & J. A.Woods (Eds.), *The knowledge management yearbook 2000-2001* (pp. 12-21). Boston, MA: Butterworth-Heinemann.

Nieto, M., & Perez-Cano, C. (2004). The influence of knowledge attributes on innovation protection mechanisms. *Knowledge and Process Management, 11*(2),117-126.

Nonaka, I., & Takeuchi, H. (1995). *The knowledge-creating company.* New York, NY: Oxford University Press.

Pan S. L., & Leidner, D. E. (2002). Bridging communities of practice with information technology in pursuit of global knowledge sharing. *Strategic Information Systems, 12,* 71-82.

Polanyi, M. (1966). *The tacit dimension.* Gloucester, MA: Peter Smith.

Price, D. J. de S. (1963). *Little science, big science.* New York, NY: Columbia University Press.

Prichard, C. (2000). Know, learn and share! The knowledge phenomenon and the construction of

a consumptive-communicative body. In C. Prichard, R. Hull, M. Chumer, & H. Wilmott (Eds.), *Managing knowledge: Critical investigations of work and learning* (pp. 176-198). London, UK: Macmillan.

Riusala, K., & Suutari, V. (2004). International knowledge transfers through expatriates. *Thunderbird International Business Review, 46*(6),748-770.

Robertson, M., Sorensen, C., & Swan, J. (2001). Survival of the leanest: Intensive knowledge work and groupware adaptation. *Information Technology and People, 14*(4), 334-352.

Roth, J. (2003) Enabling knowledge creation: Learning from an R&D organization. *Journal of Knowledge Management, 70*(1), 32-48.

Schmitz, J., & Fulk, J. (1991). Organizational colleagues, media richness and electronic mail. *Communication Research, 18,* 487-523.

Schulz, M., & Jobe, L. (2001). Codification and tacitness as knowledge management strategies: An empirical exploration. *Journal of High Technology Management Research, 12,* 139-165.

Simonin, B. L. (1999). Transfer of marketing know-how and the efficient international transfer of technology. *The Annals of the American Academy of Political and Social Science, 458,* 81-96.

Smith, E. A. (2001). The role of tacit and explicit knowledge in the workplace. *Journal of Knowledge Management, 5*(4), 311-321.

Snowden, D. (2003). Narrative patterns – the perils and possibilities of using stories in organizations. In E. Prusak & L. Prusak (Eds.), *Creating value with knowledge.* Oxford, UK: Oxford University Press.

Stoddard, L. (2001). Managing intranets to encourage knowledge sharing: Opportunities and constraints. *Online Information Review, 25*(1), 19-29.

Subramaniam, M., & Venkatraman, N. (2001). Determinants of transnational new product development capability: Testing the influence of transferring and deploying tacit overseas knowledge. *Strategic Management Journal, 22,* 359-378.

Swap, W., Leonard, D., Shields, M., & Abrams, L. (2001). Using mentoring and storytelling to transfer knowledge in the workplace. *Journal of Management Information Systems, 18*(1), 95-114.

Tsoukas, H., & Vladimirou, E. (2000). On organizational knowledge and management: A constructivist approach. *Strategic Management Journal, 17,* 27-43.

Whitley, E. A. (2000). Tacit and explicit knowledge: Conceptual confusion around the commodification of knowledge. Retrieved May 25, 2007, from http://bprc.warwick.au.uk/km093.pdf

Williams, R. (2006). Narratives of knowledge and intelligence … beyond the tacit and explicit. *Journal of Knowledge Management, 10*(4), 81-99.

Zander, U., & Kogut, B. (1995). Knowledge and the speed of the transfer and imitation of organizational capabilities: An empirical test. *Organization Science, 6*(1), 76-92.

Chapter VI
Understanding Knowledge Transfer on the Net:
Useful Lessons from the Knowledge Economy

Ettore Bolisani
University of Padua, Italy

ABSTRACT

KM is making its way among the more established branches of business management. Thus, the contribution that can come from an "economic reading" of KM practices cannot be neglected. To systematise the conceptual backgrounds and to improve the formal modelling, a more direct connection with the models and approaches of the economic disciplines would be useful, but KM and Economics have often been two too-distant areas. Recently, the attention to the economic models by KM researchers has increased. On the other hand, a growing number of economists have shown interest in the emerging field of the "Knowledge Economy," which focuses on the knowledge as an explicit object of the economic analysis. From these converging efforts, useful elements for the conceptual systematisation of KM can arise, and can give theoretical robustness to both the practice and the research. In the light of this, the chapter examines the contribution that the current studies of the Knowledge Economy can give to the clearer understanding of KM and, particularly, of Knowledge Transfer processes that are a central element of KM. The open research questions that may result from such an "economics-based" approach to KM are also analysed.

INTRODUCTION

In a broad sense, knowledge management (KM) can be intended as the set of interpretative models, methods, normative guidelines, practices, and technologies whose purpose is the deliberate, coordinated, and systematic management of knowledge as a key *asset* in organisations. In this

regard, KM is making its way among the more established branches of business management.

Indeed, managing knowledge has always been one of the major concerns of humanity, but the development of specific KM practices, and the allocation of a specific budget in companies for these, is relatively recent. The cause of this upsurge of interest is often associated to the *chal-*

lenges of the current economy, which increasingly require *new solutions*. In the growing uncertainty of markets and the globalisation of competition, the knowledge, and the capacity to acquire and exploit it, become essential. Also, the impressive advancements of ICT increases the motivation and eagerness to develop innovative solutions that can enable the full exploitation of this enormous (and, partly, still unexplored) potential.

Maybe because of its relatively young age, the background of the conceptual tools on which KM is grounded is still heterogeneous and, somewhat, jumbled. Two main fields traditionally represent the foundations of KM: Computer Science on the one hand, and Social Studies on the other hand, integrated with additional elements deriving from the business management toolbox. However, considering that the preeminent application field of KM are the firms, a more direct connection with the concepts and models of the economic disciplines would be desirable and useful.

On the other hand, the notion of knowledge in the economic studies has been, for a long time, disregarded. Recently, however, there is an upsurge of interest in the so-called "Knowledge Economy." These studies can provide useful elements for the conceptual systematisation of KM that can both give theoretical robustness to the practice, and boost the research.

In this chapter, we delineate some elements for understanding the links between KM and knowledge economy, indicate the "hot issues," and discuss the future research directions. We assume the perspective of a KM researcher that attempts to draw useful lessons from a more established discipline, in the assumption that the further development of KM as a central managerial discipline is strictly associated with the advancements of the important field of the Knowledge Economy.

In the following section, we first examine the traditional KM approaches, and give reasons for the necessity of a more direct linkage with the economic disciplines. Next, we focus on the

particular issue of knowledge transfer (KT), and discuss the contribution that the current studies of the knowledge economy can give for the clearer understanding of this essential process of KM practices. For this, we propose a simple scheme of KT that makes it possible to analyse its economic implications in a more systematic way.

KNOWLEDGE MANAGEMENT: APPROACHES AND APPLICATION FIELDS

In the attempt to find solutions to typical problems of the firms (such as how to consolidate the organisational memory and avoid the negative effects of a rapid turnover, or how to limit the negative effects of idiosyncratic *knowledge islands* into the organisation – Franz, Freudenthaler, Kameny, & Schoen, 2002), KM practical programmes have been developed as a combination of several approaches (Earl, 2001). These approaches can be referred to various distinct schools of thought, and often imply different views, but can be mostly grouped into two contrasting categories, which are:

- The *technology-oriented approach*, which is often considered the "first generation" KM. The main theme is the development and use of the most advanced ICT applications for the manipulation of knowledge in its *codified and explicit forms* (see the following). The implementation of knowledge management Systems (KMS–Maier, 2002) is the main aim and result of this approach;
- The *human-oriented approach* (the "second generation" KM) sees the management of knowledge mainly as a communicational and social problem that, well before resorting to ICT systems, first involves people and requires the organisation of their interactions. The KM solutions that can be adopted include, for example, the implementation of

communities of practice (Wenger, McDermott, & Snyder, 2002).

In accordance to the approaches mentioned, the principal reference models adopted in KM stem from the area of *computer science,* on the one hand (e.g., approaches to the codification, memorisation, and transmission of knowledge contents), and sociology and psychology on the other hand (e.g., modalities of people interaction, learning processes, etc.). Considering that the main playground of KM practices is represented by firms, it may be surprising that the economic disciplines have, for a long time, been distant from the KM field, while the linkage between the economics and the more traditional areas of business management (including e.g., marketing, operations management, accounting, etc.) is much more established and robust. The further development of KM as a managerial discipline cannot neglect the contribution of an "economic reading" of KM practices, and needs a consolidation of its economic background and an improvement of its formal modelling.

In reality, the KM literature has, to some extent, considered the economic implications, but often without a systematic approach. On the other hand, for a long time, the notion of knowledge has not found an adequate space in the economic studies, and even when it has been treated explicitly, the attempt has often been to introduce the knowledge in the traditional economic models as just a kind of good, asset, or production factor. For a long time, the economics has apparently left free range to other disciplines to analyse the role of knowledge in the economic activities (Steinmueller, 2002).

Today, things are changing in both fields. On the one hand, KM books and conference proceedings have started to publish contributions of eminent economists (just as an example, see Holsapple, 2003); on the other hand, some fields of economics, from the knowledge-based theories of the firm (Grant, 1996) to the economics

of innovation, have started to treat knowledge as a special element that plays a specific role in the economic models and thus, deserves a peculiar analysis. To indicate these contributions, here we will refer roughly to the term *Knowledge Economy* (Foray, 2004; Stiglitz 1999), which is, frequently used to identify this articulated literature.

The purpose of this chapter is to debate the economic implications of KM in light of the current studies in the field of the knowledge economy. We will particularly refer to the process of knowledge transfer (KT). KT is an essential component of KM for at least two important reasons: first, because transfers of knowledge occur continuously in any environment where there are several agents interacting; and second because, as King (2006) clearly observes, "without KT, every problem-solving approach or operating skill would have to be reinvented each time." In the firms, the problem of managing knowledge is, mainly, an issue of KT. To be managed, the knowledge needs to be retrieved from some source, processed, and then distributed to some users (Garavelli, Gorgoglione, & Scozzi, 2002). Research and practice cannot neglect the need to reach a better understanding of KT as an essential element of KM.

A SIMPLE CHARACTERISATION OF KNOWLEDGE TRANSFER

It is not easy to clearly define KT. With the attempt to distinguish it from other similar notions (such as knowledge sharing and knowledge exchange), the literature (cfr. Boyd, Ragsdell, & Oppenheim, 2007) proposes numerous definitions that, however, tend to be too complex, or focus on too detailed aspects. Here, we just need an abstract but schematic reference that can enable us to identify and discuss the main components of KT.

KT will be intended here as the process through which a "piece of knowledge" is passed from somebody (that possesses it in some form) to somebody else (that is expected to use it in some way). This process needs a medium, and occurs in a framework of *rules* and *mechanisms* that influence it. In our analysis, we thus adopt the simple scheme, depicted in Figure 1, consisting of:

- The *knowledge item*, that is, the object that is transferred;
- The knowledge *sources*, that is, people, organisations, or systems that deliver some kind of knowledge item;
- The *users/receivers*, that is, those who receive the knowledge item to make some use of it;
- The *channel or medium*, that is, the technological (or social) system through which the knowledge item is carried;
- The *enabling framework*, namely the set of rules, procedures, supporting agents, and intentional measures (or unintentional factors) that characterise the environment where the KT process occurs.

Although (as will result in this analysis as well) all these elements are mutually interdependent, this simple scheme helps to simplify the examination of the economic implications of KT by focusing on each element at a time, separately. The rest of this chapter follows this approach.

Figure 1. A simple reference scheme of knowledge transfer

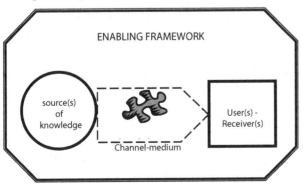

KNOWLEDGE ITEMS

A first step to understand KT is to examine what is exactly transferred, which calls for a suitable definition of knowledge. Here is not the right place to recall a debate that has occupied philosophers from the early beginnings of human history. Rather, the aim is to focalise, if possible, the economic nature of what is exchanged in a process of KT.

KM typically founds its concept of knowledge on the difference from data and information. While data are pure measures or "elementary descriptions" of facts or phenomena, and information is data that are organised and can assume a particular meaning, knowledge can be considered as something more. In this sense, knowledge builds on information (and data), but is much more than those: in KM, it is generally intended as the *capability of using information to make business decisions or take actions*, or in other words, as *workable* information (Malhotra, 2000; Tiwana, 2000). This is an "operational" definition that is often functional to the KM practices. But, it does not provide a sufficient foundation for the more formal modelling of KT and KM processes.

With regard to this, however, it is not easy to find a solution in the economic studies. One major limit of the formal economic models is that, for decades, information was assumed to be perfect (Stiglitz, 2002) and, thus, not a specially characterised object of analysis. An important step was, indeed, the development of the field of study of *information economics* that typically investigated the characteristics of economic systems from the viewpoint of elements such as "quantity, quality, symmetry among agents, distribution, access and transparency of information and communication, and their effects on the conduct of agents" (Antonelli, 2007, p. 228). It can be noted, however, that the distinction between information and knowledge does not emerge evidently, nor is it clear whether or not this distinction is important.

For this, the further step, represented by the Knowledge Economy, is essential. As Foray (2004) argues, one limit of the approaches of economists to the issue of knowledge is their attempt to remain in a "comfortable world" for their analysis. For instance, very frequently, knowledge is treated as just a product of the R&D departments, and knowledge items assume the tangible and treatable form of patents. From this viewpoint, the economic problem of KT is reduced to a question of "exchanging patents and licenses." Undoubtedly, this has provided the context for important studies and improved our understanding of these mechanisms, but it also appears a substantial reduction of the broader problem of KT. For instance, things get complicated when one considers the learning processes that individuals and organisations often perform well outside the boundaries of the R&D departments.

Indeed, treated as an economic object, there are several difficulties with knowledge. For physical assets, the economists have a rich toolbox of concepts, models, and even measurement systems that allow their observability and measurableness as economic objects. However, their application to knowledge appears often inadequate: the knowledge seems to escape the analysis conducted using these tools (Foray, 2004). Generally speaking, if we include all the "objects" that are often related to knowledge or are seen as elements of a cognitive process (i.e., documents, patents, procedures, know-how, but also experience, feelings, and even technologies), their nature appears very heterogeneous, often unique, and not uniform. Their boundaries cannot be easily traced, and it is thus virtually impossible to distinguish when one object ends and another starts.

Knowledge should not be intended as a homogeneous good that can be just the input of production (as a physical good), nor the physical outcome of a business process. Rather, knowledge items are a complex bundle of elements coming from various sources (Antonelli, 2007). A clear relationship between inputs and outputs of a process that uses or produces knowledge is, thus, quite difficult to delineate. In other words, a stable and unique *model of knowledge processing* that connects inputs and outputs, as has been done in the classic economic models of production, has not been defined yet (Foray, 2004).

Similarly, it looks sensible to affirm that "knowledge can be accumulated," but it is not clear how to measure such stocks (obviously not in terms of "number of units," nor in terms of their "acquisition cost" or "value"). Similarly, it seems obvious that there is some form of obsolescence, as happens for physical goods, but a sound measure of knowledge depreciation has not been defined.

Another aspect that is, however, related to what was previously said, is the potential *subjectivity* of knowledge. As Ancori et al. (Ancori, Bureth, & Cohendet, 2000) argue, the traditional rationalistic perspective of the economic models has typically considered knowledge as *detached* from the individuals, that is, something that can exist independently from its discoverer, observer, or user. In this sense, the difference between knowledge and information becomes meaningful, since knowledge is just the *progressive accumulation (stock) of pieces of information (flow)*.

It is just recently that economists have started to emphasise the intertwined relationships between knowledge and the subjects that manipulate it (Ancori et al., 2000). As Holsapple (2003a) argues, we can define knoweldge as a "representation" that a subject has of an object, procedure, phenomenon, and so forth. Due to this definition, a single item of knowledge is not independent from the specific "processor" that possesses, delivers, elaborates, or acquires it. The processors' cognitive background, elaboration capability, interests, behaviour, and so on, affect their "representations of the world" and thus, the nature and characteristics of knowledge items. To go even further, in a KT process, a knowledge item that is initially a specific "representation of something" possessed by the source will probably change when acquired by the user that, in other words, can have a different representation of the same phenomenon, data, fact, or whatever. Knowledge is thus not an *a priori* component that can be moved, but rather depends on the context of usage and on the learning processes that come into play (Tyre & Von Hippel, 1997).

All this challenges the way knowledge has been traditionally treated in the economic analysis, and calls for new efforts of modelisation. This debate also gives a useful lesson to the researchers in KM: a central issue that still limits our descriptive (and prescriptive) models of KT is the problem of *measurableness* and *observability* of knowledge and, more specifically, of knowledge items that are transferred.

To bypass the limitations of ambiguous or inappropriate definitions of knowledge, very frequently, an *indirect* identification is given, based on its *attributes*. This "dimensional classification" of knowledge is often useful to identify peculiar problems that may occur in specific circumstances, or, especially, to find suitable practical solutions for specific applications. The way KT can occur, and the ICT channel that can be used, are very often related to attributes of the knowledge that should be carried (see e.g., Bolisani & Scarso, 2000). The problem is that, in the literature, an impressive number of attributes of knowledge have been identified: for instance, Holsapple (2003a) is able to single out 23 different attributes, but even more can be found in the literature. In such way, a reasonably simple model that uses few variables to describe a process of KT becomes virtually impossible.

Codification of Knowledge

One particular attribute of knowledge is associated to the distinction between its tacit (i.e., not codifiable, and mostly embedded in people) vs. explicit (the one that can be codified and "detached" from its creator) form of knowledge. The existence of tacit components of knowledge is clearly connected to the previous discussion on the degree

to which the knowledge can be detached to the people that manipulate it.

It is worth noting that although this classification is evocative, it is often difficult to apply both to theoretical research and to practice. We would need an "operational" definition or procedure that allows one to identify what kind of knowledge a particular knowledge item is in the particular situation. Despite the numerous proposals, an adequate solution to this problem has not been found yet. What is more, as has been well explained by Grant (2007), all knowledge includes a degree of tacitness along a continuum in which one or the other dimension may dominate.

Having said that, this classification is probably the most cited and popular both in the KM literature and in the Knowledge Economy studies, essentially because it emphasises the core problem of KT. There is a general agreement that explicit and codified knowledge, being in a form that is very close to information and data, can be easily transferred from a source to a receiver (sometimes by means of highly automated ICT systems - Bolisani & Scarso, 1999), or can be stored in a database for subsequent reuse. All properties that tacit knowledge, instead, does not possess: it is difficult to manipulate and transfer, and tends to remain embedded in the people who possess it.

If explicit knowledge is more appropriate for KT, one might say that there are very good reasons to convert tacit knowledge into explicit knowledge every time this is possible. Indeed, to do that, a number of methods and mechanisms for *knowledge codification* (i.e., the process by means of which tacit knowledge is converted into explicit knowledge) are used in the firms, such as to translate the experience and capability of employees into manuals, procedures, best practices, guidelines, and so forth; to keep track of the work of people and teams by means of formal reports; to record the activities of the firm by measuring technical or economic parameters, and so on. In some way, we can also see codification as a process of KT itself, where knowledge passes from a person (the source, e.g., an experienced employee) to a *system* (the receiver, such as a database, a piece of writing, a series of numbers, a sequence of steps, etc.). The system becomes the support and storage of codified knowledge that can be, in turn, made available for the replicated transfers to other persons (or systems) and for a subsequent reuse. The Knowledge Economy literature highlights good reasons that can economically justify the effort of codification of knowledge by firms (Foray, 2004):

- Once codified, the knowledge tends to assume characteristics that are more similar to many physical goods: it can be described, valued, and even traded more easily (on the latter point, see the following);
- The costs of storage, replication, and dissemination of knowledge, once codified, are low;
- Globalisation requires increasing efforts of communication that, as said above, is easier when knowledge is coded;
- Innovation is today a fundamental competitive weapon; but to produce a continuous innovation flow, the firms need to exploit an "organisational memory" of old projects on which the new ones can be based, thus reducing the costs of "reinventing the wheel" any time (Argote, Beckamn, & Epple, 1990); this can be made more easily by using explicit knowledge items;
- The high turnover of today's companies requires measures to avoid the loss of useful experience of employees;
- Especially in multinational context, there is a need to set and disseminate compatible standards, best practices, and routines among all the dispersed units;
- Last, but not least, the potential of ICT technologies can be fully exploited only when knowledge is codified.

As macroeconomic investigations seem to show (see e.g., Abramovitz & David, 1996), the impressive growth of some countries (such as the USA) can be explained with their capability to exploit the potential of codified knowledge. This does not mean that tacit forms do not play a role but, rather, that the main mechanism for the economic exploitation of knowledge, and, by this means, for the economic growth, are grounded on huge investments in codification.

If there are sensible reasons to codify knowledge, where is the problem? One problem is that the process of codification of tacit knowledge into explicit knowledge implies a *loss* in the content, since a part of this remains *stuck* to its source (von Hippel, 1994). Thus, in the attempt to transfer tacit knowledge from one person, the final outcome is often something different from the initial item: codification implies the construction of a new mix of codified and tacit contents (Foray, 2004).

A second issue is that codification is, in general, very costly. Cowan and Foray (1997) indicate that this process involves three complex activities that require huge investments, namely: a) the development of a model that is appropriate for representing, in a formal way, the knowledge to be coded; b) the creation of a message that can be stored in an appropriate support; and c) the development and dissemination of a language to enable the decodification and the exploitation of knowledge by the prospective users.

SOURCES AND RECEIVERS

As mentioned before, the nature, characteristics, and behaviour of sources or receivers are not irrelevant. With regard to this, it should first be noted that a process of KT may involve completely different kinds of agents: individuals, ICT systems, organisational units in a firm, or different companies. A second important aspect is the motivation to exchange knowledge, which can vary extremely from one agent to the other. Third, KT is not only a bilateral process from one source to one receiver, but can involve a multiplicity of sources and receivers. Finally, sources and users are not fixed roles but, rather, can interchange with each other. For reasons of space, here we especially examine the two first aspects, and make some remarks about the third one in the next section.

In the very traditional literature of KM, in coherence with the two main approaches that characterise this field (i.e., the technology-oriented and the human-oriented approach – see previous), KT is generally analysed as involving two kinds of agents: individuals and/or digital repositories. This can lead to various combinations of conversion processes from tacit to explicit knowledge and vice-versa (Nonaka & Takeuchi, 1995). Organisations involved in KM programmes can thus choose among different KT solutions, and the trade-off between costs and benefits of conversion and replication of knowledge becomes fundamental. However, this evaluation is not easy: for instance, when knowledge is transferred from an individual to a system, the process of codification generally requires costly investments, but after that, the subsequent transfer from that system to another, or to a person, can be easily replicated, especially in the case of digital technologies. The effectiveness and actual benefits of such a KT process depends, however, on the degree of "stickiness" of knowledge.

Conversely, the transfer of tacit knowledge between individuals can be performed by means of various methods of direct interaction whose cost of implementation can, however, vary largely. In some cases, it is easier to allow people to exchange their tacit knowledge directly: an immediate advice given on the phone is, sometimes, the most efficient way to solve a person's problem. In others (for instance, the organisation of a company's general meeting, the implementation of a training course, or an apprentice period for new employees), the KT process can be very costly for the firm.

In these circumstances, it may become convenient to convert tacit knowledge into codified items, even though a part of the content will be lost. Producing a manual for new employees that describes the use of a machine can seriously limit the effectiveness of KT, but the costs can be much lower than a long apprentice time. In summary, the need for a cost-benefit analysis of the various KM solutions clearly emerges here.

When we consider KT as a process involving not single individuals but, rather, different organisational units (team works, departments, etc.) or distinct firms, the level of analysis changes, and other important factors arise. Here, the recent economic literature provides various useful insights. Indeed, there are good reasons to say that the ultimate aim of KT is, to some extent, the exchange of knowledge between individuals. However, especially considering that KM is mostly applied to the business environment, it is not possible to neglect the organisational context, where people share and transfer knowledge.

For instance, employees of a company are not completely free to perform KT processes "the way they like." Firms make significant efforts to organise the process of acquisition of fresh knowledge, whether or not such efforts are explicitly recognised as KM processes. As Nickerson and Zenger (2004) argue, the essential tasks of business managers can be described as follows: to select problems; to decide that there is the need for fresh knowledge to solve them; and to arrange the mechanisms or guidelines through which their subordinates will have to seek and acquire knowledge.

Thus, the existing organisational settings can seriously affect the efficacy of the KT process. As Teece (2003) argues, the process of interpretation of fresh knowledge coming from external sources ("sense-making") is an essential element that influences the absorbing capability of an organisation. Indeed, the interpretative activity is a kind of abstract model through which an agent interprets the world. The fundamental challenge here is the bounded rationality (Simon, 1982): for an organisation, even when its employees are talented and resourceful, it is very difficult to change continuously "the way it sees the world." Also, the possible actions that can derive from the knowledge acquired are selected among a limited number of alternatives, and they tend to be similar to those used in the past. Here, the weight of existing organisational routines, seen as the "memory" of the organisation, is critical. It is for this reason that the absorptive capacity is greatest when what is to be learned is related to what the firm already knows (Cohen & Levinthal, 1990).

On the other hand, the behaviour of agents may influence the efficacy of KT between firms or organisational units. An important issue here is the *motivation* of employees. Let us consider, for instance, the KT receiver: in a firm, the main reason for an employee to seek knowledge is the need to solve a problem or to make a decision. However, seeking and acquiring knowledge has a cost for the employees themselves (Antonelli, 2007). Even when, in the organisation, there is an attempt to organise the people's KT practices, such arrangements may find resistances unless they are consistent with the personal evaluations of costs and benefits.

Even more complicated is the case of sources. If knowledge has a value, why should a skilled employee be keen to share his/her precious "property" with other people inside or outside the organisation? To debate this issue, the notions of knowledge transaction and knowledge market are useful and important, and are illustrated in the next section.

ENABLING FRAMEWORK: MECHANISMS FOR GOVERNING KT

Markets for Knowledge

The awareness that knowledge can have a value, and that KT can have a cost, makes the analogy with economic transactions particularly useful.

Indeed, the notion of *knowledge transaction* is increasingly used, especially because, thanks to the concepts and models typically used by economists, the explanation of the economic use of KT processes can become clearer.

To see KT as a knowledge transaction implies, in our scheme of Figure 1, that users are the buyers and sources are the sellers of a knowledge item that represents the object of this particular kind of economic exchange (Desouza & Awazu, 2004). As in any transaction, it should be determined what goods will be bought and sold, and how the goods will be paid. Concerning the first issue, we have already discussed important elements in the previous sections. As regards the second, we can have a *barter market* where we buy "a good for a good." This is quite rare in the physical economy, but more frequent in the case of KT since it means that a source may be willing to "sell" knowledge, having, as a payback, other knowledge or, at least, the "promise" that the user will behave the same way in case of necessity (a sort of *obligation of future reciprocity*). In several practical solutions of intrafirm KM, this is what deliberately or implicitly happens.

Alternatively, payments can be exchanged for a common medium (a "currency"); in that case, a currency system has to be established (although this does not necessarily mean money), and implies a system of pricing as a way to value knowledge items. What this currency can be is, however, still debatable. Both the theory and the practice have not found an appropriate solution to relate a "money" of some kind with a consistent measure of value of the knowledge item exchanged.

The notion of knowledge transaction recalls another one; that of *knowledge market*. The practical use of this concept has two main fields of application. One is the interfirm or *external* knowledge market, while the other is the knowledge market internal to one organisation. The first type is more near to the typical ideal view of economic markets that has, until today, few attempts of application in KM. However, this area might attract the increasing attention of researchers. Indeed, as the day-by-day practice shows, it is very unlikely that the single firm can own, or internally generate, all the knowledge assets required by its business (Quintas, Lefrere, & Jones, 1997). Companies are increasingly realising that their knowledge resources derive, in significant part, from the system of interorganisational relationships established with customers, vendors, business partners, institutions, and even competitors. The implementation of formal or informal interfirm agreements to exchange knowledge and, by this way, explore innovations and exploit new ideas (Millar, Demaid, & Quintas, 1997; Peña, 2002; Warkentin, Sugumaran, & Bapna, 2001) can constitute a challenging field for KM researchers and practitioners.

The development of external knowledge markets implies that firms accept to deliberately "trade" their knowledge items with another independent organization, which involves a form of compensation in monetary or non-monetary terms. The attention is often put on the buyers of knowledge (i.e., the receivers in a process of KT), although firms can also consider the commercialization of their knowledge as proactive activity, which can be part of their business strategy. All this opens important scenarios for knowledge managers.

Knowledge markets are different from other markets. Particularly, knowledge is different from other commodities that can be traded (Teece, 2003). Here, an important distinction is between the markets for tacit or explicit knowledge. In the analysis of knowledge market, this classification recalls another one frequently used by economists, namely, the distinction between public and private knowledge. Once knowledge is discovered, coded, and made public, it becomes a public and non-rivalrous good: since knowledge is not consumed by the use, there is essentially zero marginal cost to adding more users, who, therefore, do not have to compete for the use of it. When knowledge is treated as a public good, its price should thus be equal to zero for an efficient diffusion, in accordance to the classic economic models (Foray, 2004).

A knowledge item can, however, be excludible, for instance, when it is tacit and its transfer is difficult, or when it is embodied in a "carrier" (a code, an electronic packet, a book, someone who knows, etc.) on which there may be some form of control or "property protection." Indeed, it is only purely immaterial and "disembodied" knowledge (i.e., common notions, general concepts, and other abstract objects of thought) that can be totally non-excludible. However, even in this case, it may be said that the cost of processing and disseminating knowledge is not zero to the extent that the process of assimilation by people (learning) or the embodying in things (application) is costly in time and resources.

There are also institutional mechanisms that enable a firm to turn public knowledge into an excludible good (Teece, 2003). For instance, as is well known, intellectual property rights (IPR) have been created to provide some form of protection. In such a way, knowledge is not public any more, and can become excludible. This mechanism has been introduced to provide incentives to the sources of knowledge. In fact, since the production of knowledge is not a zero-cost activity, how can the sources be convinced to spread their knowledge publicly, with no payback? For the economists, this is a crucial issue, but is well known by knowledge managers as well. For instance, in communities or practice, one major problem is how to motivate the participation, especially of those that are deemed to feed the community with their "precious" knowledge.

The use of IPR is not easy nor always useful. As Stiglitz (1999) notes, protecting the property and use of knowledge, and, thus, making it an excludible good that can have a market price, cannot be done the same way as protecting physical properties from, for instance, a thief. Due to the complex bundled nature of knowledge items, there are some reasons why protecting knowledge would be even counterproductive. For instance, new ideas build on the work of others, and often draw on the common pool of ideas. It would be impossible (and unfair) to impede the use of a mathematical theorem. Thus, a too strong intellectual property regime may render KT ineffective.

In addition, it should be noted that, from the buyer's (i.e., the KT receiver) viewpoint, public knowledge is important but, since it is public, there is no motivation to pay for it and, especially, any other competitor can acquire it easily. Seen in that way, no competitive advantage would be achieved from the use of public good while, on the contrary, it can be said that it is tacit knowledge (for instance, the one embedded in the minds and experience of employees) that represents the grounds of the competitive advantage of firms (Stiglitz, 1999). In a knowledge-based view, the essence of the firm is, thus, its ability to create, transfer, assemble, integrate, and exploit knowledge assets. Knowledge becomes a competitive asset to the extent that, as cognitive item, it becomes difficult to imitate by competitors. In this sense, the boundary of a firm can be determined, instead of transaction costs, by the tacit knowledge and its limited imitability/replicability by competitors (Teece, 2003). As is well known, assets can be the source of competitive advantage only if they are supported by a regime of strong appropriability, or they are non-easily tradable, or sticky.

In summary, the more a knowledge item is appropriable by the buyer, the more this can be interested in paying a price for it. If, in a knowledge market, only non-rivalrous knowledge items are offered, that is, those that can be easily acquired and imitated by competitors, the buyer has no incentive to pay for it.

Thus, while public knowledge is more easily transferred, it is tacit (or "non public") knowledge that can have a recognised value in a knowledge market and, thus, can give motivations to buyers and sellers for engaging in a knowledge transaction. However, at the same time, tacit knowledge cannot satisfy the essential property of homogene-

ity that characterises competitive markets. Each item of knowledge can be different from any other, and the essential elements that identify goods in physical markets become of few use: quantity does not make any sense, and price is hard to establish. Also, the markets of tacit knowledge can fail, since traders have to face several issues (Desouza & Awazu, 2004)[1]. One problem is how to "advertise" a knowledge item. To sell a good, the seller must signal its features and contents to the potential buyers. However, knowledge is an experience good (Choi et al., 1995): the buyers must experience it to gauge its value. However, if the seller allows the buyer to experience a knowledge item (i.e., to read a book, or attend a lesson), then the latter has no need to pay for it. Systems such as knowledge abstracts (i.e., a kind of "metaknowledge"), ratings (e.g., a measure of the degree of satisfaction by previous users), or counters (for instance, counting how many users downloaded a paper) can be used, and are actually used, to signal the quality of a knowledge item. However, their practical implementation and effectiveness are questionable, as the literature on the communities of practice shows.

The risk of *lemons* (Akerlof, 1970) is another problem. In a market, when buyers cannot evaluate goods, the best quality objects can suffer. Trust is an essential element for avoiding the lemons problem, but in a knowledge market, there may be the need for a regulating body that governs the establishment of a trustworthy climate.

Also, a market needs liquidity, which means convincing enough people to buy and sell their knowledge, which increases the externalities of the participation in the market. This situation becomes particularly critical at the initial establishment of the market.

In addition, the traders may try to sell or resell knowledge "illegally," namely out of the marketplace circuit. This can especially happen when a knowledge item can be easily replicated. A buyer may decide to spread it outside the organisation, or pass it on to others without rewarding the seller. This can cause a progressive mistrust in the knowledge market. Sometimes, especially in electronic-based knowledge markets, there are measures to avoid the "black market" phenomenon (such as encrypting, password protection, etc.), but these solutions may be or may be not effective, depending on the specific circumstances.

Internal Knowledge Markets

So far, we have analysed knowledge markets involving different organisations. However, from a KM viewpoint, another concept is even more interesting: that of *internal knowledge markets*, that is, the mechanisms, rules, and tools that support KT as knowledge transactions within the boundary of a single organisation. The concept of a knowledge market within an individual firm was popularised by Davenport and Prusak (1998) and is now attracting the interest of researchers (Brydon & Vining 2006; Desouza & Awazu, 2004). Indeed, it is possible to trace myriad of knowledge transactions occurring among employees and colleagues in an organisation. Many of these can be seen as "private bilateral negotiations" that are hard to capture and govern by the organisation (that cannot, for instance, reward employees for sharing their knowledge items). However, others can occur in a "regulated place," where people exchange knowledge subjected to some rules. Several current solutions of KM, from communities of practice to KMS applications, show characteristics that are similar to those of internal knowledge markets (Bolisani, Scarso, & Di Biagi, 2006), even though they have not been designed explicitly with this purpose.

The analysis of external knowledge markets, previously conducted, provides useful insights into the functioning of internal markets as well, and some issues appear particularly significant for KM. One is, for instance, the problem of "payment." What is the payment for exchanging knowledge in an internal knowledge market? Recognition? Prestige? Possibility of future reciproc-

ity? And what happens if people refuse to "make their tacit knowledge explicit," fearing that this can jeopardise their job? And since knowledge is power, even in a firm, people can try to keep it scarce in order to increase their indispensability. Or, they may tend to diminish the importance of knowledge "not invented here" and to embellish the power of the knowledge they already have.

In summary, KM initiatives that do not account for the motivations of individual employees to exchange their knowledge within structures whose functioning is similar to that of knowledge markets, are likely to fail (Brydon & Vining 2006). Successful KM programmes must recognise elements, such as the significant costs of producing knowledge, the externalities that employees face when making the decision to contribute as knowledge sources, the price of exchange of knowledge items, and so on. Even the technological implementations of an internal knowledge marketplace (e.g., an Intranet, online repository, or Web portal) require particular arrangements: just like in a physical store, for instance, somebody has to display knowledge items "on sale" in an organised way, to facilitate the exchange (Desouza & Awazu, 2004)

KT Accounting

Another economic issue that can influence the further development of KM as a managerial activity is that of how knowledge and KT processes can be *accounted*. An essential reason is that, for implementing appropriate solutions to govern KT processes, the firms need to evaluate the costs and benefits of these. Also, in an external knowledge market, the possibility to price knowledge is essential; while in internal knowledge markets, a measure of the value of knowledge exchanged can be of use both for establishing the "currency" for knowledge transactions, and for rewarding the participation in KT activities.

Although KM is increasingly considered a component of business management, its accounting is one of the most controversial and underdeveloped issues (Bose, 2004). What lacks here is the rationale to treat the problem. Traditional accounting criteria, such as reliability and relevance (Stone & Warsono, 2003), are still difficult to implement in a consistent way. As it can be easily understood, these difficulties can be directly associated to many of the issues analysed in the previous sections.

Until now, a large variety of accounting methods for KM have been developed (Liebowitz & Suen, 2000), which, however, demonstrates the lack of consensus on a general conceptual approach. Some methods are based on "indirect" estimates, such as the EVA approach, which measures the value of intangible assets of a company as its market over-evaluation compared to its actual "hard assets." The assumption here is that it is "the sum of everything everybody in the company knows" that gives it a competitive edge in the market (Grossman, 2006). This technique is of immediate understanding, but it is too rough, and fails to explain what knowledge source, receiver, or KM process is directly responsible for the creation of value. Others propose to measure the "intangible" assets (the "intellectual capital") in the same way as those that have a higher degree of tangibility. Here the core issue is, again, the lack of a coherent approach to identify and "observe" knowledge items. For KMS applications, specific non-economic metrics have also been introduced (e.g., the number of accesses, intensity of use, knowledge repository site; Kankanhalli & Tan, 2004), that do not have, however, a direct association with the idea of economic value.

CHANNEL: THE ICT SYSTEMS

Although the channels for KT are not exclusively ICT applications (other media, or direct social interactions can be used), it is the economic implication of these technologies that is mostly important for our analysis. In the previous sec-

tions, we have already highlighted various economic aspects of ICT in KT processes. Here, we will just focus on a specific point that deserves an additional examination: the nature of investments in ICT applications in relation to the different KM approaches that can be followed.

One approach to ICT investment in KM programmes is that of *hard codification*. As mentioned, to fully exploit the tremendous potential of ICT for its storage and distribution, knowledge needs to be codified. Very often, the major investment of firms is not in equipment or software but, rather, in the *codification of knowledge*. There are several examples of ICT applications that demonstrate this: EDI technologies, among the most efficient tools to exchange coded messages directly between information systems, are examples of transfers that required huge investments of codification by all the involved parties. Electronic commerce is, as well, another application that requires the efficient exchange of coded knowledge among traders, to enable the identification, selection, and payment of products online. Similar issues arise in KM programmes. As a matter-of-fact, a consistent part of the literature on KMS still focuses on the efforts to identify ways of coding knowledge effectively and efficiently. However, the codification of tacit knowledge results in a *loss of value* of the knowledge item. Thus, the cost of codification should be proportioned to the possible loss of value of knowledge. In this sense, technologies can be seen as both "friends and foes" of KM solutions (Hendricks & Vriens, 1999).

A substantially different use of ICT consists of abandoning the purpose of complete codification in favour of a *light use* of these technologies. Here, the major effort is, rather, aimed at adapting the technological system to the social and cultural features of KT processes. A frequent approach is to implement a variety of technological systems to fit the different dimensions of KT that can emerge in a particular social context (Spies, Clayton, & Noormohammadian, 2005). This, however, increases the cost of the integration of the various applications and the complexity of the systems.

A third possible approach is to *detach* the codifiable part of knowledge (and that can circulate in digital formats) from the one that is tacit. The notion of "knowledge artifact" used by Newman (2003) distinguishes between what knowledge is (cognitive artifact) and where it is embedded or "packed" (physical artifact). When the physical support can be detached from the cognitive content, the codification cost is reduced, and there is lower loss of cognitive value. For instance, some KMS applications propose "taxonomies" or "maps" as forms of "metaknowledge" that is used as a proxy of the complete knowledge content available, and helps a seeker to retrieve a particular knowledge item, to find who is the expert for a particular problem, and so forth. In this perspective, the configuration of ICT systems in KT typically comprises two integrated channels: one that carries "metaknowledge" in digital form, and the other that underpins social interactions between sources and users.

All these three configurations can be found in the current practice of KM. Here, we argue that their analysis in terms of the trade-off between codification costs and loss of knowledge value in each specific KM approach, can provide novel interpretations into the implications of ICT for KM.

CONCLUSION

The analysis conducted here aimed to stress the relevance of the economic issues in the conceptual interpretation and in the practical implementation of effective KM solutions. As a matter of fact, the development of KM has suffered from the lack of a more direct connection with the economic disciplines. Today, the results of the studies of the Knowledge Economy can provide essential insights to KM researchers, and can represent the

foundations for a robust conceptual development of this increasingly important branch of management. Here, we attempted to demonstrate this potential by analysing a central process of KM, namely knowledge transfer.

One essential point clearly emerges, and can explain some of the difficulties that KM often face, compared to other areas of management. The ultimate purpose of KM is to handle a category of goods (i.e., knowledge) that is expected to generate the most significant part of economic value, but is also *difficult to observe* and even more difficult to *measure*. As a matter of fact, a clear consensus on how to measure the value of knowledge, both in conceptual and in practical terms, has not been reached. The recent advancements in the modelisation of the economic activities that can be related to knowledge represent a promising source of ideas for KM researchers as well. With regard to this, the notions of knowledge transactions and knowledge markets are especially relevant. The models of knowledge markets can be a good representation of the relationships occurring among sources and receivers in KT. An immediate practical application of these findings is that the KM programmes that do not account for the economic motivations of individual employees to exchange their precious knowledge might fail.

As regards ICT systems, which are a core element of KM activities, here the Knowledge Economy analysis suggests a focus on the codification costs, to understand the potential and limits of these technologies. An analysis of the trade-off between codification costs and loss of knowledge value in each specific KM programme can provide novel interpretations into the implications of ICT for this field.

FUTURE RESEARCH DIRECTIONS

A number of potentially interesting research directions have already emerged from the analysis illustrated previously. In addition, there are two other promising points of a future research agenda on which it can be worth to put an emphasis.

The first point regards the mechanisms of pricing in KT processes, and more generally, how to reward participation in internal knowledge markets. This analysis can involve both theoretical aspects and empirical investigations, and might provide useful results for professional purpose as well.

Another important research area is the extension of KM programmes to interfirm environments. The management of interorganisational knowledge networks is a challenging arena for the practice of KM. The better understanding of the fundamental economic mechanisms that regulate KT between distinct firms can shed light on the potential application of KM to networked environments. Here, the concept of knowledge market becomes useful again.

ACKNOWLEDGMENT

The author gratefully thanks his colleague, Enrico Scarso, for his precious comments on the preliminary version of this chapter. This study constributes to the FIRB2003 project "Knowledge management in the Extended Enterprise: New organizational models in the digital age," funded by the Italian Ministry of University and Research.

REFERENCES

Abramovitz, M., & David, P. (1996). Technological Change and the Rise of Intangible Investments: The US Economy's Growth-path in the Twentieth Century. In D. Foray & B-A Lundvall (Eds.), *Employment and Growth in the Knowledge-based Economy*. Paris: OCDE.

Akerlof, G. A. (1970). The markets for "lemons": Quality uncertainty and the market mechanism. *Quarterly Journal of Economics*, August, 488-500.

Ancori, B., Bureth, A., & Cohendet, P. (2000). The economics of knowledge: The debate about codification and tacit knowledge. *Industrial and Corporate Change, 9*(2), 255-287.

Antonelli, C. (2007). The business governance of localized knowledge. *Industry and Innovation, 13*(3), 227-261.

Argote, L., Beckamn, S., & Epple, D. (1990). The persistence and transfer of learning in industrial settings. *Management Science, 36*(2).

Bolisani, E., & Scarso, E. (1999). Information technology management: A knowledge-based perspective. *Technovation, 19*, 209-17.

Bolisani, E., & Scarso, E. (2000). Electronic communication and knowledge transfer. *International Journal of Technology Management, 20*(1-2).

Bolisani, E., Scarso, E., & Di Biagi, M. (2006). Economic issues of online professional communities. In E. Coakes & S. Clarke (Eds.), *Encyclopedia of communities of practice in information and knowledge management.*= Hershey, PA: IDEA Group.

Bose, R. (2004). Knowledge management metrics. *Industrial Management and Data Systems, 104*(6), 457-468.

Boyd, J., Ragsdell, G., & Oppenheim, C. (2007). *Knowledge transfer mechanisms: A case study from manufacturing.* Paper presented at the 8th European Coference on Knowldege Management, Barcelona.

Brydon, M., & Vining, A. R. (2006). Understanding the failure of internal knowledge markets: A framework for diagnosis and improvement. *Information & Management, 43*, 964–974. Choi et al., 1995

Choi, S-Y., Stahl, D. O., & Whinston, A. B. (1997). The economics of electronic commerce. *Indianapolis*: MacMillan Technical Publishing.

Cohen, W. M., & Levinthal, A. (1990). Absorptive Capacity: A New Perspective on Learning and Innovation. *Administrative Science Quarterly, 35(1)*, 128-152.Cowan, R., & Foray, D. (1997). The economics of codification and the diffusion of knowledge. *Industrial and Corporate Change, 6*(3), 595-622.

Dalmaris, P., Tsui, E., Hall, B., & Smith, B. (2007). A framework for the improvement of knowledge-intensive business processes. *Business Process Management Journal, 13*(2), 279-305.

Davenport, T., & Prusak, L. (1998). *Working knowledge: How organizations manage what they know.* Boston: Harvard Business School Press.

Earl, M. J. (2001). Knowledge management strategies: Toward a taxonomy. *Journal of Management Information Systems, 18*(1), 214-233.

Foray, D. (2004). *The economics of knowledge.* Boston: MIT Press.

Franz, M., Freudenthaler, K., Kameny, M., & Schoen, S. (2002). The development of the Siemens Knowledge Community Support. In T. H. Davenport & G. J. B. Probst (Eds.), *Knowledge management case book* (pp. 147-159). Berlin: Wiley and Sons.

Garavelli, A. C., Gorgoglione, M., & Scozzi, B. (2002). Managing knowledge transfer by knowledge technologies. *Technovation, 22,* 269-279.

Grant, K. A. (2007). Tacit knowledge revisited – We can still learn from Polanyi. *The Electronic Journal of Knowledge Management, 5*(2), 173-180.

Grant, R. M. (1996). Toward a knowledge-based theory of the firm. *Strategic Management Journal, 17(Winter Special Issue),* 109-122.

Grossman, M. (2006). An overview of knowledge management assessment approaches. *The Journal of American Academy of Business, 8*(2), 242-247.

Hendricks, P.H.J., & Vriens, D.J. (1999), Knowledge-based systems and knowledge management: friends of foes? *Information and Management,* 35, 113-125.

Holsapple, C. W. (Ed.). (2003). *Handbook of knowledge management.* Berlin: Springer-Verlag.

Holsapple, C. W. (2003a). Knowledge and its attributes. In C. W. Holsapple (Ed.), *Handbook of knowledge management* (pp. 165-188). Berlin: Springer-Verlag.

Kankanhalli, A., & Tan, B. C. Y. (2004). A review of metrics for knowledge management systems and knowledge management initiatives. In *37th Hawaii International Conference on Systems Sciences (HICSS)* (pp.238-245). Computer Society Press.

King, W. R. (2006). Knowledge transfer. In D. G. Schwatz (Ed.), *Encyclopedia of knowledge management.* Hershey, PA: Idea Group.

Lichtenthaler, U. (2005). External commercialization of knowledge: Review and research agenda. *International Journal of Management Reviews, 7*(4), 231-255.

Liebowitz, J., & Suen, C. Y. (2000). Developing knowledge management metrics for measuring intellectual capital. *Journal of Intellectual Capital, 1*(1), 54-67.

Maier, R. (2002). *Knowldege management systems. Information and communication technologies for knowledge management.* Berlin: Springer Verlag.

Malhotra, Y. (2000). Knowledge management for e-business performance: Advancing information strategy to "Internet time." *Information Strategy: The Executive's Journal, 16*(4), 5-16.

Millar, J., Demaid, A., & Quintas, P. (1997). Trans-organizational innovation: A framework for research. *Technology Analysis & Strategic Management, 9*(4), 399-418.

Newman, B. (2003). Agents, artifacts, and transformations: The foundations of knowledge flows. In C.W . Holsapple (Ed.), *Handbook of knowledge management* (pp. 301-317). Berlin: Springer-Verlag.

Nickerson, J. A., & Zenger, T. R. (2004). A knowledge-based theory of the firm – The problem-solving perspective. *Organization Science, 15*(6), 617-632.

Nonaka, I., & Takeuchi, H. (1995). *The knowledge-creating company.* Oxford: Oxford University Press.

Peña, I. (2002). Knowledge networks as parts of an integrated knowledge management approach. *Journal of Knowledge Management, 6*(5), 469-478.

Quintas, P., Lefrere, P., & Jones, G. (1997). Knowledge management: A strategic agenda. *Long Range Planning, 30*(3), 385-391.

Simon, H. A. (1982). *Models of bounded rationality: Behavioural economics and business organization, vol. 2.* Cambridge MA: MIT Press.

Spies, M., Clayton, A. J., & Noormohammadian, M. (2005). Knowledge management in a decentralized global financial services provider: A case study with Allianz Group. *Knowledge Management Research & Practice, 3,* 24-36.

Steinmueller, W. E. (2002). Networked knowledge and knowledge-based economies. *International Journal of Social Science, 171,* 159-173.

Stiglitz, J. (1999). Public policy for a knowledge economy. *OECD Report.* Retrieved September 18, 2007, from http://www.worldbank.org/html/extdr/extme/knowledge-economy.pdf

Stiglitz, J. E. (2002) Information and the Change in the Paradigm in Economics. *The American Economic Review, 92(3),* 460-501.

Stone, D. N., & Warsono, S. (2003). Does accounting account for knowledge? In C. W. Holsapple (Ed.), *Handbook of knowledge management* (pp. 253-270). Berlin: Springer-Verlag.

Takeishi, A. (2002). Knowledge partitioning in the interfirm division of labor: The case of automotive product development. *Organization Science, 13*(3), 321-338.

Teece, D. J. (2003). Knowledge and competence as strategic assets. In C. W. Holsapple (Ed.), *Handbook of knowledge management* (pp. 129-152). Berlin: Springer-Verlag.

Tiwana, A. (2000). *The knowledge management toolkit.* Upper Saddle River, NJ: Prentice Hall.

Tyre, M., & Von Hippel, E. (1997). The situative nature of adaptive learning in organizations. *Organization Science, 8*(1), 71-83.

Von Hippel, E. (1994). Sticky information and the locus of problem solving: Implications for innovation. *Management Science, 40*(4).

Warkentin, M., Sugumaran, V., & Bapna, R. (2001). E-knowledge networks for interorganisational collaborative e-business. *Logistics Information Management, 14*(1/2), 149-162.

Wenger, E. C., McDermott, R., & Snyder, W. M. (2002). *Cultivating communities of practice.* Boston, MA: Harvard Business School Press.

Zander, U., & Kogut, B. (1995). Knowledge and the speed of transfer and imitation of organizational capabilities: An empirical test. *Organizational Science, 6*(1), 76-92.

ADDITIONAL READING

Adler, P. S. (2001). Market, hierarchy, and trust: The knowledge economy and the future of capitalism. *Organization Science, 12*(2), 215-234.

Alkhaldi, F. M., & Olaimat M. (2006). Knowledge conversion and transfer: A mathematical interpretation. *Interdisciplinary Journal of Information, Knowledge, and Management, 1,* 137-149.

Becker, M. C., & Knudsen, M. P. (2006). *Intra- and interorganizational knowledge transfer processes: Identifying the missing links. DRUID Working Paper no. 06-32.* Retrieved on September 18, 2007, at http://www.druid.dk/uploads/tx_picturedb/wp06-32.pdf

Castells, M. (1996). *The information age. Economy, society, and culture.* Oxford: Blackwell.

Chua, A. (2003). Knowledge sharing: A game people play. *Aslib Proceedings, 55*(3), 117-129.

Consoli, D., & Patrucco, P. P. (2004). *The economics and governance of collective technological knowledge.* Paper to be presented at the DRUID Summer Conference, Elsinore, Denmark, June 14-16.

Desouza, K., & Awazu, Y. (2004). Markets in know-how. *Business Strategy Review,* Autumn, 59-65.

Dosi, G. (1996). The contribution of economic theory to the understanding of a knowledge-based economy. In D. Foray & B. A. Lundvall (Eds), *Employment and growth in the knowledge-based economy* (pp. 81-92). Paris: OECD.

Drucker, P. (1967). *The effective executive.* New York: HarperCollins.

Drucker, P. (1969). *The age of discontinuity; guidelines to our changing society.* New York: Harper & Row.

Evans, P. B., & Wurster, T. (1999). Strategy and the new economics of information. In D. Tapscott (Ed.), *Creating value in the network economy.* Boston: Harvard Business School Press.

Grandori, A., & Kogut, B. (2002). Dialogue on organization and knowledge. *Organization Science, 13*(3), 224-231.

Hansen, M. T. (2002). Knowledge networks: Explaining effective knowledge sharing in multiunit companies. *Organization Science, 13*(3), 232-248.

Kafenzis, K., Mentzas, G., Apostolou, D., & Georgolios, P. (2004). Knowledge marketplaces: Strategic issues and business models. *Journal of Knowledge Management, 8*(1), 130-145.

Lichtenthaler, U., & Ernst, H. (2007). Developing reputation to overcome the imperfections in the markets for knowledge. *Research Policy, 36,* 37-55.

Machlup, F. (1962). *The production and distribution of knowledge in the United States.* Princeton: Priceton Univercity Press.

Markus, M. L. (2001). Toward a theory of knowledge reuse: Types of knowledge reuse situations and factors in reuse success. *Journal of Management Information Systems, 18*(1), 27-93.

Matson, E., Patiath, P., & Shavers, T. (2003). Stimulating knowledge sharing: Strengthening your organization's internal knowledge market. *Organizational Dynamics, 32*(3), 275–285.

Pyka, A. (2002). Innovation networks: From the incentive-based to the knowledge-based approaches. *European Journal of Innovation Management, 5*(3), 152-163.

Polanyi, M. (1967). *The tacit dimension.* Garden City, NY: Doubleday Anchor.

Prusak, L. (2001). Where did knowledge management come from? *IBM Systems Journal, 40*(4), 1002-1007.

Shapiro, C., & Varian, H. R. (1998). *Information rules: A strategic guide to the network economy.* Boston, MA: Harvard Business School Press.

Steinmueller, W. E. (2002). Networked knowledge and knowledge-based economies. *International Journal of Social Sciences, 171,* 159-173.

Teece, D. J. (1998). Capturing value from knowledge assets: The new economy, markets for know-how, and intangible assets. *California Management Review, 40*(3), 55-79.

Webster, F. (1995). *Theories of the information society.* London-NewYork: Routledge.

ENDNOTE

[1]   The economic analysis also explores the conditions under which knowledge markets are less effective than other solutions, such as hierarchical or centralised governance of KT.

Here, one can find similarities with the traditional economic analysis of the coordination mechanisms of economic activity. Nickerson and Zenger (2004), for example, argue that the selection between market-based or hierarchy-based KT solutions depend on the nature and characteristics of the problem to be solved. Similarly, Antonelli (2007) shows that a variety of different modes of knowledge governance can be developed even in the same organisation.

Chapter VII
Knowledge–Sharing Motivation in Virtual Communities

Jengchung V. Chen
National Cheng Kung University, Taiwan

J. Michael Tarn
Western Michigan University, USA

Muhammad A. Razi
Western Michigan University, USA

ABSTRACT

This chapter explores the motivation of virtual community members in regards to knowledge sharing and understands the underlying factors of such sharing behaviors. In order to better understand the effects of the two key factors (expectancy value and transaction cost) on the behaviors of knowledge sharing in virtual communities, this chapter presents a conceptual model to illustrate the relationship between transaction cost, expectancy value, and knowledge sharing. The knowledge transaction market is also further examined, since knowledge sharing is a form of knowledge transaction and the knowledge market provides an essential platform for knowledge transaction. This chapter is concluded with closing remarks and some suggestions for future research direction.

INTRODUCTION

Digital technology has provided a new paradigm in every corner of our society and resulted in our lives being changed through interaction over the Internet. The Internet has provided people with a new platform for social activities, thereby opening up entirely new features of social reality.

The proliferation of network access has facilitated the rapid growth of virtual communities. The impact of virtual communities is increasingly pervasive, with activities ranging from economic to marketing and social to educational. Hagel and Armstrong (1997) found that most virtual communities meet one or more of the four customer needs: interest, relationship building, transaction, and fantasy. First, communities can be created for members who share special interests. Communities that stem from particular interests are not necessarily directly connected to purchasing activities or consumer behavior. Second, communities give people an opportunity to form meaningful personal relationships without direct personal contact. Third, communities are created for people to explore new worlds of fantasy and entertainment through games and social experimentation. Individuals are able to create new identities and play in a fantasy world. Lastly, communities offer people online space to share information. For example, members share information related to the purchasing of goods and services. Prior to purchasing a product, a buyer may consult members of the community and find more information on a particular product.

This discussion explains the common characteristics of virtual communities. Focusing on knowledge sharing, many individuals participate in virtual communities, especially in professional virtual communities, to seek knowledge and solutions in favor of resolving problems at work (Hof, Browder, Elstrom, 1997). Driven by a knowledge economy, many organizations have recognized knowledge as a valuable but intangible resource

that holds the key to competitive advantages (Grant, 1996). They have begun to support the development and growth of virtual communities to meet their business needs and objectives. For example, in 1999, Caterpillar Inc., with a hundred manufacturers of construction and mining equipment, launched its knowledge network to its 12 CoPs (Communities of Practice) as a Web-based system delivered via the Internet. Today, this thriving knowledge network includes 3000 tightly focused CoPs. Based on an independent consulting firm's assessment, the tangible ROI (Return on Investment) was 200% for internal CoPs and 700% for external CoPs. Caterpillar attributes its success to the four success factors of CoPs: solid links to strategy, ingrained learning culture, user-friendly tools, and the core knowledge management support group (Powers, 2004).

Furthermore, virtual community-service providers, such as geocities.yahoo.com, who mainly focus on offering users their Web sites as a place to build virtual communities for knowledge sharing, are looking for unique, profitable, business models. It is important to understand why individuals elect to share or not to share their knowledge with other community members when they have a choice. Identifying the motivations underlying the knowl-

Figure 1. Conceptual model of knowledge sharing in virtual communities

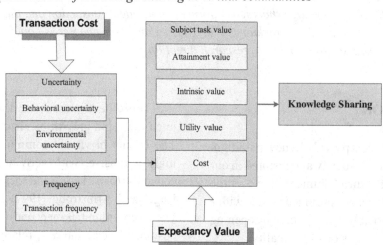

edge-sharing behaviors in virtual communities would help both academics and practitioners gain insights into how to stimulate knowledge sharing in virtual communities. To achieve this research objective, a conceptual model, as shown in Figure 1, is presented in this chapter and used to explore the theories behind knowledge sharing in virtual communities or, more specifically, the relationship of knowledge sharing with transaction cost and expectancy value. The theories and associated literature backgrounds of all components will be elaborated in the following sections.

This chapter is arranged as follows. In the first two sections, the concepts of virtual communities and knowledge sharing in virtual communities are introduced. Then, the discussion turns to transaction cost, expectancy value, and associated theories that help us understand the nature of human motivations on knowledge sharing. In the section on the knowledge transaction market, knowledge transaction and knowledge market are further examined, since knowledge sharing is a form of knowledge transaction, and the knowledge market provides an essential platform for knowledge transaction. At the end of this chapter, a discussion on findings and some suggestions for future research directions is given.

VIRTUAL COMMUNITIES

Gusfield (1975) explicated two types of virtual communities. The first is the traditional territorial or geographic community, which refers to a neighborhood, town, or region. Thus, the term of community implies the sense of belongingness to a specific spatial setting. The second is a relational community, concerned with human relationship without reference to location. For example, there are communities of interest such as hobby clubs, religious groups, and fan clubs. The above two types of communities are not necessarily mutually exclusive. Many groups of interest can also be location-based communities.

Virtual communities can be categorized on the basis of their cultural composition and the unique collective sense that members share (Leimeister, Ebner, & Krcmar, 2005). Given the definitions of virtual communities these authors found some common keywords such as members, interaction, Internet, and shared goals. In order to view it in a more comprehensive way, Adler and Christopher (1998) classified virtual communities into the following three categories:

- **Demographic:** Demographic virtual communities refer to certain groups or individuals with similar identity or background. For example, class or department boards on the Internet, job debate Web sites, and some cyber places where the discussion of local affairs is the main theme belonging to this kind of virtual community.
- **Professional:** Professional virtual communities gather groups of professionals for knowledge sharing and/or problem solving.
- **Personal interest:** Personal interest virtual communities refer to groups of people with same interests or hobbies, for example, clubs of online gaming.

Katzy and Ma (2002) further proposed the notion of virtual professional communities (VPC) based on the concept of professional virtual communities. Virtual professional communities brought different professions into virtual communities; these include professional occupations in various disciplines such as engineer, technician, doctor, lawyer, accountant, scholar, consultant, and so on. All the members that are set as a default have received formal professional education or (certified) trainings. They mutually share common value and behave with an expert's discipline. Therefore, the first step is to determine if the person has the qualified profession or expertise to become a member of a professional virtual communities. Sociologists generally consider the following rules to define professions (Cox, 1987):

- The profession owns unique knowledge.
- Knowledge can be transferred from old to new members.
- Professional practices can be monopolized.
- The distinguished members decide and estimate whether the standards for members reach the reasonable professional level.
- Ethical codes and rules are clearly listed.

Based on these rules, professional virtual communities are established and formed by groups of people who have common interests and unique knowledge to interflow, interact, and share information with each other. They teach and learn expertise constantly and, eventually, form a social relation network.

The professional virtual communities discussed previously are referred to as virtual communities throughout this chapter. It is mainly because the colleague kind of relationship in this type of virtual community provides a meaningful and more consistent base when examining the knowledge sharing behaviors in this context.

KNOWLEDGE SHARING IN VIRTUAL COMMUNITIES

Sharing is a process in which a resource is given by one party and received by another. For sharing to occur, there must be the existence of an exchange. A resource must be passed between the source and the recipient. The term "knowledge sharing" implies the giving and receiving of information within a context framed by the source. What is received is the information framed by the recipient of the knowledge. In other words, the knowledge received may not be exactly identical because the process of interpretation is subjective and framed by the existing knowledge and identity

of the recipient. Furthermore, knowledge sharing and knowledge creation are greatly influenced by cultural values of individuals (Hambrick, Davison, Snell, & Snow, 1998; Hofstede, 2001; Hutchings & Michailova, 2004; Pfeffer & Sutton, 2000).

By definition, an information system shares information. What differentiates information sharing from knowledge sharing is that the sharing of information covers a broad spectrum of exchanges and does not necessarily lead to the creation of new knowledge (Van Beveren, 2002). Knowledge sharing intrinsically implies the generation of knowledge with the recipient. In a face-to-face communication, an effective mechanism for gaining knowledge is to request help from another, such as someone who may possess the knowledge or expertise. This request may lead to a further communication that will facilitate the creation of new knowledge with the recipient.

Communication can occur electronically by e-mailing or online discussion board tools. Within the context of a virtual community, the direct mechanism for engaging another member of the group who possesses the knowledge is to post an open question or a request for assistance on the community's discussion board. Although lacking the richness of a face-to-face dialogue, the benefit of online discussion forums is that the communication becomes accessible to the whole community, and can be archived and accessed by other members. This way, a single request may generate many responses. Therefore, individuals are able to help resolve problems by sharing what they know through shared perspective, common language, and context of virtual communities.

Knowledge in virtual communities may be shared in different ways. For example, knowledge may be shared in the form of a story describing a similar experience in which a method or technique is developed or used to solve a problem. If unable to provide a solution directly, knowledge may be shared in another form by contacting someone who knows and is willing and able to help. The process of knowledge sharing involves the knowledge source using an online community system as a mechanism to convey what they know effectively. This process helps the recipient gain necessary understanding and enables them to develop a solution for the problem. In short, virtual communities are online networks in which people with common interests, goals, professions, or practices interact with each other, and a place where information and knowledge are able to be shared in the form of a social and professional way. Knowledge and information are shared in different ways, and motivations behind information and knowledge sharing in virtual communities depend on social cognition and social capital, that is, social interaction ties, trust, norm of reciprocity, identification, shared vision, and shared language (Chiu, Hsu, & Wang, 2006).

After the concepts of knowledge sharing in virtual communities are well understood, the next step is to explore the motivations of virtual community members in regards to knowledge sharing, and understand the underlying factors of such sharing behaviors, including transaction cost and expectancy value. The associated theories and concepts include transaction cost theory, transaction costs on the Internet, expectancy theory of achievement motivation, and expectancy of success. These theories and concepts are explained in the following two sections. Furthermore, they are also applied in the Knowledge Transaction Market section.

TRANSACTION COST

Transaction Cost Theory

The transaction cost theory was proposed by Coase (1937) to interpret the nature of firms. He argues that in order to carry out a market transaction, it is necessary to discover who one wishes to deal with, conduct negotiations for a bargain, draw up the contract, undertake inspection to ensure the terms of the contract being observed, and so on.

Williamson (1991) indicates that how companies determine an appropriate governance structure between the market and organizational hierarchy would clearly make a differentiation based on the characteristics of transactions. Griesinger (1990) defines a transaction as an exchange of economic or interpersonal resources, or the exchange of goods or services. Williamson (1991) argues that transactions differ in frequency, asset specificity, and uncertainty, which are explained in detail.

- **Uncertainty:** An uncertainty in conjunction with the transaction cost falls into two primary categories: behavioral and environmental uncertainties. The behavioral uncertainty arises from the difficulties associated with monitoring the contractual performance of exchange partners (Williamson, 1985). For example, there is an uncertainty in the transaction when one cannot ensure that the other party will not go out of the business or try to renegotiate the contract during the life of the contract. This uncertainty highlights the need for transacting parties to safeguard their contract in order to protect their rights. As the result, it is expected to raise the costs of writing, monitoring, and enforcing a contract. The environmental uncertainty is a two-dimensional concept that entails elements of both unpredictability and changeability (Klein, 1989; Klein, Frazier, & Roth 1990).
- **Frequency:** Frequency refers to how often a transaction occurs, either occasionally or cyclically. Therefore, it can be deduced that the frequency can be referred to as how many times a company seeks to initiate a transaction in the market. Williamson (1981) suggests that the frequency with which transactions recur is one of the critical dimensions for describing transactions. As in Internet

shopping, buying frequency has an influence on consumers' perceived transaction costs and their willingness to buy online. The reaction between an experienced and inexperienced online consumer to the same level of uncertainty in the transaction process could be different because there is a difference in their tolerance of uncertainty.

- **Asset specificity:** Asset specificity refers to the lack of ease with which the human capital, physical assets, and facilities specifically tied to the manufacturing of an item can be used by alternative users or put to alternative uses (Williamson, 1981). A central premise of the transaction cost theory is that the transaction cost increases as transactors make greater asset-specific investments. Increase specialization within a production network cannot be reached without a cost. When transactors make investments in specialization, they will put special effort (i.e., complicated contracts) to design a bilateral, or at least quasi-bilateral, and exchange for a considerable period thereafter (Williamson, 1981). As asset specificity increases, due to transactors' fear of opportunism, more complex governance structures (i.e., more complicated contracts) are required to eliminate or attenuate costly bargaining over profits from specialized assets (Williamson, 1985). Thus, transaction costs are presumed to elevate with an increase in asset specificity.

In summary, the idea of the transaction cost theory is to examine the presumable types of transaction costs (direct and opportunity costs) and potential sources (specific assets safeguarding, adaptation, and performance evaluation). Through analyzing the different principal dimensions with respect to the transactions (asset specificity, uncertainty, and frequency) under some assumptions (bounded rationality and opportunism), people try to design control mechanisms in order to minimize transaction costs according to some governance problems. From this discussion and the nature of sharing in terms with transaction, this chapter examines knowledge sharing from the perspective of transaction cost. Since virtual communities are online based, the transaction cost incurred on the Internet is further examined in the next subsection.

Transaction Costs on the Internet

Generally speaking, electronic commerce will lower the search cost but raise the examination cost, payment cost, and post-sales service cost (Liang & Huang 1998). Compared to the traditional commerce channel, the electronic channel may have higher costs in some categories but lower costs in others. For example, the electronic channel may provide a search engine that could lower the search and comparison costs by helping customers find product sources and allowing customers to compare different prices, but on the other hand, it may increase the examination cost by not letting the customer try the product physically.

According to Malone et al. (Malone, Yates, & Benjamin, 1987) and Wigand (1995), four effects may lead to reduce transaction and coordination costs on the Internet.

- **Communication effect:** Advanced information technologies allow more information to be communicated in the same unit of time, thereby reducing transaction costs.
- **Electronic integration effect:** A closer electronic linkage between the buyer and seller is enabled.
- **Electronic brokerage effect:** Occurs in an electronic marketplace where buyers and sellers come together to compare offerings.
- **Electronic strategic networking effect:** Info-communication technologies enable the design and strategic deployment of linkages and networks among cooperating firms who

intend to gain competitive advantages by achieving joint, strategic goals.

Because of the rapid growth in computing power, telecommunication services and the Internet have improved the flow of information and reduced transaction costs, especially the searching cost (Wimmer, Townsend, & Chezum, 2000). The new interactive technologies enable the "go-between service provider"; it is a kind of intermediary that can change the structure of costs. The Internet links corporations with customers and each other in a much less expensive manner than the traditional means. Since information can be transmitted onto the Internet simultaneously and globally, the "go-between service provider" can either interact with many customers or only one with few additional costs.

Moreover, as a firm gets to know customers better and does more business with them, the costs of transactions will be further trimmed down. In addition, customers can share and disseminate their know-how through virtual communities. Consumers can also train and help each other when making purchasing decisions, and eventually reduce costs of searching. As a key component of the "go-between service provider" offerings, knowledge is an abundant resource that increases with its frequency of use. In addition, it may reduce the costs of transaction. (Vandermerwe, 1999).

EXPECTANCY VALUE

Expectancy-Value Theory of Achievement Motivation

The original meaning of the Latin word "motivation" is to move. According to this concept, research on motivation is part of research on behavior (Eccles & Wigfield, 2002). Most recent theories related to this topic focus on belief, value, and goal. This chapter discusses more on

the value theory, that is, the expectancy-value theory of achievement motivation. For example, Eccles et al. (Eccles, Adler, Futterman, Goff, Kaczala, Meece, et al., 1983) modifies motivation from expectancy-value model. Atkinson (1964) connects personal choice, insistence, and performance with expectancy for success and subjective task value.

However, several differences can be pointed out between Eccles and Wigfield (2002) and Atkinson (1964). First, Eccles and Wigfield focus more on the theme, expectation, and value. They further broaden the influence of both themes in psychological, social, and cultural perspectives. Moreover, they argue that expectation and value are positively correlated, not negatively correlated, as Atkinson (1964) suggested. The expectancy-value theory of achievement motivation emphasizes more on the importance of subjective awareness.

Expectancy is related to how a person performs different tasks or activities, while value, on the other hand, is related to the motivation or reason for engaging this activity. Expectancy and task value are the cores of the expectancy-value theory of achievement motivation (Eccles & Wigfield, 2002).

Expectancy for Success

Expectancy is the prospect of success. Expectancy for success is defined as the personal belief of how well he or she can perform in the coming task, including both short- or long-term (Eccles & Wigfield, 2002; Wigfield, 1994). Those who have high expectancy for success believe that they can perform well in future or upcoming events and have a positive prospect of results.

Eccles and Wigfield (2002) pointed out that the measurement of expectancy is similar to the one used in the personal efficacy expectation (Bandura, 1997). The major difference is that Bandura's expectancy-value theory mainly concerned with the prediction of results, while

Wigfield and Eccles focus more on personal or performance expectancy, rather than the forecast results (Wigfield & Eccles, 2000).

Pajares (1996) compared self-performance and related perspective. He concludes that performance is usually measured on the task-specific level. It is measured by asking individuals how confident they are in related to achieving tasks. The expectancy-value theory, by Eccles and Wigfield (2002), prefers to measure the capability of belief and expectancy within a domain, rather than related to a specific activity. Therefore, Wigfield and Eccles (2002) argued that their measurement toward self-performance can be used more generally than Bandura's or others' (Wigfield & Eccles, 2000).

Subjective Task Value

In the past, there were different types of research on subjective task value. Some research extended Atkinson's original definition of incentive value to discuss the nature of subjective task value, and further explained it by the corelationship of task value and individual needs (Raynor, 1982). For example, when a job is viewed as valuable, it is because it satisfies individual needs, or it can benefit an individual with extra value. On the other hand, other research discussed human value in general (Rokeach, 1973). They viewed value as an output of an individual internal psychological view, estimated the influence of personal value on his or her behavior choices, and provided arguments over the link between personal value and behavior.

Eccles et al. (1983) combined these two theories; he took the influences of both personal value and subjective value on behavior into consideration, and integrated them with the expectancy-value theory of achievement motivation to define the major factors of expectancy-value; that is, attainment value, intrinsic value, utility value, and cost, as summarized.

- **Attainment value:** Based on Battle's study (1966), attainment value is defined as the importance of an individual to complete a certain task. This value usually reflects personal intention.
- **Intrinsic value:** It indicates the enjoyment gained by an individual from activities or a subjective interest from a subject, for example, experiencing the process of involvement. The more intrinsic value that individual perceived, the more personal willingness he/she can be inspired.
- **Utility value:** It can be determined by the relation between a task and other current or future tasks, such as career goals, that is, how well this task would co-relate with, and benefit to, a personal plan. A positive task means a task that benefits his or her future goal, even if he or she is not interested in the task content at all. For example, students may select courses that they do not like but are required to take for meeting their other interests such as pleasing parents or accompanying their friends.
- **Cost:** Cost can be a negative point of view in some perspectives, such as anxiety and fear toward failure. Cost is the limitation of an individual to join activities after he/she has decided to join another one. For example, if one cannot play with his/her friends due to his/her homework, this cost will let him/her put more effort to complete the work.

The level of subjective value task can be influenced by both internal and external factors at the same time. No matter that individuals take consideration in the perspective of incentives or results; the question of "Why should I do this?" reflects his or her value, which includes personal goals, utility, interest, and cost perceived. The expectancy-value theory of achievement motivation consolidates related attainment value, internal/external motivation, and need/cost perspective. It not only helps us figure out the relationship between value and successful behavior, but also allows us to realize an individual's subjective value under external environments and internal cognition perspectives.

KNOWLEDGE TRANSACTION MARKET

After the discussion of transaction cost and expectancy value, their theories help us understand the nature of human motivation in regards to knowledge sharing. In this section, knowledge transaction and knowledge market are examined, since knowledge sharing is a form of knowledge transaction and knowledge market provides an essential platform for knowledge transaction.

Knowledge Market

Knowledge differs from information in the respect that it is an intangible source that exists in the mind of an individual (Sveiby, 1997). Both information and knowledge find their origins in data, but knowledge is generated by interpreting information. A knowledge market is a medium that allows people to meet, ask, and receive knowledge. This can be informal or more formalized, as in a CoP (Community of Practice), where similarly minded people are brought together by their specialized knowledge and self interest (Wenger & Snyder, 2000). Groups of knowledge, as well as the individual parts, are expanded simultaneously (Johnson, 2001).

Knowledge Transaction and Knowledge Exchange

A knowledge transaction describes the search and acquisition of knowledge. Acquisition of knowledge requires other people to draw their own meanings for what is requested. It is conducted in an online environment where others are also allowed to benefit from and/or contribute

to. Based on the concept of knowledge transaction, knowledge exchange describes the process of knowledge sharing. To motivate members to exchange knowledge, a number of values need to be practiced. Trust that occurs in the medium of exchange will facilitate the integrity of knowledge transaction among group members, since they need to perceive that those people who exchange their knowledge with them are providing valid responses to their requests. (Sharratt & Usoro, 2003).

Relationship Between Knowledge Transactions and Virtual Communities

Virtual communities are groups of similarly minded individuals. They get online together by proxy. Knowledge exchange occurs in virtual, but socially relevant environments. Conversations conducted online allow all other participating group members to see the nature of knowledge exchange and therefore, increase their input (Sharratt & Usoro, 2003). It is quite special, as group members from diverse geographical locations and time zones can go online and enter into a same context to exchange knowledge. Thus, in this context, by having conversation, the knowledge then can be "transferred" (Zeldin, 1998).

Knowledge differs greatly from information because information is merely used to inform people. Knowledge requires a person to identify it and perceive some kind of meaning from it. It is a very personal process that requires a number of conditions to make a contributor or recipient comfortable during a knowledge exchange (Andematten, Bettoni, & Mathieu, 2007).

Effect of Knowledge Transactions on the Internet

Some online communities have their basis grounded in an existing physical face-to-face network, which helps to overcome the need to develop trust online as people already know each other. This type of online community is known as a Hybrid Physical Virtual Community (Gaved & Mulholland, 2005). This hybrid aspect means that knowledge transactions have an unprecedented level of rapport and social relevance between members, which allows them to support each other during a personal or community crisis. In some cases, people with acute medical conditions or disabilities can use such social networks to support each other. This takes knowledge transactions to a higher level of effectiveness since people can share and learn how others cope with their health problems and disabilities.

Cultural differences among virtual community members can act as barriers to effective knowledge transactions (LeBaron, Pulkkinen, & Scollin, 2000). This highlights the very nature of virtual communities and knowledge transactions because people are brought together by common interests that transcend their national and cultural identities. Personal- or work-related interests can motivate people to interact with others in a virtual community. This virtual community may have a common language and shared culture that also related to the concept of cyber citizens who develop a new online culture for their members with a common interest (Flavian & Guinaliu, 2005).

Knowledge Sharing in a Knowledge Market

Davenport and Prusak (1998) think people pursue knowledge sharing because they desire to finish their tasks by using this knowledge, which is the same when they face uncertainties. However, they also expect to obtain some benefits when providing knowledge for sharing. In a professional virtual community, this kind of transaction usually does not involve money reward. Nevertheless, the fact of market price mechanisms cannot be ignored. Knowledge market is similar to a typical market, where a participant's intent is to exchange rare

resources for current or future benefits. In the transaction cost theory, the transaction means that buyers and sellers both have independent techniques and the view of positive self-absorption. For the goods or services that people want to exchange, both parties can establish a certain contract and complete the exchange activity at a condition that buyers and sellers can accept.

In virtual communities, the flow of knowledge is always two-way or multiway. This knowledge exchange process must have knowledge demanders and suppliers, and it can even happen without a physical place or certain form to display. Thus, in the knowledge sharing process, knowledge suppliers are sellers. Although knowledge suppliers and demanders obtain different forms of rewards from exchange processes, they still need to satisfy the conditions that both parties accept, and unfortunately, the market mechanisms still have faults. Thus, a virtual community's knowledge transaction market often experiences insufficient or inadequate phenomenon.

Davenport and Prusak (1998) stated that "knowledge buyers look for support to solve problems, while knowledge sellers have knowledge and ability to resolve problems." Both parties possess different expectancies because of their different roles. Then, knowledge is driven by the market power, which operation is similar to that of a service market. The knowledge market also involves buyers and sellers who determine and agree upon a satisfied price after communication and negotiation.

According to Davenport and Prusak (1998) and Teece's (1998) studies, the reasons that a knowledge transaction market is insufficient can be summarized as follows:

- **Incomplete information:** It means that a buyer does not know the physical location of the seller and whether the knowledge that the seller provides matches his or her need.

- **Knowledge distributed unfairly:** Knowledge is always collected or controlled by a few people or certain groups, which monopoly of knowledge market can occur.
- **Localization of knowledge:** People may have a psychological distance due to distrust. Thus, even if people have proper knowledge, they are still unwilling to communicate with strangers or people who they do not trust. This is an important reason that leads to an insufficient knowledge market.
- **Human barrier:** In the knowledge market, knowledge is expensive and may be difficult to obtain. It means that sellers are not willing to sell or share with others, and their counterparts have "Not Invented Here" syndrome or "Class Barrier." In other words, upper-social-class people do not share knowledge with lower-social-class people. This type of insufficient knowledge transaction market will eventually lead to a condition that increases the knowledge transaction cost and seriously impedes the sharing behavior.

This chapter deems that knowledge transaction market exists, and it has the same characteristics of transaction cost as those of general commodities or service market. The problem that occurs in knowledge market brings up an unjustifiable transaction cost or the impeding factors that will result in insufficiency in a knowledge market. It is one of the main reasons why this study employs transaction-cost theory to analyze the characteristics of knowledge sharing among virtual community members..

From this discussion, this study recognizes that expectancy value theory of achievement motivation and transaction cost theory encompass the same concept of cost. The definition of cost in the transaction-cost theory is based on an economic view. The transaction-cost theory defines cost as a kind of price for completing transaction in the market, and also classifies cost

as several kinds, such as search cost and monitor cost. The cost of expectancy-value theory in achievement motivation is defined as how much effort is needed to complete the selected activity. The main difference between these two theories is the cost concepts in which one establishes on the economic base and another is on psychological base. From one view, it stands for the amount of money needed to pay. On the other hand, it means an effort, loss, or damage takes place in order to compensate or achieve something. Therefore, the generic concept of cost is applicable. Generally speaking, cost stands for a certain payoff that is used to complete or achieve something such as a transaction or behavior.

CONCLUSION

This chapter has been dedicated to provide a better understanding of whether the expectancy value and transaction cost can affect the behavior of knowledge sharing in virtual communities, or specifically, in professional virtual communities. Virtual communities cannot be classified by Hagel and Armstrong's (1997) four basic categories because the subjects involved are widely dispersed. It implies that the development of virtual communities tends to complicate the management issue. Nevertheless, the capacity of professional virtual communities for providing a common platform for sharing expertise or knowledge is probably more appealing. To ensure a successful experience on either a service provider or community member's perspective, the theoretical linkages between the critical factors, transaction cost, and expectancy value, and knowledge sharing or transaction, have been addressed in this chapter. For a service provider, a unique business model can be established. For community members, their decision to share knowledge and interact with other members can be reasonably justified, based on the cost and value of their knowledge sharing, to help other members or receive professional assistance from other members. Finally, identifying the motivations underlying the knowledge-sharing behavior in virtual communities would help both academics and practitioners gain insights into how to stimulate knowledge sharing in virtual communities.

FUTURE RESEARCH DIRECTIONS

Several outcomes can result from virtual community activities while sharing knowledge, for example, group cohesion and unity, members' feeling of the virtual community ownership, members' loyalty to the community, and organizational citizenship behaviors (Organ, 1988). These outcomes are not directly related to commercial performance, but to social performance that may lead the commercial performance in the long run. Future research can be done by examining the relationship between these outcomes and knowledge sharing in virtual communities.

Second, the current research can be extended to investigate the effect of trust, privacy, and culture on knowledge sharing in virtual communities. Undoubtedly, "trust or privacy" is one of the most controversial issues in online communities. The profit motive may indeed create new forms of virtual communities with strong commercial elements that will enhance and expand the basic requirements of community; that is, trust and commitment to each other. There should be more investigation on how trust is related to transaction cost and expectancy value, therefore, the interaction of trust and other factors (i.e., cost and value) and its relationship with knowledge sharing in virtual communities should be examined. Regarding issues about online privacy, the nature of the Internet and its global reach has created some interesting issues that have crossed national and cultural boundaries. With few debates, some say that the advance in information technology runs ahead then lays down the laws. Politicians and policymakers debate on what kinds of online behaviors are acceptable and what are not. At present, no theoretical framework exists for examining cultural differences in relation with online privacy issues. In reality, research shows that people are not always as concerned with Internet privacy as they proclaim. This is probably because their actions are often contrary to what they have said (Hsu, 2006). Cultural differences have great impacts on the issues related to online privacy. When moving towards virtual communities, it shows a social context in which the group members determine their online security practices by the influence of culture within that community. Cultural influences are strong, but research can only give a general comparative view of what a person in a given culture will do with regards to his or her privacy practices. While culture may heavily influence knowledge behaviors, the privacy issues in virtual communities will also not be a simple case. As discussed, this study does have room for future research; the effects of trust, privacy, and culture on knowledge sharing in virtual communities are some interesting topics.

REFERENCES

Adler, R. P., & Christopher, A. J. (1998). *Internet community primer – overview and business opportunity*. Retrieved from http://www.digiplaces.com/

Andenmatten, S., Bettoni, M., C., & Mathieu, R. (2007). Knowledge cooperation in online communities. *The Electronic Journal of Knowledge Management, 5*(1), 1-6.

Atkinson, J. W. (1964). *An introduction to motivation*. Princeton, NJ: Van Nostrand.

Bandura, A. (1997). *Self-efficacy: The exercise of control*. New York, NY: Freeman.

Battle, E. (1966). Motivational determinants of academic competence. *Journal of Personality and Social Psychology, 4*, 534-642.

Chiu, C-M, Hsu, M-H,, & Wang, E. T. G. (2006). Understanding knowledge sharing in virtual communities: An integration of social capital and social cognitive theories. *Decision Support Systems, 42*(3), 1872-1888.

Coase, R. H. (1937). The nature of the firm. *Econometrics, 4*, 18-33.

Cox, D. E. (1987). Programmatic factors associated with effective occupational education programs in community colleges. *Community/Junior College Quarterly of Research and Practice, 11*(1), 11-17.

Davenport, T. H., & Prusak, L. (1998). *Working knowledge: How organizations manage what they know.* Boston: Harvard Business School Press.

Eccles, J. S., Adler, T. F., Futterman, R., Goff, S. B., Kaczala, C. M., Meece, J. L., et al. (1983). Expectancies, values, and academic behaviors. In J. T. Spence (Ed.), *Achievement and achievement motives* (pp.75-146). San Francisco, CA: W.H. Freeman.

Eccles, J. S., & Wigfield, A. (2002). Motivational beliefs, values, and goals. *Annual Review of Psychology, 53*(1), 109-132.

Flavian, C., & Guinaliu, M. (2005). The influence of virtual communities on distribution strategies in the Internet. *International Journal of Retail & Distribution Management, 33*(6), .405-425.

Gaved, M., & Mulholland, P. (2005). *Grassroots initiated networked communities: A study of hybrid physical/virtual communities.* Paper presented at the 38th Hawaii Conference on System Sciences, Big Island, Hawaii.

Grant, R. M. (1996). Toward a knowledge-based theory of the firm. *Strategic Management Journal, 17*(10), 109–122.

Griesinger, D. (1990). The human side of economic organization. *Academy of Management Review, 15*(3), 478-499.

Gusfield, J. (1975). *The community: A critical response.* New York: Harper Colophon.

Hagel, J., & Armstrong, A. (1997). *Net gain: Expanding markets through virtual communities.* Boston, MA: Harvard Business School Press.

Hambrick, D., Davison, S., Snell, S., & Snow, C. (1998). When groups consist of multiple nationalities: Towards a new understanding of implications. *Organization Studies, 19*(2), 181-205.

Hof, R. D., & Browder, P. E. (1997). Internet communities-forget surfers. A new class of netizen is settling right. *Business Week,* 38–45.

Hofstede, G.. (2001). *Culture's consequences: Comparing values, behaviors, institutions and organizations across nations* (2nd ed.). Thousand Oaks, CA: Sage Publications.

Hsu, C. (2006). Privacy concerns, privacy practices and Web site categories: Toward a situational paradigm. *Online Information Review, 30*(5), 569-86.

Hutchings, K., & Michailova, S. (2004). Facilitating knowledge sharing in Russian and Chinese subsidiaries: The role of personal networks and group membership. *Journal of Knowledge Management, 8*(2), 84-94.

Johnson, C. M. (2001). *A survey of current research on online communities of practice. The Internet and Higher Education, 4*, 45-60.

Katzy, B. R., & Ma, X. (2002). Virtual professional communities – definitions and typology. In K. Pawar, F. Weber, & K. Thoben (Ed.), *Proceedings of the The 8th International Conference on Concurrent Enterprising,* Rome, Italy (pp.311-318). Nottingham: Nottingham University Press.

Klein, S. (1989). A transaction cost explanation of vertical control in international markets.

Journal of the Academy of Marketing Science, 17(3), 253-260.

Klein, S., Frazier, G. L., & Roth V. J. (1990). A transaction cost analysis model of channel integration in international markets. *Journal of Marketing Research, 27*(2), 196-208.

LeBaron, J., Pulkkinen, J., & Scollin, P. (2000). Promoting cross-border communication in an international Web-based graduate course. *Electronic Journal of Computer Enhanced Learning, 2*(2). Retrieved February 6, 2001, from http://imej. wfu.edu/articles/2000/2/01/index.asp

.Leimeister, J., Ebner, W., & Krcmar, H. (2005). Design, implementation and evaluation of trust supporting components in virtual communities for patients. *Journal of Management Information Systems, 21*(4), 101-135.

Liang, T.-P., & Huang, J.-S. (1998). An empirical study on consumer acceptance of products in electronic markets: A transaction cost model. *Decision Support System, 24*, 29-43.

Malone, T., Yates, J., & Benjamin, R. (1987). Electronic markets and electronic hierarchies. *Communication ACM, 6*, 485-497.

Organ, D. W. (1988). *Organizational citizenship behavior: The good soldier syndrome.* Lexington, MA: Lexington Books.

Pajares, F. (1996). Self-efficacy beliefs in academic settings. *Review of Educational Research, 66*, 543-578.

Pfeffer, J., & Sutton, R. (2000). *The knowing doing gap: How smart companies turn knowledge into action.* Boston, MA: Harvard Business School Press.

Powers, V. (2004). Virtual communities at Caterpillar foster knowledge sharing. *Training & Development, 58*(6), 40-45.

Raynor, J. O. (1982). Future orientation, self-evaluation, and achievement motivation: Use of an ex-

pectancy-value theory of personality functioning and change. In N. T. Feather (Ed.), *Expectation and actions: Expectancy-value models in psychology* (pp. 97-124). Hillsdale, NJ: Lawrence Erlbaum Associations, Inc.

Rokeach, M. (1973). *The nature of human values,* New York: Free Press.

Sharratt, M., & Usoro, A. (2003). Understanding knowledge sharing in online communities of practice. *Electronic Journal on Knowledge Management, 1*(2), 187-196.

Sveiby, K. E. (1997). *The new organizational wealth.* San Francisco: Berret-Koehler.

Teece, D. J. (1998). Capturing value from knowledge assets: The new economy, markets for know-how, and intangible assets. *California Management Review, 40*(3), 55-79.

Van, Beveren J. (2002). A model of knowledge acquisition that refocuses knowledge management. *Journal of Knowledge Management, 6*(1), 18-22.

Vandermerwe, S. (1999). The electronic "go-between service provider": A new "middle" role taking centre stage. *European Management Journal, 17.*

Wenger, E., & Snyder, W. M. (2000). Communities of practice: The organizational frontier. *Harvard Business Review,* 139-145.

Wigand, R. T. (1995). Electronic commerce and reduced transaction costs: Firms' migration into highly interconnected electronic markets. *Electronic markets, 16*, 1-5.

Wigfield, A. (1994). Expectancy-value theory of achievement motivation: A developmental perspective. *Educational Psychology Review, 6*, 49-78.

Wigfield, A., & Eccles, J. S. (2000). Expectancy-value theory of achievement. *Contemporary Educational Psychology, 25*, 68-81.

Williamson, O. E. (1981). The economics of organization: The transaction cost approach. *American Journal of Sociology 87*(3), 548–77.

Williamson, O. E. (1985). *The economic institutions of capitalism*. New York: Free Press.

Williamson, O. E. (1991). Comparative economic organization: The analysis of discrete structural alternatives. *Administrative Science Quarterly, 36*, 269-296.

Wimmer, B. S., Townsend, A. M., & Chezum, B. E. (2000). Information technologies and the middleman: The changing role of information intermediaries in an information - rich economy. *Journal of Labor Research, 21*, 407-416.

Zeldin, T. (1998). *Conversations: How talk can change our lives*. London: Harville Press.

ADDITIONAL READING

Ardichvili, A., Maurer, M., Li, W., Wentling, T., & Stuedemann, R. (2006). Cultural influences on knowledge sharing through online communities of practice. Journal of *Knowledge Management*, 10(1), 94-107.

Baek, E-O., & Schwen, T. (2006). How to build a better online community: Cultural perspectives. *Performance Improvement Quarterly*, 19(2), 51-68.

Ballantine, P., & Martin, B. (2004). Forming parasocial relationships in online communities. *Advances in Consumer Research, 32*, 197.

Choi, D., & Perez, A. (2007). Online piracy, innovation, and legitimate business models. *Technovation*, 27(4), 168-178.

Dumont, G., & Candler, G.. (2005). Virtual jungles: Survival, accountability, and governance in online communities. *American Review of Public Administration*, 35(3), 287-299.

Eccles, J. S., & Wigfield, A. (1995). "In the mind of the actor: the structure of adolescents' achievement task values and expectancy-regulated beliefs." *Personality and Social Psychology Bulletin*, 21(3),215-225.

Farquhar, J., & Rowley, J. (2006). Relationships and online consumer communities. *Business Process Management Journal*, 12(2), 162-179.

Flor, N. (2006). Addressing the problem of content restrictions in online community forums. *Journal of Information Technology Case and Application Research*, 8(1), 7-33.

Füller, J., Bartl, M, Ernst, H., & Mühlbacher, H. (2006). Community based innovation: How to integrate members of virtual communities into new product development. *Electronic Commerce Research*, 6(1), 57-73.

Grace-Farfaglia, P., Dekkers, A., Sundararajan, B., Peters, L., & Park, S-H. (2006). Multinational Web uses and gratifications: Measuring the social impact of online community participation across national boundaries. *Electronic Commerce Research*, 6(1), 75-101.

Graff, M. (2006). Constructing and maintaining an effective hypertext-based learning environment: Web-based learning and cognitive style. *Education & Training*, 4(2-3), 143-155.

Greenfield, G.., & Campbell, J. (2006). Communicative practices in online communication: A case of agreeing to disagree. *Journal of Organizational Computing and Electronic Commerce*, 16(3-4), 267.

Hemetsberger, A., & Reinhardt, C. (2006). Learning and knowledge-building in open-source communities: A social-experiential approach. *Management Learning*, 37(2), 187-214.

Johnson, G.., & Ambrose, P. (2006). Neo-tribes: The power and potential of online communities in health care. *Communications of the ACM*, 49(1), 107-113.

Kidane, Y., & Gloor, P. (2007). Correlating temporal communication patterns of the Eclipse open source community with performance and creativity. *Computational and Mathematical Organization Theory, 13*(1), 17-27.

Kling, R., & Courtright, C. (2003). Group behavior and learning in electronic forums: A sociotechnical approach. Information Society, 19(3), 221.

Maloney-Krichmar, D., & Preece, J. (2005). A multilevel analysis of sociability, usability, and community dynamics in an online health community. *ACM Transactions on Computer-Human Interaction, 12*(2), 201-232.

Nahapiet, J., & Ghoshal, S. (1998). Social capital intellectual capital and the organizational advantage. *Academy of Management Review, 23*(2).

Neumann, M., O'Murchu, I., Breslin, J., & Dekker, S. (2005). Semantic social network portal for collaborative online communities. *Journal of European Industrial Training, 29*(6), 472-524.

Nolan, T., Brizland, R., & Macaulay, L. (2007). Individual trust and development of online business communities. *Information Technology & People, 20*(1), 53-71.

Nonnecke, B., Andrews, D., & Preece, J. (2006). Non-public and public online community participation: Needs, attitudes and behavior. *Electronic Commerce Research, 6*(1), 7-20.

Ren, Y., Kraut, R., & Kiesler, S. (2007). Applying common identity and bond theory to design of online communities. *Organization Studies, 28*(3), 377-408.

Ridings, C., Gefen, D., & Arinze, B. (2006). Psychological barriers: Lurker and Poster motivation and behavior in online communities. *Communications of the Association for Information Systems, 18*, 26.

Schoberth, T., Heinzl, A., & Preece, J. (2006). Exploring communication activities in online communities: A longitudinal analysis in the financial services industry. Journal of Organizational *Computing and Electronic Commerce, 16*(3-4), 247.

Sternberg, D. (2003). Online community options. *Marketing Health Services, 23*(3), 48 -51.

Wiertz, C., & Ruyter, K. (2007). Beyond the call of duty: Why customers contribute to firm-hosted commercial online communities. *Organization Studies, 28*(3), 347-376.

Williams, R. L., & Cothrel, J. (2000). Four smart ways to run online communities. *Sloan Management Review, 41*(4), 81–91.

Williamson O. (1975). *Market and hierarchies.* New York: Free Press.

Ziegler, C-N., & Golbeck, J. (2007). Investigating interactions of trust and interest similarity. *Decision Support Systems, 43*(2), 460-475.

Section II
Applications

Chapter VIII
Opportunities and Obstacles to Narrow the Digital Divide:
Sharing Scientific Knowledge on the Internet

Margarita Echeverri
University of Maryland, USA & Tulane University, USA

Eileen G. Abels
Drexel University, USA

ABSTRACT

Access to scientific information is considered a competitive advantage to foster knowledge, research, and development; improve quality of education; and advance professional practices. Although, the Web was conceived to encourage information sharing, restrictions to some publications reduce access to knowledge, especially to those in developing countries. This chapter presents a conceptual framework of the knowledge transfer cycle, and examines key factors affecting the dissemination of scientific information. Current challenges facing the open-access initiative of making scientific information free and available worldwide are also discussed. This chapter examines key factors affecting the dissemination of scientific information and current challenges posed by the open-access initiative of making scientific information free and available worldwide.

INTRODUCTION

Information and communication technologies (ICT) have transformed the way scientific knowledge is shared nowadays. Scientific communities have moved from being centered on a physical location (universities, colleges, research institutes, laboratories, or professional organizations), to being centered on a particular focus or topic of interest. Researchers work collaboratively at international level using Internet, e-mail, online chats, electronic forums, mailing lists, Web sites, FTP sites, blogs, and wikis. Knowledge and information are shared within seconds around the world, and are available around the clock through remote databases, digital libraries, and electronic journals.

The Internet has provided a new channel for disseminating electronic journals, which have long been central to scientific communication. Electronic journals and the Internet together play an important role in the new paradigms of creating and sharing scientific knowledge: access through the Internet is currently the fastest and least expensive way to distribute scientific information worldwide. New models in the publication and codification of scientific knowledge have transformed the way people search for information. Now one has the ability to find articles by title, author, topic, and keywords, independently of the journals in which they are published. Then, there is a possibility that the article will be freely available on the Web or if not, one has the option to pay for the article through pay-for-view rather than subscribing to the entire publication. Furthermore, hypertext links within articles, extended bibliographic references including articles that cite and have been cited, and links to databases and related articles are changing the concept of "journals" as they have been known.

Electronic publishing has been considered as important to science as was the invention of printing, and is viewed as an innovation producing profound changes in scholarly communication. Used effectively, electronic resources and the Internet are fostering a new research paradigm that empowers researchers, authors, students, and the general public with richer communication at lower costs. In the same way as e-commerce, e-learning and e-government have eliminated the barriers of distance and time, e-research has provided a way to create, access, understand, use, and share knowledge with new ICT available in a networked society.

However, as a contradiction, inadequate access to scholarly scientific information is still considered an important barrier to research, especially in less developed countries (LDC) (Echeverri, 2006). Scholarly publishing has been criticized as being more focused on discussing restrictions than opportunities for dissemination when considering the potential offered by the Internet (Echeverri, 2006; Open Access, 2003). For example, licensing agreements are commonly required for access to documents, journals, books, and databases available on the Web, with layers of protection such as encryptions and password-protected subscriptions. Although information may be available in electronic format on the Web, this does not mean that it is "freely accessible" anytime, anyplace, and by everyone, which runs counter to an important principle of the Web: "free access to information for all" (Echeverri, 2006; Tenopir et al., 2003).

Even though, the power of the publishing industry is such that academic libraries are expected to pay whatever is necessary to obtain the material (Thomes, 2000), the critics of the high cost of scientific journals have taken action. In 2003, scientists at University of California organized a worldwide boycott of six scientific journals published, by Reed Elsevier, in molecular biology because of the prohibited costs of subscribing to the electronic versions of those journals, which in turn impedes the dissemination of scientific knowledge (Foster, 2003).

As one solution to the exorbitant costs of scientific journals, the Scholarly Publishing and Academic Resources Coalition (SPARC), a coalition of academic and research libraries and organizations, was created to correct the dysfunctions in the scholarly publishing system through the Open Access Initiative (OA). Although, more and more organizations and authors are joining the OA initiative, this is still in the early stages of adoption. In a study on open access to medical literature, McVeigh and Pringle (2005) found that less than 60% of articles published since 1992 in

174 medical journals indexed in the Thomson Scientific ISI Citation Databases are electronically available, and only 21% of those articles were available through open access.

One of the initial reasons that have delayed the adoption of OA journals has been the lack of quality due to the absence of a peer-review process. Fortunately, in June 2004, the Institute of Scientific Information (ISI) had classified 239 OA journals as adhering to high publishing standards and favorably competing with similar journals in their fields (Testa & McVeigh, 2004).

Open access to scientific journals, however, is only a partial solution to wider dissemination of scientific information. Other barriers include poor research and English skills, restricted access to the Internet and scholarly scientific information, limited online library services, and a lack of interlibrary loans (Echeverri, 2006). As noted in the following quote, competition at international level is not possible without appropriate services and education: *Even if all the people in developing countries were to be wired up to all the knowledge in all the libraries and databases of the world, not much would necessarily change unless people in developing countries had the education and skills to use this knowledge* (World Bank, 2002).

This relates directly to the digital divide dilemma. Resolution of the digital divide would contribute to the elimination of the vicious cycle among poverty, inequity, unemployment, poor education, lack of literacy skills, and lack of or poor access to and use of ICT. Mossberger et al. (Mossberger, Tolbert, & Stansbury, 2003) "divided" the digital divide into four different types: access divide (access points, and frequency of computer and Internet use); skills divide (technical competence and information literacy); economic opportunity divide (experiences, beliefs, and attitudes regarding computers and economic advancement); and the democratic divide (attitudes and experiences regarding using Internet for political activities or searching information). Using multivariate statistical analysis, the authors concluded that

computer and Internet access are insufficient to encourage use of technology, and that technical and literacy skills are also required.

The digital divide, defined as ". . . the gap between individuals, households, businesses and geographic areas at different socio-economic levels with regard both to their opportunities to access information and communication technologies (ICTs) and to their use of the Internet for a wide variety of activities" (OECD, 2001, p.5) has been highlighted as one of the main obstacles for the participation of developing countries in the modern economy (World Bank, 2002b).

A more recent study supports both statements by Mossberger and the Word Bank, and refers more specifically to the existence of divides in access and skills that influence knowledge transfer, research, and development. Limitations in access to computers, the Internet, and printers, as well as limitations in English and research skills still represent important barriers in developing countries (Echeverri, 2006).

This chapter begins with the presentation of a conceptual framework for knowledge transfer, and examines key factors affecting the dissemination of scientific information. Then, key barriers to access to scholarly scientific information in developing countries, and the coping mechanisms used to overcome those barriers are identified based upon empirical evidence. In conclusion, the authors encourage the advancement of open-access initiatives to make scientific information freely available worldwide.

CONCEPTUAL FRAMEWORK

During the knowledge transfer cycle in which information and knowledge are exchanged, there are several players, each assuming different roles. These players include, among others, members of the scientific community such as researchers, faculty, and graduate students involved in research activities, libraries, and publishers. The conceptual framework includes four components represented at the top in Figure 1:

- **Knowledge acquisition:** Mechanisms used by scholars and libraries to acquire knowledge such as signing licenses agreements, contacting the authors, exchanging information, attending conferences, and so forth. Acquisition refers to having access to the knowledge; it does not mean to absorb and apply it.
- **Knowledge absorption:** Mechanisms used by scholars to absorb and apply knowledge such as pursuing an academic degree, attending online courses, doing tests in labs, applying knowledge in new settings, and so forth. Absorption refers to using the knowledge acquired; it does not mean to create new.
- **Knowledge creation:** Mechanisms used by scholars to create or generate new knowledge such as researching, innovating, proposing new models, and so forth. Creation refers

to the generation of new knowledge; it does not mean to disseminate it.

- **Knowledge dissemination:** Mechanisms used by scholars, libraries, and publishers to communicate the new knowledge created such as posting documents on the Web, publishing articles in a journal, publishing new books, and so forth. Dissemination implies to make new knowledge accessible to other people so they can acquire it to begin again the cycle and doing that, to move forward the topic under consideration.

Players in the exchange of scholarly scientific information are represented in boxes below the knowledge components in Figure 1, and the interactions among them are shown by the arrows:

- Scholars, as the users of information, who send requirements to libraries and publishers to acquire information, and also send them new information to be published,

Figure 1. Conceptual framework (Adapted from Echeverri, 2006)

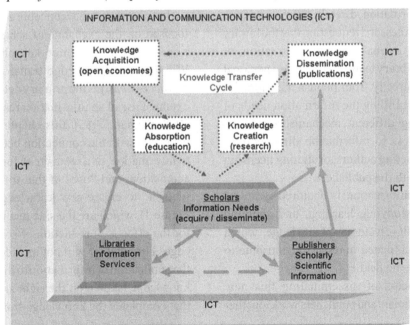

- Libraries, as intermediaries to the research process, facilitate communication between librarians, scholars, and publishers to satisfy demands for acquisition and publication of new information, and
- Publishers, as the owners of scholarly scientific information, who use different mechanisms to acquire new information to publish, such as contacting libraries and scholars for new articles, papers, or books to be published

Scholars are the central point connecting the *knowledge acquisition* (left side) with the *knowledge dissemination* (right side) in the framework and during this process, they interact with libraries and publishers in different ways.

In the process of acquiring knowledge, scholars and libraries work together (their interactions are represented on the left side of the diagram through arrows to both scholars and libraries in Figure 1), and receive either freely available or fee-based information directly from authors, publishers, or personal contacts. In addition, scholars use different mechanisms such as accessing information directly from the Web or contacting authors; receiving information directly from academic programs or professors; requesting that the library subscribe to a journal, buy the information, or order an interlibrary loan; or obtaining a personal subscription directly from publishers. Libraries contribute to fulfilling the information needs of scholars' using different mechanisms such as providing access to information directly from the Web, contacting authors, or signing licensing agreements with the publishers.

Once the information is acquired, scholars absorb it by studying, learning, and applying and, as a result, create new knowledge, which has to be disseminated in order to contribute to the advance of the field.

In the process of disseminating this new knowledge, scholars and publishers work together

(their interactions are represented on the right side of the diagram as leaving arrows from both the scholars and publishers boxes in the figure 1), and publish information either in open access or fee-based scientific journals. Scholars publish their new developments through commercial publishers, open access journals, or other outlets like personal Web sites, wikis, and blogs, the new self-publishing mechanisms transforming the way knowledge is disseminated nowadays. Publishers make the new articles, papers, and books received from scholars available to the public, using the traditional journals and books on paper and/or creating new formats such as e-journals and e-books.

Throughout the process, publishers, libraries, and scholars interact with each other to satisfy the supply and demand of scholarly information; ICT is shown in Figure 1 as a border surrounding the process, indicating that this is the primary mechanism fostering knowledge transfer. ICT plays an important role in facilitating access to information and reducing obstacles to the acquisition of information, thereby, creating better conditions for learning, researching, and sustainable development, specifically in developing countries.

In summary, the conceptual framework is focused on the exchange of scholarly scientific information among three key players utilizing ICT to foster knowledge transfer. Considering that *accessibility* is the primary determinant of the extent of *use* of an information resource (Bishop, 1998; Culnan, 1985), this chapter is concerned primarily with the connection between "access" to information, as a requisite to foster knowledge acquisition, and "use" of that information, as a requisite to create new knowledge (left side of Figure 1), which are the sine qua non conditions for the effective production of scientific knowledge. This chapter will not include discussion of the publication of information to disseminate new knowledge (shown on the right side of Figure 1) that completes the knowledge transfer cycle.

Perceived *Access to* Scholarly Scientific Information and *Use of* Online Electronic Resources

Although, access and use of information are two concepts closely related (we cannot use what we cannot access), they have to be clearly differentiated when studying "access" to information and "use" of information. One study on the factors affecting *access to* and *use of* scientific information considers *access* to information as a subjective concept, and defines **perceived access to scholarly scientific information** as the perception of the ease of obtaining the *full text* of an information source; the higher the score, the more accessibility perceived (Echeverri, 2006). Further, **use of online electronic resources** is defined as a combination score of the frequency of using eight electronic resources that offer rich possibilities for research activities; the higher the score, the more overall use of these electronic resources for research purposes.

The eight resources can be categorized as either (a) Web sites and search engines or (b) electronic publications and services.

Web sites and search engines used for research by scholars include much information that is freely available. Despite the ongoing debate about the use of information freely available on the Web as formal resources for research, the advantages of the Web as a publishing medium has been recognized by the Institute for Scientific Information (ISI), which has been building *Current Web Contents*, a collection of reviewed scholarly Web sites providing information in the fields of science, social science, technology, and arts & humanities (Trolley, 1999). The following are resources and tools within this category:

- **General purpose search engines:** Web search engines, such as Google, Yahoo, or AltaVista, provide the ability to conduct searches quickly, which has been seen by some authors as a point of concern because

most of the scientific literature is copyrighted and not available in the "publicly indexable Web" (Graham, 2003).

- **Institutional/scholarly Web sites:** Scholarly, research-oriented Web sites are those created by individuals or institutions to provide scientifically relevant content on services, products, or other issues related to a specific topic, for example the National Institute of Health (NIH).

- **University library Web sites:** When comparing Web sites of universities in developing and developed countries, Silvio (1998) points out that "the least sophisticated kinds of interactivity prevail in the former... while in developed countries, universities have Web sites with a greater degree of interactivity," which was confirmed by Echeverri (2006). A greater degree of interactivity in a library's Web site refers to having remote and around the clock access to the library's services and resources licensed by the library, the ability to make online requests for interlibrary loans, and the possibility to ask questions directly of a librarian.

- **Other library Web sites:** Independent of the degree of interactivity and the use or nonuse of a library Web site affiliated with a university, on occasion, scholars may use other library Web sites (e.g., the Library of Congress and Library of Medicine) for different reasons such us better access, services, or coverage of a topic, or more convenience of use.

Electronic publications and services include electronic journals, electronic databases, and online alert services.

- **Electronic journals:** Scholars need access to current research very quickly, particularly in science and technology. Online electronic journals make research articles available relatively quickly, and many publishers provide online tables-of-contents to facilitate browsing journal issues.

- **Electronic databases:** Many Electronic databases contain publications and other resources that can be found in print versions of a magazine, journal, or other credible source. Two types of databases fall into this category: Full-text databases that contain complete articles; and bibliographic databases that contain only citations and/or abstracts. Hybrid databases, with both full-text and bibliographic records, are becoming more common. Electronic databases are differentiated from general Web searches because databases involve access through keywords and subjects to improve the searching (Witten & Bainbridge, 2001). Usually, CD-ROM databases are restricted to use directly in the libraries. This restriction has the advantage of not requiring Internet access, but the disadvantage that these resources are not available from home or work.

- **Online Citation Indexes:** The proliferation of digital libraries and Web-based abstracting and indexing databases and electronic journals is revolutionizing the way researchers conduct research (Ke et al., 2002; Witten, 2003) and facilitating interdisciplinary thinking and understanding of topics and ideas within the context of other disciplines. However, some authors have demonstrated that searching for information about journals and locating journal articles is still an extremely difficult task (Mack et al., 2004).

- **Online alert services:** Awareness of the availability of a specific information source or channel is crucial to its use (Vakkari & Pennanen, 2001). Alert services provide a mechanism for users to become aware of current research topics and new trends in research. The low use of databases other than MEDLINE and journals other than the Ovid collection was considered an indicator of the low awareness of available online databases

and full-text journals in the health sciences (De Groote & Dorsch, 2003).

FACTORS AFFECTING BOTH *ACCESS TO* AND *USE OF* SCHOLARLY SCIENTIFIC INFORMATION ON THE WEB

Even though there have been ongoing efforts to examine electronic publishing and the Internet's impact on the scholarly community, there is still much to learn in order to exploit fully the immense potential of the Internet and e-publishing. Recent studies on the information seeking behavior and research process, as well as a literature review on the impact of electronic publishing and the Internet on the dissemination of information, indicate that attention has been given to describing how scholars are using Internet-based resources instead of examining the factors that affect their use (Echeverri, 2006; Zhang, 1999). Four dimensions have been identified as having an influence on both *access to* and *use of* scholarly scientific information. These dimensions were derived from the framework presented in Figure 1: scholars form the basis of the **user dimension** since, they are representative of one group of information users; libraries and their information services form the **library dimension**; publishers providing scholarly scientific information form the **information dimension**; and information and communication technology forms the **ICT dimension**.

Through a literature review, more than 200 items were identified that influence *access to* and/or *use of* scholarly scientific information on the Web, and fit within the four dimensions of the framework. Grasping the impact of these items is difficult, given the large number and the fact that the interrelationship between these items is not specified in the literature. However, it seems evident that the influence of many of these items is more intense in developing countries where the digital divide is more evident.

Table 1. Summary of factors explaining each dimension (adapted from Echeverri, 2006)

DIMENSION	FACTOR	ITEMS
Users	Research Project	Research process, Months working in a research project, and Number of grants obtained
	Information Literacy Skills	Computer skills, Internet skills, and Research skills
	Language Skills	Influence of content strictness, and Influence of language
	Students Anxieties	Literature review anxiety and Research design anxiety
	Willingness to Pay for Information	Willingness to pay for a journal, and Willingness to pay for an article
Library	Level of Services	Respondents' expectations about: Subscriptions to print journals; Subscriptions to electronic journals; OPAC; Reference services; Document delivery services; Remote access to library; Training; and Library hours of service
	Online Resources	Frequency of using: *OPAC*s (online public access catalogs); Online-journals subscribed to by the library; Online-databases
	Interlibrary Loans	Frequency of: Visiting the library for Interlibrary loans; Using online interlibrary loans services; Using online library help
Information	Access to Information	Findability and Accessibility
	Use of Information	Currency, Reliability, and Relevance
	Distinct Conditions	Timeliness, Affordability, and Permanence
	Type of Sources	Importance of seminars, institutional Web sites, and thesis
ICT	ICT at Work	Access to and Use of computer, Internet, and printer at work
	ICT at Home	Access to and Use of computer, Internet, and printer at home
	ICT at the Library	Access to and Use of computer, Internet, and printer at the library
	ICT at Other Places	Access to and Use of computer, Internet, and printer at other places
	ICT	Configuration of computer, Internet connections, and printer

To begin to understand how these items can be grouped into factors and how they interact with each other in developing countries, a study with graduate students in health sciences in public universities in Colombia was conducted (Echeverri, 2006). Graduate students are important to study because they represent the new generation that has been more exposed to new technologies, and many will become future faculty and researchers. Information behaviors acquired during graduate studies will likely continue as professionals. In order to be successful, graduate students must conduct research and publish in journals. This requires having easy access to up-to-date and reliable scientific information, as well as the skills needed to use this information. Without these,

graduate students will be at a disadvantage to compete in the new international economic order. Research without reliable and current information risks drawing faulty conclusions that could decrease the quality of research in the academic environment. With appropriate resources and skills, graduate students in less developed countries have the potential one day to raise the level of scientific and technological research in their countries and deal effectively with knowledge transfer at the international level. Caution has to be taken in considering these findings as they are limited to graduate students in one discipline in one developing country. However, these findings can be validated through additional research to confirm their generalizability to other countries and to other user groups, such as scholars. Initially, the results are useful to provide updated data relating to sharing scientific information on the Internet.

A questionnaire containing more than 100 of the items identified in the literature as influencing *access to* and/or *use of* scientific information was administered to 886 graduate students doing research in PhD, Master's, and Specialization programs in health sciences in Colombia. Factor analysis was used to aggregate 107 of the items from the survey into 27 groups or "factors" within the dimensions of the framework. Following is the discussion of the items associated with each dimension and the results of the factor analysis.[1] The factors associated with each dimension are summarized in Table 1.

User Dimension

The User dimension refers to the differences associated with individuals that have been identified as important factors affecting both *access to* and *use of* scholarly scientific information. The User dimension initially included 15 items: research process; months working in the research project; grants awarded; computer skills; English skills; Internet skills; research skills; literature review anxiety; research design anxiety; influence of format; influence of price; influence of content strictness; influence of language; willingness to pay for a subscription; and willingness to pay-per-view. During the factor analysis, 12 of these items grouped on 5 factors, explaining 73.18% of the total variance. The items *influence of price* and *influence of format* did not group within any factor, meaning that they should be considered independently as single factors. The item *English skills* exhibited an interesting behavior that it is discussed next.

Research project factor: This factor relates to the level of respondents' involvement in the research project, and measures whether or not the person was engaged in research, as one of

the greatest predictors of electronic use (Nelson, 2001 cited by Tenopir et al., 2003; Vakkari, 2000). Three items grouped together in this factor: *research process*, *months working in the project*, and *number of grants obtained*.

Research process includes both the stage of research as well as the research style as factors influencing information use. Kennedy et al. (Kennedy, Cole, & Carter, 1999) defined three research stages: prefocus, focus, and post-focus. Palmer (1991) defined five research styles ; non-seekers; lone-wide rangers; unsettled-self conscious seekers; confident collectors; and hunters. Echeverri (2006) combined research stages and styles: (1) non-seeker: not involved in any important research activity yet; (2) lone-wide rangers, prefocus: reading/scanning a wide variety of literature to select the topic of research; (3) unsettled-self conscious seekers, prefocus: having a wide topic selected and trying to narrow it; (4) confident collectors, focus: having a topic with clear boundaries and searching for very specific information; and (5) hunters, post-focus: keeping up with new developments on specific information about the topic. According to Echeverri, scholars in an advanced research process are more confident in searching for information and more successful in finding the most relevant one.

Length of time spent on research activities has been considered a predictor of use of electronic information (Nelson, 2001 cited by Tenopir et al., 2003), meaning that users with more experience in research are more familiar with where to look for information and have more personal contacts to find the information needed.

Projects funded by grants usually include a budget to buy the information required, which minimizes problems of access. Projects funded by small organizations or personal funds are likely to face more difficulties in accessing information.

Information literacy skills factor: Three items grouped together in this factor: *Computer skills*, *Internet skills*, and *research skills*. They represent three issues that are directly related to people's educational background and computer and information literacy (Chen et al., 2000; Eisenberg & Johnson, 2002; NSF, 2002). Information literacy skills contribute to the effective use of ICT to find and access information, and to process and evaluate the information found.

A lack of computer skills is an important barrier to the effective use of ICT to find, access, process, and evaluate information (NSF, 2002). The USA Computer Literacy Initiative defines four basic computer skills as "the essential knowledge needed to function independently with a computer: using word processing and spreadsheets, managing files, maintaining the computer system, and using the Internet and other networks."

Scholars need complex analytical skills and capabilities to identify, locate, and access the most appropriate information sources; and to evaluate, organize, and use effectively the information obtained (Eisenberg & Johnson, 2002). Several problems have been identified when using search tools on the Internet: retrieving too much or not enough information; getting lost on a tangent; and not knowing when to stop searching (Epic, 2001 cited in Tenopir et al., 2003). For non-English speakers, the lack of English comprehension and writing skills results in ineffective use of key words and search engines, which obstructs the research process and makes the evaluation and selection of sources difficult. Having too much or too little information leads to stress and anxiety. Dealing with these search issues requires the use of complex analytical skills and capabilities that are components of information literacy (Case, 2002; Eisenberg & Johnson, 2002).

Language skills factor: Several authors have linked user's preferences and information behaviors to the use of information services and sources (Abels, et al., 2004; Larsen, 1997; Stanford University Libraries, 2002; Tenopir et al., 2003; Thomes, 2000). The following four items have been identified as the key characteristics shaping users' preferences when searching for scholarly information on the Web: *format* (print or electronic); *price* (free or paid); *content strictness* (peer-reviewed or non peer-reviewed); and *language* (English, non English). First, since the mid-1990s, much scientific and scholarly information has shifted from print to digital format, and with this shift has come a preference for the digital formats; studies have shown that many researchers utilize online formats almost exclusively because of their convenience, currency, and searchability (Tenopir et al., 2003). Second, price increases over the last 20 years have led to a significant decrease in personal subscriptions to journals and a bigger impact in developing countries, where currencies are very weak when compared to the U.S. dollar. Furthermore, electronic subscriptions available for free on the Web (open access) or subsidized by the library have become more common (Tenopir & King, 2000; Tenopir et al., 2003). Third, the perception that electronic journals are of lower quality than print journals has been changing with the increased number of peer-reviewed print journals that have been digitalized and are available on the Web (Tenopir et al., 2003). Also, there has been an increase in the inclusion of *open access journals,* available freely on the Web, in the *Science Citation Index* (Testa & McVeigh, 2004). And fourth, poor English skills have an important impact in the information seeking process, especially for non-English speakers who have to narrow their array of information sources to those written in their native language, thus, eliminating much valuable information (Echeverri, 2006).

Although, these four items were included in the factor analysis, only two of them, *influence of content strictness* and *influence of language,* grouped together. Additionally, the item *English Skills* showed high cross-loads with *influence of language* with a high and an inverse relationship meaning that the lower the *English skills*, the higher the *influence of language* when searching for information. A deeper analysis of these items revealed that *English Skills* is highly related to the respondents' use of online resources (p=.006), and that there is also an inverse relationship between *influence of language* and the *influence of content strictness,* meaning that limitations in *English skills* have a negative influence on the use of peer-reviewed journals, most of which are written in English. Because much of the scientific information available on the Web is in English, language barriers are very important; especially in countries whose native language is not English (Echeverri, 2006; Goldstein, 1985). Although, writing, reading, and listening are essential language skills, English reading comprehension is the skill that most relates to knowledge sharing on the Internet.

Students anxieties factor: Two items, *literature review anxiety* and *research design anxiety,* grouped together confirming that high levels of anxiety are considered unfavorable to the information-seeking process. Onwuegbuzie (1997) found that scholars experienced high *research anxiety* during the selection of a research topic and the associated methodology to use, as well as high *library anxiety* during the literature review in a research project. An analysis of the effects of these anxieties in the information-seeking process confirms that poor library and research skills engage users in negative feelings and insecurities that interfere with the information search process (Case, 2002; Kuhlthau, 1991; 1993).

Willingness to pay for information factor: Two items grouped in this factor: *willingness to pay for a journal* and *willingness to pay for an article.* Roughly half of respondents in this study were not willing to pay for information required for their research projects. When asked about their willingness to pay for articles that were critical for their research, 50 % of the respondents indicated a preference to work without the article than to pay for it. Furthermore, when asked how much they would be willing to invest annually for a personal subscription to one of the most important journals in their research area , 42% of the respondents indicated that they would not pay for a personal subscription under any circumstance.

These results are similar to findings obtained by Stanford University Libraries (2002) in the Electronic Journal User Study (eJUST), where the U.S. and Canadian scholars also stated that they would do without the article rather than pay any amount for online access. This seems to imply that the reluctance to pay for information is not related to culture or economic development.

Library Dimension

The Library dimension refers to the scholars' use of the library services that relate directly to their research activities. Also included are ratings of the perceived level of quality and cost of services. Studies of academic libraries generally focus on the information resources available and services provided. Common findings include: a *decrease* in the number of visits to the library, use of physical collections, and number of reference transactions; an *increase* in the use of online services provided by the library, interlibrary borrowing, and demand for user education; and a preferred use of general search engines over library interfaces (Covey, 2002; 2003; Hiller, 2002; Kyrillidou & Young, 2003, 2004; Tenopir et al., 2003).

Important barriers in the use of certain library services relate to the access to scholarly scientific information in developing countries. Interlibrary loan agreements or resources are often lacking, impose restrictions in time periods and quantity of documents that may be borrowed, and impose complicated procedures that discourage the use of the service. An increase in interlibrary borrowing has been noted as a result of the serial crisis (Kyrillidou & Young, 2003, 2004), which has had an impact on developing countries where there are few libraries focused on research, most of them funded by the government with budgetary constraints, and with a high percentage of information to be acquired overseas and under unfavorable conditions including negative currency exchanges, high taxes, strict regulations, and complex procedures. Remote access to library services may not be available or may be limited because of low connectivity speeds for downloads and unreliable service. Due to the low degree of interactivity of library Web pages in developing countries, users do not have access to the library's information everywhere and anytime and usually, the library' services are restricted to its facilities within library hours (Echeverri, 2006; Silvio, 1998).

The items identified in this dimension grouped into six factors: frequency of using physical library services; perceived costs of library services; distance to library; level of services; online resources; and interlibrary loan. The following discussion focuses only on the last three ones that are more relevant for this chapter and that, in turn, influence important information behaviors.

Level of services factor: This factor measures how respondents' expectations of the services related to research purposes offered by the library are met. Eight items grouped together in this factor: (1) subscriptions to print journals; (2) subscriptions to electronic journals; (3) OPAC; (4) reference services; (5) document delivery services; (6) remote access to library; (7) training; and (8) library hours of service.

Online resources factor: This refers to the respondents' frequency of using online resources, available through the library Web page, for research activities. Three items grouped in this factor: Frequency of visiting the library Web site for using (1) *OPACs* (online public access catalogs), (2) online journals subscribed to by the library, and (3) online databases subscribed to by the library, which are the most common e-resources available in academic libraries.

Interlibrary loans factor: This factor reflects the frequency of using interlibrary loans. It includes three items: (1) Frequency of visiting the library for interlibrary loans, (2) frequency of using online interlibrary loans services, and (3) frequency of using online library help (e-mail/chat to the librarian). The fact that the last item grouped in this factor could mean that the library's online

help is used more frequently for issues related to interlibrary loans.

Information Dimension

This dimension refers to the information attributes influencing users' *access to* and *use of* sources of information. The "value" given to specific characteristics of information is an important issue when considering the use or lack of use of a specific source of information.

Several authors have studied the users' criteria to select information resources. Using factor analysis, Bateman (1999) defined *quality, credibility,* and *completeness* as the three main constructs underlying the concept of relevance for graduate students, and suggested three additional constructs for consideration: *availability, topicality,* and *currency.* In a similar study, Zhang (1999) found the following four main constructs to explain how scholars evaluate electronic resources: *content and archive* (accuracy; authority; consistency; and permanence); *access* (accessibility and availability); *use* (flexibility and ease of use); and *distinct features* (timeliness and uniqueness). Prior to this research, Pinelli (1991) identified accessibility, relevance, ease of use, expense, familiarity, and reliability as the most compelling factors influencing the use of information sources by engineers and scientists. Noguera (2003) found that graduate students in mathematics give more importance to reliability of access; convenience of use; browsability; access to full content; ease of use; and remote access to journals. Although, these studies contribute to an understanding of the key factors influencing users' selection of sources, they do not discuss the meaning of the attributes analyzed, nor do they look for possible relationships among the attributes.

This dimension included 10 items related to attributes of information: awareness; findability; accessibility; usability; reliability; currency; relevance; timeliness; affordability; and permanence; and 5 items related to the importance of the fol-

Table 2. Information dimension: items and factors related to information attributes (Adapted from Echeverri, 2006)

Knowledge transfer elements	Factor	Item	Definition	Condition
Knowledge acquisition	None	Awareness	Ease of knowing of the existence of a specific information	Knowing that a document exists does not imply to be able to find it
	Access to Information	Findability	Ease of finding the full text of a document	Finding the document the first time does not guarantee that it will be found again
	Distinct Conditions	Permanence	Capability of being found again	Finding the document every time does not imply to have its full text
	Distinct Conditions	Affordability	Free or reasonable price to obtain the information	Free or affordable information does not imply access to the full text
	Access to Information	Accessibility	Ease of obtaining the full text of an information source	Having the full text of a document does not imply to have it on time
	Distinct Conditions	Timeliness	Fast or immediate access to the full-text	Having the full text on time does not imply its usage
Knowledge absorption	None	Usability	Ease of using, reading, and understanding the content of the full text of an information source	Using, reading, and understanding the information does not imply satisfaction with the content; it has to be reliable
	Use of Information	Reliability	Trusting the authority, methods, and procedures	Being reliable does not imply being current
		Currency	Up-to-date content reflecting the latest information and advance in the topic	Being current does not imply to be relevant
		Relevance	Applicability to the topic of interest	**Success!**

lowing types of sources: thesis, institutional Web sites, seminars, books, and journals.

Table 2 presents the attributes in the Information Dimension, explains the relationship between them, identifies the factor with which they are associated (if any), and shows how they fit into the knowledge transfer cycle shown in the framework.

The following factors were obtained during the factor analysis. The items *usability* and *awareness* were dropped because of their low factor loadings, meaning that they were not of concern to respondents during the search for, and use of, information for research purposes.

Access to information factor: Refers to the attributes influencing the acquisition of information required for the research project: *findability* and *accessibility*.

Use of information factor: Includes the characteristics influencing the use of a document as a bibliographic reference: *reliability, currency,* and *relevance*.

Distinct conditions factor: Groups the characteristics that differentiate between the electronic and print resources of information in the research process: *timeliness, affordability,* and *permanence*. The fact that these three items grouped together is an important result that integrates the principle concerns involved in the new models of electronic publishing: fast access, low cost, and long-term storage of information.

Type of sources factor: During the factor analysis, the items *importance of seminars* (proceedings, white papers, technical reports, etc.), *importance of institutional Web sites* (reports, papers and information posted in the Web sites

Figure 2. Ranking on importance of information attributes (N=854) (Echeverri, 2006)

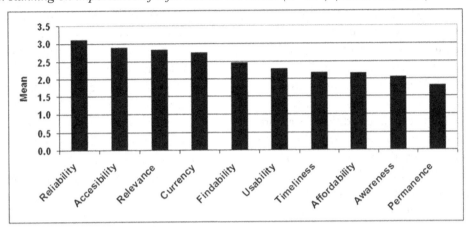

of international organizations and well known research in institutions), and *importance of thesis* (master or doctoral thesis) grouped together. The finding of the factor analysis reinforced the survey findings. The low loading in the factor analysis of *importance of books* confirmed the finding that books are considered less important by the majority of the population under study. Also, journals/articles were the type of document considered most important by the majority of the population under study, and the item *importance of journals/articles* had high cross-loads with most of all items included in the barriers faced to access information, meaning that respondents think on e-journals when talking about access to information.

Respondents ranked the importance given to the information attributes when selecting sources for their research. Figure 2 shows the various attributes ranked with *currency of information* being rated among the more important attributes. This means that although some publishers have a policy to provide open access to old issues of their journals, this does not solve the access problem, specifically when we are talking about information on topics that are very highly sensitive and require access to state-of-the-art information

such as health sciences, environmental changes, and genetics.

ICT Dimension

The ICT dimension refers to the availability and use of specific Information and Communication Technologies (ICT) by scholars during their research activities, and includes computers, the Internet, and printers as those most used for research activities. The ICT dimension included 27 items that were initially classified in three factors: *ICT access, ICT use,* and *ICT type.*

Access to ICT is one of the critical variables in the generation, acquisition, dissemination, and utilization of knowledge (Sagasti, 2001), and lack of access to ICT is still an important barrier limiting the use of information available on the Web (Echeverri, 2006). Barriers such as lack of access to computers, Internet, or printers; costly and restricted online connections; long connecting times; and ICT unreliability discourage the use of resources available on the Web.

Although studies on the use of electronic resources have concluded that access to computers, the Internet, and printers, along with the number of access points (home, work, library, and other places) shape usage frequency (Echeverri, 2006; Stanford University Libraries, 2002; Zhang, 1999), access alone to ICT does not translate into use. ICT use refers to how often scholars use computers, Internet, and printers in their home, work, library, and other place for research activities. While studies have shown that Internet users prefer e-journals over printed editions (Stanford University Libraries, 2002), that is true only when the conditions to use ICT are favorable and not problematic for the users (Echeverri, 2006).

ICT type–configuration of computers, Internet connections, and printers available for research-impacts access to scientific information on the Web because of the heavy use of graphics and data. Low speed connections and long delays in response time discourage the use of electronic resources, in particular, when restrictions of time and cost exist, as is common in developing countries.

However, during the factor analysis, the items did not group as classified; they grouped instead by place (home, work, library, and other places). This means that respondents did not differentiate between access and use because they tend to use places with better access to ICT to work on their research project. As a result, five factors, instead of three, explain the ICT dimension:

- **ICT at work factor:** Grouped the six items measuring "access" to and "use" of computer, printer, and Internet at work
- **ICT at home factor:** Grouped the six items measuring "access" to and "use" of computer, printer, and Internet at home
- **ICT at the library factor:** Grouped the six items measuring "access" to and "use" of computer, printer, and Internet at the library
- **ICT at other places factor:** Grouped the six items measuring "access" to and "use" of computer, printer, and Internet at other places

- **ICT type factor:** Three items grouped together during the factor analysis: configuration of the computer, configuration of the Internet connection, and configuration of the printer used more often for research purposes. Although the Alpha coefficient (.53) is not reliable enough to reach firm conclusions, positive relationships were found between ICT configuration and use of e-resources. According to the data, more than half of the respondents had unrestricted access to a computer (81.0%), the Internet (62.1%), and a printer (71.5%) at home. However, more than one-third of the respondents (36.5%) used a modem to connect to the Internet from home, with a very low speed to search and download electronic journals and other sources. Deeper analysis of data showed positive relationships between computer and Internet configurations and the use of online resources at the work place (p=.000), meaning that the faster Internet connections respondents had were at work. In summary, data confirmed that the lack of adequate access to ICT, specifically to

Figure 3. Use of online electronic resources (N=885) (Echeverri, 2006)

Electronic resources	Mean
General purpose search engines	3.87
Online electronic journals	3.50
Online citation indexes	2.79
Institutional websites	2.45
University library website	2.12
Other libraries websites	1.65
Online alert services	1.64
Electronic databases	1.52

the Internet, is still an important barrier to access electronic resources available on the Web.

BARRIERS AND COPING MECHANISMS FOR BOTH ACCESS TO AND USE OF SCHOLARLY SCIENTIFIC INFORMATION

Although ICT, specifically the Internet, digital libraries, and electronic journals have provided open access, to some extent, and facilitated the sharing of information worldwide, there are still significant barriers that impede connecting information to users, especially in less-developed countries.

In the study described, in addition to the factor analysis, data were gathered to measure perceived accessibility and use. Again, the study is limited in that it focuses on students in one country, so caution should be taken in generalizing. However, the findings support other findings reported in the literature.

In this study, the average score for the *use of online electronic resources* for research activities—defined in the conceptual framework—was 19.54 out of a total possible score of 40, which

Figure 4. Perceived access to scholarly scientific information (N=882)

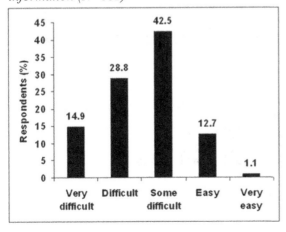

translates to moderate *use* of electronic resources for research purposes. In total, 2% of the respondents were classified as non-users; 30% as low users; 58% as moderate users; and 10% as high users of electronic resources for research purposes. Figure 3 shows the electronic resources listed, in descending order, by their mean scores. Data confirm that respondents prefer the use of general search engines (mean=3.87) over the library Web site (mean=2.12) to search for scholarly information. This result is similar to findings in a national study conducted in 392 doctoral research universities in the United States in which 47.4% of faculty members and 39.9% of graduate students selected "search engines" as the top response to the question "how do you usually get pointed to the right information sources?" (Marcum & Gerald, 2003)

Additionally, the average score of *perceived access* to scholarly scientific information—defined in the conceptual framework—was 2.56 from a range of 1 to 5. Figure 4 shows that 87% of the respondents found *access* to be at least somewhat difficult. Only 1.1% of the respondents indicated that they perceived access to scholarly information to be very easy.

During the factor analysis described, the following barriers were identified, and help to explain the high percentage of respondents who find access to be difficult. These barriers can be categorized as personal, technical, and politico-economic.

The personal barriers found included limited user skills needed for research purposes. These are limitations in searching strategies, evaluation skills (difficulty to select and evaluate information), computer skills, and English skills.

Technical barriers found related to limited access to ICT and library services. Items included relate to a lack of or restrictions to access to computers, Internet ,and printers; lack/limitation of remote access to library services; low speed of answer/downloads; and unreliability of the service, which confirms that access to ICT

Figure 5. Barriers to access scholarly scientific information (N=885) (Rank 1 to 5) (Echeverri, 2006)

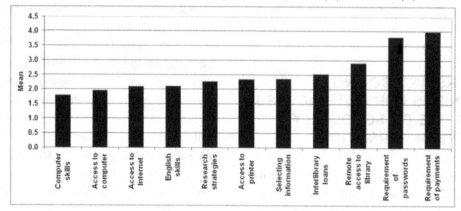

is still an important concern in the information seeking process.

Politico-economic barriers found were those barriers created based on policies or procedures: limiting interlibrary loan services and restrictions imposed by publishers to access information. Limitations in interlibrary loan (ILL) service included items related to restrictions/lack of agreements with other libraries nationally and at the international level; restrictions/lack of information systems to handle the loan process; restrictions in loans such as limitations in the time/quantity of documents to borrow and requirements of payment for document delivery (photocopies, faxes, phone calls, e-mails, scanning, etc.); and complicated procedures that discourage the use

of the service. Publishers restrictions included two items related to access to information that is already available on the Web: requirements of passwords (registration, membership, affiliation to a specific group), and requirement of payments (pay-per-view or journal subscription).

These barriers restrict the capacity of people to access the information already available on the Web, and affect the manner in which students and scholars utilize the resources and technology for their research. In this study, respondents ranked the barriers in order of importance (Figure 5), ranking the restrictions imposed by publishers to access electronic journals as the most important ones: payment and password.

Figure 6. Coping mechanisms used to overcome barriers (N=883) Echeverri (2006)

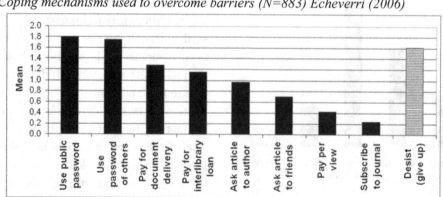

When respondents are faced with restrictions to access the information they require, they use coping mechanisms to resolve their information needs. As a response to the barriers described, and in light of the real need for relevant and up-to-date and timely information, the following coping mechanisms were identified.

A strategy used by some respondents to access information is to find others to pay for the subscription to the journals or pay-per-view the article. The most common sponsors willing to provide payment are the departments/organizations in which the respondent is working, the granting agency that funds a project, and laboratories or businesses that are interested in promoting the use of their products in specific settings. Some respondents opted for the option to pay for inter-library loan services (paying the fees imposed by the lender library or institution), and pay for document delivery services (paying the cost of mail, fax, and photocopies) on their own, which is less expensive than subscribing to the journals or paying per view.

Another mechanism to obtain documents of interest is approaching personal contacts, peers, or friends in other universities or abroad, who have access to a needed document and are able to download or print the document and send it via e-mail or mail. Others prefer to approach the author directly, explaining their need for the document and difficulty in paying for it. In the study described, these mechanisms were dropped during the factor analysis because of their low loading factors, which could be explained by the small percentage of respondents using these strategies.

In order to avoid publisher imposed restrictions, some respondents used publicly known passwords or obtaining authorization to use borrowed passwords from a person/institution that has legal access to the publication.

As can be seen in Figure 6, the mechanisms most used to avoid publishers' restrictions are to obtain publicly available passwords or to obtain passwords through colleagues (means 1.80 and 1.75 respectively). In contrast, pay-per-view and subscribe to journals, were the mechanisms least used (mean =0.43 and mean=0.24 respectively). Interestingly, the third most used coping mechanism was to desist or give up (mean 1.62). This suggests that if respondents do not have access to passwords, they prefer to give up before using other strategies to obtain the information needed.

CONCLUSION

The use of electronic resources has changed the way scholars conduct research because of the convenient 24-hour-a-day access, full-text searching capabilities, interdisciplinary connections, availability of the most current research, and increasing awareness of new information resources available on the Web (Echeverri 2006; Roger, 1995; Zhang, 1999).

Even though the use of electronic journals has grown considerably in the last decade, barriers to access and use of scientific information on the Internet continue to exist. Apparently, the most problematic issue relates to publishers. Password requirements and restrictions to full-text access discourage the use of online journals and citation indexes. Ease of accessibility often wins out over authoritativeness and Zipf's Law of Least Effort (1949), which states that when choosing among several paths to a goal, individuals will adopt the course of action that involves the expenditure of the least amount effort, still holds true. It is common to find that publishers' restrictions to access to scholarly scientific information are an issue of concern even in developed countries. In a study in Canada, Willinsky (2006a, p.43) clearly states that:

"Policymakers were frustrated by the hefty subscription rates and pay-per-view costs.... When they were not able to locate open access studies, they had to depend on freely available research from institutes, think tanks, and other government agencies, which did not always reflect the same level of quality or rigor found in peer-reviewed scholarly literature"

No specific mechanisms were identified as being used by scholars to deal with their personal barriers, specifically in their limitations in English and research skills; however, due to the time constraints related to research projects, it is unlikely that there is time to acquire new skills, such as English language learning. Options available might include hiring some one to conduct research or to request translation services. It is also possible to hire information professionals to assist with copyright issues or to handle subscription problems. However, all of these options are costly, and studies have shown that scholars are likely to go without needed information rather than spend out of pocket.

While technical barriers of limited access to Internet are being dealt with through access at work, this may not be a long-term solution. Currently, it is common to find that employers are limiting the use of Internet for issues not directly related to their job, and firewalls are being installed in organizations that may block certain activities such as searching resources on the Web, receiving e-mails, and downloading files.

The use of general search engines to find information on the Web, instead of using the library services because of the limitations in remote access, is another common solution that needs to be used with caution. Not all scientific and technical information is available for free on the Web, and many free resources are not found with search engines, but rather are available through the invisible Web. For example, patents are freely available on the Web, but one must know to go to patent office Web sites to access them.

Some projects are helping to close the digital divide and provide free access to scientific and scholarly information. Being cognizant of the importance of access to scholarly scientific information, at the end of year 2004, Google launched its new search engine, "Google Scholar," designed specifically to search for scholarly literature (peer-reviewed papers, theses, books, abstracts, and articles, from academic publishers, professional societies, preprint repositories, universities, and other scholarly organizations) located across the Web. Google Scholar includes material that "wouldn't ordinarily be accessible to search spiders, because it is locked behind subscription barriers" (Sullivan, 2004). The inclusion of this material was possible because Google worked with publishers to allow the searching and indexing of their material.

Although, Google Scholar is having a positive impact on the scholars search process, it does have its limitations. Many of the articles found provide citations and abstracts only, and access to full-text would require fee-payment databases. The search process has been facilitated, but the full-text access remains an issue due to restrictions from publishers.

As discussed earlier in the chapter, libraries in developing countries still face serious limitations in economic and technical resources that restrict them in the negotiation and implementation of interlibrary loan services such as the ILLiad (interlibrary loan internet accessible database), and in the development of library Web sites with high level of interactivity (remote and round the clock access to the library's services and its resources). Definitely, restrictions to journals reduce access to knowledge, especially to "those who work outside of the privileged sphere of well-endowed research libraries," which is the case of most developing countries (Willinsky, 2006, p.119). Being faced with these library restrictions and the ones imposed by publishers, scholars in developing countries have found it necessary to satisfy their information needs by sharing passwords among select groups of users.

Aware of this situation, some organizations and publishers, such as the *MIT OpenCourseWare*[2] and the *Developing Countries Oxford Journals Online Collection*[3], are offering free or greatly discounted access to their electronic journals to not-for-profit organizations and individuals in less developed countries. Although, the discounts offered are significant, they usually are restricted to academic institutions in "low income" countries, under the World Bank's GNP-based classification. This policy does not consider that scholars and libraries have restricted budgets to cover their expenses, and are facing day-to-day struggles to survive, either in the most developed countries as the United States where libraries are cancelling subscriptions to journals because of their exorbitant prices that cannot be covered with current budgets. In many cases, the issue is not the price so much as the lack of funds in budget.

Publishers are also contributing to the solution of the problem by offering access to old issues of their journals, usually a 6-month delay. However, this does not solve the problem of access; instead, this policy reinforces the digital divide, where scholars in less developed countries (LDC) will never have access to the up-to-date information and will not be able to include the latest developments in their research. In essence, with these policies, scholars' research in LDC is always "left behind." A policy that will have an important impact, once fully implemented, is the 2005 NIH *Policy on Enhancing Public* Access to Archived Publications Resulting from NIH-funded Research, which requires that all NIH-funded investigators submit their final publications to the National Library of Medicine's (NLM) PubMed Central (PMC). This policy has been expanded as the 2006 *Federal Research Public Access Act* that mandates all major agencies to open access to all articles 6 months after publication.

Recommendations to foster both *access to* and *use of* electronic scholarly scientific information worldwide are summarized below:

- Make mandatory the attendance to workshops and training to build research and information literacy skills. Most of the time the attendance to these events is voluntary.

Educational programs should consider mandatory the attendance to this kind of training and include it as part of the curriculum.

- Extend training to build research and information literacy skills to all education levels, including elementary school.
- Implement online interlibrary loan systems, such as ILLiad, with partners worldwide and include services in other languages.
- Guarantee 24X7 remote access to library services, and encourage users learning about the library services available and how to access them from everywhere. Easy URL or names to remember are of great importance when accessing services from public computers when the user does not have access to ones own bookmarks and/or favorite sites.
- Strengthen existing consortia of academic libraries to empower them to negotiate subscriptions to journals as a block for the whole academic sector in the country.
- Engage to the open access initiative through learning about the process, being active in the discussion groups, and creating links to open journals in the library Web sites.
- Empower publication of university peer-reviewed journals and offer free access to those journals as exchange of information or collaboration in research.
- Expand the NIH's initiative to open access to all publications resulting from NIH-funded research to other organizations such as NASA, National Sciences Foundation, World Bank, and so forth, and also extend the initiative to publications produced by professional associations such as the Institute of Electrical and Electronic Engineers (IEEE), American Psychological Association (APA).
- Build virtual communities engaged in specific research topics through the use of blogs and wikis, free tools that are of easy implementation.

Opportunities and Obstacles to Narrow the Digital Divide

- Decrease the time delayed, "embargoed" access, to full open access to published research.
- Transform the library to be the "gateway" of information.

FUTURE RESEARCH DIRECTIONS

Taking full advantage of the advances of ICT would not only make it possible to transfer, almost immediately, information and knowledge worldwide, but would also bring unlimited new possibilities of multidisciplinary research and international collaboration. The economic powers are neglecting human development by imposing restrictions to the access to information; information that could contribute to the advance of sciences for the well being of people and society.

Open access seems to be the most promising solution to the restrictions imposed by publishers to the dissemination of scientific knowledge worldwide, and is considered the "most important scientific gain afforded by the Internet" (Willinsky, 2006b, p.9078). Fortunately, the academic community is attempting to declare their independence from publishers, which will make it possible to have freed access to information. The Scholarly Publishing and Academic Resources Coalition (SPARC) is fostering the Open Access (OA) initiative, which strives for completely free worldwide electronic distribution of peer-reviewed journal literature in all academic fields with unrestricted access for all. According to Peter Suber, publisher of the SPARC Open Access Newsletter:

All we need is the consent of the copyright holder to waive some of the rights given by the statute, and to permit the unrestricted reading, downloading, copying, sharing, storing, printing, searching, linking, and crawling of their work. (Interview with Peter Suber, 2003)

Initiatives, such as governments making mandatory open access to publicly funded research, such as the National Institute of Health's Public Access Plan; initiatives to provide access to health information for free or at discounted costs, such as PubMed, HINARI, and the Health InterNetwork Access to Research Initiative; collaborative worldwide projects to complete open access journal publishing, such as the Public Library of Sciences (PLoS), Scientific Electronic Library Online (SCIELO), Bioline International, and Research Papers in Economics; open source publishing software, such as Open Journal Systems; and strong advocates, such as John Willinsky, Director of the Public Knowledge Project, and Peter Suber, Publisher of the SPARC Open Access Newsletter, will all contribute to narrowing the digital divide. Each time an author, professional, researcher, organization, journalist, politician, or civil servant embraces open access philosophy, it is a new step towards this goal.

ACKNOWLEDGMENT

The first author would like to acknowledge the guidance provided by the members of her Doctoral Committee and especially, to Dr. William Bertrand and Dr Janet C. Rice during the development of the conceptual framework and statistical analysis completed during her doctoral studies in the Payson Center for International Development and Technology Transfer at Tulane University

REFERENCES

Abels, E., et al.. (2004). If you build it, will they come? *Marketing, 8*(10), 13-17.

Bateman, J. (1999). Modeling the importance of end-user relevance criteria. In *ASIS '99, Proceedings of the 62nd ASIS Annual Meeting: Vol 36. Knowledge Creation, Organization and Use* (pp. 396-406). Washington, DC.

Bishop, A. P. (1998). Logins and bailouts: Measuring access, use, and success in digital libraries. *The Journal of Electronic Publishing, 4(2).*

Case, D. O. (2002). *Looking for information: A survey of research on information seeking, needs, and behavior.* Lexington, KY: Academic Press, Elsevier Science.

Chen, C., et al. (2000). Individual differences in virtual environments – Introduction and overview. *Journal of American Society for Information Science, 51(6),* 499-507.

Covey, D. T. (2002). Usage and usability assessment: Library practices and concerns. In *Digital Library Federation and Council on Library and Information Resources,* Pub 105, Washington, D.C.

Covey, D. T. (2003). The need to improve remote access to online library resources: Filling the gap between commercial vendor and academic user practice. *Libraries and the Academy, 3(4),* 577-599.

Culnan, M. (1985). The dimensions of perceived accessibility to information: Implications for the delivery of information systems and services. *Journal of the American Society for Information Science, 36(5),* 302-308.

De Groote, S. & Dorsch, J. (2003). Measuring use patterns of online journals and databases. *Journal of Medical Library Association. 91(2),* 231-241.

Echeverri, M. (2006). *Factors affecting access to and use of scholarly scientific information: A model for health science graduate students in Colombia.* Unpublished doctoral dissertation, Tulane University, New Orleans, Louisiana

Eisenberg, M., & Johnson, D. (2002). Computer skills for information problem-solving: Learning and teaching technology in context. *Eric Digest* EDO-IR-2002-04. Retrieved September 10, 2007, from http://www.eric.ed.gov/ERICWebPortal/ contentdelivery/servlet/ERICServlet?accno=ED465377

EPIC. (2001). *Online use & cost evaluation program: The use of electronic resources among undergraduate and graduate students.* Retrieved September 10, 2007, from http://www.epic.columbia.edu/eval/find03.html

Foster, A. (2003). Scientists at the U. of California at San Francisco call for a boycott of 6 biology journals. *The Chronicle of Higher Education: Information Technology Section, 50(10),* Page A34. Retrieved September 10, 2007, from http://chronicle.com/weekly/v50/i10/10a03403.htm

Goldstein, E. (1985). *The use of technical information by engineers of the electrical sector in Mexico.* University of California, Los Angeles, UMI Doctoral Dissertation.

Graham, J. (2003). The search engine that could. *USA TODAY,* August 26, 2003.

Hiller, S. (2002). The impact of information technology and online library resources on research, teaching and library use at the University of Washington. *Performance Measurement and Metrics, 3(2),* 134-139.

Interview with Peter Suber, publisher of SPARC Open Access Newsletter. *Library Journal Academic Newswire,* The Publishing Report, July 24, 2003.

Ke, H.-R. et al. (2002). Exploring behavior of e-journal users in science and technology: Transaction log analysis of Elsevier's Science Direct Onsite in Taiwan. *Library & Information Science Research, 24(3),* 265-291.

Kennedy, L., Cole, C., & Carter, S. (1999). The false focus in online searching: The particular case of undergraduates seeking information for course assignments in the humanities and social sciences. *Reference & User Services Quarterly, 38(3),* 267-273.

Kuhlthau, C. (1991). Inside the search process: Information seeking from the user's perspective. *Journal of the American Society for Information Science, 42*(5), 361-371.

Kuhlthau, C. (1993). *Seeking meaning: A process approach to library and information services.* Norwood, NJ: Ablex Pub. Corp. Kyrillidou, *M., & Young, M. (2003).* ARL Statistics 2001-02. *Association of Research Libraries –ARL, Washington, D.C.*

Kyrillidou, *M., & Young, M. (2004).* ARL Statistics 2002-03. *Association of Research Libraries –ARL, Washington, D.C.*

Larsen, V. (1997). *Exploring user behavior utilizing statistical analysis of WWW HTTPD access logs:Aan enquiry employing Net-Frog.* Doctoral Dissertation, University of Virginia.

Mack, T. et al. (2004). Designing for experts: How scholars approach an academic library Web site. *Information Technology and Libraries* (ITAL), *23*(1).

Marcum, D., & Gerald, G. (2003). Who uses what? Report on a National Survey of Information Users in Colleges and Universities. *D-Lib Magazine, 9*(10). Retrieved September 10, 2007, from http://www.dlib.org/dlib/october03/george/10george.html

McVeigh, M., & Pringle, J. (2005). Open access to the medical literature: How much content is available in published journals? *Serials, 18*(1), 45-50.

Mossberger, K., Tolbert, C., & Stansbury, M. (2003). Virtual inequality: Beyond the digital divide. Washington, DC: Georgetown University Press.

National Science Foundation –NSF. (2002). *Science and engineering: Indicators 2002,* volume 1. Arlington, VA: NSF.

Nelson, D. (2001). The uptake of electronic journals by academics in the UK, Their attitudes towards them and their potential impact on scholarly communication. *Information Services & Use, 21*(3/4), 205-214.

Noguera, E. (2003). Usability of e-journals and preference for the virtual periodicals room: A survey of mathematics faculty and graduate students. *Electronic Journal of Academic and SpecialLibrarianship, 4*(2-3).

OECD. (2001). *Understanding the digital divide.* Organisation for Economic Co-operation and Development. Retrieved February 15, 2004 from http://www.oecd.org/dataoecd/38/57/1888451.pdf

Onwuegbuzie, J. (1997). Writing a research proposal: The role of library anxiety, statistics anxiety, and composition anxiety. *Library & Information Science Research, 19*(1), 5-33.

Open Access to Scientific Research Editorial. (2003). *New York Times,* August 7, 2003, p. A27. Published on February 10, 2007 by the Society of Scholarly Publishing (SSP). Retrieved August 31, 2007, from http://www.sspnet.org/custom/news/details.cfm?id=141

Palmer, J. (1991). Scientists and information: I. Using cluster analysis to identify information style. *Journal of Documentation, 47*(2), 105-129.

Pinelli, T. (1991). NASA/DoD Report Number 6: The relationship between the use of U.S. Government Technical Reports by U.S. Aerospace Engineers and Scientists and selected institutional and sociometric variables. *Aerospace Knowledge Diffusion Project.* NASA Technical Memorandum 102774, Department of Defense, Indiana University.

Roger, E. M. (1995). *Diffusion of innovations* (4th ed.). New York, NY: Free Press.

Sagasti, A. (2001). The knowledge explosion and the digital divide. United Nations Development Programme (UNDP), *Human Development Reports,* background papers. Retrieved September

10, 2007, from http://hdr.undp.org/docs/publications/background_papers/sagasti.doc

Silvio, J. (1998). The virtualization of higher education: Scope, possibilities and limitations. UNESCO, Regional Centre for Higher Education in Latin America and the Caribbean (CRESALC). *Rufis'98, International Congress.* Universidad Regiomontana. Monterrey N.L., México.

Stanford University Libraries. (2002). *Electronic journal user study: eJUST.* Retrieved September 10, 2007, from http://ejust.stanford.edu/index.html

Sullivan, D. (2004). Google Scholar offers access to academic information. *SearchEngineWatch* (Nov 18, 2004). Retrieved September 10, 2007, from http://searchenginewatch.com/searchday/article.php/3437471

Tenopir, C., & King, D. (2000). *Towards electronic journals: Realities for scientists, librarians, pnd Publishers.* Washington, D.C.: Special Libraries Association.

Tenopir, C. et al. (2003). *Use and users of electronic library resources: An overview and analysis of recent research studies.* Council on Library and Information Resources. Retrieved September 10, 2007, from http://www.clir.org/pubs/reports/pub120/contents.html

Testa, J., & McVeigh, M. (2004). *The impact of open access journals: A citation study from Thomson ISI.* The Thomson Corporation. Retrieved September 10, 2007, from http://www.isinet.com/media/presentrep/acropdf/impact-oa-journals.pdf

Thomes, K. (2000). *The economics and usage of digital library collections.* Bevier Engineering Library, University of Pittsburgh, The Association of Research Libraries (ARL)

Trolley, J. (1999). New wine and old vessels: The evaluation and integration of Web-based information in well established resources. *Asis '99*

Proceedings of the 62nd Asis Annual Meeting: V36. Knowledge Creation, Organization and Use, (pp. 628-632), Washington, DC

Vakkari, P. (2000). Relevance and contributing information types of searched documents in task performance. Proceedings of the 23rd annual international ACM SIGIR conference on Research and Development in Information Retrieval (pp. 2-9). Athens, Greece.

Vakkari, P. & Pennanen, M. (2001). Sources, relevance and contributory information of documents in writing a research proposal: A longitudinal case study. *The New Review of Information Behavior Research, 2*(November), 217 – 232

Willinsky, J. (2006). *Altering the material conditions of access to the humanities. Tasks for the new humanities: Professing with Derrida* (pp. 118-136). London: Palgrave Macmillan. . Retrieved September 10, 2007, from http://pkp.sfu.ca/node/456

Willinsky, J. (2006a). Access to power: Research in international policymaking. *Harvard International Review*, summer 2006, 42-45. Retrieved September 10, 2007, from http://pkp.sfu.ca/node/432

Willinsky, J. (2006b). Why open access for research and scholarship? *Journal of Neuroscience, 26*(36), 9078-9079. Retrieved September 10, 2007, from http://www.jneurosci.org/cgi/reprint/26/36/9078

Witten, I. (2003). *Digital libraries and society: New perspectives on information dissemination.* Department of Computer Science, University of Waikato, New Zealand. Retrieved September 10, 2007, from http://www.cs.waikato.ac.nz/~ihw/DLs.and.society.pdf

Witten, I. & Bainbridge, D. (2001). *How to build a digital library.* New Zealand Digital Library Project, University of Waikato, New Zealand, Morgan Kaufmann Publishers.

World Bank. (2002). *Harnessing knowledge for development.* III World Knowledge Forum, World Bank Plenary, Seoul, October 18, 2002. Retrieved September 10, 2007, from http://lnweb18.world-bank.org/eap/eap.nsf/Attachments/speech/$File/WKF+Speech.pdf

World Bank. (2002b). *Information and communication technologies: A World Bank Group Strategy, Executive Summary.* The World Bank Group, Washington, D.C.

Zhang, Y. (1999). *Scholarly use of Internet-based electronic resources.* Doctoral Dissertation, University of Illinois at Urbana-Champaign. UMI Digital dissertation AAT 3013240.

Zipf, G. (1949). *Human behavior and the principle of least effort; An introduction to human ecology.* Cambridge, MA: Addison-Wesley Press.

ADDITIONAL READING

Web Sites

Association of College & Research Libraries (ACRL): http://www.ala.org/ACRLTemplate.cfm

Centre for Knowledge Transfer: http://www.ckt-ctc.ca/

Digital Divide: http://en.wikipedia.org/wiki/Digital_divide

Directory of Open Access Journals (DOAJ): http://www.doaj.org /

International Federation of Library Associations and Institutions (IFLA): http://www.ifla.org/index.htm

Knowledge Utilization Studies Program–KUSP: http://www.nursing.ualberta.ca/kusp/index.htm

Public Access to Science Act (HR 2613): http://thomas.loc.gov/cgi-bin/query/z?c108:H.R.2613

Public Knowledge Project–PKP: http://pkp.sfu.ca/

UN World Summit on the Information Society (WSIS): http://www.itu.int/wsis/index.html

World Bank. Knowledge for Development (K4D) Framework: http://www.worldbank.org/wbi/knowledgefordevelopment/k4dcommunity.html

Articles, Reports, and Books

European Technology Assessment Network –ETAN. (1999). *Transforming European science through information and communication technologies: Challenges and opportunities of the digital age.* ETAN Working Paper prepared for the Directorate General for Research, European Commission, Final Version, September 1999.

Harnad, S. (2003). *For whom the gate tolls? How and why to free the refereed research literature online through author/institution self-archiving, now.* Retrieved September 10, 2007, from http://users.ecs.soton.ac.uk/harnad/Tp/resolution.htm

Knott, J., & Wildavsky, A. (1980). If dissemination is the solution, what is the problem? *Science Communication, 1,* 537 – 578.

Kwasik, H., & Fulda, P. (2005). Open access and scholarly communication—A selection of key Web sites. *Issues in Science and Technology Librarianship,* Summer 2005. Retrieved September 10, 2007, from http://www.istl.org/05-summer/internet.html

Shadbolt, N., Brody, T., Carr, L. & Harnad, S. (2006). *The open research Web: A preview of the optimal and the inevitable.* In N. Jacobs (Ed.), *Open access: Key strategic, technical and economic cspects.* Retrieved September 10, 2007, from http://eprints.ecs.soton.ac.uk/12369/01/shadbch.htm

Suber, P. (2003). Removing barriers to research. *College & Research Libraries News, 64*(2), 92-4, 113.

Tamber, P. S. (2003). Open access to peer-reviewed research: making it happen. *The Lancet, 362*(9395):1575-7.

Willinsky, J. (2006). *The access principle: The case for open access to research and scholarship.* Cambridge, MA: MIT Press. Retrieved September 10, 2007 from http://pkp.sfu.ca/node/457

WHO. (2004). *Galvanising mental health research in low- and middle-income countries: Role of scientific journals.* A Joint Statement issued by Editors of Scientific Journals Publishing Mental Health Research and Department of Mental Health and Substance Abuse World Health Organization, Geneva. Retrieved September 10, 2007, from http://www.who.int/entity/mental_health/evidence/en/final_joint_statement.pdf

ENDNOTES

[1] Details on the factor analysis may be found in Echeverri, 2006

[2] A large-scale, Web-based electronic publishing initiative that provides free access to 1,550 MIT courses materials in 33 academic disciplines, to educators, students, and individual learners around the world. http://ocw.mit.edu/OcwWeb/ [Retrieved August 15, 2007]

[3] An Oxford University's program that allows free or discounted electronic access to over 160 titles of their professional journals to "not-for-profit organizations from qualifying countries whose mission involves education and/or health". Oxford University, *Developing Countries offer – Journals*, http://www.oxfordjournals.org/access_purchase/developing_countries.html [Retrieved August 15, 2007]

Chapter IX
Knowledge Exchange in Electronic Networks of Practice:
An Examination of Knowledge Types and Knowledge Flows

Molly Wasko
Florida State University, USA

Samer Faraj
McGill Unversity, Canada

ABSTRACT

This study examines knowledge exchange in a worldwide, extra-organizational, Usenet-based electronic network of practice. Participation in such networks is voluntary, globally distributed, and network participants generally do not have personal or organizational ties. The purpose of the study was to investigate two questions: first, what type of knowledge is being transferred in these networks, and second, how is knowledge transferred across individuals in electronic networks. To address these questions, we observed and saved all messages posted to comp.lang.C++ for a period of 7 weeks. Our analyses include content analysis of 1,562 messages, survey responses from 593 participants, and objective data from the electronic message postings. The study illuminates how people use computer-mediated communication to support knowledge transfer, the types of knowledge transferred, as well as how knowledge flows in this network.

INTRODUCTION

Recent advances in information and communication technologies have led to the emergence of virtual social spaces where individuals self-organize electronically to discuss and debate issues based on shared interests. Internet-based technologies have enabled the development of thousands of freestanding open-membership forums focused on discussing the problems of practice (Butler, 2001; Sproull & Faraj, 1995;). In these networks, an unlimited number of geographically dispersed individuals who come from diverse organizational, national, and demographic backgrounds (Sproull & Faraj, 1995) are able to share knowledge by helping each other solve problems, telling stories of personal experiences, and debating issues relevant to the network (Wasko & Faraj, 2000). An enduring characteristic of these networks is the propensity of individuals to provide their valuable knowledge and insights to strangers (Kollock and Smith, 1996; Rheingold, 1993; Wasko & Faraj, 2000). Individuals benefit from these networks since they gain access to new information, expertise, and ideas that are often not available locally.

We refer to these informal electronic communication networks as "electronic networks of practice" or ENoPs. Following Brown and Duguid (2000) in their use of the term "networks of practice," we add the term "electronic" to highlight that communication within this type of network of practice occurs through asynchronous computer-based communication technologies, such as bulletin boards, listservs, and Usenet newsgroups. We define an electronic network of practice as a self-organizing, open, activity system focused on practice that exists through electronic communication. These defining characteristics have some unique technical and social features that influence how knowledge is created and exchanged. Conceptually, electronic networks of practice share characteristics with virtual teams, communities of practice, and networks of practice. They share with virtual teams a distributed membership and reliance on computer networks to bridge distance and time. However, an electronic network of practice differs from virtual teams in that there is no established performance goal or recognized end point. In electronic networks of practice, participation is voluntary, and its form left entirely to the individual. In contrast, in most virtual teams, membership is controlled; it is either assigned or approved by some authority. Additionally, an

electronic network of practice is self-organizing in the sense that no organizational mandate or sponsorship is required for its sustenance.

An electronic network of practice shares with a community of practice the focus on shared practice, learning, and joint problem solving. However, participants in an electronic network of practice typically do not share a common geographic and organizational setting, and these networks can become extremely large due to their open worldwide membership and reliance on electronic communication technology. Such networks differ from communities of practice in that their members are typically strangers and do not share a common organizational or geographical setting. Communities of practice are characterized by strong personal ties and reciprocal interactions related to mutual engagement, mentoring, and learning (Orr, 1996; Wenger 1998). In contrast, electronic networks of practice are characterized by weak electronic ties that connect strangers worldwide, and interactions are limited by the technological infrastructure.

Electronic networks of practice are similar to what Brown and Duguid (2000, 2001) refer to as networks of practice. Individuals in networks of practice have practice and knowledge in common, but individuals may never get to know one another. Knowledge flows through newsletters, Web sites, meetings, and professional conferences. As a result, exchanges tend to be highly reliant on text representations of knowledge, which also holds true for electronic networks of practice. However, electronic networks of practice differ in that they exist primarily through computer-mediated, asynchronous exchange. Communication between members occurs through message threads, which resemble conversations, rather than static documentation.

Electronic networks of practice play an important role in the transfer of knowledge. For example, electronic networks are supporting distributed R&D efforts (Ahuja et al., 2003; Orlikowski et al., 1995) and enabling cooperation around open source software development (Lakhani & von Hippel, 2000). ENoPs provide an opportunity for individuals interested in a specific practice to congregate and share knowledge through activities, such as helping each other test and debug computer code (Butler, 2001; Wasko & Faraj, 2000), and frequently emerge in fields where the pace of technological change requires access to knowledge and resources that are unavailable within any single organization (Powell et al., 1996).

However, while interest in how individuals and organizations can leverage the Internet to facilitate knowledge transfer continues to grow, there is surprisingly little theoretical and empirical development that addresses knowledge transfer through the use of large, openly available electronic networks on the Internet (Butler, 2001; Fulk et al., 1996). While researchers have examined why individuals share knowledge with strangers, using theories such as weak ties (Constant et al., 1996), the resource-based view of resource availability and benefit provision (Butler, 2001), and generalized gift exchange (Kollock, 1999), researchers have yet to examine what types of knowledge are conducive to transfer via the Internet, and how knowledge flows across individuals. The availability of communication technology to sustain group interactions does not necessarily translate into the creation of electronic networks focused on practice. Even though there is evidence that active knowledge transfer in electronic networks of practice can occur, high levels of online interactivity are largely the exception, not the rule (Cummings et al., 2002). While the creation of a virtual social space for sharing knowledge is technically relatively easy, there is no guarantee that knowledge transfer between individuals will actually take place (Alavi & Leidner, 1999; Orlikowski, 1996).

Therefore, the first objective of this chapter is to explore two research questions. First, what type of knowledge is being transferred in these electronic networks? Information technologies have been categorized as a lean medium of exchange (Daft & Lengel, 1986; Daft et al., 1987). This implies that the type of information conveyed through electronic channels is limited, and the technology may not support complex knowledge transfer. To examine this issue, we perform content analysis of the messages posted to one electronic network to empirically investigate the types of knowledge exchanged in this network.

The second research question looks at how knowledge flows in electronic networks. This analysis examines the dynamics of knowledge transfer in electronic networks by looking at who asks for help, who provides help, and the underlying individual motivations to engage in these different activities. We examine this issue two ways: first, how does knowledge flow between individuals, based on level of expertise and message activity. Second, how does knowledge flow, based on the underlying individual motivations for why people ask questions vs. post responses.

The second objective of this chapter is to offer examples of how a variety of analysis techniques and methods can be leveraged to better understand knowledge transfer via the Internet. In addressing the research questions posed, our first analysis describes a process for performing content analysis on message postings. Our second analysis combines the results from content analysis with survey data to see if we can predict how and why individuals participate. The goal of presenting our multimethod approach in this chapter is to encourage researchers to pursue multiple methods in their investigations of knowledge transfer on the Internet. The advantage of Internet-based research is the ability to actually observe knowledge transfer in practice by examining message dynamics. Combining objective data available from the electronic network and subjective data from network participants themselves enables researchers to develop a deeper understanding of knowledge transfer across multiple levels of analysis, such as how individuals participate in electronic networks, how message content facilitates knowledge transfer, and how networks are sustained over time. We end the chapter by discussing the findings, highlighting the study limitations, noting future trends and other possible methods for studying electronic networks of practice, and final conclusions.

BACKGROUND

For the purposes of this chapter, we do not distinguish between knowledge and information. From our perspective, knowledge is defined simply as "that which is known" (Grant, 1996), and the knowledge of interest is the codified knowledge (e.g., knowledge expressed through written text) contained in the messages. However, even though our focus is on knowledge that is codified, one of our main interests is the examination of this codified knowledge in order to determine whether it varies along a tacit-explicit dimension. Thus, we are not making the assumption that codified knowledge can only consist of explicit knowledge.

In addition, we use the word transfer to mean knowledge that has been codified and made available to others electronically. We examine knowledge transfer in terms of message postings that are questions and message postings that are responses. We do not explore whether actual "transfer" occurs, meaning we do not know if receivers actually absorb, understand, and integrate the knowledge posted to the electronic network. Prior studies have conceptualized knowledge transfer as a process that depends on five factors: 1) receiver's perception of the value of the knowledge, 2) motivational disposition of the source (e.g., willingness to share), 3) existence and richness of the communication channel, 4) motivational disposition of receiver, and 5) absorptive capacity of the receiver (Alavi & Leidner 2001; Gupta & Govindarajan, 2000;). In this chapter, our approach to examining transfer focuses on the content of the questions and responses, and

how knowledge flows from those who respond to those who ask questions.

KNOWLEDGE TYPES

Knowledge exchange in electronic networks of practice is similar to what Nonaka terms "Cyber Ba" (Nonaka & Konno, 1998). According to these authors, "Ba" is conceived as the frame (made up of the borders of space and time) in which knowledge is activated as a resource for creation (Nonaka & Konno, 1998). Based on the work of Polanyi (1962), Nonaka defines two classifications of knowledge: explicit and tacit. Explicit knowledge can be expressed in words and numbers, and shared in the form of data, specifications, and manuals. This kind of knowledge can be transferred between individuals formally and systematically. Tacit knowledge, on the other hand, is highly personal and hard to formalize, making it difficult to communicate or share with others. This form of knowledge is deeply rooted in an individual's actions and experiences, and encompasses "know-how" (Nonaka & Konno, 1998).

In a two-by-two matrix, Nonaka and Konno (1998) propose that new knowledge is created through the transformation from tacit to tacit, tacit to explicit, explicit to tacit, and explicit to explicit. Cyber Ba is represented by the last quadrant, the combination of explicit to explicit knowledge (Nonaka & Konno, 1998). Cyber Ba is defined as "a place of interaction in a virtual world instead of real space and time; and represents the combination phase. Here, the combining of new explicit knowledge with existing information and knowledge generates and systematizes explicit knowledge throughout the organization" (Nonaka & Konno, 1998). According to this conceptualization, knowledge transfer in electronic networks should be limited to explicit knowledge, such as specialized facts, definitions, and data.

Winter (1987) presents an alternative view, and suggests that tacit/explicit should be considered a dimension along which knowledge can vary. From this perspective, tacitness is the degree to which the knowledge can be codified. Even knowledge that is primarily tacit can be codified and expressed through language. Tacit knowledge can be verbalized and expressed through the use of metaphors, stories of personal experience, and the use of context. From this point of view, much of what we know is a combination of both tacit and explicit knowledge, and to the extent that knowledge is tacit, has implications for how difficult the knowledge is to codify.

Research on knowledge transfer in organizations has often focused on selecting the appropriate communication media for the type of knowledge to be transferred. Media richness theory (Daft et al., 1987; Daft & Lengel, 1986) describes organizational communication channels as having objective characteristics that determine the channels' capacity for conveying information. These characteristics consist of: immediacy of feedback, language variety, number of cues, and personalization. Daft and Lengel (1986) argued that managers could improve performance by matching communication media to the complexity (based on either uncertainty or equivocality) of the organizational information processing task. According to the theory, messages should be matched to communication channels with sufficient and appropriate media richness capacities to avoid misinterpretation and maximize efficiencies. Because information conveyed through computer channels is typically restricted to text only, according to media richness theory, computer-mediated communication represents a less rich form of exchange.

However, media richness has had limited success when tested empirically, and has become a popular "straw man" theory, set up to be easily refuted. Media richness has been referred to as a "cues filtered out" approach because it predicts that the richness of the communication media "will result in predictable changes in intrapersonal and interpersonal variables" (Culnan & Markus, 1987). Media richness has been interpreted to suggest that since media forms differ in their ability to convey information, technology imposes constraints that restrict and ultimately determine the outcomes of actors. This objective, deterministic view of technology is not generally appropriate, and is particularly inadequate in the case of information technologies (Orlikowski, 1992). According to Dennis and Kinney (1998), the limiting factor may not be the communications media, but "rather our preconceived perceptions of their limitations" based on media richness theory.

Communication media have objective characteristics that determine the capacity of the media to carry information, but in using technology, individuals interpret, manipulate, and appropriate technology in different ways. Technology is physically constructed, but is also socially constructed by users through the various features they emphasize and use, as well as the meanings that individuals attach to the technology (Orlikowski, 1992). This use of technology as a social practice is well illustrated by how people have adapted asynchronous, text-based communication, such as used on the Usenet. Even though individuals communicating on the Usenet are limited to text only, individuals have found ways to adapt this technology to convey a variety of signals and symbols. Individuals create faces using colon and parentheses keys (emoticons) to convey emotion. Individuals SHOUT AT EACH OTHER using capital letters to convey anger, frustration, or gain attention. Individuals translate common sayings through the use of the symbols available in text, such as "let me add my $1/50 worth," or by creating shorthand symbols (FWIW, BTW, IMHO). Individuals build complex pictures using text characters to imitate the drawing of lines. And even though the technology was designed to support written communication, individuals in the technical groups use the technology to exchange computer code. So although there is an objective aspect of the technology that limits communication to text only, the use of the technology is socially constructed, based on the social context of the individuals communicating and the communication practices that are adopted to meet the various needs of these individuals.

Therefore, one question is whether the knowledge being transferred in electronic networks is limited to explicit, specialized facts and definitions due to difficulties of codification, or does the knowledge vary along a tacit/explicit dimension. This leads to our first set of research questions:

RQ1: Is the knowledge, although codified, primarily explicit, or a combination of tacit and explicit?

RQ2: How do members convey tacit meaning through codified exchange?

KNOWLEDGE FLOWS

The second phase of this research looks at how knowledge flows in electronic networks of practice. This analysis examines the dynamics of knowledge transfer in electronic networks by looking at who asks for help, who provides help, and the underlying individual motivations to engage in these different activities. Research shows that individuals gravitate towards communities of practice to have increased access to knowledge resources. This includes having access to more experienced colleagues, leveraging existing knowledge through stories, and passing on personal experience to others in the network. Increasing access to knowledge resources should increase the productivity of the network as a whole. But how does knowledge flow between individuals within the network, and do people benefit differentially? On the one hand, people may receive equivalent flows and benefits. This would assume that all people request and respond knowledge at an equivalent level, regardless of personal differences, such as level of expertise.

However, another perspective supported by the research of Hesse et al. (1993) suggests that knowledge flows differentially. They found that when networks were used to support oceanographic research, scientists on the periphery and core scientists benefited differentially from network participation (Hesse et al., 1993).

Additionally, individual level motivations are factors that may affect participation and knowledge transfer in electronic networks of practice. Based on previous literature, there appears to be three primary motivations as to why people interact with strangers in electronic networks of practice: personal gain, social affiliation, and professional affiliation (Constant et al., 1996; Wasko & Faraj, 2005). Sources of personal gain include a desire to improve one's reputation and status in the network, or to leverage participation in the network for professional gain (Lakhani & von Hippel, 2003). Another source of personal gain is to find answers to a specific question of interest (Wasko & Faraj, 2000). Social affiliation indicates that individuals may participate in order to socialize and create friendships with others who share similar interests. There is early evidence that the Internet is making it possible for people to create and sustain new relationships, thus, fulfilling a need for social affiliation and belonging with others (Walther, 1995; Wellman et al., 1996). Thus, participation may be based on a prosocial orientation and wanting to meet and socialize with others.

Alternatively, individuals may participate due to an intrinsic motivation based on professional affiliation, and a desire to engage in intellectual exchange. For many knowledge workers, a social space is at the core of their work and their professional identity, where they can collaborate, narrate stories, and construct joint solutions and understanding (Brown & Duguid 1991). Knowledge work requires the open discussion of topical issues and the expression of multiple perspectives away from any hierarchical constraints. Whether face-to-face (Van Maanen & Barley, 1984) or online

(Pickering & King, 1995), knowledge workers in a fast changing field are intrinsically motivated to keep up with latest trends in the field, and increase their stock of knowledge by asking questions and providing help when they can.

Therefore, the other question investigated in this chapter is how knowledge flows among individuals in the network. As noted previously, while prior research has investigated why people participate and help others, investigating the issues of who benefits most from participation, and why individuals participate in certain ways, has not been fully investigated. This leads to our second set of research questions:

RQ3: Do all participants benefit equally or are there differential returns to participation?

RQ4: Do the underlying individual motivations for participation affect whether or not individuals seek answers or post responses?

RESEARCH SETTING

The study was conducted on the Usenet. The Usenet is a distributed conferencing system, or bulletin board, where individuals can post and respond to messages. The Usenet consists of over 30,000 different discussion areas organized around issues and topics that participants want to discuss. The focus of the group and the nature of the topics under discussion are conveyed to users by the group name. There are six major domain categories: alternative (alt.), computer (comp.), recreation (rec.), societal (soc.), science (sci.), and miscellaneous (misc.), and the category is typically identified at the beginning of the group name. For example, some popular group names are soc.women, comp.lang.c, rec.humor, and misc.forsale.

Newsgroups are of special research interest because they are open and lively forums where people combine and exchange knowledge using a relatively unsophisticated information technology. We view technical (as opposed to social or recreational) Usenet newsgroups as examples of what we refer to as electronic networks of practice. Members of such newsgroups are oriented around a specific knowledge practice; they communicate, sensemake, exchange ideas, and help each other with technology topics such as computer languages, hardware platforms, and complex applications. This narrow common interest defines the boundary of the group and helps differentiate the group from others.

We picked one, high-volume, technical Newsgroup, comp.lang.c++, and collected all of the messages posted to this group for a period of 7 weeks. A total of 9,952 different messages were posted during this period by 3,284 individuals. The individuals participating in this electronic network are globally distributed, although the majority of members originate from domain names from the United States (Appendix A lists country of origin, number of individuals by country, and how individuals participated in terms of posting questions or responses). We sent out an electronic survey to every individual who posted during that period. Of these, 310 did not reach their recipient due to a changed or invalid address. We received a total of 593 usable responses from the 2,974 people who received the survey, for a response rate of 20.0%.

INVESTIGATING KNOWLEDGE

We used content analysis to categorize the messages submitted to the group, for those people who responded to the survey. Content analysis is a standard methodology in the social sciences for studying the content of communication. For the purposes of this study, we focused on textual content analysis, indicating that we are dealing exclusively with the analysis of text. Ole Holsti (1969) offers a broad definition of content analysis as any technique for making inferences by objectively and systematically identifying specified characteristics of messages. We developed a content coding schema (see Appendix B), defining how messages were to be coded. Messages were coded along three separate dimensions: message purpose, knowledge type, and message form. A total of 1,562 messages were included in the analysis, of which 1,136 were responses and 426 were questions. There were over 9,000 messages posted to the group during the study time period, and only the messages posted by survey respondents were analyzed.

Message purpose indicates why the message was sent to the group. Message purpose fell into one of eight categories: (1) questions, (2) responses, (3) announcements (e.g., job openings, upcoming events, and calls for papers), (4) messages that addressed group behavior, (5) messages that addressed professional community standards, (6) junk mail (spam), and (7) thank you replies. If a message did not fall into one of these categories, the message was classified as (8) other. Table 1 summarizes the message purpose categories and the number of messages that fell under each category. The message purposes of interest to this study are questions and responses. Although all messages represent some kind of knowledge codification and transfer, the vast majority of messages are questions and responses. Thus, we are looking at the dynamics underlying the exchange between people who look for knowledge and the people that contribute knowledge to others. Messages that are coded as questions indicate that the message purpose is to request information. Responses indicate that the message was an answer to a request for information.

Knowledge content was determined through a two-step process. First, categories were developed a priori, based on the idea that knowledge varies along a tacit/explicit dimension. We defined five knowledge types that vary from explicit knowledge forms to more tacit knowledge forms: knowledge source, know-what, know-how, technical assessment, and professional assessment. A knowledge source was determined if the message requested or provided either an electronic, text-based, or personal information source. This category represents messages that identify a specific location to find tools, books, or more information about a specific subject. Examples of a knowledge source are "does anybody know where I can find…," "check out this Web site for more information," "refer to this book for steps on how to do it," or "talk to this person."

Messages that fall under the know-what category are requests/answers to technical questions that are specific and definable. In order to qualify as know-what, responses must have a specific, clear answer to the question "who knows what," and not be subject to opinion or multiple interpretations. Typical know-what questions/responses provided definitions of terms such as "does anyone know what this means," explanations of certain failure codes, and relaying specific facts about some event.

Know-how also refers to questions/responses that contain specific, technical knowledge, but asks/answers the question "does anyone know how." This category is similar to know-what, in that there must be an objective, specific response that does not require multiple interpretations. However, unlike know-what, know-how requires that people be able to link know-what type events together to form meaning in a procedural way. Examples of know how are "does anyone know

Table 1. Message purpose

Questions	426
Responses	1136
Announcements	19
Community standards	33
Professional standards	2
Other	10
Spam	6
Thank yous	41

how to build…," "this is how to fix your code," and/or "this is how to accomplish that specific task."

Technical assessments were coded as those messages that are opinion-based, could have multiple potential responses, and do not have one specific answer. Technical assessments are expertise-based opinions, typically stemming from personal experience or comprehension of multiple interacting variables. Assessments typically address issues of "why something is happening" or "can someone compare these things." Examples of technical assessments are asking/offering an assessment of the advantages/disadvantages of different technical systems, posting/solving a complex problem that requires different levels of know-how and know-what in combination with context/environmental variables, and requesting/providing experience-based opinions on complex problems.

Professional assessments are similar to technical assessments in that they are messages that are opinion-based and subject to multiple interpretation. However, professional assessments deal with issues that occur in the professional community at-large, and not restricted to technical matters. Due to their general nature, professional assessments are debatable. Topics of professional assessments are typically the likelihood of product or company success/failure, and the future of the community at-large.

These categories are meant to represent practical knowledge, or knowledge that would be useful in a person's work. However, practical knowledge was not the only knowledge contributed to the group. In addition, some of the messages in the group conveyed pastime knowledge such as jokes and gossip, or requested/provided additional information and clarification for an earlier message. These messages were not included in this analysis.

Media richness theories would suggest that due to the lean medium of exchange, the majority of knowledge transferred would consist primar-

ily of explicit knowledge that is more readily codified. Therefore, this would suggest that the majority of messages should consist of pointers to a knowledge source (e.g., a book or Web site), and know-what. Due to the tacitness of the knowledge related to know-how and assessments, this type of knowledge is more difficult to transfer via lean, text-based communications; thus, we would expect to see fewer messages containing this type of knowledge content.

Message form - Finally, messages were coded for form. Form categories indicate whether or not additional information, in addition to knowledge type, is conveyed. Three message forms were of interest to this study: the addition of context, the use of embedded messages, and the transfer of computer code. Context is defined as data that provides additional information used to frame the issue at hand. Examples of context include extraneous information such as the office environment, the technology requirements, and current technical equipment, where to specifically look within a source to find an answer, or under what conditions a solution will hold.

Embedded messages are those responses that included a copy or snippet from a previous post, typically the question being addressed. Finally, the inclusion of code indicates that computer code was included in the message. Examples of response messages from each of the categories are presented in Appendix B. Table 2 presents the results of the content analysis.

RESULTS

From the content analysis summary, practical knowledge was the most common knowledge type requested and contributed to the group (there were 276 messages posted that requested clarifications, and 58 messages that were jokes, gossip, or humor). The summary includes only the 1,562 messages that were practical knowledge questions and practical knowledge responses. Questions that contained a pointer to a knowledge source were posted 13.1% of the time, and responses 10.8% of the time. Know-what knowledge was requested 22.8% compared to 25% of total responses. Know-how was contributed 34.1%, and requested 53.3% of the time. Finally, 20% of people requested assessments, and people provided assessments 25.3% of the time.

Explicit knowledge, consisting of knowledge source and know-what, were only 35.8% of response volume. Messages that integrated tacit knowledge, indicated by know-how and technical/professional assessments, were contributed 60% of the time. This seems to indicate that although text-based and a lean medium of exchange, people are using these networks to transfer knowledge that has tacit dimensions. This lends support to the conceptualization of knowledge as varying on a tacit/explicit dimension, and that knowledge transfer in "Cyber Ba" is not limited to explicit/concrete exchange, but rather represents the combination of codified with codified knowledge that varies along a tacit/explicit dimension.

Table 2. Types of knowledge transfer

	Questions		Responses	
	Frequency	Percent	Frequency	Percent
Source: electronic	18	4.2	68	6
Source: book, other	9	2.1	42	3.7
Source: multiple	29	6.8	13	1.1
Know what	97	22.8	284	25
Know how	227	53.3	387	34.1
Technical assessment	65	15.3	237	20.9
Professional assessment	3	.7	50	4.4
Context	402	94.4	1009	88.8
Embedded message	6	1.4	1027	90.4
Includes code	189	44.4	474	41.7
Total	426		1136	

In addition, 44.4% of questions and 41.7% of the responses contained computer code, which indicates that electronic exchange is a useful medium for collaborative programming. Surprisingly, even though 35.8% of responses were more explicit, close to 90% of the response messages relied on the use of context (88.8) and embedded messages (90.4) in order to convey additional meaning. This gives some indication as to how codified, text-based communication is used to convey knowledge that has tacit elements. This also indicates that these networks are useful for the transfer of computer code; however, context is still used to convey more specific meaning for interpreting the code. Thus, the people in this electronic network have overcome the inherent limitations of electronic exchange and are not limited to explicit knowledge exchange, but are able to codify tacit meaning as well.

INVESTIGATING KNOWLEDGE FLOWS

To investigate how knowledge flows among individuals, we first divided our sample into three groups: novices, professionals, and experts, based on level of expertise obtained from the survey data. Level of expertise was estimated by asking respondents to provide their level of expertise on the subject matter of the group, based on a seven-point scale (1 or 2 - novice, 3, 4, or 5—professional, and 6 or 7—expert). Message activity for each individual was aggregated so each individual obtained one message activity score. Members who posted more than once in the group were assigned an aggregated score to represent type of participation. For example, if a member posted five messages, and all of the messages were responses, this member received a "1" for message responses. If the group member asked one question, but responded to four questions, this was scored as .2 message questions and .8 message responses. In this way, we were able to reduce message data down to an individual level of analysis. We then divided the messages into question and response categories. ANOVA was used to determine if there were significant differences between the groups. Included in the comparisons are levels of expertise and type of knowledge transfer.

In order to examine why people participate, in the survey, we asked people seven questions about their reasons for participating in the newsgroup, reflecting personal gain motivations, social motivations, and professional motivations (using a seven-point Likert scale from strongly disagree to strongly agree). We then use linear regression to see which motivations were significant predictors of posting questions and posting responses (the same variables as described previously).

RESULTS

Results from the ANOVA provide support for differential benefit (Table 3). Novices were more likely to ask questions (F=18.89, $p<.001$), and experts were more likely to provide answers (F=25.93, $p<.001$). However, professionals were just as likely to post questions as responses. This seems to indicate that knowledge flows in a stepwise fashion between individuals. One possibility is that novices ask easier questions that professionals are able to answer. Then, when professionals have questions, presumably more technically advanced and complicated, the ex-

perts are available to respond. Experts also seem to benefit from the exchange with other experts. Even though experts were three times more likely to respond, occasionally experts also asked for advice. This seems to indicate that the majority of knowledge is flowing from the experts to the professional and then from professional to the novices. This also provides some indication that electronic networks help to elevate the non-experts in the field, thereby leveling the field.

The results for the motivation analysis are presented in the Table 4. The items are listed in terms of order of general relevance in terms of motivation (the mean of the survey responses). Two of the top three most important motivations are those associated with personal gain. Thus, it appears that the personal gain motivations related "practice" related gains, as opposed to reputation gains are more important. The professional affiliation motivations were ranked quite a bit higher than social affiliation motivations.

In terms of actually predicating participation, however, we find that people who post questions do so primarily to solve a specific problem, and then for social affiliation motivations. People who post responses are significantly less likely to be motivated to solve a specific problem, but rather to help others and keep abreast of innovations in the practice. The two personal gain motivations, to enhance personal and professional goals and status, were not significantly related to actual participation in the network.

The results of this analysis suggest some interesting findings. In order to understand why

Table 3. ANOVA analysis of knowledge flows

	Questions		Responses			
	Frequency	Aggregate	Frequency	Aggregate	F	Sig
Novice – N=84	90	56.85	82	24.62	18.89	0.001
Professional – N=302	242	140.25	514	155.89	0.789	ns
Expert – N=162	69	43.18	486	112.17	25.93	0.001
Aggregate scores were used in one-way ANOVA						

Table 4. Motivations predicting participation

	One of my reasons for participating in the newsgroup is:	Mean	SD	Post questions	Post responses
1	To solve a specific problem of direct concern to me	5.61	1.77	.42**	-.38**
2	To keep abreast of new ideas and innovations	5.48	1.63	-.18**	.15**
3	To enhance my personal and professional goals	5.07	1.91	-.07	0.07
4	To help other group members with their problems	4.96	1.67	-.15**	.16**
5	To meet new and different people	2.15	1.52	.14**	-.14*
6	To build friendships with others	2.14	1.51	.15**	-.15**
7	To increase my status and prestige	1.65	1.33	-.08	0.08
	R^2adj			.27**	.24**

people participate in electronic networks of practice, it is important to distinguish among types of participation. Simply counting the number of messages posted to a network may result in spurious findings, given the variations in message purpose, indicating that different people participate in different ways and for different reasons. Therefore, having a diversity of members in the electronic network of practice that includes novices, professionals, and experts, as well as encouraging participation from people with different motivations, are two important underlying dimensions for how knowledge flows in these networks.

CONCLUSION

This chapter examined the role of electronic networks of practice for supporting the transfer of knowledge in electronic networks of practice. In spite of the lean communication medium, lack of colocation and members being primarily strangers, we found that electronic networks of practice are supporting knowledge exchange between members. Recently, researchers noted the emergence of electronic networks of practice and expressed skepticism that such networks could ever develop the strong ties, local embeddedness, and identity that so strongly characterizes success-

ful communities of practice (Brown & Duguid, 2000, 2001; Cohen & Prusak, 2001). Our study provides early evidence that electronic networks of practice can successfully adapt the message-based communication technology to sustain their practice. Thus, in line with the predictions of technology structuration theories (DeSanctis & Poole, 1994; Orlikowski et al., 1995) and channel expansion theory (Carlson & Zmud, 1999), the low richness medium, by itself, does not prevent individuals from building and sustaining an electronic network of practice.

In this study, we find that Cyber Ba is more accurately described as the combination of codified knowledge with codified knowledge, rather than the combination of explicit with explicit knowledge. Even in instances where specific, explicit knowledge was contributed, group members preferred to provide additional information in the forms of context and embedded messages. So, while text-based communication may lend itself well to explicit knowledge transfer, such as computer code, know-what and knowledge sources, it is not limited to only explicit knowledge transfer. It appears that group members prefer to respond with complex contributions that display their personal level of expertise. In addition, group members also rely heavily on additional, contextual information (implying a higher tacit dimension) even in cases where explicit knowledge may have been sufficient. This would indicate that we need to change our thinking about tacit and explicit knowledge being definitional categories of knowledge types. We argue that tacit/explicit should be conceptualized as a dimension along which knowledge can vary, and that Cyber Ba should be conceptualized as the combination of codified knowledge with codified knowledge that contains both tacit and explicit characteristics.

The second phase of our study appears to demonstrate that knowledge flows from experts to professionals to novices in a stepwise fashion. It seems that all group members, regardless of level of expertise, benefit from participation in the newsgroup, and that experts play a central role by providing knowledge to others. Similar to the findings in Hesse, et al (1993), people seem to benefit differentially from participation in electronic networks. We also find that individual motivations differ in terms of why people participate. This indicates that having a diversity of individuals participating with varying motivations is important for encouraging knowledge flows. Without individuals seeking answers and interested in building social ties with others, there would not be an audience for others interested in sharing their knowledge. Additionally, without individuals who are intrinsically motivated to keep abreast of new ideas and innovations and help others with their problems, seekers would not be able to receive answers.

FUTURE RESEARCH DIRECTIONS

The second purpose of this chapter was to present a multimethod approach to the study of electronic networks of practice. In our analysis, we combined message level data using textual analysis of the message content with survey data from network participants. One of the great advantages of studying knowledge transfer on the Internet is that the technology makes it possible for researchers to actually observe knowledge transfer objec-

tively, by investigating the pattern of message postings, along with the author of the message. Some Web sites even make it possible to collect personal profiles of the individuals participating, ratings of individual participants based on past participation, and member ratings of the quality of responses. This makes it possible to employ a variety of methodologies across multiple levels of analysis to investigate issues of knowledge transfer. In terms of objective data, researchers can investigate issues at the individual level. For instance, by tracking individual participation in electronic networks, researchers can determine who is interacting with whom and to what extent. Methods, such as social network analysis, that examine the pattern of dyadic relationships between people (indicating who is responding to whom), enable researchers to identify individuals who are central, active participants in the network (Grewal et al., 2006; Wasko & Faraj 2005).

In addition to the individual level of analysis, research, has examined dynamics at the network level. For instance, Butler (2001) examines the sustainability of electronic networks of practice by objectively assessing network size in terms of its membership, message volume, and thread dynamics to determine the attraction and retention of members over time. Jones et al. (2004) use objective data to examine how the pattern of communication changes in electronic networks in response to higher communication loads. Using social network analysis, other researchers have examined the underlying structures of electronic networks of practice, and found a pattern resembling scale-free networks, where the vast majority of contributions are sustained by a small minority of participants (Faraj & Johnson, 2005).

However, when objective data is combined with survey data, researchers can also include issues such as why people participate and to what effect. For instance, event-driven survey methodologies have been used to examine the perceived value of the knowledge exchange, by surveying seekers upon posting a question to assess the quality of the responses (Constant et al., 1996). Another study examines the perceptions of trust that form between members of network (Ridings et al., 2002). Adding content analysis enables researchers to determine who says what to whom. The combination of all four methods: objective, survey, social network analysis, and content analysis data has been used to investigate why people participate and help others, and the value of the help provided (Wasko & Faraj, 2005). By taking a multimethod approach to the investigation of knowledge transfer on the Internet, researchers move beyond examining questions related to "what is happening" to more complex questions, such as why and how knowledge transfer takes place.

Of course, Internet technologies have now advanced to the point that Web sites such as secondlife.com and there.com enable knowledge exchange across geographic distance, but provide the appearance of being in the same virtual place through synchronous communications and a shared 3-D experience. People interact with one another through their avatars, which are electronic representations of themselves. While the potential of these new Internet-based "metaverses" to support knowledge exchange is just now being explored, many major corporations and universities are creating initiatives on Second Life that support global knowledge transfer.

Currently, high-tech companies, including Sun Microsystems, Dell, HP, Cisco, Oracle, Accenture, and IBM, have all staked a claim in Second Life. For instance, Sun launched its Sun Pavilion in Second Life, featuring interactive kiosks and an outdoor theater where an avatar representing Sun's chief researcher, John Gage, held a press conference. IBM has purchased 24 Second Life islands (when viewed from above, it forms their logo), more than 3,000 IBM employees have acquired avatars in Second Life, and about 300 routinely use it to conduct company business. IBM has used one of its islands to set up a virtual store for retailer Circuit City, where avatars can move furniture around to find best placements for their electronics at home. On Dell island, an avatar can fly through a gigantic digital version of the Dell SP700, a computer geared at the gaming market. Cisco has built an eight-room house to showcase its networking products, and its research unit holds team meetings in Second Life, bringing together globally dispersed project teams.

Second Life has also emerged as one of the cutting-edge platforms for online education, having sold more than 100 islands for educational purposes, including institutions such as Harvard, Pepperdine, and New York University. The senior editor of the Harvard Business Review gave a talk on marketing in Second Life, in Second Life. Reuters has established a news agency to report on events in Second Life. Sweden has opened an embassy in Second Life, and the United States "Capitol Hill Island" was unveiled earlier this year. Toyota sells cars in Second Life and clothing designer American Apparel sells virtual clothes for avatars.

Future research of knowledge transfer on the Internet will include investigations about how to create "virtual" face-to-face communities of practice on the Internet, mapping the evolution of the community of practice to the electronic network of practice (as we discuss in this chapter), and then its "de-evolution" back towards the initial conceptualizations of communities of practice, and how technology is able to replace physical face-to-face interactions with virtual face-to-face interactions.

REFERENCES

Ahuja, M., Galletta, D., et al. (2003). Individual centrality and performance in virtual R&D groups: An empirical study. *Management Science, 49*(1), 21-38.

Alavi, M., & Leidner, D. (1999). Knowledge management systems: Issues, challenges and benefits. *Communication of the Association for Information Systems, 1,* 1-28.

Alavi, M., & Leidner, D. (2001). Review: Knowledge management and knowledge management systems: Conceptual foundations and research issues. *MIS Quarterly, 25*(1), 107-136.

Argote, L., & Ingram, P. (2000). Knowledge transfer: A basis for competitive advantage in firms. *Organizational Behavior and Human Decision Processes, 82*(1), 150-169.

Brown, J. S., & Duguid, P. (1991). Organizational learning and communities-of-practice: Toward a unified view of working, learning, and innovation. *Organization Science, 2*(1), 40-57.

Brown, J. S., & Duguid, P. (2000). Balancing act: How to capture knowledge without killing it. *Harvard Business Review, May-June*: 73-80.

Brown, J. S., & Duguid, P. (2000). *The social life of information.* Boston, MA: Harvard Business School Press.

Brown, J. S., & Duguid, P. (2001). Knowledge and organization: A social-practice perspective. *Organization Science, 12*(2), 198-213.

Butler, B. (2001). Membership size, communication activity, and sustainability: A resource-based model of online social structures. *Information Systems Research, 12*(4), 346-362.

Carlson, J., & Zmud, R. (1999). Channel expansion theory and the experiential nature of media richness perceptions. *Academy of Management Journal, 42*(2), 153-170.

Cohen, D., & Prusak, L. (2001). *In good company: How social capital makes organizations work.* Boston, MA: Harvard Business School Press.

Constant, D., Sproull, L., et al. (1996). The kindness of strangers: The usefulness of electronic weak ties for technical advice. *Organization Science, 7*(2), 119-135.

Culnan, M. J., & Markus, M. L. (1987). Information technologies. In F. M. Jablin, L. L. Putnam, K. H. Roberts, & L. W. Porter (Eds.), *Handbook of organizational communication: An interdisciplinary perspective* (pp. 421-443). Newbury Park, CA: Sage.

Cummings, J. N., Butler, B., et al. (2002). The quality of online social relationships. *Communications of the ACM, 45*(7), 103-108.

Daft, J. E., Lengel, R. H., et al. (1987). Message equivocality, media selection, and manager performance: Implication for information systems. *MIS Quarterly, 11,* 354-366.

Daft, R. L., & Lengel R. H. (1986). Organizational information requirements, media richness and structural design. *Management Science, 32*(5), 355-366.

Dennis, A., & Kinney, S. (1998). Testing media richness theory in the new media: The effects of cues, feedback and task equivocality. *Information Systems Research, 9*(3), 256-274.

DeSanctis, G., & Poole, M. S. (1994). Capturing the complexity in advanced technology use: Adaptive structuration theory. *Organization Science, 5*(2), 121-147.

Faraj, S., & Johnson, S. L. (2005). Reciprocity or generalized exchange? Structuring of electronic knowledge networks. *Academy of Management Conference,* Honolulu, HI.

Fulk, J., Flanagin, A. J., et al. (1996). Connective and communal public goods in interactive communication systems. *Communication Theory, 6*(1), 60-87.

Grant, R. (1996). Prospering in dynamically competitive environments: Organizational capability as knowledge integration. *Organization Science, 7*(4), 375-387.

Grewal, R., Lilien, G. L., et al. (2006). Location, location, location: How network embeddedness affects project success in open source systems. *Management Science, 52*(7), 1043-1056.

Gupta, A., & Govindarajan, V. (2000). Knowledge flows within multinational corporations. *Strategic Management Journal, 21,* 473-496.

Hesse, B., Sproull, L., et al. (1993). Returns to science: Computer networks in oceanography. *Communications of the ACM, 36*(8), 90-100.

Holsti, O. (1969). *Content analysis for the social sciences and humanities.* Reading, MA: Addison-Wesley.

Jones, Q., Ravid, G., et al. (2004). Information overload and the message dynamics of online interaction spaces: A theoretical model and empirical exploration. *Information Systems Research, 15*(2), 194-210.

Kollock, P. (1999). The economies of online cooperation: Gifts, and public goods in cyberspace. In M. A. Smith and P. Kollock (Eds.), *Communities in cyberspace* (pp. 220-239). New York: Routledge.

Kollock, P., & Smith, M. A. (1996). Managing the virtual commons: Cooperation and conflict in computer communities. In S. Herring (Ed.), *Computer-mediated communication: Linguistic, social and cross cultural perspectives* (pp. 109-128). Amsterdam: John Benjamins.

Lakhani, K., & von Hippel, E. (2000, May). How open source software works: Free user-to-user assistance. *The 3rd Intangibles Conference.* Knowledge: Management, Measurement and Organization, Stern School of Business, NYU.

Lakhani, K., & von Hippel, E. (2003). How open source software works: Free user-to-user assistance. *Research Policy, 32*(6), 923-943.

Nonaka, I., & Konno, N. (1998). The concept of Ba: Building a foundation for knowledge creation. *California Management Review, 40*(3), 40-54.

Orlikowski, W. J. (1996). Learning from notes: Organizational issues in groupware implementation. In R. Kling (Ed.), *Computerization and controversy* (pp. 173-189). New York: Academic Press.

Orlikowski, W. J., Yates, J., et al. (1995). Shaping electronic communication: The metastructuring of technology in the context of use. *Organization Science, 6*(4), 423-444.

Orr, J. (1996). *Talking about machines: An ethnography of a modern job.* Ithaca, NY: ILR Press.

Pickering, J. M., & King, J. L. (1995). Hardwiring weak ties: Interorganizational computer-mediated communication, occupational communities, and organizational change. *Organization Science, 6,* 479-486.

Polanyi, M. (1962). *Personal knowledge: Towards a post-critical philosophy.* New York: Harper & Row.

Powell, W. W., Koput, K., et al. (1996). Interorganizational collaboration and the locus of innovation: Networks of learning in biotechnology. *Administrative Science Quarterly, 41,* 116-145.

Rheingold, H. (1993). *The virtual community: Homesteading on the electronic frontier.* Reading, MA: Addison Wesley.

Ridings, C. M., Gefen, D., et al. (2002). Some antecedents and effects of trust in virtual communities. *Journal of Strategic Information Systems, 11,* 271-295.

Sproull, L., & Faraj, S. (1995). Atheism, sex and databases: The net as a social technology. In B. K. J. Keller (Ed.), *Public access to the Internet* (pp. 62-81). Cambridge, MA: MIT Press.

Van Maanen, J., & Barley, S. R. (1984). Occupational communities: Culture and control in organizations. In B. M. Staw & L. L. Cummings (Eds.), *Research in organizational behavior* (pp. 287-365). Greenwich, CT: JAI Press.

Walther, J. B. (1995). Relational aspects of computer-mediated communication: Experimental observations over time. *Organization Science, 6*(2), 186-203.

Wasko, M., & Faraj, S. (2000). It is what one does: Why people participate and help others in electronic communities of practice. *Journal of Strategic Information Systems, 9*(2-3), 155-173.

Wasko, M. M., & Faraj, S. (2005). Why should I share? Examining knowledge contribution in electronic networks of practice. *MIS Quarterly, 29*(1), 1-23.

Wellman, B., Salaff, J., et al. (1996). Computer networks as social networks: Collaborative work, telework, and virtual community. *Annual Review of Sociology, 22,* 213-238.

Wenger, E. (1998). *Communities of practice.* Cambridge, UK, Cambridge: University Press.

Winter, S., (Ed.) (1987). *Knowledge and competence as strategic assets. The competitive challenge-Strategies for industrial innovation and renewal.* Cambridge, MA: Ballinger.

ADDITIONAL READING

Bagozzi, R. P., & Dholakia, U. M. (2006). Open source software user communities: A study of participation in Linux user groups. *Management Science, 52*(7), 1099-1115.

Blanchard, A., & Horan, T. (2000). Virtual communities and social capital. In G. D. Garson (Ed.), *Social dimensions of information technology: Issues for the new millenium* (pp. 6-21). Hershey, PA: Idea Group.

Donath, J. S. (1999). Identity and deception in the virtual community. In M. A. Smith & P. Kollock (Eds.), *Communities in cyberspace* (pp. 29-59). New York: Routledge.

Hagel, J., & Armstrong, A. G. (1997). *Net.gain: Expanding markets through virtual communities.* Boston, MA: Harvard Business School Press.

Preece, J. (2002). Supporting community and building social capital. *Communications of the ACM, 45*(4), 37-39.

Tapscott, D., & Williams, A. D. (2006). *Wikinomics: How mass collaboration changes everything.* New York: Portfolio.

Teigland, R., & Wasko, M. (2004). Extending richness with reach: Participation and knowledge exchange in electronic networks of practice. In P. Hildreth & C. Kimble (Eds.), *Knowledge networks: Innovation through communities of practice* (pp. 230-242). London: Idea Group Publishing.

APPENDIX A—SUMMARY OF GLOBAL PARTICIPATION

Figures in the top line are sums of aggregate scores of individual level data. Figures on the second line are averages, sums divided by the total number of participants from that nation.

Table 1.

		Members	Tenure	Personal ties	Expertise	Total mssgs	Questions	Responses
1	**Australia**	17	210.00	9.00	69.00	38.00	8.20	8.10
			13.13	0.53	4.06	2.24	0.49	0.48
2	**Belgium**	5	37.00	0.00	19.00	7.00	4.00	0.00
			7.40	0.00	3.80	1.40	1.00	0.00
3	**Brazil**	3	74.00	0.00	16.00	12.00	1.00	2.00
			24.67	0.00	5.33	4.00	0.33	0.67
4	Canada	25	321.00	2.00	110.00	75.00	9.80	15.16
			12.84	0.08	4.40	3.00	0.39	0.61
5	Chile	1	36.00	0.00	4.00	1.00	0.00	1.00
6	China	2	12.00	8.00	9.00	2.00	2.00	0.00
			6.00	4.00	4.50	1.00	1.00	0.00
7	Croatia	1	3.00	0.00	4.00	8.00	0.13	0.88
8	Cyprus	1	6.00	1.00	4.00	1.00	1.00	0.00
9	Denmark	2	13.00	5.00	9.00	2.00	2.00	0.00
			6.50	2.50	4.50	1.00	1.00	0.00
10	Finland	2	9.00	0.00	7.00	2.00	1.00	1.00
			4.50	0.00	3.50	1.00	0.50	0.50
11	France	15	318.30	10.00	67.00	31.00	10.00	5.00
			22.70	0.71	4.79	2.20	0.67	0.33
12	Germany	28	574.00	46.00	121.00	53.00	14.33	13.47
			22.10	1.84	4.84	1.90	0.51	0.48
13	Hong Kong	6	27.00	0.00	18.00	9.00	5.67	0.33
			4.50	0.00	3.00	1.50	0.94	0.06
14	India	2	12.00	3.00	6.00	8.00	2.00	0.00
			6.00	1.50	3.00	4.00	1.00	0.00
15	Ireland	1	5.00	1.00	3.00	7.00	0.00	1.00
16	Israel	5	53.00	3.00	26.00	22.00	1.33	3.67
			13.25	0.60	5.20	4.40	0.27	0.73
17	Italy	4	40.00	4.00	19.00	6.00	3.50	0.50
			10.00	1.00	4.75	1.50	0.88	0.13

continued on following page

Table 1. continued

18	Japan	3	23.00	0.00	11.00	8.00	0.50	2.50
			7.67	0.00	3.67	2.67	0.17	0.83
19	Jordan	1	4.00	0.00	5.00	1.00	0.00	1.00
20	Korea	1	18.00	0.00	5.00	1.00	0.00	0.00
21	Malaysia	1	3.00	0.00	4.00	1.00	1.00	0.00
22	Netherlands	15	206.00	6.00	68.00	47.00	5.67	9.00
23	New Zealand	3	46.00	0.00	9.00	3.00	3.00	0.00
			15.33	0.00	3.00	1.00	1.00	0.00
24	Norway	2	7.00	0.00	8.00	2.00	1.00	1.00
			3.50	0.00	4.00	1.00	0.50	0.50
25	Portugal	3	36.00	14.00	11.00	10.00	2.88	0.13
			12.00	4.67	3.67	3.33	0.96	0.04
26	Romania	1	4.00	0.00	4.00	1.00	1.00	0.00
27	Russia	5	21.00	17.00	26.00	7.00	2.00	3.00
			4.20	3.40	5.20	1.40	0.40	0.60
28	Singapore	2	38.00	0.00	10.00	2.00	2.00	0.00
			19.00	0.00	5.00	1.00	1.00	0.00
29	South Africa	3	13.00	3.00	8.00	7.00	1.80	1.20
			4.33	1.00	4.00	2.33	0.60	0.40
30	Spain	5	81.00	2.00	20.00	11.00	1.75	3.25
			16.20	0.40	4.00	2.20	0.35	0.65
31	Sweden	8	111.00	0.00	24.00	8.00	4.00	4.00
			15.86	0.00	3.00	1.00	0.50	0.50
32	Switzerland	2	10.00	3.00	9.00	2.00	1.00	1.00
			5.00	1.50	4.50	1.00	0.50	0.50
33	Taiwan	1	5.00	15.00	4.00	2.00	1.00	0.00
34	Thailand	1	5.00	0.00	2.00	1.00	1.00	0.00
35	United Kingdom	22	240.00	8.00	87.00	60.00	7.70	14.15
			11.40	0.40	4.14	2.70	0.35	0.64
36	U.S.	2	72.00	6.00	12.00	8.00	0.50	1.50
			36.00	3.00	6.00	4.00	0.25	0.75
	U.S. comm	223	3481.50	282.00	967.00	737.00	79.40	134.30
			16.40	1.32	4.65	3.30	0.36	0.60

continued on following page

Table 1. continued

	U.S. gov	3	30.00	2.00	10.00	7.00	1.40	0.60
			10.00	0.67	3.33	2.33	0.47	0.20
	U.S. network	83	854.00	51.00	231.00	210.00	43.25	38.70
			10.54	0.62	4.00	2.50	0.52	0.47
	U.S. org	8	147.00	6.00	40.00	40.00	0.93	7.07
			18.38	0.75	5.00	5.00	0.12	0.88
	Edu	58	492.00	10.00	225.00	135.00	29.40	28.20
			8.95	0.18	4.10	2.33	0.51	0.49
37	**Yugoslavia**	1	8.00	0.00	6.00	1.00	0.00	1.00

APPENDIX B—EXAMPLES OF RESPONSE MESSAGES

Professional Assessment with context, and embedded message

XXX wrote:
..snip..

> Read the word *long-term*. Did you seriously think that Digital, a HUGE
> company second to IBM would not see the threat of UNIX and someday be
> bought for chump change by a PC company that has been around since the '80's?

ok, i read *long-term*. Could you translate it into some meaningful like
3-years,5-years, 10-years ? Does it matter how long that PC company is around ?
The
simple fact is that this 'PC company' is doing 24B$ a year and is looking to
double
that figure withing the next 2-3 years. Apparently they came to the conlcusion
that
this only would be possible by buying another big name operating in the
enterprise IT segment. So they certainly would fail to become a 50B$ company
by throwing away what Digital could bring in.

>
>
> Things change. I'm a UNIX person, but I can see NT moving into the
> Enterprise in the future. Will UNIX be there (Solaris,HP-UX, & AIX)
> of course - but the NT market will be more than enough for Compaq.

Is that your wish or did Compaq tell you? All predictions for theUNIX market in
years

to come show that it will continue to grow and it will do so in the
enterprise segment. In $ volume it will stay well ahead of NT. Both
Gartner and IDC for the years to come predict that in revenue
UNIX will by 50%+ of the enterprise market while
both see NT's share at 15-20%.

> Again. Read long-term. If UNIX is so important to Compaq, tell me why
> I've never seen Compaq promote UNIX on their servers? Why all I ever
> see is Compaq/Intel/Microsoft NT ads

Because that's where they do their current business. But to grow where theywant
to they have to do something additional. And as far as i understand,
in number of systems Compaq sells quite some UNX.
Compared to NT of course small. And SCO of today is not an enterprise
unix platform.

> IS that the UNIX Compaq is now supporting? They also have Tandem UNIX
> and SCO UnixWare 7.0 Enterprise.

Remember, the Compaq/DIGITAL deal is not done as of yet (FTC and
shareholderapproval pending, EC gave ok). As long as this is, there are some
rules (quiet period)
which prohibit to communicate a lot of things. I don't know how big Tandem's unix
market is, SCO's revenue for last FY was around 180M$. Put that in contrast with
Digital's multi-B$ unix business.

Technical Assessment with context, and an embedded message

>>
>> XXX writes:
>>
>> >In fact, a lot (all?) of the Motorola Suns had Sun's own MMU in. Memory
>> >fades, but either the Motorola chips were late, or didn't do what Sun
>> >wanted, or both.
>>
>> All accept the 68030 based systems.
>
>Did they use the MMU that the '030 had onboard, or did they use the
>external one designed for the '020 (the 68851, as I recall)? I was
                          68451
>involved in a SVR3 port that was running on a '020 board that had the
>off-chip MMU and moved onto a '030 board that used the on-chip MMU, and
>I was struck by how much smaller the cache was (20 contexts rather than
>60? Something like that).

As far as I remember the 68451 did have 96 page table entries

which was the reral limitation. The company where I worked when this

MMU as actual, made a UNIX system with 7 68451 type MMU's for this reason

before they switched from a selfmade UNIX like to Sun systems in 1985.

An example of know-how with context, but no embedded messages

Bill,

Two approaches, both require modeling

1. Top down. Start with a fresh examination of your requirements and then model them. Fit the existing data in at the physical level and only use what you need. If your incumbent solution really is that disparate you are probably doing the safest thing.

2. Reverse engineering. Get every data item in every place you currently have, document them. Then group them into like descriptions. Use this grouping as draft entities and begin an ER process.

You want to do the same for function definitions and processes. In the meantime you need to architect the new system so it all fits together.

I don' t know of any books that can explain all this. I've tried to find a publisher so I could write on but without luck. The only thing that comes close are the chapters I wrote in Oracle Data Warehousing Unleashed by Sams Pub.

An example of know-what with context and embedded messages

In article <35225CF5.8999BCCE@sol.co.uk>,
  XXX writes:
> Arn't they all made by IBM / Motorolla ?
>
> (if wrong please enlighten)

No, TI has been Sun's primary processor foundry for a long time.

An example of source (electronic) with an embedded message, no context

>Beca XXX wrote:
>>
>> If anyone knows of any accounting databases on the web, could you please
>> post them? I would really appreciate it!! Thanks! :-))

>
>
Try looking at www.ardent.com

Good Luck!

Message Content Coding Scheme

Indices	Message #	This is the identifier number for the message posting
	E-Mail	This is the personal identifier for the member posting the message
	Location	This is the last part of the e-mail address identifying the domain of the server
	Original message	1 original post, 0 a response
	Reference message	e-mail of person responding to the message

Message Purpose	Question	This indicates if the post was a request for information
	Response	This indicates if the post was a response to a request
	Announcement	This indicates that the post was neither a request nor a response, but rather the posting of information helpful to the group
	Community std	This refers to a post that tries to set community/group standards
	Professional std	This refers to a post that tries to set standards in the professional community
	Technical alternative	This indicates that the post is giving another point of view
	Other	This indicates that the post does not fall into a previous category
	Spam	This refers to a post that does not contain information that falls within the domain of the group
	Thank you	A specific thanks for receiving help

Knowledge Type	Reference to knowledge source	Does the post contain a specific reference to a person, written materials, electronic source, book
	Clarification	Request for more technical and/or contextual information
	Know-How	Refers to a specific technical procedure "Does anyone know how to.."
	Know-What	Refers to specific technical information "Does anyone know what.."
	Technical assessment	Opinions based on expertise about features/advantages/disadvantages relating to the technology
	Professional assessment	Opinion based on professional expertise about the profession or community as a whole
	Pastime knowledge	Jokes, humor, gossip or news of relevance to the group.

Chapter X
Knowledge Sharing Through Interactive Social Technologies:
Development of Social Structures in Internet–Based Systems Over Time

Isa Jahnke
Dortmund University of Technology, Germany

ABSTRACT

How do the Internet and new interactive Web-based tools, for example, wikis and discussion boards, affect people and their behavior in organizations? This chapter will show the emergence of social structures in Internet-based systems over time. Based on results of an empirical investigation of an Internet-based knowledge-sharing system, the author demonstrates the change of roles, expectations, and activities in online communities. Finally, the author sketches some essential process criteria for introducing online communities, which are extended parts of organizations (e.g., companies and institutions), characterized by a large size and supplemented the formal company.

INTRODUCTION

New buzzwords have become part of our daily lexicon: Web 2.0, social software, and social web, often used as synonyms. These concepts focus on new or existing software systems that are influenced by human communication and collaboration. Web 2.0 is heavily reliant on social interaction, so, social Web-based applications generate a human-centered design approach. Web 2.0 is, as O'Reilly (2005) said, a *"second genera-tion of Internet-based services."* The common idea is to enable people to collaborate and share information online in new ways, such as in wikis, communication tools, social networking sites, and, for example, in Folksonomies. Folksonomy consists of "folk" and "taxonomy."[1] Folksonomy is a 21st century practice of collaboration and taxonomy. People categorize content such as Web pages, online photographs, or Web links. However, they do not do it on their own as a lonesome rider, they generate "tags" (labels) in collaboration with others. This social process is known as social or collaborative tagging. The underlying idea is that many Internet users find more suitable classifications and keywords than a computer or a limited number of people at a company can.

To describe such new concepts and new forms of Internet-based applications, it is appropriate to compare Web 1.0 and the newer Web 2.0. When we do so, we see, for example, that "personal Web sites" disappear and blogging becomes the favored interaction of Internet users. Individual publishing has evolved in the direction of participation. Wikis replace pure "content management systems." Whereas Web 1.0 was focused more on the downloading of prepared information, Web 2.0 transfers the process into communication about the information (for example blogs). The behavior of users is changing from being readers

Figure 1. Shift from Web 1.0 to Web 2.0 (similar to O'Reilly, 2005)

Web 1.0 (mainly 1992-2002)	Web 2.0 (shift since 2003)
Encylopedia Britannica Online / German Brockhaus etc.	Wikipedia.com
Personal Websites	Blogging (e.g., IBM developerWorks Blogs[1])
Publishing	Participation (e.g., pepysdiary.com[2] and many discussion boards)
Content management systems	Wikis
Directories (creating a taxonomy top-down)	Social tagging (Folksonomy': bottom-up), social bookmarking (e.g., del.icio.us[3])
Telephone	Instant Messaging (e.g., ICQ), VoIP (e.g., Skype)
GPS non Internet-based	New location-based services (mobile devices, e.g., Dodge-ball[4])
Newsgroups	Social networking (e.g., facebook.com and xing.com[5]) / online communities
→ Download of information (download of prepared content): one-to-many users	→ Communication & collaboration about the information, creating new knowledge: many-to-many users

[1]   *Retrieved September 9th, 2007, from http://www.ibm.com/developerworks/blogs/*

[2]   *Pepysdiary.com site "is a presentation of the diaries of Samuel Pepys, the renowned 17th century diarist who lived in London, England. A new entry written by Pepys will be published each day over the course of several years; 1 January 1660 was published on 1 January 2003." (Retrieved September 9th, 2007, from http://www.pepysdiary.com/). People discuss Pepys' life and his diary entries by posting own annotations.*

[3]   *Del.icio.us is a social bookmarking site. By using tags, people can organize their own bookmarks and see what other people with similar tags have. This supports the idea to find information from the Internet easier. "Tags are one-word descriptors that you can assign to your bookmarks on del.icio.us to help you organize and remember them. Tags are a little bit like keywords, but they're chosen by you, and they do not form a hierarchy. You can assign as many tags to a bookmark as you like and rename or delete the tags later. So, tagging can be a lot easier and more flexible than fitting your information into preconceived categories or folders." Retrieved September 9th, 2007, from http://del.icio. us/help/tags*

[4]   *Dodgeball site helps to find friends when people are at different places: "Tell us where you are and we'll send messages to all your friends letting them know, so you can meet up. (...) we'll locate friends of friends within 10 blocks (...) find venue locations and broadcast messages to all your friends." Retrieved September 9th, 2007, from http://www. dodgeball.com/*

[5]   *"Facebook is a social utility that connects you with the people around you." Retrieved September 9th, 2007, from http://www.facebook.com/ Similar to Facebook (especially in USA), Xing.com is popular in Europe.*

and consumers (Web 1.0) to authors and producers (Web 2.0). Figure 1 displays both concepts.

In this chapter, we will focus on Web-based groups and communities that are a part of Web 2.0. Many empirical studies and practical projects give insights into the initiation, support, or cultivation of communities (in particular, Preece, 2000; Wenger, McDermott, & Snyder, 2002). Our analysis focuses on communities that predominantly depend upon computer-supported communication, and ask if and how people build forms of social structures (e.g., how the community members collaborate). Our analysis is particularly concerned with social structures, for example: How do they interact and will they build roles (formal/informal roles)? What relevance do computer-mediated social relations have on trust and social capital for online groups in Web 2.0? Does the technical system help to create social proximity? Our in-depth case study of the online community "InPUD," gives indicators about such social structures of virtual groups. These indicators are based on an empirical investigation of the mentioned case.

We will first define the concept of online communities as socio-technical systems, define what an online community is, and highlight the social structures of online communities. An essential indicator of social structures is the development of roles (Section 2). In Section 3, we describe the case study of the empirical investigation of the InPUD Community, as an example of Web 2.0 applications, and describe what InPUD actually is. In Section 3, we describe also the research method. Section 4 derives empirical results from the case, and shows aspects of social structures that have been developed, based on interactive social technologies (such as Web 2.0). Section 5 sketches some essential process criteria for introducing online communities supplemented to formal organizations. Section 6 offers a conclusion, and Section 7 looks forward to possible future areas of study.

INTERNET-BASED COMMUNITIES AND SOCIAL STRUCTURES

Online communities are good examples of typical socio-technical systems (cf. Coakes, 2002): On the one side, such Internet-based communities consist of actors who use technical systems to communicate and share knowledge. On the other side, the technical system influences the communication of the community members. An online community owes its existence to the fact that the technical system exists. People who participate and interact in Internet-based communities share knowledge and communicate "through" the technical systems (for example, discussion boards, instant messaging, or networking tools). Such socio-technical phenomena were investigated especially by Preece (2000), Kim (2000), Williams and Cothrel (2000) and, Wenger et al. (2002), who give design criteria for cultivating pure online communities as well as communities of practice (as internal part of business companies).

Definitions of Online Communities

Our contribution follows the definition of "*communities of practice*" created by Lave and Wenger (1991, p. 98) and Wenger et al. (2002, p. 4). Web-based communities are generated through social relationships among individuals "*who share a concern, a set of problems, or a passion about a topic, and who deepen their knowledge and expertise in this area by interacting on an ongoing basis.*" Similar to Preece et al. (Preece, Abras, & Maloney-Krichmar, 2004), we use the term "*online communities*" to describe all online groups that have some kind of online presence, but these groups differ in the following four areas:

- The size (small groups with just 25 people (members); big groups with hundreds or thousands of people (members).
- The primary content (e.g., discussion boards about specific books or movies; discussions

about sports like marathon training; communication about stock exchanges; information sharing about classes at universities).

- The lifespan (several years or just for one topic).

- The type of communication: "*Whether the community exists only virtually, or has a physical presence, or exists primarily through physical connections, for example a networked neighborhood*" (Preece et al., 2004, p. 3).

Value of Participation in Online Communities

In contrast to companies and organizations, where the members are rather formally bound (e.g., by work contracts), online communities consist of informal connections between members, however, with strong ties (Granovetter, 1973). "*Communities are defined as collections of individuals bound by informal relationships*" says Snyder (1997, in Lesser & Prusak, 1999). Koch (2002) reported online communities as a set of people who are willing to help each other in order to accomplish their own goals. Wenger et al. (2002) add that the members form a "*joint enterprise and the community continually renegotiates itself through its members.*" The members act in good faith, they trust each other, although they may not normally act in such a way: *I will help you, even if you do not help me immediately because I know you, or another community member, will assist me when I need support* (cf. Putnam, 1995). This underlying idea of altruism[7] affects active participation and mutual support as well as collaborative knowledge sharing. Mutual support is given for example through feedback, annotations, and comments, sharing ideas, answering questions, mutual reviews, and so forth.

However, this view on computer-mediated social interaction neglects the role of the "lurker": just a few community members, in relation to the whole group, answer questions of the others, while the majority of the community members only read the information and do not actively participate. The description of such members who "*observe what is going on but remain silent*" is "*lurker*" (cf. Preece, 2000, p. 87).

Further investigations about roles in online settings, such as elders, leaders, regulars, novices, and visitors, did particularly Kim (2000) and Preece et al. (2004). These kinds of denotations (of the term "role") are focused on the number of postings of the community members and the date of registration. It neglects the difference between formal and informal roles, how the members interact with others, and the dynamic change of roles and social structures.

Social Structures and Roles

Mackinnon (2006) reviewed the literature on the concept of social structures. He comes to the conclusion that different definitions emphasize "*social structures as a set of elements in mutual relation to each other*– also known as social networks. Instead of just mutual relations, Jary and Jary (1991, p. 465) describe the term "social structures" as a "*relatively enduring pattern or interrelationship of social elements,*" that is, expectations, social interaction and relationships within social systems. This notion of social structures, as relationships between different members of groups or as enduring and relatively stable patterns of relationships, emphasizes the idea that social and socio-technical systems, for example online communities, are grouped into sets of patterns often defined as roles with different functions, meanings, or purposes. Lave and Wenger (1991) give similar results from their analysis of "*legitimate peripheral participation.*" Hence, the analysis of social systems as well as online communities needs, besides the analysis of social networks, especially the analysis of social roles. The emergence and change of social roles in virtual communities are essential observable aspects that influences and forms the social structure of communities and vice versa.

Social roles are often defined as sets of expected activities performed by individuals. According to Dahrendorf (1958), a role is the sum of all behavior expectations of a social system (all different members) towards a concrete role actor. From this viewpoint, a role is a set of descriptions defining the expected behavior of a position (Biddle & Thomas, 1966).

Instead of roles in social systems, roles in socio-technical systems (e.g., online communities) depend primarily on technically mediated communication. Therefore, the development of roles in online communities can be particularly observed through the written communications of community members. Then, a role is a perceivable interaction pattern created through the repetition of social interaction[8]. Such repeated and anticipated behavior leads to expectations that characterize a role.

A role consists of the following aspects with four observable factors (cf. especially our prior publication that includes a full description of roles for designing community systems: Herrmann, Jahnke, & Loser, 2004):

1. **Position:** Members' position in the online community in relation to the others (also known as network position): How many and what social/communicative contacts has a member to others?
2. **Tasks/Activities:** what primary activity is conducted by the member? (e.g., moderating, lurking, contributing)
3. **Expectations:** How do community members communicate to others the expectations they have about behavior in online discussions (rules of online behavior)? Do members communicate just factual information (aspect of content) and/or could we observe indices of information about their relationships to the others (aspect of relationship)?
4. **Online interactions (Role-playing):** A role is built and changed by individuals by way of their communication and social interaction. Roles are gradually developed in online communities by perceiving the repetition of social interaction patterns. Such repeated and anticipated behavior leads to expectations that characterize a role. These patterns can metaphorically be described as *role-mechanisms*. Role-mechanisms describe how people take a role or assign someone a role. The role-mechanisms are, for example, role-assignment, role-taking, to allow someone's role-taking, role-changing, role-making, role-(re)defining (Herrmann et al., 2004, p.169). Herrmann et al. (2004) explain the role mechanisms, and describe empirically how to find and support such role mechanisms in Internet-based community systems.

CASE STUDY: THE INPUD COMMUNITY—AN EXAMPLE OF WEB 2.0

What was the Problem?

In 2001, the Department of Computer Science at the University of Dortmund in Germany had about 2,000 students. However, in the years between 1996 and 2001, problems occurred. A lot of students did not achieve the degree of computer science (statistic report from 2001). This report made clear that many students ended their computer science courses after three or four semesters without degree[9] or even moved to another the university; others did not take the written examinations. But we did not know exactly why the students were failing and so we wanted to find out why the students were dropping their computer science studies. Our assumption was based on the "organizational problem." We assumed that the problem was not just related to the content of the courses but with the study management. So, the primary question for our research was: How do German students organize their studies at a university? Do they have enough information about how to organize their studies successfully?[10]

Additionally, the university has a wide diversity of roles: students who are beginners, who are experts, there are tutors for course guidance, study management advisors, lecturers, an examinations office, a registry office, and so on. To conclude, there are many people in different roles who support student's activities. Each of them has a lot of information and knowledge about study management. However, the problem seems to be their joint collaboration. Do they really cooperate and share knowledge as well as they could in order to help and promote students?

What Exactly is the InPUD Community?

The InPUD community[11] can be described as an "online knowledge sharing community" for computer science students at the University of Dortmund, Germany. The InPUD community differs from other communities that are built in spare time and that are not a part of a company.

According to the characteristics from Preece et al. (2004, see also Section 2), the InPUD community is characterized by a large size (more than 1,500 people), and is an extended part of the Department of the mentioned university supplemented to the formal organization. The primary content of InPUD is knowledge (and its

Figure 2. Screenshot of InPUD (in more detail: http://www.inpud.de)

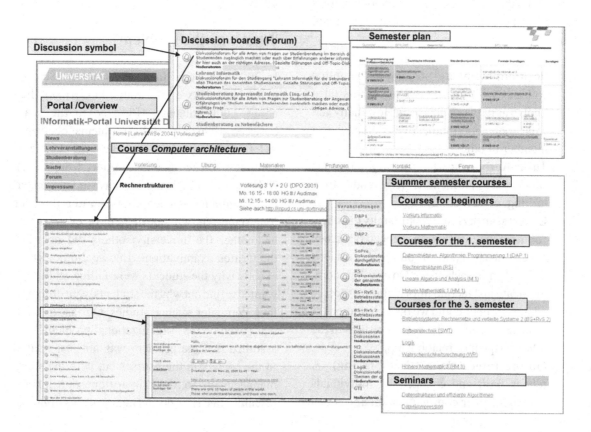

collaborative creation) about the study of computer science, its courses, and study management. The students get information about how to study successfully, and the opportunities to discuss study management, content, and exercises of lectures as well as seminars. Thus, InPUD helps to share information to improve the practice. The community exists primarily online, but has also a physical presence through physical connections, for example, networked students in different courses. InPUD was launched in 2002.

In detail, the InPUD Community includes an overview of all classes and lectures that are offered during the course of a semester. The way that the information is structured is the same for each lecture or seminar. The information about the lectures, including any tutorials that are being held (and when they are being held), course materials, notices for examinations, lecturer contact information, and often a free discussion forum are included, as well as news and search functions.

The information and content about the study management domain were integrated with online discussion boards. These enabled the potential members to build active social interactions. The discussion boards exist for each lecture as well as for study management. They are embedded into an information Web site that includes facts about course guidance, as well as graphical maps of how to study which course at which time.[12] The discussion boards include discussions about selected lectures. (At the time of writing, 30 boards are online, each with their own moderator.) It is possible to discuss exercises and their solutions on the discussion boards. Furthermore, there is information, and discussion boards, that have been initiated by study management advisors, course guidance, or counseling services. The discussion boards include questions and answers referring to course guidance, for example, *"how to study successfully," "how and where to register for written examinations," "where to find the university calendar (timetable)," "what are the contents of computer science courses," "which semester is best suited for studying abroad,"* and so forth. Figure 2 shows a screenshot of InPUD.

Many members participated. The community members are primarily people (in particular students) from the Department of Computer Science at the University of Dortmund, Germany, but also people who are interested in studying at the department (e.g., high school students). The community members are also made up of advisors

Figure 3. Continuous flow to more usage (dark bars show beginning of new semesters)

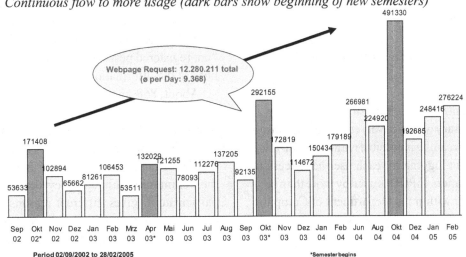

Figure 4. InPUD discussion board—Number of contributions per individual

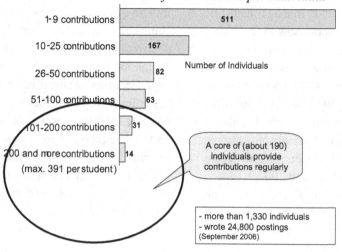

from counseling services, course guidance, and the examinations office. The initiated and empirically investigated community InPUD currently has more than 1,300 members.

The InPUD community consists of students who could theoretically meet at lectures. However, this face-to-face communication is, in fact, unlikely due to the fact that the courses are oversubscribed; sometimes there are as many as 600 students in a single course; direct social interaction with each person seems to be not realistic.

Stages of Development of the InPUD Community

The InPUD community is continuously increasing. Since the launch in May 2002, more than 1,330 registered participants have written more than 24,000 contributions. Registration and login is only necessary when actively contributing. Observation and reading is possible without registration and without logging in; each user has access to all information. InPUD is used by more than 60% of students within the Department of Computer Science at the University of Dortmund.

The number of requests has grown consistently, and the access rate usually peaks at the beginning of a new semester. In October 2002 there were only 171,408 requests. A year later, in October 2003, there were 292,155 requests and in October 2004, this had increased to 491,330 requests. To this day, requests are continually increasing (see Figure 3).

Figure 4 shows the analysis of the communication structure: About 2,000 students (100%) are enrolled at the Department of Computer Science at the German University of Dortmund. More than 1,330 (66.5%) were registered in September 2006. About 670 students (33.5%) are not registered at the InPUD community. We do not know if these "not registered persons" are lurkers or if they do not use the information portal.

About 868 members (of 1,330 registered members) contribute actively. The other 462 members are registered but did not post. We assume that these registered InPUD lurkers (23.1% of 2,000 students) want to show their interest in the community although they did not actively participate. It gives different reasons why they do not post (e.g., motivation, no personal need, curiosity without exposure; see Section 2; cf.

Preece, 2000). Maybe they are waiting for "the right" moment for posting.

A core (of about 190) individuals regularly provide contributions: ranging from 26 to 391 postings (questions/answers) per individual. That is a significant number. The core members are the elders, leaders, and partly the regulars (cf. Kim, 2000). The other 678 active members (167 and 511) make postings in the range from 1 to 25. These members can be described as regulars, too, but include also novices and visitors (cf. Kim, 2000).

The InPUD discussion board provides an awareness tool (provides information about activities of the users, formal roles. and current status) that shows who and how many users are online at a given time.[13] The large number of participants indicates that a significant number of students appreciate this form of knowledge sharing. They discuss, ask questions, answer the questions of others, come up with new ideas, and help each other.

As already stated, the community also includes lecturers and tutors as well as study management advisors. Therefore, it is possible to say that the success of the InPUD community can be measured by the significant number of students who actively participate. More than 60% of computer science students participate and use the community contents.

How we Analyzed the Problem: The Action Research Process (An Exploratory Research Method)

Starting from the problem of the organization of the study management, we started the WIS-project[14] in 2001. The aim was both first to find out, on the one hand, what the barriers to studying were and to establish which factors lead to success for students of computer science and second, to give the results back to the students in order to initiate a discussion about these issues. To sum-

marize, the purpose of the empirical procedure was to help students build their online community about study management. Besides the practical purposes, we used the project in order to study people's behavior, as well as emerging changes of social structure and social roles in that online community.

Thus, the project was based on an empirical exploratory research method including ethnographic observations and qualitative interviews and questionnaires as well as action research processes. The exploratory method was essential since we did not have sufficient theses in order to explain why the students dropped their studies. Action research is an iterative process that enables us to understand a social or sociotechnical phenomenon or to improve its quality. It consists of several phases of analysis (reflection) and action (interventions) that are alternate and interwoven. Avison et al. (Avison, Lau, Neilsen, & Myers, 1999) calls it a cycle of activities: "*Action research involving researchers and practitioners acting together on a particular cycle of activities, including problem diagnosis, action intervention, and reflective learning (...) in real situations, gain feedback from this experience, modify the theory as a result of this feedback, and try it again*" (Avison et al.,1999, pp. 94-95). Our empirical procedure included the following phases of action research:

Part 1: Main Steps of Implementation Process

Identifying the problem(s): Based on semistructured interviews, we found out the student's main problems with study management. The interviews, held between 2001 and 2002 with an open-ended interview guide, included 14 people face-to-face (8 students and 6 professors/lecturers). The diversity of how students manage their studies was summarized in the following nine areas (main problems):

1. Students know the importance of attending lectures and learning groups, though they do not attend courses.[15]

2. Informal learning groups: students know how helpful a learning group is, but a lot of them do not create or participate.

3. The city of residence of the students is often not the same as the place where they study (many students travel to university each day by car or bus).

4. The majority of students take on jobs to fund their studies; consequently, they have less time to attend courses.

5. New students at German universities need a high degree of self-organization, but they have not learnt (and it has not been taught) to organize themselves prior to attending university.

6. There is a significant amount of information available about computer science courses; however, there is no single portal organizing this information. As a result, students are forced to search through a jungle of information to find a suitable course.

7. A large number of students say they become disoriented during the regular nine semesters (4-5 years), becoming unsure of when to attend which lectures and seminars and when to register for which examinations.

8. New students have a false impression of what a course in computer science really entails.

9. The university experience is not just about studying, many students want to find out about themselves and develop their own personalities.

Based on the empirical-based main problems, a standardized questionnaire was sent out to the computer science students at the University of Dortmund. Three hundred and eighty four completed questionnaires were returned. This represented a total of about 20% of all computer science students enrolled in the bachelor courses. The results confirmed the thesis: The majority of students know theoretically how to organize themselves for a successful computer science course, but they did not practice it.

In addition, the interviews and the questionnaire should also find answers about "how to" spread the main problems into the students' groups in order to create awareness and to encourage discussions about possible solutions. Hence, we decided to use Internet-based tools for two reasons: (1) due to the large number of students that would be involved and (2) to document the process for the next generation of students. Thus, the way to an Internet-based information portal was built.

Creating an information portal: The interview results gave the idea to create an Internet-based information portal that would offer an overview of each lecture, seminar, and course per semester, a graphical plan of the first four semesters (according to a bachelor degree). Second, the portal would enable information from the study management advisors and other university roles. In May 2002, the first prototype of the community system called "InPUD" (Informatic Portal University of Dortmund: http://www.inpud.de) was launched.

Support ways of active communication and collaboration: Based on empirical insights into the InPUD prototype, we added a discussion board about study management, the nine areas (which see), and selected courses in September 2002. The aim was to improve the transparency of the study management factors that are critical for success. Information about study management and seminar content was interwoven with online discussion boards. Thus, a computer-mediated knowledge-sharing system was created. The knowledge-sharing process was based upon voluntary participation. As we will describe later, that was the beginning of an online community.

Continuous improvement: From 2002 to 2006, the project team enhanced the technical system and changed some things, for example, to improve the performance of the technical system. Meanwhile, a lot of new discussion boards were added, likewise more information about study management was included. The InPUD community grew.

Part 2: Analyzing the Implementation Process in Order to Study Emerging Social Structures

Especially from 2002 to 2006, we analyzed the InPUD community and its emerging social structures based on the following research methods.

First in 2003-2004, interviews with eight experts were held face-to-face. The experts came from the area of study management, had experiences of "university management," and knew Web-based IT-Systems very well. We asked what the crucial factors for successful study management were, in order to compare the experts' statements with InPUD's development. Based on the empirical results of the interviews with the experts, we supported the InPUD community with new ideas, for example, giving members with formal roles a role name and making roles visible; for instance, the study management advisors were labeled explicitly. Furthermore, we conducted participant observation of the online discussions in InPUD from 2002-2006. Moreover, the analysis also regarded user statistics, communication structures, as well as qualitative content analysis that focused on social relationships, to understand the social interactions.

As a result, in this exploratory action research process, we identified empirically based theses about the emergence of social structures through social interactive technologies. The results can be found in the next Section, number 4.

SOCIAL STRUCTURES OF THE InPUD COMMUNITY

Our empirical analysis focuses on social structures and in particular, the development and dynamic of (existing and new) roles in Internet-based communities that depend on technically mediated communication. In the InPUD case, we have analyzed how people build social structures in online communities. We subdivided social structures with four criteria: network position, task/activities, expectations, and role-playing (cf. Section 2). From our exploratory case study about the online community InPUD (from 2001 to 2006), we can derive the following results. These results, empirical-based theses, were derived from our exploratory study. Hence, the results are not representative, but can spark off new ideas and innovative new theses about further visions of social structures of Internet-based knowledge sharing systems and online communities.

(1) The Member's Position in the Online Community and Changing of Position

(1.1) Members Of Online Communities Build Different Qualities Of Social Relationships, Just in Time When Needed

We observed that the members of the InPUD community, particularly students, develop social relationships online. Some people even build social ties, for example, the same people met habitually at the same discussion board at the same time. Wenger et al. 2002 call these members "*the core of the community*," what Kim (2000) differentiates as elders, leaders, und regular members. (Novices and visitors are outside of the core; rather on the edge; cf. Kim, 2000). The emergences of social ties were affected by following aspects:

First, the analysis shows that it was not necessary to create a face-to-face communication among students before the online community was created. The students did not take advantage of the opportunity to build social relationships at face-to-face meetings (e.g., seminars, lectures) because of the fact that there can be more than several hundred students at lectures. Although the interviewed experts said it would be important to promote face-to-face communication before cultivating a Web-based community, we know today that this is not correct for every online setting: we explain these differences with homogenous and heterogeneous groups.

Homogenous groups: The students of InPUD build homogenous interests and therefore, a face-to-face workshop is unnecessary. The underlying idea is that homogenous groups have same (or similar) interests and therefore, the members act truthful and rely on the others (in more detail, see point 3.1).

Heterogeneous groups include people who work in hierarchical dependences, for example, in the investigated case people work in different formal roles, for instance, they are advisors, part of the counseling services, at the examination office, at the registry office, and they are lecturers and so on. Such people, in different formal roles, do not have the same goals (although they may have many similar interests in the context of student support).[16] Consequently, it might be better to create a trust-building face-to-face workshop before you support their knowledge sharing with IT. For example, the "central office for study management at the university" creates a face-to-face workshop for advisors at each department.

Second, the analysis of InPUD shows that the online communication, through the medium of the technical system, gives the community members the opportunity to find people with the same topic, problem, or passion. A person can find people with the same interests within a large rather anonymous group. From the individual's viewpoint, a community helps her/him to become *"someone with a (new) name"*: a person who needs information from others but also has information for other people.

Third, the InPUD members could foster their collaborative knowledge sharing under the condition of a minimum of formal regulations and limited university control. For instance, without registration, every person, also external people,

can read all of the InPUD content. Registration is just required when anyone wants to give answers or pose questions. Additionally, the registration needs just a username and an e-mail address.

Finally, InPUD is open 24 hours a day, and people are able to connect to others. Some students really answered questions and helped other students at night. Instead of one-to-many users' communication, InPUD is able to support the communication from many-to-many users, and promote the *"wisdom of the crowds"* (Surowiecki, 2004).[17]

In summary, these settings enable the InPUD community and its members to build different qualities of social relationships online, right at the moment when people need knowledge. Therefore, the InPUD members combine their knowledge and may develop their own understanding in a collaborative effort.

As mentioned in Section 2, each community includes also the role of lurkers: the majority of the community members just read the information and do not actively participate. We could observe this phenomenon also in the investigated InPUD community during the community stages of development; start (in 2002), phase of initial growth (2002-2004), and phase of sustainable development (2005-2006). The InPUD lurkers did not give an active input. These people gain knowledge from other active members without sharing. The high number of lurkers seems to be a problem. However, that is not a problem, since they have the essential function of spreading information about the existence of the community into other groups. The specific relationship that is developed between active members and lurkers decides if the knowledge-sharing system works successfully.

Furthermore, in contrast to usual lurkers, some of the InPUD lurkers did not post but they were registered. We explain this phenomenon as follows. These registered lurkers want to show they are part of the community and they want to support the community, but there are many individual reasons why they do not post. Based on Preece's (2000, p. 89) research, this can include, for example, personal factors, desire for privacy, interaction mechanisms (fear of embarrassing oneself), and the time for posting. She lists further reasons, based on empirical analysis, given by lurkers for not posting. It might be that such registered lurkers become active users later.

(1.2) The Visible Value Of Benefit; Providing Immediate Support and Building More Social Capital

Meeting on a virtual community platform has not the same quality as participating in a *"bowling team"* (Putnam, 1995). Nevertheless, for people who are unable to find other people with the same interests in face-to-face situations, meeting in an online community is better than not meeting at all. That is one essential and easy-to-know benefit.

The Internet-based InPUD community gives its members easy access to many people and their knowledge, this is called "social capital" of a group. *"Social capital is the sum of the resources, actual or virtual, that accrue to an individual or a group by virtue of possessing a durable network of more or less institutionalised relationships of mutual acquaintance and recognition"* (Bourdieu, & Wacquant, 1992, p. 119). In other words, social capital is the access to people, their knowledge, and possibly immediate support. A person knows someone, or someone of someone, who can help. Such immediate help, for instance, a person's problem can be solved immediately through other people, is one of the added values of an online community. To conclude, the access to a large social group is the potential for cultivating more social capital and knowledge sharing.

Nahapiet and Goshal (1998) distinguish the concept of social capital into three dimensions: The structural dimension identifies the *"patterns of connections between actors - that is who you reach and how you reach them"* (p. 244). Second, the relational dimension describes the form of

"personal relationship people have developed with each other." In the InPUD community, the relationships are built through computer-supported communication over a period of time. Trust plays an important role. Fukuyama says that social capital is the social capability that develops when trust in a social system exits (Fukuyama, 1995, p. 26). Finally, the cognitive dimension identifies the *"shared representations,"* norms, and *"systems of meaning."*

In summary, the more members actively participate, with personal relationships as well as similar social values and meanings, the more social capital will be created. According to Wellman et al. (Wellman, Hasse, Witte, & Hampton, 2001), who demonstrated that the Internet is increasing interpersonal connectivity and organizational involvement, the empirical analysis show that In-PUD leads also to an increase in social capital.

The building of social capital depends also on the quality of social ties. But the *"development of weak ties is better than not meeting at all"* (Preece, 2000, p.24). The analysis gave some hints about the core members of InPUD who built rather strong ties. The members do not share just pure information, but they also wrote some emotional sentences to create social relationships (cf. point 1.1 as well as point 1.3 about online presence and social proximity). For example, the members *"wish good luck for the exams"* and said *"thank you"* when other people helped them.

(1.3) Online Presence and Social Proximity Through Technical Systems

Based on the InPUD analysis, some members are better visible than others because of their numbers or quality of contributions to online discussions (similar to Kim, 2000: elders, leaders, and regulars vs. novices and visitors). The degree of online presence affects the perception of the people, their expectations, and finally, their behavior. For instance, such students who made postings more frequently and more regularly gave answers than others (e.g., who are just one time contributors) are more and better visible within the Web-based community (cf. Section 3, statistic analysis: several members post contributions every day).

The people's motivation behind this social interaction, degree of online presence by written contributions, is similar to aspect 1.1 (which see): to build social ties. Furthermore, interviews with students showed that some of them wanted to "*break out*" from the anonymous mass (from the large student's group of about 2,000 members). The online community gives the students the chance to keep in touch with people with the same problems. A second argument is the "self-profiling" (self-expression) of those people. Third, other members respect members more when they are more present in InPUD. In other words, in the minds of the users the more regular online presence is connected with a higher degree of competency that can result in a higher status assigned by others to such "leaders." To conclude, some interviewees assume a connection between the frequency and quality of contributions, on the one hand, and a higher social status and acceptance in the community, on the other hand. Moreover, such a higher online status also has impacts on their lives outside of InPUD. These people might feel more confident in their face-to-face communication as a result of their increased online social status. For instance, interviews with some students at the Department of Computer Science showed that some students also know the strong members personally, behind their usernames, and when they want they could meet them face-to-face.

The online presence also influences kinds of "online social proximity" through the technical system (what we describe as computer-mediated social proximity). Indicators for such online proximity are emotional interaction patterns, for example, they say "thank you" or wish "good luck" with exams and further hints. In summary, some contributions drift from the main topic, just pure information, to questions about personal interests, for example, "*where do you live?*" that

have positive influences on the building of social proximity.

(2) Tasks/Activities in Online Communities

The InPUD community has many participating members; hundreds of people who give ideas or share their knowledge online. The differences between communities and organizations, such as companies and institutions, are the established formal processes, work roles, and tasks. The InPUD community is successful due to the fact that it has less formal roles. That means for organizations with knowledge sharing problems, they are not so successful since their processes are more formalized. They might need the support of more informal communication, for example, computer-supported communities or communities of practice.

During the initial stages (in 2002), the majority of the InPUD community's members occupied the same position. Tasks were transparent for each new member. At the outset of InPUD, the main tasks were following:

- Posting/contributing (function: provides information for the community or asks questions)
- Only reading (function: takes the information and spreads it to the outside world)
- Formal facilitating by academic staff (function: gives rules, checks conventions)

In the initial growth phase (from 2002-2004), we observed that the members began to employ new forms to communicate. We define these new forms as "informal posting activities." For example, some core members took the part of the informal moderator. They did not have the formal role of a moderator, but guided the other members with words. The following points illustrate the differentiation of those informal posting activities (in more detail see Herrmann et al., 2004):

- **Author:** Contributes information, communicates own ideas by writing short statements. InPUD members add own contributions and ideas, for example, *"It would be nice, if the Department had a central Web site with all information about the computer science courses. Inpud is a good idea. Unfortunately some people in the department do not work sufficiently with Inpud."*

- **Scaffolding:** Person who gives structure to the discussion, for example: *"Please, look at the thread of study management, before you ask the same questions like the others before"*; *"This question was already answered in thread 19."*

- **Reading as visitor (cf. Kim 2000):** Reads contributions of other users; visitor: only interested in getting an orientation without making own contributions (gets inspiration), for example, one member wrote: *"I am not a member of this university."*

- **Conflict mediator:** Acts as mediator in emotional conflicts (e.g., when two people or more have a dispute); intervention in emotional discussions (to enable the discussion to continue), for example: *"I understand your problem, and it is good that you want to change something, but this thread is not the right way to solve your problem. Would you mind talking with the professor face-to-face?"*

- **Technical supporting:** Solves technical problems (e.g., a person has problems with the discussion board since it is off-line at the weekend; the technical-supporter helps and explains the use of the technical system), for example: *"Why is the board so often off-line at the weekend?"* The answer of a different user in the informal role of technical-helper was: *"I just asked the technical project team and they said they had upgraded the software. The new version should work in two weeks. Hopefully they are right."*

- **Conclusion making:** Adds comments to the process of communication; has an essential influence on the content discussion, for example: *"From my point of view, it looks like ..."* or *"Summarized... ."*

- **Promoter of the procedure:** Makes the current procedure more transparent; supports task completion; positively promotes the discussion or activities; motivates to participate, for example: *"Yes, I could explain the seven answers of the exam after the exam – when there are enough students who will participate. I suggest Wednesday, 14 February, 10am in room E28. I will not do this if there are just 3 or 4 people, so, come on, and all come to the meeting."*

- **Organizational supporter:** Helps to give another view of the activities (metalevel: communication about the communication), support to think about organizational conventions (e.g., how to communicate), for example: *"Why have you written this posting three times? Please, wait a moment before you write it again"* or *"You say that someone says the script would be online, but where is it and who said this?"*

- **Decision initiator:** Combines diverging contributions by relating them to a summarizing statement; if the discussion diverges, the person calls for an informal vote to reach consensus, for example: *"Do we share this view of the problem?"*

To conclude, during the growth phase, the InPUD community was able to build new informal roles. These developments are continuing.

In the phases of sustainable development of InPUD (from 2005-2006), the analysis showed particularly a lot of new members who were in formal roles, for example, moderating tasks by lecturers, academic staff, and professors). These new formal members started a lot of new topics on the discussion boards (e.g., studying abroad, women in computer science, discussions about new courses of bachelor and master).

Nevertheless, the students, and not the formal members, were the driving force behind InPUD. Because of their high number as well as good practice, they pushed the academic staff and other students to become involved in this online collaboration and communication.

(3) Expectations Affecting the Behavior of Other Members

(3.1) Trust (Implicit Expectation)

All online communities build their potential on the basis of trust. Shneiderman (2000, p.58) says that trust is *"the positive expectation a person has for another person, organization, tool, or process that is based on past performance and truthful future guarantees made by a responsible person or organization."* The process of trust building in the Internet-based InPUD community is computer-mediated and based only on online communication with little face-to-face contact. Hence, the InPUD members who communicate with other InPUD users do not generally know them outside of this virtual space. Furthermore, anonymity can also be maintained, if desired, by the use of a discreet username. Similar to Schmidt (2000), we distinguish between four areas of trust. These are design criteria for facilitating trust:

1. Trust in the identity of the others: who is the person behind the name that I see on my computer screen?
2. Trust in the interests and motives of others: Which interests/motives does she/he follow/have? Why does she/he communicate with me? Is the person acting faithfully and giving honest statements?
3. Trust in the expertise of others: Does she/he know enough about these things to help me?

4. Trust in others' played roles: which role does she/he play?

Internet-based communities (like the InPUD community) need particularly *pre*trust in the beginning. Betrayal of trust can have a significant negative impact on the online community, and can limit or dissolve collaborative learning. *"When there is trust among people, relationships flourish; without it, they wither"* (Preece, 2000, p. 191). Therefore, the question is how to encourage trust in computer-mediated communities?

Similar to Shneiderman's model (2000) to facilitate trust, we *clarified the context;* for example, we made transparent that InPUD is part of the Department of Computer Science. Second, it was important to *"make clear commitments,"* for instance, each board has a description about possible content and the announcement that *"off topic discussions will be deleted."* And finally, the trust building was supported by ensuring that each discussion board had one or more formal moderators, a task that is obligatory taken by academic personnel. The static information in InPUD is also checked by the academic personnel, in particular, by the administrators. Therefore, the formal moderators, although they act as facilitator moderately and not often, also gave the InPUD community the context for facilitating trust.

(3.2) How Online Role Naming Affects Expectations

In the case of the InPUD community, the formal role of the moderator and others with responsibilities, such as study management advisors, counseling services, or people offering course guidance, are integrated into the community by an "online role presence," for example, *"Mr. Miller, Advisor of Study Management"* or *"Mrs. Smith, Lecturer for Computer Science Study: Human-Computer-Interaction."* To summarize, the formal roles were visible when people communicated online.

This formal role presence also helps new community members who can easier assess the quality of information through the member's role (e.g., formal moderator and advisors). The members, in particular students, ascribe more expertise and knowledge to those members who have formal roles. So, the empirical investigation shows that online role presence is essential when checking the quality of the given information. In conclusion, the visible presence of role names improves the ability to assess the quality of the information given, and this may improve the frequency and quality of requests that finally encourage the members and affects the evolution of a community (cf. trust, in point 3.1).

(4) Role-Playing: The Emergence of Online Interaction Patterns (Roles)

The InPUD analysis illustrated the development of roles over a period of time, for example, the interaction pattern of active people, the promoter, the conclusion maker, the decision initiator, and the conflict mediator (cf. point 2: differentiations of informal activities). These perceivable interaction patterns provided a structure for a joint online communication. We describe this by the following examples:

- Our analysis of the InPUD community provides indices for the importance of a moderator (cf. point 3.2) and a promoter: a person who feels responsible for the growth of the community. During the first stage of InPUD's development of a common culture (in 2002), the formal role of a moderator, as well as a promoter, was essential. However, the frequency of their comments is less important than the fact that the other (or new) members know that a moderator exists and she/he can delete contributions or comment on false contributions. If there is a moderator's role, it is also essential to make the rules and (off)topic contents vis-

ible. The moderators *"must learn to achieve a balance,"* (Preece, 2002, p. 291). In the InPUD case, "balance" means that the moderator should act in a moderate way, for example, delete off-topic remarks, comment on factually incorrect answers, clarify which content may be discussed, which topics are not required, and make them visible. To summarize, the InPUD moderators have a very moderate position; they only provide answers when other students had no idea or provided incorrect answers.

- Other members, often students, also took part in informal moderation activities. In InPUD, the formal moderator role is often supported by students as informal moderator. These informal moderators help other members and tell them *"how to ask questions"* or tell them that *"this question has already been answered on board 6"* (cf. in particular point 2, the beginning of the development of tasks).

Besides these positive aspects of roles, community members can, however, also restrict the joint enterprise of knowledge sharing. The behavior of the community members, especially the moderators, affects the development of the community: either the community will grow better, or the roles have a negative influence on the community and cause problems. For example, some people communicate in a negative way when they act carelessly with their choice of words. In such cases, the members prevent the cultivation of a common culture and even more, they can destroy trust. In some of such cases in InPUD, other members either did comment the behavior as "not okay" or they ignore such behavior, they did not answer or opened new discussion threads. It is important to be aware of these problems. In the case of "danger," for example, too much negative influence, it is important to intervene, for example, as formal moderator, in order to support the "good" community members.

ATTRACTIVENESS OF ONLINE COMMUNITIES: DESIGN CRITERIA

The success of online communities depends upon the interplay of social structures and technical systems: the attractiveness of the socio-technical system promotes the online communication. A socio-technical system, such as the InPUD community, needs to be given the opportunity to develop itself, and give people the opportunity to share their information. The members should be able to organize context, create online spaces for discussions, and be able to cultivate a common culture of knowledge sharing.

Resulting from our observations of the InPUD community (cf. Section 4), in this section, we draw some general aspects for the attractiveness and designing of online communities. This conclusion might be applied to communities that are characterized by a large size and supplemented to the formal company. However, we also suggest these ideas for firm's internal communities.

1. Identify the Group and their Problems

According to most designers and researchers, we have no doubt that it is essential to understand the group for whom you are designing a community. Hence, the possible community members should be consulted and involved in the design process from the start (cf. Preece et al., 2004, p. 4).

The first "To Do" is to identify the group. Furthermore, it is necessary to answer at least following questions: What problem is the group faced with? Why do they have insufficient contact, communication, and/or collaboration? Second, if the group and the problems are clearer, you can ask what technical system(s), for example Web2.0 applications, are appropriate to support the "new way" of communication, cooperation, or the social networking. From our empirical analysis, we suggest to ask some people who could be participants at the new community. Finally, it is

necessary to make your personal goals, as well as your role, clear, and to compare it with the community's need.

2. Integration of Web 2.0 Applications and Critical Mass

If it is clear what kind of technical systems the group needs, Web 2.0 applications (or new forms of them) should be integrated to the group as quickly as possible in order to support the interests and formal tasks of the users at their organizations or companies. From the InPUD case, we know that it is important to support many-to-many communication, and the possibility that users can discuss about information when they want. Hence, information and communication must be combined to enable questions and answers. Thus, the creation of new knowledge is possible.

Second, it is essential to have a critical mass in the beginning. This is the number of people at online communities who use the technical system in order to communicate with each other. It attracts other people to invest time at the same community. This phenomenon is also discussed as the "*cold start problem.*" Markus and Connolly (1990) showed that in cooperative settings, the use of the technical system increases with the number of users, while the cost for an individual's use stays stable and individual benefit increases. If there are not enough users, the cost/benefit balance is negative. An indicator for a well-designed community system is the growth without external marketing. For example, the InPUD community grew without marketing or any external advertising. Although we did not make external marketing, we already had a lot of participants in the beginning.

In addition, the project team should ensure just a minimum of formal regulations. That means low level of control by project team and company leaders. A knowledge-sharing process, which is based on the willingness of individual users and participation is not obligatory, might work better than other communities. Furthermore, a success factor is also the support of rather less formal roles, but more members in informal roles (in more detail see Section 4). This factor is closely linked with the next aspect, which is called as "facilitate the social dynamic" (see point 3).

3. Interviewing the People, Support Communication About the Community

Whilst the whole process of cultivating of an online community, conduct interviews with possible community members about "what is good" and "what could be better.Such a continuous evaluation leads to a better understanding of the community, and gives ideas for redesigning, not only in the case or problems.

Similar to the success factor "minimum of formal regulations," also the aspect "facilitate the social dynamic" includes the support of interactions and communication. Following questions might help: Could participants constantly read *new* documents, annotations, and so forth? Do members reply relative immediately to questions from others? How can actors and new members react to contributions of other actors? Is the interaction between new user and actors, or among actors in general, rather complicated, emotional, or just okay? To conclude, the support of social dynamic also means to give people the possibility to create relationships and the opportunity for social networking to enable collaboration and knowledge sharing.

Furthermore, ensure a "sufficient quality of content." Following questions might be helpful to achieve that goal: What information is presented? Do the members comment on wrong information? Which different roles have been created over time and who takes part? Once again, are content and discussion about it integrated in order to promote active interactions? A further aspect is to facilitate the assessment of the quality of the given information. One success factor is to give participants, who take formal roles, for example, staff of the

organization, role names. To conclude, make the less formal roles present in order to show what posting comes from what role. Such explicit role names (which should comprehensible and not too artificial) might help to assess the given information. This also affects trust and reliability for the community members.

4. Ensure Sustainable Development by Enabling Possible Changes

From our InPUD analysis, we suggest to support social integration, for example: Are the members able to exchange their knowledge amongst different communities and does the technical system of the community offers the building of diverse networks? This is important also with regard to Davenport (2005, p.162f.). His research confirmed that knowledge workers who are high performers have larger, "*stronger and more diverse networks to which they can turn for information*" than lower performers. To summarize, it seems to be essential to support diverse networks, as well as possible changes at the community: Are the members able to influence the structure of the community in accordance with their needs? Does a person have the opportunity to develop personally, for example to get more prestige, and have the community members the possibility to create new social networks?

Finally, from our 5-year research about the InPUD case, we also recommend an action research process with iterative learning cycles. For this, Preece (2000, p. 291) provides further design criteria: a checklist with eight heuristics (usability and sociability concerns) for guiding the development process and planning evaluations.

CONCLUSION

Knowledge management studies reveal that online communities or communities of practice (Wenger, 1998) positively promote knowledge sharing in organizations. They initiate and enhance information exchange among many people in different departments (e.g., Lesser & Prusak, 1999; Wenger et al., 2002). Our empirical study, mentioned in this publication, also confirmed this thesis. However, our viewpoint focused on the dynamic development of social structures in the computer-mediated communications of a big group.

Although the InPUD community is different from a community created in a firm or from a large international community, we assume that the results (Section 4) as well as the design criteria (Section 5) may be applied for resembling communities with similar attributes, that is, rather large communities, lifespan of several years or more, especially online communication than face-to-face.

Section 4 confirms that members of an online community develop new social structures, although the InPUD community was only supported by a minimum of formal regulations (e.g., few formal roles, easy log in).

Furthermore, the explanation of the ongoing quantitative development of InPUD users refers to the continuing evolution of social relationships and ties between its users, which is mirrored in their interactions and written contributions. A clear willingness to be helpful to others has been observed. The students developed an interest in the careers of others, although they often only knew them through InPUD. Due to the activities of its users, InPUD has become a continuously growing and helpful database for successfully organizing and answering questions about the study of computer science.

Moreover, the analysis of the InPUD case showed the evolution of social structures. Active social interactions and communication about information led to new "behavior settings," rules, and conventions. In the stages of growth, the online community InPUD formed new social structures that depend on computer-mediated communication, and led to technically mediated

regulation. For example, the InPUD community is beginning to create new social conventions, for example, new activities and new informal roles could be observed (cf. Section 4). However, as mentioned in Section 4, these social mechanisms can also lead to more social control. These results are in accordance with Giddens' (1984) theory of the "*duality of structures*": on the one side the structures are composed by those who interact, and simultaneously, on the other side, the rules, values, and social relationships are produced and reproduced during social interaction. Both sides influence each other.

Additionally, we have observed that on the one hand, computer-mediated communication can lead to new social structures (e.g., new informal activities), and on the other hand, the initially established structures do affect the online communication. The members built social structures through the use of the technical system.

Nevertheless, the emergence of social structures in online settings leads to a similar differentiation as in "physical" societies. The observed roles affect social distinctions. Therefore the line of thought that "all people are the same" when they communicate in online communities must be rejected. The dynamic of social structures in online communities does make a difference. However, the difference between online and face-to-face settings is following: People who have had bad experiences in online settings, for instance, unexpected behavior in contrast to the self-description of the online community, are able to participate again by using another nickname, that is not (so easily) possible in the "real" world.

Summarized, the empirical aspects (of Section 4), emergence of informal roles; visible formal roles, providing immediate support and building social capital online; enabling social presence, building social proximity and trust "through" the technical system, are characteristics of the *developed results of the social structure over time* at the InPUD community.

Although the InPUD case did not include

all technical features as discussed with respect to Web 2.0 (cf. Section 1), the success of this community was evidently driven by the spirit underlying of Web 2.0: The evolution of reliable, social relationships and the development of a valuable basis of content and communication "through" user-generated content are highly interweaved. This process was based on a minimum of formal regulations and control, and on only a very moderate intervention by moderators. We strongly believe that these ingredients are the fundamentals upon fundaments on which the further emergence of Web 2.0, a socio-technical phenomenon, is based.

FUTURE RESEARCH DIRECTIONS

In further research, we will more deeply evaluate the quantitative network of the InPUD members, for example, analyzing who persons communicate with whom and how often. Furthermore, the question of how strong the InPUD's relationships really are should be investigated in further research.

Moreover, further research should focus also on the question of community boundaries in relation to online networks and their affects on the Internet-based society. Do online communities build new social boundaries or will they build a free-open network where everybody is able to participate without boundaries? Will system boundaries be dissolved or will they emerge on a higher level?

In addition, further research should also investigate if and how the development of social structures in online communities leads to new social boundaries (e.g., new members could be excluded; closed vs. open system) or if and how the social dynamic leads to new forms of sociotechnical phenomena and the potential for business companies.

To summarize, we want to find answers to these research questions to enable us to learn more about the Web 2.0 phenomenon and the next generation (e.g., Web 3.0) when we move from a social to a socio-technical society.

ACKNOWLEDGMENT

I would like to thank Thomas Herrmann for giving me the opportunity to work and carry out research in the field of socio-technical systems and roles. I gratefully acknowledge and thank him for his supervision, help, and advice not only throughout my work on the InPUD project, but also in developing my own role. I also would like to thank Volker Mattick, who I worked together with on this project, and to everyone who made my research studies such a fulfilling experience.

REFERENCES

Avison, D., Lau, F., Neilsen, P. A., & Myers, M. (1999). Action research. *Communications of ACM, 42*, 94-97.

Bales, R. F. (1950). *Interaction process analysis. A method for the study of a small group.* Chicago: The University of Chicago Press.

Biddle, B. J., & Thomas, E. J. (1966): *Role theory: Concepts and research.* New York: John Wiley.

Bourdieu, P., & Wacquant, L. (1992). *An invitation to reflexive sociology.* Chicago: University of Chicago Press.

Coakes, E. (2002). Knowledge management: A sociotechnical perspective. In E. Coakes, D. Willis, & S. Clarke (Eds.), *Knowledge management in the sociotechnical world. The graffiti continues* (pp.4-14). London: Springer.

Dahrendorf, R. (1958). *Homo sociologicus.* Opladen, Germany: Westdeutscher Verlag.

Davenport, T. H. (2005). *Thinking for a living. How to get better performance and results from knowledge workers.* Boston: Harvard Business School Press.

Fukuyama, F. (1995). *Trust. The social virtues and the creation of prosperity.* New York: The Free Press.

Giddens, A. (1984). *The constitution of society.* Cambridge: Polity Press.

Granovetter, M. S. (1973). The strength of weak ties. *American Journal of Sociology, 78*(6), 1360-1380.

Herrmann, T., Jahnke, I., & Loser, K. U. (2004). The role concept as a basis for designing community systems. In F. Darses, R. Dieng, C. Simone, & M. Zackland (Eds.), *Cooperative systems design. Scenario-based design of collaborative systems* (pp. 163-178). Amsterdam: IOS Press.

Jary, D., & Jary, J. (Eds.). (1991). *The Harper Collins directory of sociology.* New York: Harper Collins.

Kim, A. J. (2000). *Community building on the Web. Secret strategies for successful online communities.* Berkeley: Peachpit.

Koch, M. (2002). Interoperable community platforms and identity management in the university domain. *The International Journal on Media Management, 1,* 21-30.

Lave, J., & Wenger, E. (1991). *Situated learning. Legitimate peripheral participation.* Cambridge: Cambridge University Press.

Lesser, E., & Prusak, L. (1999). Communities of practice, Social capital and organizational knowledge. *Information Systems Review, 1*(1), 3-9.

Mackinnon, L. (2006). *Questioning the level of correspondence between structure in economic theory and the structure in real world economic systems.* University of Queensland, Australia. Retrieved June 10th, 2007, from http://eprint.uq.edu.au/archive/00004559/01/Structure_in_economic_systems.pdf

Markus, M. L., & Connolly, T. (1990). Why CSCW applications fail: Problems in the adop-tion of interdependent work tools. In *Proceedings of the ACM conference on Computer-supported cooperative work* (pp. 371-380). Los Angeles: ACM Press.

Nahapiet, J., & Goshal, S. (1998). Social capital, intellectual capital and the organizational advantage. *Academy of Management Review, 23*(2), 242-266.

O'Reilly, T. (2005): *What Is Web 2.0? Design patterns and business models for the next generation of software.* Retrieved June, 25th, 2007, from http://tim.oreilly.com/

Preece, J. (2000). *Online communities. Designing usability, supporting sociability.* Chichester: Wiley & Sons, Ltd.

Preece, J., Abras, C., & Maloney-Krichmar, D. (2004). Designing and evaluating online communities: Research speaks to emerging practice. *International Journal Web based Communities, 1*(1), 2-18.

Putnam, R. D. (1995). Bowling alone: America's declining social capital. *Journal of Democracy, 6*(1), 65-78.

Schmidt, M. P. (2000). *Knowledge communities.* Munich, Germany: Addison-Wesley.

Shneiderman, B. (2000). Designing trust into online experiences. *Communication of ACM, 43*(12), 57-59.

Snyder, W. M. (1997). Communities of practice: Combining organizational learning and strategy insights to create a bridge to the 21st century. Presented at the 1997 *Academy of Management Conference,* p. 3.

Surowiecki, J. (2004). *The wisdom of crowds: Why the many are smarter than the few and how collective wisdom shapes business, economies, societies and nations.* Doubleday, Random House inc.

Wellman, B., Hasse, A., Witte, J., & Hampton, K. (2001). Does the Internet increase, decrease or supplement social capital? Social networks, participation and community commitment. *American Behavioral Scientist, 3*(45), 437-456.

Wenger, E. (1998). Communities of practice. Learning as a social system. *Systems Thinker, 9*(5- June).

Wenger, E., McDermott, R., & Snyder, W. M. (2002). *Cultivating communities of practice. A guide to managing knowledge.* Boston, MA: Harvard Business School Press.

Williams, R. L., & Cothrel, J. (2000). Four smart ways to run online communities. *Sloan Management Review, Summer,* 81-91.

ADDITIONAL READING

Herrmann, T., Kunau, G., Loser, K.-U., & Menold, N. (2004). Sociotechnical walkthrough: Designing technology along work processes. In A. Clement, F. Cindio, A. M. Oostveen, D. Schuler, & P. van den Besselaar (Eds.), *Artful integration: Interweaving media, materials and practices. Proceedings of the Eighth Participatory Design Conference 2004* (pp. 132-141). New York: ACM Press.

Strijbos, J. W., Martens, R., & Jochems, W. (2004). The effect of functional roles on group efficiency. In *Small Group Research, 35*(2), 195-229.

Wellman, B. (1997). An electronic group is virtually a social network. In S. B. Kiesler (Ed.), *Cultures of the Internet* (pp. 179-205). Hillsdale, NJ: Lawrence Erlbaum,

ENDNOTES

1   Taxonomy is the practice and science of classification of data, photos, pictures, and so on.

2   Altruism usually means helping another person without expecting material reward from that person, although it may include the intrinsic motivated benefit of a "good feeling" (as sense of satisfaction).

3   We got inspirations of the "*interaction process analysis*" of Bales (1950). He developed a method for the study of small groups in face-to-face situations.

4   The standard length of an undergraduate computer science degree in Germany is nine semesters (4-5 years). The majority of students take 12-14 semesters to complete their course (6-7 years).

5   German students have often a high degree of freedom: the decision of when to attend lectures or seminars (in which semester) or even when to take examinations (in which semester) is left to the discretion of each student.

6   InPUD is an acronym for Informatics Portal University of Dortmund (Germany) and can be found at http://inpud.cs.uni-dortmund.de

7   German universities offer multitudes of lectures and students have to create their own semester plan for lectures; meaning they can choose which lectures they attend and when to attend them.

8   The community grew without marketing or any external advertising.

9   WIS is an abbreviation for the project "Development the Computer Science" at the University of Dortmund (Prof. Dr. Thomas Herrmann). It was promoted by the state of North Rhine Westphalia (Germany) from 2001-2004.

10   It is not obligatory for German computer science students to attend lectures in order to take the examinations.

11   People have not the same goals since the role "study management advisors" is perceived as "*just an add-on job*" that must be conducted

by the academic staff from the Department of Computer Science. This job is an add-on job besides research activities, lectures, and doctoral thesis. Hence, from the viewpoint of such people, the job "study management" is not their priority.

12   Surowiecki argues that the aggregation of information in groups, resulting in decisions, is often better than by any single member of the group.

Chapter XI
Information Technology in Times of Crisis:
Considering Knowledge Management for Disaster Management

Kalpana Shankar
Indiana University, USA

Sam Shoulders
Indiana University, USA

David J. Wild
Indiana University, USA

Sheetal Narayanan
Indiana University, USA

Jaesoon An
Indiana University, USA

ABSTRACT

Crisis and disaster management requires the sharing of complex information among numerous entities and individuals. Traditional knowledge management techniques are being used in government agencies responsible for disaster management, but many new technologies and practices, particularly the Internet and Web 2.0, are creating opportunities for individuals, responders, and trainers to share what they know and to acquire needed information, and prepare for the next crisis. However, the use of networked technologies, like the Internet, is still in its infancy, and the use of them diffuse, with very little cohesion among researchers and practitioners in disaster management. We argue that although the Internet is already in extensive use in disaster management, knowledge management will only be effected if top-down and bottoms-up approaches to information gathering, organization, and dissemination are implemented. The aim of this chapter is to provide an introduction to some of the many technologies, practices, and open problems for knowledge sharing in disaster situations, outline some persistent challenges, and suggest venues for exploration and practice.

INTRODUCTION

Information and knowledge are at the heart of disaster preparation, response, mitigation, and recovery. Large-scale crises require the coordination of local, regional, and national agencies, getting information to and from affected individuals and channeling the efforts of volunteers and private entities. Increasingly, the coordination of community-based organizations, individual volunteers, major disaster-relief organizations, and government and corporate entities is accomplished through the use of the Internet and other networked technologies. The sheer quantity of information that is needed to handle the impact of both human-made and natural disasters, manage situations on the ground during such crises, and learn enough to make the aftermath smoother and the "next one" less traumatic, presents numerous possibilities for knowledge management technologies and practices, where. The Internet, as in so many other contexts, is both a blessing and a curse in this regard. Its scope and immediacy make it extremely useful for disseminating information over wide areas, courting feedback, sharing information, and presenting information in multiple languages and formats (video, images, and sound, among others). At the same time, the Internet cannot necessarily be relied on in times of crisis, as it is dependent upon the persistence of other infrastructural technologies, it is not universally accessible or usable, and still presents challenges for the secure verification and validation of information.

Nevertheless, the Internet and knowledge management (KM), in general, have an increasing role to play in disaster mitigation and recovery at all levels, local to global. Both will be essential in coordinating the actions of human beings with no common authority who must cooperate around hastily formed networks (Denning, 2006). However, making the most of these technologies will require some rethinking of KM, which has primarily been shaped by and for the needs of the private sector. Such efforts have been characterized by the boundedness of the organization in which KM is deployed, relative coherence of goals and plans, and the ability to take for granted the kinds of knowledge and skills to be captured and disseminated. However, the Internet, and disasters themselves, of course, are not bounded. Since KM has traditionally been tied to specific organizational objectives, it is a challenge to consider how its tenets and technologies can be used in different cross-organizational and informal contexts. It is also necessary to reconsider the context of design and use, since most approaches to KM have relied on static processes and knowledge basis of metadata and described documents (Butler, 2003), neither of which holds in the context of disasters.

For example, capturing and displaying the kinds of information needed by officials who are charged with mobilizing resources and assessing impacts require large quantities of free-text data and text drawn from reliable sources. Secure transmission of classified data may be required and is not always possible over the Internet. At the other end of the scale, families and individuals affected by a disaster may need to use the Internet to contact family and friends, apply for benefits, or scan and post photos of missing friends or family members. In some cases, the affected individuals may not be at all familiar with accessing the Internet. In short, disasters and disaster recovery challenge human and technical systems and what we know about infrastructural technologies, social technologies (those that are designed and used specifically for collaboration and communication), systems and information design, and the organization of information.

At first glance, KM in the disaster management setting may seem most applicable to formal organizational structures (such as local, regional, and national government), but we argue that it is a valuable technology for the kinds of grassroots engagement in disaster preparedness, mitigation, response, and recovery. This particular area of disaster management, the use of information and the communication of it in crisis, has a short history as a research field, with many empirical studies and little theoretical framing (Falkheimer & Heide, 2006). Many of the studies have focused on description with little overlap with the engineering literature on infrastructure and technology. Not surprisingly, there has been even less theoretical literature in this arena integrating knowledge management practices into the discourse of community-based approaches to disaster management, although there has been more descriptive and anecdotal work.

However, some recent research has been conducted towards the aim of creating an appropriate framework for data collection and analysis in the role of local knowledge networks in disasters (Dekens 2007). Dekens suggests that local knowledge for disaster management can be assessed on four dimensions: observation of a disaster, anticipation through monitoring, communication strategies, and adaptation. All of these dimensions of knowledge can be augmented through the use of the Internet. Kitamoto (2005) posits an information aggregation model that models information systems as a network of information sources, mediators of that information, and the recipients of that information, with or without a hub.

Thinking about how information is shared across networks like the Internet in crisis and disaster management requires a good understanding of human computer interaction design (HCI). HCI is complex due to the unpredictable nature of human behavior. These interactions usually occur in dynamic situations in which the outcomes and expectations are constantly being renegotiated by the status of the situation. The environment is generally very chaotic and often life threatening. HCI designers have to be aware of these characteristic constraints. The nature of

the Internet has made context-sensitive design difficult, however.

In this chapter, we argue that the Internet, and other networked technologies in service of disaster management, require top-down technology development and implementation through the development and deployment of standards and technologies, but that knowledge cannot be fully utilized without grassroots engagement. While this may seem obvious, considering knowledge management in crises requires an integration of networked technologies, social technologies, and practices that draw out tacit knowledge from both to inform future learning.

We provide the reader with an overview of the state of the art by discussing the context of disaster management, and some of the issues that make it challenging for traditional KM. We derive strategies of managing disaster knowledge, outline promising Internet technologies and bottom-up practices of disaster management, communication technologies that aggregate useful information, and strategies of transforming the collated information into disaster knowledge (i.e., KM strategies, perhaps the most intriguing uses of the Internet for disaster management). The chapter concludes with discussion of some of our current research efforts in this arena, and some open challenges for using the Internet and KM in disaster situations.

Disasters and Crises: Understanding Context

Turoff et al. (Turoff, Chumer, Van de Walle, Yao, 2004) argue that an emergency system not used on a regular basis before an emergency will never be of use in an actual emergency. Hence, a system must be used frequently, in prior, in training and simulation. Related to this is the importance of aggregating crisis memory for the improvement of response processes. Instead of remaining static, the system must be evolved and improved by capturing history of what took place and learning from the history.

Their second premise emphasizes the importance of attaining situation information that allows responders to picture the full context surrounding the emergency situation. The system must allow for free communication and information exchange among many individuals dealing with interpretation and actions at different levels of the operation. In addition, the system must be able to refine the communicated data into valid and timely information about the developing situation to help responders make execution decisions appropriate for the situation. Knowing what data is current and what the source is (i.e., accuracy and status of the data) is as important as the data itself.

Turoff et al.'s third premise is that almost everything in a crisis is an exception to the norm, that is, things no one thought of and prepared for occur in an emergency situation. It is impossible to predict who will undertake what specific role in a crisis situation. This implicates the importance of ensuring flexibility of the system so that individuals of appropriate talent and background can be formed into a response team for each incident. Furthermore, roles often need to change during the response process; the system must allow for apt coordination of changes in responsibility and accountability.

Given these exigencies, it is not surprising that most technologies in support of disaster management are usually very formalized, and revolve around traditional communication technologies (two way radios, and so on). However, they form the backbone of knowledge management for both formal organizations and citizens engaged in disaster management. Networked technologies (which can be used on any network, including the Internet) are now starting to be used in addition to these traditional technologies. In the next section, we review some of the existing technologies and introduce some of the recent network technologies that could change practices in the future.

FORMALIZED COMMUNICATION IN DISASTERS

Traditional Communication Technologies

Two-Way Radios

Two-way radios are extremely well established, and are the primary means of local communications for public safety and volunteer agencies in routine and disaster work for voice, and increasingly digital, information. Radios may be handheld (small portable units than can be carried on the person, sometimes known as HTs, or portables), mobile (higher power radios designed for installation in vehicles), or base stations (designed for installation in buildings). These radios work in one of a number of bands based on the parts of the radio frequency spectrum in which they operate. The most common are HF (high frequency, also known as shortwave), VHF (very high frequency), and UHF (ultra high frequency).

Radio communications are either simplex or repeater based. Simplex communications are direct radio-radio communications, and with the exception of HF band radios, are typically very short range. Handheld and mobile radios working in simplex mode have a maximum range of only a few miles in ideal conditions; often the practical range is much less. Thus, repeaters are widely used to extend the range of handheld and mobile radios. Repeaters are units that listen on one (input) frequency and transmit what they receive on another (output) frequency. They typically have receive-and-transmit antennas on high locations (e.g., antenna towers). Handheld and mobile radios are set to transmit on the repeater input frequency, and receive on the repeater output frequency, so all radio communications are picked up by the repeater and are retransmitted from the high vantage point for other radios to receive. Repeaters generally increase the coverage of handheld and mobile units to tens of miles, enough to cover an area of jurisdiction or a small- to medium-sized area. However, when operating in this mode, radios are critically dependent on the repeater(s), and in disaster scenarios, fixed repeaters often are knocked out of service.

In order that frequencies be used more efficiently, trunked radio systems (TRSs) have emerged, and have become popular for public safety and some business use. In a TRS, a small number of input-output frequency pairs (typically 3-20) are allocated and licensed, and a repeater is set up to operate on each frequency pair. Conventionally, this would allow as many user groups to have "private" communications as there were frequency pairs. However, in a trunked system, user groups (and radios) are assigned talkgroup ID's, and the radios will only replay communications tagged for that particular talkgroup. When a radio transmits, a trunking controller allocates the radio broadcast to a repeater frequency. Radios on the system scan all of the frequencies, and will respond to communications broadcast for the talkgroup(s) they are programmed to receive. Thus, many hundreds of user groups can share a system using only a few frequencies, and the number of repeaters can be adjusted based on demand. Popular trunking systems are LTR (mainly for business users), EDACS, a variety of systems by Motorola, and TETRA (in Europe). The TRS concept has been recently expanded to create statewide public safety radio networks (with multiple repeater sites throughout the state) that operate in a similar manner to a cell phone network.

In the United States, as well as around the world, there is a thriving community of amateur radio operators who are tested and licensed to operate a variety of two-way radios. This community has demonstrated consistent utility in emergency situations, often being able to establish short- and long-range voice and digital communications when other methods have failed (for example in 9/11 (Lindquist & Ortiz, 2001) and

Hurricane Katrina (Krakow, 2005)). Amateur radio communications are generally the first to be restored and the last to be destroyed in a disaster (Townsend & Moss, 2005). In the United States, the establishment of the Amateur Radio Emergency Service (ARES) and the Radio Amateur civil emergency service (RACES) has meant that most communities have groups of amateur radio volunteers ready to establish emergency communication networks with their own equipment, should the need arise.

Land-Line Phones

The public switched telephone network operates very reliably in normal situations. However, the network capacity is designed for normal loads, and so, in disaster situations, it can quickly be overloaded (Bell, 1993; Townsend & Moss, 2005). Because of this, the Government Emergency Telecommunications Service (GETS) has been established to permit certain government and non-governmental phone users to have priority in times of national, regional, or serious local emergency (Townsend & Moss, 2005) This system did seem to work effectively in the aftermath of Hurricane Katrina, with 94% of GETS calls being completed successfully (McGregor, Craighill, & Mosley, 2006).

Cellular and Satellite Telephones

Cellular phones are now ubiquitous, and thus, when they operate reliably, have proved to be an excellent way of communicating emergency information routinely (911 calls, communication with family, and so on). However, they have also been shown to have two problems in disaster situations: cellular networks tend to become overloaded in widespread emergencies, and cellular towers can be easily disabled by adverse conditions (such as loss of power or high winds). The former problem can, to some degree, be subverted by the use of text messaging (which see), although 911 centers are not currently set up to receive text messages. Despite these problems, it was interesting that in the aftermaths of 9/11 and Hurricane Katrina, cellular networks were among the first infrastructure elements to be restored, due to the deployment of temporary, mobile towers by the cellular network companies. A wireless equivalent of GETS, the wireless priority service (WPS) also seemed to work reasonable well during Katrina, with 84% of calls being completed successfully (McGregor et al., 2006)

Satellite phones can be used in almost any situation, and so long as a connection can be made with a satellite, they are generally very reliable for point-to-point communications. However, they are expensive.

Emergency Alerting Systems

Several systems exist in the U.S. for alerting people to local and national hazards. The most widely used and employed is the National Weather Service's All-Hazards Radio (recently renamed from weather radio to reflect its use for non-weather related emergencies). The all-hazards radio system employs radio towers, covering most of the U.S., that routinely broadcast weather forecast and condition information on VHF frequencies, and in case of a local or national weather or other emergency, broadcast an alert tone (including digitized county information) followed by the emergency message. All hazards radio decoders/receivers can be bought by members of the public for U.S. $20-$100.

A related system is the emergency alert system (EAS), administered by the FCC and based on the prior cold-war Emergency Broadcast System. Through arrangements with local radio and cable TV stations, EAS messages are distributed through a network of primary and secondary radio stations using decoders at the station sites. EAS was developed primarily for use for presidential address during a national emergency such as a nuclear attack, but it has been also widely used to alert the public about local emergencies. EAS

and All Hazards Radio are often interlinked, broadcasting each others' messages.

Other local systems may be employed in communities, including dedicated radio receivers for schools, companies, and other key installations that receive local emergency broadcasts, warning sirens, and so on.

Emerging Network Technologies

Meissner et al. (Meissner, Luckenbach, Risse, Kirste, & Kirchner, 2002) describe three kinds of communication networks that are likely to be of importance in future disaster situations: wide area networks, linking the disaster area to the outside world (such as government authorities), local area networks, linking command posts and personnel in the disaster area, and "personal area networks," linking sensors and displays on the bodies of first responders. These networks would properly integrate together, permitting all kinds of information, from small granularity (e.g., sensor readings on first responders) to large granularity (e.g., strategic decisions), to be accessed at any point.

There exist two major barriers to implementing networks of varying granularities: reliability of information communication performance (e.g., transmitting images over low-bandwidth radio systems), and lack of integration of information sources. The latter is likely to be the most difficult problem, as there are so many kinds of sources, proprietary formats, and kinds of communications media to be considered. However, it is possible that standards will develop for the communication of disaster information. One example of this is the common alerting protocol (CAP) for transmission of alert messages. Because of their lack of critical dependence on terrestrial infrastructure, satellite systems are also likely to play a greater role in disasters, particularly after successes during 9/11 and Katrina (Taylor & Skjei, 2002), although cost still precludes widespread use by first responders, volunteer groups, and so on.

While effective "top down" planning for the use of these newer network technologies is necessary for disaster preparation, it is clearly not sufficient. It has become apparent that each major disaster has unique technology issues, and often, groups have to be involved that were not part of the planning process (Marcy, 2005). Further, the pace of technological innovation means that new technologies are often available that can help in disasters (such as WiMAX in Hurricane Katrina (Jordan, 2006)) that have not had time to be included in plans. Simply investing in immature technologies is not in itself effective, as these technologies have not had time to be tested in real situations (Townsend & Moss, 2005). Thus, there is much interest in ways of harnessing "bottom up" innovative technological use in a timely manner during actual disasters, and researching ways in which this activity can be encouraged and supported.

Ad-Hoc Wireless Networks, Mesh, and Peer-to-Peer Networks

Local area wireless networks are now widely used in metropolitan areas. Wireless routers that establish these local wireless networks over a range of typically 100 feet are widely available, and are used in many homes and small businesses to connect multiple computers to the Internet. More advanced networks are deployed in large buildings (such as airports) and common spaces that have multiple access points that allow wider coverage of the network. A further development on this theme is the MESH network, which uses specially modified routers that work together in an extensible ad-hoc network (Akyildiz, Wang, & Wang, 2005; Bruno, Conti, & Gregori, 2005). This network can be a fully connected network (full mesh), where every node in the network is connected to every other node in the network, or a partial mesh, where few nodes would be fully connected and the other few would be connected to only few other nodes.

The wireless mesh networks have wireless mesh routers and clients connected through the mesh topology, and are a mix of fixed and mobile nodes. Multihop technique is used to forward data to and from the Internet; only one of the mesh nodes needs to have an Internet connection for this to work. The routers perform the role of the backbone, and also have the gateway/bridge functionality, which makes it easier to connect it to other networks such as the Internet, Cellular, Wi-Fi, and so forth. Each node can dynamically join the network, and can act as both a client and a router. Deploying wireless mesh networks is relatively easy, as most of the components are available and have been used in the wireless network protocols.

Redundancy is very high, but scalability and quality of service of real-time services are difficult to achieve. Self-healing and dynamic reconfiguration (updating of connection information and optimization of the connections) are two important features of the MESH networks that make them very useful in emergency situations.

Related to MESH networks are the more generalized Peer-to-Peer networks in which a group of computers can collaborate and share information without the need for a centralized server. Whilst developed primarily for file sharing, such systems are clearly robust and redundant and thus, provide a good model for information sharing in disasters.

Voice Over IP (VOIP)

Voice over IP is a technology that enables sending of voice, like data packets, over the Internet using the Internet Protocol (IP) (Robins, 2006). The voice data is first converted to a digital signal that is then compressed and broken down into small packets. Each packet contains the destination address, and can be routed in different directions; they are then reassembled at the destination. VoIP has many applications, of which Internet Telephony is the most popular (Jordan, 2006), followed by Conferencing and Fax over

IP. Various technologies are also emerging for interfacing two-way radios with the Internet using VoIP (Kaluta, 2006).

Distributed Sensors

The establishment of personal area networks can allow individuals to participate in data collection and communication. However, to establish a network in hostile environments, such as emergency situations, robust and scalable technologies are necessary. Disasters not only create human casualties, but also hamper technological networks and infrastructures. In addition, existing technologies need to expand or alter to cope with dynamic changes occurring during the emergencies.

Such robust and scalable networks can be made available by utilizing the distributed sensor networks (DSN) technology. DSN is an ad-hoc mobile network that includes sensor nodes with limited computation and communication capabilities. It senses or collects data from the environment, processes the data, and then communicates the results (Eschenauer & Gligor, 2002). DSN differs from traditional embedded wireless networks in two important aspects. Firstly, its scale is larger: tens of thousands of nodes can be connected as opposed to just tens. Secondly, it allows addition and deletion of sensor nodes, after deployment, to extend the network or replace failing or unreliable nodes without physical contact. This characteristic makes DSN especially suitable for hostile areas where sensor nodes may be captured, manipulated, or destroyed by human or natural adversaries. (Eschenauer & Gligor, 2002)

SOCIAL TECHNOLOGIES: USING THE INTERNET TO SHARE LOCAL KNOWLEDGE

Many of the technologies discussed in the previous section require training, licensing, or other mechanisms that make them suitable for organizational use. The bottoms-up approach to disaster management is one that relies heavily on local knowledge, informal networks, and transmission of context and content: arenas in which the Internet has long been employed to connect disparate communities of interest, and share information without extensive training. This kind of information has always been the most difficult to capture and use, but perhaps is the most useful to victims and potential victims of disasters. For example, the large impact of the Indian Ocean Tsunami in 2004 was made worse by the lack of effective warning systems, and by a lack of understanding on the part of the general public of danger signals.

Many recent technologies, such as blogs, wikis, and other social networking technologies, have first found widespread use in bringing people together for entertainment, networking, and sharing information in the context of play. A blog, short for Web log, uses widely available applications to provide individuals with the ability to create a chronologically organized commentary, with the ability to integrate text and other media, and receive feedback. A similar collaborative technology, the wiki, allows many to collaborate to organize information, but is not organized chronologically. As implementations of these uses, they have also found utility in disaster situations, not the least because social networks become extremely important, and are a natural way for humans to find security in disasters. For example, a group of local bloggers, in the city of Mumbai, India, used blogs to help individuals share information and pictures on missing relatives during the unprecedented flooding, in the summer of 2005, that displaced and killed thousands of people. The same blogs were used in the summer of 2006 during the multiple bomb attacks to the subway system in that city. Similar blogs were in use during Hurricanes Katrina and Rita in the United States as well (Rodriguez, Trainor, & Quarantelli, 2006). These updatable, highly interactive systems also serve as an archive of information, about the development of events, that can be mined for useful information for improving management of future disasters.

To date, there are no empirical studies that validate or evaluate the use of blogging or similar technologies in disaster management. It is clear, though, that social technologies are problematic for use in disaster settings. One of the most obvious issues is a lack of systematic approaches to their use, or best practices. As mentioned previously, sporadic incidents of blogging during the events of disaster have shown usefulness in sharing information and helping victims, indicating a need for researching and developing more organized approaches of exploiting them. How Internet (and related) technologies and informal use can be harnessed in systematic ways requires human intervention. We will now discuss how these approaches can be integrated into knowledge management.

INTEGRATIVE KNOWLEDGE MANAGEMENT APPROACHES

From the previous discussion, it is clear that there are two distinct communities, each with their own practices: official entities that generally use traditional communication techniques with formal practices, and grassroots citizens using Internet social computing techniques in disaster situations. Both of these communities provide highly useful information and personnel networks in disasters. We believe that a successful knowledge management approach in disasters will be one that integrates the information and practices of both. To tackle this comprehensively would be a large undertaking. We therefore offer some examples that are of limited scope, but, nevertheless, approach knowledge management in an integrative way.

When researching knowledge management approaches that can be truly useful for disaster management, it is necessary to consider them in the context of disaster situations and management processes. Characteristics of disaster contexts imply that to manage disaster situations, it is necessary to have adaptable information systems that allow for ongoing training, communication, and information exchange. Functions necessary for communicating, training, and sharing information must be provided in the system, and the functions must be able to evolve by satisfying unique requirements of each disaster event, and by accommodating changes and additions in both content and structure over time. In addition, the system must be used and rehearsed regularly to become useful in actual emergencies. Indeed, Gillespie and Colignon (1993) explain that training is one of the three important processes through which emergency preparedness is achieved, along with planning and exercising.

Traditionally emergency training has been provided through transitory workshops and brochures that lack the urgency occurring in actual emergencies. In addition, the practice of knowledge management has scarcely been implemented in the sharing, transferring, or archiving of disaster knowledge. Knowledge mostly resided in the head of individuals, and practices of externalizing and sharing knowledge with a broader population were lacking. Two-way radios, telephone, and alerting systems tended to be distrusted: they have limitations in the number of people who can use them, and are often rigid. In brief, traditional disaster management practice has tended to be disconnected, closed, and brittle; hence, it could be improved by incorporating more integrated, open, and robust approaches.

In this section, we introduce disaster management approaches that can reach, and involve, the general public, as well as emergency professionals, by organizing trusted reporters and asking them to communicate through a Web-based application called bloomington emergency collaborative information system (BECIS). Second, we discuss two infrastructural knowledge management practices, service learning and online communities of practice, that can provide effective means for organizing volunteers and general public through network technologies. Lastly, we discuss strategies more specific than these infrastructural practices that can inform us of the kinds of knowledge management systems appropriate for grassroots approaches of managing disasters. Storytelling, modeling, and simulation are considered to be engaging, cognitively effective, realistic, and safe modes of sharing information. These characteristics make them suitable for community-based or bottom-up disaster management approaches.

Integration of Traditional and Other Information Sources Using Social Computing Techniques

We (the authors of this article) have begun putting many of the ideas outlined in this chapter into action by creating a local area Internet application for exchanging and capturing critical information in times of emergencies. This research project is currently titled the Bloomington Emergency Collaborative Information System, or BECIS. Using simple-to-use collaboration software on the Internet, our test system links local volunteers and individuals who are already involved in emergency response, either through their professional roles or amateur interest, in a network of "trusted reporters" (our term). In cases of emergencies, this group can scan weather and public service radio frequencies, news sources, Internet resources (such as weather radar), and other information sources, and "blog" the information in a common resource. We are currently in the process of evaluating the system's design, infrastructure, and training aspects to elicit requirements for a future system that would incorporate more requested features and be infrastructure independent.

Shneiderman and Preece (2007) recently noted that technologies in disaster management must support information sharing among the "true" first responders: average citizens who are involved in, and affected, by crises situations. To this end,

Shneiderman and Preece call for developing a national social networking site based on Web technologies.

Knowledge Management Practices: Adding Value to Learning

Since the 1990s, many service learning programs and sponsoring organizations emerged and proved to be beneficial in promoting the wellbeing of community, and increasing participants' learning gains in areas such as career development, citizenship skill, interpersonal development, learning motivation, and so forth. (Strom & Miller, 2002) Learning gains are achieved because, by definition, service learning strives to achieve defined learning objectives while having students participate in community service activities (Stanton, Giles, & Cruz, 1999). Added value of learning gain makes community service activities more appealing to educators, students, and parents. Such an appeal increases participation; community needs, such as bottom-up disaster management, can be better fulfilled by the increased participation.

Campus Compact, the coalition of higher education institutions for building civic engagement into campus and academic life, lists its member institutions' relief activities in response to Hurricane Katrina on its Web site. Many of the activities demonstrate service learning practices such as a university campus functioning as a training center, culinary students providing home-cooked meals for victims staying at a facility, and veterinary students caring for rescued pets and farm animals. (Campus Compact, 2007)

Steiner and Sands (2000) specifically report service learning experiences of medical students in responding to Hurricane Floyd. The authors describe how much the students felt it was rewarding to provide medical services to the victims and participate in other recovery activities. They indicate that the immediate rewards of the short-term experience may prove to be a powerful incentive to students to continue long-term service activities, hence, achieving the instructional objective of instilling an ethic of community service and social responsibility in medical students.

If educators and students participating in service learning programs each year, or each semester, start building communities where they exchange experiences and reflections as well as disaster information, the synergy between education and disaster management could prove beneficial to both communities. Although a community of practice (Wenger, 1998) is considered to be informally created and managed, organized programs, such as service learning, can play a vital role in nurturing a healthy growth of the community. For example, incentives and rewards can be established in terms of education credits and certificates to reinforce the members' voluntary, informal contribution to disaster management. At the same time, technology infrastructure can be enhanced to provide time and space for collaboration, and to support the process of distributed information sharing and subsequent knowledge generation. Particularly, using emerging Web technologies and social networking phenomena on the Internet, people can be organized, connected, and facilitated through online communities.

Online communities of volunteers participating in service learning programs can play a role as the consistently focal point for sharing disaster information and preparing community members for disasters. They can provide open and sustainable methods of managing disasters by making it possible to organize a large number of participants continuously and create information redundancy. In addition, systems, processes, and knowledge acquired and used during these community-based and real-time educational practices are immediately transferable to those actually responding to and recovering from emergencies. Social and technological infrastructures used in ongoing education can be used during the response and recovery phases, increasing effectiveness of overall disaster management.

Knowledge Management Systems

In order to expand upon the sociotechnical infrastructure discussed, our current BECIS system needs to be enhanced with the capabilities of knowledge management. When planning for knowledge management systems, perspectives on knowledge sharing modes give us ideas on the kind of system appropriate for given contexts and users. The context and user of our interests are disaster management contexts and volunteers from the community. Sole and Wilson (2002) give a list of knowledge sharing modes that includes storytelling, modeling, simulations, codified resources, and symbolic objects. Codified resources, such as manuals, instructions, textbooks, and so forth, and symbolic objects, such as maps, signs, prototypes, and so forth, have been traditionally utilized much in the disaster management practice. In fact, knowledge management systems, in general, have been considered as a tool for exchanging codified knowledge. However, balancing these static strategies with more dynamic and engaging strategies of storytelling, modeling, and simulations can facilitate knowledge sharing more effectively. Our target users, members of the general public, do not necessarily have the motivation to share and generate knowledge actively. Hence, it is important that knowledge management systems, to be used in the disaster management context, utilize more facilitative knowledge sharing modes.

Storytelling Systems

Stories tell personal or collective experiences by recounting what happened, why, and what might happen next, in a vivid, engaging, and entertaining manner by employing characters, plots, and drama (Bruner, 1992). Stories often offer the listener an opportunity to experience the narrated situation in a surrogate fashion (Sole & Wilson, 2002). Information resulting from a direct or surrogate experience is encoded in the episodic memory and becomes readily available for retrieval (Swap, Leonard, Shields, & Abrams, 2001). Stories also include rich contextual details that they are ideal carriers of tacit dimensions of knowledge such as values and norms, trust and commitment, internalized expertise, and emotional connection (Sole & Wilson, 2002). Easy acquisition and retrieval of knowledge, and effectiveness in building personal connection and commitment to intended values and norms, make stories a very strong strategy for raising awareness and preparedness toward disasters among general public. Indeed, in the event of the Indian Ocean Tsunami, one of the few coastal areas to evacuate ahead of the tsunami was on the Indonesian island of Simeulue, where its folklore recounted an earthquake and tsunami in 1907 (Wikipedia, 2007).

The Indigenous Knowledge in Disaster management Web site (RAIPON & UNEP, 2006) shows a good example of incorporating stories in systematic management of disaster knowledge. Stories about how indigenous peoples in Russia perceive and cope with natural disasters and extreme weather events are archived. Each story has an identification number, and items can be sorted by the categories of region, disaster type, knowledge theme, and story type. By reading the stories, the reader learns about strategies for early detection of coming events, coping strategies, and perceptions of short- and long-term impacts of these events on biodiversity, without even realizing that they are acquiring such knowledge.

To be useful, such stories must be part of a technical and organizational framework such that the knowledge they incorporate can be processed and acted upon. This requires, among other features, appropriate indexing and searching features. The system must have information processing functions that will quickly recognize content of each incoming story and assign it to relevant repositories in real time. A rigorous search and index engine, such as semantic blogging (Cayzer, 2004), can expedite the process by either augmenting human controllers or by autonomously performing

the recognition and categorization tasks. In order for emergency responders to make use of the real-time stories in their decision making, the system must have information-processing functions that will quickly recognize content of each incoming story and assign it to relevant repositories in real time. A rigorous search and index engine such as semantic blogging (Cayzer, 2004), can expedite the process by either augmenting human controllers or by autonomously performing the recognition and categorization tasks.

Modeling and Simulation Systems

Modeling and simulation have been recognized as appropriate means for managing emergency tasks in recent years. First of all, they increase preparedness toward emergencies by exposing first responders in simulated scenarios, and having them experience model behaviors and acquire them. According to Jain and McLean (2003), these strategies have been suggested as the key ingredient for preparing emergency response, especially since the September 11, 2001 terrorism. Modeling and simulation strategies also play useful roles in conducting other emergency management tasks. In the report of the Committee on Science and Technology for Countering Terrorism (National Research Council, 2002), for example, they were identified as necessary tools for assessing threat, identifying infrastructure vulnerabilities and interdependencies, planning and coordinating response, and supporting research on disaster preparedness. Situations, such as the dispersion of hazardous atmospheric release, fire dynamics inside building, bio-terror attack, and tornado-causing thunderstorms, have been modeled and simulated to study and project impact of the disaster events, improve capabilities for emergency response, analyze and develop techniques for identifying possibility of occurrence prior to the event, and so forth. (Jain & McLean, 2003)

Knowledge sharing through modeling refers to the learner's exposure to behavior of others, particularly experts, as in the activities of mentoring, apprenticeship, demonstration, and observation. Simulation refers to learning through experiential situations that recreate the complexities of action, as in case studies, role playing, and technology-supported simulations (Sole & Wilson, 2002). Modeling often precedes or occurs as a part of simulation; hence, the two strategies usually appear together in the discussion of knowledge management strategies. The combination of experiential situations and expert modeling allows people to experience aspects of disasters often dangerous in the real situation, and learn from the simulated experience in a safe manner.

One of the most engaging and immersive forms of simulation is Virtual reality (VR). It provides virtual environments that represent highly realistic simulations of the actual environments, and allows users to explore and interact within the created reality. A virtual experience is acknowledged to evoke the same reactions and emotions as a real experience, a concept known as presence. (Schuemie, Ver Der Straaten, Krijn & Van Der Mast, 2001) This sense of presence has a significant impact on how successfully the skills learned in VR will be transferred to the real world, because the performance simulated with a sense of presence is more likely to represent the competence in the actual task than the performance executed in unrealistic settings. Presence also supports effectiveness of VR systems for the purpose of knowledge sharing and learning about "affectively intense behaviors" such as driving a car, flying an airplane, treating psychological and mental health disorders, and managing a disaster event (Tichon et al., 2003). It allows the user to experience and learn, in a simulated environment, of those behaviors that otherwise would be too dangerous, hostile, or expensive to explore. Examples of online VR systems for disaster management include the First Responder Simulation and Training Environment (FIRSTE, 2007) and Play2Train (Play2Train, 2007).

CONCLUSION

As this review suggests, the use of KM in disaster/crisis management, particularly in knowledge sharing, is in its infancy, as is the use of the Internet. There are indications that integrating information shared in traditional, formalized systems with local knowledge and emerging social interaction networks (particularly on the internet) has the potential to greatly improve information flow in all stages of disaster management; yet it is unclear how this relates to traditional KM or indeed, whether it is useful to attempt to create a cohesive KM system for handling. Since KM is generally predicated upon shared goals and meanings, it may work best in bounded organizational settings with specific outcomes to be derived from the KM initiative. To some extent, successful initiatives will rely on some of the following keystones:

- Appropriate choice of sustainable infrastructural technologies
- Trust in the information that is being gathered and managed
- Appropriate and reliable mechanisms for transfer of information
- Manageable scope

There are also a number of potential problems with this approach. First, when using these leading-edge technologies, there is the danger of creating a "rich get richer" scenario (Quarantelli, 1997), where resource-rich communities are favored with access to information. Second, traditional disaster management takes a "top down", highly controlled approach to disaster planning and management, and it is not clear that this approach would work well with "grassroots" technologies. Third, the all-too-common tendency to throw technology at social problems exacerbates a widespread organizational problem: to focus on problems that can be solved with new technologies and downplay those that cannot.

For these reasons, the authors of this piece are approaching the KM problem from a "bottoms up" approach: using infrastructure, HCI, and social technologies to integrate fine-grained information from "trusted reporters" to provide information to first-responders and others in the position of acting upon information. They are also exploring the role of practice, information sharing, and design in creating appropriate interfaces for such work.

These issues aside, taking a knowledge management approach to disaster management entails tackling many of the same issues that executives face in the corporate sector with respect to KM initiatives. The size and complexity of even the largest structured database or content management system that most KM implementers are used to working with are nothing in comparison to the multimedia environments represented by blogs and Wikis. Technical knowledge, or access to the Internet, cannot be assumed, much less literacy. Again, consider the case of Hurricane Katrina: refugees could find information on benefits and disaster recovery on the Internet, but many of these people had no computer knowledge. In the formal entities that are implementing KM strate-gies, unwillingness to share information or display ignorance impede collaboration and information sharing, a situation that is often reported in KM evaluation. These challenges suggest that, at least for the near term, we need to consider the Internet as an intriguing possibility for knowledge sharing in terms of crisis, but not necessarily as a formal KM system.

FUTURE RESEARCH DIRECTIONS

Disaster management is a large area of research and practice that requires the integration of technological infrastructures with social and educational practices to be effectively carried out. It is also one with (as yet) few overlaps in the KM field, although appropriate KM strategies will essentially help achieve the integration. As mentioned in the previous section, the discussion of KM strategies can derive insights by identifying general directions of system functions implicated by contexts and necessary user tasks: context-aware computing that is sustainable, secure, and trustworthy. Context-aware is a term for the emergent trend toward computing that is:

Table 1.

Disaster phase	Technologies	Practices
Mitigation	Storytelling Modeling and simulation Communications Infrastructure Deployment	Use of modeling and simulation to identify mitigation steps Establishing community activities that will help during disasters (e.g., neighborhood organizations)
Preparedness	Storytelling Modeling and simulation Social computing and the Internet	Community planning Understanding of risks and threats Prediction of disasters and community responses
Response	Personal, local- and wide-area networks Sensors Ad hoc networks Voice and data communications Alerting systems Predictive Modeling Decision making tools	Communication amongst volunteers and first responders Communication of information to citizenry Aggregation of information from the disaster area Decision making Prediction of the development of a disaster
Recovery	Social Computing and the Internet Ad hoc networks Voice and data communications	Reconnection if displaced citizenry Rebuilding of communities Emotional and practical support Dissemination of aid

- Casually accessible, often invisible.
- Frequently mobile or embedded in the environment.
- Connected to an increasingly ubiquitous network infrastructure composed of a wired core and wireless edges.

Making computation useful in the various situations that can be encountered in the real world requires that technology responds to the ever-changing context of use and meaning (Dey, Salber, & Abowd, 2001; Moran & Dourish, 2001). One might tabulate the technologies and practices relevant to phases of disasters:

Clearly, there is overlap in the phases, and it is of particular interest how technologies and practices used in one phase might positively or negatively impact another; for example, a community blog or Web site used by a neighborhood organization in a preparedness phase might be gainfully employed for information sharing in response and recovery phases. However, if the Internet infrastructure is unavailable in those phases, the dependence of the community on the Web site as a source of information might mean citizenry are less aware of other ways of finding information.

The characteristics of disaster contexts thus imply a need for adaptable systems that allow for ongoing training, communication, and information exchange. In turn, these issues must be dealt with such that the information exchanged can be trusted, is secure, and sustainable: three qualities that are frankly not represented in the current Internet. We suggest potential avenues for exploration in these three arenas, though there are many others.

Information Sharing and Security (Securing Information and Networks)

During a crisis, organizations often have a need to share information with selected members of other organizations. For example, the Department of Homeland Security mandates that its constituent

organizations, like the U.S. Secret Service and the U.S. Coast Guard, may need to share information related to particular leads on a continuing basis. However, this sharing must also be restricted. (Pan, Mitra, & Liu, 2006).

Historically there have been three approaches to information sharing: DAC or discretionary access control—access to the information is controlled at the discretion of the owner; MAC or mandatory access control- allows information to flow in one direction in a lattice of security labels; ORCON or originator control- each object and each user can be treated differently and is discretionary in that the owner is the principal source of the policy to be enforced (Sandhu, Ranganathan, & Zhang, 2006). Within the domain of information sharing and KM, how can we have secure fault tolerant transmission of information, ability to detect intrusion on a distributed system, and reliability of information delivery?

In context-aware computing, that is, ubiquitous/pervasive computing, in which information is omnipresent, migrating seamlessly through the environment to be accessible whenever and wherever needed. We are confronted with tremendous challenges to information security and privacy protection. Enabling secure information sharing among diverse organizations faces two fundamental challenges: one, interoperating among semantically heterogeneous information sources in an omnipresent manner and two, maintaining the integrity of each organization's security policies (Dragovic & Crowcroft, 2004). Implementing security for systems that citizens and officials can share and use requires balancing needs for access and ease of use with filters for spurious or damaging "noise" and security from hacking or other malicious attack.

Sustainable Design (Context-Aware Devices vs. Context-Aware Infrastructures)

Hong and Landay (2001) have suggested that the services component of the context-aware conceptual framework be abstracted out into a service infrastructure. By providing uniform abstractions and reliable services for common operations, such service infrastructures could make it easier to develop robust applications; even on a diverse and constantly changing set of devices and sensors. A service infrastructure would also make it easier to incrementally deploy new sensors, new devices, and new services as they appear in the future, and as well, scale these up to serve large numbers of people. Last, a service infrastructure would make it easier for sensors and devices to share sensor and context information, placing the burden of acquisition, processing, and interoperability on the infrastructure instead of on individual devices and applications (2001). Disaster management needs to concern itself with the medium and long-term, and that concern extends to the sustainability of designs from concept to inception. Sustainable design can be defined as the creation of artifacts that have a minimal environmental and negative social impact on the user and the society at-large. Two, if the service components and the sensors are embedded in the device upgrades and repairs are device dependant. This can be both financially costly and impractical, if devices are constantly not available due to upgrade. When and where and how to disburse limited resources can be defined resource allocation dynamics. Three, this minimizes the issues of operability, by creating standardization based on the context-aware infrastructure. The general inspiration behind this idea is the Internet and the various layers of protocol that make it possible for computers to interoperate. Each layer would be an interactional snapshot of events in the field. The context-layered design could be real-time diagram of various contextual information such as time-relevant data, geospatial data, and data for various non-governmental organizations, NGOs, governmental organizations, GOs, and volunteer groups (Hong & Landay, 2001). As the crisis evolves, the context of relevance of data at any given time will change and therefore,

the information would change. A context-aware service infrastructure is just another high-level abstraction of the conceptual framework of context-aware computing, services component, but far more robust and sustainable.

REFERENCES

Akyildiz, I. F., Wang, X., & Wang, W. (2005). Wireless mesh networks: A survey. *Computer Networks, 47*(4), 445-487.

Bell, J. K. (1993). How to plan to keep communications open after disaster strikes. In *Proceedings of the 1993 national earthquake conference: Earthquake Hazard Reduction in the Central and Eastern United States: A Time for Examination and Action* (pp. 339-348).

Bruner, J. S. (1992). The narrative construction of reality. In H. Beilins & P. B. Pufall (Eds.), *Piaget's theory: Prospects and possibilities* (pp. 229-248). Hillsdale, NJ: Erlbaum.

Bruno, R., Conti, M., & Gregori, E. (2005). Mesh networks: Commodity multihop ad hoc networks. *IEEE Communications Magazine, March*, 123-131.

Butler, T. (2003). From data to knowledge and back again: understanding the limitations of KMS. *Knowledge and Process Management, 10*(3), 144-155.

Campus Compact. (2007). *Higher education responds to Katrina*. Retrieved January 18, 2007, from http://www.compact.org/resources/downloads/Katrina.pdf

Cayzer, S. (2004). Semantic blogging and decentralized knowledge management. *Communications of the ACM, 47*(12), 47-52.

Denning, P. J. (2006). Hastily formed networks. *Communications of the ACM, 49*(4), 15-20.

Dekens. J. (2007). Local knowledge on disaster preparedness: A framework for data collection and analysis. *Sustainable mountain development, 52,* 20-23. Retrieved from http://www.disasterpreparedness.icimod.org/publications.php

Dey, A. K., Salber, D.. & Abowd, G. D. (2001). A conceptual framework and a toolkit for supporting the rapid prototyping of context-aware applications. *Human-Computer Interaction (HCI) Journal, 16*(2-4), 97-166.

Dourish, P. (2001). Seeking a foundation for context-aware computing. *Human-Computer Interaction, 16*(2, 3, & 4), 229-241.

Dourish, P. (2003). Speech-gesture driven multimodal interfaces for crisis management. In *Proceedings of the IEEE 91* (pp. 1327-1354).

Dourish, P. (2004.) What we talk about when we talk about context. *Personal and Ubiquitous Computing, 8*(1), 19-30.

Dragovic, B., & Crowcroft, J. (2004). Information exposure control through data manipulation for ubiquitous computing. In *Proceedings of the 2004 workshop on New security paradigms* (pp. 57-64).

Eschenauer, L., & Gligor, V. (2002). A key-management scheme for distributed sensor networks. In *Proceedings of ACM Conference on Computer and Communication Security (CCS'02)*, Washington DC.

Falkheimer, J., & Heide, M. (2006). Multicultural crisis communication: Towards a social constructionist perspective. *Journal of Contingencies and Crisis Management, 14*(4), 180-189.

FIRSTE. (2007). Retrieved January 18, 2007, from http://campus.umr.edu/firste/

Gillespie, D., & Colignon, R. (1993). Structural change in disaster preparedness networks. International *Journal of Mass Emergencies and Disasters, 11*(2), 143–62.

Hong, J. I., & Landay, J. A. (2001). An infrastructure approach to context-aware computing. *Human-Computer Interaction, 16*(2, 3, & 4), 287-303.

Ivefors, G. M. (1995). Emergency information management and disaster preparedness on the Internet. *IDA Fifth Annual Conference on Computer and Information Science*, Lingköping, Sweden, November 1995. Retrieved January 10, 2007, from http://hb.se/bhs/ith/2-97/gi.htm

Jain, S., & McLean, C. (2003). A framework for modeling and simulation for emergency response. In *Proceedings of the 2003 Winter Simulation Conference* (pp. 1068-1076).

Jasanoff, S. (1994). *Learning from disaster: Risk management after Bhopal*. Philadelphia: University of Pennsylvania Press.

Jordan, B. (2006). The Katrina response that worked. *Homeland Defense Journal, 4*, 8-12.

Kaluta, R. W. (2006). Organizing community-level emergency response with interoperable communications. *Homeland Defense Journal, 4*, 20-22.

Kitamoto, A. (2005). Digital Typhoon: Near real-time aggregation, recombination and delivery of typhoon-related information. *Proceedings of the 4th International Symposium on Digital Earth*, pp. (CD-ROM), 2005-03. Available: http://agora.ex.nii.ac.jp/~kitamoto/research/publications/kisde05.pdf

Krakow, G. (2005). *Ham radio operators to the rescue after Katrina*. Retrieved December 10, 2006, from http://www.msnbc.msn.com/id/9228945/

Leland, E. (2001). *Voice over IP: Is your telephone system outdated?* Retrieved January 12, 2007, from http://www.techsoup.org/learningcenter/internet/page5256.cfm

Lindquist, R., & Ortiz, D. (2001). 9/11/01: This is Not a Test. *QST, 11*, 28-34, 59.

Marcy, J. (2005). Communicating after Katrina. *Homeland Defense Journal, 11*, 10-11.

McGee, D. R., Cohen, P. R., & Wu, L. (2000). Something from nothing: Augmenting a paper-based work practice via multimodal interaction. In *Proceedings of the ACM Designing Augmented Reality Environments (DARE)* (pp. 71-80). New York: ACM Press.

McGregor, P., Craighill, R., & Mosley, V. (2006). Government Emergency Telecommunications Service (GETS) and Wireless Priority Service (WPS) performance during Katrina. In M. H. Hamza (Ed.), *Communications, Internet, and Information Technology*, St. Thomas, U.S. Virgin Islands.

Meissner, A., Luckenbach, T., Risse, T., Kirste, T., & Kirchner, H. (2002). In *Design Challenges for an Integrated Disaster management Communication and Information System, First IEEE Workshop on Disaster Recovery Networks*, New York.

Moran, T. P. & Dourish, P. (2001). Introduction to special issue on context-aware computing. *Human-Computer Interaction, 16*(2, 3, & 4), 87-95.

National Research Council. (2002). *Making the nation safer: The role of science and technology in countering terrorism*. Washington DC: National Academies Press.

Oviatt, S. L. (1996). Multimodal interfaces for dynamic interactive maps. In *Proceedings of the Conference on Human Factors in Computing Systems (CHI'96)* (pp. 95-102). New York: ACM Press.

Pan, C. C., Mitra, P., & Liu, P. (2006). Semantic access control for information interoperation. In *Proceedings of the eleventh ACM symposium on Access control models and technologies* (pp. 237-246).

Play2Train. (2007). Retrieved January 18, 2007 from http://irhbt.typepad.com/play2train/

Quarantelli, E. L (1997). Problematical aspects of the information/communication revolution for disaster planning and research: ten non-technical issues and questions. *Disaster Prevention and Management, 6*(2), 94–106.

RAIPON & UNEP. (2006). *Indigenous knowledge in disaster management*. Retrieved January 18, 2007, from http://www.raipon.org/ikdm/Default.aspx

Rauschert, I., Agrawal, P., Sharma, R., Fuhrmann, S., Brewer, I., & MacEachren, A. (2002). Designing a human-centered, multimodal GIS interface to support emergency management. In *Proceedings of the 10th ACM International Symposium on Advances in Geographic Information Systems (GIS '02)* (pp. 8-9). New York: ACM Press.

Robins, M. (2006). New IP telephony solutions for the government enterprise. *Homeland Defense Journal, 1*, 22-27.

Rodriguez, H., Trainor, J., & Quarantelli, E. L. (2006). Rising to the challenges of a catastrophe: the emergent and prosocial behavior following Hurricane Katrina. *The Annals of the American Academy of Political and Social Science, 604*(1), 82-101.

Sandhu, R., Ranganathan, K., & Zhang, X. (2006). Secure information sharing enabled by Trusted Computing and PEI models. In *Proceedings of the 2006 ACM Symposium on Information, computer and communications security* (pp. 2-12).

Schuemie, M., Ver Der Straaten, P., Krijn, M., & Van Der Mast, C. (2001). Research on presence in virtual reality: A survey. *Cyberpsychology and Behavior, 4*(2), 183-201.

Shneiderman, B., & Preece, J. (2007). 911.gov. *Science, 315*(5814), 944.

Sole, D., & Wilson, D. (2002). *Storytelling in organizations: The power and the traps of using stories* to share knowledge in organizations. Learning Innovations Laboratory (LILA), Graduate School of Education, Harvard University. Retrieved January 18, 2007, from http://lila.pz.harvard. edu/_upload/lib/ACF14F3.pdf

Stanton, T. K., Giles, D. E., & Cruz, N. I. (1999). *Service learning: a movement's pioneers: Reflections on its origins, practice, and future.* San Francisco: Jossey-Bass Publishers.

Steiner, B., & Sands, R. (2000). Responding to a natural disaster with service learning. *Family Medicine, 32*(9), 645-649.

Strom, T. Q., & Miller, C. (2002). *Service learning. What works in preventing school violence: The safe and responsive fact sheet series.* Safe & Responsive Schools Project, Indiana Education Policy Center, Indiana University. Retrieved January 18, 2007, from http://www.indiana. edu/~safeschl/service_learning.pdf

Swap, W., Leonard, D., Shields, M., & Abrams, L. (2001). Using mentoring and storytelling to transfer knowledge in the workplace. *Journal of Management Information Systems, 18*(1), 95-114.

Taylor, A., Skjei, S. M. (2002). A disaster-recovery plan for local municipalities using currently available communication satellite facilities and services, *National Conference on Digital Government, ACM International Conference Proceeding Series,* 1-11.

Tichon, J., Hall, R. H., Hilgers, M. G., Leu, M. C., & Agarwal, A. (2003). Education and training in virtual environments for disaster management. In *Proceedings of the World Conference on Educational Multimedia, Hypermedia & Telecommunications* (EdMedia) (pp. 1191 – 1194).

Townsend, A. M., & Moss, M. M. (2005). Telecommunications infrastructures. In *Disasters: Preparing cities for crisis communications.* Retrieved January 18, 2007, from http://hurricane. wagner.nyu.edu/report1.pdf

Turoff, M., Chumer, M., Van de Walle, B., & Yao, X. (2004). The design of a dynamic emergency response management information system (DERMIS). *Journal of Information Technology Theory and Application (JITTA), 5*(4), 1-36.

Upkar Varshney, A. S., McGivern, M., & Howard, C. (2002). Voice over IP. *Communications of the ACM, January, 45*(1), 88-96.

Wenger, E. (1998). *Communities of practice: Learning, meaning, and identity.* New York: Cambridge University Press.

Wikipedia. (2007). *2004 Indian Ocean earthquake: Signs and warnings.* Retrieved January 18, 2007, from http://en.wikipedia.org/wiki/2004_Indian_Ocean_earthquake

Wildavsky, A. (1988). *Searching for safety.* New Brunswick, NJ: Transaction Press.

ADDITIONAL READINGS

Amdahl, G. (2002). *Disaster response: GIS for public safety.* Redlands, CA: ESRI Press.

Bankoff, G., Frerks, G., & Hilhorst, D. (2004). *Mapping vulnerability: Disasters, development and people.* Earthscan Publications

Battista, F., & Baas, S. (2004). *The role of local institutions in reducing vulnerability to recurrent natural disasters and in sustainable livelihoods development.* Consolidated report on case studies and workshop findings and recommendations prepared by Rural Institutions and Participation Service (SDAR), Food and Agriculture Organization of the United Nations (FAO).

Bellotti, V, & Edwards, K. (2001). Intelligibility and accountability: Human considerations in context-aware systems. *Human-Computer Interaction, 16*(2, 3, & 4), 193-212.

Bernsen, N.O. (1994). Modality theory in support of multimodal interface design. In *Proceedings of*

1993 Intelligent MultiMedia MultiModal Systems (pp. 37-44).

Bødker, S. (2006). When second wave HCI meets third wave challenges. In *Proceedings of the 4th Nordic conference on Human-computer interaction: changing roles* (pp. 1-8).

Bornträger, C., Cheverst, K., Davies, N., Dix, A., Friday, A., & Seitz, J. (2003). Experiments with multimodal interfaces in a context-aware city guide.In *Proceedings of Mobile HCI* (pp. 116-130).

Cassell, J., Bickmore, T., Billinghurst, M., Campbell, L., Chang, K., Vilhjálmsson, H., et al. (1999). Embodiment in conversational interfaces: Rea. In *Proceedings of the SIGCHI conference on Human factors in computing systems: the CHI is the limit* (pp. 520-527).

Chittaro, L. (2003). Human-computer interaction with mobile devices and services. In *5th international Symposium, Mobile HCI 2003,* Udine, Italy, September 8-11, 2003. Springer.

Comfort, L. K., et al. (2002). *Complex systems in crisis: Anticipation and resilience in dynamic environments.* Retrieved December 26, 2006, from http://www.blackwell-synergy.com/links/doi/10.1111/1468-5973.00164/abs/

Cowan, D. D., Mayfield, C. I., Tompa, F. W. & Gaspani, W. (1998). New role for community networks. *Communications of the ACM, April, 41*(4), 61-63.

Dey, A. K., & Abowd, G. D. (1999). *Towards a better understanding of context and context-awareness.* GVU Technical Report GIT-GVU-99-22, College of Computing, Georgia Institute of Technology. (ftp://ftp.cc.gatech.edu/pub/gvu/tr/1999/99-22.pdf)

Disaster preparedness and local knowledge knowledge base. Prepared by International Centre for Integrated Mountain Development (ICIMOD).

Retrieved from http://www.disasterpreparedness.icimod.org/knowledge.php

Fischer, G. (2001). Articulating the task at hand and making information relevant to IT. *Human-Computer Interaction, 16*(2, 3, & 4), 243-256.

Frincke, D., & Wilhite, E. (2001). Distributed network defense. In *Workshop on Information Assurance and Security United States Military Academy* (pp. 236–238).

Gurstein, M. (2005). Tsunami warning systems and the Last Mile: Towards community based and ICT enabled disaster response systems. *Journal of Community Informatics, 1*(2). Available: http://ci-journal.net/index.php/ciej/issue/view/

Horowitz, M., Martonosi, M., Mowry, T., & Smith, M. (1996). Informing memory operations: providing memory performance feedback in modern processors. In *Proceedings of the 23rd annual international symposium on Computer architecture* (pp. 260-270).

Kaptelinin, V. (2003). Learning with artefacts: integrating technologies into activities. *Interacting with Computers, 15*(6), 831-836.

Kim, S., Vasireddy, V., & Harfoush, K. (2007a). *Scalable coordination for sensor networks in challenging environments.* Seoul, Korea: ACM Press.

Lennon, J. A. & Maurer, H. (2001). Can knowledge management help in poverty-stricken countries and crisis situations? *Journal of Universal Computer Science, 7*(4), 327-334. Retrieved from http://www.jucs.org/jucs_7_4/can_knowledge_management_help/Lennon_J.pdf

Lyles, M. A., & Easterby-Smith, M. (2003). *The Blackwell handbook of organizational learning and knowledge management.* Malden, MA; Oxford, UK: Blackwell Publishing.

Lyytinen, K., & Yoo, Y. (2002). The next wave of nomadic computing: A research agenda for information systems research. *Information Systems Research, 13*(4), 377-388.

MacEachren, M., Cai,G., McNeese, M., Sharma, R., & Fuhrmann, S.In press. GeoCollaborative crisis management: Designing technologies to meet real-world needs. In *Proceedings of the 7th Annual National Conference on Digital Government Research*, San Diego, California. Retrieved from http://www.geovista.psu.edu/publications/2006/MacEachren_dgo2006.pdf

MacEachren, A., Cai, G., Sharma, R., Rauschert, I., Brewer, I., Bolelli, L., et al. (2005). Enabling collaborative geoinformation access and decision-making through a natural, multimodal interface. *International Journal of Geographical Information Science, 19*(3), 293-317.

Mcallister, S., Ravenscroft, A., & Scanlon, E. (2004). Combining interaction and context design to support collaborative argumentation using a tool for synchronous CMC. *Journal of Computer Assisted Learning, 20*(3), 194-204.

Nardi, B. (1995). Some reflections on the application of activity theory. *Context and consciousness: activity theory and human-computer interaction table of contents*, 235-246.

Nardi, B., & Whittaker, S. (2002). The place of face-to-face communication in distributed work. *Distributed Work*, 83-110.

Olson, G., & Olson, J. (2003). Human-computer interaction: Psychological aspects of the human use of computing. *Annual Review of Psychology*, 491-517.

Peters, R., Pak, R., Abowd, G., Fisk, A., & Rogers, W. (2004). *Finding lost objects: Informing the design of ubiquitous computing services for the home*. Georgia Tech GVU Technical Report: GIT-GVU, 04-01.

Puccinelli, D., & Haenggi, M. (2005). Wireless sensor networks: applications and challenges of ubiquitous sensing. *Circuits and Systems Magazine, IEEE, 5*(3), 19-31.

Putnam, L. (2002). By choice or by chance: How the Internet is used to prepare for, manage, and share information about emergencies. *First Monday 7*(11). Retrieved from http://www.firstmonday.org/issues/issue7_11/index.html

Ren, K., & Lou, W. (2007). Privacy-enhanced, attack-resilient access control in pervasive computing environments with optional context authentication capability. *Mobile Networks and Applications, 12*(1), 79-92.

Schafer, W. A., Carroll, J. M., Haynes, S. R., & Abrams, S. (2005). Emergency management as collaborative community work. *ECSCW 2005: Ninth European Conference on Computer-Supported Cooperative Work*. Retrieved from http://cscl.ist.psu.edu/public/users/jcarroll/Self/PapersOnline

Shneiderman, B. (1992). *Designing the user interface: strategies for effective human-computer interaction*. Boston, MA: Addison-Wesley Longman Publishing Co., Inc.

Sorensen, C., Yoo, Y., Lyytinen, K., & Degross, J. (2005). *Designing ubiquitous information environments: Sociotechnical issues and challenges*. Berlin: Springer.

Srivastava, Sanjay K. Bandyopadhayay, S. Manikiam, B. Hegde, V. S, &. Jayaraman, V. (2006). A geo-informatics based approach for disaster risk assessment: a perspective analysis. Disaster forewarning diagnostic methods and management. In F. Kogan, S. Habib, V. S. Hegde, & M. Hegde (Eds.). *Proceedings of the SPIE, Volume 6412, pp. 641214*. Retrieved May 18, 2007, http://www.science.gov/scigov/link.html?redirectUrl=http%3A%2F%2Fadsabs.harvard.edu%2F%2Fabs%2F2006SPIE.6412E..25S

Stephenson, R., & Anderson, P. S. (1997). Disasters and the Information Technology

Revolution. *Disasters, 21*(4), 305-334. Retrieved from http://www.blackwell-synergy.com/doi/abs/10.1111/1467-7717.00065

Wallace, W. A., & Balogh, F. D. (1985). Decision support systems for disaster management. *Public Administration Review, 45*(Special Issue: Emergency Management).

Winograd, T., & Flores, F. (1986). *Understanding computers and cognition.* Norwood, NJ: Ablex Publishing Corporation.

Zhu, S., Setia, S., & Jajodia, S. (2003). LEAP: efficient security mechanisms for large-scale distributed sensor networks. In *Proceedings of the 10th ACM conference on Computer and communication security* (pp. 62-72).

Chapter XII
Managing Knowledge-Based Complexities Through Combined Uses of Internet Technologies

Cécile Godé-Sanchez
Research Center of the French Air Force, France

Pierre Barbaroux
Research Center of the French Air Force, France

ABSTRACT

This chapter introduces a theoretical framework to study how Internet technologies provide organizations with additional capabilities to handle various forms of communication and decision-making complexities. In particular, we investigate how specific use-based combinations of Internet technologies emerge within operational contexts. Principal illustrations are drawn from the U.S. military uses of Tactical Internet during recent operations in Afghanistan and Iraq. Military contexts offer relevant illustrations of organizations using Internet within complex decision environments for which short-term responsiveness and tactical adaptability are critical. Within this framework, we discuss the conditions for which combined uses generate additional value for organizations, and we underline the active role played by final users in exploiting the benefits of tactical Internet. Finally, we examine their additional value in the formulation of an effective technological strategy.

INTRODUCTION

Information and Communication Technologies (ICTs) provide organizations with major technological solutions to manage decision-making and communication processes (Gittell & Weiss, 2004; Pickering & King, 1995). Exploiting the benefits of ICTs often requires deep organizational transformations. Organizations have to select an appropriate technological strategy (and implement associated technological tools) with regard to the decisions and problems they face. Therefore, understanding the impact of ICTs on an organization involves a close examination of its uses. This issue goes far beyond technical aspects to be related to a socio-organizational "use-based" approach of technology (Barley, 1986; De Sanctis & Poole, 1994; Orlikowski, 1992). There is a need to discuss the uses of ICTs in terms of contextualized work practices, and to understand how uses emerge through the actions of final users within organizational contexts (Brown & Duguid, 1991; Orlikowski, 2000).

In this chapter, we focus on the use of Internet technologies within organizations, and analyze their impact on decision making and knowledge sharing. We develop a theoretical framework to study how Web-based tools provide organizations with additional capabilities to handle various information and knowledge problems. According to our framework, people assimilate technologies with regard to their technical features while satisfying their own needs. Uses are driven by the logic of adaptation of final users to uncertain and complex conditions. Hence, technologies might trigger the emergence of unexpected uses, and generate mitigated results. We suggest that combinations of technology uses enable organizations to control and foster decision making and communication processes. Therefore, we investigate how specific use-based combinations of technological functions, knowledge types, and knowledge processes emerge within operational contexts, and we discuss the conditions for which use-based combinations generate additional value for organizations.

Principal illustrations are drawn from the recent U.S. military operations in Afghanistan and Iraq. These operations have been the opportunity for U.S. military organizations to experiment with a new model of warfare that consists in exploiting network-centric technologies to develop information superiority on the battlefield (Alberts, Gartska, & Stein, 1999). At the tactical level of warfare, this new doctrine consists in using digital Web-based tools (Tactical Internet, TI) to communicate and to make decisions. Tactical Internet comprises various functions related to distinct knowledge processes: decision making and communication. In using decision-support and communication tools, war fighters learn to combine knowledge-based functions and processes, which, in turn, enable them to solve operational problems.

We now develop a theoretical framework that describes the ways ICTs enable organizations to manage various forms of complexity. Then, we provide empirical illustrations, and analyze how Tactical Internet affects knowledge sharing and decision making within military organizations. Finally, we suggest that combined uses of Web-based tools are one of the main sources of value for the organization, and enable decision makers to manage complexities. The last section is conclusive.

THE USE OF INFORMATION AND COMMUNICATION TECHNOLOGIES TO MANAGE UNCERTAINTY AND COMPLEXITY

Organizations are confronted to increasing paces of technological and socio-organizational changes that are major sources of uncertainty and complexity. In seeking to adapt their products and services to changing circumstances, organizations develop technological solutions to deal with multiple forms of complexity. Before discussing the various types of knowledge and processes involved in the development of such technological solutions, the next section focuses on the concepts of uncertainty and complexity.

Complexity and Uncertainty

Complexity is a cross-disciplinary research topic that is firmly rooted in systems theory and information theory. It is often associated with such core concepts as uncertainty, non-linearity, chaos, and emergence (Simon, 1969b). Complexity is widely used in economics and management science as a theoretical concept able to cope with the analysis of individual and organizational decision making and learning (Anderson, 1999; March, 1991; Nonaka, 1994). Complexity is also currently used by evolutionary, as well as institutional economists, to study how patterns of interactions emerge and evolve within and across markets and firms (Arthur, Durlauf, & Lane, 1997).

Following Herbert Simon, complexity refers to situations in which a great number of entities interact in a non-simple way (Simon, 1969a; Simon, 1969b). Many conceptions of complexity in social sciences, as well as in natural sciences, consider that complex phenomena might emerge from frequent interactions between simple entities. All complexity theorists share the same view that a system is complex when its macrobehaviours cannot be explained simply by referring to micro-level interactions and behaviours. This statement reflects the idea that within complex systems the whole is more than the sum of the parts. Such a definition is widely accepted by scholars who assume that complex system dynamics emerge from inextricable microinteractions between simple entities. Further, scholars acknowledge that the behaviour of a complex system is highly unpredictable. Even when a complex system is deterministic, it might be highly sensible to initial conditions, and generates unexpected macrobehaviours. On the one hand, a complex system can be chaotic, evolutionary, or self-organizing by virtue of its structure and dynamics and, on the other hand, it can exhibit radical uncertainty.

For the purpose of this chapter, we suggest that complexity is a core concept from which a theoretical framework can be developed in order to cope with organizational behaviours. Before analysing how organizations manage complexity, the conceptual difference between uncertainty and complexity must be established. Consider a deci-

sion maker who starts collecting and computing information and data about her/his environment. Confronted to uncertainty, the decision maker cannot have access to any exhaustive and complete set of information and data. Her/his rationality is limited by incomplete and/or imperfect information sets that make rational decision making hard to achieve (Shackle, 1961). By contrast, in situations of complexity, the decision maker might well have collected all the relevant information about her/his environment and still be unable to develop a relevant understanding. Complexity appears when a decision maker feels cognitively uncomfortable with the interpretation of a particular data or event. This might reflect her/his ambiguous and/or equivocal understanding of the behaviours and interactions that characterize her/his environment and its components.

Discriminating between uncertainty and complexity is thus critical because they rely on different phenomenological perceptions of the relationships between the organization and its environment. According to Zack (2001), uncertainty corresponds to situations for which organizations do not have enough information (1) to make rational decisions, and (2) to predict events that have an impact on current and future decisions. Organizations might need the kind of information related to the variety of elements and relationships that must be simultaneously considered in order to decide effectively. The variety of interactions between heterogeneous and often dispersed events and components is a key characteristic of organizations' decision-making environment. Therein, the goal of organizations is to develop a relevant representation of the complex relationships between the elements that have an impact on its own decisions. Confronted to uncertainty, organizations collect, analyze, and contextualize a variety of data in order to accumulate information, and create knowledge about external conditions. These processes extend organizations' responsiveness and strategic capabilities (Davenport, Harris, De Long, & Jacobson, 2001), and reduce uncertainty.

Complexity is quite different. Complexity emerges when organizations experiment interpretive failures. If organizations effectively reduce uncertainty by continuously collecting and processing additional information about their environment, it does not mean they have a unique or convergent interpretation of this information. The accumulation and processing of information do not provide organizations with appropriate conceptual framework to interpret information in an unambiguous and/or univocal way (Zack, 2001). We propose that ambiguity and equivocality are more likely to emerge in organizational contexts within which the diversity of decision makers' mental models can induce divergent, multiple, and/or contradictory interpretations of common information. Therefore, interpretive failures are more likely to occur when different decision makers interact, communicate, and share common goals, but fail to correctly interpret information about their environment.

We suggest that uncertainty and complexity require specific capabilities to collect and exploit additional information about critical elements and events, and to assess the nature of their relationship. In particular, organizations must have the capability to identify, develop, and improve appropriate knowledge, expertise, and skills in order to reduce information and knowledge gaps. Problems of interpretation cannot be simply handled by collecting and integrating more information. To deal with interpretive forms of complexity, organizations must improve their sense-making capabilities, and develop appropriate communication contexts that enhance cooperation and knowledge sharing. When organizations are confronted with complexity, they need to improve their sense-making capability (Weick, 1995; Weick, Sutcliffe, & Obstfeld, 2005).

The concepts of complexity and uncertainty provide a useful typology that relates to various knowledge-based problems. In situations of complexity and uncertainty, organizations must be able to collect, store, transform, and communicate a variety of knowledge types within a variety of decision-making contexts. Next section investigates the various types of knowledge the organization deals with in order to make effective decisions under conditions of complexity and uncertainty.

Taxonomies of Knowledge

Conceptually, knowledge splits into two broad categories: explicit and codified knowledge *vs.* implicit and tacit knowledge. There is a vast literature on the distinction between codified and tacit knowledge and its implications for organizations' managers and decision makers (Cowan, David, & Foray, 2001; Häkanson, 2007; Johnson, Lorenz, & Lundvall, 2002; Nonaka, 1994). Knowledge is made explicit through its codification on a particular support. Explicit forms of knowledge are congenial since they can be stored, absorbed, and disseminated easily within and across organizations. However, even when knowledge has been made explicit and codified, it remains highly subjective. Codified knowledge needs to be complemented with tacit forms of knowledge that are embodied in knowledge workers' experience and expertise. The absorption and interpretation of codified knowledge depend on prior skills and competences. Further, the codification of knowledge does not automatically enhance the organization's capacity to share knowledge (Jensen, Johnson, Lorenz, & Lundvall, 2007). The diffusion and sharing of codified knowledge depend on the codification process *per se*. The code used to write knowledge down, and the resulting levels of knowledge abstraction and generalization, contribute to its effective diffusion among individuals and communities (Boisot, 1998).

Lundvall and Johnson (1994) have proposed a useful set of distinctions that digs more deeply into the variety of knowledge organizations deal with. This set is based on four types of knowledge: know-what, know-why, know-how, and know-who. As Jensen et al. (2007) argue, "while important aspects of know-what and know-why may be obtained through reading books, attending lectures and accessing data bases, the two other categories are more rooted in practical experience" (p. 3).

One should consider that the former two types of knowledge, know-what and know-why, are usually related to explicit knowledge that have been codified (or could be "easily" codified with reasonable costs) and stored on particular supports. By contrast, the latter two types of knowledge, know-how and know-who, are characterized by implicit and tacit forms of knowledge that have been mainly acquired through learning, experimentation, and social practices. Subsequently, know-how and know-who are embodied in people's skills and experiences, and cannot be shared easily without additional cognitive efforts.

The previous taxonomies provide useful insights on the distinction between complexity and uncertainty. While uncertainty is conceptually related to the decision maker's inability to build an exhaustive and complete set of information (codified knowledge) about a particular situation, complexity is associated with ineffective cognitive activities that might lead the decision maker to develop ambiguous and/or equivocal perception and interpretation of this set of information. This means that the reduction of uncertainty is logically concerned with the accumulation of explicit and codified knowledge, while complexity is effectively managed through the development of tacit knowledge, and learning by experimentation. However, the coupling of uncertainty and complexity with two ideal types of knowledge does not mean that the perception of uncertainty by the decision maker is exclusive and free from any form of ambiguity or equivocality. As codified and tacit knowledge, uncertainty and complexity appear in a much more mixed form in real organizational life.

Four Forms of Complexity

The organization can be simultaneously confronted to many forms of **knowledge-based complexity**. Building on the previous analysis, we suggest that organizations have to manage four "ideal forms" of knowledge-based complexity. The four forms are respectively oriented toward one particular dimension of organizational context: environment, information, cognition, and communication.

- Environment forms of complexity are associated with physical features of organizations' external and internal environment; in particular (1) the number of actors involved in decision-making and coordination, (2) the geographical dispersion of their activities, and (3) the integration of contingent behaviours within organizations' plans and decisions. These forms of complexity relate to the intricacy of the internal and external interactions between the various units and actors that make up the organization and its environment as a whole.

- Information forms of complexity emerge when organizations are confronted with information incompleteness. These forms of complexity are also related to the architecture of the decision-making models that have been implemented and employed by the organization.

- Cognitive forms of complexity are associated with decision makers' psychological states (e.g., stress, emergency, crisis management) and mental models' diversity, which make up the cognitive structure of the organization.

- Communication forms of complexity appear when formal and informal communications between units and partners involved in collaborative projects require rich interactions and strong knowledge-sharing mechanisms.

Within this framework, two categories of information and knowledge-processing problems are particularly significant: **information gaps** and

knowledge gaps. We define information gaps as the lack of information (codified knowledge) about a given situation, and the variety of interactions between facts, events, and actors. Information gaps are related to environment and information forms of knowledge-based complexity. By contrast, knowledge gaps are related to communication failures due to divergent mental models and misinterpretations (or multiple interpretations) of the same data, circumstances, and events. Knowledge gaps are associated with communication and cognitive forms of knowledge-based complexity (tacit knowledge). Together, information and knowledge gaps can cause biased decisions and create coordination failures. Moreover, these two categories of problems often occur simultaneously within organizations' decision-making environment. In many cases, decision-makers cannot clearly discriminate between information shortcomings and interpretive failures. Table 1 presents the four forms of complexity that characterize organizations' decision-making environment.

In implementing information and communication technologies, organizations seek to hamper the effects of complexity. ICTs tend to improve the quality of both communication and decision-making processes (Huber & Crisp, 2003) by providing organizations with additional capacities to deal with knowledge-based complexities. However, ICTs cover a large spectrum of heterogeneous tools and support various knowledge processes. Next section develops a use-based perspective on information and communication technologies, and discusses how combined uses emerge and improve organizational capabilities.

The Use of ICTs: A Combination-Based Approach

Many scholars have proposed classifications to link knowledge processes to sets of dedicated technologies. For instance, Marwick (2001) associated ICTs with the four different phases of the knowledge life cycle formalized by Nonaka and Takeuchi (1995). Alavi and Tiwana (2003) identified the key technologies that support the creation, the storage/retrieval, the transfer, and the application of knowledge in organization. Despite the interest of these classifications, they are primarily focused on knowledge management processes. Subsequently, the basic functions of ICTs, such as communication and decision support, remain in the background. In order to grasp the effect of ICTs on both information and knowledge gaps, it is critical to define a framework that associates knowledge processes with basic

Table 1. Four forms of knowledge-based complexity

	KNOWLEDGE GAPS
Environment Number of actors Geographical dispersion of activities Contingent behaviors Physical features	**Cognitive** Psychological states Diversity of mental models
Information Information completeness/ exhaustiveness Decision models	**Communication** Formal and informal communications Collaboration Knowledge sharing
INFORMATION GAPS	

functions of technologies. This could clarify the mechanisms through which ICTs enable organizations to process a variety of knowledge types and to deal with uncertainty and complexity issues. In that way, the classification proposed by Zack (1999) is helpful in making ICTs' functions easy to identify. Zack distinguished two main knowledge processes: integrative and interactive. He associated each knowledge process with (1) a specific type of knowledge and (2) a set of technologies.

Integrative knowledge process refers to the management of existing stocks and sequential flows of explicit knowledge in organization. As we previously mentioned, explicit knowledge is related to declarative knowledge (know-what and know-why) that is formal and can be packaged as information. Declarative knowledge is codified, documented, transferred, and easily shared. Hence, the set of ICTs dedicated to integrative process provides a way to integrate and manage declarative knowledge. We suggest calling these tools "decision-support" technologies. Decision-support technologies are upgrading databases, expert systems, online management information systems, tactical navigation aids, information repositories, and so forth. As Huber and Crisp (2003) argued, decision-support tools allow the organization to (1) store and retrieve large amounts of knowledge, (2) combine and reconfigure knowledge so as to create new knowledge, and (3) use the decision models developed in experts and decision makers' mind and stored as expert systems. We consider that decision-support technologies enable organizations to handle problems related to environment and information forms of knowledge-based complexity.

The second knowledge process is called interactive. It concentrates primarily on supporting interactions among individuals holding tacit knowledge. Since tacit knowledge is developed from experiences and action, it is difficult to articulate and share. However, tacit knowledge can be made explicit, in particular through knowledge exchanges and rich communications among peo-

ple. ICTs that focus on communication, such as e-mail, text-chat, and videoteleconferencing, generate interactive knowledge processes in allowing individuals to share a part of their tacit knowing. Such dedicated ICTs refer to "communication" technologies. They facilitate (1) communication across time and geographical location with greater precision to target groups, and (2) participation and control in networks (Huber & Crisp, 2003). As collaborative and communication tools, such technologies make the conversion of tacit knowing into explicit knowing easier, and reduce the probability of misinterpretation to emerge. We suggest that communication technologies may efficiently reduce knowledge gaps related to communication and cognitive forms of knowledge-based complexity.

In associating integrative and interactive knowledge processes with basic functions of ICTs, the previous framework points out the ways technologies help to manage and create knowledge. Nevertheless, this classification tends to establish a rather deterministic link between knowledge processes and basic functions of technologies. Even when Zack introduced combinations of knowledge processes, he always associated a specific set of ICTs with a single knowledge process. This perspective promotes a linear cause-effect relationship in which technology systematically produces the desired (or near desired) effect on knowledge management goals.

In this chapter, we seek out to avoid technological determinism since it plays down contextual effects and human factors on technologies. In order to develop our framework, we adapt the typology of Zack to a "use-based" perspective. Structurational models (Barley, 1986; De Sanctis & Poole, 1994; Orlikowski, 1992; Orlikowski & Robey, 1991) fit well with our purpose since they are inherently dynamic and grounded in ongoing human action. According to the authors, people appropriate the "embodied structures" inscribed in technologies during their uses. Structures are here understood as the set of rules and resources developed in recurrent social practices (Giddens, 1984). When people interact regularly with technologies, they are engaged with some of these rules and resources that shape their actions by facilitating some outcomes and constraining others (Orlikowski & Robey, 1991). Then, different types of appropriation might occur that preserve, substitute for, combine, enlarge, contrast, constrain, affirm, or negate the structures provided by ICTs (De Sanctis & Poole, 1994, p. 135). Orlikowski (2000) went deeper into the idea of appropriation in focusing on "emergent structures" of technologies. Through their regularized and contextualized engagement with ICTs, final users enact a set of rules and resources that structure their ongoing interactions with technologies. The concept of enactment represents the ability of final users to translate technologies into action and to transform them during action. In their recurrent and situated practices, final users shape the technologies' structures that shape their uses. Orlikowski stressed on the recursive nature of users' interactions with technologies. Further, she highlighted that when people use ICTs, they draw on (1) technologies' structures gradually inscribed by designers and users in their previous interactions, (2) their skills, knowledge, expectations about technologies and their uses, and (3) their knowledge and experiences concerning the organizational and social contexts in which they live and work, including cultural values and social conventions (Orlikowski, 2000, p. 410).

Technologies' uses are, thus, strongly affected by situated practices. That is the reason why the impact of ICTs' implementation is difficult to anticipate. People are able to enact a single technology in different ways, depending on their needs, their situation, the context of use, and so forth. Such an insight is critical for our framework since it stresses on the non-linear relationship between ICTs functions and knowledge processes. For instance, Benghozi (2002) reported that the implementation of workflow generates two different types of uses. On the one hand,

workflow is implemented to sustain repetitive tasks, dealing with a large amount of information and following rigorous procedures. In that case, it represents a production-assisting tool, and supports an integrative knowledge process. On the other hand, workflow is deployed in order to facilitate a project management or an innovation process. In this case, procedures are not decided beforehand. Individuals contribute to their definition through collaborative exchanges during the project life cycle. Therefore, workflow supports cooperation, among individuals, in articulating disseminated knowledge and activities. It can be assimilated to a collaborative tool and generates interactive knowledge process. The different uses of workflow depend on the particular ways and conditions final users deal with.

A given technology enables organizations to process declarative as well as procedural knowledge. The contribution of technology as integrative or interactive knowledge process depends on its effectiveness, at a given time, in fulfilling organizational goals. Final users adopt a technology with regard to their needs, at a given time and within a given context. More precisely, they combine their uses to adapt their actions to uncertain and complex circumstances. Such combinations are situated since they fulfill particular needs in particular ways.

We refer to the concept of use as the combination of knowledge processes, knowledge types, and basic functions of technologies, in order to study how organizations exploit decision support and communication tools. However, we consider that combined uses can generate mitigated results. On the one hand, they might enable organizations to reduce both information and knowledge gaps. On the other hand, combined uses might create additional and unexpected decision making and communication problems.

The use of tactical Internet (TI) by U.S. military organizations provides a relevant example to grasp the impact of combined uses on decision making and communication. Indeed, military organizations act within highly demanding environments where time pressures are severe and errors only tolerated at minimum rates. Tactical Internet is considered by the military as an effective set of decision-making and communication technologies that enables dispersed units to achieve tactical goals within highly austere conditions. As such, the TI example provides significant insights for a variety of distinctive organizational contexts (medical health care, fire brigades, nuclear plants, etc.) within which responsiveness and adaptability are decisive success factors (Faraj & Xiao, 2006). Therefore, we focus on military organizations since they offer illustrations of organizations that use Internet technologies within complex decision environments. Examples are drawn from recent military operations in Afghanistan (Operation Enduring Freedom – 2001) and Iraq (Operation Iraqi Freedom – 2003). We have chosen to investigate these two operations since they represent the first operations in history where a truly digital force has been deployed in real war situations.

THE USE OF TACTICAL INTERNET WITHIN THE U.S. MILITARY ORGANIZATIONS

Tactical internet (TI) consists of various Web-based tools as modern collaboration systems (chat, e-mail, videoteleconferencing, voice over Internet protocol), computer decision-support aids (Tactical navigation aids, automated interfaces to training and simulation systems), and upgrading databases (modification, filtering, and storage of graphics, text files, tactical environment, and target data). Such Internet technologies tend to improve the common operational picture (COP) that enables war fighters to access the same information and knowledge and to obtain a clear picture of the tactical situation (Seymour & Cowen, 2006).

Next sections focus on text-chat, upgrading databases (as the positioning location guidance system—PLGS), and videoteleconferencing (VTC) to study how combined uses of Web-based tools provide the military with effective capacities to reduce both information and knowledge gaps. We stress on the unexpected effects of such combinations, especially problems of misunderstanding and information overload.

Using Tactical Internet to Reduce Information and Knowledge Gaps: Insights from the Text Chat

Text-chat is widely used tactically on U.S. Navy ships and by Special Forces (U.S. Army and U.S. Marine Corps), and is a key communication tool for all military services (Seymour & Cowen, 2006). Chat tools can be very useful for conversing and sharing files with remote war fighters. This technology allows multiple users synchronous participation within various chat rooms. Since text-chat enables collaboration as well as real time information dissemination, it is used by the military to coordinate disseminated units, but also to supplement (or in some cases replace) other Command and Control systems (Eovito, 2006). During Operation Iraqi Freedom, 4th Air Support Operation Group (ASOG from the US Army) used chat tool to combine operations (the so-called close air support —CAS) between Special Forces on the ground and Air Force planes. Uses of chat were wide-ranging. On the one hand, it appeared useful to task Unmanned Aerial Vehicles (UAVs) and others sensors in order to collect and disseminate intelligence to all units requiring information for CAS execution. Imagery from UAVs, weather forecasts, and other target information, were easily distributed among soldiers. This extra information about environment features and evolution of tactical goals helped to manage information gaps. On the other hand, chat tool allowed real-time collaboration between CAS key actors for questions on strike-related, target, and coordination with other parallel agencies. Chat helped to monitor the mission in preparation and to send debrief/mission report once pilots returned. As a result, chat enhanced efficient collaborative interactions.

Despite the lack of non-verbal cues (Scott, Cummings, Graeber, Nelson, & Bolia, 2006; Wainfain & Davis, 2004), text chat provided war fighters with frequent occasions to exchange know-how as experiences, stories, viewpoints, and more conceptual knowledge. In sharing procedural knowledge and creating new know-how, chat supports the externalization of knowledge through the conversion of tacit knowledge to explicit knowledge (Nonaka & Takeuchi, 1995). One of chat critical properties for users is to access multiple rooms simultaneously. It gave to 4th ASOG the opportunity to manage information from sensors while communicating with other key actors involved in the operation: soldiers were dealing with declarative and procedural types of knowledge at the same time. They developed combinations of uses that generated both interactive and integrative knowledge processes. Such combined uses improved their situational awareness with no additional cost in time and effort. Eovito (2006) reported that soldiers felt their situational awareness without chat could be strongly diminished, and information dissemination and coordination would be a struggle.

This illustration suggests that the efficiency of Internet technologies comes from combinations of uses developed by final users on the battlefield. War fighters assimilated chat's technical features, and adapted them to their operational needs and constraints. They looked beyond chat's initial collaborative functions, and also used it as a decision-support tool. A single Web-based tool allowed war fighters to develop and to exploit both interactive and integrative knowledge processes. Such combined uses improved knowledge-sharing and decision-making processes on the battlefield. However, despite significant improvements, many information gaps and knowledge gaps remained unsolved. Further, combined uses generated unexpected effects that increased organizational decision making and communication problems.

Creating Unexpected Information and Knowledge Gaps: Insights from the Text Chat, the Positioning Location Guidance System (PLGS) and the Videoteleconferencing (VTC)

Many officers and scholars reported suboptimal results of text-chat uses (Akavia & Gofer, 2006; Eovito, 2006; Scott et al., 2006). Its promises were not fully realized due to some unexpected issues. Since knowledge-sharing occured in real-time, war fighters had to remain focused and watchful in order to hold the right information at the right moment. The situation could become very stressful since they did not want to miss out critical information. The problem was to determine the moment where soldiers stopped collecting information and concentrated exclusively on mission execution. Therefore, soldiers quickly felt themselves under pressure and overloaded by information flow. Such a result illustrates a problem related to the lack of skills in managing information spaces. Recent researches and experiments into human performance (Cummings, 2005) suggest that subjects remain fixated on the chat interface, and ignore the task of retargeting missiles in urgent and stressful situations. Even when instructors repeat that the primary mission is retargeting, subjects are still focused on chat; answering all queries before dealing with retargeting problems. Even if time and effort are saved from repeating questions (previous conversations are written and time stamped), the multiple rooms property tends to increase the amount of information available at a given time. Such a situation can be explained since we consider the volume and the time-sensitive nature of chat traffic.

After-action reports from Afghanistan and Iraq stressed additional information-space management problems concerning the use of

Web-based decision-support tools. The **Positioning Location Guidance System (PLGS)** provides a relevant example of such problems. The U.S. Army uses PLGS in order to capture tactical information in real time: opposing and allied forces locations appear on the display(s) as coloured icons on a digitized map. Information is related to troop movements, speed of moving, battle development (level of fuel, ammunitions, etc.). PLGS also provides e-mail communication to exchange procedural knowledge on tactical situation. War fighters reported that they could feel overloaded with the amount of information, and that sometimes much of it may have had little bearing on their missions (Wilson, 2005). They received messages and images from too many different networks, leading them to operate a large number of selections that involved additional pressure. Reports also indicated that soldiers tended to automatically transmit data from sensors to the highest level of command. Problems arose when numerous sensors detected a single vehicle, at the same time. In that case, the threat was overestimated. All these examples illustrate the limitation of Web-based tools combined uses. Even if uses tend to generate integrative as well as interactive knowledge processes, information and environment forms of complexity are not fully handled. Information gaps still subsist, mainly due to a lack of skills dedicated to information space management.

Further, problems of misinterpretation and sense-making still persist despite extended exchange opportunities through Tactical Internet. Knowledge gaps arose because war fighters attribute different interpretations to the same cue, the same message, or the same tactical situation. Cues, like conversational pauses during chat exchanges, could be misinterpreted, and introduced unwarranted confusion. When a team failed to answer to a text message, the sender could misinterpret this lack of response as a disagreement with its statement, while it was just as likely that the message receiver was concentrated on another

task (Scott et al., 2006). Clarifying the situation from the receiver introduces significant costs: it requires effort, and may be disruptive if information is provided at an inopportune moment (Dabbish & Kraut, 2004). As a result, the ability of knowing when and how to communicate with a remote team (if it is available for conversation or not) has to be acquired by final users in order to avoid communication failures. Such misinterpretations of non-verbal cues can produce more challenging situations.

After-action reports from Operation Iraqi Freedom also indicated that the use of **videoteleconferencing (VTC)** by U.S. military often led participants to question the commander intent. As Wainfain and Davis (2004) pointed out, VTC often challenges the attendees in interpreting each one's body language and gestures, especially as the number of participants increases. VTC limits non-verbal, para-verbal, and status cues, and reduces the quality of the knowledge exchanged. Participants are also less willing to engage a discussion and find a solution. VTC appears less persuasive than face-to-face, in part because of the poor image resolution and the delays in VTC's audio. During mission preparation, such disadvantages constrained the commanders to clarify their objectives through more detailed e-mails, but in most cases, by face-to-face meetings. As a result, the time required to prepare operation was longer than expected (Fox, 2004; White, 2002). Such a knowledge gap between commanders and war fighters on the ground illustrates the limitation of explicit communication Web-based technologies. If chat and VTC promise efficient collaboration, they lack the richness of face-to-face interactions. This is the reason why knowledge sharing through Tactical Internet tools must be accompanied by more subtle group interactions to help the military communicate and coordinate during joint operations (Scott et al., 2006).

Illustrations from operations Enduring Freedom and Iraqi Freedom highlight one main result: in generating integrative and interactive knowledge processes, combined uses of Web-based tools improve knowledge sharing and decision making on the battlefield. However, they often trigger the emergence of additional information and knowledge-related problems. This point raises the more general question of Web-based tools' net value for organizations. While Internet technologies inspire organizations' strategy to leverage knowledge, they themselves cannot fully explain their organizational value. Technologies might provide efficient solutions to knowledge-based problems if both technological and socio-organizational factors are taken into account by managers who seek out to develop an effective technological strategy.

THE ADDITIONAL VALUE GENERATED BY COMBINED USES OF ICTS IN ORGANIZATIONS

Analysing combined uses of Internet technologies within organizations, the first thing that comes into views is that we need to identify the various domains for which ICTs are likely to generate additional value. We identify two organizational areas: (1) decision making and (2) knowledge sharing. Since the effects of the implementation of ICTs are non-linear, issues concerning technologies enactment by final users must be addressed to ensure organizational benefits. This perspective might affect the strategic management of technological change in organization.

Articulating Decision Making and Knowledge Sharing through ICTs: An Ambivalent Relationship

Successful organizations are able to develop valuable competences dedicated to decision making and knowledge sharing under conditions of uncertainty and complexity. Many of these valuable competences are dependent on the technological attributes of modern Internet technologies. For example, ICTs generate an exponential increase of knowledge-processing speed, volumes, and memorization capacities. On the one hand, the introduction of decision-support and communication tools triggers the generalization of automated command and control loops for a wide range of well-structured repeated decisions. The result is a continuous trend toward optimized decision loops because the rate of interactions increases both vertically and horizontally, reducing decision time lags, and allowing for a selective control of decision-making tempo. On the other hand, the number and variety of available communication tools are extended. The quality of communications increases significantly, thanks to the variety of communication supports (e.g., voice, texts, images, videos) that can be transmitted. By promoting horizontal communications within a hierarchically organized system, Web-based tools facilitate the decentralization of decision making. This suggests that ICTs create additional autonomy within the organization's hierarchy, enhancing organizational flexibility and adaptability. However, the organizational impact of decision-support and communication tools remains ambivalent. ICTs can turn the chain of command into a decentralized network of interacting decision nodes, but they can also reinforce a trend toward centralization and direct supervision of subordinates that might impede intermediate decision makers' initiatives, and create a climate of distrust.

Another critical issue concerning the net value of ICTs relates to knowledge sharing. While technological attributes affect both the collective storing and sharing of knowledge and the ability for individuals to communicate frequently (Fulk & DeSanctis, 1995), they should be mixed with socio-organizational factors to better appreciate the role played by ICTs in the process of knowledge sharing. Among these factors, van den Hooff et al. (van den Hooff, Elving, Meeuwsen, & Dumoulin, 2003) regard interindividual trust and community-based identification as major determinants since they affect individuals' ability and willingness to share knowledge and cooperate. As Faraj and Xiao (2006) argued, knowledge sharing "is one of the most difficult aspects of expertise coordination. Technological solutions provide redundancy but cannot replace the human element" (p. 1163). It is therefore critical to keep in mind that a great deal of knowledge sharing depends on people's willingness to share what they know, often through verbal, informal, and face-to-face interactions. Pickering and King (1995) also suggested that cooperation in the digital work place depends on a particular category of individuals who provide loose connections between members of strong-tie communities. This need for a weak-tie communication network as a complement to Web-based tools is reinforced within organizations exhibiting high levels of geographical dispersion of operations. Such organizations are indeed dependent on long-distance intra- and interorganizational communications to ensure effective coordination. They can exploit Web-based technologies to connect organizational units within loosely coupled cooperative structures. Therein, weak ties might serve as "bridges" between strong-tie networks, and provide organizationally useful information.

The organizational value of Internet technologies for organizations is not straightforward. ICTs cannot be managed only through preconceived technological standards and routines. Combined uses of ICTs cannot be fully expected because decision making cannot be specified in sufficient detail to be carried out, repeated, and standardized.

The Additional Value of ICTs: A Strategic Perspective

As Malhotra (2005) reminded us, investing in the most advanced technologies does not ensure real business-performance improvements. Most of the leader organizations in a wide range of industries did not massively invest in ICTs. In contrast, they have adopted a well-designed trans-formation strategy (or business model) to drive technology deployment and utilization. Hence, the implementation of ICTs should be motivated by organizational expectations about their strategic value for the organization. The conditions for success reside in the attributes and qualities of the strategy-driven model of technological change adopted by the organization.

The issues of technology appropriation by users, technology integration within specific work-contexts, and organizational transformation need to be addressed together to ensure that technology can deliver upon the promise of organization performance. There is a need to discuss the combined uses of ICTs in terms of a contextualized set of practices that remains emergent and tacit. Therefore, combined uses refer to work practices that emerge from an ongoing stream of activities and are enacted through the actions of individuals within specialized contexts (Brown & Duguid, 1991; Brown & Duguid, 1998; Orlikowski, 2000).

We suggest that a balanced integration of formal and informal decision-making and communication mechanisms, based on combined uses of ICTs, should be privileged in order to enhance organizations' adaptation to uncertain and complex circumstances. By focusing on combinations of formal and informal communications, tangible and intangible assets, and interactive and integrative processes, organizations are able to leverage strategic value from the deployment of ICTs.

Our perspective has a natural affinity with the resource-based view of competitive advantage in the strategy field (Barney, 1991; Grant, 1991). The resource-based view states that a firm develops a competitive advantage by combining, and effectively deploying, its physical, human, and organizational resources in ways that add unique value (Barney, 1991). This perspective draws attention to the role played by individual and collective skills, knowledge, routines, and learning mechanisms. Theses resources result from complex social structures (as rules and resources) built over time and, thus, difficult to understand and imitate (Colbert, 2004). Our **combined uses framework** is connected to the resource-based view since it promotes such combinations of physical, human, and organizational resources. Final users improve the basic functions of ICTs by combining and deploying routines, skills, and knowledge processes and types. Value comes from these capacities of combination and recombination of tangible and intangible resources, depending on contextual and working circumstances.

Despite its focus on the role played by managers in the selection, development, combination, and deployment of a firm's resources, the resource-based view offers little in the way of prescriptions. It does not specifically deal with how an organization can develop and support the efficient combinations of tangible and intangible resources to create and sustain competitive advantage (Delery, 1998). Our concept of combined uses might be useful for building and maintaining a competitive advantage. By focusing on the need to reconcile planned uses with unexpected ones, this concept offers a practical view on the way organizations can effectively manage what Sanchez et al. (Sanchez, Heene, & Thomas, 1996) called "the coordinated deployment of resources." In particular, our concept of combination insists on the role played by both centralized and decentralized coordination mechanisms in the generation of appropriate technology uses. This means that organizations should reconcile two competitive approaches of organizational change: a top-down strategy-based approach and a bottom-up mode of management. Amin and Cohendet (2004) called these two competing perspectives "management by design" and "management by communities." The first mode (management by design) focuses on organizational design issues and coordination mechanisms. The governance of the organization is conceptualized from a top-down approach, suggesting the dominance of hierarchical relationships and a routine-based architecture for

coordinating inter individual knowledge and actions. However, designing an effective strategy for deploying and exploiting ICTs cannot ensure organizational value. According to our approach, the core problem of Internet technologies management relates to the evolving social practices that fold together the planned and the unexpected, the tacit and the codified, into a complex combination of uses. For ICTs to generate value, it is therefore critical to combine the top-down approach with a localized mode of management that focuses on how knowledge is formed and made explicit, how it is created and shared, and how it is disseminated. Here, the governance of the organization follows a bottom-up mode of management that seeks to exploit "enactive" socio-organizational dynamics.

CONCLUSION

This chapter developed a theoretical framework to analyze how Internet technologies help organizations to handle various forms of complexity related to decision making and knowledge sharing. First, it built on the concept of combination of ICTs' uses to study how individuals learn to mix different knowledge processes and technological functions to manage both information gaps and knowledge gaps. Second, it developed illustrations that highlighted the role played by combined uses emerging from the exploitation of Tactical Internet by the U.S. military in Afghanistan and in Iraq. Within this framework, we underlined the active role played by final users in exploiting the benefits of ICTs, and we focused on both the expected and unexpected effects of ICTs uses on various organizational processes. This view led us to examine the additional value of ICTs in terms of the role played by combined uses in the formulation of an effective technological strategy that reconciles a top-down approach of technology with a bottom-up mode of management.

FUTURE RESEARCH DIRECTIONS

The greatest barriers to the effective uses of Web-based tools are not technical: they relate to individual as well as organizational competences that are encapsulated in daily work practices. These practices emerge in a particular context, and remain tacit. Within this framework, two research issues can be explored:

- The acquisition and coordination of core technological and organizational capabilities through various modes of individual and organizational learning.
- The definition of organizational change as a coevolutionary process between the organization's architecture and its communication interfaces.

Core Capabilities and Learning Processes

In the field of strategic management, the main challenge for organizations is to acquire, exploit, and adjust core capabilities in responding to complex circumstances. We argue that two types of capability are likely to become core. The first one is concerned with the reduction of information gaps, and relates to the development of information space management capabilities. The second one should facilitate the reduction of knowledge gaps, and is linked to the development of knowledge-sharing capabilities. Each type of capability is associated with distinct knowledge activities (knowledge sharing and information processing), and requires appropriate learning processes. To understand how organizations acquire and exploit both information space management and knowledge-sharing capabilities, it is critical to focus on the nature of the learning mechanisms involved. This future research path shall insist on the variety of individual and organizational learning mechanisms that must be articulated in

order to provide knowledge intensive organizations with effective core capabilities.

Transformation of Organizational Architecture and Communication Interfaces

This chapter raises a number of issues related to organizational change. In particular, it insists on two critical dimensions that underlie the transformation of organizations. The first dimension is concerned with the exploitation of networking communication technologies and its impact on organizations' communication structures. The second dimension is more related to the evolution of organizational structures induced by the deployment of network-centric technologies. By and large, these dimensions relate to the coevolution of organizations' architecture, and interfaces. This future research path could build on the theory of complex products and systems (CoPS, Prencipe, Davis, & Hobday, 2003) and modularity (Langlois, 2002) to understand organizational transformation and technological change.

ACKNOWLEDGMENT

The authors would like to thank Ettore Bolisani and the three anonymous referees for their helpful suggestions and comments on this chapter. Ideas expressed in this chapter are those of the authors and do not reflect the position of the French Ministry of Defense nor of the French Air Force.

REFERENCES

Akavia, G., & Gofer, E. (2006). *Two weeks with a network-centric infantry company in an urban warfare trial.* Paper presented at the Command and Control Research and Technology Symposium, San Diego, CA.

Alavi, M., & Tiwana, A. (2003). Knowledge management: The information technology dimension. In M. Easterby-Smith & M. A. Lyles (Eds.), *Handbook of organizational learning and knowledge management* (pp. 104-121). Oxford: Blackwell Publishing.

Alberts, D. S., Gartska, J. J., & Stein, F. P. (1999). *Network-centric warfare: Developing and leveraging information superiority.* Washington D.C: Department of Defense C4ISR Cooperative Research Program.

Amin, A., & Cohendet, P. (2004). *Architectures of knowledge: Firms, capabilities, and communities.* Oxford: Oxford University Press.

Anderson, P. (1999). Complexity theory and organization science. *Organization Science, 10*(3), 216-232.

Arthur, W. B., Durlauf, R., & Lane, D. (1997). *The economy as an evolving complex system II.* Reading, MA: Addison-Wesley.

Barley, S. R. (1986). Technology as an occasion for structuring: Evidence from observation of CT scanners and the social order of radiology departments. *Administrative Science Quarterly, 31*, 78-108.

Barney, J. B. (1991). Firm resources and sustained competitive advantage. *Journal of Management, 17*, 99–120.

Benghozi, P. J. (2002). Technologie et organisation : le hasard et la nécessité. *Annales des Télécommunications, 57*(3-4), 289-305.

Boisot, M. (1998). *Knowledge assets. Securing competitive advantages in the information economy.* Oxford: Oxford University Press.

Brown, J. S., & Duguid, P. (1991). Knowledge and organization: A social-practice perspective. *Organization Science, 12*(2), 198-213.

Brown, J. S., & Duguid, P. (1998). Organizing knowledge. *California Management Review, 40*(3), 90-111.

Colbert, B. (2004). The complex resource-based view: Implications for theory and practice in strategic human resource management. *Academy of Management Review, 29*(3), 341-358.

Cowan, M., David, P., & Foray, D. (2001). The explicit economics of knowledge codification and tacitness. *Industrial and Corporate Change, 9*(2), 211-253.

Cummings, M. (2005). *The need for command and control instant message adaptive interfaces: Lessons learned from tactical Tomahawk human-in-the-loop simulations.* Cambridge, MA: Massachusetts Institute of Technology, Humans and Automation Laboratory.

Dabbish, L., & Kraut, R. (2004). Controlling interruptions: Awareness displays and social motivation for coordination. In *Proceedings of ACM Conference on Computer Supported Cooperative Work* (pp. 182-191). ACM Press.

Davenport, T. H., Harris, J. G., De Long, D. W., & Jacobson, A. L. (2001). Data to knowledge to results: Building an analytic capability. *California Management Review, 43*(2), 117-138.

Delery, J. E. (1998). Issues of fit in strategic human resource management: Implications for research. *Human Resource Management Review, 8*, 289–309.

De Sanctis, G., & Poole, M. (1994). Capturing the complexity in advanced technology in use: Adaptive structuration theory. *Organization Science, 5*(2), 121-47.

Eovito, B. (2006). *The impact of synchronous text-based chat on military Command and Control.* Paper presented at the 11th International Command and Control Research and Technology Symposium, Cambridge, UK.

Faraj, S., & Xiao, Y. (2006). Coordination in fast-response organizations. *Management Science, 52*(8), 1155-1169.

Fox, G. (2004). *Virtual collaboration: Advantages and disadvantages in the planning and execution of operations in the information age*, Newport: Naval War College.

Fulk, J., & DeSanctis, G. (1995). Electronic communication and changing organizational forms. *Organization Science, 6*(4), 337-349.

Giddens, A. (1984). *The constitution of society: Outline of the theory of structure*. Berkeley, CA: University of California Press.

Gittell, J., & Weiss, L. (2004). Coordination networks within and across organizations: A multilevel framework. *Journal of Management Studies, 41*(1), 127-153.

Grant, R. M. (1991). The resource-based theory of competitive advantage. *California Management Review, 33*(3), 114–135.

Häkanson, L. (2007). Creating knowledge: The power and logic of articulation. *Industrial and Corporate Change, 16*(1), 51-88.

Huber, G., & Crisp, C. (2003). Organizations, information systems impact on. In. H. Bidgoli (Ed.), *Encyclopedia of information systems* (pp. 413-26). San Diego: Elsevier Science Publishers.

Jensen, M. B., Johnson, B., Lorenz, E., & Lundvall, B.A. (2007). Forms of knowledge and modes of innovation. *Research Policy*.

Johnson, B., Lorenz, E., & Lundvall, B. A. (2002). Why all this fuss about codified and tacit knowledge? *Industrial and Corporate Change, 11*(2), 245-262.

Lundvall, B-A., & Johnson, B. (1994). The learning economy. *Journal of Industry Studies, 1*(2), 23-42.

Malhotra, Y. (2005). Integrating knowledge management technologies in organizational business processes: Getting real time enterprises to deliver real business performance. *Journal of Knowledge Management, 9*(1), 7-28.

March, J. G. (1991). Exploration and exploitation in organizational learning. *Organization Science, 2*(1), 71-87.

Marwick, A. (2001). Knowledge management technology. *IBM Systems Journal, 40*(4), 814-830.

Nonaka, I. (1994). A dynamic theory of organizational knowledge creation. *Organization Science, 5*(1), 14-34.

Nonaka, I., & Takeuchi, H. (1995). *The knowledge creating company: How Japanese companies create the dynamics of innovation?* New York: Oxford University Press.

Orlikowski, W. (1992). The duality of technology: Rethinking the concept of technology in organizations. *Organization Science, 3*(3), 398-427.

Orlikowski, W. (2000). Using technology and constituting structures: A practice lens for studying technology in organizations. *Organization Science, 11*(4), 404-428.

Orlikowski, W., & Robey, D. (1991). Information technology and the structuring of organizations. *Information Systems Research, 2*(2), 143-169.

Pickering, J., & King, J. (1995). Hardwiring weak ties: Interorganizational computer-mediated communications, occupational communities, and organizational change. *Organization Science, 6*(4), 479-486.

Sanchez, R., Heene, A., & Thomas, H. (1996). Toward the theory and practice of competence-based competition. In R. Sanchez, A. Heene, & H. Thomas(Eds.), *Dynamics of competence-based competition: Theory and practice in the new strategic management* (pp. 1-36). London: Elsevier Science.

Scott, S., Cummings, M., Graeber, D., Nelson, W., & Bolia, R. (June). *Collaboration technology in military team operations: Lessons learned from the corporate domain*. Paper presented at the

Command and Control Research and Technology Symposium, San Diego, CA.

Seymour, G., & Cowen, M. (2006). *A review of team collaboration tools for crisis response in the military and government*. Paper presented at the Command and Control Research and Technology Symposium, San Diego, CA.

Shackle, G. L. S. (1961). *Decision, order and time in human affairs*. Cambridge: Cambridge University Press.

Simon, H. A. (1969a). The architecture of complexity. In H. A. Simon (Ed.), *The Science of the artificial* (pp. 192-229). Cambridge, MA: MIT Press.

Simon, H. A. (1969b). *The science of the artificial*. Cambridge, MA: MIT press.

Van den Hooff, B., Elving, W., Meeuwsen, J. M., & Dumoulin, C. (2003). Knowledge sharing in knowledge communities. In M. Huysman, E. Wenger, & V. Wulf (Eds.), *Communities and technologies* (pp. 119-141). Boston: Kluwer Academic Publishers.

Wainfain, L., & Davis, P. (2004). *Challenges in virtual collaboration: Videoconferencing, audioconferencing and computer-mediated communications*. Santa Monica, CA: Rand Corporation, National Defense Research Institute.

Weick, K. E. (1995). *Sensemaking in organizations*. Thousand Oaks, CA: Sage Publications.

Weick, K. E., Sutcliffe, K. M., & Obstfeld, D. (2005). Organizing and the process of sensemaking. *Organization Science, 16*(4), 409-421.

White, J. (2002). *Retrospect of information technology's impact on society and warfare: revolution or dangerous hype?* Newport: Naval War College.

Wilson, C. (2005). *Network centric warfare: Background and oversight issues for Congress*, Wash-ington, D.C.: Report for Congress, Congressional Research Service, The library of Congress.

Zack, M. (1999). Managing codified knowledge. *Sloan Management Review, 40*(4), 45-58.

Zack, M. (2001). If managing knowledge is the solution, then what's the problem? In Y. Malhotra (Ed.), *Knowledge management and business model innovation* (pp. 16-36). Hershey, PA: Idea Group Publishing.

ADDITIONAL READING

Andreu, R., & Ciborra, C. (1996). Organisational learning and core capabilities development: the role of IT. *Journal of Strategic Information Systems, 5*, 111-127.

Argyres, N. S. (1999). The impact of information technology on coordination: Evidence from the B-2 "stealth" bomber. *Organization Science, 10*(2), 162-180.

Argyris, C., & Schön, D. (1978). *Organizational learning*. Reading, MA: Addison-Wesley.

Boland, R. J., Tenkasi, R. T., & Te'eni, D. (1994). Designing information technology to support distributed cognition. *Organization Science, 5*(3), 456-475.

Brown, J. S., & Duguid, P. (1996). Organizational learning and communities of practice. In M. D. Cohen & L. S. Sproull (Eds.), *Organizational learning* (pp. 58-82). London: Sage Publication.

Brusoni, S., Prencipe, A., & Pavitt, K. (2001). Knowledge specialization, organizational coupling, and the boundaries of the firm: Why do firms know more than they make? *Administrative Science Quarterly, 46*, 597-621.

Chandler, A. (1966). *Strategy and structures*. Cambridge: MIT Press.

Crowston, K. (1997). A coordination theory approach to organizational process design. *Organization Science, 8*(2), 157-175.

Davenport, T., & Prusak, L. (1998). *Working knowledge: How organizations manage what they know.* Cambridge, MA: Harvard University Press.

Davis, A., & Hobday, M. (2005). *The business of project: Managing innovation in complex products and systems.* Cambridge: Cambridge University Press.

Dodgson, M. (1993). Organizational learning: A review of some literatures. *Organization Studies, 14*(3), 375-394.

Henderson, R. M., & Clark, K. B. (1990). Architectural innovation: The reconfiguration of existing product technologies and the failure of established firms. *Administrative Science Quarterly, 35*(1), 9-30.

Hobday, M. (1998). Product complexity, innovation and industrial organization. *Research Policy, 26,* 689-710.

Kogut, B., & Zander, U. (1996). What firms do? Coordination, identity, and learning. *Organization Science, 7*(5), 702-718.

Langlois, R. N. (2002). Modularity in technology and organization. *Journal of Economic Behavior and Organization, 49,* 19-37.

Lave, J., & Wenger, E. (1991). *Situated learning: Legitimate peripheral participation.* Cambridge: Cambridge University Press.

Leonard-Barton, D. (1990). Core capabilities and core rigidities: A paradox in managing new product development. *Strategic Management Journal, 13,* 111-125.

Levitt, B., & March, J. G. (1988). Organizational learning. *Annual Review of Sociology, 14,* 319-340.

March, J. G., & Simon, H. A. (1958). *Organization.* New York: Wiley.

McDermott, R. (1999). Why information technology inspired but cannot deliver knowledge management. *California Management Review, 41*(4), 103-117.

Mintzberg, H. (1983). *Structure in fives: Designing effective organizations.* Englewood Cliffs NJ: Prentice-Hall.

Orton, J. E., & Weick, K. E. (1990). Loosely coupled systems: A re-conceptualization. *Academy of Management Review, 15*(2), 203-223.

Prahalad, C., & Hamel, G. (1990). The core competence of the corporation. *Harvard Business Review,* 79-91.

Prencipe, A., Davis, A., & Hobday, M. (2003). *The business of systems integration.* Oxford: Oxford University Press.

Sanchez, R., & Mahoney, J. T. (1996). Modularity, flexibility, and knowledge management in product and organization design. *Strategic Management Journal, 17,* 63-76.

Schilling, M. (2000). Toward a general modular systems theory and its application to interfirm product modularity. *Academy of Management Review, 25*(2), 312-334.

Teece, D., Pisano, G., & Schuen, A. (1997). Dynamic capabilities and strategic management. *Strategic Management Journal, 18,* 509-533.

Wang, Q., & Majchrzak, A. (1996). Breaking the functional mindset in process organizations. *Harvard Business Review, 74*(5), 92-99.

Zander, U., & Kogut, B. (1995). Knowledge and the speed of the transfer and imitation of organizational capabilities: An empirical test. *Organization Science, 6*(1), 76-92.

Zollo, M., & Winter, S. G. (2002). Deliberate learning and the evolution of dynamic capabilities. *Organization Science, 13*(3), 339-351.

Chapter XIII
Leading Firms as Knowledge Gatekeepers in a Networked Environment

Deogratias Harorimana
Southampton Solent University, UK

ABSTRACT

This chapter introduces the role of the knowledge gatekeeper as a mechanism by which knowledge is created and transferred in a networked environment. Knowledge creation and transfer are essential for building a knowledge-based economy. The chapter considers obstacles that inhibit this process and argues that leading firms create a shared sociocultural context that enables the condivision of tacit meanings and codification of knowledge. Leading firms act as gatekeepers of knowledge through the creation of shared virtual platforms. There will be a leading firm that connects several networks of clients and suppliers who may not interact directly with one another, but are, indeed, connected indirectly though the leading firm that acts as a gatekeeper. The chapter argues that a large firm connecting several clients and suppliers at the multinational level represents a gatekeeper, but even individuals and focal firms in industrial districts can be gatekeepers. The author hopes that, through this discussion, academics, researchers, and doctoral students will have a comprehensive theoretical and practical basis on which to study the role of leading firms in building innovations and virtual teams of knowledge sharing in a highly networked and competitive environment.

INTRODUCTION

This chapter discusses the role of leading firms in knowledge sharing practices in networked environments. In a global economy, distant relationships can be a source of novel ideas and expert insights useful for innovation processes. Firms can develop global channels and create platforms not only to exchange products or services, but also in order to benefit from outside knowledge inputs and desire for growth. Recent indications also are that, in a global knowledge economy, organisational success can no longer be measured based on its internal interactions alone. Rather, corporate success can be derived from its capacity and its ability to identify and access external knowledge sources located far away, and to convert this knowledge into an explicit format that can be transferred and reused.

On the one hand, this is an indication that knowledge is an external factor that can have an effect on firms' innovative processes, and that the extent of the effect is more or less dependent on the extent of relationships with other firms. On the other hand, the author acknowledges that many of the developed countries have successfully integrated information and computer technology to support business processes, but research into knowledge creation and knowledge transfer processes remains subdivided along several lines; and this subject still lacks focus and consistency. The value of the availability of the Internet to Organisation for Economic Cooperation and Development (OECD) nations can be related to cultural understanding as well as scientific development. However, codified knowledge can be shared on the net, whilst much of the tacit knowledge cannot. In this chapter, the author introduces perspectives of knowledge-sharing practice under the support of leading firms, and discusses how this is supported by social interactions as well as technological tools such as the Internet. Using knowledge gatekeeper theories, we are able to show that the practices of both sharing knowledge and, more specifically, sharing knowledge through networking and virtual places offered by leading and focal firms, may be directly linked to existing social relationships that characterise communities' members. Social relationships are sophisticated and they may include several networks that, in a broad sense, act as knowledge gatekeepers. In this process, identity and learning culture of recipients play an important role in building trust and long-term

relationships that are perceived to be essential to distance networking and knowledge sharing. The indications are that the value of knowledge building can be maximised where social ties seem to exist; and above all, the identity of the source plays a greater part. This chapter uses theories that may be borrowed from different subject domains to enrich the debate. This is because, on the one hand, there continues to be what can be seen as technology-led knowledge management research that appears to sideline social tools such as communities of practice, social networks, gatekeepers, and alike. On the other hand, we continue to observe research into knowledge management that is inclined more to the social tools named, but does not bring in a technology perspective. In particular, in such research, the Internet-supported knowledge sharing is not talked about. These are two interrelated areas, and they complement each other. Even in distant knowledge sharing, relationships are built and sustained over time. In this chapter, the author will not present further new empirical research; rather, he aims to provide food for thought, and a new way of thinking that would seek to bring together knowledge-creation and knowledge-transfer (KT) research to an intersection with technology-supported knowledge-sharing practices.

THE CONTEXT IN KNOWLEDGE-BASED ECONOMY RESEARCH

.... Ultimate limits to growth may lie not so much in our abilities to generate new ideas, as in our abilities to process to fruition an ever-increasing abundance of potentially fruitful ideas. (Weitzman, 1998, p. 331)

This statement underlines the need to have this debate on how and why building the knowledge society and enabling the extraction of value from knowledge exchange constitutes an integral part of today's leadership and academic concerns. The foundation for the knowledge economy was first introduced by Drucker (1966) in *The Effective Executive*, in which he described the difference between the manual worker (1966, p.2) and the knowledge worker. A manual worker works with his hands and produces things. A knowledge worker (Drucker 1966:3) works with his head and produces ideas, knowledge, and information. For OECD countries, the rules and practices that determined success in the industrial economy of the 19th and 20th centuries need rewriting for an interconnected world where resources, such as know-how, are more critical than other economic resources (Bell, 1973)[1], and this chapter can be seen as one of a series of contributions towards achieving this goal. Research into how these rules can be rewritten at the level of firms and industries in terms of networking, knowledge creation, knowledge transfer, and knowledge-management processes is subdivided and lacking an integrated approach, while there is an increasing role and significance of knowledge as an input to economic processes leading to fundamental changes (OECD, 1996).

Some of these changes rest on advances in information technology that are leading to a paradigm shift. This paradigm shift is linked to the fact the world is experiencing basic changes in economic functioning, and changes in the economic rules, for both business and policymakers (Smith, 2000). In fact, Drucker predicted that in the age of social transformation:

... How well an individual, an organization, an industry, a country, does in acquiring and applying knowledge will become the key competitive factor. The knowledge society will inevitably become far more competitive than any society we have yet known—for the simple reason that with knowledge being universally accessible, there will be no excuses for non-performance... (Drucker, 1994, p.9).

This suggests two things that businesses are faced with. (1) Developing innovative tools for collecting appropriate information, and (2) being able to translate this information into knowledge that sustains their competitive advantage. Moreover, knowledge that sustains competitive advantage is often that which is implicit and sticky (Von Hippel, 2005, p.8, p.67). This is the form of knowledge perceived as the source of innovation (Nonaka & Takeuchi 1995). Drucker (1994, p. 9) emphasises that "How well an individual, an organization, an industry, a country, does in acquiring and applying knowledge" is a reflection on the conditional requirements to achieving firm competitive advantage through continuous internalisation of knowledge both at firm and individual levels

PRELIMINARY CONCEPTS

The author will introduce concepts that will require our readers concur as to their meanings as we set out in this chapter. In the first instance, readers can be alerted to the fact that knowledge sharing is not the same as "information sharing." Similarly, "knowledge sharing" is not the equivalent of "knowledge transfer." The United States Department of Defense research team that introduced the concept of knowledge sharing suggested that the goal of knowledge sharing would be to develop techniques, methodologies, and software tools for knowledge sharing and knowledge *reuse*, design, implementation, or execution time (Patil, 1992). Knowledge sharing is therefore more complex than information sharing, and much closer to knowledge transfer. However, knowledge sharing requires communication that, in turn, requires a common language (Neches et al 1990). Thus, "information sharing" becomes a subpart of knowledge sharing in itself.

Knowledge sharing goes much further to include an unspoken aim to achieve a continuous application of what one already knows. This process becomes much more complex in its process because it entails knowledge transfer (KT). The Office of Science and Technology (OST) (2007) of the British Government defines KT as "the process of transferring good ideas, research results and skills between universities, other research organisations, business and the wider community to enable innovative new products and services to be developed," (http://www.ost.gov.uk). In addition, KT may involve the effective sharing of ideas, knowledge, or experience between units of a company or from a company to its customers. At the organisational level, KT is defined as "the practical problem of getting a packet of knowledge from one part of the organisation to another (or all other) part(s) of the organization" (Argote & Ingram, P., .2000). This is the definition Argote and Ingram (2000) built on in their study of the context of organisational studies within which KT was described as the sole basis for competitive advantage. Argote and Ingram's study defined KT in terms of observed changes in experiences, both at the organisational recipient units as well as the source. Changes in organisational knowledge (that is, routine or best practices) can be observed through changes in the knowledge or performance of recipient units.

This variety of definitions constitutes a starting point to realising the complexity of knowledge transfer. Several studies (Bresman *et. al.* 1999, p. 447; Garavelli *et. al.* 2002, p. 271; Simonin 1999b, p. 596-7; Szulanski 2000, p. 10) point out that KT is a complex, time-consuming, and difficult process. What we essentially have is a subject that, so far, has not been completely studied from its epistemological foundations up to its deep conceptual analysis, which is typically characterised by a variety of models. Attempts made to define KT link (1) the types of knowledge being transferred: knowledge being perceived as tacit or codified), and (2) physical and social factors: the source and recipient, the distance knowledge travels, and cultural differences, and identity. All these are but elements that have featured in knowledge

creation and knowledge-transfer research that attempt to provide a definition in the first place, and the models in the second ranking. As we set out this chapter, we will refer to knowledge sharing and extracting value from knowledge exchange. Readers are advised that the author willingly accepts that the two concepts are not interchangeable, as knowledge sharing is a continuation from information sharing, and it is much more complex than information sharing.

KNOWLEDGE CONVERSION MODELS

Among the several models that exist with regard to KT, some have been developed more than others. Among those successful models, many appear to concentrate at organisational levels. At organisational levels, they include studies on (1) knowledge gatekeepers (Allen & Cohen, 1969), which is explored later on in this chapter, (2) Communities of Practice (CoPs) (Lave & Wenger, 1991), (Lave & Wenger, 1991),(3) Nonaka (1994) and Nonaka and Takeuchi 's(1995) knowledge conversion model, widely known as the "SECI model."

In a Community of Practice, members are involved in a set of relationships over time (Lave & Wenger 1991, p. 98), and communities develop around things that matter to people (Wenger 1998, p.8). The fact that they are organising around some particular area of knowledge and activity gives members a sense of joint enterprise and identity. For a CoP to function, it needs to generate and appropriate a shared repertoire of ideas, commitments, and memories. It also needs to develop various resources such as tools, documents, routines, vocabulary, and symbols that, in some way, carry the accumulated knowledge of the community. In other words, it involves practice (ways of doing and approaching things that are shared to a significant extent among members). The interactions involved, and the ability to undertake larger or more complex activities and projects though cooperation, bind people together and help to facilitate relationship and trust. Although CoPs can offer a culturally homogeneous space and a set of shared interpretative elements that facilitate knowledge exchange, even by means of ICT tools, their implementation is limited by their specific scope. Also, these are useful inside the single organisation, but are less effective for connecting different organisations.

Another model often referred to is the Socialisation, Externalisation, and Internalisation model (known as the SECI model). Nonaka (1994, p.19) was the architect of the SECI model, but this was yet to be fully developed (see Nonaka & Takeuchi, 1995). The later study provides the detailed accounts of the knowledge creation process, which allows us to understand the dynamic nature of knowledge creation, and offers advice on how to fruitfully manage such a process. For Nonaka (1994) and Nonaka and Takeuchi (1995), in the SECI model, knowledge creation is a continuous dialogue between tacit and explicit knowledge (see Figure 1). This interaction is represented in a spiral knowledge creation diagram that becomes larger in scale as it moves up through the organisational levels. Along this process, the circle can trigger new spirals of knowledge creation and the circle starts again (Figure 2).

This model has prerequisites if it is to be successful: (1) the organisational leadership must be actively involved in motivating employees to dynamically support this culture of knowledge development, as well as being able to manage unstoppable changes and make adjustments to required changes; (2) the ability of a company to identify its knowledge capabilities and assets; and (3) the learning culture of employees. This already indicates potential problems that need further studies, for instance, we already know that Nonaka's model was developed in the Japanese culture where there is a "one job for life" ethic.

A legitimate question, for example, as to whether this model is applicable to western organisational cultures remains to be evidenced. Secondly, the SECI model appears to be linear, and evidence of its flexibility is still lacking. Can it change direction to start at any of its steps (see Figure 2)? Can it respond to changing patterns of a learner's needs during the KT process?

Cumming and Teng (2003) also proposed a KT practice based on relationships' interdependency. This model gives a view of what goes on when KT involves many organisations. While Nonaka's SECI model aims to study knowledge creation and KT processes within the sociological context of an organisation, Cumming and Teng's model takes us a step further to understanding the

Figure 1. SECI, knowledge conversion model, as described in Nonaka & Takeuchi (1995)

	Tacit Knowledge	**Tacit Knowledge**	
Tacit Know.	**Socialization:** Empathizing This is where people share tacit knowledge through a face-to-face communication and shared experiences.	**Externalization:** Articulating People are able to build up concepts. These concepts are combined with tacit knowledge, consequently facilitating its communication via interactions and recordings	Explicit Know.
Tacit Know.	**Internalization:** Embodying Less experienced learn from those who are most experienced and knowledgeable. People share experiences and external knowledge becomes part of individuals' knowledge base, and finally, creating an organizational asset.	**Combination** :Connecting This is a result of combining a choice of elements of explicit knowledge such as building archetype.	Explicit Know.
	Explicit Knowledge	**Explicit Knowledge**	

Figure 2. Knowledge conversion process according to Nonaka & Takeuchi (1995)

relationships and interdependency of knowledge and the environment, both at the source and at the recipient site. This is essential in any study of KT, given that both the type of knowledge and the nature of relationships that facilitate KT would dictate the outcome.

Cummings and Teng's (2003) proposed model tells us that it is necessary to identify which knowledge is needed (that can be transferred). Both the source of the knowledge and the recipient site must be able to understand one another. Cultural similarities must be greater than their differences. If people's cultures are similar, this will be reflected in terms of trust, mutual engagement, and clarity of knowledge-sharing activities.

The majority of KT studies seem to agree that where an element of trust is strong, knowledge to be transferred can be identified, and the context and extent of its application can be agreed upon with both the source and the recipient. In the absence of trust, knowledge identification becomes more subjective, and less likely to achieve change, which must be reflected in terms of changing behaviour (or at least changing practice) at the recipient unit. The importance of having social relationships in knowledge transfer is that people are able to identify areas of tacit lacuna with one

another. Thus, trusting one another becomes an important tool in identifying tacit knowledge to be transferred. Social relationships are perceived as important in this process of identification; it is even better when people have similar cultures and understanding.

CULTURAL INFLUENCE IN THE BUILDING OF KNOWLEDGE ECONOMY

Cultures heavily influence what is perceived as useful, important, or valid knowledge in an organisation. Culture shapes what a group defines as relevant knowledge, and this will directly affect which knowledge a unit focuses on (De Long & Fahey, 2000, p. 120).

The degree of cultural distance is widely considered as one of the major obstacles to successful performance in cross-cultural business relationships. Most results, derived from previous studies of knowledge creation and KT, concluded that cultural differences in a network of knowledge constitute just one of many other barriers. The main argument is that common identity, as opposed to the cultural distance between cultures, impacts on knowledge sharing and transfer (Shenkar, 2001). Johanson and Vahlen (1977, p.24) define cultural distance as the result of culture-based factors that impede the flow of information between the firm and its partners. Cultural distance matters, with regard to knowledge, because it raises barriers for understanding other members of the organisation elsewhere. Maximising return using the net will require the addressing of such issues and undoubtedly, very little, or nothing at all, will be achieved before such issues of cultural difference, trust, and identity are addressed.

For this study to contribute towards the understanding of issues that may effect knowledge sharing practices, the argument is supported that someone better informed would act as a gatekeeper to facilitate knowledge creation and the KT processes (Allen 1977; Allen & Cohen, 1967). Alternatively, technology, and particularly the Internet, has taken a greater role in replacing copresence via either virtual relationships or more commonly, in increasing and creating virtual networks without human beings having to meet one another.

THE TACIT-CODIFIED KNOWLEDGE INFLUENCE

Several studies (particularly Chartrand, 2002:12) described the "know-why" as that knowledge which is associated with scientific theories of the principles and laws of nature. This is the kind of knowledge that underpins the advancement of t the technological development of products and processes in most industries. The production and reproduction of "know-why" (Chartrand, 2002, p.12) is often organised in specialised organisations, such as research laboratories and universities. To gain access to this kind of knowledge, firms have to interact with those organisations who own this knowledge; using any possible mechanism that is available to them. There are several mechanisms, ranging from recruiting scientifically trained labour, engaging in direct contact, and joint activities, such as developing virtual platforms where knowledge sharing activities is conducted. With regards to "know-how," this refers to skills or the ability to do something; it includes insight and personal judgment that, so far, have been linked to undocumentable knowledge (Nonaka & Takeuchi, 1995). For example, "know-how" has to be employed when judging market prospects for a new product or recruiting and training staff. The same is true for the skilled workers operating complicated machine tools. It is also true for highly specialised services, such as those that are consultancy based. "Know-how"(Chartrand, 2002, p.12) is typically a kind of knowledge developed and kept within

the boundaries of an individual's experiences, intuitions, and feelings, and involves trust and confidence when imparting it from one person to another. However, this raises the further question of how can businesses maximise their knowledge-sharing practices that involve tacit knowledge? On analysing the latest research, however, we start to uncover some practices that are a target of gathering mechanisms that would facilitate tacit knowledge sharing. These have been identified as a combination of tools ranging from videos, online chat rooms, recording of workshops, and networking.

THE ISSUE OF CODIFICATION AND TRANSFER OF KNOWLEDGE

The process by which knowledge evolves and spreads through an organisation involves interchanging its nature between tacit and codified forms. The way this is achieved has been demonstrated at large in Nonaka's (1994, p.19) spiral model, in which knowledge is created as well as transferred through socialisation. The act of interacting with people does allow people to learn from one another. Through this interaction, people can come up with new insights and ideas that may lead to new knowledge development and application (externalisation). Socialisation can help people to determine what knowledge can be codified, and that which cannot. The process of codification includes three aspects; these are model building, language creation, and the writing of messages. With the development and change in several technologies, these three activities have been affected by changes in costs and benefits in particular, and technological development has cut down the costs of codification (Cowan & Foray, 1997). Technical change is another area that facilitates the diffusion of codified knowledge, for example, via Web spaces; this is increasing the value of codified knowledge. There are, however, some issues that can be raised here, for example, the effects of temporal relations between the three aspects of codification suggested that, in some cases, are inevitable, given the nature of advances in technological changes. The codification process may be dependent on language and the context of the knowledge being codified; moreover, there has been a suggestion that the ongoing process in which codification would take place may be path dependent (Cowan & Foray 2000, p.241).

The path dependency of knowledge is very much related to the type of knowledge itself. Codified knowledge has been defined as that which can be transmitted in formal, systematic language. From a technological point of view, however, codified knowledge is discrete or "digital" (Snowden, 2002). It is also referred to as "codified" because it has been captured in records of the past, such as libraries, archives, and databases, and is assessed on a sequential basis. Codified knowledge can be expressed in words and numbers, and it can be shared in the form of data, scientific formulae, specifications, manuals, and the like. This kind of knowledge can be readily transmitted using the Internet and manuals systematically. Unlike codified knowledge, it has been said that it is not possible to codify or document tacit knowledge in manuals (Polanyi, 1966).

Polanyi (1966) is, by tradition, the authoritative source for the concept of tacit knowledge. Many regard tacit knowledge as personal, private knowledge, thus, appropriately treated only at the individual level (Ambrosini & Bowman, 2001; Boiral, 2002; Johannessen, & Olaisen, 2001). Others refer to collective or organisational tacit knowledge linking this with organisational capabilities, routines, and procedures (Colis, 1996; Johannessen, & Olaisen, 2001; Leonard & Sensiper, 1998; Nelson & Winter, 1982; Spender, 1996). Collins (2001) claims that tacit knowledge is manifested in the form of the life of a group, and he also points to a supra-individualistic if not collective form.

There is general agreement that tacit knowledge is acquired through an individual's direct experience of whatever his tacit knowledge concerns through, for example, on-the-job training and informal learning at work (Herbig, Büssing, & Ewert, 2001; Marchant & Robinson, 1999; Patel, Arocha, & Kaufman, 1999; Wagner, Sujan, Sujan, Rashotte, &Sternberg, 1999). Others, however, suggest that we are biologically predisposed towards certain kinds of tacit knowledge thus minimising the role of experience (Patel *et al.,* 1999; Torff, 1999).

One issue that has aroused much interest, particularly following Nonaka and Takeuchi's (1995) thesis about the knowledge creation process, has been whether *tacit* knowledge can be converted into *explicit* knowledge. Here, we find widely and strongly differing opinions. Patel *et al.,* (1999), Ambrosini and Bowman (2001), Herbig & Büssing (2003), and Tsoukas (2003) argue that tacit knowledge is, by definition, non-verbal, inarticulable, unconscious, or ineffable. However, Wagner and Sternberg (1985, 1986), Spender (1996), Torff (1999), and Boiral (2002) argue that it is rarely expressed, or difficult to express, or to simply assume that it can be made explicit. Difficulties include the fact that it is, by definition, personal and context based on the holders' fear that making it explicit entails losses, and that extraction requires a supportive environment involving trust and appropriate social structures. It is probably of little surprise to tacit-knowledge theorists that it is widely accepted among academics of knowledge management that tacit knowledge cannot be codified; therefore implying that if this knowledge could be codified, it could no longer be considered as tacit knowledge. However, one simple question has to be asked: When does one's knowledge cease to be tacit? And, when and where do we move from tacit knowledge to codified knowledge?

During social gatherings, people translate personal and team experiences to develop knowledge databases. These databases are retrievable in a form of codified knowledge. However, this is an attempt to elicit somebody else's experiences. We can also see people using video conferencing, pod casts, and so on. These are tools in themselves that aim at facilitating social interactions, where one can see the body language as well as hear the person speaking. What does a person learn from this process? In my view, this is codified knowledge being shared, but also a semitacit knowledge.

Tacit knowledge is thus said to be both an individual and a collective type of knowledge; individuals acquire it through experience, from live chats and distant videoconferencing. This is, however, still somewhat innate. The presence of others is generally regarded as essential for its acquisition. Some recent authors, such as Busch et al (2002: 10), suggested that eventually, tacit knowledge becomes codified in practice as individuals, organisations and finally, all of us learn by its successful application. If we can take this argument further, we can see that tacit knowledge may become codified during its reduction into simple underlying principles, but not all of it can be codified. Gourlay (2006) even goes as far as to say that this knowledge facilitates routine behaviours (in both negative and positive senses), but, it is simultaneously a source of innovation. Clearly, there is no one who acclaims confidently whether this type of knowledge may be convertible into explicit knowledge. This of course raises the question of how technology can facilitate the sharing of this type of knowledge. Perhaps these difficulties arise because tacit knowledge is unconscious (Easterby-Smith & Lyles, 2003) or even ineffable (Tsoukas, 2003) and difficult (or impossible) to investigate using empirical methods per se. The need to translate and transfer tacit knowledge constitutes a driving force to create an environment where tacit knowledge can be codified and transferred. One of many solutions to this is building up a favourable environment where networking can allow knowledge conversion from tacit to explicit form.

GATEKEEPERS AND THEIR ROLE IN KNOWLEDGE CONVERSION

Knowledge gatekeepers create a shared sociocultural context that enables the condivision of "tacit" meanings, knowledge codification, and transmission. According to the pioneer of the concept of the "knowledge gatekeeper" (Allen, 1977, p.145), a "gatekeeper" is a key person (or a group of people) who facilitates knowledge transfer by informal communication by taking an intermediary role. Gatekeepers differ from their colleagues in their orientation toward outside knowledge sources. On average, gatekeepers read, advise local communities, search online, and present and publish papers more than researchers, scientists, academics, and local leadership do. Initially, Allen (1977, p. 145) identified gatekeepers as

... A small number of key people to whom others frequently turned for information. These key people differ from their colleagues in the degree to which they exposed themselves to sources of technological knowledge outside their organization. Their features are such as they constitute a small community of individuals, they are at the core of an information network, they overexposed to external sources of information, and the linkages they develop with external actors are more informal. (Allen, 1977, p. 145)

Whilst early studies of knowledge gatekeeper research focussed on individuals or a group of peoples' role in knowledge conversion, these studies have moved on to include the role of leading firms (Malpiero, Munari, & Sobrero, 2005) who play similar roles to that initially envisaged by Allen (1967). Leading firms can create shared virtual platforms to avoid rigidity of fixed configuration by decentralising the interface into a virtual meeting place into which part or all of the partners have to make their way. Interactions do not require physical presence or durable colocation. Physical interaction may follow as a result, but this type of interaction requires partners' identification and an established common base of interest. Wherever partners are not located in the same site, this would require a physical meeting in order to initiate further interactions. However, interfirm interactions are generally part time and do not require continuous face-to-face interaction.

As gatekeepers expand their networks of interactions, they can access valuable knowledge from their networks and bring it into the operation of daily formal or informal businesses, including intranet and extranet, or human beings such as individuals or a group of professional associations. In particular, gatekeepers can be seen as an essential element of boundary spanning that is informal and increasingly Internet-based, which reduces distant relationship barriers. In the foreseeable future of technological developments, this kind of virtual relationship may be likely to increase.

Gatekeepers, in the form of leading firms, may contribute to the articulation of internal and external resources, allowing local actors to benefit from their own external relations, but also giving external actors access to local resources. As evidence, Gannon (2005, p.22), who used the case of the Bologna automatic packaging machinery district in Emily-Romagna (Italy), the "Packaging Valley," has shown how some enterprises (commitenti) organise their networks of subcontractors and coordinate the work of highly specialised small and medium enterprises (terzisti) to whom they pass on the requirements and specifications of external customers. In a similar move, in the textile district of Prato, the role is played by the "impannatori," who may specialise in this function, so much so, as to abandon production tasks in order to exclusively devote themselves to this unique activity (Gannon, 2005, p.22).

Gatekeepers and their networks are also regarded as an especially significant strategy for managing long-term exchange relationships between firms. They combine autonomy often

offered by ICT facilities and flexibility with increasing control and efficiency. Leading firms may emphasise the importance of partnerships between firms, and depend on relationship management instead of market transactions (Webster & Frederic, 1992). They depend on negotiation, rather than market-based processes, as principal bases for conducting business. These organisations, acting as gatekeepers through creating platforms of knowledge sharing, can fulfil several functions at a time. First, in addition to some intangible benefits associated with information collected from participants, organisations are able to strengthen their internal capacity of knowledge development and knowledge translation. Secondly, they can develop interorganisational strategies arising through shared platforms.

Leading firms set up a shared resource centre connecting several of their partners and alliances through a single intranet. In doing so, they created a platform that brings together several parts of the worldwide organisation, incorporating customers, suppliers, and users, including the parent company, from around the world. Indeed, this could be a question of technicality, but it is increasingly becoming a part of corporate social responsibility, allowing people to learn from what they do, and by doing so, to attract customers who understand their products better. As such, anyone on the supplier, buyer, and manufacturer network can be allowed to have access to the intranet. This adds value knowledge of products, but of course, a leading firm acting as a gatekeeper is able to collect information on customers' needs, and the product development teams are able to plan ahead for market demands. In introducing his work on democratising innovation, Von Hippel (2005) argued:

"Users aided by improvements in computer and communications technology, increasingly can develop their own new products and services. These innovating –users both individuals and firms-often freely share their innovations with others, creating user-innovation communities and a reach intellectual commons." ibid (p1)

The point the author wants to make here is that organisations are increasingly allowing consumers and suppliers to access their inside knowledge. In doing so, companies are breaking the conventional approach to the development of innovative products by focusing instead on the users' knowledge of goods and services companies have on offer. Conventionally, customers (or consumers) and buyers have different profiles as well as different needs. Consumers are also distributed across geographical boundaries and cultures. This heterogeneous aspect of consumers makes it difficult to for them to share their implicit knowledge, resulting from membership heterogeneity in terms of cultures, languages, and physical distance.

In order to be successful, those firms that are providing a platform of knowledge sharing ensure that knowledge conversion from *tacit* to *explicit* takes place. In the leading firm, the role of the research and development (R&D) teams is to ensure that product specifications are responding to consumers' and customers' expressed needs. Such an approach has generated active participation of network members and, in some circumstances, this has led to the birth of innovative communities.

Another aspect that is so far yet to be studied is the distribution of possible "differing" innovative ideas, which may result from a heterogenic membership of these innovative communities that emerges along one line of business. In some cases, knowledge collected may not necessarily fall within the core mission of the gatekeeper firm. In fact, Von Hippel (2005) says that: "When users needs are heterogeneous and when information drawn by innovators is sticky, it is likely that product-development activities will be widely distributed among users, rather than produced by just a few prolific user innovators"(Ibid p93). Moreover, "individual users and user firms tend to develop innovations that serve their particular needs…" (ibid p.94). The underlying issue here is that, where such a knowledge-sharing platform

using virtual platforms provided by leading gatekeeper firm leads to knowledge translation, not all knowledge resources can be translated from their tacit forms. Knowledge shared on the company's platform, which was not relevant to its core businesses, can only be translated by those who find it relevant, and this may spark new innovations, of which some, if not all, lead to new business start-ups. Innovation activities and knowledge production only require limited moments of face-to-face interactions and do not necessarily give rise to related and similar businesses. Moreover, Torre's (2006), study finds that geographical proximity limitation can be adequately achieved through virtual spaces or at the most, through temporal interactions, knowledge sharing, and services, through individuals or staff travelling to each others' locations. In each of these situations, knowledge conversion into tangible results is supported by two things: (1) trust, where company directors, locally and at the parent company level, encourage knowledge sharing and new products developments involving customers, and (2) by social relationships and products that are tailored to meet local and individual needs.

GATEKEEPERS OF KNOWLEDGE AS A MECHANISM OF KNOWLEDGE CREATION, NETWORKING, AND KNOWLEDGE TRANSFER

The literature reveals that there is currently an increasing interest in the use of gatekeepers of knowledge for management, and for the transfer of knowledge both at the local and increasingly at the international level. Those who prefer to employ "gatekeepers" are mainly motivated by the fact that, like knowledge intermediaries, KT domains involve an inherent distribution of sources, problem-solving capabilities, and responsibilities. Interactions in KT environments are fairly sophisticated. These include negotiation, information sharing, and coordination, which all require complex social skills that gatekeepers can often apply.

Based on the nature of their role of imparting knowledge within the local knowledge system, knowledge gatekeepers can be seen as "knowledge senders." These are distinguished by their knowledge of technological advancement that stimulates other local organisations to approach them for advice (Pinch, Henry & Tallman, 2003). Some organisations have individuals who act as networkers, who motivate others and/or who promote the sharing of knowledge within the communities and local firms (Malpiero *et al,* 2005). Knowledge gatekeepers appear to behave like boundary spanners; they are able to access information from other firms. Allen (1977) identified gatekeepers according to the degree of interconnectivity with other colleagues in other organisations. He undertook a study of the communication network within the R&D division of a large aerospace firm in which gatekeepers brought their knowledge contribution into the organisation. Some of the gatekeepers' contributions included bringing new information to the project from outside their own organisations. Because bringing new information to the project from outside can be valuable, organisations that are aware of this should support and use technical gatekeepers in the most efficient ways.

Although gatekeepers have been described as mediating individuals or knowledge brokers, not everyone agrees. Persson (1981) argues against Allen's studies of gatekeepers in research and development organisations. In his view, Allen's flow model of gatekeepers does not inform us of who the gatekeeper is communicating what is being discussed to, or what effect the gatekeeper has on internal informal dissemination of information. Using an empirical study of an R&D organisation, Persson presented a thesis that gatekeepers can contribute to an elitist pattern of distribution rather than to a reduction of the information gap.

Particularly, this study refers to Aloni (1985), whose investigations into the literature review of studies of informal communication of scientific and technical information were published in the American Management literature between 1976 and 1982. These included Tushman and Katz, (1980) who has extended and developed Allen's (1969) approach to gatekeepers of knowledge. Aloni's (1985) literature survey demonstrates that the subject has been mentioned only infrequently in the management literature and abstracts of information science of recent years. What Aloni's literature survey reveals is that even management scientists view the informal KT as a special type of organisational communication arrangement. This attracts the question of whether there is enough empirical evidence to sufficiently identify the role of the gatekeeper.

GATEKEEPERS IN ORGANISATIONS

Gatekeepers of knowledge have been given several appellations to include knowledge seekers/knowledge senders (Ali, Pascoe, & Warne, 2002), knowledge brokers (Sverisson, 2001), and knowledge intermediaries (Howells, 2002; Max Lock Centre, 2000). Knowledge brokers are people who facilitate the creation, sharing, and use of knowledge in an organisation. Many organisations have created knowledge broker roles such as a "knowledge coordinator" or a "chief knowledge officer." The term "knowledge broker" is also sometimes used to describe companies or individuals that operate commercially as knowledge traders or provide knowledge-related services. Sverisson (2001) uses the concept of knowledge brokers in an analysis of the opportunities for, and the obstacles to, entrepreneurial activities, which are posed by a pragmatic environmentalism in Sweden. Sverisson argues that knowledge brokers can identify an opportunity to network. The opportunities in a network of people and businesses are such that there may be obstacles to knowledge sharing. In asserting the opportunity, obstacles are seen as the driving force behind the need for networking brokerage, knowledge-oriented (or "translation") brokerage, and brokerage of organisational or technological novelties. Sverisson's (2001) work suggested that the obstacles are rooted in the inertia of prevailing technological structures and in the fragmentation of practical environmental knowledge, both of which can be turned into opportunity by environmental brokers. The resulting opportunity space is a collective or "'networked" type of entrepreneurial practice that has developed in the openings provided by pragmatic environmentalism. Knowledge brokerage activity is not necessarily profit oriented or focused on creating new businesses, as knowledge brokers tend to do more than they are paid for, and often have no formal responsibility for carrying out the role. They are often at the core of information; they continuously seek to understand the implications of research results for their communities, even when communities do not require them to provide knowledge contribution.

KNOWLEDGE GATEKEEPERS OUTSIDE FIRMS' BOUNDARIES

The knowledge transfer process should be considered as an adaptive process of interactions that relies partly on spatial proximity to spread and create knowledge. Though it is not supposed that gatekeepers in local networks can be efficient if they become isolated from the rest of the world, per se, their work is such that separating them from their outside connections could drain them of their meaning. The role of gatekeepers within wider networks is a key feature of the process of knowledge creation and transfer that opens knowledge renewal and possible recombination. Local arrangements (for example, the introduction of a gatekeeper) within a global network can allow firms to take advantage of spatial proximity

while retaining outside access to a large variety of resources and opportunities. Another advantage of course is that knowledge gatekeepers can be very good boundary-spanning mechanisms that are not necessarily subject to strict control and rules that may apply elsewhere if the firm, as a whole, attempted to access the information from elsewhere. In fact, Allen Scott (2006) points out that in a network economy, there is a fundamental difference between innovation that comes from R&D programmes and innovation that occurs by coincidence. In the first case, we know who is participating and what the aim is. The latter may occur when firms engage in mutual discussions and assessment; individuals caught up in this discussion will often arrive at insights that would otherwise have remained hidden from them. Scott (2006) argues that this is where a gatekeeper can be an essential element. As a member of such an informal negotiation, he/she can create a holistic picture of where innovation is likely to come from. It is therefore much easier to predict the best candidate to conduct such highly socially driven, but skillfully approached, negotiations.

Local/global tradeoffs can be solved by exploring the new organisational configurations of those networks that rely on the design of interfaces between local and global networks, such as networks of practice or intermediaries that resemble knowledge brokers' behaviours. As this chapter shows, one of many other ways put forward to build an interface is by setting up two different types of mechanisms; the first, around a key-actor, or "gatekeeper," that ensures the linkages between local and global interactions; the second, through the concept of "temporary proximity," which would permit agents to set up and mobilise links without requiring actors' durable colocation. This temporary proximity can be realised by actors moving for a limited duration from their location to those areas that need training, support in developing business processes, and assistance in setting up systems with the ultimate intention of the locals being able to run these systems independently. In this case, however, locals would still have access to the benefits provided through the network of experts (that is, the gatekeepers). Knowledge gatekeepers, therefore, play a diffusion role; a linkage role, and they are a source of knowledge and specific information to businesses.

KNOWLEDGE GATEKEEPERS PERCEIVED AS "BOUNDARY SPANNERS"?

Well-explained and further-explored works on the role of gatekeepers are those which are associated with "boundary spanners" (Sonnenwald, 1995, 1996; Sonnenwald & Lievrouw, 1997). These authors characterised design as a process of "contested collaboration" (1995, p.873), and specified the types of boundary spanning roles in engineering teams: "organisational boundaries, task boundaries, discipline boundaries, personal boundaries, and multiple boundaries" (1996, p.180) Based on Sonnenwald's study, she argued that boundary spanning must occur across boundaries of organisations as well as within a project. The study by Sonnenwald and Lievrouw (1997) was conducted, in a high technology firm, to examine the applicability of those boundary roles. From the questionnaires and extensive interviews, they found that there exist certain types of communication roles or multiple roles in the design team, and individual work performance is strongly related to the communication among team members.

CAN LEADING FIRMS BE KNOWLEDGE GATEKEEPERS?

In an attempt to study the role of the gatekeeper in manufacturing firms in the Murge district, Southern Italy, Morrison's (2004) study investigated to what extent leading firms, located within

a successful Italian furniture district, behave as gatekeepers of knowledge. While their empirical analysis was carried out on a small sample of technicians working within firms' knowledge-intensive units, findings can serve as an indication of the role of leading firms in knowledge creation and knowledge-sharing practices within the contexts of industrial districts in Southern Italy. The study adopted social network techniques to trace linkages between technicians and external sources of knowledge, and to evaluate their relevance for innovative activities. Morrison's findings suggest that leading firms absorb external knowledge and only disperse it to their own network of clients, and to those who are exclusively perceived as partners. Within this theoretical framework, Morrison (2004) concluded that leading firms cannot necessarily serve as knowledge gatekeepers.

On the one side leaders may behave as district's screening actors. That is they incorporate within their networks the best providers and subcontractors. A creative-destruction mechanism then favours the survival of the most efficient ones. On the other side they could produce perverse effects. They may strengthen internal asymmetries and in turn exasperate conflicts, in particular between large and medium firms. (2004, p.30)

It is, therefore, believed that in some regions, companies may present asymmetric structures that limit the extent to which they can share knowledge outside their boundaries of networks. Firms do use their buying influence to incorporate, within their networks, the best suppliers and subcontractors or "portage." These leading firms can create and develop destructive mechanisms, inhibiting and sometimes preventing knowledge flow to the outside world. Moreover, Von Hippel (2005) in "Democratizing innovation" has argued that leading firms incorporate subcontractors, and create subnetworks of suppliers, as well as an end-user-supplier relationship. In doing so, firms are able to collect information they need from their customers. Firms are, in return, able to develop products that meet customers' aspirations and standards, and the ownership of the acquired (both old and new) knowledge remains the property of the firm.

In the context of leading firms, however, Porter (1990) has suggested that firms may prevent their knowledge from freely circulating, particularly if they believe that this is the source of their competitiveness. Moreover, firms may not want to share knowledge because of the costs and risks involved. Huber's (1991) and Pan and Scarborough's (1998) research has shown that because time is a scarce resource in organisations, extrinsic rewards signal to employees that time spent sharing knowledge is deemed important by the organisation. Indeed, practitioners and researchers have identified nontrivial extrinsic rewards for knowledge sharing as an important motivator to knowledge transfer (Davenport & Prusak, 1998; Gupta & Govindarajan, 2000; Knowledge Partnership Management Group (KPMG), 2000), but surprisingly, surveys have found that the majority of organisations' executives do not believe that their organisations reward or recognise knowledge transfer and knowledge sharing (KPMG, 2000). Moreover there is an almost total lack of "hard evidence" available to support the claim that large firms cannot be gatekeepers for those new or relatively weak and small firms. Rather, there is evidence that suggests that some large firms may help to train local human capacity, particularly where weak governments are unable to provide the skilled labour needed by firms investing in their countries. In this regard, some large companies engage in supporting local businesses through initiatives, and by investing in research and development activities, as well as in training staff.

CONCLUSION

This chapter argued that in the process of building knowledge economy, knowledge transfer (KT)

constitutes an essential element. However, there is an initial significant obstacle to KT that is represented by the the impossibility of codifying it, and to convey knowledge through ICT channels. Secondly, there is another barrier, associated with the cultural distance between players, that hinders an effective knowledge-sharing flow among both individuals and organisations. The cultural distance hinders the codification of knowledge that is required in order to be able to transfer knowledge through various means. While tacit knowledge is accepted as the source of innovation, it is codified knowledge that is easier to transfer.

The chapter introduced theories and practices of knowledge creation, knowledge conversion, and transfer models that have been developed in the literature. Against this background, and from the understanding of existing models, the chapter concludes that in order to solve knowledge-sharing problems that hinder the process of knowledge conversion and knowledge sharing, there is an inevitable need to create a "shared" sociocultural context that enables the condivision of "tacit" meanings. This shared sociocultural context allows knowledge translation from an implicit form to an explicit form. However, this is best supported through the implementation of networked environments, where networking can occur.

The solution is represented by "gatekeepers." The presence of gatekeepers can be found even in interorganisational networks. Also, there may be a leading firm that connects a network of clients and suppliers that may not interact with one another directly, but are indeed connected through the leading firm that, in this way, acts as knowledge gatekeeper. In such a way, a gatekeeper represents an element that resolves the problem of cultural homogeneity, and provides functions of "meaning translation," trust building, and tacit-explicit conversions.

Thus, a large firm, connecting several clients and suppliers at a multinational level, represents a knowledge gatekeeper. But, even focal firms in local industrial districts can represent gatekeepers.

Virtual enterprises are forms of networks where a gatekeeper enables the condivision of knowledge by means of information and computer technologies tools as well.

FUTURE RESEARCH DIRECTIONS

The concept of the "knowledge gatekeeper" may not have received a great deal of research interest in the field of management and knowledge transfer, but this trend is changing. At the time, the management view of the concept was limited purely to an internal communication issue. From the early 1980s, however, the concept was revived, with many research studies conducted in the areas of R&D and technology transfer (see Allen, 1966; Herzog, 1981; Malpiero *et al,* 2005; Morrison, 2004; Persson, 1981; Pinch & Henry, 1999; Pinch *et al,* 2003; Tushman & Katz, 1980;). The most interesting part of the recent studies is that there is a clear shift from an informal communication system to a much more serious economic matter for organisations. Also, there is growing confidence among researchers that knowledge gatekeepers are essential for positive business performance and delivering of results. Probably one of the most striking issues is the shift from the subject domain of the research. Initially, conceptualisation of the knowledge gatekeeper seemed to be led by technology transfer (see Allen, 1977; Allen, 1996; Allen & Cohen, 1969). Recent studies, however, do suggest a significant shift from perceptions of the subject as management and technology issues alone to being included more in the economic and human geography research, receiving much more attention from economic geographers (see Scott, A. 2006; Malpiero *et al,* 2005; Morrison, 2004; Pinch & Henry; 1999; Pinch *et al,* 2003, just to mention a few). It is not clear from the evidence in this study whether this change could be associated with an increased focus on knowledge management research, or whether it could be associated with subject diversification.

ACKNOWLEDGMENT

Dr. Carol Bulpett (Southampton Solent University) for her advice, reviews, and tireless support and encouragement.

Dr. Ettore Bollisani, (Book Editor) for his reviews and advice.

Sophie N'jai (Postgraduate Research Administrator at Southampton Solent University) for her efforts in the editing of the submitted version of this chapter.

REFERENCES

Ackoff, R. L. (1989). From data to wisdom, *Journal of Applies Systems Analysis*, *16*, 3-9.

Ali, I., Pascoe, C., & Warne, L. (2002). Interactions of organizational culture and collaboration in working and learning. *IEEE Journal of Educational Technology and Society*, *5*(2).

Allen, T. J. (1970). Communication networks in R & D laboratories. *Journal of R & D Management*, *1*(1), 14-21.

Allen, T. J. (1977). *Managing the flow of technology; Technology transfer and the dissemination of technological information within the Research and Development organization*. Cambridge, MA: MIT Press.

Allen, T. J. (1966) *Managing the flow of scientific and technological information*. Cambridge, Mass.: M.I.T. (Ph D thesis).

Allen, T. J., & Cohen, S. I. (1969). Information flow in research and development laboratories. *Administrative Science Quarterly*, (4), 12-19.

Allen, T. J. & Cohen, S. I. (1969). Information flow in research and development laboratories. *Administrative Science Quarterly*, *14*(1), 12-19.

Aloni, M. (1985). Patterns of information transfer among engineers and applied scientists in complex organizations. *Scientometrics*, *8*, 5-6.

Ambrosini, V., & Bowman, C. (2001). Tacit knowledge: Some suggestions for operationalization. *Journal of Management Studies, 38*(6), 811–829.

Argote, L., & Linda, P.(2000). KT: A basis for competitive advantage in firms. *Organizational Behavior and Human Decision Processes, 82*(1), 150-169.

Bell, D. (1973). *The coming of post-industrial society: A venture in social forecasting.* New York: Basic Books.

Benedict, B. M. (1996). *Making the modern reader cultural mediation in early modern literary anthologies.* Princeton: Princeton University Press. Retrieved from http//www.pupress.princeton.edu/books/benedict/

Birkinshaw, J. (2001). Why is knowledge management so difficult? *Business Strategy Review, 12*(1) 11-18.

Boiral, O, (2002). Tacit knowledge and environmental management. *Long Range Planning, 35,* 291–317.

Bresman, J., Birkinshaw, J., & Nobel, R. (1999). Knowledge transfer in international acquistions. *Journal of International Business Studies, 30,* 439-462.

Busch, P., & Richards, D. (2000). Graphically defining articulable tacit knowledge. *ACM International Conference Proceeding Series, 9,* 51 – 60.

Busch, P., Richards, D., Dampney, C., Galloway, J., (2002). *Selected tacit knowledge observations within two organisations.* Sydney Area Workshop on Visual Information Processing December University of Sydney, (pp. 5-11).

Chartrand, H. H. (2002). *The competitiveness of nations in a global knowledge-based economy: An individual interdisciplinary studies.* Unedited PhD Dissertation, University of Saskatchewan.

Chen, C. H., & Shish, H. T. (2005). *High-tech industries in China.* Edward Elgar Publishing.

Colis, D. (1996). Organizational capability as a source of profit. In B. Moingeon & A. Edmondson (Eds), *Organizational learning and competitive advantage.* London: Sage.

Collins, H. M. (2001). Tacit knowledge, trust and the Q of sapphire. *Social Studies of Science, 1*(31), 71-85.

Cowan, R., David, P. A., & Foray, D.(2000). The explicit economics of knowledge: Codification and tacitness. *Industrial and Corporate Change, 9*(2), 211-253.

Cowan, R., & Foray D. (1997). The economics of codification and the diffusion of knowledge. *Industrial Corporate Change, 6,* 595-622.

Cummings, J. L., & Teng, B.S. (2003). Transferring R&D knowledge: The key factors affecting knowledge transfer success. *Journal of Engineering and Technology Management, 20*(1) 39-68.

Davenport, T. H., & Prusak, L.(1998). *Working knowledge: How organizations manage what they know.* Boston, MA: Harvard Business School Press.

De Long, D. W., & Fahey, L. (2000). Diagnosing cultural barriers to knowledge management. *The Academy of Management Executive, 14*(4), 113 - 127.

Doz, Y. L. (1988). Technology partnerships between larger and smaller firm: Some critical issues. In F. Contractor & P. Lorange (Eds), *Cooperative strategies in international business.* Lexington, MA.

Drucker, P. (1966). *The knowledge worker.* New York: Harper Collins.

Drucker, P. (1994). The age of social transformation. *The Atlantic Monthly, 274*(5), 53-80. Retrieved 02/03/2007, from http//www.providersedge.com/docs/leadership_articles/Age_of_Social_Transformation.pdf

Easterby-Smith M., & Lyles M. A. (2003). Introduction watersheds of organizational learning and knowledge management. In M. Easterby-Smith, & M. A. Lyles (Eds.), *The blackwell handbook of organizational learning and knowledge management* (pp 1–15). Blackwell Publishing Ltd, Oxford.

Easton, G. (1992). Industrial networks. A review. In B. Axelsson & G. Easton, (Eds.), *Industrial networks*, *A new view of reality*. London: Routledge.

Garavelli, A. C., Gorgoglione, M., & Scozzi, B. (2002). Managing knowledge transfer by knowledge technologies. *Technovation*, 22, 269-279.

Ghauri, P. N., & Prasad, B. (1995). A network approach to probing Asia's interfirmlinkages. Advances, *International Comparative Management, 10*, 63-77.

Gourlay, S. N. (2006). Towards conceptual clarity concerning "tacit knowledge": A review of empirical studies. *Knowledge Management Research and Practice, 4*(1), 60-69.

Granovetter, M. S (1983).The strength of weak ties: A network theory revisited. *Sociological Theory,* (1), 201-233.

Griffith, D. A., & Harvey, M. G. (2001). Executive insights: An intercultural communication model for use in global interorganizational networks. *Journal of International Marketing, 9*(3), 87-103.

Gupta, A. K., & Govindarajan, V. (2000). Knowledge management social dimension lessons from Nucor steel. *Sloan Management Review,* 71-80.

Hakansson, H. (1989). *Corporate technological behaviour: Cooperation and networks.* London: Routledge.

Harorimana, D. (2006), Knowledge networks: A mechanism of creation and transfer of knowledge in organisations? In P. Feher (Ed.), *European conference of knowledge management* (pp. 213-222). ACI.

Hedlund, G., & Nonaka, I. (1993). Models of knowledge management in the West and Japan. In P. Lorange (Ed.), *Implementing strategic processes: Change, learning and cooperation.* Oxford: Basil Blackwell.

Herbig, B., & Büssing, A.(2003). Comparison of the role of explicit and implicit knowledge in working. *Psychology Science, 45*(3), 165–188.

Herbig, B., Büssing, A., & Ewert, T. (2001). The role of tacit knowledge in the work context of nursing. *Journal of Advanced Nursing, 34*(5), 687–695.

Herzog, A. J. (1981). The gatekeeper hypothesis and the international transfer of scientific knowledge .*The Journal of Technology Transfer, 6*(1).

Hildreth, P., & Kimble, C. (2004). *Knowledge networks innovation through communities of practice.* London, Hershey: Idea Group Inc.

Hong, J., Pöyhönen, A., & Kyläheiko, K. (2006). Cultural and communicative interaction and the development of dynamic capabilities. In P. Feher (Ed.), *European conference of knowledge management* (pp241-249). ACI.

Howells, J. L.(2002). Tacit knowledge, innovation and economic geography. *Urban Studies, 39*(56), 871-884.

Huber, G. P. (1991).Organizational learning: The contributing processes and the literature. *Organization Science, 2*(1), 88–115.

Johannessen, J. A., & Olaisen, B. (2001). Mismanagement of tacit knowledge the importance of tacit knowledge, the danger of information technology, and what to do about it. *International Journal of Information Management, 21,* 3–20.

Johanson, B., Karlson, & Stough. (2004). The emerging digital economy entrepreneurship. In *Clusters and olicy.* Berlin: Springer-Verlag.

Johanson, J., & Vahlen, J. E. (1977). The internationalization process of the firm - A model of knowledge development and increasing foreign market commitments. *Journal of International Business Studies, 8*(1), 23–32.

KPMG Consulting. (2000). *Knowledge Management Research Report.* KPMG.

Kraut, R. E., & Streeter, L. A. (1995). Coordination in software development. *Communications of the ACM, 38*(3), 69-81.

Lave, J., & Wenger, E. (1991). *Situated learning legitimate peripheral participation.* Cambridge University Press.

Leonard, D. & Sensiper, S. (1998). The role of tacit knowledge in group innovation. *California Management Review 40(3)*, 112-132.

Lissoni, F. (2001). Knowledge codification and the geography of innovation the case of Brescia mechanical cluster. *Research Policy, 30,* 1479-1500.

Lundvall, B-Å., & Foray, D.(1996). *The knowledge-based economy from the economics of knowledge to the learning economy: OECD Employment and Growth in the Knowledge- Based Economy.* Paris: OECD.

Malipiero, A., Munari, F., & Sobrero, M..(2005). *Focal firms as technological gatekeepers within industrial districts: Knowledge creation and dissemination in the Italian packaging machinery industry.* DRUID Working Paper N°05-05.

Malperio, F. (2005). *Local firms and technological gatekeepers within industrial districts knowledge creation and dissemination in real-estate industry.* DRUID Research paper 15 (5)55

Marchant G., & Robinson J. 1999. Is knowing the tax code all it takes to be a tax expert? On the development of legal expertise. In Sternberg RJ & Horvath JA (Eds.) *Tacit Knowledge in Professional Practice,*(pp. 3–20). Mahwah, NJ: Lawrence Erlbaum Associates.

Max Lock Centre. (2000). *Communication for development: Comments from peer review.* London: Max Lock Centre, University of Westminster.

Morrison, A. (2004). *Gatekeepers of knowledge within industrial districts: Who they are, how they interact.* Milan: Centro di Ricerca Sui Processi di Innovazione e Internazionalizzazione, CESPRI.

Muller, E., & Zenker, A. (2001). Business services as actors of knowledge transformation: The role of KIBS in regional and national innovation systems. *Research Policy, 30,* 1501-1516.

Neches,R., Fikes, R., Finin,T., Gruber,T., Patil, P.,Senator, T., & Swartout,W.(1991). Enabling technology for knowledge sharing. *AI Magazine, 12*(3), 37-56.

Nelson, R., & Winter, S. (1982). *An evolutionary theory of economic change.* Cambridge, MA: Belknap Press.

Nonaka, I. (1994). A dynamic theory of organizational knowledge creation. *Organization Science, 5*(1) 14-37.

Nonaka, I. (2005). *Knowledge management critical perspectives on business and management.* Routledge.

Nonaka, I., & Takeuchi, H. (1995). *The knowledge-creating company.* New York, Oxford: Oxford University Press.

OECD (1996). *The knowledge-based economy.* OECD: Paris. Retrieved from http://www.oecd.org/dataoecd/51/8/1913021.pdf

OST. (2007). Knowledge transfer. In *British Library's strategy (2005 – 2008) glossary.* Retrieved 20/07/2008, from http://www.bl.uk/about/strategic/glossary.html

Pan, S., & Scarbrough, H. (1998). A sociotechnical view of knowledge-sharing at Buckman laboratories. *Journal of Knowledge Management, 2*(1) 55-66.

Patel, V., Arocha, J., & Kaufman, D. (1999). *Expertise and tacit knowledge in medicine*. In R. J. Sternbern & J. A. Horvath (Eds.), *Tacit knowledge in professional practice*. Mahwah, NJ: Lawrence Erlbaum Associates.

Patil, S. R, Fikes, R., Patel-Schneider, P., McKay, D. P., Finin,T., Gruber,T., & Neches R.(1992). *The DARPA knowledge sharing effort: Progress report*. Washington DC: United States Department of Defense.

Persson, O. (1981). Critical comments on the gatekeeper concept: Science and technology. *R& D Management, 11*(1), 37-40.

Pinch, S., Henry, J. M., & Tallman, S. (2003). From industrial districts to knowledge clusters: A model of knowledge dissemination and competitive advantage in industrial agglomerations. *Journal of Economic Geography, 31*, 665-682.

Pinch, S..,& Henry, N. (1999). Discursive aspects of technology innovation from knowledge sharing perspective. *Environmental planning,* 373-388

Polanyi, M. (1996). *The tacit dimension*. Garden City, NY: Doubleday.

Porter, M. (1990). *The competitive advantage of nations*. New York: Free Press.

Prahalad, C. K. & Hamel, G. (1990). The core competence of the corporation. *Harvard Business Review, 68*(3) 79-92.

Scott, A., (2006). *Geography and economy: The Clerendon Lectures in Geography and Environmental Studies*. Oxford: Oxford University Press.

Shenkar, O. (2001). Cultural distance revisited towards a more rigorous conceptualization and measurement of cultural differences. *Journal of International Business Studies, 32(*3), 519-535.

Simonin, B. (1997). The importance of developing collaborative know-how: An empirical test of the learning organization. *.Academy of Management Journal, 40*(5), 1150–1174.

Simonin, B. L. (1999a). Ambiguity and the process of knowledge transfer in strategic alliances. *Strategic Management Journal, 20*(7), 595-623.

Simonin, B. L. (1999b). Transfer of marketing know-how in international strategic alliances :An empirical investigation of the role and antecedents of knowledge ambiguity. *Journal of International Business Studies, 30*(3), 463-490.

Singley, M. K., & Anderson, J. R. (1989). *The transfer of cognitive skill*. Cambridge, MA: Harvard Univ. Press.

Smith, K. (2000). W*hat is the knowledge economy? Knowledge-intensive industries and distributed knowledge bases. The Learning Economy - Firms, Regions and Nation Specific Institutions*. DRUID Summer Conference. June 15-17.

Snowden, D. (2002). Complex acts of knowing; Paradox and descriptive self awareness. *Journal of Knowledge Management, 6*(2), 1-14.

Sonnenwald, D. H. (1995). Contested collaboration: A descriptive model of intergroup communication in information system design. *Information Processing and Management, 31*(6) 859-877.

Sonnenwald, D. H. (1996). Communication roles that support collaboration during the design process. *Design Studies, 17*, 277-301.

Sonnenwald, D. H., & Lievrouw, L. (1997). Collaboration during the design process: A case study of communication, information behavior, and project performance. In R. Savolainen, G. Taylor, & B. Dervin (Eds.), *Information seeking in context* (pp. 179-204).

Spender, J-C. (1996). Competitive advantage from tacit knowledge? Unpacking the concept and its strategic implication. In B. Moingeon & A. Edmondson (Eds.), *Organizational learning and competitive advantage.* London: Sage.

Spender, J.C. (1996). Making knowledge the basis of a dynamic theory of the firm. *Strategic Management Journal, Special Issue,* (17), 45-62.

Spender, J. C., & Grant, R. M.(1996). Knowledge and the firm: Overview. *Strategic Management Journal, 17*(Winter Special Issue), 5–9.

Sverisson, (2001). Translation networks, knowledge brokers and novelty construction: Pragmatic environmentalism in Sweden. *Acta Sociologica, 44*(4), 313-327.

Szulanski, G. (1996). Exploring internal stickiness: Impediments to the transfer of best practice within the firm. *Strategic Management Journal, 17,* 27-43.

Szulanski, G. (2000). The process of knowledge transfer: A diachronic analysis of stickiness. *Organization Behavior and Human Decision Processes, 82* (1), 9-27.

Torff, B. (1999). Tacit knowledge in teaching folk pedagogy and teacher education. In R. J. Sternberg & J. A. Horvath (Eds.), *Tacit knowledge in professional practice.* Mahwah, NJ: Lawrence Erlbaum Associates.

Tsoukas, H. (2003). Do we really understand tacit knowledge? In M. Easterby-Smith & M. A. Lyles (Eds.), *Blackwell handbook of organizational learning and knowledge management.* Oxford: Blackwell Publishing Ltd.

Tushman, M. L., & Katz, R. (1980). External communication and project performance: An investigation into the role of gatekeepers. *Management Science, 26,* 1071-1085.

Van de Ven, A., & Ferry, D.L. (1980). *Measuring and assessing organizations.* New York: John Wiley.

Von Hippel, E. (2005).*Democratizing innovation.* MIT Press.

Wagner, R. K., & Sternberg R. J. (1985). Practical intelligence in real-world pursuits the role of tacit knowledge. *Journal of Personality and Social Psychology 49*(2) 436–458.

Wagner, R. K., & Sternberg R. J. (1986). Tacit knowledge and intelligence in the everyday world. In R. J. Sternberg, & R. K. Wagner (Eds.), *Practical Intelligence,* (pp. 51–83). Cambridge University Press, Cambridge.

Wagner, R. K., Sujan, J., Sujan, M., Rashotte, C. A., & Sternberg, R. J. (1999). Tacit knowledge in sales. In R. J. Sternberg & J. A. Horvath (Eds.), *Tacit knowledge in professional practice.* Mahwah, NJ: Lawrence Erlbaum Associates,.

Webster, J., & Frederic, E. (1992). The changing role of marketing in the corporation, *Journal of Marketing, 56*(4), 17-37.

Weitzman, M. L. (1998). Recombinant growth. *The Quarterly Journal of Economics, 113*(2) 331-360.

Wenger, E. (1998). *Communities of practice. Learning, meaning and identity.* Cambridge: Cambridge University.

Williams, J. D., Han, S.-L., & Qualls, W. J. (1998). A conceptual model and study of cross-cultural business relationships. *Journal of Business Research, 42,* 135-143.

Zander, U., & Kogut B. (1995). Knowledge and the speed of the transfer and imitation of organizational capabilities: An empirical test. *Organization Science, 6*(1) 76–92.

ADDITIONAL READING

Cunningham, P., Cunningham, M., & Fatelnig, P.(2003). *Building the knowledge economy - Is-*

sues, applications, case studies(Part 1 & 2). Amsterdam, The Netherlands: IOS Press.

Gannon, F. (2005). Le district des machines automatiques pour l'emballage de la région de Bologne: logique industrielle et interaction sociale, A working paper in *Une approche interactioniste de la complexité* (Zimmermann J.B. Coord.) ACI « Systèmes complexes en SHS »

Henry, N., & Pinch, S. (2000). (The) Industrial agglomeration (of Motor Sport Valley): A knowledge, space, economy approach. In J. Bryson, P. Daniels, N. Henry, & J. Pollard (Eds.), *Knowledge, space, economy.* London: Routledge.

Malipiero, A., Munari, F., & Sobrero, M. (2005). *Focal firms as technological gatekeepers within industrial districts: Knowledge creation and dissemination in the Italian packaging machinery industry.* Communication to the DRUID, DRUID Working Paper N°05-05.

Malmberg, A., & Maskell, P. (2002). The elusive concept of localization economies: towards a knowledge based theory of spatial clustering. *Environment and Planning, 34,* 439-449.

Morisson, A. (2004). *Gatekeepers of knowledge within industrial districts: Who they are, how they interact.* Paper presented at the 4th Proximity Conference, Proximity, Networks and Coordination, Marseille, June 2004.

Rychen, F., & Zymmermann, J. B. (2007). *Industrial clusters and the knowledge-based economy: From open to distributed structures?* Ecole des Hautes Etudes en Sciences Sociales Universités d'Aix-Marseille II et III, working paper n°2007-07.

Torre, A. (2006). Clusters et systèmes locaux d'innovation. Un retour critique sur les hypothèses naturalistes de la transmission des connaissances à l'aide des catégories de l'économie de la proximité, *Regions et Développement, 24.*

Vale, M. (2004). Innovation and knowledge driven by a focal corporation: The case of the AutoEuropa Supply Chain. *European Urban and Regional Studies, 11*(2), 124-140.

Zimmermann, J. B. (2002). Grappes d'entreprises et petits mondes: une affaire de proximités. *Revue Economique, 53*(3 Mai), 517-524.

ENDNOTE

[1] Danie Bell put forth the concept of a *post-industrial society* or *information age* in his book *The Coming of Post-Industrial Society* (1973). Later, he renamed this concept the information society, for which he is generally considered as the creator of the term (1979). By an information society, Bell means that we move from a producer of goods (manufacturing) to a service economy, and that theoretical knowledge, technology, and information become the major mode of commodity.

Chapter XIV
The Role of Knowledge Mediators in Virtual Environments

Enrico Scarso
University of Padua, Italy

ABSTRACT

This chapter discusses the role of online knowledge mediator, an entity that occupies an intermediate position in a knowledge transfer/exchange between a source and a receiver, and whose task is to assist and facilitate the knowledge transfer process, when performed through the use of Internet-based technologies to a significant degree. In the present rapidly evolving world of Internet, many types of virtual knowledge mediators continue to come out with different features and functions. Despite their growing diffusion, little effort has been devoted to examine their practices thoroughly. In light of this, the chapter aims to develop an analytical framework that could be of use to a deeper and more systematic investigation of these new economic agents. It is a two-dimensional framework, since it is based on two complementary, conceptual views of the knowledge transfer process, that is, the cognitive and the economic one.

INTRODUCTION

Although knowledge has, for a long time, been recognised as a key resource for achieving and sustaining competitive advantage, only in recent years the need to efficiently and effectively manage it has emerged clearly, especially as a consequence of the increased possibilities offered by the Internet–related information and communication technologies (ICTs). Actually, such technologies have dramatically reduced costs and increased speed, spatial reach, and amount of information and knowledge flows (Becerra-Fernandez & Sabherwal, 2006; Kim & Trimi, 2007).

In that context, the discipline of Knowledge Management (KM) has developed, and has attracted the increasing interest of both scholars and practitioners. According to Coakes et al. (Coakes, Bradburn, & Sugden, 2004), KM entails any process or practice of creating, acquiring, capturing, sharing, and using knowledge, wherever it resides, to enhance learning and performance in organisation. Similarly, Holsapple and Joshi (2006) define KM as an entity's (e.g., an individual, group, organisation, etc.) deliberate and organised efforts to expand, cultivate, and apply available knowledge in ways to add value to the entity, in sense of positive results in accomplishing its goals or fulfilling its purpose. To sum up, KM involves several processes[i] whose ultimate aim is to make the relevant knowledge available where it can be usefully applied to enhance the performance of the organisation, thus, generating economic value.

Even if all the different KM activities give their specific contribution to the value generation, the KM literature has always devoted particular attention on the knowledge transfer process (Riege, 2007). The reason is the fact the actual challenge organizations have to deal with is not incrementing the existing knowledge pool, but locating and capturing the needed piece of knowledge and transferring it where it is of use. Knowledge transfer is important also because it allows avoiding the need to reinvent an already successfully applied solution. To this point, it can be recalled the famous saying of an HP top executive, "if we only knew what we already know" (Sieloff, 1999), that exactly indicates where the heart of the matter resides. It must be specified that the literature makes a distinction between the terms knowledge transfer, sharing, and exchange (Boyd, Ragsdell, & Oppenheim, 2007; King, 2006a, 2006b; Lindsey, 2006). In particular, while knowledge transfer is one directional, since the knowledge flows from the sender to the recipient(s), knowledge sharing is a multidirectional process that usually occurs between several actors, who can be senders and receivers at the same time. Conversely, knowledge

exchange is similar to knowledge transfer, but it takes place between two parties and is reciprocal in that the recipient will reward the sender by transferring to him/her a different piece of knowledge (or by paying him/her for the knowledge received). Given the theme of the chapter, in the following pages, the three terms will be used interchangeably, as often done in the literature.

At the beginning, during the so-called first generation KM that mainly considered knowledge as an object that can be possessed and exchanged (Huysman & Wulf, 2006), ICTs were deemed to be able to overcome most of the difficulties and obstacles related to the knowledge transfer process. In reality, those technologies, especially the Internet-based, may have a double effect, may be friends or foes, as rightly said by Hendriks and Vriens (1999). On the one side, in fact, they make possible to have access to a vast amount of information, to communicate without space and time constraints, to store, retrieve, and manipulate a large quantity of data and documents rapidly and effectively. On the other side, the same technologies are making it even easier to get lost in a sea of chaotic, and even dangerous, information, as well depicted by the term "information overload," which has been recently coined to denote such a situation. Furthermore, they may induce the belief that the success of the knowledge transfer process is only a matter of having an adequate technological infrastructure, an idea that many experiences have revealed to be completely wrong (Desouza, 2003; Walsham, 2001).

On the contrary, according to the recently emerged second generation KM that considers knowledge as constructed through joint experience in social networks and groups (Newell et al., 2006), technology is a still necessary (Holsapple, 2005) but not sufficient tool, while it is essential to implement appropriate organisational structures (e.g., communities of practice, knowledge networks, etc.), processes, and mechanisms able to facilitate the sharing of experience, ideas, and suggestions directly among individuals.

Among the various organisational solutions that can be employed to favour the knowledge transfer process, specific attention deserves the resort to a particular kind of third party, here designated as knowledge mediators. A knowledge mediator is an entity (individual, team, organisation) that occupies an intermediate position in a knowledge exchange between the source (sender) and the user (receiver), and whose task is to assist and facilitate the knowledge transfer. This role seems to be particularly useful in the case of virtual exchanges of knowledge, that is, performed through the use of Internet-based ICTs (e.g., e-mail, Web site, knowledge portal, online meeting space, bulletin boards, common databases, groupware, wikis, and so on) to a significant degree. In such circumstances, in fact, the sender and the receiver are not directly connected, but communicate via Internet-based tools whose design, implementation, and management is usually in charge of an external agent that acts as online knowledge mediator.

In the present rapidly evolving world of Internet, many new types of virtual knowledge mediators continue to come out with different features that can operate both inside and between organisations. Our attention will be about those latter, since KM is progressively shifting towards an interorganisational use, aimed at bringing together and effectively integrating knowledge coming from a variety of external and dispersed sources. In this case, a specific company assumes the role of interorganisational knowledge broker, and performs its job by means of Internet-based technologies. Interesting examples of such kinds of companies are Monster, in the area of job recruitment; FindLaw and Legalco in that of legal services; HotDispatch, devoted to the need of IT/IS professionals. Despite the growing diffusion of those new economic actors, little effort has been devoted to describe and classify their practices, and to investigate and analyse their role to support interorganisational knowledge exchanges. Actually, the literature is lacking

in both empirical investigation and theoretical thought on this matter, so it could be useful to attempt to fill that gap.

This is the aim of the present chapter that examines the key aspects of knowledge mediators in virtual environments. It opens by giving some basic notions about organisational knowledge, in particular, the distinction between explicit ant tacit knowledge is addressed, as well as its impact on knowledge transferability. Next, the chapter focuses on the knowledge transfer process. In particular, three different models of that process are illustrated and discussed, as well as the related issues and problems. Then, after recalling what extant KM literature says about the knowledge mediator role, an integrated framework, to describe this emerging role is proposed, that combines the basic elements of the three models. The chapter closes with some summarizing considerations and indications on possible future research directions.

ON THE CONCEPT OF ORGANISATIONAL KNOWLEDGE

Before analysing the knowledge transfer process, the notion of organisational knowledge, that is, knowledge created and circulating inside an organization, is recalled, given that a proper understanding of this concept is crucial in order to consider the transfer process. In this connection, it is worth noting that the literature is full of definitions of knowledge and of classifications concerning its different kinds. As far as the definition of the term is regarded, a commonly agreed and mentioned one is that of "justified true belief," meaning that individuals justify the truthfulness of their beliefs based on their observations of the world. Justification hinges on unique viewpoints, personal sensibility, experience, and history (Nonaka, von Krogh, & Voelpel, 2006), and is highly influenced and shaped by the socio-organisational context the individuals belong to.

Another frequently quoted definition is that of "actionable or workable information" (Malhotra, 2000; Tiwana, 2000), that is, information that has been organised and analysed to convey meaning, experience, learning, and expertise so that it is understandable and applicable to problem solving and decision making (McKinnel Jacobson, 2006). This more pragmatic working definition has the merit of highlighting the business orientation of the organisational knowledge. Also, it is more suited to the case of electronic knowledge transfer, since ICTs can only handle data and information (Albino, Garavelli, & Gorgoglione, 2004; Bolisani & Scarso, 1999). Thus, we will refer to it here, but without overlooking the role the context plays to understand and use that actionable information correctly.

About the different kinds of knowledge, the most mentioned and used classification refers to the widely known distinction popularised by Nonaka and Takeuchi (1995) that differentiates between tacit and explicit knowledge[2]. It is worth analysing this issue thoroughly, since it is widely acknowledged that the more or less tacit nature of knowledge directly affects its transferability.

According to most KM literature, explicit knowledge represents the *knowing about* (the *objective* knowledge), while tacit knowledge the *knowing how* (or the *subjective* knowledge). Explicit knowledge comes from a rationalisation of the information about facts, and can be codified in the form of formulas, designs, reports, and so on; for that reason, it is relatively easy to obtain, store, and transfer. On the contrary, tacit knowledge is directly connected with ideas, perceptions, and experience, and therefore, is quite impossible to codify. Generally, it can only be observed when applied, acquired through practice and experience, and is consequently difficult to transfer. In reality, as underlined by Keane and Manson (2006) and by Grant (2007), referring to the seminal works of Polanyi (1958, 1967), tacit and explicit are not two distinct types but two inseparable dimensions of knowledge (see also McAdam, Mason, & McCroy,

2007). In light of this, information (i.e., what is actually transferred through any communication channel) can be considered as the explicit representation of knowledge, while the tacit dimension comes into play when the user interprets, interacts, and applies information in a context. Again, this means that information always requires a tacitly constructed cognitive background to be correctly understood and employed.

As well explained by Grant (2007), all knowledge includes a degree of tacitness along a continuum in which the one or the other dimension may dominate. As clearly depicted in Figure 1 (derived by Grant from Polanyi, 1958), the continuum ranges from a situation where there is little tacitness, and the knowledge can be held by many people with a limited common background and experience (this is, e.g., the case of the knowledge needed to cook a dish); through a situation where only experts (of a certain domain) can completely share the knowledge given their common background, specific training, and experience; to the situation where there is a strong personal component, and the knowledge results very difficult to articulate and share; and finally, reaching the point that knowledge is impossible to codify/articulate (the "ineffable" knowledge, as that needed to play golf). The degree of explicitness closely affects the language (spoken, written, symbolic) that has to be used to transmit one's own knowledge to another individual. When knowledge is highly explicit to the most, it can be articulated by means of a generic language; on the contrary, as the level of tacitness increases, a more specific language is needed to fully articulate it. This is the case of a jargon used by the members of a particular professional business group, whose meaning is quite impossible to understand outside that group. In this area, the concept of implicit knowledge might be positioned, that is, knowledge that having a prevailing tacit dimension requires significant efforts to be codified. In such a circumstance, articulation can be done only in favour of a community that shares a specialized cognitive background, that is, having a common language, shared visions and mental models, similar practices, and so on. Since codification is very expensive in this case, implicit knowledge remains unarticulated very often, and thus has a limited circulation.

Highly personal knowledge pertains to the sphere of natural aptitudes, intuition, and skills of the single individual, and thus is very difficult to translate in explicit forms. Ineffable knowledge, which is virtually impossible to articulate, is positioned at the maximum degree of tacitness. This is the case of something that one is able to do (e.g., riding a bicycle) without really knowing why. In such situations, he/she knows perfectly how to do those things, though he/she knows the particulars of what he/she knows only in a subsidiary/instrumental manner and is quite ignorant of them. Thus, he/she may say that he/she knows these matters even though he/she cannot tell clearly, or hardly at all, what it is that he/she knows. Subsidiary or instrumental knowledge is not known in itself, but in terms of something focally known, to the quality of which it contributes, and to this extent it is unspecifiable (Polanyi, 1958, p. 88).

In short, when the tacit dimension becomes predominant, knowledge articulation becomes more difficult, rises in incompleteness, requires more specialised and richer languages and representation forms, and often calls for additional context

and background knowledge to be transferred to other people. On the other hand, since it is a more individual and instrumental knowledge, probably has a limited applicability outside its original context, and thus, less need to be transferred.

Another interesting classification that supplements the previous one is that recently proposed by Schwartz (2006), who, following Aristotle's way of thinking, distinguishes among five "virtues" (i.e., types) of thought:

- Epistémé, that is, factual or scientific knowledge. It is pure knowledge such as of mathematics and logic;
- Tèchné, that is, skill-based technical and action-oriented knowledge. It deals with things that change rather than with constant relationships found in epistémé;
- Phrónésis, that is, experiential self-knowledge or practical wisdom based on experience. It deals with action and getting things done;
- Noûs, that is, intuition. It embodies the perception side of knowledge, and thus, it is largely personal and tacit;
- Sophía, that is, theoretical knowledge of universal truths or first principles, and thus, is less interesting from the KM point of view.

Figure 1. The tacit/explicit dimension (from: Grant, 2007)

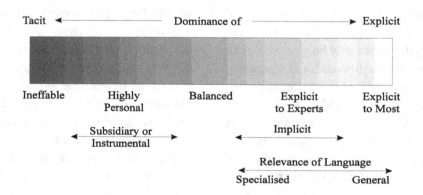

As underlined by the author, the different types of knowledge raise specific demands to the knowledge management activities and in particular, appear more or less suitable to be handled by means of computer-based tools. In particular, factual knowledge (epistémé) can be organised in knowledge bases, databases, documents, and so on, and hence, can be enabled and exchanged by IT and computer-mediated communications quite easily. Skill-based and action-oriented knowledge (tèchné), in that it belongs to the sphere of the individual physical abilities, is more difficult to encapsulate and reuse. Attempts have been done to replicate and implement it by artificial intelligent and decision support systems, but those technologies seem to be still undeveloped. Insofar as it can be narrated and described (in case histories, best practices, and the like), experiential self-knowledge or practical wisdom based on experience (phrónésis) can be stored, replicated, and delivered through rich media-based computer technologies. Lastly, intuition (noûs) is very difficult to share, but it is possible to have a digital representation of where it can be found (who possesses it) and how it might be applied. Furthermore, Internet-based applications can enable the social network through which noûs is uncovered. Again, possible use of computer-based technologies to transfer a specific type of knowledge seems to depend on the weight assumed by the tacit dimension: the smaller its incidence, the easier it will be to articulate and hence, exchange it by means of ICTs.

Given our interest in online environments, in the rest of the chapter, when we will consider the knowledge transfer process, we will refer to knowledge whose explicit component is prevailing (i.e., knowledge placed in the right side of Figure 1). This is also in line with the definition of knowledge as actionable or workable information, assumed in the first section.

MODELS OF THE KNOWLEDGE TRANSFER PROCESS

To identify and discuss the possible role played by a virtual knowledge mediator, a representation of the *knowledge transfer* process is of use. In the literature, there exist several models of this process, which are helpful to recall here. In general, all the models refer to the simple case of a "single" transfer involving two subjects: the sender and the recipient. As said in the introduction, real circumstances are much more complex since more subjects may be involved[3], and knowledge exchanges may be reciprocal, more or less simultaneous, and so forth. In any case, if it is a knowledge transfer, or a knowledge sharing, or a knowledge exchange, the basic question concerns the actual transmission of a piece of knowledge from a source to a receiver. Thus, the following models, which represent the knowledge transfer process, describe a single step of a more complex process that generally may be multistep, bidirectional and involve several actors.

The Communication-Like Model

We first refer to the communication-like perspective borrowed by the Shannon and Weaver (1949) transmission model of communication, that considers the knowledge transfer process as a form of communication (Figure 2), where a sender (the knowledge source) transmits a message (containing the transferred knowledge) to a receiver (Linsdey, 2006; McKinnel Jacobson, 2006). In order to be transferred, knowledge is firstly encoded in a message, and then sent through a communication channel. Once arrived at the destination, the message is decoded by the receiver, who may also send a feedback to the sender through the same (or another) channel. The model highlights that all the various steps/tasks of the communication/transfer process are disturbed by noise, whose effect is to distort the whole communication. The success of

Figure 2. The communication-like model of the knowledge transfer process (from: Lindsey, 2006)

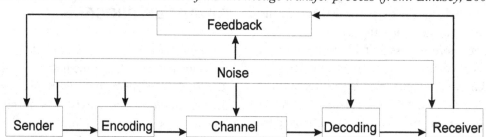

the knowledge transfer process is also influenced by some relevant characteristics of the various elements (McKinnel Jacobson, 2006). As regards the knowledge source, they are the perceived value of the owned knowledge, its credibility, and motivation. The effectiveness of the message is affected by the kind of knowledge that is being shared, its scope, and the nature (routine or non-routine) of the task that the transmitted knowledge intends to support. As far as the receiver is concerned, his motivation and absorptive capacity play a crucial role. Lastly, as to the communication channel, key factors are its features (related to the employed means), its degree of formality, and direction.

This model offers a simple but fundamental starting point to analyse the main elements that constitute the knowledge transfer process, and to identify the communication barriers that may affect its success. However, essentially because of its technical derivation, it overlooks some aspects that deeply affect the knowledge transfer process; the most important ones are the cognitive and social context in which the transfer occurs, and the cognitive features of the message itself (McKinnel Jacobson, 2006). Both these issues are taken into account by the cognitive view that is largely adopted by the KM literature (Albino et al., 2004; Garavelli, Gorgoglione, & Scozzi, 2002; Hendriks & Vriens, 1999; Mentzas, Apostolou, Kafentzis, & Georgolios, 2006; Tuomi, 2000).

The Cognitive Model

According to the cognitive perspective (Figure 3), a piece of knowledge, owned by some source, is firstly *externalised*, that is, represented in a message through an appropriate format, language, and so forth. As previously said, the degree of explicitness, that is, the extent to which knowledge can be verbalised, written, drawn, and the like, reflects on its transferability. The resulted message is then transmitted by various means, ranging from electronic channels to verbal communications. Once received, the message is *internalised*, that is, read, understood, assimilated, and exploited by the recipient. Internalisation consists in applying the tacit (contextual) dimension to the respective explicit representation (the message) in order to reconstruct the original meaning. The success of this process requires an "interpretative context" (or background) shared by the interacting parties (i.e., the sender and the receiver should give the same meaning to the message); a reciprocal interest in transferring knowledge; and a mutual "trust," since the parties should not doubt the quality of the knowledge transferred and its "proper" use. The cognitive model underscores some relevant issues, as follows:

- Knowledge is formed and resides inside human beings, who are its very producers and users. Consequently, any knowledge transfer process starts and finishes with an individual;

- Especially in the case of virtual knowledge exchanges, what is really transferred are the data (numbers, words, images, sounds, etc.) that constitute the fixed representation of the message. Communication may be synchronous or more often asynchronous; in the latter case the message has to be temporarily stored somewhere;

- There are several barriers that hinder the reception and the internalisation of the cognitive content of the message, and thus, the full and accurate absorption of the transmitted knowledge (see: Disterer, 2001; Riege, 2005; Yih-Ton Sun & Scott, 2005 for a complete list). Those barriers intervene at the individual, organisational, and technology level, and regard both cognitive and social/cultural aspects, as well as technical factors;

- A key role is played by the knowledge gap (cognitive distance) that separates the source from the receiver. It is worth noting that there is an always-existing gap, since two individuals will never share exactly the same values, beliefs, observations, and viewpoints (Nonaka et al., 2006). Strictly related with the former is the concept of stickiness that denotes the costs of transferring knowledge between two parts. Stickiness will be relatively low when the source and the recipient share the same context and are engaged in the same practice; on the contrary, stickiness will be very high in case of different contexts and practices. However, while knowledge redundancy and overlapping facilitate knowledge exchanges, relevant benefits notably reduce as the gap between the participants narrows;

- Trust is a necessary condition to make the transfer possible. People, in fact, are will-

Figure 3. The cognitive model of the knowledge transfer process

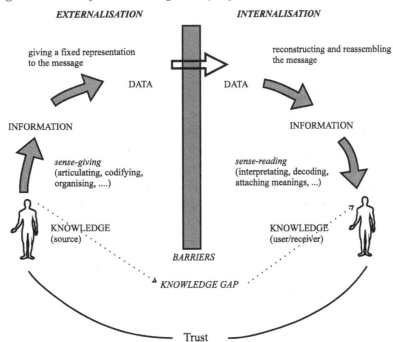

ing to exchange their knowledge only if they trust each other. This is particularly the case of virtual exchanges, where the two parties are not colocated, and cannot control themselves directly. Real-life experience shows that trust derives from different bases and is of different types, and this has a different impact on the extent and nature of the knowledge shared (see: Ford, 2003 for a broad discussion). Usually, the level of trust increases with the enhancement of the cooperative relationship that links the different parties.

Since it explicitly incorporates the context in which the knowledge transfer occurs and better specifies the cognitive phases (externalisation and internalisation) of the transfer process, the cognitive-like model gives a more complete representation than the communication-like one. Its main limit consists in the fact that (likewise the communication-like model) this model focuses on the transfer/exchange stage, without considering those preceding and following the single transfer, and which are decisive for its execution. Also, the previous perspectives put the economic aspects of a knowledge exchange in the background, and this is clearly not the case of knowledge exchanges that involve business organisations.

The Transaction-Like Model

To include the economic aspects of a knowledge transfer, it is of use to refer to a quite different, but complementary, approach that consists in equating the exchange of a piece of knowledge to a business transaction, where knowledge is the object of the transaction. This perspective is adopted by some authors (Desouza & Awazu, 2003; Kafentzis, Mentzas, Apostolou, & Georgolios, 2004; Matson, Patiath, & Shavers, 2003) who embrace an economic reading of knowledge exchanges, and develop the notion of "knowledge

markets." According to the transaction-like view, a knowledge exchange can be represented as consisting of the following phases (Kafentzis et al., 2004):

- The *contact/matching* phase, where the participants are searching the necessary information about receivers, senders, and their knowledge. This phase ends when the two parties come into contact and the actors develop concrete intentions of exchanging knowledge. The result is a precise request and offer of knowledge;
- In the *contracting* phase, the negotiation takes place, and the economic and other conditions of the transaction are settled;
- The *execution* phase, when the settlement of the knowledge exchange occurs. This phase involves the effective transfer of the piece of knowledge, as well the respective payment (or other types of reward), and other related services.

The transaction-like perspective highlights some factors that the previous two views partially overlooked:

- As any business transaction, a knowledge transaction may also involve three different kinds of players: the buyer (i.e., the receiver and user), who is looking for a required piece of knowledge; the seller, who possesses the searched knowledge; and the broker, who helps buyers and sellers to meet, and facilitates the knowledge exchange;
- In order that the exchange occurs, its "economic" requirements have to be fulfilled. In other word, all the involved parties must have an (direct or indirect) economic motivation and interest to participate in the exchange. To this point, it must be remembered that a knowledge exchange generates value, since it allows making a business use of the ex-

changed knowledge. It must also be noted that the knowledge transfer process produces costs that must be borne by someone;

- The matching phase is strongly based on metaknowledge, that is knowledge about the exchanged knowledge. Metaknowledge, in fact, is required to locate the knowledge the user is searching for, to analyse its content, to assess its value, and so on. Metaknowledge does concern both the piece of knowledge and its sources, and can be owned by single individuals, as well as articulated in several forms. Directories of experts, yellow pages, knowledge maps, abstracts, and taxonomies are typical examples of different kinds of metaknowledge.

What is of interest here is that knowledge markets (here considered as the physical, or better, the virtual places where the knowledge exchanges occur) show the typical market problems, such as the market of lemons effect, due to information asymmetries between sellers and buyers; the chicken-and-egg dilemma, originating from the need that the market reaches a minimal size; the possible existence of black markets that appear when one of the participants makes an illegal use of the exchanged knowledge (e.g., by transferring the acquired knowledge to another user without informing and rewarding the original provider); and the need of advertising strategies that take into account that knowledge objects are experience good, whose value to the potential receiver is not unknown until the knowledge is revealed, and after revelation, the potential acquirer has no need to pay for it, and can resell it at near-zero marginal cost (Desouza & Awazu, 2003). Furthermore, as any market, a knowledge market is subjected to failures[4] that may concern the previously recalled three market players as well as the market-wide conditions (Matson et al., 2003).

THE ROLE OF VIRTUAL KNOWLEDGE MEDIATORS: TOWARDS A DESCRIPTIVE FRAMEWORK

The Knowledge Mediator Task: Evidence from the KM Literature

Although from different, but surely complementary, perspectives, the former models put the accent on the fact that the knowledge transfer process is bristling with difficulties and barriers, so that its accomplishment cannot be taken for granted. Often, in fact, when knowledge is transferred, it may get "damaged," resulting in depreciated value. It is just to overcome those problems that new agents, that is, the knowledge mediators, have emerged in everyday life, as testified by the large number of references the KM literature makes to individuals, teams, and also business organisations that occupy an intermediary (supporting) position in the knowledge-exchanging processes. Since there is no room here for a complete overview, in that follows, only some influential KM authors will be recalled.

To begin with, Davenport and Prusak (1998) discuss knowledge brokers, or gatekeepers, as individuals who act as a link between knowledge senders and receivers. In particular, they consider document managers as a special kind of broker whose task is to direct searchers to relevant information. As for him, Teece (1998) identifies the function of knowledge translator, that is, an individual who is able to express the interests of a group according to the interpretative frameworks and languages used by another group of people. Also, Brown and Duguid (2001) consider translation as a typical job of a knowledge broker.

Maier (2002) affirms that the knowledge broker is one of the various roles, established within KM projects, whose task consists in surfing, that is, helping people in moving inside the company's knowledge repositories; searching, that is, collecting documents and locating experts belonging to a specific knowledge domain; analysing, that is, writing reports and studies, by evaluating, synthesising documents, and referring to the located experts. Knowledge mediators may also fulfil other functions. For example, they may act as knowledge-matter specialists, having in charge the development/management of a particular field of knowledge, or, they may be managers of a specific network or community of practice.

On this subject, Markus (2001) deserves a particular mention. He is probably the KM scholar who analysed the notion of knowledge mediator the most thoroughly when dealing with the topic of knowledge reuse, that is, the process through which knowledge is captured (i.e., documented), packaged (i.e., selected, cleaned, structured, formatted, and indexed for future reuse), distributed (i.e., sent to the potential user by means of push and/or pull mechanisms), and reused. In his opinion, knowledge reuse involves three roles: the knowledge producer (the originator and documenter of knowledge); the knowledge intermediary, who prepares knowledge for successive reuse by eliciting it, indexing it, summarising it, packaging it, and who performs various functions in distribution and facilitation; and knowledge reuser, who retrieves the knowledge content and applies it in some way. He also notes that the three roles can be performed by the same individual(s) or group(s), different individual(s) or groups, or some combination. Different knowledge reuse situations, according to the knowledge distance that separates the reuser from the producer, can be encountered, each one raising different questions to the knowledge intermediary. The most challenging one occurs when knowledge has to be documented for users who are very dissimilar (in cognitive terms) to producers. In such circumstances, it must be taken into account that the reuser may be completely outside the original context, and thus, he/she runs the risk of not being able to understand the relevance, or not correctly applying the acquired knowledge. In this cases,

the intervention of an intermediary is particularly useful to improve the intelligibility and usability of the knowledge received by the end user.

The mentioned literature strictly focused on the role of knowledge mediator inside a single organisation, where this role can be played by one or more individuals belonging to the same organisation, and performing the task of favouring the transfer and sharing of knowledge between the different parties (employees, teams, divisions) of the organisation.

More recently, given the increased attention put to the external sources of knowledge, the interest has moved towards mediators that enable the exchanges of knowledge between different organisations. It is quite superfluous to point out that exchanges that take place between organisations raise additional challenges, the first and foremost one pertains to trust (Oshri, 2006). Mentzas et al. (2006) give several examples of intermediaries who support interorganisational knowledge sharing. In these cases, the knowledge mediator is not a single individual or group, but a distinct company that does its business connecting two or more companies willing to exchange knowledge. Those companies usually make an intense use of Internet-based technologies in their daily work, and thus, they can be rightly defined virtual mediators.

The Knowledge Mediator Task: A Cognitive and Economic Reading

As underlined by the empirical evidence, many kinds of knowledge mediators exist who perform a variety of rather different functions and roles. This could be the reason why the relevant literature results is quite fragmentary and lacking in a common vision. Furthermore, since the literature deserves less attention to interorganizational knowledge sharing, a similar little interest is devoted to interorganizational knowledge mediators. In point of this, in the following sections, we will try to better understand, discuss, and classify the possible role of a virtual knowledge mediator; at this aim we will refer to the previously discussed models of the knowledge transfer process.

In accordance with the communication-like model (Figure 2), the main function of the mediator is to reduce (or limit) the noise that disturbs each step of the transfer process. Thus, they may get involved in all the phases of the process, but especially in the arrangement and management of the appropriate communication channels, and in elaborating (amending, integrating, storing, etc.) the message in order to increment its intelligibility; thus, adding value to the recipient. In light of this, two main roles can be identified for a mediator: *channel manager* and *content manager*. While the former essentially works on the technical side, the latter is responsible for the cognitive matter of the exchanged messages, in particular, for its capturing, storing, manipulating, updating, validation, and so on. Clearly, this is a quite simple and simplifying classification that, however, may be a useful starting point to deepen the analysis of the role of knowledge mediator, and in particular, of the skills and capabilities they are requested to have.

Referring to the cognitive view, the role of knowledge mediator seems to be primarily influenced by the two elements that affect the transfer process mostly, that is, the *tacit, complex, specific, and systemic nature* of the exchanged knowledge, and the *cognitive distance* (the knowledge gap) that separate users from sources (Figure 3). When knowledge is substantially tacit, complex, and specific, externalisation becomes very hard and consequently, only a limited part of the knowledge possessed by the source can be expressed in a message and then transmitted. Moreover, in case of systemic knowledge, it requires complementary knowledge to be usefully applied. The notion of cognitive distance refers to people who, operating in different contexts, have different languages, interpretative frameworks, and the like. In those conditions, internalisation is very difficult, and this prevents the receiver from fully understanding and absorbing the transmitted knowledge. Based on these two elements, Cillo (2005) suggests a classification of four types of internal knowledge mediators that can directly extend also to the cases of external (i.e., interorganisational) and virtual knowledge mediators (Figure 4):

- *Information broker*, who transfers simple information between two parties belonging to closely related context and with sporadic

Figure 4. Types of knowledge mediators (adapted from: Cillo, 2005)

	Complexity of knowledge	
High	***Knowledge Coder*** Selecting the knowledge to be transferred and codifying it in a coherent language	***Pure Knowledge Broker*** Interpreting and manipulating knowledge
Cognitive distance between the contexts	***Information Broker*** Pure transfer of information	***Integrated Knowledge Broker*** Accessing and transferring knowledge by directly interacting with the two parties needing to share knowledge
Low	Low	High

interactions. Probably in the long run, this type of broker will be strongly supported (and partially replaced) by technological devices;

- *Knowledge coder*, who selects the knowledge to be transferred and codifies it in a coherent language. This mediator operates essentially as an information translator when the contexts of the two parties are very distant, but the knowledge is not complex. An example is the exchange of information between different departments of the same organisation. Generally, they are sporadic interactions;

- *Integrated knowledge broker*, who operates in the case of complex knowledge and similar contexts. Such a broker accesses and transfers knowledge by continuously interacting with the two parties. A typical situation is that of an intermediary acting inside a community of practice;

- *Pure knowledge broker*, who interprets and manipulates knowledge. They act in situations where cognitive distance is great, knowledge is very complex, and interactions are continuous. Brokers between two differ-

ent communities of practice well represent such a situation.

The transaction-like model gives a complementary view, since it focuses on the roles that a virtual knowledge mediator can assume during the different phases of a knowledge transaction. To this point, it is of use to refer to the literature about virtual mediators, where five roles are identified, as follows (Barnes & Hinton, 2007):

1. **Informational:** This role involves the provision of information about receivers, sources, and related knowledge, and results to be crucial during the contact/matching phase;

2. **Transactional:** The mediator might participate in the transaction directly as either a knowledge buyer or a seller; or alternatively, it might act to facilitate the transaction, for example, by giving assistance to the participants during the contractual phase;

3. **Assurance:** This role is that of providing assurance of the quality of the exchanged knowledge, and of ensuring the correct behaviour of participants. This function is

Figure 5. Business and knowledge intermediation: A comparison

Functions	Business intermediation	Knowledge intermediation
Physical (concerning the exchanged good)	• Grouping or subdivision of homogeneous goods • Assortment of heterogeneous goods • Physical storage • Transportation • Conditioning	• Assembling or splitting of homogeneous knowledge • Integration of fragmented and heterogeneous knowledge • Storage and updating • Translation/contextualization • Transfer
Commercial	• Demand and supply connection • Purchase and selling • Assistance and consulting • Commercial risk • Warranty	• Source and recipient connection • Acquisition and selling • Certification of sources • Content validation and certification
Economics/Financial	• Price setting • Funding	• Price setting • Costs allocation
Communication	• Information • Promotion	• Information • Promotion

Figure 6. A two-dimensional framework of the cognitive and transactional role of knowledge mediators

Cognitive roles Transactional roles	Information broker	Knowledge coder	Integrated knowledge broker	Pure knowledge coder
Informational				
Transactional				
Assurance				
Logistical				
Customisation				

performed both during the information and the settlement phase. Mediators can choose to enhance their assurance role by providing some kind of legal guarantee, and/or by deliberately building and reinforcing their reputation;

4. **Logistical:** It consists in delivering the needed knowledge to the end user. In case of virtual transactions, the delivery is made through online distribution channels;

5. **Customisation:** It involves the tailoring of the knowledge objects to meet the needs of individual users. The tailoring process increases the value of knowledge transaction, notably, in that it aims to make the exchanged knowledge of better use for the recipient.

An analogous transaction-like way to categorize the activities carried out by a knowledge mediator consists in drawing a parallel with the main functions performed by a business mediator (Figure 5).

Those functions are directly associated with the roles previously discussed. For instance, the informational roles generally require an intense communication effort to give the participants the information needed for their contact. As formerly recalled, metaknowledge plays a crucial role here, in that it facilitates demand getting in touch with supply. The "physical" functions, in particular, those related to knowledge manipulation, allow better fulfilling the end users' requirements, and hence, pertain to the customisation role. The most these needs are user and context specific, the most will be the knowledge manipulating activity performed by the intermediary. Knowledge storage and transfer pertain to the logistical role, and are especially crucial when knowledge transfer is asynchronous, that is, when the piece of knowledge has to be stored somewhere and somehow before being sent to the recipient. Lastly, transactional roles involve the commercial and economics/financial functions of costs allocation and price setting.

What is worth noting here is that, given the complexity and multifaceted nature of the intermediation function, as a commercial broker may offer a more or less complete service, also a knowledge mediator may perform all, some, or only one of the enumerated functions. This means that one or more mediators may assist a knowledge transfer, each specialised in a set of knowledge intermediation functions.

Developing a Descriptive Framework

In the light of what up to here discussed, an integrated interpretative framework of the virtual knowledge mediator role is developed that combines the cognitive with the economic view. It is a two-dimensional framework (see Figure 6) that considers both the cognitive and the transactional role at the same time, and identifies 20 possible different specific roles that a knowledge mediator may assume. In our intention, the framework should be a useful tool to analyse and classify real cases of virtual knowledge mediators. In this sense, it can be seen as a first step towards a deeper and more systematic investigation of this new phenomenon.

The framework offers some food for thought about the knowledge mediator role. In particular, it raises some interesting research questions about the actual nature of such a role. For instance, are all the cognitive and transactional roles compatible to one another? That is, are there any empty (not viable) cells in the matrix of Figure 6? Also, are some kinds of knowledge mediator more widespread than others? Is there an extreme specialisation in this sector? Are operators vertically integrated (i.e., along the cognitive dimension) or horizontally integrated (along the transactional dimension)? How much is this role affected by the kind of industry where the mediators act? Answering these questions could certainly be a first step towards a better understanding the role of knowledge mediators in virtual environments.

CONCLUSION

As strongly confirmed by both the every day practice and the theoretical thinking, the knowledge transfer process is at the basis of the KM activities, since it makes it possible to transfer the available knowledge from where it resides to where it can be economically exploited. Unfortunately, this process is bristling with several difficulties and barriers that increase when knowledge is exchanged through virtual channels and involves different organisations. To overcome such problems, the presence of a knowledge mediator is required, who acts as a bridge between the involved parties, that is, source and receiver. Given the recent origin of such phenomenon, little is still known about which functions the knowledge mediator role consists of. In the present chapter, some

preliminary indications about the nature and the key features of this new economic agent have been given. In particular, a descriptive framework has been developed that by combining the cognitive and the transactional dimension of virtual knowledge mediators, should allow examining some key aspects of their business strategies and behaviours. The framework intends to provide an analytical tool that should be of help in explaining and thoroughly understanding the practice of knowledge intermediation in virtual environment. Clearly, ongoing empirical investigation is needed in order to test and refine the framework. This is not a simple task, since the Internet world is very dynamic, and new types of knowledge mediators seem to continue to emerge.

FUTURE RESEARCH DIRECTIONS

Despite its two-dimensional nature, the framework leaves in the background some important aspects that deserve particular attention in the future. A crucial one concerns the competitive factors of the knowledge intermediation activity. Since it is a new business model on the Internet, its key components should be deeply investigated, with special attention on the related economic aspects. In this connection, the transactional nature of the knowledge intermediation business should be considered more thoroughly, with direct reference of knowledge as the object of economic exchange. Assuming that perspective should allow one to tackle two crucial and interrelated questions, that is, what is the value generated by the exchanged knowledge (and the related costs), and who (and how much) is willing to pay for that value. Answering those questions should allow better understanding the conditions of the economic sustainability of the virtual knowledge mediator business model (Scarso, Bolisani, & Di Biagi, 2006). Unfortunately, the economic and market-like view, which seems to be useful to analyse knowledge transfer and sharing processes, still represents a marginal approach inside the KM literature, and hence, it should be further developed.

Another question, which could be an interesting future research topic, concerns the impact of the technological evolution on the knowledge mediator role. Without doubt, in the future, KM will benefit from continual and even more dynamic progress in ICT, and thus, the future of KM will be very different from the present (Becerra-Fernadez & Sabherwal, 2006). But, what about knowledge mediators? Will the new technological tools replace the intermediation role or call for new kinds of mediators? Probably upcoming technologies will automate a good part of the mediator's job, till to substitute the simplest functions, as affirmed by Cillo (2005). This will occur especially if it will be possible to develop new representations able to make the transferred knowledge more suitable to the virtual communication channels and to enhance the absorptive capability of the receivers. However, since interorganisational knowledge exchanges will continue to intensify, the knowledge intermediation needs will continue to increase and to become even more sophisticated. To sum up, probably does not exist a univocal answer to such a question, and the effects of technological advancements will depend on each specific situation, in terms of the more or less tacit, and more or less systematic nature of exchanged knowledge, kind of involved participants and their relationships, width of the cognitive gap, and so on.

ACKNOWLEDGMENT

The chapter contributes to the FIRB 2003 project "Knowledge management in the extended enterprise: New organizational models in the digital age," funded by the Italian Ministry of University and Research.

REFERENCES

Alavi, M., & Leidner, D. E. (2001). Knowledge management and knowledge management systems: Conceptual foundations and research issues. *MIS Quarterly, 25*, 107-136.

Albino, V., Garavelli, A. C., & Gorgoglione, M. (2004). Organisation and technology transfer. *Benchmarking: An International Journal, 11*(2), 584-600.

Apostolou, D., Papailiou, N., & Mentzas, G. (2007). Developing knowledge networks: A practical methodology and experiences from cases. *International Journal of Knowledge Management Studies, 1*, (3/4), 330-355.

Barnes, D., & Hinton, M. (2007). Developing a framework to analyse the roles and relationships of online intermediaries. *International Journal of Information Management, 27*, 63-74.

Becerra-Fernandez, I., & Sabherwal, R. (2006). ICT and knowledge management systems. In D. G. Schwartz (Ed.), *Encyclopedia of Knowledge Management* (pp. 231-236). Hershey, PA: Idea Group.

Bolisani, E., & Scarso, E. (1999). Information technology management: A knowledge-based perspective. *Technovation, 19*, 209-217.

Boyd, J., Ragsdell, G., & Oppenheim, C. (2007). Knowledge transfer mechanisms: A case study from manufacturing. In B. Martin & D. Remenyi (Eds.), *Proceedings of the 8th European Conference on Knowledge Management* (Vol. I, pp. 139-146). Reading, UK: Academic Conferences Limited.

Brown, J. S., & Duguid, P. (2001). Structure and spontaneity: Knowledge and organization. In I. Nonaka, & D. J. Teece (Eds.), *Managing Industrial Knowledge. Creation, Transfer and Utilization* (pp. 44-67). London: SAGE.

Cillo, P. (2005). Fostering market knowledge use in innovation: The role of internal brokers. *European Management Journal, 23*(4), 404-412.

Coakes, E., Bradburn, A., & Sugden, G. (2004). Managing and leveraging knowledge for organisational advantage. *Knowledge Management Research & Practice, 2*, 118-128.

Davenport, T. H., & Prusak, L. (1998). *Working knowledge: How organizations manage what they know.* Boston: Harvard Business School Press.

Desouza, K. C. (2003). Knowledge management barriers: Why the technology imperative seldom works. *Business Horizons*, January-February, 25-29.

Desouza, K. C., & Awazu, Y. (2003). Constructing internal knowledge markets: Considerations from mini cases. *International Journal of Information Management, 23*, 345-353.

Disterer, G. (2001). *Individual and social barriers to knowledge transfer.* Paper presented at the 34th Hawaii International Conference on System Sciences, Maui, Hawaii.

Ford, D. P. (2003). Trust and knowledge management: The seeds of success. In C. W. Holsapple (Ed.), *Handbook on knowledge management* (Vol. 1, pp. 553-575). Berlin: Springer.

Garavelli, A. C., Gorgoglione, M., & Scozzi, B. (2002). Managing knowledge transfer by knowledge technologies. *Technovation, 22*, 269-279.

Grant, K. A. (2007). Tacit knowledge revisited – We can still learn from Polanyi. *The Electronic Journal of Knowledge Management, 5*(2), 173-180.

Hendriks, P. H. J., & Vriens, D. J. (1999). Knowledge-based systems and knowledge management: Friends or foes? *Information & Management, 35*, 113-125.

Holsapple, C. W. (2005). The inseparability of modern knowledge management and computer-based technology. *Journal of Knowledge Management, 9*(1), 42-52.

Holsapple, C. W., & Joshi, K. D. (2006). Knowledge management ontology. In D. G. Schwartz (Ed.), *Encyclopedia of knowledge management* (pp. 397-402), Hershey, PA: Idea Group.

Huysman, M., & Wulf, V. (2006). IT to support the knowledge sharing in communities, towards a social capital analysis. *Journal of Information Technology, 21*, 40-51.

Kafentzis, K., Mentzas, G., Apostolou, D., & Georgolios, P. (2004). Knowledge marketplaces: Strategic issues and business models. *Journal of Knowledge Management, 8*(1), 130-146.

Kankanhalli, A., Tan, B. C. Y., & Wei, K-K. (2006). Knowledge producers and consumers. In D. G. Schwartz (Ed.), *Encyclopedia of Knowledge Management* (pp. 459-466). Hershey, PA: Idea Group.

Keane, B. T., & Mason, R. M. (2006). *On the nature of knowledge. Rethinking popular assumptions.* Paper presented at the 39th Hawaii International Conference on System Sciences, Maui, Hawaii.

Kim, S-K, & Trimi, S. (2007). IT for KM in the management consulting industry. *Journal of Knowledge Management, 11*(3), 145-155.

King, W. R. (2006a). Knowledge sharing. In D. G. Schwartz (Ed.), *Encyclopedia of Knowledge Management* (pp. 493-498). Hershey, PA: Idea Group.

King, W. R. (2006b). Knowledge transfer. In D. G. Schwartz (Ed.), *Encyclopedia of Knowledge Management* (pp. 538-543). Hershey, PA: Idea Group.

Lindsey, K. L. (2006). Knowledge sharing barriers. In D. G. Schwartz (Ed.), *Encyclopedia of Knowledge Management* (pp. 499-506). Hershey, PA: Idea Group.

Maier, R. (2002). *Knowledge management ay-stems. Information and Communication Tech-nologies for knowledge management.* Berlin: Springer.

Malhotra, Y. (2000). Knowledge management for e-business performance: Advancing information strategy to "Internet time." *Information Strategy: The Executive's Journal, 16*(4), 5-16.

Markus, M. L. (2001). Toward a theory of knowl-edge reuse: Types of knowledge reuse situations and factors in reuse success. *Journal of Manage-ment Information Systems, 18*(1), 27-93.

Matson, E., Patiath, P., & Shavers, T. (2003). Stimulating knowledge sharing: Strengthening your organization's internal knowledge market. *Organizational Dynamics, 32*(3), 275-287.

McAdam, R., Mason, B., & McCroy, J. (2007). Exploring the dichotomies within the tacit knowledge literature: Toward a process of tacit knowing in organisation. *Journal of Knowledge Management, 11*(2), 43-59.

McKinnel Jacobson, C. (2006). Knowledge shar-ing between individuals. In D. G. Schwartz (Ed.), *Encyclopedia of Knowledge Management* (pp. 507-504). Hershey, PA: Idea Group.

Mentzas, G., Apostolou, D., Kafentzis, K., & Geor-golios, P. (2006). Interorganizational networks for knowledge sharing and trading. *Information Technology Management, 7,* 259-276.

Newell, S., Bresnen, M., Edelman, L., Scarbrough, H., & Swan, J. (2006). Sharing Knowledge Across Projects. Limits to ICT-led Project Review Prac-tice. *Management Learning, 37*(2), 67-185.

Nonaka, I., & Takeuchi, H. (1995). *The knowl-edge-creating company,* Oxford, UK: Oxford University Press.

Nonaka, I., von Krogh, G., & Voelpel, S. (2006). Organizational knowledge creation theory: Evolu-tionary paths and future advances. *Organization Studies, 27*(8), 1179-1208.

Oshri, I. (2006). Knowledge reuse. In D. G. Schwartz (Ed.), *Encyclopedia of knowledge management* (pp. 487-492). Hershey, PA: Idea Group.

Papoutsakis, H. (2007). Sharing knowledge in the organisation: A retrospective analysis and empiri-cal studies. *The Electronic Journal of Knowledge Management, 5*(2), 231-244.

Polanyi, M. (1958). *Personal knowledge. Towards a post-critical philosophy.* Chicago: University of Chicago Press.

Polanyi, M. (1967). *The tacit dimension,* Garden City, NY: Doubleday Anchor.

Riege, A. (2005). Three-dozen knowledge-shar-ing barriers managers must consider. *Journal of Knowledge Management, 9*(3), 18-35.

Riege, A. (2007). Actions to overcome knowledge transfer barriers in MNCs. *Journal of Knowledge Management, 11*(1), 48-67.

Scarso, E., Bolisani, E., & Di Biagi, M. (2006). Knowledge intermediation. In D. G. Schwartz (Ed.), *Encyclopedia of Knowledge Management* (pp. 360-367). Hershey, PA: Idea Group.

Schwartz, D. G. (2006). Aristotelian view of knowledge management. In D. G. Schwartz (Ed.), *Encyclopedia of Knowledge Management* (pp. 10-16). Hershey, PA: Idea Group.

Seufert, A., von Krogh, G., & Bach, A. (1999). Towards knowledge networking. *Journal of Knowledge Management, 3*(3), 180-190.

Shannon, C. E., & Weaver, W. (1949). *The math-ematical theory of communication.* Chicago: University of Illinois Press.

Sieloff, C. G. (1999). If only HP knew what HP knows: The roots of knowledge management at Hewlett-Packard. *Journal of Knowledge Manage-ment, 3*(1), 47-53.

Teece, D. J. (1998). Capturing value from knowledge assets: The new economy, markets for know-how, and intangible assets. *California Management Review, 40*(3), 55-79.

Tiwana, A. (2000). *The knowledge management toolkit.* Upper Saddle River, NJ: Prentice Hall.

Tuomi, I. (2000). Data is more than knowledge: Implications of the reversed knowledge hierarchy for knowledge management and organizational memory. *Journal of Management Information Systems, 16*(3), 103-117.

Walsham, G. (2001). Knowledge management: The benefits and limitations of computer systems. *European Management Journal, 19*(6), 599-608.

Yih-Ton Sun, P., & Scott, J.L. (2005). An investigation of barriers to knowledge transfer. *Journal of Knowledge Management, 9*(2), 75-90.

ADDITIONAL READINGS

Bolisani, E., & Scarso, E. (2000). Electronic communication and knowledge transfer. *International Journal of Technology Management, 20*(1/2), 116-133.

Chen, S., Duan, Y., & Edwards, J. S. (2006). Inter-organisational knowledge transfer process model. In E. Coakes, & S. Clarke (Eds.), *Encyclopedia of Communities of Practice in Information and Knowledge Management* (pp. 239-245). Hershey, PA: Idea Group.

du Plessis, M. (2007). Knowledge management: What makes complex implementation successful? *Journal of Knowledge Management, 11*(2), 91-101.

Goh, S. C. (2002). Managing effective knowledge transfer: An integrative framework and some practice implications. *Journal of Knowledge Management, 6*(1), 23-30.

Griffith, T. I., & Sawyer, J. E. (2006). Supporting technologies and organizational practices for the transfer of knowledge in virtual environments. *Group Decision and Negotiation, 15*, 407-423.

Holsapple, C. W. (Ed.). (2003). *Handbook on knowledge management.* Berlin: Springer.

Hutzschenreuter, T., & Listner, F. (2007). A contingency view on knowledge transfer: Empirical evidence from the software industry. *Knowledge Management Research & Practice, 5*, 136-150.

Maier, R., & Händrich, T. (2006). Knowledge management systems. In D. G. Schwartz (Ed.), *Encyclopedia of Knowledge Management* (pp. 442-450). Hershey, PA: Idea Group.

Priestley, J. L. (2006). Knowledge transfer within interorganizational networks. In E. Coakes & S. Clarke (Eds.), *Encyclopedia of Communities of Practice in Information and Knowledge Management* (pp. 307-316). Hershey, PA: Idea Group.

Scott, J. E. (2003). The role of trust in e-business knowledge management. *International Journal of Electronic Business, 1*(2), 187-210.

Tsoukas, H., & Vladimirou, E. (2001). What is organizational knowledge? *Journal of Management Studies, 38*(7), 974-993.

ENDNOTES

[1]   Although the various scholars make use of different terms, there is substantial agreement on the main processes that characterise KM, and that can be summarised as follows: knowledge generation (creation or acquisition), which entails the internal development or the external acquisition of new knowledge; knowledge storage and retrieval, needed to preserve, organise, and make accessible existing knowledge; knowledge transfer and sharing, which consists of the transmission of

the knowledge where it is of use; knowledge application, which involves the exploitation of the previously generated, organised, and transferred knowledge (Alavi & Leidner, 2001; Holsapple & Joshi, 2006; Maier, 2002; Schwartz, 2006).

2   Other classifications, less significant here, are based on the content and the owner of the knowledge. The former distinguishes among (Alavi & Leidner, 2001): descriptive knowledge (know-about), procedural knowledge (know-how), causal knowledge (know-why), knowledge of the sources of knowledge (know-who), and relational knowledge (know-with). The latter differentiates between individual and collective (organisational) knowledge, with the second being constructed and existing in the joint action of a group of individuals engaged in a common effort. According to Tsoukas and Vladimirou (2001), any business knowledge, including the individual one, has an organisational dimension, since its creation, dissemination, and use occur inside a specific organisational environment.

3   As a matter of fact, collaboration is always more at the heart of the KM processes (Apostolou, Papailiou, & Mentzas, 2007), and it generally occurs within the so-called knowledge networks, that is, a set of actors, resources, and social relationships among them who interact in order to accumulate and use knowledge mainly by means of knowledge creation and sharing processes, for purpose of creating value (Seufert, von Krogh, & Bach, 1999). Knowledge sharing networks are types of networks among individuals, communities or organisations that serve as a locus for facilitating knowledge sharing and effective knowledge work (Papoutsakis, 2007). Such networks are denoted by multidirectional and intense knowledge flows that link the various participants, who can be at the same time knowledge senders, receivers, and manipulators.

4   In particular, Matson et al. (2003) identify nine market failures: three related to the supply side (i.e., lack of external knowledge sources; lack of codification mechanisms, lack of incentives to codify/share); three to the demand-side (i.e., ineffective delivery mechanisms, perception that knowledge is not valuable, lack of external awareness); three to the market enabler (i.e., lack of intermediaries, inconsistent knowledge architecture, uncoordinated knowledge systems); and three to the market itself (i.e., redundant initiatives, inadequate measures, unprotected intellectual property).

Chapter XV
Knowledge Management in Virtual Enterprises:
Supporting Frameworks and Enabling Web Technologies

Stavros T. Ponis
National Technical University Athens, Greece

George Vagenas
National Technical University Athens, Greece

Ilias P. Tatsiopoulos
National Technical University Athens, Greece

ABSTRACT

The new globalized and demanding business environment of the 21st century has created a shift from traditional organizations to more loose and flexible business schemes shaped in the form of Virtual Enterprises. This transformation would never have been successful without the support of Information Technologies and particularly the Web. Internet, in the last decade, has become the universal medium of interactions between distributed entities. In this chapter, the issue of Knowledge Management support for Virtual Enterprises is discussed. Building upon the current state of the art, this chapter aims to identify the major knowledge requirements of VEs, in an effort to provide a roadmap towards a holistic Knowledge Management framework that will satisfy the excessive knowledge needs of Virtual Enterprises at the interorganizational level. In that context, the role of supporting Web and Semantic Web technologies for the enactment of KM in VEs is described in detail.

INTRODUCTION

The 21st century's unstable and highly competitive business environment is calling for a fundamental reassessment of the way enterprises are doing business. Modern business entities, more like world-class competing athletes that are constantly asked to run faster, jump higher, and throw further, are continuously stressed, by both competitors and customers, to produce more customized products in low costs and high quality. Competition is relentless and according to Zwegers et al. (Zwegers, Wubben, & Hartel, 2002), three are the major factors that put additional requirements to enterprises, namely the globalization of market, production and supply; the emergence of outsourcing activities; and the turn of customers' demand towards highly customized products.

This new and demanding environment has created an enterprise management shift from well-defined, stable enterprises having limited relationships with other companies and focusing on internal efficiency and effectiveness, toward loose enterprise formations, tightly integrated with their suppliers and customers, pursuing overall optimization. In a nutshell, one can argue that nowadays, there is a well-recognized change of management direction, from "self-centered" closed enterprises to global, open enterprises (Browne & Zhang, 1999), cooperating and forming interenterprise organizations in order to achieve a sustainable position in the market, and ensure their survival and business success.

In this new networked business reality, the 30-years old slogan "knowledge is power," by the ACM (Association for Computing Machinery) Turing Award winner, Ed Feigenbaum (Feigenbaum & McCorduck, 1983, p.8), has proved more than accurate. As Peter Drucker (1993) and others have claimed, Western organizations are not becoming more labor, material, or capital-intensive, but more knowledge intensive, an observation that holds particularly true in the case of the competency-oriented networked-enterprise formations of the new era. As a result, there is an unambiguous recognition by academics, researchers, and practitioners about the importance of knowledge and knowledge management (Drucker, 1968; Nonaka, 1991; Wiig, 1997), which displays all the characteristics of a nascent megatrend (Bair, Fenn, Hunter, & Bosik, 1997).

Especially in the case of virtual enterprises (VEs), one of the most dominant contemporary organizational schemes, knowledge and its interorganizational management, is a crucial factor for gaining and sustaining competitive advantages (Preiss, Goldman, S& Nagel, 1996). This chapter aims to address the issue of Knowledge Management (KM) support for virtual enterprises with the use of IT, and particularly, Web technologies. Our perspective on KM, as presented in this section, is not static. Knowledge is generated, passed on, used, and in turn, contributes to its regeneration. In order for this to happen, an intensive cooperation and an open real-time knowledge exchange between participants in the global information environment are required, so that the right knowledge from distributed sources can be integrated and transferred to the right person within the right context at the right time for the right purpose. The aggregate of these interrelated activities is found in the literature under the term, Knowledge Logistics-KL (Ponis, Tatsiopoulos, & Vagenas, 2006; Smirnov, Pashkin, Chilov, & Levashova, 2004). An often critique on KL goals is that they describe mostly an "ideal world." Still, in the highly demanding reality of VEs, in which excellence is the prime requirement, Knowledge Logistics and the constant pursue of its optimistic goals is an imperative, even though most of the time the road to their achievement is harsh and the results often dubious.

In the next section, a brief literature review on KM, and existing state of the art on KM frameworks, is conducted. This section provides the reader with the necessary theoretical background, and enables the better understanding of the next section dealing with VEs' particular knowledge characteristics and needs.

KNOWLEDGE MANAGEMENT: DEFINITIONS AND APPROACHES

A fundamental issue in providing a complete definition of knowledge and its management is to understand its differences in comparison to information and data. The distinction between data, information, and knowledge already appears in the CODASYL report of 1971 (CODASYL, 1971) on general features of database systems. On the one hand, data comprises a set of discrete and objective facts concerning events (Joia, 2000), while information is the result of analyzing and interpreting data (Bourdreau & Couillard, 1999). On the other, hand knowledge is "a justified belief that increases an entity's capacity for effective action" (Nonaka, 1994, p. 15). However, it is difficult to draw a discrete line separating these concepts, a reality reflected in the interchangeable use of the terms information and knowledge in the KM literature. This is mainly because of the dynamic relationships among the triple of data information and knowledge. In the same spirit, Spiegler (2000) suggests a recursive and spiral model of linking the triple, according to which "yesterday's data are today's information, and tomorrow's knowledge, which in turn recycles back through the value chain into information and then into data"(p. 3). It is clear that in a subjective field such as KM, strict and rigid approaches do not apply, and restricting a philosophical concept, such as knowledge, in the confinement of an inflexible definition has nothing to offer. As a result, while we have tried to use the concepts of information and knowledge in a distinct way, the reader has to be aware that this was not always possible. In this sense, Holsapple's and Joshi's (2004) definition for KM is adopted, according to which KM is an entity's systematic and deliberate efforts to expand, cultivate, and apply the available knowledge in ways that add value to the entity. Added value is regarded as the production of positive results that support the entity in accomplishing its objectives or fulfilling its purpose.

A detailed look in the literature proves that knowledge management (KM) attracts the interest of scientists from a wide range of disciplines, mainly organizational science, strategy and management science, computer science, as well as management information systems that have attempted to define and structure the KM domain and thus, provide guidance to practitioners. This multidisciplinary focus has resulted in an abundance of perspectives on KM. First, there are those that adopt a mechanistic view of KM, focusing on intellectual capital and treating knowledge resources in an ordinary resource management fashion. Second, approaches exist that concentrate on knowledge processes, determining and analyzing the activities that can be performed on knowledge itself. And finally, few are the approaches that percept KM in an integrated manner and based on that, provide a holistic description of the KM paradigm in an applicable form. An exhaustive literature review, conducted by the authors, presented in the remainder of this section, proves (at least to our extensive knowledge of the field) that KM theoretical frameworks addressing VEs' specific needs in an applicable form simply do not exist. It is the aim of this chapter to address this shortcoming by identifying the major knowledge characteristics and needs of VEs, and providing a roadmap towards a holistic knowledge management framework in the context of VEs.

The perspectives on KM (Intellectual Capital, IT, processes, and holistic), mentioned previously, are also evident in existing framework approaches found in literature. In this chapter, we utilize the definition of frameworks provided by CEN (2004) in the *European Guide of Good Practice in Knowledge Management*. According to that definition, a KM Framework is a structure relating the various components of knowledge management (processes, activities, and enablers) to each other. It provides a schematic picture of how these various aspects depend on each other, and how they are positioned within KM activities and projects. A detailed literature review (of at least 30 KM frameworks and numerous KM papers), in existing research efforts that support knowledge management, has provided us with a list of KM frameworks, organized into four distinct categories, depending on the perspective of their approach to knowledge and its management, shown in the following Table. It should be

Table 1. KM frameworks

Framework	Short Description
IC frameworks	
The intangible assets monitor (Sveiby, 1997)	The IAM is a technique for measuring intangible assets, and a presentation format that displays a number of relevant indicators for measuring intangible Assets, according to the company strategy. The framework identifies three kinds of intangible assets: external structures, internal structures, and employee competence.
The skandia navigator (Edvinsson & Malone, 1997)	The Skandia Navigator is a technique for evaluating the soft assets of an organization, as well as a management reporting system that helps managers visualize and develop measures that reflect intangible assets, and guide them into the future. It identifies company goals along five focus areas: financial, process, renewal/ growth, human, and costumer.
IT frameworks	
KM IT architecture (Mühlbauer & Versteegen, 2000)	The KM IT architecture is based on the assumption that technology is indispensable for knowledge management processes, and shows what kind of components can be integrated into a KM IT architecture.
The CommonKADS methodology (Schreiber, Akkermans, Anjewierden, de Hoog, Shadbold, van der Velde,. & Wielinga, 1999)	CommonKADS is the leading methodology to support structured knowledge engineering. It now is the European de facto standard for knowledge analysis and knowledge-intensive system development. It enables the analysis of opportunities and bottlenecks in how organizations develop, distribute, and apply their knowledge resources.
Process frameworks	
The knowledge creation process – The SECI model (Nonaka & Takeuchi 1995)	Nonaka and Takeuchi developed a theoretical model set, analyzing, in detail, the knowledge-creation process through the elaboration of a five-phase model. Furthermore, they provided a model qualifying the conversion of knowledge between the two identified knowledge modes (tacit and explicit).
Building blocks of knowledge kanagement (Probst, Raub, & Romhard, 1997)	The building blocks of KM model claims to support the implementation of KM by dividing it into eight modules. These modules/ building blocks represent activities that are directly knowledge related (identification, acquisition, development, distribution, preservation, and use of knowledge, goal-setting, and measurement.
The knowledge chain model (Holsapple & Singh, 2001)	The knowledge chain model identifies five primary (acquisition, selection, generation, internalization, and externalization) and four secondary KM activities (leadership, coordination, control, and measurement).
Holistic frameworks	
Model of organizational knowledge management (Andersen & APQC, 1996)	The APQC model identifies seven KM processes (create, identify, collect, adapt, organize, apply, and share) that manipulate corporate knowledge, and four organizational enablers (leadership, measurement, culture, and technology) that facilitate that manipulation. The model does not characterize in detail the nature and the interrelationships of its constructs.
The know-Net approach (Mentzas, Apostolou, Abecker, & Young, 2003)	The Know-Net claims to be a total knowledge-management solution that provides a holistic knowledge-management framework. This framework defines the main components of KM; a KM methodology, supporting the implementation of KM initiatives; and an intranet-based KM tool, supporting the collection, organization, and sharing of knowledge.
European knowledge management framework (CEN, 2004)(http://www.cenorm.be)	This European KM Framework aids organizations towards the successful implementation of a KM project. It sees three KM dimensions, a) value-adding processes that should be in the centre of any KM initiative, b) core knowledge activities (identify, create, store, share, and use), which form an integrated KM process, and c) enablers that support knowledge activities.

noted that this list is not exhaustive. There are other studies that could be included in the list; still, the ones described in this table constitute, to our opinion, the predominant and most complete research efforts for each identified category.

From the quite exhaustive literature review, which produced the results of the following table, it was made obvious to the research team that the situation regarding KM in modern organizations is still blurry and highly unstructured. There are no standardization bodies providing a set of commonly accepted guidelines to researchers or practitioners. As a relatively new scientific field, KM is still dominated by several research proposals, and is receiving strong fluctuations. As a result, literature regarding KM frameworks is highly fragmented, generating a gap between the theoretical approaches of KM and the practical challenges of coping with knowledge in the every day business practice. This situation is amplified by the immaturity of the available KM applications that have, up to now, failed to provide holistic support to KM business practice, leaving organizations struggling to effectively use and integrate knowledge management tools. Such assertions describing the inefficiency of KM to connect theoretical guidelines with tangible business practice, as well as the inadequacies of KM Systems, have been proved by a large number of testimonials and empirical studies (Chase, 1997; KPMG, 2003).

In addition, one can argue that a gap between theory and business practice is more intense in the business context of distributed and networked enterprises. Existing frameworks provide no actual support for the enactment of KM in the context of virtual enterprises. Indeed, in this respect, few proposals have been documented, such as the KnowNet approach (Mentzas et al., 2003), which includes a rough specification of an interorganizational KM approach, and even fewer have been successfully implemented. In summary, literature reveals that although VEs, by common assent, are considered knowledge-driven organizations (Filos, 2005), still, KM has not managed to address their particular needs adequately.

As for KM tools, a research of the available, so labeled, KM Systems (KMS) reveals the immaturity of the respective market. For one thing, there is no integrated and complete KM IT solution (Lindvall, Rus, & Suman Sinha 2003; Maier, 2002; Marwick, 2001; Schmaltz, Hagenhoff, & Kaspar, 2004), but rather isolated tools capable of supporting specific KM tasks. According to Maier (2002), the basic categories of KM applications include (a) intranet infrastructures providing basic functionality for communication, e-mail, teleconferencing, as well as storing, exchanging, searching, and retrieving of data and documents, (b) document and content management systems handling electronic documents or Web content respectively, (c) workflow management systems supporting the execution of well-defined workflows, (d) artificial intelligence technologies supporting search and retrieval of distributed knowledge, user profile management, text, and Web mining, (e) business intelligence tools and data warehouses, supporting the transformation of fragmented organizational and competitive data into goal-oriented "knowledge," (f) visualization tools assisting the relationships between knowledge, people, and processes (g) groupware tools supporting time management, discussions, meetings, or creative workshops of work groups and teams, and finally (h) e-learning systems offering specified learning content to employees in an interactive way and thus, supporting the teaching and/or learning process. An effort to integrate these disparate KM tools into a complete KM solution is the KM Architecture Model, presented in Figure 1 (Lindvall et al., 2003 based on Lawton, 2001). However, up to now we have not been able to identify a documented implementation of this architecture.

Literature reveals the fact that the most prominent use of IT in the support of KM is mostly documented in the extensive use of mere Content and

Figure 1. The KM architecture model, adopted by Lindvall et al., 2003

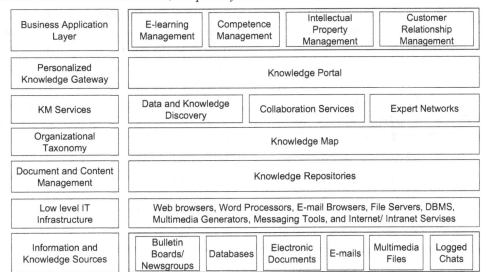

Document Management Systems, which provide some support for knowledge work but nevertheless, offer limited capabilities, and suffer from severe weaknesses in the semantic level, providing low accuracy of search results. Semantic features of KMS are of great importance, especially in the context of networked organizations, in order to enable and support cross-industry enterprise collaboration, systems interoperation, and last but not least, unstructured knowledge extraction from the dispersed organizational knowledge bases or the Web.

In this chapter, the glass is seen half full and therefore, the identified shortcomings in current state of the art are viewed as a significant research opportunity. This optimism mainly stems from the positive and encouraging results of the initial, and thus immature and partial to some extent, attempts to address the issue of managing knowledge in VEs. To draw an example from current literature, we cite the EnerSearch AB case of implementing an ontology and Semantic Web based knowledge management approach (Mika, Iosif, Sure, & Akkermans, 2003). EnerSearch AB (http://www.enersearch.com) is an industrial

research Consortium investigating new IT-based business strategies and customer services in deregulated energy markets. EnerSearch operates with the minimal number of permanent staff, and projects are carried out by a network of researchers geographically spread across the continent. The goal of the initiative was to improve the management of both information items and domain knowledge used to organize information, while minimizing the additional effort required from content managers and knowledge workers. Research and development was carried in the framework of the European On-To-Knowledge project. The outcome was a major decrease in the mistakes during search tasks, as well as a minor reduction of the time required to complete information-finding tasks.

This real-life example proves both the necessity and the feasibility of effectively addressing KM in VEs, while at the same time points out the need for a more structured approach capable of enhancing knowledge management performance. The first step towards a successful KM implementation for VEs is the identification and clear understanding of their particularities, and the determination of the specific requirements they produce. The successful outcome of this initial challenge will constitute the cornerstone of the developed KM structure.

CURRENT TRENDS ENABLING KNOWLEDGE MANAGEMENT IN VIRTUAL ENTERPRISES

The identification of the VE organizational paradigm, and a first reference on its core operational characteristics, can be traced back to the 1980s (Miles & Snow, 1986). Still, a more elaborated approach of the concept appeared later on, in the early 1990s, in high impact publications by Drucker (1990) and the Iacocca Institute in 1991 (Nagel & Dove, 1993), which placed the loose enterprise concept within the context of wider and already accepted management movements like Lean Production and Agile Manufacturing. The term "virtual" made its first appearance in literature in 1992 (Davidow & Malone 1992), followed by the solid definition of Byrne (1993), who states that a Virtual Enterprise can be defined as a temporary network of independent companies, suppliers, customers, and rivals, linked by information technology (IT) to share skills, costs, and access to one another's market.

Further developments and parallaxes of the VE concept, based mostly on the strength of the bond and level of formalism of the relationship between participating business entities, originated in a number of proposals for new organizational models, such as the extended enterprise (Browne, Sackett, & Wortmann, 1995), smart organizations (Filos, 2005), and Supply Chains (Stevens, 1998). The result of applying those models can be anything from a rather stable alliance between partners, as in a supply chain (Li, Cabral, Doumeingts, & Popplewell 2006), on one end, to a more transitory cooperation, as in a Virtual Enterprise, on the other.

The common ground of almost all definitions for Virtual Enterprises in the current literature is their strong dependence on information and communication technologies (ICT) that are primarily responsible for interconnecting geographically distributed business partners and thu,s enabling knowledge flow and collaboration. Although not a panacea, in the case of managing knowledge in the context of virtual enterprises, ICT, and particularly Web technologies, seem to promise one reliable and effective remedy based on a well defined IT infrastructure and architecture, and the use of standards. Current trends in infrastructures are moving from client/server over the Intranet towards P2P (peer to peer) over the Internet, while for architectures, there is a significant transition from transaction/layer-based approaches towards service-based and agent-based ones. Finally, the use of standards is widely accepted as a mechanism for the relief of heterogeneity symptoms in virtual enterprises. Standards can be used for elements and their meanings (semantic heterogeneity), data models, languages and exchange formats (syntax heterogeneity), and communication mechanisms (system heterogeneity). In the remainder of this section, the issues of Web technologies and standards that can be used for enabling KM, in the context of VEs, are going to be discussed in detail.

The open and dynamic environment of a VE calls for a well-defined IT architecture capable of supporting information exchange between the geographically dispersed partners of the collaborative VE network, sharing resources among multiple organizations, and organizing tasks executed in a collaborative manner by more than one partner. Unfortunately, this statement is far from the real-life business situation, where information exchange, not to mention knowledge, between different enterprise information systems, is very difficult. This deficiency, when viewed from a strict IT perspective, becomes an interoperability issue mostly attributed to heterogeneity. Heterogeneity is a term used to describe differences in hardware, operating systems, data models, data semantics, and data quality. Sheth (1998) classifies heterogeneity into four categories: (a) system heterogeneity, which includes incompatible hardware and operating systems, (b) syntax heterogeneity, which refers to different languages and data representations, (c) structure heterogeneity, which includes different data models such as relational and object-oriented models, and (d) semantic heterogeneity, which refers to the meaning of terms. Up to now, many technological approaches have been proposed aiming to support the universal communication of information, such as electronic data interchange (EDI) systems that are based on highly structured messages and middleware technologies using remote procedure calls (RPCs) between CORBA and DCOM objects. However, these approaches are too rigid, do not address heterogeneity at all levels, and most important, could not be used efficiently over HTTP, raising compatibility and security issues. Therefore, alternative approaches have been investigated, with the most prominent one being SOAP (simple object access protocol (SOAP). SOAP is an XML-based protocol that works over HTTP, enabling communication between applications running on different operating systems, technologies, and programming languages (http://www.w3c.org.).

One of the most challenging system heterogeneity issues for Virtual Enterprises is openness. Openness can be achieved by establishing a system capable of dynamically changing, and still being able to communicate with other systems. The distributed nature of KM processes in the VE context requires technologies that can support open systems (Hewitt, 1986) reality. Agent systems technology emerged as a possible solution, and it has generated lots of excitement in recent years because of its promise for implementing software systems that operate in open and distributed environments, such as the Internet. Currently, the majority of agent-based systems on the Internet

consist of a single agent mostly performing information retrieval and filtering. However, as the technology matures and addresses increasingly complex applications, it is expected that the next generation of agent technology will perform information gathering in context and sophisticated reasoning in support of user problem-solving tasks. These capabilities create the need for systems that consist of multiple agents that communicate in a peer-to-peer fashion. Such functions will require techniques, based on negotiation or cooperation, that lie firmly in the domain of Multi Agent System (MASs) (Bond & Gasser, 1988; O'Hare & Jennings, 1996). A multiagent System can be defined as a loosely coupled network of problem solvers (agents) that interact to solve problems that are beyond the individual capabilities or knowledge of each problem solver (Durfee & Lesser, 1989). The characteristics of MASs (Sycara, 1998) are that (a) each agent has incomplete information or capabilities for solving the problem and, thus, has a limited viewpoint, (b) there is no system global control, (c) data are decentralized, and (d) computation is asynchronous.

The use of the agent paradigm and technologies in order to support KM in VEs is motivated by the specific needs of a distributed and dynamic knowledge management system that demands a flexible, scalable, and highly customizable IT infrastructure. Camarinha-Matos (2005) provides an exhaustive list of arguments in favor of using MAS to address virtual enterprise interoperability issues, such as the distributed, autonomous, and heterogeneous composition of VEs easily mapped by MAS, the dynamic nature of VEs requiring a flexible modeling paradigm, and so forth. MAS applications (Chaib-draa, 1995; Durfee, 1996; Durfee & Lesser, 1989), show that despite some difficult challenges (Bond & Gasser, 1988), they can provide many potential advantages if solutions to these identified problems are intertwined (Gasser, 1991). Still, and despite these motivating elements, it is true that the application of MAS technology to support VE infrastructures is mostly limited to research projects, most of them using agents to represent VE network members, and to support relatively simple processes, such as partner search and team formation. The failure of MAS to establish themselves through large, commercial, working applications has created a negative image, forcing well-known scientists of the field, such as Rzevski, to wonder whether MAS are a myth or a practical reality (Rzevski, 2003). Currently, the disappointment by the technology seems to have been relaxed, and the "hype" stigma that had been created has worn off. This can partly be attributed to the close relation of the MAS and the widely accepted Web services concepts. Cultivating that relationship, Web service support by multi agents systems, and new synthetic concepts, such as Service Agents (Petrie, & Bussler, 2003), are gaining acceptance by the research community, and have the potential to become the new trend in the VE technology scientific area.

However, while overcoming system heterogeneity is a good start, it is certainly not enough in the VE context. In order to address the fundamental barrier of structural and semantic heterogeneity, we propose ontologies as a knowledge representation means for agents (Weiss, 2000). Current knowledge-oriented IT solutions, such as content and document management systems, have severe semantic weaknesses in core knowledge intensive processes, such as

- **Searching information:** Existing keyword-based suffers from limited precision (how many retrieved documents are really relevant?) and recall (has all relevant information/ knowledge been found?).
- **Presenting information:** The format of a query response is a list of hyperlinks; textual and graphical information that is denoted by them. As a result, human browsing and reading is required to extract relevant information from information sources (Fensel, 2001).

- **Information integration:** Currently, the ad hoc integration of different pieces of knowledge that lay in a network's disparate KBs in order to respond to a user's query is practically impossible.

Ontologies promise to resolve these problems by moving from a document-oriented view of KM to a content-oriented view, where knowledge items are semantically enriched, mapped, and interlinked. The emerging hype around ontologies is mainly due to what they promise, that is, sharing a common understanding of the structure and meaning of information among people or software agents (Musen, 1992). Ontologies grew out of being a philosophical endeavor of finding the top-level categories of existence (those appear in the works of Aristotle, Kant, and Heidegger) into an important tool in domain-knowledge representation, and recently, for information-systems modelling and knowledge engineering (Raban & Garner, 2001). In the VE context, with many different legacy applications, database systems, operating systems, and data formats, ontologies are considered as the only means in order to overcome structural and semantic heterogeneity, by providing dynamic and flexible maps of the information contained in the disparate data sources.

The combined use of agents and ontologies addresses heterogeneity at the system, structure, and semantic levels. In an effort to overcome syntax heterogeneity referring mostly to communication issues in a multiagent System, the use of Web services Architectures and technologies, in order to orchestrate and coordinate the different agents, seems as the appropriate solution. Web services can be described as self-contained, self-describing, modular applications that can be published, located, and invoked across the Web. Once a Web service is deployed, other applications (and other Web services) can discover and invoke the deployed service. W3C Web Services Architecture Group (W3C, 2003) provides a

Figure 2. The Web services' conceptual ladder- two overlapping approaches

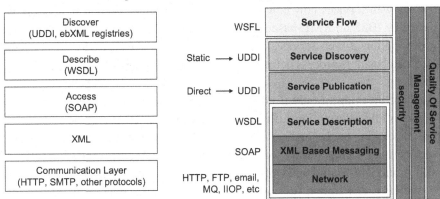

Dacota et al., 2003

Kreger, 2001

concrete definition of Web services according to which "A Web service is a software system designed to support interoperable machine-to-machine interaction over a network. It has an interface described in a machine-processable format (specifically WSDL)". In an effort to draw a line between the concepts of agents and Web-services the W3C declares (W3C, 2003) that "A Web service is viewed as an abstract notion that must be implemented by a concrete agent. The agent is the concrete entity (a piece of software) that sends and receives messages, while the service is the abstract set of functionality that is provided. Other systems interact with the Web service in a manner prescribed by its description using SOAP-messages, typically conveyed using HTTP with an XML serialization in conjunction with other Web-related standards." In summary, we conclude that Web services are software applications that operate on the Web, providing a specific service by exploiting distributed computing and informational resources, based on Web standards such as XML. The following Figure presents two overlapping approaches describing the stack of Web services' standards.

The upper layers of both approaches build upon the capabilities provided by the lower layers. Since Web Services must be network accessible, the foundational layer in every case is the network

infrastructure that facilitates real-time accessibility of the services, and communication among them and between them and human agents. While HTTP is the de facto standard network protocol for Web services, other protocols can also be supported, including SMTP and FTP.

The next level addresses communication issues between Web services, or else the syntax of the transmitted messages. For this purpose, the eXtensible Markup Language (XML) standard is used as the messaging protocol, addressing the request for syntactic interoperability. In particular, SOAP, developed as the Simple Object Access Protocol, but no longer an acronym, is the XML-based message protocol utilized. SOAP is a unidirectional envelope syntax for passing XML compliant information among Web services. Currently, SOAP is combined with HTTP and SMTP as underlying communication protocols, but others are still also possible, according to the specification.

One step up the Web services' conceptual ladder lies the description layer. At this level, web service definition language (WSDL) is the de facto standard for XML-based service description. WSDL is 'an XML format for describing network services as a set of endpoints, operating on messages containing either document-oriented or procedure-oriented information (W3C, 2001).

An extension to WSDL aiming to support this collaboration is the web services flow language (WSFL), designed by IBM, an XML-based language, for the description of Web Services compositions as part of a business process definition (Leymann, 2001).

Web services are meaningful only if potential users are able to find information sufficient to permit their execution, so the highest level of the Web service stack caters exactly for this issue. The most prominent technologies of this layer include universal description, discovery, and integration (UDDI) and ebXML registries. Simply put, UDDI is a directory where organizations can register their Web services, making them globally available and allowing for their dynamic discovery. The information provided in a UDDI business registration consists of three components (Daconta, Obrst & Smith2003): (a) white pages of company contact information, (b) yellow pages that categorize businesses by standard taxonomies, and (c) green pages that document the technical information about services that are exposed.

Although the hype about Web services is on its prime, it is true that they are still in the adoption phase, and successful business cases that prove their value are few. Nevertheless, according to Beznosov et al. (2005), Web services have many characteristics that set them apart from solutions that came before them, and make Web services more likely to succeed. First of all, Web services enjoy the active involvement of major software vendors, such as Microsoft, IBM, and Sun, that few other distributed technologies enjoy. Secondly, Web services are based on the loose coupling of applications, not requiring a common application environment at both ends of a transaction, and thus, allowing the subscriber and provider to adopt the technology that is most suited to their needs. Moreover, by using XML, Web services have a flexible model for data interchange that is independent of the computing environment. Finally, the use of Internet standard protocols means that most organizations already have much of the communications software and infrastructure needed to support Web services. As for their limitations, according to Beznosov et al. (2005), these mostly fall into two categories. First, Web services are not proven technology, and there is some suspicion that Web services are the fashionable solution of the day, the same way that MAS were in the end of the previous decade. The second reservation about Web services has to do with their heavy reliance on XML. While there are many advantages to XML, size is not one of them, since using XML expands the size of data several times.

Despite some current limitations of ontologies, MAS, and Web services, we believe that their combined use has great potential in supporting KM in the VE context. First of all, they can deal with the knowledge sharing need of VEs, by addressing geographical distribution issues and language variety, through their distributed Web nature, and the use of ontologies that can provide a multilingual knowledge environment. Furthermore, they are applicable in the VE environment since they can deal with the disparate computing environment (system heterogeneity) through the use of agents that can act independently of the different legacy applications, database systems, and operating systems that might exist in a VE, and thus, enable interoperability and integration, which are considered crucial issues for knowledge management. Finally, the modular nature of Web Technologies enables the efficient inclusion and exclusion of new members (and their systems) into the network, which is absolutely necessary, given the temporal and project-oriented character of a VE.

KNOWLEDGE MANAGEMENT IN VIRTUAL ENTERPRISES: A HOLISTIC APPROACH

So far, in this chapter, the need for a holistic approach towards KM, in the context of virtual enterprises, has been determined, and a technological toolset, consisting of Web services, Multiagent Systems, and ontologies to enable this approach, has been defined. What remains to be seen is the actual approach that can benefit from this IT infrastructure. Holistic approaches toward any problematic or underexplored area of business presuppose a common consent of stakeholders on the importance of the subject. Unfortunately, in the unstable business environment of the 21st century, the emphasis on operational aspects, and the stress for achieving "quick and dirty" results on financial indicators, usually leads to the underestimation or overlooking of "soft processes," such as knowledge management, with a long and cloudy horizon of return on investments. This phenomenon is further enhanced in the case of small and medium enterprises that, on the one hand, lack know-how and resources, but still constitute the majority of the participants in virtual enterprise formations, on the other. In order to overcome this jeopardy, the establishment of a knowledge-sensitive business ecosystem that will favor the establishment and operation of a knowledge-breeding environment is essential. In this chapter, we utilize the notion of the KM ecosystem, and we highlight its major constituents,

Figure 3. The KM ecosystem

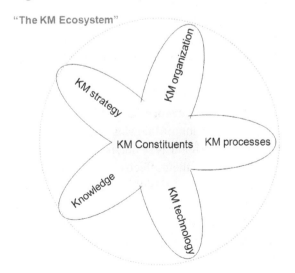

which include the KM strategy, organization, processes, technology, and the knowledge that is processed, used, and stored during the lifecycle of a virtual enterprise (see Figure 3).

Providing a sense of direction for KM is considered fundamental in order to successfully embody such a complicated business discipline. The strategic component intents to deal with this need by specifying the high-level goals of KM, coupled with directions guiding their achievement. However, the long-term perspective of strategy conflicts with the rather short horizon of VEs. As a result, from a strategic viewpoint, we consider essential the existence of a business network responsible for designing and controlling soft, managerial operations, such as knowledge management. Naturally, the business network is not limited to supporting KM; nonetheless, it is a major strategic enabler of KM in VEs. In detail, the business network is "a cooperative alliance of enterprises established to jointly exploit business opportunities through setting up virtual enterprises. The main purpose of a network is to prepare and manage the life cycle of VEs and to prepare product life cycles. The network is thus to be seen as a potential, from which different VEs can be established in order to satisfy diverse customer demands. The network will seek out and await customer demands, and when a specific customer demand is identified the business potential is realized by forming a VE. Compared to a virtual enterprise, a network can accordingly be perceived as a relative long-termed cooperation since it typically sets up multiple VEs" (Vesterager Pedersen, & Tølle, 1999).

It is now evident that strategic planning cannot be subjected to the extreme time pressure that rules the operation of VEs and thus, is to be executed at the network level. Of course for an enterprise network that aims at flexibility, numerous and complex strategic declarations are not a desired option. On the contrary, we claim that the network's business strategy, defining the type of projects and the business opportunities that are to be pursued, should be enriched and extended with the respective knowledge aspects. In detail, the business strategy can provide a valuable source for analyzing the necessary competencies that should be possessed by the partner of the network, generating substantial support for the recruitment of new network partners. In this way, KM strategy becomes perfectly aligned with the overall network's objectives.

A major issue that has to be resolved at the strategic level is the protection of each company's intellectual rights, and the resolution of relative trust, cultural, and legal issues. However, this strategic goal is extremely complicated due to intrinsic characteristics of VEs. On the one hand, VEs rely on knowledge sharing in order to excel their current expertise and enhance their competitive position, adopting a perspective with emphasis on the dynamic, regenerative, and infinite nature of knowledge. On the other hand, though, there are many factors setting barriers to knowledge diffusion. For one thing, each individual company has a natural tendency to protect their own knowledge from both rivals and partners, in an effort to secure their competitive advantage. At the same time, in the VE business context, companies unify their resources in order to produce a more complex or innovative product. Such projects ,though, for most of the participating firms, do not constitute their sole business activity. On the contrary, it is almost certain that many of them would be participating, in the past or the future, in other competing strategic formations, or they would simply be doing business by competing with the established network. This form of competition between VE members creates significant security, privacy, and confidentiality issues, especially regarding knowledge assets that have to be handled/ managed in a coherent and mutually agreed manner.

The KM organization component aims at specifying and describing the required KM roles, thus, providing a concrete structure for implementing KM in VEs. The major task,related to the organization component is competency management, which requires the description of both the available and required business skills in order to carry out the networks current projects and future strategy. The concept of core competences was introduced by Prahalad and Hamel (1990), and according to Fletcher (2001), is defined as the answer to the question: "What does an organization need for future successes?". This reality has already been identified by the Globeman21 project (Vesterager, Pedersen, & Tølle, 1999), which proposes the competency manager as one of the fundamental roles in the network of business partners. Taking it one more step further, we believe that a knowledge manager is also essential, and should be responsible for monitoring the whole KM initiative, and providing the required guidance for its successful application.

As for the VE KM roles and responsibilities, things are somewhat more complicated, due to the different, ad hoc forms that a VE can take (Thoben & Jagdev, 2001). In this chapter, we utilise the established "star" formation for virtual enterprises (Thoben & Jagdev, 2001) as a basis for our analysis. According to the "star" formation, a dominant enterprise is sited in the centre of the star topology, playing the role of the VE leader. This enterprise is responsible for managing all the leading phases of the VE life cycle, starting from project initiation and team formation to the final VE dissolution. From a KM perspective, this central enterprise should be responsible for the internal monitoring and control of KM, and work in close cooperation with the networks competency and knowledge managers.

The knowledge processes component focuses on the description of knowledge processes that take place, consciously or not, in every organization, but also on their effective embodiment into the business activity. Within the context of this study, seven core, knowledge processes have been identified: (a) knowledge identification, which traces and maps the required knowledge to support business processes execution and enterprise strategy implementation, (b) knowledge capture, which is the process during which existing internal or external knowledge is represented in a formalized way, (c) knowledge acquisition, from external environment through interaction with customers, suppliers, competitors, and partners, (d) new knowledge creation, through R&D, experimentation, lessons learned, creative thinking, and innovation. In detail, Knowledge creation is the task that complements knowledge acquisition and focuses on generating new skills, new products, better ideas, and more efficient processes, (e) organization and storage of all the available knowledge, in order to support its effective use and reuse. Organization and storage includes the selective retention of information and knowledge in properly indexed and interlinked knowledge repositories, (f) knowledge sharing is the extent to which people share their knowledge through its effective access and distribution to users on the basis of their needs and interests, (g) knowledge use and reuse is the application of knowledge to support effective decision making, problem solving, and customer service. Next, we will focus on the most important knowledge processes in the VE context, these being knowledge sharing, organization, and storage.

The most important process at the interorganizational level, which constitutes the base of the collaboration between VE partners, is knowledge sharing. Participating business entities join capacities and expertise in order to cover a market need by producing a usually highly complex product that no participating firm is capable or willing to produce by itself. As a result, sharing and integrating knowledge and information, and making it visible throughout the organization, is a vital, yet complex task. The main reason for this complexity is the distributed nature of VEs. The geographical distribution and the task variety and complexity of partners create a set of differences (workflow, business rules, language, cultural, etc.) that jeopardize effective knowledge sharing.

What is more, effective knowledge sharing is realized when each organization, and the VE as a whole, utilize the shared knowledge in order to improve their know-how and fulfill the VE mission successfully. Thus, a major factor that has to be considered is the trade-off between the value gained by sharing knowledge against protecting and internally using it. In this respect, Loebecke et al. (Loebecke, Van Fenema, & Powell, 1999) identified three dimensions of interorganizational knowledge transfer, which are synergy, leveragability, and negative reverse impact. Synergy denotes the value added to the cooperation from the interdependent knowledge sharing. Leveragability refers to the potential of each partner, separately, to capitalize value from utilizing the shared knowledge. Finally, negative reverse impact describes the sender's lost knowledge value due to its use by the receiver (e.g., sharing a patent has a huge negative reverse impact).

As for knowledge organization and storage, they are considered as fundamental processes, since they constitute a safe pathway in reassuring that most of the information and knowledge generated will not be lost following the VE's dissolution. Furthermore, people, in making decisions, are called to analyze large amounts of knowledge/information that originates from different enterprise domains, such as product specifications and designs, project management reports, marketing researches, customer needs and feedback, and so forth. In this information-overloaded environment, knowledge organization is a decisive prerequisite for its effective reuse. The reuse of stored past experience can be very useful in several situations, for example, for speeding up the VE formation phase and the selection of partners, of for implementing similar projects with different partners.

The knowledge component of the VE KM ecosystem refers to the actual content that is created, shared, and used during the VE lifecycle. One of the most critical issues regarding the knowledge content relates to variety of linguistic patterns and content. It is inevitable that linguistic differences and terminology gaps, especially those identified in business terminology, would lead to misunderstandings, even in the case VE partners that share the same dialect/language. Furthermore, the project-oriented nature of VEs denotes their reliance on non-routinized, highly contextual, and situational knowledge. In response to the requirements that this situation raises, the main goal of the content view of KM in VE is to exhaustively structure the available knowledge, providing a semantic unification space that is necessary in overcoming ambiguity and the communication barriers that it imposes. In doing so, knowledge has to be formally represented through the use of structured approaches, such as knowledge maps, taxonomies, Entity Relationship diagrams, and especially, ontologies.

Last but not least, the technology component, including the technological infrastructure and especially ICT (Information and Communication), plays a critical role in successful knowledge management. Particularly in the VE context, interoperability and integration between heterogeneous hardware and software platforms of the VE members are the most crucial issues regarding ICT. It is not rare, the phenomenon of data produced by an application of one VE partner that cannot easily be integrated in the information system of another. In addition, the obstacles of integrating different back-end or legacy applications and information or databases from multiple sources are, most of the time, costly and time consuming. To address these issues, semantic web technologies and ontology engineering come to play, in an attempt to create a modular environment and thus, permit, to the furthest possible extent, the efficient inclusion and exclusion of new members (and their systems) into the network. The situation gets even harder in run-time mode, when different systems are called not only to identify each other, but also to operate and collaborate in an effective and efficient manner. In that case, current state of the art suggests multiagent Systems and Web services heavily relying on XML constructs as the best possible solution.

Figure 4. Obstacles to a successful use of knowledge in virtual organizations (Neumann, 1999, p. 28)

Individual Perspective	Collective perspective	Organizational perspective
• Anger to lose position	• Intragroup conflicts	• Missing organizational slack
• The wanting of power	• Power fights	• Hierarchic principals
• Few knowledge concerning the own	• Groupthink	• Defensive routines
• Competencies and potentials	• Missing trust	• Cultural differences
• Single orientation on competition	• Barriers of language	• Inadequate incentives
• Living in the past	• Psycho and socio dynamic effects	• Intransparent systems for decision making, information and communication
• Conservatism	• Single orientation on competition and egoism	• Unused technical possibilities in ICT
• Emotional and motivational aspects	• Missing awareness on responsibility	• Undefined functions, jobs and competencies
• Limited capacity of observation, processing and learning		• High degree of specialization and centralization
• Paradigm		• Conservatism and orientation on the past
• The loss of sense		• Strong value system and myth
		• Blocking dominant coalitions
		• Missing possibilities for sanctions
		• Inadequate thinking and doing in internal relationships of suppliers and customers
		• Demotivation
		• Destructive, unlearning management of mistake

What is more, a VE relies on knowledge coming from a variety of sources including knowledge of existing and potential partners, as well as knowledge of the customers and the market. Thus, the availability of an effective knowledge management system, capable of scanning both the intranet and the Web, is considered a strong advantage over competition, especially when it comes to opportunity identification and team formation. Finally, one general issue in VEs' operation that puts additional pressure to supportive ICT solutions is that of trust. Business partners may be known only from electronic contacts, and this fact imposes significant security requirements from an IT solution in order to protect each company's intellectual property and to secure the data sent over the network.

In conclusion, it is inarguable that virtual enterprises are overwhelmed with particular knowledge needs that traditional enterprises do not have, or at least not at this level of importance. This fact is also evident in the work of Neumann, presented in Figure 3, who identified the foremost obstacles to the successful use of knowledge in Virtual Organizations. In an effort to establish the foundations for the development of a holistic and sound KM framework in support of VEs, in this section, we tried to analyze these VE specific characteristics and needs along the five major components of the KM ecosystem of VEs.

PROPOSAL OF A HOLISTIC KM FRAMEWORK

Throughout this chapter, we have argued that the nature, dynamics, and operational characteristics of VEs demand a holistic approach towards knowledge management that is inevitably heavily relied on IT, and especially the Web. One of the main research goals supported by these arguments is the development of such a framework, tailor it to the Greek industrial reality, and practically evaluate it through a series of pilot projects. The major

Figure 4. The characteristics of the KM framework

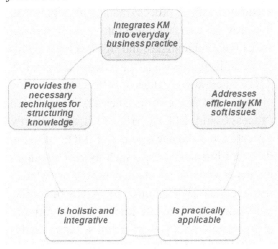

characteristics of this framework that development has to achieve are shown in Figure 4.

The initial goal of the framework is to provide the means to define and structure the set of organizational KM concepts required for the building of a knowledge intensive enterprise capable of efficiently managing knowledge management in its internal and its external (intra-enterprise) environment. In doing so, we propose the integration of enterprise modeling and knowledge management in an effort to provide a holistic yet process-oriented framework (Ponis, Tatsiopoulos, Vagenas, & Koronis in press). This objective will be achieved through the utilization of existing and well-established enterprise-modelling techniques that support virtual enterprises in their heavy task of constantly readjusting their way of doing business and particularly, the rapid inclusion, analysis, and dissemination of new products, new processes, and new organizational structures into the system.

The framework utilizes ARIS Architecture (architecture of integrated information systems) (Scheer, 1999), and its enterprise modeling (EM) and Knowledge modeling capabilities, in an effort to provide structure to the KM ecosystem and overcome modeling deficiencies troubling similar research efforts identified in the literature. ARIS is a leading business process management platform that provides users with an intuitive user interface, smart Web technologies, and high level of scalability (visit http://www.ids-scheer.com for details). ARIS integrates a range of different modelling methods and frameworks, such as, Event-driven Process Chain (EPC), UML, BPEL, and so forth, which enable the deployment of ARIS in many different business areas, such as risk management, performance management, and knowledge management. By exploiting the ARIS enterprise modeling capabilities, the knowledge practitioner is provided with a powerful and scalable ready-to-use KM toolset that addresses the analysis and modeling requirements of the knowledge management processes thus, enhancing the rapid communication of knowledge logistic activities within the entire enterprise. An indicative list of methodological tools ARIS provides the analyst includes extended Event-driven Process Chain diagrams (eEPCs), organizational charts, knowledge maps, and knowledge network diagrams.

As for the technological counterpart of the KM framework the combined use of agents, Web technologies, and ontologies seem to be the solution, as analyzed earlier in this chapter. In previous research efforts by the authors (Ponis et al., 2006), the general scheme of the required IT infrastructure has been determined. The main operational actors in this infrastructure are software agents that fall into two main categories, namely content (wrapper agents, translation agents, ontology Agents) and system agents (broker agents, monitoring agents, security agents, user agents). The first are responsible for manipulating knowledge assets at the content and metacontent (metadata) layer while on the other hand, system agents are responsible for administration issues such as the coordination, control, security, and effectiveness of the multiagent system. All software agents are registered as Web services through the use of UDDI, WSDL, and WSFL repositories, which

contain the necessary information required for tracing an agent, understanding its operation, and if necessary, integrate it with one, or more than one, other agents into one single workflow sequence.

FUTURE RESEARCH DIRECTIONS

It is true that the basic concepts of this approach are attractive, but as with all theoretical constructs, their actual implementation hides challenges and issues that, in essence, they constitute the limitations of the approach, at least for the present time. The main issues of the proposed approach are the following: (a) creating industry-wide, ready-to-use ontologies in a machine-readable format to address language and terminology issues thus, boosting team formation and enhancing cooperation and production performance and efficiency, (b) utilizing techniques based on semantic Web and rich media concepts to support integration and interoperability issues throughout the network (c) creating smart, flexible, and efficient workflow enactment based on sophisticated service choreography, (d) enabling secure and trusted communication protocols, for the Internet, based on public key encryption schemes and the development of access controls, (e) elaborating coherent and functional user management models able to support the complex relationships between VE members, the efficient management of user identities, policies, and passwords. Apparently, this list will grow even bigger if one will add non-IT related issues of the cultural, legal, and socioethical nature, such as resistance to change, intellectual property rights and trust, and personal relationships within the VE, respectively. Still, this would go out and beyond the scope of this chapter.

To address those mentioned shortcomings of the approach, future research actions are currently in plan, with the most imminent ones being the enrichment of the elaborated ontology library with the required system ontologies (e.g., agent description ontology), the expansion of current ontologies to more sectors in collaboration with industrial partners, and the elaboration of reference knowledge service workflows on a per industry basis. These actions are expected to increase the framework's generality and enhance its flexibility and dynamic amorphousness enabling VEs to pursue business opportunities in other vertical industries.

CONCLUSION

It is inarguable that virtual enterprises are overwhelmed with particular knowledge needs that traditional enterprises do not have, or at least not at this level of importance and time pressure. However, as literature proves, the area of knowledge management in the VE context is still in the initial stages of evolution, lacking structured approaches and holistic frameworks that will unite concepts together into a solid application roadmap.

Toward this objective, although not a panacea, information technologies play a rather significant role. Even for the skeptics among the researchers who claim that ICT are not the magic wand, one can say that maybe it is, since they can make the VE construct disappear by simply withdrawing from it. In our opinion, ICT are embedded in the very core of cotemporary virtual enterprises that try to compete in a global environment. IT infrastructures and standards are necessary to ensure interoperability, syntactic conformity, and workflow enactment within the VE enterprise network.

The need for technology support, if not self-justifiable, becomes evident by the advancements achieved in the design and development of IT infrastructures, support frameworks, and services for VEs in the last 15 years. A critical role in these efforts has been played by the World Wide Web, which is already established as the almost de facto standard platform for information exchange in distributed environments. Despite these advance-

ments, the respective market is still fragmented and immature, since most of the efforts in the area have been conducted by research projects that, and it hurts to admit so, very rarely find their way to the commercial software market in the form of a viable product. To heal this trauma, knowledge engineers, and IT systems that support them, have to work closely together; evolve, and by evolving, finally manage to resolve a number of critical issues before knowledge management can fully exploit the numerous possibilities that IT, and in particular the Web, can provide them. In an attempt to contribute to these efforts and establish the foundations for the development of a holistic and sound KM framework in support of VEs, in this chapter, we tried to analyze these VE specific needs along the five major components of the KM ecosystem described earlier in this chapter: KM strategy, KM Organization, KM Processes, KM Technology, and processed knowledge itself.

What remains to be seen is how VE formations can be persuaded into making the necessary investments in budget and resources that are needed for the deployment and implementation of a structured approach for managing their knowledge. Major reasons for their current cautious attitude seem to be the lack of the required level of IT know-how, the absence of hard core empirical validation of the current approaches in real-life working environments, and the difficulty of determining the actual cost and time needed to implement such approaches and infrastructures.

REFERENCES

Andersen, A., & The American Productivity and Quality Center. (1996). *The knowledge management assessment tool: External benchmarking version.* Winter.

Bair, J., Fenn, J., Hunter, R., & Bosik, D. (1997). *Foundations for enterprise knowledge manage-*

ment (Report R-400-105). Stamford: Gartner Group.

Beznosov, K., Flinn, D., Kawamoto, S. and Hartman, B. Extended and virtual enterprises - similarities and differences. *Information Security Technical Report*, 10, 2-14.

Bond, A. H., & Gasser, L. (1988). *Readings in distributed artificial intelligence*. San Francisco, CA: Morgan Kaufmann.

Bourdreau, A., & Couillard, G. (1999). System integration and knowledge management. *Information Systems Management, 1*(3), 24–32.

Browne, J., & Jagdev, H. S. (1998). The extended enterprise - A context for manufacturing. *Journal of Production, Planning & Control, 9*(3), 216 -229.

Browne, J., Sackett, P. J., & Wortmann, J. C. (1995). Future manufacturing systems - towards the extended enterprise. *Computers in Industry, 25*(3), 235-54.

Browne & Zhang, (1999). Extended and virtual enterprises - similarities and differences. *International Journal of Agile Management Systems,* 1(1), 30-36.

Byrne, J. (1993). The virtual corporation. *Business Week, 26*(3), 36–41.

Camarinha-Matos L. M. (2003). Infrastructures for virtual organizations - where we are. In *Emerging Technologies and Factory Automation: Vol. 2. Proceedings of ETFA '03* (pp. 405- 414).

Camarinha-Matos L. M. (2005). ICT infrastructures for VO. In L. M. Camarinha-Matos, H. Afsarmanesh, & M. Ollus(Eds.), *Virtual organizations: Systems and practices* (pp. 89-110). Boston: Springer Science and Business Media.

CEN. (2004). *European guide to good practice in knowledge management - Part 1: Knowledge management framework* (ICS 03.100.99, CWA 14924-1). CEN, The European Committee for Standardization.

Chaib-draa, B. (1995). Industrial applications of distributed AI. *Communications of the ACM, 38*(11), 49–53.

Chase, R. (1997). The knowledge based organisation: an international survey. *Journal of Knowledge Management, 1*(1), 38-49.

CODASYL. (1971). Feature analysis of generalized data base management systems. *ACM,* May.

Daconta, M. C., Obrst, L. J., & Smith, K. T. (2003). *The semantic Web: A guide to the future of XML, Web services, and knowledge management.* Indianapolis, IN: John Wiley & Sons Inc.

Davidow, W. H., & Malone M. S. (1992). *The virtual corporation.* New York: Harper Business.

Drucker, P. F. (1968). *The age of discontinuity guidelines to our changing society.* New York: Harper & Row.

Drucker, P. F. (1993). *Post-capitalist society.* New York: HarperBusiness.

Drucker, P. F. (1990). The emerging theory of manufacturing. *Harvard Business Review, 68*(3), 94-102.

Durfee, E. (1996). Planning in distributed artificial intelligence. In G. M. P. O'Hare & N. R. Jennings (Eds.), *Foundations of distributed artificial intelligence* (pp. 231–246). New York: Wiley.

Durfee, E. H., & Lesser, V. (1989). Negotiating task decomposition and allocation using partial global planning. In L. Gasser & M. Huhns M. (Eds.), *Distributed artificial intelligence, volume 2* (pp. 229–244). San Francisco, CA: Morgan Kaufmann.

Edvinsson, L., & Malone, M. (1997). *Intellectual capital: Realizing your company's true value by finding its hidden brainpower.* New York: Harper Business.

Feigenbaum, E. A., & McCorduck, P. (1983). *The fifth generation: Artificial intelligence and Japan's computer challenge to the world.* MA: Addison-Wesley.

Fensel, D. (2001). *Ontologies: Silver bullet for knowledge management and electronic commerce.* Berlin: Springer-Verlag.

Filos, E. (2005). Virtuality and the future of organisations. In G. Putnik & M. M. Cunha (Eds.), *Virtual enterprise integration: Technological and organizational perspectives.* Hershey, PA: Idea Group Publishing.

Fletcher, S. (2001). *Competence-based assessment technique.* London: Kogan Page.

Gasser, L. (1991). Social conceptions of knowledge and action. *Artificial Intelligence, 47*(1–3), 107–138.

Hewitt, C. (1986). Offices are open systems. *ACM Transactions of Office Automation Systems, 4*(3), 271–287.

Holsapple C. W., & Joshi K. D. (2004b). A formal knowledge management ontology: Conduct, activities, resources, and influences. *Journal of the American Society for Information Science and Technology, 55*(7), 593 – 612.

Holsapple, C. W., & Singh, M. (2001). The knowledge chain model: Activities for competitiveness. *Expert Systems with Applications, 20*(1), 77-98

Joia, L. A. (2000). Measuring intangible corporate assets: Linking business strategy with intellectual capital. *Journal of Intellectual Capital, 1*(1), pp. 68-84.

KPMG. (2003). Insights from KPMG's European Knowledge Management Survey 2002/2003. *KPMG Knowledge Advisory Service Amsterdam.* Retrieved March 10, 2007, from http://ep2010.sal-zburgresearch.at/knowledge_base/ kpmg_2003.pdf

Kreger, H., & IBM Software Group. (2001). *Web services conceptual architecture (WSCA 1.0).* Retrieved November 1, 2006, from http://www-306.ibm.com/software/solutions/ webservices/pdf/WSCA.pdf

Lawton, G. (2001). Knowledge management: ready for prime time? *IEEE Computer, 3*(2), 12-14.

Leymann, F. (2001). Web services flow language (WSFL 1.0). *IBM Software Group.* Retrieved April 10, 2007, from http://xmlcoverpages.org/WSFL-Guide-200110.pdf

Li, M., Cabral, R., Doumeingts, G., & Popplewell K. (2006). *Enterprise interoperability – Research roadmap (Final Version).* Retrieved November 11, 2006, from http://cordis.europa.eu/ist/ict-ent-net/ei-roadmap_en.htm

Lindvall, M., Rus, I., & Suman Sinha S. (2003). Software systems support for knowledge management. *Journal of Knowledge Management, 7*(5), 137-150.

Loebecke, C., Van Fenema, P. C., & Powell, P. (1999). Coopetition and knowledge transfer. *The DATABASE for Advances in Information Systems, 30*(2), 14-25.

Maier, R. (2002). State-of-practice of knowledge management systems: Results of an empirical study. *Upgrade, 3*(1). Retrieved October 10, 2006, from http://www.upgrade-cepis.org

Marwick, A. D. (2001). Knowledge management technology. *IBM systems journal, 40*(4), 814-900.

Mentzas, G., Apostolou, D., Abecker, A., & Young, R. (2003). *Knowledge asset management – Beyond the process-centred and product-centred approaches.* London: Spinger-Verlag.

Mika, P., Iosif, V., Sure, Y., & Akkermans, H. (2003). Ontology-based content management in a virtual organization. In S. Staab & R. Studer (Eds.), *Handbook on ontologies* (pp. 455-476). Heidelberg: Springer.

Miles, R., & Snow, C. (1986). Organizations: New concepts for new forms. *California Management Review, 28*(2), 68-73.

Mühlbauer, S., & Versteegen, G. (2000). *Wissensmanagement. Empirische Untersuchung, beste Praktiken und Evaluierung von Werkzeugen.* Höhenkirchen: IT Research.

Musen, M. (1992). Dimensions of knowledge sharing and reuse. *Computer and Biomedical Research, 25*(5), 435-467.

Nagel, R., & Dove, R. (1993). *21st century manufacturing enterprise strategy.* Bethlehem, PA: Iacocca Institute, Lehigh University.

Neumann, R. (1999). *Die Organisation als Ordnung des Wissens.* Habilitation-Thesis, University of Klagenfurt.

Nonaka, I. (1991). The knowledge creating company. *Harvard Business Review, 69*(November-December), 96-104.

Nonaka, I. (1994). A dynamic theory of organizational knowledge creation. *Organization Science, 5*(1), 14-37.

Nonaka, I., & Takeuchi, K. (1995). *The knowledge creating company: How Japanese companies create the dynamics of innovation.* Oxford: Oxford University Press.

O'Hare, G., & Jennings, N. (1996). *Foundations of distributed artificial intelligence.* New York: Wiley.

Petrie, C., & Bussler, C. (2003). Service agents and virtual enterprises: A survey. *IEEE Internet Computing, July-August.*

Ponis, S., Tatsiopoulos, I. & Vagenas, G. (2006). Ontology support for virtual organisations: A proposed framework for knowledge management. *The International Journal of Knowledge, Culture and Change Management, 6*(8), 89-100.

Ponis, S., Tatsiopoulos, I. P., Vagenas, G., & Koronis, E. (in press). A process-based knowledge management framework supported by ARIS Enterprise Modelling architecture. *International Journal of Applied Systemic Studies.*

Prahalad, C. K., & Hamel, G. (1990). The core competition of the corporation. *Harvard Business Review, May-June*, pp. 79-91.

Preiss, K., Goldman, S. L., & Nagel, R. N. (1996). *Cooperate to compete. Building agile business relationships.* New York: Van Nostrand Reinhold.

Probst, G., Raub, S., & Romhard, K. (1997). *Wissen Managen.* Wiesbaden: Gabler Verlag.

Raban, R., & Garner, B. (2001). *Ontological engineering for conceptual modelling.* Paper presented at the 9th Austrian Conference on Artificial Intelligence, Vienna, Austria.

Scheer, A. W. (1999). *ARIS - Business process framework.* Berlin: Springer-Verlag.

Schmaltz, R., Hagenhoff, S., & Kaspar, C. (2004). *Information technology support for knowledge management in cooperations.* Paper presented at The Fifth European Conference on Organizational Knowledge, Learning and Capabilities.

Schreiber, G., Akkermans, H., Anjewierden, A., de Hoog, R., Shadbold, N., van der Velde, W., & Wielinga, B. (1999). *Knowledge engineering and management, the common KADS methodology.* Cambridge: MIT Press.

Sheth, A. P. (1998). Changing focus on interoperability in information systems: From system, syntax, structure to semantics. In M. F. Goodchild, M. J. Egenhofer, R. Fegeas, & C. A. Kottman (Eds.), *Interoperating geographic information systems.* Norwell, MA: Kluwer Academic Publishers.

Spiegler, I. (2000). Knowledge management: A new idea or a recycled concept. *Communications of the AIS, 3*(14), 1–24.

Stevens, J. (1998). Integrating the supply chain. *International Journal of Physical Distribution and Materials Management, 13*(1), 37-56.

Sveiby, K. (1997). *The new organizational wealth.* San Francisco: Berrett-Koehler.

Sycara, K. P. (1998). Multiagent systems. *AI magazine, 19*(2), 79-92.

Thoben, K. D., & Jagdev, H. (2001). Typological issues in enterprise networks, *Journal of Production Planning and Control, 12*(5), 421–436.

Vesterager, J., Pedersen, J. D., & Tølle, M. (1999). *Virtual enterprise reference architecture and methodology*, a modified for publication extract of deliverable 1.3 "Final Report on Models" of IMS 95001/ESPRIT 26509 Globeman21 (Global Manufacturing in the 21st Century).

Weiss, G. (Ed.) (2000). *Multiagent systems: A modern approach to distributed artificial intelligence.* London: MIT Press.

Wiig, K. M. (1997). Integrating intellectual capital and knowledge management. *Long RangePplanning, 30*(3), 399-405.

W3C. (2003). *Web Services Architecture, W3C Working Draft 8 August 2003.* Retrieved November 13, 2006, from http://www.w3.org/TR/2003/WD-ws-arch-20030808/

Zwegers, A., Wubben, H., & Hartel, I. (2002). Relationship management in enterprise networks. In V. Marik, L. M. Camarinha-Matos, & H. Afsarmanesh (Eds.), *Knowledge and technology integration in production and services – Balancing knowledge and technology in product and service life cycle* (pp. 157-164). Boston: Kluwer Academic Publishers.

ADDITIONAL READING

Alavi, M. (1997). *KPMG Peat Marwick U.S.: One giant brain.* Boston, MA: Harvard Business School.

Antoniou, G., & Harmelen, F. V. (2004). *A semantic Web primer* (Cooperative Information Systems). London: The MIT Press.

Aricon Consortium. (2004). Aricon handbook of virtual enterprises – Business advantage through collaboration.

Bayardo, R. J., Bohrer, W., Brice, R., Cichocki, A., Fowler, G., Helal, A., Kashyap, V., Ksiezyk, T., Martin, G., Nodine, M., Rashid, M., Rusinkiewicz, M., Shea, R., Unnikrishnan, C., Unruh, A., & Woelk, D. (1997). InfoSleuth: Agent-based semantic integration of information in open and dynamic environments. In *SIGMOD '97, Proceedings ACM SIGMOD International Conference on Management of Data. ACM SIGMOD Record, 26*(2), 195-206. Tucson, AZ: ACM Press.

Davies, J., Fensel, D., & van Harmelen, F. (Eds.) (2003). *Towards the semantic Web: Ontology-driven knowledge management.* Chicester, UK: John Wiley & Sons.

Davies, J., Studer, R., & Warren, P. (Eds.). (2006). *Semantic Web technologies: Trends and research in ontology-based systems.* John Wiley & Sons.

Forbairt. (1996). *Virtual corporation defined.* Summary Section for Forbairt Internet Report, Forbairt, Ireland.

Fowler, A. (2000). The role of AI-based technology in support of the knowledge management value activity cycle. *Journal of Strategic Information Systems, 9*(1), 107-128.

GLOBEMEN - Global Engineering and Manufacturing in Enterprise Networks. IMS 99004, IST-1999-60002. Retrieved from http://globemen.vtt.fi, 2000-2002.

Goldman, S. L., Nagel, R. N., & Preiss, K. (1994). *Agile competitors and virtual organizations: Strategies for enriching the customer.* New York: Van Nostrand Reinhold.

Gray, P. D. M., Preece, A., Fiddian, N. J., Gray, W. A., et al. (1997). KRAFT: Knowledge fusion from distributed databases and knowledge bases. In *Proceedings of the 8th International Workshop on Database and Expert Systems Applications (DEXA '97)* (pp. 682- 691). Toulouse, France: IEEE.

Guarino, N. (1998). Formal ontology and information systems. In N. Guarino (Ed.), *Proceedings of FOIS'98* (pp. 3-15). Amsterdam: IOS Press. Retrieved from http://www.loa-cnr.it/Papers/FOIS98.pdf.

Hendler, J. (2001). Agents and the semantic Web. *IEEE Intelligent Systems, 16*(2), 30–37.

Kucza, T. (2001). *Knowledge management process model.* Technical Research Centre of Finland, VTT Publications 455.

Lin, S., & Lu, D. (2003). *Web services based supporting platform for virtual enterprise.* Paper presented at the 8th International Conference on Computer Supported Cooperative Work in Design Proceedings.

Mariotti, J. L. (1996). *The power of partnerships - the next step beyond TQM. Reengineering and lean production.* Cambridge, MA: Blackwell Publishers.

O'Leary, D. E. (1998). Using AI in knowledge management: Knowledge bases and ontologies. *IEEE Intelligent Systems, 13*(3), 34-39.

Remus, U. (2002). *Prozessorientiertes Wissensmanagement. Konzepte und Modellierung.* (Dissertation). Regensburg: Universitat Regensburg, Wirtschaftswissenschaftliche Fakultät.

Rzevski, G. (2003). *Multiagent systems: The myth or practical reality?* Keynote paper, Volga Conference on Complex Adaptive Systems, Samara, Russia.

Smirnov, A., Pashkin, M., Chilov, N., & Levashova, T. (2004). Knowledge logistics in information grid environment. *Future Generation Computer Systems, 20*(1), 61–79.

Staab, S., Studer, R., Schnurr, H. P., & Sure, Y. (2001). Knowledge processes and ontologies. *IEEE Intelligent Systems, 16*(1), 26-34.

Taniar, D., & Rahayu, J. W. (Eds.) (2006). *Web semantics and ontology.* Hershey: Idea Group Publishing.

Taylor Small, C., & Tatalias, J. (2000). Knowledge management model guides KM process. *The Edge Newsletter.* Retrieved April 7, 2002, from www.mitre,org/pubs/edge/april_00.htm

Uschold, M., & Gruninger, M. (1996). ONTOLOGIES: Principles, methods and applications. *Knowledge Engineering Review, 11*(2), 93-155.

Weggeman (1997). *Kennismanagement, inrichting es besturing vas kennisintensieve organisaties.* Schiedam: Scriptum management.

Chapter XVI
Sharing and Protecting Knowledge:
New Considerations for Digital Environments

G. Scott Erickson
Ithaca College, USA

Helen N. Rothberg
Marist College, USA

ABSTRACT

*As **knowledge management (KM)** practice increasingly moves onto the Internet, the field is changing. The Internet offers new opportunities to use knowledge assets, defines new types of knowledge assets, and readily spreads knowledge beyond the borders of the organization to collaborators and others. This potential is tempered, however, by new threats to the security of proprietary knowledge. The Internet also makes knowledge assets more vulnerable to competitive intelligence efforts. Further, both the potential and the vulnerability of knowledge on the Internet will vary according to the nature of knowledge assets (tacitness, complexity, appropriability). Those looking to practice KM must, more than ever, understand their knowledge assets and how to best employ them.*

INTRODUCTION

Knowledge management (KM), even though a young discipline, has already passed through a number of stages. From the recognition that personal, tacit knowledge has unique value to the organization to systems for measuring and managing knowledge assets, and now to information technology (IT) KM installations, we have seen the field grow in its sophistication and applications.

In this chapter, we will look at some specific trends in KM related to the Internet. Initially, there are ways in which KM, as it is traditionally understood, is changing, as new methods and techniques come online. The Internet has opened up the use of knowledge and knowledge-related assets, allowing greater and more effective sharing, and it has also expanded the number of tools we can apply to KM processes.

Secondly, if one takes a broader view of what constitutes valuable knowledge within an organization, as well as a broader view of organizational boundaries, the increasingly tight Web-based ties between a firm and its e-network also create new opportunities for knowledge management. Rather than just considering the core organization in a network and its knowledge assets, a more complete perspective now includes all collaborators with whom firms exchange knowledge or information. Established Internet-based systems for immediate exchange of such assets have contributed to this broad trend.

Thirdly, an often overlooked part of KM is protection of these valuable proprietary knowledge assets. While KM theorists and practitioners typically recommend ever more knowledge sharing, few in the field ever talk about keeping these valuable proprietary assets protected. The

Internet has raised all sorts of new concerns about knowledge protection, as it and other information technology advances have amplified competitive intelligence (CI) threats. Digital knowledge is an issue in and of itself, and when digital knowledge is available through the Web, protection becomes an issue.

KNOWLEDGE MANAGEMENT

The basic concepts of KM, and its companion field **intellectual capital (IC)**, have been with us for some time. From Drucker's (1991) knowledge workers to Edvinsson's (Edvinsson & Sullivan, 1996) attempts to measure the knowledge assets of the firm, we have been talking about the management of these intangible resources for almost two decades. A full discussion of KM/IC and their underlying theory requires defining some basic terminology, as described in Table 1. Let us start with IC.

Intellectual capital (IC), as the name implies, grew out of an interest in **intellectual property (IP)**. IP includes formalized knowledge assets that can be structured and then protected by

Table 1. Knowledge definitions

Preknowledge	Data are "observations or facts out of context" and information is "data within some meaningful context" (Zack, 1999, p.46).
Knowledge	"That which we come to believe and value on the basis of the meaningfully organized accumulation of information (messages) through experience, communication, or inference" (Zack, 1999, p.46). Also sometimes termed know-how, learning that takes place leading to individual expertise (Zander & Kogut, 1995).
Knowledge assets	Intangible assets of the firm. Personal knowledge, corporate culture, social capital with those outside the organization, intellectual property, or any other valuable organizational knowledge.
Intellectual property (IP)	Formalized knowledge assets, qualifying for a patent, copyright, trademark, or other institutionalized protection mechanism.
Intellectual capital (IC)	Knowledge assets of the firm. The field of intellectual capital focuses on the identification, measurement, and management of these intangible assets. Includes IP (in most treatments, not all) as well as less formalized knowledge (Edvinsson & Malone, 1997).
Knowledge management (KM)	The practice of managing knowledge assets, focusing on identification, capture (when possible), organization, sharing, and analysis. Closely related to IC, the differences are more in emphasis on measurement (IC) vs. management (KM).

Table 2. Knowledge variables

Tacit knowledge	Knowledge assets that are personalized and difficult (perhaps impossible) to communicate (Nonaka & Takeuchi, 1995, Polanyi, 1967).
Explicit knowledge	Knowledge assets that can be captured by the organization, more easily communicated, and perhaps stored in a formalized manner in an IT system or elsewhere (Choi & Lee, 2003).
Human capital Structural capital Collaborative/relational capital	Personal knowledge assets pertaining to job performance. Organizational knowledge assets including corporate culture, information technology systems, and other ingrained knowledge. Knowledge concerning relationships with those outside the core firm (suppliers, customers, regulators, and so forth.) (Bontis, 1998; Edvinsson & Malone, 1997).
Complexity	Does the knowledge draw upon "distinct and multiple kinds of competencies" in order to be understood (Zander & Kogut, 1995)?
Appropriability	Ability of the firm to keep the knowledge to itself, including observability (Zander & Kogut, 1995), stickiness, and causal ambiguity.

mechanisms such as patents, copyrights, trademarks, and trade secrets. A great deal of theory has developed around IP, and the field is relatively well understood in terms of developing technology and protecting it with the standard mechanisms. Technology transfer, leakage, licensing, and other such issues also have a history in the literature, as we shall discuss.

The field of IC grew out of efforts by accountants and other practitioners to treat softer, less definable intangible assets in a manner similar to IP. Again, patented knowledge can be identified, described in a patent application, and valued for licensing purposes. All sorts of other knowledge exists within organizations that cannot be formalized in such a manner, but is valuable or potentially valuable (Hansen, Nohria, & Tierney, 1999; Nahapiet & Ghoshal, 1998). Getting a handle on such assets so that they can be more effectively managed is the point of IC/KM. If they can be identified and measured (the IC/accounting point of view), then they can be better managed (the KM point of view).

As **KM** theory has developed, knowledge has been more specifically defined as data or information subjected to reflection. Data, as the table notes, is basic observations and/or facts, while information is data with context. The authors have taken to referring to data and information

as "**preknowledge,**" referencing their potential to become knowledge assets and their value in the hands of others (as we will discuss later). This is not a common reference, but we believe it critical to the concept of managing knowledge sharing and protection.

As noted earlier, intellectual capital is made up of knowledge assets; the full knowledge of the organization. Part of this is intellectual property; part, less well-defined knowledge assets. Knowledge management is the process of trying to better utilize these knowledge assets, through identification, capture by the organization (when possible), sharing, and analysis (Davenport & Prusak, 1998). Numerous tools exist for better managing knowledge, from information technology (IT) installations to person-to-person techniques such as communities of practice and storytelling.

A number of key concepts have been developed having to do with managing knowledge. Some of the most important are summarized in Table 2. Essentially, the type of knowledge and its environment can have a substantial effect on an organization's ability to manage the assets. These variables can also impact the choice of tools for collecting and sharing knowledge.

The distinction between **tacit** and explicit knowledge predates interest in KM (Polanyi,

1967). As applied in KM, and for our purposes, the distinction is particularly important (Nonaka & Takeuchi, 1995). Tacit knowledge is typically personal and difficult, perhaps impossible, to express or explain. Explicit knowledge is easier to communicate and share and, as a result, easier for the firm to capture and codify. These differences are critical for how KM systems are organized and administered, as tacit-to-tacit sharing is much different from explicit to explicit (or the other possible combinations) (Boisot, 1995; Nonaka & Takeuchi, 1995). At its simplest, explicit knowledge can be digitized and spread widely with modern IT systems. Tacit knowledge remains more of a personalized one-to-one or one-to-small group process (Denning, 2000; Wenger, 1998).

Another common distinction in the literature is between human, structural, and collaborative or relational capital (Bontis, 1998; Edvinsson & Malone, 1997). Human capital refers to individual job-specific knowledge, whether running a machine, delivering a service, or managing an operation. Structural knowledge has to do with knowledge assets embedded within the organization such as the IT structure, corporate culture, and other such system-wide elements. Collaborative capital relates to knowledge about interacting with those outside the firm, matters such as taking care of a key supplier, satisfying the wishes of a customer, working well with an R&D partner or key regulator, and so forth. Some treatments have also added competitive capital, knowledge concerning competitors' activities, and strategies, though this piece is far from universal (Rothberg & Erickson, 2002).

The literature also addresses other variables related to how knowledge might be managed. Two that continually recur in studies are **complexity** and **appropriability** (Kogut & Zander, 1993; Reed & DeFillippi, 1990; Zander & Kogut, 1995). Complexity of knowledge can make it more difficult to transfer; among other things, recipients must be prepared to understand it and employ it properly, fitting it in with existing knowledge assets,

a concept referred to as combinative capabilities (Kogut & Zander, 1992), absorptive capacity (Cohen & Levinthal, 1990), or knowledge integration (Grant, 1996). Appropriability refers to the ability of an organization to keep valuable knowledge to itself. Patents, for example, have been valued by firms for decades because of their potential for conferring appropriability to a technology. With a patent, an organization can keep the technology to itself, preventing others from using the product or process. Hence, the firm can appropriate the gains from a valuable technology. Other types of KM can be harder to appropriate, and concepts, such as the stickiness of the knowledge (are there elements in place that make the knowledge usable only in its current circumstance?) (Teece, 1998; von Hippel, 1994) and causal ambiguity (how much of the application of the knowledge can be kept hidden?) (Lippman & Rumelt, 1982; Reed & DeFillippi, 1990), are also relevant to the discussion. Both complexity and appropriability can affect the ability of an organization to share its knowledge assets.

This background is key to understanding how the Internet affects knowledge development and protection. As we further develop the framework of this chapter, the place of these concepts will become clear. The key point is that KM is complex, varying by circumstances, and that a number of factors will affect the success or failure of a KM program. Further, KM/IC is a different concept than traditional IP, requiring different strategies and different treatment. We are just beginning to explore how to better manage knowledge, and its practice has already been complicated by the rapid growth of the Internet.

THE INTERNET

Over the past few years, the Internet has had a significant impact on the traditional practice of KM. Most major consulting organizations and IT services firms have standard, but customizable, Web-based KM installations allowing the collection and dispersion of knowledge from throughout the firm (Matson, Patiath, & Shavers, 2003). These systems allow accessible data storage throughout the globe, search capabilities, usage rankings, usefulness ratings, and so forth. They can also develop competency and skills catalogs, identifying experts in particular knowledge areas. As a result, although the knowledge of these experts might not be captured, per se, the experts are made available to the full organization as resources when the need or opportunity arises. In a number of ways, these Web-based systems can become IT-supported influence networks, recording and compiling the individuals most in demand from colleagues for help, including the type of help requested.

Most of these applications are not new. They have improved over the past few years, but the basic concepts and applications have been around for a while. Note that just about all have to do with explicit knowledge or cataloging those with tacit knowledge. The newest Internet advances have more to do with **tacit** knowledge. With the growth of collaborative tools in the consumer realm, there is little surprise that a number of these mechanisms are being applied to knowledge management (Vara, 2006). From Wikis collaboratively building knowledge stores to social networking tools similar to MySpace, from downloadable audio/video playable on an iPod to internal blogs and Web pages that allow easy sharing of perceptions and perspectives, these tools provide mechanisms to publish and share more personal, tacit knowledge throughout organizations. Firms that know how to employ these mechanisms can enhance their KM capabilities.

These changes and trends are of interest to those in the KM field, but they are not as striking as some other aspects of KM and the Internet. To properly understand the impact of these other aspects, we need to extend the boundaries of what we consider KM to be. Initially, KM system extensions beyond the core firm are common but

not often recognized by scholars or theorists. Firms engaged in KM will typically both collect knowledge from and share knowledge with a range of collaborators, sometimes only close ones, sometimes more distant partners. Knowledge may be available from or useful to suppliers, operations partners, distribution partners, research partners, marketing partners, and others. Thus, e-networks exist that routinely move knowledge around between collaborators.

Secondly, the infrastructure supporting these e-networks and/or entirely independent information and data-sharing networks have proliferated over the last decade as Enterprise Resource Planning, Supply Chain Management, Customer Relationship Management , and similar systems have moved onto the Web (Economist, 2000). Operational requirements for inputs and labor, inventory levels, sales data, customer data, and similar information and data are exchanged by network partners every day. These systems both move around and store the massive amounts of information and data we previously referred to as preknowledge. Again, basic data and information are preknowledge, but can become valuable knowledge assets, if subjected to analysis through data mining, business intelligence, or similar methods.

Dell, of course, has always been one of the first firms noted when discussing these e-networks. Although the firm's pioneering efforts are not as much of a differentiator as they were 5 years ago (chiefly because competitors have copied their supply chain and production systems), the firm's quick move to the Web still illustrates the value of these systems (Park & Burrows, 2001). When a Dell customer pushes the key to order a customized laptop over the Internet, the production and supply requirements are simultaneously routed to all suppliers throughout the e-network, who know immediately what they need to supply and where. At the bottom of these systems is a lot of knowledge (what are Dell's best-selling models?) and preknowledge (what parts do I need to deliver on Tuesday?) flying around between collaborators.

Similarly, Wal-Mart is renowned for its IT-driven logistics, and has particularly close relations with large suppliers such as Procter & Gamble (P&G) (Economist, 2000). The two are so connected that one product manager at P&G voiced a desire that when a customer picked up a package of Bounty paper towels from the store shelf, he wanted the tree for a replacement roll to be dropping simultaneously in a forest in Georgia. Wal-Mart and P&G are tied together closely enough that this is almost possible, exchanging price, volume, promotional, operational, and customer preknowledge and knowledge in real time.

Another example is UK retailer Tesco, well known for its Clubcard customer loyalty program (Rohwedder, 2006). With its massive Web-created database of consumer preknowledge, the grocer is able to build knowledge not only about customer segments, but about individual customers. This knowledge allows Tesco to tailor merchandise, pricing, and even promotional offers to each unique consumer. The firm is able to share and even sell its preknowledge and knowledge to collaborators and other consumer goods providers.

DISCUSSION: KM AND THE INTERNET

What do these trends mean in terms of the conceptual structure developed earlier in this chapter? The issue is knowledge sharing and transfer. In general, explicit knowledge is more easily spread. Once it is captured and codified, the organization can share it with whomever it likes. The Internet, of course, makes this even easier. Moreover, explicit knowledge can be shared through the Internet across the boundaries of the firm with all sorts of collaborators.

But the Internet also impacts **tacit** knowledge. Personalized knowledge was often hard to transfer from one individual to another, requiring direct contact and, at times, specialized techniques. While still harder to communicate than explicit knowledge, sharing of tacit knowledge has certainly been made easier with Web-based systems. As noted earlier, identifying the individual who holds the key knowledge, even if they are located on the other side of the globe or in another part of the e-network, is possible with today's KM systems. It is then just a matter of communication.

Complexity typically makes knowledge harder to share, as well. But again, the Internet has had a role in making the process easier. At the heart of the complexity issue, as noted earlier, is the difficulty in locating and transferring the full range of intellectual capital necessary to understand and use a particular knowledge asset. Web-based systems more easily transfer, or at least allow access to, the complete set of assets needed for understanding and application.

When **appropriability** is high, knowledge is more specific to an original application and harder to transfer to different circumstances; therefore, it is again more difficult to share. And again, the Internet plays a part in making knowledge sharing more effective. When the conditions of use are more easily accessed in the KM system or subject to easy identification and transfer when questions arise, knowledge sharing is more effective. The ability of systems to store the full range of knowledge necessary for application, to quickly provide answers to follow-on questions, or to provide immediate access to the original knowledge holder is critical to effective management. All these aspects are provided by the Internet.

To summarize, not only KM systems, but also Web-based data and information systems are routinely transferring tremendous quantities of knowledge and preknowledge throughout e-networks. These knowledge assets are important to the successful operations of contemporary organizations and their network partners, and the more the assets are shared, the more effective the network can be. The Internet has already had an impact on effectiveness by directly changing the influence of the variables determining KM success. Regardless of the level of tacitness, complexity, and appropriability, the move to Web-based KM and preknowledge systems has made any particular combination of these variables more effective in managing knowledge assets.

PROTECTION

The move to the Internet becomes even more important, however, when one adds the vulnerability of knowledge assets to competitive incursions. There is growing recognition among both scholars and practitioners that KM and **competitive intelligence (CI)** are two sides of a coin. Knowledge or preknowledge that is valuable to an organization will be equally valuable to its competitor(s) if they can obtain it (Liebeskind, 1996). CI operations are a growing means to obtain knowledge about competitors, including their critical knowledge assets (Fuld, 1995; Gilad, 1994).

Once again, when we talk about the more established discipline of **intellectual property**, these matters are more settled. Well-understood mechanisms for protection (patents, copyright, etc.) exist, and are routinely applied. Indeed, some organizations have explicit strategies for managing the release of IP, either through technology transfer (with stacks of legal documents and careful framing concerning what IP is to be shared and what not) or leakage (allowing access, often in order to set an industry standard) (Teng & Cummings, 2002). Because of the established nature of IP and its management tools, firms understand what they are dealing with, and are able to make strategic decisions about what gets disseminated and how. However, KM is still much less structured, harder to protect (though trade secret law holds potential), and thus, competitive intelligence becomes more of an issue.

CI traditionally utilizes numerous methods to gather and analyze knowledge and preknowledge, both explicit and tacit (Bouthillier & Shearer, 2003; Fleisher & Bensoussan, 2007). These methods can generally be grouped into four categories (Rothberg & Erickson, 2005). Initially, publicly available information can be used. Published sources, regulatory filings, public appearances by a competitor's employees, and other such methods can be quite fruitful. Secondly, human intelligence within the organization is available. Employees often know things about competitors. Sources can include salespeople who have heard about competitive offerings, scientists who know what is going on in competitive R&D labs, or even employees who have previously worked for the competitor. Indeed, a common technique is to simply hire away a key employee, provided it can be done without violating non-compete and non-disclosure agreements. Thirdly, human intelligence may be available from sources outside the firm. Suppliers, vendors, research partners, production partners, marketing partners, and so forth, may all also have knowledge concerning a competitor. And of course, all may have employees who might have previously worked at the competitor, or for someone within the competitor's extended network of collaborators. Finally, CI initiatives may seek to actively gather information or knowledge through observation, simply calling up and asking, or more ethically challenged methods, such as dumpster diving, surreptitious picture taking on tours, and pretexting. Mainstream CI professionals would disavow ethically or legally questionable methods, but economic espionage does occur as well, and only reinforces the point that competitive intelligence is an important and growing trend.

Once preknowledge or knowledge is captured by a CI operation, it is gathered, analyzed, and, ideally, acted upon. Knowledge of competitive activities or strategies can be extremely useful in building one's own strategic and tactical plans. Consequently, any type of competitor data, information, or knowledge can be useful to a CI operation attempting to build an understanding of a competitor and its actions. The preknowledge we discussed in the previous section can be just as valuable as better-developed knowledge assets when analyzed correctly. Indeed, a CI operation may be better able to create knowledge from preknowledge, through analysis, than would the originating firm.

The key point is that as KM systems have proliferated, so has the vulnerability of organizations to competitive intelligence. This is particularly true with the simultaneous expansion of knowledge and preknowledge sharing on the Internet. Consider first the ways in which traditional **CI** methods have been made more effective by these trends. In terms of human intelligence, CI operations have many more potential targets, each with access to much more knowledge and/or preknowledge, from both their own organization and, potentially, a wealth of collaborators. This is a direct result of Web-accessible KM and preknowledge systems. So, when an employee is hired away from a competitor, the potential is there for them to bring not only the tacit knowledge in their heads, but additional knowledge or preknowledge to which they might have been exposed. Further, the individual would likely have had access to the KM system of the previous employer, raising the possibility of file downloads and transfer of explicit organizational knowledge or preknowledge via e-mail, portable storage devices, or other mechanisms. This raises a classic issue concerning who owns what knowledge and what the exiting employee is entitled to take with them. Whether or not the employee is legally entitled to specific knowledge, with widespread access to KM and other Web-based systems, the potential for something substantive leaving with an employee is present.

Some firms, for example, have even taken to hiring away entire teams holding targeted knowledge (McGregor, 2006). Well-functioning groups not only have typical knowledge about how to perform their own jobs (and knowledge or preknowledge concerning their specific organization), but they also have social capital built up within the team. They have knowledge about how

to work with one another most effectively, who can perform what functions best, and who to go to for problem solving. KM is essentially based on the concept of the most valuable resources of the firm being found in employee heads, and hiring away the employee or employees remains one of the simplest and most effective methods of obtaining those knowledge assets, both explicit and tacit.

Further, these same issues now spread beyond the boundaries of the firm. As noted earlier, KM and related systems extend to collaborators. As a result, CI operations have many more potential targets than might have been the case previously. Whether publicly available information, human intelligence, or active gathering, any e-network member can be a target, and CI efforts can choose whatever individual or group appears to be the weak point. The core firm may not even be aware of some of the poorly protected access points to its proprietary knowledge if they are situated a long way out along the e-network; in some cases, the collaborator itself might be interested in the knowledge.

Recent examples of this phenomenon include advertising agencies utilizing employees with experience from client A to work on projects for a direct competitor, client B (Vranica, 2001, 2005). Law firms have been an issue because of client-specific knowledge in some cases (Terhune, 2006). Suppliers, vendors, research partners, and others are all fair game, too. Essentially, the most vulnerable point of an e-network is the one most likely to be attacked. A very recent suit filed by Oracle against SAP had to do with the latter entering the former's KM system through customers and technical support (Vara, 2007). CI attacks on Microsoft have gone through public relations and other non-profit affiliates of the firm (Simpson & Bridis, 2000). A pointed CI action against HP went through both retailers and suppliers (Tam, 2002)

As noted, sometimes the collaborator itself can be a concern. Earlier, we discussed the close working relationship between P&G and Wal-Mart. Based on that relationship, a tremendous amount of preknowledge (sales volume, pricing information, promotional tactics, and results) and knowledge (P&G's consumer research) pass between them. In the mid-nineties, when P&G's trademark on White Cloud toilet tissue expired, Wal-Mart snapped up the rights and started selling the brand as a private label (Ellison, Simmerman, & Forelle, 2005). As a result, the retailer was now using previously shared knowledge to directly compete with P&G in the toilet tissue market.

The use of Internet-based KM and similar systems also poses some new opportunities for infiltration. Some are technology related, others have more to do with individuals. However, they create new threats and are likely to be in the vanguard of ever-increasing challenges to protecting proprietary knowledge and preknowledge.

Initially, the simple fact that much knowledge and preknowledge is stored digitally opens up new opportunities for CI operations. We have already covered this in relation to individuals accessing more knowledge, but it also creates issues with protecting computer systems themselves. Although the methods of attack are often illegal and certainly unethical, Web-based KM and similar systems are open to hacking, theft, wireless eavesdropping, and other basic computer security issues. Further, the past few years have seen a sharp rise in the loss of laptops, personal digital assistants, portable storage devices, and other such hardware potentially holding valuable knowledge or preknowledge. Just in 2006, well-publicized episodes occurred involving Equifax and the US Department of Veterans Affairs (McQueen, 2006), Ameriprise Financial and Fidelity Investments (Levitz, 2006), and Towers Perrin (Wall Street Journal, 2007). Discarded hard drives and other computer security issues are becoming ever bigger concerns (Ilett, 2006)

A related, but different, threat is found in system users. Not just exiting employees, but also those employees failing to follow procedures,

or with a grudge, can expose the organization to infiltration (Allison, 2006). In some cases, it may be employees or others with good intentions. Regardless of the motivation for releasing knowledge or preknowledge, the Internet is an extremely effective dispersal mechanism. Apple, for instance, is a company that seemingly does everything right in terms of security, both in its systems and in how it manages employee behavior (Wingfield, 2006). But Apple has been pursuing a "John Doe" case against an apparently internal individual who leaked new product information to blogging Web sites attracting Apple fans. Once a secret of that sort is out, the Web allows it to be quickly and easily spread, including to competitors. There may be little a firm can do about it if its security procedures are considered partially at fault (*O'Grady v. Superior Court*, 2006). Of course, if the blogger or a Web site is hostile, the problem only intensifies.

DISCUSSION: CI AND THE INTERNET

A wave of anecdotal evidence suggests that more knowledge and preknowledge is available online, open to direct or indirect incursion by CI efforts. Easily referenced numbers on enterprise system spending, IT security spending, and competitive intelligence employment and spending show tremendous growth in all areas over the past decade. How do these trends fit into our theoretical framework?

In the same way that the Internet enhances the ability of an organization to share knowledge more widely, so it makes that same knowledge more vulnerable. Explicit knowledge is readily available and can be directly targeted by CI operatives through IT incursions or by individuals with IT access, who may themselves be subject to CI manipulation. Similarly, tacit knowledge is more vulnerable, as the knowledge identification databases we have discussed earlier are apt to be targeted. Further, a number of CI techniques are specifically designed to piece together a profile of a competitor, product, or individual based on snippets of information. If a great number of tacit hints (not full knowledge) are available on the Internet, they may mean nothing to the originating organization, but a CI team could find something interesting through proper analysis.

Just as complex knowledge is easier to share through the Internet, so it is easier to lose, as the full knowledge base can disappear in the blink of an eye. Similarly, appropriation is harder, as the knowledge is not kept only by the firm holding the knowledge, and the circumstances of its use are more likely to be transferred with it.

The conceptual picture of what we have discussed can be summarized in Figure 1. The impact of the Internet can be captured in some function with the components discussed earlier:

- Number of users (N)
- Amount of organizational knowledge available to each user (A)
- Degree of digitization of knowledge base (D), and
- Range of network partners with access (R)

Whether a positive or a negative, the Internet affects KM systems by dramatically increasing the potential number of users, making huge amounts of knowledge available to each, digitizing explicit knowledge (or guides to where to find tacit knowledge), and extending beyond the borders of the firm to include all partners of an e-network. Thus, the impact of the Internet can be captured in the equation in Figure 1: $f(N,A,D,R)$.

The effectiveness of a knowledge management initiative, as we have discussed repeatedly, is impacted by the variables:

- Tacitness (the more tacit knowledge is, the harder it is to share)
- Complexity (the more complex knowledge is, it is harder but more beneficial to share)
- Appropriability (the more appropriable or specific knowledge is, it is harder but more beneficial to share)

One could also add type of knowledge (human capital, structural capital, or relational capital) though we have not discussed that aspect at any length in relation to the Internet. Therefore, these knowledge components will help to determine

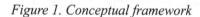

Figure 1. Conceptual framework

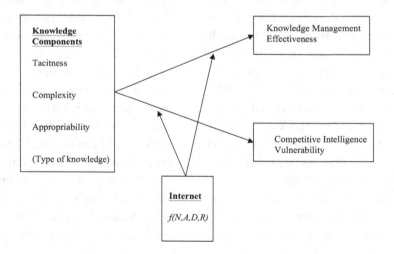

the effectiveness of a program to develop and share knowledge.

The risk from competitive intelligence activities is affected by the same variables, as the tacitness (tacit knowledge is less vulnerable), complexity (complex knowledge is less vulnerable), and appropriability (appropriated or specific knowledge is less vulnerable) of the knowledge impact the CI threat. Again, these knowledge components will help to determine the vulnerability of a program to protect knowledge.

However, the impact of the Internet will be felt in both the knowledge component, effectiveness relationship and the knowledge component, vulnerability relationship. The Internet enhances the underlying components, expanding their potential for KM use and increasing their impact on susceptibility to CI incursion. The Internet, then, has raised the stakes concerning the security of knowledge and preknowledge management systems. All sorts of proprietary knowledge assets are dispersed digitally throughout e-networks, and are accessible to many, many individuals both inside and outside the organization. Digital knowledge or preknowledge is much easier to move. Weak points in the security system can be targeted and infiltrated; once the knowledge or preknowledge is out, it can be spread much more easily, raising the possibility that even competitors not actively practicing CI might come across pertinent secrets.

What to do? The specifics of protection of knowledge and counterintelligence have been covered in depth, including the new complication of the Internet, in other venues (DeGenaro, 1996; Rothberg & Erickson 2005). Further, the appropriate answer depends on vulnerability, risk, and other firm-specific considerations. However, some common principles are fairly straightforward. Obviously, the basics of computer security are critical, with hardware protections, firewalls, encryption, and all the other IT network security prescriptions. Probably not as obvious are the softer parts of security, basically, the behaviors of the people with access to proprietary knowledge. Proper training, incentives to follow appropriate procedures, and so forth, are important to getting individuals to use, transfer, and store knowledge assets appropriately. It is fairly well known, especially in hacking circles, that the cleanest way into a system is not a direct technical attack, but rather "social engineering," essentially manipulatng people to get the knowledge or to get access to the knowledge or preknowledge you want. Finally, as should be clear from the previous discussion, it is important to have all your collaborators on board, too. If you are going to share knowledge and preknowledge with them, you need some level of comfort that they are taking the same precautions, both hard and soft, that you are. Indeed, compliance standards similar to those for quality or environmental protection may be the way to go (Carr, Erickson, & Rothberg, 2004).

CONCLUSION

What we see, then, are a variety of changes coming together to make the environment within which KM is practiced both much more promising and much more challenging. The Internet has allowed KM systems to become an organized part of the daily life of numerous organizations, with employees entering, searching for, and retrieving relevant knowledge on a routine basis. Moreover, a more comprehensive view of the knowledge assets of firms also brings the preknowledge contained in Web-based information systems, such as ERP, SCM, and CRM, into the discussion. Although not part of our classic view of knowledge (and certainly not IP), this preknowledge can become valuable either in the hands of the firm or in the hands of one of its competitors. The unprocessed preknowledge has the potential to be just as useful as the processed knowledge. Further, all of this knowledge and preknowledge is increasingly being shared across the Web with collaborators of all kinds.

All aspects of this scenario make KM a more effective tool, but they also make organizations much more vulnerable to CI incursions. Digital preknowledge or knowledge, stored in massive amounts, accessible to many more individuals, inside and outside the core organization is much harder to protect. Moreover, CI techniques are also adapting to the opportunities provided by the move of knowledge and preknowledge systems onto the Internet.

As a result, organizations seeking to establish a competitive advantage from KM need to look to the Internet and collaborators for the fullest collection and dispersion of knowledge and preknowledge assets. They also need to take appropriate steps to protect these assets. IT security systems, employee training, counterintelligence, and other steps are all important; these steps need to be taken throughout the e-network. It is not enough to ensure knowledge is secure within one's own firm, it needs to be secure in the hands of collaborators as well. A balance needs to be struck between the benefits of sharing and the risks of infiltration. That is the increasingly formidable challenge facing today's users of KM and systems.

FUTURE RESEARCH DIRECTIONS

The most obvious and useful direction for additional research is in developing formal hypotheses and testing the relationships illustrated in the figure. Kogut and Zander (1993) have developed some measures for the knowledge variables (tacitness, complexity, appropriability), so the trick will be to define and measure KM effectiveness and CI vulnerability. The former should not pose too much of a problem, as there are standard (though unsettled) definitions of IC, such as market/book value or Pulic's VAIC method. The latter is the sticky part, and to fully explore the framework, the measures for the Internet function need to be

defined and measured as well, something that may be possible within a specific firm.

An even more interesting direction from our point of view is exploring the balance and tension between how far to share knowledge and how far to protect knowledge. These aspects clearly operate in opposing directions, as more knowledge spread among more individuals implies more CI vulnerability. Further, this balance is unlikely to be the same for all firms, operating in all industries, in all nations. Numerous variables at each level are likely to affect the tension. Determining a method to measure the balanced factors, as well as measuring pertinent variables at the firm, industry, and national level would be invaluable to firms trying to make these sorts of decisions.

REFERENCES

Allison, K. (2006). How to unearth the IT moles. *Financial Times*, (September 5), 10.

Boisot, M. (1995). Is your firm a creative destroyer? Competitive learning and knowledge flows in the technological strategies of firms. *Research Policy, 24*, 489-506.

Bontis, N. (1998). Intellectual capital: An exploratory study that develops measures and models. *Management Decision, 36*(2), 63-76.

Bouthillier, F., & Shearer, K. (2003). *Assessing competitive intelligence software: A guide to evaluating CI technology.* Medford, NY: Information Today.

Carr, C., Erickson, G. S. & Rothberg, H. (2004). Intellectual capital, competitive intelligence and the economic espionage act. *International Journal of Learning and Intellectual Capital, 1*(4), 460-482.

Choi, B., & Lee, H. (2003). An empirical investigation of KM styles and their effect on corporate performance. *Information & Management, 40*, 403-417.

Cohen, W. M., & Levinthal, D. A. (1990). Absorptive capacity: A new perspective on learning and innovation. *Administrative Science Quarterly, 35*(1), 128-152.

Davenport, T. H., & Prusak, L. (1998). *Working knowledge: How organizations manage what they know.* Boston: Harvard Business School Press.

DeGenaro, B. (1996). Counterintelligence. In B. Gilad & J. Herring (Eds.), *The art and science of business intelligence.* Greenwich, CT: JAI Press.

Denning, S. (2000). *The springboard: How storytelling ignites action in the knowledge-era organization.* Woburn, MA: Butterworth-Heinemann.

Drucker, P. F. (1991). The new productivity challenge. *Harvard Business Review, 69*(November-December), 69-76.

Economist. (2000). Inside the machine: A survey of e-management. *The Economist,* (November 11).

Edvinsson, L., & Malone, M. S. (1997). *Intellectual capital: Realizing your company's true value by finding its hidden brainpower.* New York: Harper Business.

Edvinsson, L. & Sullivan, P. (1996). Developing a model for managing intellectual capital. *European Management Journal, 14*(4), 356-364.

Ellison, S., Simmerman, A. & Forelle, C. (2005). P&G's Gillette edge: The playbook honed at Wal-Mart. *Wall Street Journal,* (January 31), A1.

Fleisher, C. & Bensoussan, B. (2007). *Business and competitive analysis: Effective application of new and classic methods.* Upper Saddle River, NJ: FT Press.

Fuld, L. (1995). *The new competitor intelligence.* New York: John Wiley & Sons.

Gilad, B. (1994). *Business blindspots.* Chicago: Probus Publishing.

Grant, R. M. (1996). Prospering in dynamically-competitive environments: Organizational capability as knowledge integration. *Organization Science, 7*(4), 375-387.

Hansen, M. T., Nohria, N., & Tierney, T. (1999). What's your strategy for managing knowledge? *Harvard Business Review, 77*(2), 106-116.

Ilett, D. (2006). Out damned data—the lingering dangers of a hard disk's memory. *Wall Street Journal,* (October 4), 6.

Kogut, B. & Zander, U. (1992). Knowledge of the firm, combinative capabilities, and the replication of technology. *Organization Science, 3*(3), 383-397.

Kogut, B., & Zander, U. (1993). Knowledge of the firm and the evolutionary theory of the multinational corporation. *Journal of International Business Studies, 24*(4), 62-645.

Levitz, J. (2006). Ameriprise, Massachusetts settle over company's loss of laptop. *Wall Street Journal,* (December 12), B2.

Liebeskind, J. P. (1996). Knowledge, strategy, and the theory of the firm. *Strategic Management Journal, 17*(Winter), 93-107.

Lippman, S. A., & Rumelt, R. P. (1982). Uncertain imitability: An analysis of interfirm differences in efficiency under competition. *Bell Journal of Economics, 13*(2), 418-438.

Matson, E., Patiath, P., & Shavers, T. (2003). Strengthening your organization's internal knowledge market. *Organizational Dynamics, 32*(3), 275-285.

McGregor, J. (2006). I can't believe they took the whole team. *Business Week,* (December 18), 120-122.

McQueen, M. P. (2006). Laptop lockdown. *Wall Street Journal,* (June 28), D1.

Nahapiet, J., & Ghoshal, S. (1998). Social capital, intellectual capital, and the organizational advantage. *Academy of Management Review*, *23*(2), 242-266.

Nonaka, I., & Takeuchi, H. (1995). *The knowledge-creating company.* New York: Oxford University Press.

O'Grady v. Superior Court (2006). 139 Cal. App. 4Th 1423.

Park, A., & Burrows, P. (2001). Dell, the conqueror. *Business Week*, (September 24), 92-102.

Polanyi, M. (1967). *The tacit dimension.* New York: Anchor Day Books.

Reed, R., & DeFillippi, R. J. (1990). Causal ambiguity, barriers to imitation, and sustainable competitive advantage. *Academy of Management Review*, *15*(1), 88-102.

Rohwedder, C. (2006). No. 1 retailer in Britain uses "clubcard" to thwart Wal-Mart. *Wall Street Journal*, (June 6), A1.

Rothberg, H. N, & Erickson, G. S. (2002). Competitive capital: A fourth pillar of intellectual capital? In N. Bontis (Ed.), *World Congress on Intellectual Capital Readings* (pp.94-103). Woburn, MA: Butterworth-Heinemann,

Rothberg, H. N., & Erickson, G. S. (2005). *From knowledge to intelligence: Creating competitive advantage in the next economy.* Woburn, MA: Elsevier Butterworth-Heinemann.

Simpson, G. R., & Bridis, T. (2000). Oracle hired firm to probe Microsoft allies. *Wall Street Journal*, (June 28), A3.

Tam, P. (2002). High-technology giant duels with nimble knock-off artists. *Wall Street Journal*, (September 25), A1.

Teece, D. J. (1998). Capturing value from knowledge assets: The new economy, markets for know-how, and intangible assets. *California Management Review*, *40*(3), 55-79.

Teng, B-S., & Cummings, J. L. (2002). Trade-offs in managing resources and capabilities. *Academy of Management Executive*, *16*(2), 81-91.

Terhune, C. (2006). Coke legal battle with bottlers stalls on lawyer-conflict claim. *Wall Street Journal*, (August 10), A2.

Vara, V. (2006). Offices co-opt consumer Web tools like "wikis" and social networking. *Wall Street Journal*, (September 12), B1.

Vara, V. (2007). Oracle's SAP suit casts light on technical support. *Wall Street Journal*, (March 23), B4.

Von Hippel, E. (1994). "Sticky information" and the locus of problem solving: Implications for innovation. *Management Science*, *40*(4), 429-439.

Vranica, S. (2001). Foote Cone loses two accounts from Coke in wake of Pepsi suit. *The Wall Street Journal*, (November 12), B3.

Vranica, S. (2005). Lowe's old gang flocks to new shop; string of former colleagues join still-unnamed agency; defections hurt Interpublic. *The Wall Street Journal*, (December 13), B11.

Wall Street Journal. (2007). Towers Perrin laptops, client data stolen. *Wall Street Journal,* (January 9), A17.

Wenger, E. (1998). *Communities of practice: Learning, meaning and identity.* Cambridge: Cambridge University Press.

Wingfield, N. (2006). At Apple, secrecy complicates life but maintains buzz. *Wall Street Journal*, (June 28), A1.

Zack, M. A. (1999). Managing codified knowledge. *Sloan Management Review*, (Summer), 45-58.

Zander, U., & Kogut, B. (1995). Knowledge and the speed of transfer and imitation of organizational capabilities: An empirical test. *Organizational Science*, *6*(1), 76-92.

ADDITIONAL READING

Argyris, C. (1992). *On organizational learning.* Cambridge, MA: Blackwell.

Birkinshaw, J., & Sheehan, T. (2002). Managing the knowledge life cycle: Knowledge isn't static, but it often gets managed as if it were. *Sloan Management Review, 44*(1), 75-83.

Bontis, N. (1999). Managing organizational knowledge by diagnosing intellectual capital: Framing and advancing the state of the field. *International Journal of Technology Management, 18*(5-8), 433-462.

Brooking, A. (1996. *Intellectual capital: Core assets for the third millennium enterprise.* London: Thomson Business Press.

Choo, C. W., & Bontis, N. (Eds.). (2002). *The strategic management of intellectual capital and organizational knowledge.* New York: Oxford University Press.

Davenport, T. H., DeLong, D. W., & Beers, M. C. (1998). Successful knowledge management projects. *Sloan Management Review,* (Winter), 43-57.

Diereckx, I., & Cool, K. (1989). Asset stock accumulation and the sustainability of competitive advantage. *Management Science, 35,* 1504-1513.

Eells, R., & Nehemkis, P. (1984). *Corporate intelligence and espionage.* New York: MacMillan.

Fuld, L. (2006). *The secret language of competitive intelligence.* New York: Crown Business.

Ghoshal, S., & Westney, D. E. (1991). Organizing competitor analysis systems. *Strategic Management Journal, 12*(1), 17-31.

Gilad, B., & Herring, J. (1996). *The art and science of business intelligence.* Greeenwich, CT: JAI Press.

Grant, R. M. (1996). Toward a knowledge-based theory of the firm. *Strategic Management Journal, 17*(Winter), 109-122.

Lesser, E. L. (2000). *Knowledge and social capital.* Boston: Butterworth-Heinemann.

Montgomery, D. B., & Weinberg, C. B. (1998). Toward strategic intelligence systems. *Marketing Management, 6*(4), 44-52.

Norling, P. M., Herring, J. P., Rosenkrans, W. A., Stellpflug, M., & Kaurman, S. B. (2000). Putting competitive technology intelligence to work. *Research-Technology Management,* (November-December), 18-24.

Saint-Onge, H. (1996). Tacit knowledge: The key to the strategic alignment of intellectual capital. *Strategy and Leadership,* (March/April), 10-14.

Schultz, M., & Jobe, L. A. (2001). Codification and tacitness as knowledge management strategies: An empirical exploration. *Journal of High Technology Management Research, 12,* 139-165.

Sveiby, K.E. (1997). *The new organizational wealth: Managing and measuring knowledge-based assets.* New York: Berrett-Kohler.

Winter, S. G. (1987). Knowledge and competence as strategic assets. In D. J. Teece (Ed.), *The competitive challenge: Strategies of industrial innovation and renewal* (pp.159-184). Cambridge, MA: Ballinger Publishing Co.

Zack, M. A. (1999). Developing a knowledge strategy. *California Management Review, 41*(3), 125-145.

Chapter XVII
Identifying Knowledge Values and Knowledge Sharing Through Linguistic Methods:
Application to Company Web Pages

June Tolsby
Ostfold University College, Norway

ABSTRACT

How can three linguistical methods be used to identify the Web displays of an organization's knowledge values and knowledge-sharing requirements? This chapter approaches this question by using three linguistical methods to analyse a company's Web sites; (a) elements from the community of practice theory (CoP), (b) concepts from communication theory, such as modality and transitivity, and (c) elements from discourse analysis. The investigation demonstrates how a company's use of the Web can promote a work attitude that actually can be considered as an endorsement of a particular organizational behaviour. The Web pages display a particular organizational identity that will be a magnet for some parties and deject others. In this way, a company's Web pages represent a window to the world that need to be handled with care, since this can be interpreted as a projection of the company's identity.

INTRODUCTION

The aim of this chapter is to analyse a company's **Web pages** to see if this could provide some answers to the following question: How can linguistical methods be used to identify what the Web display in terms of an organization's knowledge values and knowledge sharing requirements? The answers to this question were found by doing a text analysis, using tools within the field of language theory, and by applying concepts from a **community of practice theory** (CoP) (Wenger,

1998). Still, an analysis of a set of Web pages cannot give a complete picture of the different aspects of an organization since their main purposes lie in their commercial value. Web pages published by companies can have a variety of aims, like attracting new customers or investors by displaying their products, the knowledge, and the achievements of the company. Furthermore, Web pages could aim at attracting new employees, display the legal and political values of the company, and provide an easy way to gain access to the company's financial information and product portfolio updating.

The use of a set of linguistical methods does not pay attention to the graphical elements of the Web pages, only the written text. This is, of course, a weakness when the choice is to analyse a set of Web pages, since design and layout are such important elements of Web pages. Nevertheless, in this chapter, one has deliberately omitted the elements of design and layout as part of the data interpretation, first and foremost because the aim was to do a textual analysis that would not be influenced by any design and layout considerations.

The organizational image that Web pages display is most likely a result of a refinement process, created through interpretations and reinterpretations, as results from negotiations between members within the organization. When the Web pages of a company are analysed linguistically, caution should be made with respect to how these results are interpreted and applied. My perspective is that Web pages reflect how the organization works, not only how organizational phenomena can be read from the Web pages. By using three selected **linguistical approaches,** it is demonstrated how Web pages can be analysed for a first understanding of how an organization works. Web pages analysed in this way will then provide a useful tool for further in-depth investigations of a company, and as a frame of references to whether the Web pages actually display how an organization works.

Knowledge of how and why the text was produced would require additional empirical data from the inside of the organization, but this was beyond the aim of this study. Rather, this chapter demonstrates how some linguistic concepts and a social theory on learning can be applied to uncover how a set of Web pages present how the organization works, and what knowledge values and sharing requirements can be identified using such methods. This chapter is about knowledge value and knowledge sharing. It refers to how knowledge gets its value from being shared with others. Partly this perspective is a result of social interaction (Lave & Wenger, 1991; Wenger, 1998). Wenger (1998) explored, in detail, how a practice is more than just a learning process, but also how the practice is created as a continuous process of negotiation and renegotiation of meaning, and how this process forms our identity. His idea is that members of a community of practice participate in a shared activity or enterprise. He emphasises that participation embraces all kinds of relations, controversial ones as well as harmonious ones, intimate as well as political, competitive as well as cooperative, and our ability (or inability) to shape the practice. He also highlights that "participation goes beyond direct engagement in specific activities with specific people. It places the negotiation of meaning in the context of our forms of membership in various communities. It is a constituent of our identity" (Wenger, 1998, p. 57).

Anyone interested in organizational behaviour might find the methods and the results of this chapter worthwhile in providing a different entrance to how an organization's knowledge values and knowledge management practices can be interpreted and understood.

What is presented in this chapter is a historical snapshot of company Web pages at a particular place in time, and which are no longer accessible. The reason for choosing Web pages as empirical data was that a company's Web pages provide easy accessible data, useful for developing a first understanding of the image the company is projecting to the world. By studying these Web pages, we are able to draw useful information about how the organization works.

BACKGROUND

Putnam, Phillips, and Chapman have pointed out that **communication theory** has failed to "uncover the subtle and complex ways that communication and organization are interrelated," and, "do not account for new developments in discourse and language analysis that set forth what communication is and how it operates as organizing" (Putnam, Phillips, & Chapman, 1996, p. 77). As an answer to this challenge, this chapter demonstrates how a linguistical analysis of a company's Web pages' can tell us something about how the organization works.

A threefold approach was used to achieve the results discussed in this chapter. Firstly, modality and transitivity, as linguistic forms, were applied in order to identify the company's own relationship to the knowledge-sharing process. Secondly, elements from a theory of communities of practice were applied to understand how the company stimulates knowledge-sharing practices. Thirdly, elements from discourse analysis were used to place the studied text in context. Such an approach was adopted here for three reasons.

Primarily, to demonstrate if, by studying a company's Web pages, we are able to produce any information about how the organization works. To accommodate this, the research in this chapter applies the linguistic concepts of **modality** and **transitivity.** Modality is not an agreed concept within the field of language theory, and is still discussed among theorists. It can be intended as "what properly belongs to the semantics of modal verbs and what belongs to pragmatic inference proceeding from the semantics of modal verbs in specific discourse contexts" (Wald, 1993, p. 61). The search for modality and transitivity in a text can indicate tautology, as authors analyse a

text focusing on these forms, and tend to discuss them from a narrow textual perspective, without paying attention to the textual setting, and how the textual setting imbeds content, context, and meaning. Halliday points out, in his functional grammar, how "a language is interpreted as a system of meanings, accompanied by forms through which meanings can be realized" (Halliday, 1994, p. xiv). Within this functional grammar, Halliday defines modality as the way a statement refers to "the judgement of the speaker" (Halliday, 1994, p. 75). On the other hand, she defines transitivity as "representational meaning, what the clause is about, which is typically some process with associated participants and circumstances" (Halliday, 1994: 179). When talking about discourse analysis, Halliday is concerned both with explaining, through the linguistic analysis, how and why the text means what it does mean, and if and how the text is effective in achieving its purpose. The latter point requires attention to the context of the text (Halliday, 1994: p. xv). In this chapter, transitivity and modality have functioned as instruments of identifying what is being said by analysing the text according to Halliday's functional grammar. Modality and transitivity should, within the context of this chapter, be interpreted as the degree of affinity between the teller/speaker and the sentence, and as the connections between grammatical subjects and objects (Jørgensen & Phillips, 1999: p. 95). Modality focuses upon the degree of relation between the speaker and the sentence. Typically, in sentences such as "it is cold," "I find it cold," "perhaps it is a bit cold," different ways of talking about the temperature, and different modalities, whereby the speaker relates himself/herself with the expression, are shown. Transitivity, on the other hand, focuses upon how events and processes are connected (or not connected) with grammatical subjects and objects, and are used to uncover ideological consequences that different presentations may have. In a sentence like "50 nurses were given the sack yesterday," a passive form is used, and the sacking of the nurses is presented as a natural phenomenon, something just happening without an agent being responsible. Using such a sentence emphasises the effects, ignoring the actions and processes leading to them (Jørgensen & Phillips, 1999, p. 95).

The second purpose is to see if and how elements used by Wenger (1998), in his **CoP theory,** appear or could be revealed from studying the company's Web pages. Hence, Etienne Wenger's (1998) concepts of meaning and identity in a community are applied to understand how these concepts can be found in the company's Web pages. His concept of identity embeds both the idea of learning as an individual and a collective process, and the idea that we create our identities through a learning process. Accordingly, identity should be viewed as an individual, as well as collective element, shaped through a negotiation "in the course of doing the job and interacting with others" (Wenger, 1998, p. 146). In order to analyse the Web pages using Wenger's concepts of identity, the text will be analysed with an emphasis upon how the text presents the employee performance, and the skills that the employees were expected to have when they entered the company, or were expected to achieve while they worked there.

The third purpose is to see if a particular **organizational discourse** can be inferred from the company's Web pages. One of those who used Halliday's functional grammar, as a tool for understanding texts and the textual context, is Norman Fairclough (1992), in his critical discourse analysis. Critical discourse analysis should be understood as an analysis applied for investigating the relations between discursive practices, as well as social and cultural development in different social connections (Fairclough, 1992). There is, according to him, a need for an interdisciplinary perspective, combining text analysis and social analysis, to understand how people actively create a rule-bound world of daily practices (Fairclough, 1992). Doing only a text analysis as part of a discourse analysis is, for Fairclough (1992),

not sufficient, since it does not shed any light on the connections between texts and the societal and cultural processes and structures. Jørgensen and Phillips (1999) argue that discourse could be understood as the way we talk about and perceive the world (or parts of the world). Despite this, attention should be paid to the fact that discourse is a "dubious" word, and, as a concept, has been criticised. Alvesson and Karreman (2000) claim that the term discourse sometimes incorporates everything, and thus, stands for nothing. Their explanation to the multitude of interpretations of discourses and discourse analysis is, to many researchers, a question of balance between the terms emphasised. It is questionable if the focus should be on the language interpretation, or meaning, or both. Additionally, consideration should be paid to how the language used relates to other issues (meaning, practices). For some types of discourses, this may represent a shift from traditional concerns (values, cognition, practices, and events) to a strong interest in the language in action/social context, without paying attention to meaning (Alvesson & Karreman, 2000). A reasonable interpretation of Alvesson and Karreman is that discourse analysis needs to incorporate not only language and meaning, but also ideas, conceptions, and so forth. This illustrates how difficult the discourse analysis is, and attention should be paid to the fact that a discourse analysis will never unveil the total picture, but only fragments of it.

As indicated, it is worth reflecting on the interpretation of empirical data, as expressed through a company's Web pages. New knowledge and new methods equip us with a new set of tools for analysing the data as time passes (Bloch, 1998). This could induce the awareness of new facets of the data, and thus, might change the way we approach and interpret them. Nevertheless, the interpretation of a set of Web pages will only give an instant view of the company, since Web pages are intended to be updated regularly, and they will change according to how the organization develops. Therefore, their dynamic character only enables us to give a snapshot of how the organization presents itself at the time of the analysis. From another point of view, rather than demonstrating how Web pages, over time, reflect organizational development, the goal of this chapter was to demonstrate *if it is possible to identify an organization knowledge sharing values by linguistical analysis of its Web pages*. It should be mentioned that Web pages of the company studied in this chapter are no longer available on the Internet. Therefore, the findings presented here will only demonstrate how a linguistical analysis can be done, and its results. Nevertheless, I hope researchers will be inspired to conduct similar studies using a broader spectrum of company Web pages, and thereby provide a better approach to how Web pages can be analysed, and what they tell us about the organization.

The three analytical perspectives, linguistic, communities of practice, and discourse, fit with the interpretative orientation of this research. The interpretative approach was chosen in order to give a just representation of the studied object (Holloway & Jefferson, 2000).

This analysis deals with "ambiguous representations" that potentially could yield a variety of accounts, but considering the methods used in this chapter, the aim is to give a viable representation (Riessman 1993, p. 8). Hence, it is insignificant for the results produced in this chapter that the representations are ambiguous.

THE LEARNING PROCESS WITHIN THE KNOWLEDGE MANAGEMENT DEBATE

Since the focus of this book is knowledge values and knowledge sharing, as displayed via the Internet (the World Wide Web), it is important to define

Figure 1. The root of knowledge management (from Mårtensson, 2000).

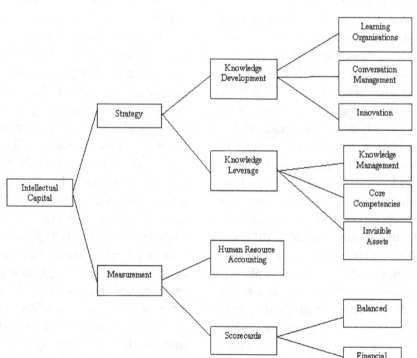

a few issues concerning the importance of viewing knowledge as a result of a learning process. Learning within an organizational landscape can be split into two main areas: **knowledge development** and **knowledge measurement.** Mårtensson (2000) made a literature review of the origins of knowledge management, and how this concept can be understood. Her claim is that knowledge management is considered as a "prerequisite for higher productivity and flexibility in both the private and the public sectors" (Mårtensson, 2000, p. 204). She claims that knowledge management deals with how the "intellectual capital" of the company can be administrated and facilitated. Accordingly, knowledge management is about strategy and measurement, as illustrated in Figure 1.

As seen in Figure 1, Mårtensson (2000) illustrates that strategy deals with how knowledge production occurs and how it is linked to measurement. In her model, Mårtensson (2000) shows that **intellectual capital** consists of the two elements, strategy and measurement. Measurement deals with building new information systems to measure knowledge creation. The latter element thus treats knowledge creation as other financial approaches do, that is, by counting and measuring (Roos, Roos, Dragonetti, & Edvinsson, 1997).

This brings us to how learning is defined, from an organizational point of view, and, for obvious reasons, to the concepts of "**organizational learning**" and "**learning organizations.**" Simplified, an organization can be defined as a collaboration between different individuals to solve specific tasks, where the tasks are divided into several subtasks distributed to the individuals. In large organizations, this process can be very complex (Rasmussen, Dahl, Mølbjerg Jørgensen, Laursen, & Rasmussen, 2001). Additionally, customers, suppliers, and external cooperating partners will influence the process. An organization can be interpreted as a collaboration between individuals, related to a set of defined tasks and goals. The

two latter (tasks and goals) define the structural conditions for any organization.

Organizational learning is an overall joint designation that describes how the organization handles its knowledge and experiences. This attitude is characterized by the fact that, to perform organizational learning, it is important to consider the "contrasts and interaction between the competence potentials which are available in the organization and how to use them in a learning perspective" (Rasmussen *et. al.*, 2001, p. 10).

Hence, organizational learning, viewed as a learning process, is thus a coplay of many small actors' know-what, know-how, attitude, and learning.

The two dominating views of organizational learning are the technical view and the social view (Easterby-Smith, Burgoyne, & Araujo, 1999). The technical view assumes that organizational learning is about how to respond and process information, both inside and outside the organization, in an efficient way. Argyris and Schön (1996) are two of the major contributors to this school. When Argyris and Schön (1996) talk about learning, they define this as a result of an inquired action, and claim that the performance of an action new to the organization is the most decisive test to understand whether a particular instance of organizational learning has taken place. This is based upon two considerations. First, that a collective, in the form of an organization with members that learn for it, exists; and secondly, that these members are able to carry out, on behalf of the organization, a process of inquiry that results in a learned product. Argyris and Schön (1996) define a collective as an organization capable of acting, based on a rule-governed way of deciding, delegating, and setting the boundaries of membership. The members of an organization carry out a process of inquiry resulting in a learned product. A process of inquiry is, thus, defined as a process going from thought to doubt, to resolution of doubt, and to action. Argyris and Schön (1996) claim that an inquiry cannot become part of an organizational inquiry unless it is undertaken by individuals who function as agents of the organization, in accordance with the roles and rules that prevail in that organization. When individual and organizational inquiries intersect, individual inquiry helps to shape organizational inquiry. A new organizational inquiry emerges, which then feeds back to shape the further inquiry carried out by individuals. In this way, organizations are sources of knowledge, and knowledge is either in the minds of individual members or recorded in the organization's files, through which the organization becomes understandable (to itself and others).

Once recorded and embedded in routines and practices, organizational knowledge can be inspected and decoded, even when the individuals who perform these routines are unable to pronounce it. In this sense, any organization, in itself, both represents answers and solutions to a set of questions or a set of problems.

Applying a social view to organizational learning means focusing on how people develop their work experiences. Such a view sees learning as something emerging from social interactions. The authors that contributed to develop this notion of organizational learning come from three different schools of thought that see learning a) as socially constructed, b) as a political process, or c) as implicated in the culture of the organization (Easterby-Smith *et. al.*, 1999). Seeing **learning as socially constructed** emphasises that data have no significance unless people define what they mean. Therefore, people have to be engaged in a **sense-making process**.

Researchers who consider organizational learning from a **political perspective** are concerned with how learning, as a social interaction, will be influenced by people's interest. Thus, a particular interpretation of information will suit some people's interest and harm others (Easterby-Smith *et. al.*, 1999; Wenger, 1998). A **social approach** to the learning organization focuses on the individuals' capability to learn from their work experiences and from working with others. Also, within this approach to the learning organization, there is an emphasis on how learning can be improved, that is, the development of methods to enhance learning. One example is the "dialogue" method, used to improve the quality of communication between people. By using a structured method for intervention into workgroups, the members are required to allow space for everybody to speak, avoid evaluating each other's comments, and be willing to speak out their views (Senge, 1990).

Hence, a learning organization that emphasises a technical view is oriented towards designing the learning process in order to achieve an improved performance in the company, and therefore emphasises the value of knowledge for the organization. A social approach to the learning organization focuses on how the individuals' experience can be optimised. Thus, both perspectives are based on the design of learning processes, but focus on different aspects of the organization to achieve this: on the organizational value of knowledge rather than the individual value of knowledge, respectively.

CHOOSING THE OBJECT OF STUDY

The Web pages studied in this chapter were chosen because of three criteria. Firstly, to use a more novel approach for analysing how an organization's knowledge sharing values can be identified from its Web pages. Secondly, the Web pages should contain a broad spectrum of information about the company's policies, expectations, and requirements of employees. Thirdly, they should provide a rich text to which the application of the chosen methods could be feasible. In this way, the analysing methods, more than the case, would be decisive for selecting the Web pages.

At the time of the study, spring 2000, I was working at Aalborg University, Denmark, and based on these criteria, the Web sites of the local Science Park (NOVI PARK), situated next to Aalborg University, emerged as sources to identify potential companies (Novi Park Web pages, 2006). The companies located at the Novi Park, at that time a handful of software companies, complied with the criteria. The one selected, Cadcam Consult, emerged as the most interesting, judging from its Web pages.

Cadcam Consult was, at the time of the study, a 10-year-old consulting company, offering business advice and software to businesses. During these years, the company had developed and implemented IT solutions for production companies within four main areas: development of automatic order systems, strategic planning of technology and information technology, system development, and standard products of technical information technology.

The approach used in this chapter is explorative. The aim is to apply a set of methods on a single case, in order to see what insights this gives in terms of interpreting the organizational image displayed. Therefore, the applied methods and their results are the main focus in this study. It is important to bear in mind that this investigation was undertaken to demonstrate the application of a set of analysing tools in order to interpret what Web pages can tell us about an organization. The approach applied should not be considered as an objective method, but rather as a starting point for a more coherent approach to analysing Web pages. This will provide us with the possibility to illustrate the organizational image without having to do interviews or read official company literature.

The data to be analysed consisted of eight Web pages forming a description of the company's profile, its products, and its employee requirements. The Web pages were in Danish and, for the purpose of this book, they were translated into English.

To what extent this caused loss of linguistical structure and meaning is hard to tell, but it could not be ignored. Nevertheless, the translations were done with an aim of being as true as possible to the original structure and meaning.

As previously described, the analysis of the Web pages was motivated by this research aim: to understand what organizational knowledge sharing values are displayed on the company's Web pages, by using a set of specific methods within linguistical theory in combination with CoP theory and discourse analysis.

Analysing Modality and Transitivity

The first element examined in Cadcam Consult's Web pages was the way the company valued their employees. Cadcam Consult declared they emphasised the organization's ability to solve complex tasks and therefore, they preferred to employ people with higher education.

Cadcam Consult put emphasis on the organization's ability to solve complex tasks, and thus employ preferably highly educated personnel.

In terms of modality and transitivity, this sentence shows high modality, since Cadcam Consult related themselves to the context of the sentence, and placed themselves in the sentence as the grammatical subject. In terms of transitivity, it is shown that Cadcam Consult's ability to solve complex tasks was related to holding personnel with higher education. Thus, both this effect, and the actions or events leading to this effect, could be found in the sentence.

When writing about how the company worked and collaborated to produce their products, the degree of modality becomes high, since Cadcam relate themselves strongly to this , by using the term "we," which was supported by the adjectives "considerable," "large," and "best," as can be seen in the following sentences.

We have a considerable level of knowledge, inside both production- and information technology. We put large emphasis on the collaboration between our customers, their products, their production technology and their information technology. The organization functions as a well collaborative team, giving us the best conditions for solving many different tasks.

In terms of transitivity, an agent (i.e., "the organization," "we"') can be identified in all of these statements. It was less obvious to identify the effects, except for being able to "solve many different tasks." In terms of how events and processes are connected, the text emphasises the combination of a high knowledge level, a close collaboration with customers, and collaboration inside the company, but it does not show the effects of this. Some actions and some processes in their relationships were identified, but with a rather fuzzy connection to their effects.

Further, in the text, it was possible to identify what the aim of the relationship to the customers was.

Our aim is to create productivity for our customers through the development and use of advanced information technology. We wish to build collaboration with our customers, based upon the necessary trust required to establish and carry out the necessary changes in the customer's company.

A high degree of modality is achieved by placing the company in the sentences as a grammatical subject, that is, "our" referring to Cadcam Consult, combined with an expected effect, "create productivity" and "change customer's company," based on "development and use of technical information technology" and "trust." This demonstrates that events and processes are connected with the grammatical subjects and objects. In short, that "technology changes how we do our jobs and live our lives" (Tolsby, 2000, p. 2)

It was not possible to infer, from the Web pages, conclusively to what extent Cadcam Consult were able to achieve these effects, but some indications were found. By emphasising their closeness to the NOVI Science Park, they promote a view where they can provide their customers with the latest technology, by their peer existence in a science park.

By establishing the company at NOVI (the NOVI Science Park), we have gained a location close to Aalborg University, AAU. Through this, we accomplish close contact with AAU's research activities and thus can support our customers with the most recent new knowledge.

Another indication can be found, where all the different requirements required from their customers through the years were listed, and the company concluded that this made them experts: *technical/administrative efficiency – an area in which Cadcam Consult are specialists.*

And finally, it is stated that applying *an automatic order handling system* would provide companies with a "substantial competitive advantage."

An automatic order handling system will give order producing companies a substantial competitive advantage. At the same time the customers' specific products will be offered with efficiency corresponding to that of serial producing competitors. This is documented through several assignments we have been, and continually is, involved in.

When Cadcam Consult, in their Web page, talked about how they supported the development of their customers, a high degree of modality and transitivity can be found: the text analysis shows that the development of customer companies is associated with the integration of information technology and traditional technology. This is illustrated in the next two paragraphs.

We perform strategic planning and development of Your Firm's technology based on an integration of information technology and traditional technology. Both in production - and information technology have we much knowledge, and particularly we have expertise of the use of electronic data processing to support the production tasks. We develop technical and administrative systems based on the customer's specifications.

In conclusion of this text analysis, attention should be paid to the aspects related to a functional grammar, by identifying how and why the text means what it does, and if it is effective in achieving its purpose. A set of Web pages might be designed to achieve several goals. The text analysis shows that Cadcam Consult wanted to attract particular employees, and to do that, they described their capabilities by listing in what fields they operated, what they achieved, and how this could accommodate the customers' requests. Then, it can be said, we know something about how and why by interpreting the text. On the other hand, whether the text was effective in achieving its purpose is not so easy to reveal. That would depend on both how well a message is communicated through the Web pages, and on the specific results obtained by the organization and resulting from reading the pages. This would require knowledge about how easy the company was able to recruit new employees, and whether or not new customers had been reached since the launch of these Web pages.

Another aspect to be considered in a textual analysis, the way it was conducted here, is the reflection about what was in the mind of the text creator. The Web pages should function both as a window of opportunities for new recruits, but at the same time, display a serious image of hardworking organization, offering robust solutions based on customer requests. A restricted, rather neutral design and layout, without moving objects and commercials, focused at presenting a text message that is aimed at building up a picture of a serious organization achieving its goals.

When analysing the Web pages of Cadcam Consult, their high profile on team cooperation became apparent; this was considered one of the best requirements needed to solve a multitude of tasks. The company spoke of the organization's ability to solve complex tasks that require highly educated personnel. Cadcam Consult's home page illustrated quite well what the aim of this company was: *Compact solutions for complex tasks.*

Application of Concepts from CoP Theory

In order to understand the learning process taking place in Cadcam Consult, the Web pages were analysed with the concepts of identity and meaning in mind (Wenger, 1998). In his CoP (Community of Practice) theory, Wenger (1998) emphasises how practice is more than just a learning process, but also that the community of practice is created as a continuous process of negotiation and re-negotiation of meaning, and this process forms our identity. Since we are looking at the learning process as it is displayed on a set of Web pages, we need to contextualise the definition of learning.

Illeris (1999) tried to tie together some of the different notions of learning. He affirms that learning basically consists of two related processes influencing each other: firstly, the coplay between the individual and his/her surroundings, including the interaction with different types of media (e.g., a book, a tape, a computer); and secondly, the internal cognitive acquisition and preparation process leading to something being learned, a learning result (Illeris, 1999, p. 15-16). Thus, learning involves some negotiation of meaning, made tacit (i.e., internalised by the individual) and materialised (Easterby-Smith *et. al.*, 1999; Polanyi, 1983; Wenger, 1998). This implies that learning occurs through social interaction (Lave & Wenger, 1991; Wenger, 1998). If we look at how Cadcam Consult's Web pages comply with this, we find the following: *The work climate is free and informal, focusing on technology, development and implementation. If you are a sharp programmer, this is an advantage, but if you are not, we will be helpful with further education. We work with the following platforms: SAP, Baan, Solid Works, Pro/E, AutoCAD, ME10, Microsoft, C, C++, Java, Visual Basic, Xpress.*

This tells how Cadcam Consult stressed their informal work atmosphere, but at the same time, since the focus was be on work, they stressed that the purpose (meaning) of creating a somewhat relaxed environment, was the "focusing on technology, development and implementation." In order to create such an environment, Cadcam Consult declared they used several strategies "to recruit highly educated personnel," which would ensure a minimum of knowledge relevant for solving the company's projects. Another strategy was to educate the employees as part of making them equipped to use the "shared repertoire" necessary to work in this company (Wenger, 1998). The message, displayed via the Web pages, leaves an impression of a company that gives considerable freedom to the employees, since the text tells us that they were made responsible for the completion of their assigned projects, all the way from sales until delivery, ending in the maintenance phase of the delivered product. Furthermore, the text on the Web pages tells us that if employees convey to these circumstances and are enthusiastic about the artefacts necessary to produce the products according to customer's satisfaction, the employees will be able to explore their engineering knowledge and *participate in the development of the latest IT technologies.* Furthermore, what the Web pages promise the employees is *the most stimulating, best paid, and most attractive career-related jobs, both now and in the future.*

You are responsible for your assignments, and to accomplish them, of a sequence of activities from sales, development, implementation, delivery and maintenance. We do not expect you to have a deep *knowledge of the technologies we are working with, but we expect you to think that development and implementation using World Class-IT should be exciting. By us, you will be allowed to use your technical knowledge and participate in the development of the most recent IT technologies. With a technical IT career you will get access to the most stimulating, the most stimulating, best paid, and most attractive career-related jobs, both now and in the future.*

This text illustrates how learning in Cadcam Consult was based upon teamwork and a close collaboration with the customer, where a prerequisite for this was created through an informal atmosphere by employing highly educated personnel with similar background, knowledge and skills. If we apply Wenger's (1998) theory, the text tells us that this will only be achieved if employees learn the "shared repertoire" of the company, something which was considered a precondition for completing their assignments (as shown in the previous paragraph).

In contrast to the emphasis on teamwork, the investigation also showed how Cadcam Consult, through their Web pages, projected the image of an organization that valued autonomous employees who were able to work on an individual basis, if required. However, despite the apparent freedom the Web pages claim is offered to employees in the company, some signs found in the Web pages show that employees wanting to work for this company needed to be able to use, or adapt to, the tools used for developing the learning product of the company. Therefore, autonomous employees are seen as those able to conform to the prevailing requirements of the company. Thus, these contrasting requirements and expectations were regarded as equally important in the relationship between the employees and the company.

A way to achieve this was to recruit employees with a similar background. In this case, similar background not only referred to employees with the same education, but, more specifically, to the skills they were required to have. In this way, the company's Web site illustrated how the company created a uniform knowledge level facilitating a particular learning process.

For the survival of the company, it was not enough to have an even knowledge level, but equally important was to build on the learning traditions of the company. Building on existing learning traditions would enable the company to remain competitive and profitable.

According to the message conveyed by the Web pages, the company considered themselves having a high level of knowledge, both within production and information technology. Additionally, their technical solutions needed to be compatible with the customers' products, production technology, and information technology. In order to solve their assignments and to make reliable solutions for complex tasks, the Web pages of Cadcam Consult display that the company gave priority to a set of knowledge and skill to which employees had to fulfill.

The aim for Cadcam Consult, as laid out on the company Web pages, was to create productivity for their customers through the development and use of advanced technical information technology. They wanted to build collaboration with their customers, based upon the necessary trust required to start and go through with the required changes in the customer's company.

On their Web pages, Cadcam Consult presented their location in the NOVI Science Park and thus, their closeness to the university is an argument for being able to provide their customers with the latest up-to-date knowledge. The learning process reveals itself on a set of Web pages, through the requirements and expectations it poses to potential employees. The employees have to be able to possess particular knowledge/skills (programming and strategic planning), which poses particular requirements upon the employees involving cooperation, teamwork, and collaboration with the customers. The customers' requests indicated, as described on the Web pages,

some of the capabilities and learning processes the company need to comply to, such as *faster throughput, faster order handling, increased capacity, less mistakes, increasing demand for data, need for production times, increasing demand for documentation,* and *increasing standardisation.* All these requirements demanded that Cadcam Consult was able to find appropriate solutions, and thus, they imbedded a process of problem solving and learning, according to their Web pages.

According to Wenger (1998), learning occurs through a socialisation process, normally when an employee is getting acquainted with how the work should be done. On Cadcam Consult's Web pages, this happens through formal training and through practical experiences in the organization. The processes taking place between employees in the company happen through negotiation and unlearning in teams, and solving work tasks. This demonstrated how Cadcam Consult's Web pages possess some of the elements defining a community of practice. An important element within this theory is that a true community of practice may extend beyond project groups and organizational settings, and thus does not cease to exist when a project is over, or when people change to another organizational setting when they change jobs. These elements cannot be read from the Web pages studied here; accordingly, it cannot be concluded that Cadcam Consult is a community of practice, nor can it be concluded that it is not.

Using a Discourse Approach

If a discourse analysis, as claimed by Fairclough (1992), includes going beyond a pure textual analysis, and takes both societal, cultural processes, and structure into consideration, then it is not possible to infer from the Web pages what discourse they belong to. On the other hand, one could argue that it is possible to look at the broader context of the produced text, taking the company operative environment and its characteristics into consideration. It could be argued that the Web pages have another important role, namely, spreading and sharing relevant information to be used by the company's employees. Thus, the Web pages become a tool for knowledge distribution within the company. When spreading knowledge, they also spread a particular behaviour, as in the case of the Web pages studied in this chapter. The result of this is that the Web pages promote what traditions the company stands fo,r and how they want these traditions to be continued by a homogeneous work force with particular skills and education. The latter could then be a relevant description of the dominating organizational discourse of Cadcam Consult.

Trust is an element emphasised in Cadcam Consult's Web pages. *Our aim is to create productivity for our customers through development and use of advanced technical information technology. We wish to build collaboration with our customers, based upon the necessary trust required to establish and go through with the necessary changes in the customer's company.*

Furthermore, employees need to learn how to establish a climate of trust, with customers, that allows them to access their organization. Trust and confidence are considered as important prerequisites for establishing a mutual learning process between the company and its customers. Trust must also be considered in a discussion of the elements that make the social practice between superiors and subordinates occur.

According to Karen Jones (1996), trust consists of two elements: 1) a cognitive element and 2) an affective element. The first element, cognition, is based on the understanding of the conditions that make us trust in the other. This is based upon "optimism about the goodwill and competence of another" (Jones, 1996, p. 7). The affective element of trust is based on how emotions "are distinctive ways of seeing a situation" (Jones, 1996, p. 11). Therefore, the affective element influences "one's willingness to rely on the other seems reasonable" (Jones, 1996, p. 11).

Trustworthiness is the basis for creating trust (Hardin, 1996, p. 29). Hardin's background is the field of political sciences, and his ideas about trust must be considered from an institutional perspective. Acting trustworthy depends on individuals' commitment and interest, but can be supported by a "network of laws and conventions" or self-interest in "maintaining particular relationships" (Hardin, 1996, p. 42). Nevertheless, any discussion about trustworthiness deals basically with a relationship between two individuals. It is from this perspective that Hardin (1996) discusses trustworthiness, and therefore, his ideas get a generic resonance applicable to any situation where trustworthiness results. Trust, as is displayed as a discourse on Cadcam Consult's Web pages, could, therefore, be defined as trustworthiness. From the explanations provided by Jones (1996) and Hardin (1996), we can infer that trustworthiness builds on goodwill, competence, commitment, and interest, but that laws, conventions, norms, and rules can back that trustworthiness.

It should be noted that a vital element in Cadcam Consult discourse is to have employees capable of establishing trustworthy relationships to customers. However,trust is something that is not acquired, but is a result of commitment and interest (Hardin, 1996). When Cadcam Consult includes trust as part of their Web discourse, they are taking both societal, cultural processes, and structure into consideration: societal processes, since trust extends beyond the borders of the company and into the wider society, to customers; and cultural processes, since the organizational discourse is promoting this as an integral part of what an employee is expected to be, according to the Web pages of Cadcam Consult.

As such, this employee involvement initiative is aimed at increasing productivity and organizational success (Marchington, 2001). Employees can take on different roles involving different degrees of authority and decisive power, something that can be difficult to turn off once the employees are expected to be ordinary team members. Shifting roles from one project to the next can cast the team into a wait-and-see position, not knowing how to relate to other employees that formerly had more authority and responsibility. A wait-and-see position signals that trust is at stake here, and the potential of distrust towards the attitudes and beliefs the former project leader bring back with him as an ordinary project member. It is fair to say that "optimism about the goodwill and competence of another" is under threat (Jones, 1996, p. 7). Hence, according to Alvesson and Karreman (2000), the way trust manifests itself, in the studied Web pages, has a structuring effect on employees in terms of framing their action. This qualifies it for "a close-range/determination notion of discourse" (Alvesson & Karreman, 2000, p. 1138).

CONCLUSION

In this chapter, a company's Web pages have been linguistically analysed. This was done to see if application of a set of methods, taken from learning and communication theory, is a feasible approach to identify how an organization works. It has been revealed that the identification of modality and transitivity, in combination with CoP concepts and discourse analysis, can be viable tools for identifying how the Web pages of the company is projected, and what this can tell us about the way the organization works. Additionally, the research showed that knowledge of learning processes of a company could be obtained even from its Web site, which provides a useful amount of material to identify elements of such processes. Based on these elements, we are able to describe how and why the company learns, the aspects involved in these processes, the requirements of the employees, and the expected learning product. Furthermore, by using linguistic elements to analyse the Web pages, it is possible to discover what particular organizational behaviour is promoted. This is achieved through communicating about

the company in a way that emphasises a particular learning element aimed at producing particular products. Analysing the Web pages shows that Cadcam Consult had a high degree of awareness of the importance of interaction in the learning process. The company emphasises values such as close collaboration through teamwork, both inside the company and with their customers. The research shows that the company values this as a prerequisite for completing their assignments. Part of the learning process is to establish trust with customers, to allow the company access to their organization. Trust and confidence are considered important prerequisites for establishing a mutual learning process between the company and its customers. Contrasting the emphasis put on teamwork, my investigation also shows that the company values autonomous employees who also are able to work on an individual basis, if required. Despite the apparent freedom offered to the employees, I find signs showing that employees who want to work in this company have to be able to use, or adapt to, the tools used for developing the learning product of the company. Autonomous employees are therefore intended as employees that are able to conform to the, at any one time, prevailing requirements of the company. Thus, both requirements and expectations are equally important in the relationship between the employees and the company.

This study of these Web pages also showed that the development of a particular learning product is associated with a high degree of uniformity in the company's organization. An element that allows this is the recruitment of employees with a similar background. In this case, similar background not only refers to the same education, but more specifically, to the skills employees are required to have. The text on the studied Web pages demonstrated what types of problem the customers face, and the different set of solutions the company has chose to develop to deal with these problems. Thus, the company's Web site illustrated how the homogeneous level of knowledge that the company created facilitated a particular learning process.

In order to understand some of the long-term impacts of company Web pages on employees understanding of an organization, more investigations are needed. When a company's Web pages promote a particular discourse, it will limit the pool of potential employees. The Web pages end up advocating a perfect view of how the organization works. The Web becomes a new courier for the stories, talk, and action in the company and thus, contribute to uphold a particular organizational identity, through communication of the company in a way that emphasises a particular knowledge-sharing practice aimed at producing particular products. This will deprive the company from getting a more heterogeneous work environment that promotes collaboration, engagement, and creativity. A fallacy would be the promotion of elite employee identities "internally, elite identity develops through a process of reflexivity amongst organizational members with reference to cultural artefacts, norms and values which are shaped through a variety of symbolic, strategic, and discursive media which in turn embeds identity in organizational culture" (Alvesson & Robertson, 2006, p. 200).

Therefore, when Web pages are designed, their content needs to be analysed in order to understand the effect of the messages they send. This is necessary if one wants to be considered a dynamic and employee-friendly organization. It does not help to put emphasis on teamwork if the real message is autonomous employees who are able to work on an individual basis. Nor does it matter to emphasis learning and knowledge values if this only means adapt to the tools used by the company. Consequently, the message to employees was you should be able to work on an individual basis, but we expect you to adjust to our practice. Autonomous employees were those able to conform to the, at any time, prevailing requirements of the company.

FUTURE RESEARCH DIRECTIONS

By studying a set of Web sites, this chapter frames some of the knowledge-sharing and knowledge-management practices that can be promoted using the Internet, and how these affect potential recruitment policies and organizational behaviour. For future researchers, more detailed studies, using the analytical tools from learning and communication theory, are needed. As shown in this chapter, these analytical tools will be beneficial in uncovering some of the knowledge values that can be identified through a linguistical analysis of a company's Web pages. This will provide the research community with a useful amount of material that allows us to understand how knowledge management and sharing is presented via a company's Web pages. Moreover, we are able to create a sensible description of how the World Wide Web displays how these processes take place. Furthermore, managers and companies need to understand that the Web has a major impact on what image the outside world gets of the company, not only through sophisticated layout and good design, but also through the messages imbedded in the text. Only by analysing the text on the Web pages is itpossible to fully understand what company image is projected to the outside world.

ACKNOWLEDGMENT

I am extremely grateful for the feedback and help from Dr. Ettore Bolisani in finishing this chapter. Much appreciation also goes to the three anonymous reviewers. Invaluable language help has come from my colleague Ester Log.

REFERENCES

Alvesson, M., & Karreman, D. (2000). Varieties of discourse - On the study of organizations through discourse analysis. *Human Relation, 53(9)*, 1125—1149.

Argyris, C., & Schon, D. A. (1996). *Organizational learning II theory, method, and practice.* Reading, MA: Addison Wesley-Publishing Company Inc.

Bloch, M. E. F. (1998). *How we think they think anthropological approaches to cognition, memory and literacy.* USA: Westview Press.

Cadcam Consult Web pages. (2000). Retrieved February – March, 2000, from http://www.novi.dk/cadcam/

Easterby-Smith, M., Burgoyne, J., & Araujo, L. (1999). *Organizational learning and the learning organization developments in theory and practice.* Gateshead: SAGE Publications Ltd.

Fairclough, N. (1992). *Discourse and social change.* Cambridge: Polity Press.

Halliday, M. A. K. (1994). *An introduction to functional grammar.* New York: Arnold.

Hardin, R. (1996). Trustworthiness. *Ethics, 107(1)*, 26-42.

Holloway, W., & Jefferson, T. (2000). *Doing qualitative research differently free association, narrative and the interview method.* Wiltshire: Sage Publications Ltd.

Illeris, K. (1999). *Læring - aktuell læringsteori i spenningsfeltet mellom Piaget, Freud og Marx (Learning – Current Learning Theory between Piaget, Freus and Marx).* Gylling: Roskilde Universitetsforlag.

Jones, K. (1996). Trust as an affective attitude. *Ethics 107(1)*, 4-25.

Jørgensen, M. W., & Phillips, L. (1999). *Diskurs analyse som teori og metode. (Discourse analysis as theory and method).* Gylling: Roskilde Universitetsforlag.

Lave, J., & Wenger, E. (1991). *Situated learning: Llegitimate peripheral participation.* Cambridge: Cambridge University Press.

Marchington, M. (2001). Employee involvement at work. In J. Storey (Ed.), *Human resource management, a critical text (2nd. ed)*. Cornwall: Thomson Learning.

Mårtensson, M. (2000). A critical review of knowledge management as a management tool. *Journal of Knowledge Management, 4(3)*, 204-216.

Novi Park Web pages. (2006). Retrieved January 15, 2006, from http://www.novi.dk

Polanyi, M. (1983). *The tacit dimension.* USA: Peter Smith.

Putnam, L L., Phillips, N., & Chapman, P. (1996). Metaphors of communication and organization. In R. Stewart, C. H. Clegg, & W. R. Noord (Eds.), *Handbook of organization studies* (pp. 375-408). London: Sage Publications Ltd.

Rasmussen G. J., Dahl, P. N., Mølbjerg Jørgensen, K., Laursen, E., & Rasmussen, P. (2001). *Perspektiver på organisatorisk læring* (VCL-serien nr. 28, ISSN 1399-7300). Aalborg, Denmark: Aalborg University, Center for Organisatorisk Læring Videncenter for Læreprocesser.

Riessman, K. C. (1993). *Narrative analysis.* CA: Sage Publications.

Roos, J., Roos, G., Dragonetti, N., & Edvinsson, L. (1997). *Intellectual capital: Navigating in the new business landscape.* London: MacMillan Business.

Senge, P. M (1990). *The fifth discipline: The art & practice of the learning Organization.* London: Century Business.

Tolsby, J. (2000). Taylorism given a new hand: How an IT system changed employees flexibility and personal involvement in their work. *Journal of Organizational Change Management, 13(5)*, 482-492.

Wald, B. (1993). On the evolution of would and other modals in the English spoken in East Los Angeles. In N. Dittmar & A. Reich (Eds.), *Modality in language acquisition* (pp. 59-96). Berlin: Walter de Gruyter.

Wenger, E. (1998). *Communities of practice learning, meaning, and identity.* Cambridge: Cambridge University Press.

ADDITIONAL READING

Addleson, M. (2001). Stories about companies: Boundaries, structures, strategies, and processes. *Managerial and Decision Economics, 22*, 169-182.

Alvesson, M., & Robertson, M. (2006). The best and the brightest: The construction, significance and effects of elite identities in consulting firms. *Organization, 12(2)*, 195-224.

Berners-Lee, T. (2000). *Weaving the Web: The original design and ultimate destiny of the World Wide Web.* San Francisco, Ca: HarperBusiness.

Dainton, M., & Zelly, E. D. (2004). *Applying communication theory for professional life: A practical introduction.* Thousand Oaks, CA: Sage Publications Ltd.

Duguid, P. (2005). The art of knowing: Social and tacit dimensions of knowledge and the limits of the community of practice. *The Information Society 21(2),* 109-118.

Epple, D., Argote L. & Devadas R. (1991). Organizational learning curves; A method for investigating intra-plant transfer of knowledge acquired through learning by doing. *Organization Science, 2*, 58-70.

Gee, J. P. (2005). *Introduction to discourse analysis: Theory and method.* New York: Routledge.

Greyling, M. A., (1998). Mental models of the Internet - theory and application in human factors. *International Journal of Industrial Ergonmics, 22*(4), 299-305.

Harman, K., & Ackermann, E. (2004). *Searching & researching on the Internet & World Wide Web.* London: Franklin Beedle & Associates Inc.

Hawisher, G. (1999). *Global literacies and the World Wide Web.* London: Routledge.

Holloway, W., & Jefferson, T. (2000*). Doing qualitative research differently free association, narrative and the interview method.* Wiltshire: Sage Publications Ltd.

Hudson, R. (1999). The learning economy, the learning firm and the learning region: A sympathetic critique of the limits to learning. *European Urban and Regional Studies, 6*(1), 59-72.

Illeris, K. (2000). *Tekster om Læring. (My translations: Texts about Learning)* Gylling: Roskilde Universitetsforlag.

Iverson, J. O., & McPhee, R. D. (2002). Knowledge management in communities of practice: Being true to the communicative character of knowledge. *Management Communication Quarterly, 16*(2), 259-66.

Littlejohn, S. W, & Foss, K. A. (2007). *Theories of human communication.* England: Wadsworth Publishing Company.

Martin, T. L. (2004). *Poiesis and possible worlds: A study in modality and literary theory.* Canada: University of Toronto Press.

Miller, K. (2004). *Communication theories: Perspectives, processes, and contexts* (2nd ed.). McGraw-Hill Humanities/Social Sciences/Languages.

O'Halloran, K. (2004). *Critical discourse analysis and language cognition.* Edinburgh: Edinburgh University.Royce T. D., & Bowcher, W. L. (2006).

New directions in the analysis of multimodal discourse. USA: Lawrence Erlbaum Associates.

Shedletsky, L., & Aitken, J. E. (2003). *Human communication on the Internet.* England: Allyn & Bacon.

Trevino, L. K., Lengel, R. K., & Daft, R. L. (1987). Media symbolism, media richness and media choice in organizations. *Communication Research, 14(5)*, 553-574.

Trevino, L., Lengel, R., Bodensteiner, W., Gerloff, E., & Muir, N. (1990). The richness imperative and cognitive style: The role of individual differences in media choice behavior. *Management Communication Quarterly, 4(2)*.

Wooffitt, R. (2005). *Conversation analysis and discourse analysis: A comparative and critical introduction.* London: Sage Publications Ltd.

Compilation of References

Abels, E., et al.. (2004). If you build it, will they come? *Marketing, 8*(10), 13-17.

Abidi, S. S. R., & Pang, X. (2004). Knowledge sharing over P2P knowledge networks: A peer ontology and semantic overlay driven approach. *International Conference on Knowledge Management*, Singapore, 13-15.

Ackerman, M. S. (1994). Augmenting the organizational memory: A field study of Answer Garden. In R. Furuta & C. Neuwirth (Eds.), *Proceedings of CSCW'94* (pp. 243–252). Chapel Hill, NC: ACM.

Ackoff, R. L. (1989). From data to wisdom, *Journal of Applies Systems Analysis, 16*, 3-9.

Adler, R. P., & Christopher, A. J. (1998). *Internet community primer – overview and business opportunity.* Retrieved from http://www.digiplaces.com/

Ahuja, M., Galletta, D., et al. (2003). Individual centrality and performance in virtual R&D groups: An empirical study. *Management Science, 49*(1), 21-38.

Ai-Alawi, A. I., Al-Marzooqi, N. Y., & Mohammed Y. F. (2007). Organizational culture and knowledge sharing: Critical success factors. *Journal of Knowledge Management, 11*(2), 22-42.

Akavia, G., & Gofer, E. (2006). *Two weeks with a network-centric infantry company in an urban warfare trial.* Paper presented at the Command and Control Research and Technology Symposium, San Diego, CA.

Akerlof, G. A. (1970). The markets for "lemons": Quality uncertainty and the market mechanism. *Quarterly Journal of Economics*, August, 488-500.

Akyildiz, I. F., Wang, X., & Wang, W. (2005). Wireless mesh networks: A survey. *Computer Networks, 47*(4), 445-487.

Alavi, M., & Leidner, D. (1999). Knowledge management systems: Issues, challenges and benefits. *Communication of the Association for Information Systems, 1*, 1-28.

Alavi, M., & Leidner, D. (2001). Knowledge management and knowledge management systems: Conceptual foundations and research issues. *MIS Quarterly, 25*(1), 107-136.

Alavi, M., & Leidner, D. E. (2001). Knowledge management and knowledge management systems: Conceptual foundations and research issues. *MIS Quarterly, 25*, 107-136.

Alavi, M., & Leidner, D. E. (2001). Review: Knowledge management and knowledge management systems: Conceptual foundations and research issues. *MIS Quarterly, 25*(1), 107-136.

Alavi, M., & Tiwana, A. (2003). Knowledge management: The information technology dimension. In M. Easterby-Smith & M. A. Lyles (Eds.), *Handbook of organizational learning and knowledge management* (pp. 104-121). Oxford: Blackwell Publishing.

Alberts, D. S., Gartska, J. J., & Stein, F. P. (1999). *Network-centric warfare: Developing and leveraging information superiority.* Washington D.C: Department of Defense C4ISR Cooperative Research Program.

Albino, V., Garavelli, A. C., & Gorgoglione, M. (2004). Organisation and technology transfer. *Benchmarking: An International Journal, 11*(2), 584-600.

Ali, I., Pascoe, C., & Warne, L. (2002). Interactions of organizational culture and collaboration in working and learning. *IEEE Journal of Educational Technology and Society, 5*(2).

Allee, V. (2000). Knowledge networks and communities of practice. *OD Practitioners: Journal of the Organization Development Network, 32*(4). Retrieved May 25, 2007, from http://www.odnetwork.org/odponline/vol32n4/knowledgenets.html

Allen, T. (1977). *Managing the flow of technology.* Cambridge, MA: MIT Press.

Allen, T. J. & Cohen, S. I. (1969). Information flow in research and development laboratories. *Administrative Science Quarterly, 14*(1), 12-19.

Allen, T. J. (1966) *Managing the flow of scientific and technological information*. Cambridge, Mass.: M.I.T. (Ph D thesis).

Allen, T. J. (1970). Communication networks in R & D laboratories. *Journal of R & D Management, 1*(1), 14-21.

Allen, T. J. (1977). *Managing the flow of technology; Technology transfer and the dissemination of technological information within the Research and Development organization*. Cambridge, MA: MIT Press.

Allen, T. J., & Cohen, S. I. (1969). Information flow in research and development laboratories. *Administrative Science Quarterly*, (4), 12-19.

Allison, K. (2006). How to unearth the IT moles. *Financial Times*, (September 5), 10.

Aloni, M. (1985). Patterns of information transfer among engineers and applied scientists in complex organizations. *Scientometrics, 8*, 5-6.

Alvesson, M., & Karreman, D. (2000). Varieties of discourse - On the study of organizations through discourse analysis. *Human Relation, 53*(9), 1125—1149.

Ambrosini, V., & Bowman, C. (2001). Tacit knowledge: Some suggestions for operationalization. *Journal of Management Studies, 38*(6), 811–829.

Amin, A., & Cohendet, P. (2004). *Architectures of knowledge: Firms, capabilities, and communities*. Oxford: Oxford University Press.

Ancona, D., & Caldwell, D. (1992). Bridging the boundary: External activity and performance in organization teams. *Administrative Science Quarterly, 37*(4), 634-665.

Ancori, B., Bureth, A., & Cohendet, P. (2000). The economics of knowledge: The debate about codification and tacit knowledge. *Industrial and Corporate Change, 9*(2), 255-287.

Andenmatten, S., Bettoni, M., C., & Mathieu, R. (2007). Knowledge cooperation in online communities. *The Electronic Journal of Knowledge Management, 5*(1), 1-6.

Andersen, A., & The American Productivity and Quality Center. (1996). *The knowledge management assessment tool: External benchmarking version*. Winter.

Anderson, A., Mullin, J., McEwan, R., Bal, J., Carletta, J., Grattan, E., & Brundell, P. (2005). Exploring why virtual teamworking is effective in the lab but more difficult in the workplace. In R. Bromme, F. Hesse & H. Spada (Eds), *Barriers and biaes in computer-mediated knowledge communication. And how they may be overcome* (pp. 119-142). NY, NY: Springer-Verlag.

Anderson, P. (1999). Complexity theory and organization science. *Organization Science, 10*(3), 216-232.

Andres, H. P. (2002). A comparison of face-to-face and virtual software development teams. *Team Performance Management, 8*(1/2), 39-48.

Andrews, K. M., & Delahaye, B. L. (2000). Influences on knowledge processes. In Organizational learning: The psychosocial filter. *Journal of Management Studies, 37*(6), 797-810.

Ang, Z., & Massingham, P. (2007). National culture and standardization vs. adaption of knowledge management. *Journal of Knowledge Management, 11*(2), 5-21.

Antonelli, C. (2007). The business governance of localized knowledge. *Industry and Innovation, 13*(3), 227-261.

Apostolou, D., Papailiou, N., & Mentzas, G. (2007). Developing knowledge networks: A practical methodology and experiences from cases. *International Journal of Knowledge Management Studies, 1*, (3/4), 330-355.

APQC: American, Productivity & Quality Center. (1999). Creating a knowledge-sharing culture: Consortium benchmarking study best-practice report. *APQC International Benchmarking Clearinghouse*.

Archer, N., & Wang, S. (2002). Knowledge management in network organizations. *Michael G. DeGroote School of Business,* working paper #456.

Ardichvili, A., Mauner M., Li, W., Wenting, T., & Stuedemann R. (2006). Cultural influences on knowledge sharing through online communities of practice. *Journal of Knowledge Management, 10*(1), 94-107.

Argote, L., & Ingram, P. (2000). Knowledge transfer: A basis for competitive advantage in firms. *Organizational Behavior and Human Decision Processes, 82*(1), 150-169.

Argote, L., & Linda, P.(2000). KT: A basis for competitive advantage in firms. *Organizational Behavior and Human Decision Processes, 82*(1), 150-169.

Argote, L., Beckamn, S., & Epple, D. (1990). The persistence and transfer of learning in industrial settings. *Management Science, 36*(2).

Argote, L., McEvily, B., & Reagans, R. (2003). Managing knowledge in organizations: An integrative framework and review of emerging themes. *Management Science, 49(4)*, 571-582.

Argote, L., McEvily, R., & Reegans, R. (2003). Managing knowledge in organizations: An integrative framework and review of emerging themes. *Management Science, 49*(4), 571-582.

Argyris, C., & Schon, D. A. (1996). *Organizational learning II theory, method, and practice*. Reading, MA: Addison Wesley-Publishing Company Inc.

Arthur, W. B., Durlauf, R., & Lane, D. (1997). *The economy as an evolving complex system II*. Reading, MA: Addison-Wesley.

Atkinson, J. W. (1964). *An introduction to motivation*. Princeton, NJ: Van Nostrand.

Avison, D., Lau, F., Neilsen, P. A., & Myers, M. (1999). Action research. *Communications of ACM, 42*, 94-97.

Baeza-Yates, R., & Ribeiro-Neto, B. (1999). *Modern information retrieval*. Wokingham: Addison-Wesley.

Bair, J., Fenn, J., Hunter, R., & Bosik, D. (1997). *Foundations for enterprise knowledge management* (Report R-400-105). Stamford: Gartner Group.

Bal, J., & Teo, P. K. (2000). Implementing virtual teamworking. Part 1: A literature review of best practice. *Logistics Information Management, 13*(6), 346-352.

Baldwin, N. S., & Rice, R. E. (1997). Information-seeking behavior of securities analysts: Individual and institutional influences, information sources and channels and outcomes. *Journal of the American Society for Information Science, 48*(8), 674-693.

Bales, R. F. (1950). *Interaction process analysis. A method for the study of a small group*. Chicago: The University of Chicago Press.

Balstrup, B. (2004). *Leading by detached involvement – Success factors enabling leadership of virtual teams*. MBA Dissertation, Henley Management College, UK.

Bandura, A. (1997). *Self-efficacy: The exercise of control*. New York, NY: Freeman.

Barley, S. R. (1986). Technology as an occasion for structuring: Evidence from observations of CT scanners and the social order of radiology departments. *Administrative Science Quarterly, 31*, 78-108.

Barley, S. R. (1986). Technology as an occasion for structuring: Evidence from observation of CT scanners and the social order of radiology departments. *Administrative Science Quarterly, 31*, 78-108.

Barley, S. R., & Tolbert, P. S. (1997). Institution and structuration: Studying the links between action and institution. *Organization Studies, 18*(1), 93-117.

Barnes, D., & Hinton, M. (2007). Developing a framework to analyse the roles and relationships of online intermediaries. *International Journal of Information Management, 27*, 63-74.

Barney, J. B. (1991). Firm resources and sustained competitive advantage. *Journal of Management, 17*, 99–120.

Bateman, J. (1999). Modeling the importance of end-user relevance criteria. In *ASIS '99, Proceedings of the 62nd ASIS Annual Meeting: Vol 36. Knowledge Creation, Organization and Use* (pp. 396-406). Washington, DC.

Battle, E. (1966). Motivational determinants of academic competence. *Journal of Personality and Social Psychology, 4*, 534-642.

Becerra-Fernandez, I., & Sabherwal, R. (2006). ICT and knowledge management systems. In D. G. Schwartz (Ed.), *Encyclopedia of Knowledge Management* (pp. 231-236). Hershey, PA: Idea Group.

Bechky, B. (1999). *Creating shared meaning across occupational communities: An ethnographic study of a production floor*. Paper presented at the annual meeting of the Academy of Management, Chicago, IL.

Bechky, B. (2003). Sharing meaning across occupational communities: The transformation of understanding on a production floor. *Organization science. 14*(3), 312-330

Becker, M. (2001). Managing dispersed knowledge: Organizational problems, managerial strategies, and their effectiveness. *Journal of Management Studies, 38*(7), 1037-1051.

Becker, M. C. (2004). Organizational routines: A review of the literature. *Industrial Corporate Change, 13*(4), 643-677.

Bell, D. (1973). *The coming of post-industrial society: A venture in social forecasting*. New York: Basic Books.

Bell, J. K. (1993). How to plan to keep communications open after disaster strikes. In *Proceedings of the 1993 national earthquake conference: Earthquake Hazard Reduction in the Central and Eastern United States: A Time for Examination and Action* (pp. 339-348).

Benedict, B. M. (1996). *Making the modern reader cultural mediation in early modern literary anthologies*. Princeton: Princeton University Press. Retrieved from http//www.pupress.princeton.edu/books/benedict/

Benghozi, P. J. (2002). Technologie et organisation : le hasard et la nécessité. *Annales des Télécommunications, 57*(3-4), 289-305.

Bennett, B. R., & Theodoulidis, B. (1998). *Towards a notion of personal ontology*. University of Manchester.

Berends, H. (2005). Explore knowledge sharing: Moves, problem solving and justification. *Knowledge Management Research & Practice, 3*, 97-105.

Berger, C. J. (1979). Organizational structure, attitude and behavior. *Research in Organizational Behavior, 1*, 169-208.

Beznosov, K., Flinn, D., Kawamoto, S. and Hartman, B. Extended and virtual enterprises - similarities and differences. *Information Security Technical Report*, 10, 2-14.

Bhagat, R. S., Kedia, B. L., Harveston, P. D., & Triandis, H. C. (2002). Cultural variations in the cross-border transfer of organizational knowledge: An integrative framework. *The Academy of Management Review, 27*(2), 204-221.

Biddle, B. J., & Thomas, E. J. (1966): *Role theory: Concepts and research*. New York: John Wiley.

Biemann, C. (2005). Ontology learning from texts: A survey of methods. *LDV-Forum 20*(2), 75-93.

Biggart, N. W., & Hamilton, G. (1984). The power of obedience. *Administrative Science Quarterly, 29*, 540-549.

Birkinshaw, J. (2001). Why is knowledge management so difficult? *Business Strategy Review, 12*(1) 11-18.

Bishop, A. P. (1998). Logins and bailouts: Measuring access, use, and success in digital libraries. *The Journal of Electronic Publishing, 4(2).*

Bisson, G. (1992). Learning in FOL with a similarity measure. *AAAI*, 82–87.

Bisson, G., Nedellec, C., & Canamero, D. (2000). Designing clustering methods for ontology building - The Mo'K Workbench. In S. Staab, A. Maedche, C. Nedellec, & P. Wiemer-Hastings (Eds.), *Proceedings of the Workshop on Ontology Learning, 14th European Conference on Artificial Intelligence*, Berlin, Germany.

Blankenship, R. L. (1980). *Colleagues in organization*. Huntington, NY: Robert E. Krieger Publishing Company.

Bloch, M. E. F. (1998). *How we think they think anthropological approaches to cognition, memory and literacy*. USA: Westview Press.

Block, H. D. (1962). The perceptron: A model for brain functioning. *Reviews of Modern Physics, 34*, 123-135.

Blood, R. (2002). *We've got blog. How Web logs are changing our culture*. Cambridge, MA: Perseus Publishing.

Boase, J., Horrigan, J. B., Wellman, B., & Rainie, L. (2006). *The strength of Internet ties. The Internet and e-mail aid users in maintaining their social networks and provide pathways to help when people face big decisions*. PEW Internet and American Life Project Report, Report Number 202-419-4500. Retrieved May 25, 2007, from http://www.pewinternet/org

Boiral, O, (2002). Tacit knowledge and environmental management. *Long Range Planning, 35*, 291–317.

Boisot, M. (1995). Is your firm a creative destroyer? Competitive learning and knowledge flows in the technological strategies of firms. *Research Policy, 24*, 489-506.

Boisot, M. (1998). *Knowledge assets. Securing competitive advantages in the information economy*. Oxford: Oxford University Press.

Bolisani, E., & Scarso, E. (1999). Information technology management: A knowledge-based perspective. *Technovation, 19*, 209-17.

Bolisani, E., & Scarso, E. (2000). Electronic communication and knowledge transfer. *International Journal of Technology Management, 20*(1-2), 116-133.

Bolisani, E., Scarso, E., & Di Biagi, M. (2006). Economic issues of online professional communities. In E. Coakes & S. Clarke (Eds.), *Encyclopedia of communities of practice in information and knowledge management.=* Hershey, PA: IDEA Group.

Bond, A. H., & Gasser, L. (1988). *Readings in distributed artificial intelligence*. San Francisco, CA: Morgan Kaufmann.

Bontis, N. (1998). Intellectual capital: An exploratory study that develops measures and models. *Management Decision, 36*(2), 63-76.

Bose, R. (2004). Knowledge management metrics. *Industrial Management and Data Systems, 104*(6), 457-468.

Bourdieu, P., & Wacquant, L. (1992). *An invitation to reflexive sociology*. Chicago: University of Chicago Press.

Bourdreau, A., & Couillard, G. (1999). System integration and knowledge management. *Information Systems Management, 1*(3), 24–32.

Bouthillier, F., & Shearer, K. (2003). *Assessing competitive intelligence software: A guide to evaluating CI technology.* Medford, NY: Information Today.

Boyd, J., Ragsdell, G., & Oppenheim, C. (2007). *Knowledge transfer mechanisms: A case study from manufacturing.* Paper presented at the 8th European Coference on Knowldege Management, Barcelona.

Boyd, J., Ragsdell, G., & Oppenheim, C. (2007). Knowledge transfer mechanisms: A case study from manufacturing. In B. Martin & D. Remenyi (Eds.), *Proceedings of the 8th European Conference on Knowledge Management* (Vol. I, pp. 139-146). Reading, UK: Academic Conferences Limited.

Brannen, M.Y., & Salk, J. (2000). Partnering across borders. *Human Relations, 53*(4), 451–487.

Brass, D. J., & Burkhardt, M. (1993). Potential power and power use: An investigation of structure and behavior. *Academy of Management Journal, 36*(3), 441-460.

Bresman, J., Birkinshaw, J., & Nobel, R. (1999). Knowledge transfer in international acquistions. *Journal of International Business Studies, 30*, 439-462.

Brown, J. (2000). Growing up digital, the Web and the new learning ecology. *Change, the Magazine of Higher Learning,* March/April, 11-22.

Brown, J. S., & Duguid, P. (1991). Knowledge and organization: A social-practice perspective. *Organization Science, 12*(2), 198-213.

Brown, J. S., & Duguid, P. (1991). Organizational learning and communities-of-practice: Toward a unified view of working, learning, and innovation. *Organization Science, 2*(1), 40-57.

Brown, J. S., & Duguid, P. (1998). Organizing knowledge. *California Management Review, 40*(3), 90-111.

Brown, J. S., & Duguid, P. (2000). Balancing act: How to capture knowledge without killing it. *Harvard Business Review, May-June*: 73-80.

Brown, J. S., & Duguid, P. (2000). *The social life of information.* Boston, MA: Harvard Business School Press.

Brown, J. S., & Duguid, P. (2001). Knowledge and organization: A social-practice perspective. *Organization Science, 12*(2), 198-213.

Brown, J. S., & Duguid, P. (2001). Structure and spontaneity: Knowledge and organization. In I. Nonaka, & D. J. Teece (Eds.), *Managing Industrial Knowledge. Creation, Transfer and Utilization* (pp. 44-67). London: SAGE.

Brown, J. W., & Utterback, J. (1985). Uncertainty and technical communication patterns. *Management Science, 31*(3), 301-311.

Brown, J., & Duguid, P. (2002). *The social life of information.* Boston, MA: Harvard Business School Press.

Browne & Zhang, (1999). Extended and virtual enterprises - similarities and differences. *International Journal of Agile Management Systems, 1*(1), 30-36.

Browne, J., & Jagdev, H. S. (1998). The extended enterprise - A context for manufacturing. *Journal of Production, Planning & Control, 9*(3), 216 -229.

Browne, J., Sackett, P. J., & Wortmann, J. C. (1995). Future manufacturing systems - towards the extended enterprise. *Computers in Industry, 25*(3), 235-54.

Bruner, J. S. (1992). The narrative construction of reality. In H. Beilins & P. B. Pufall (Eds.), *Piaget's theory: Prospects and possibilities* (pp. 229-248). Hillsdale, NJ: Erlbaum.

Bruno, R., Conti, M., & Gregori, E. (2005). Mesh networks: Commodity multihop ad hoc networks. *IEEE Communications Magazine, March,* 123-131.

Brydon, M., & Vining, A. R. (2006). Understanding the failure of internal knowledge markets: A framework for diagnosis and improvement. *Information & Management, 43*, 964–974. Choi et al., 1995

Burger, P. L., & Luckman, T. (1966). *The social construction of reality.* Garden City, NY: Doubleday & Company.

Burgoon, J. K., Bonito, J. A., Ramierez Jr., A. Dunbar, N. E., Kam, K., & Fischer, J. (2002). Testing the interactivity principle: Effects of mediation, propinquity, and verbal and nonverbal modalities in interpersonal interaction. *Journal of Communication, 52*(3), 657-678.

Burns, T., & Flam, H. (1987). *The shaping of social organization.* London: Sage.

Busch, P., & Richards, D. (2000). Graphically defining articulable tacit knowledge. *ACM International Conference Proceeding Series, 9,* 51 – 60.

Busch, P., Richards, D., Dampney, C., Galloway, J., (2002). *Selected tacit knowledge observations within two organisations.* Sydney Area Workshop on Visual Information Processing December University of Sydney, (pp. 5-11).

Butler, B. (2001). Membership size, communication activity, and sustainability: A resource-based model of online social structures. *Information Systems Research, 12*(4), 346-362.

Butler, T. (2003). From data to knowledge and back again: understanding the limitations of KMS. *Knowledge and Process Management, 10*(3), 144-155.

Byrne, J. (1993). The virtual corporation. *Business Week, 26*(3), 36–41.

Cabrera, A. & Cabrera, E. F. (2002). Knowledge-sharing dilemma. *Organization Studies, 23*(5), 687-710.

Cadcam Consult Web pages. (2000). Retrieved February – March, 2000, from http://www.novi.dk/cadcam/

Camarinha-Matos L. M. (2003). Infrastructures for virtual organizations - where we are. In *Emerging Technologies and Factory Automation: Vol. 2. Proceedings of ETFA '03* (pp. 405- 414).

Camarinha-Matos L. M. (2005). ICT infrastructures for VO. In L. M. Camarinha-Matos, H. Afsarmanesh, & M. Ollus(Eds.), *Virtual organizations: Systems and practices* (pp. 89-110). Boston: Springer Science and Business Media.

Campus Compact. (2007). *Higher education responds to Katrina*. Retrieved January 18, 2007, from http://www.compact.org/resources/downloads/Katrina.pdf

Caraballo, S. A. (1999). Automatic construction of a hypernym-labeled noun hierarchy from text. *Proceedings of the 37th Annual Meeting of the Association for Computational Linguistics*, 120-126.

Carlson, J., & Zmud, R. (1999). Channel expansion theory and the experiential nature of media richness perceptions. *Academy of Management Journal, 42*(2), 153-170.

Carmichael, D. J., Kay, J., & Kummerfeld, B. (2004). Personal ontologies for feature selection in intelligent environment visualisations. In *Proceedings of the Workshop on Artificial Intelligence in Mobile Systems*.

Carr, C., Erickson, G. S. & Rothberg, H. (2004). Intellectual capital, competitive intelligence and the economic espionage act. *International Journal of Learning and Intellectual Capital, 1*(4), 460-482.

Case, D. O. (2002). *Looking for information: A survey of research on information seeking, needs, and behavior*. Lexington, KY: Academic Press, Elsevier Science.

Cayzer, S. (2004). Semantic blogging and decentralized knowledge management. *Communications of the ACM, 47*(12), 47-52.

CEN. (2004). *European guide to good practice in knowledge management - Part 1: Knowledge management framework* (ICS 03.100.99, CWA 14924-1). CEN, The European Committee for Standardization.

Chaffee, J., & Gauch, S. (2000). Personal ontologies for Web navigation. *Proceedings of the Ninth international Conference on information and Knowledge Management*, 227-234.

Chaib-draa, B. (1995). Industrial applications of distributed AI. *Communications of the ACM, 38*(11), 49–53.

Chartrand, H. H. (2002). *The competitiveness of nations in a global knowledge-based economy: An individual interdisciplinary studies*. Unedited PhD Dissertation, University of Saskatchewan.

Chase, R. (1997). The knowledge based organisation: an international survey. *Journal of Knowledge Management, 1*(1), 38-49.

Chen, C. H., & Shish, H. T. (2005). *High-tech industries in China*. Edward Elgar Publishing.

Chen, C., et al. (2000). Individual differences in virtual environments – Introduction and overview. *Journal of American Society for Information Science, 51*(6), 499-507.

Chiu, C-M, Hsu, M-H,, & Wang, E. T. G. (2006). Understanding knowledge sharing in virtual communities: An integration of social capital and social cognitive theories. *Decision Support Systems, 42*(3), 1872-1888.

Choi, B., & Lee, H. (2003). An empirical investigation of KM styles and their effect on corporate performance. *Information & Management, 40*, 403-417.

Choo, C. (1996). The knowing organization: How organizations use information to construct meaning, create knowledge, and make decisions. *International Journal of Information Management, 16*(5), 329-340.

Choo, C., Detlor, B., & Turnbull, D. (2000). *Web work: Information seeking and knowledge work on the World Wide Web*. NY, NY: Springer.

Chua, A. (2001). Relationship between the types of knowledge shared and types of communication channels used. *Journal of Knowledge Management Practice* October, 2001. Retrieved May 25, 2007, from http://www.tlainc.com/articl26.htm

Ciborra, C. U., & Andreu, R. (2001). Sharing knowledge across boundaries. *Journal of Information Technology, 16*(2), 73-81.

Cillo, P. (2005). Fostering market knowledge use in innovation: The role of internal brokers. *European Management Journal, 23*(4), 404-412.

Clarke, L. (1994). *The essence of change*. London, UK: Prentice-Hall.

Clarke, R. (2002). Trust in the context of e-business. *Internet Law Bulletin, 4*(5), 56-59.

Coakes, E. (2002). Knowledge management: A sociotechnical perspective. In E. Coakes, D. Willis, & S. Clarke (Eds.), *Knowledge management in the sociotechnical world. The graffiti continues* (pp.4-14). London: Springer.

Coakes, E., Bradburn, A., & Sugden, G. (2004). Managing and leveraging knowledge for organisational advantage. *Knowledge Management Research & Practice, 2*, 118-128.

Coase, R. H. (1937). The nature of the firm. *Econometrics, 4*, 18-33.

Cobb, A. T. (1980) Informal influence in the formal organization: Perceived sources of power among work unit peers. *Academy of Management Journal, 23*, 155-161.

CODASYL. (1971). Feature analysis of generalized data base management systems. *ACM*, May.

Cohen, D., & Prusak, L. (2001). *In good company: How social capital makes organizations work*. Boston, MA: Harvard Business School Press.

Cohen, W. M., & Levinthal, D. A. (1990). Absorptive capacity: A new perspective on learning and innovation. *Administrative Science Quarterly, 35*(1), 128-152.

Cohen, W., & Levinthal, D. (1990). Absorptive capacity: A new perspective on learning and innovation. *Administrative Science Quarterly, 35*(1), 128-152.

Colbert, B. (2004). The complex resource-based view: Implications for theory and practice in strategic human resource management. *Academy of Management Review, 29*(3), 341-358.

Colis, D. (1996). Organizational capability as a source of profit. In B. Moingeon & A. Edmondson (Eds), *Organizational learning and competitive advantage*. London: Sage.

Collins, H. M. (2001). Tacit knowledge, trust and the Q of sapphire. *Social Studies of Science, 1*(31), 71-85.

COM 229. (2005). *i2010 – A European Information Society for growth and employment*. Communication from the commission to the council, the European parliament, the European economic and social committee and the committee of the regions, Brussels, 1.6.2005.

Constant, D., Sproull, L., et al. (1996). The kindness of strangers: The usefulness of electronic weak ties for technical advice. *Organization Science, 7*(2), 119-135.

Cook, S. N., & Brown, J. S. (1999). Bridging epistemologies: The generative dance between organizational knowledge and organizational knowing. *Organization Science, 10*(4), 381-400.

Covey, D. T. (2002). Usage and usability assessment: Library practices and concerns. In *Digital Library Federation and Council on Library and Information Resources*, Pub 105, Washington, D.C.

Covey, D. T. (2003). The need to improve remote access to online library resources: Filling the gap between commercial vendor and academic user practice. *Libraries and the Academy, 3*(4), 577-599.

Cowan, M., David, P., & Foray, D. (2001). The explicit economics of knowledge codification and tacitness. *Industrial and Corporate Change, 9*(2), 211-253.

Cowan, R., & Foray D. (1997). The economics of codification and the diffusion of knowledge. *Industrial Corporate Change, 6*, 595-622.

Cowan, R., David, P. A., & Foray, D.(2000). The explicit economics of knowledge: Codification and tacitness. *Industrial and Corporate Change, 9*(2), 211-253.

Cox, D. E. (1987). Programmatic factors associated with effective occupational education programs in community colleges. *Community/Junior College Quarterly of Research and Practice, 11*(1), 11-17.

Craven, M., DiPasquo, D., Freitag, D., McCallum, A., Mitchell, T., Nigam, K., & Slattery, S. (2000). Learning to construct knowledge bases from the World Wide Web. *Artificial Intelligence, 118*, 69-113.

Cray, D., & Mallory, G. R. (1998). *Making sense of managing culture*. London, UK: International Thomson Business Press.

Cremer, D. D. (2002). Respect and cooperation in social dilemmas: The importance of feeling included. *Personality and Social Psychology, 28*(10), 1335-1341.

Cross, R., & Baird, L. (2000). Technology is not enough: Improving performance by building organizational memory. *Sloan Management Review, 41*(3), 69-78.

Culnan, M. (1985). The dimensions of perceived accessibility to information: Implications for the delivery of information systems and services. *Journal of the American Society for Information Science, 36*(5), 302-308.

Culnan, M. J., & Markus, M. L. (1987). Information technologies. In F. M. Jablin, L. L. Putnam, K. H. Roberts, & L. W. Porter (Eds.), *Handbook of organizational communication: An interdisciplinary perspective* (pp. 421-443). Newbury Park, CA: Sage.

Cummings, J. (2004). Work groups, structural diversity, and knowledge sharing in a global organization. *Management Science, 50*(3), 352-364.

Cummings, J. L., & Teng, B.S. (2003). Transferring R&D knowledge: The key factors affecting knowledge transfer success. *Journal of Engineering and Technology Management, 20*(1) 39-68.

Cummings, J. N., Butler, B., et al. (2002). The quality of online social relationships. *Communications of the ACM, 45*(7), 103-108.

Cummings, M. (2005). *The need for command and control instant message adaptive interfaces: Lessons learned from tactical Tomahawk human-in-the-loop simulations.* Cambridge, MA: Massachusetts Institute of Technology, Humans and Automation Laboratory.

Cyert, R. M., & March, J. G. (1963). *A behavioral theory of the firm.* Englewood cliffs, NJ: Prentice-Hall.

Dabbish, L., & Kraut, R. (2004). Controlling interruptions: Awareness displays and social motivation for coordination. In *Proceedings of ACM Conference on Computer Supported Cooperative Work* (pp. 182-191). ACM Press.

Daconta, M. C., Obrst, L. J., & Smith, K. T. (2003). *The semantic Web: A guide to the future of XML, Web services, and knowledge management.* Indianapolis, IN: John Wiley & Sons Inc.

Daft, J. E., Lengel, R. H., et al. (1987). Message equivocality, media selection, and manager performance: Implication for information systems. *MIS Quarterly, 11,* 354-366.

Daft, R. L. & Lengel, R. H. (1984). Information richness: A new approach to managerial behaviour and organizational design. *Research in Organizational Behaviour, 6,* 191-233.

Daft, R. L., & Lengel R. H. (1986). Organizational information requirements, media richness and structural design. *Management Science, 32*(5), 355-366.

Dahlin, K., Weingart, L., & Hinds, P. (2005). Team diversity and information use. *Academy of Management Journal, 48*(6), 1107-1123.

Dahrendorf, R. (1958). *Homo sociologicus.* Opladen, Germany: Westdeutscher Verlag.

Dalkir, K., & Wiseman, E. (2006). Knowledge elicitation, organization and dissemination in a knowledge network: The role of knowledge brokers. In V. Guerrero-Bote (Ed.), *Current research in information sciences and technologies.*

Dalmaris, P., Tsui, E., Hall, B., & Smith, B. (2007). A framework for the improvement of knowledge-intensive business processes. *Business Process Management Journal, 13*(2), 279-305.

Darr, E., Argote, L., & Epple, D. (1995). The acquisition, transfer, and depreciation of knowledge in service organizations: Productivity in franchises. *Management Science, 41*(11), 1750-1762.

Davenport, T. H. (2005). *Thinking for a living. How to get better performance and results from knowledge workers.* Boston: Harvard Business School Press.

Davenport, T. H., & Prusak, L. (1997). *Working knowledge.* Boston, MA: Harvard Business School Press.

Davenport, T. H., & Prusak, L. (1998). *Working knowledge: How organizations manage what they know.* Boston: Harvard Business School Press.

Davenport, T. H., Harris, J. G., De Long, D. W., & Jacobson, A. L. (2001). Data to knowledge to results: Building an analytic capability. *California Management Review, 43*(2), 117-138.

Davenport, T., & Glaser, J. (2002). Just-in-time delivery comes to Knowledge Management. *Harvard Business Review, 80*(7), 107-111.

Davenport, T., & Prusak, L. (1998). *Working knowledge: How organizations manage what they know.* Boston: Harvard Business School Press.

Davenport, T., & Prusak, L. (2000). *Working knowledge: How organizations manage what they know*. Boston, MA: Harvard Business School Press.

Davidow, W. H., & Malone M. S. (1992). *The virtual corporation*. New York: Harper Business.

Davis, J. G., Subrahmanian, E., & Westerberg, W. (2005). The "global" and the "local" in knowledge management. *Journal of Knowledge Management*, (1), 101-112.

Davis, R., Shrobe, H., & Szolovits, P. (1993). What is a KR? *AI Magazine, 14(1)*, 17-33.

De Groote, S. & Dorsch, J. (2003). Measuring use patterns of online journals and databases. *Journal of Medical Library Association. 91*(2), 231-241.

De Long, D. W., & Fahey, L. (2000). Diagnosing cultural barriers to knowledge management. *Academy of Management Executive, 14*(4), 113-127

De Sanctis, G., & Poole, M. (1994). Capturing the complexity in advanced technology in use: Adaptive structuration theory. *Organization Science*, 5(2), 121-47.

DeGenaro, B. (1996). Counterintelligence. In B. Gilad & J. Herring (Eds.), *The art and science of business intelligence*. Greenwich, CT: JAI Press.

Dekens. J. (2007). Local knowledge on disaster preparedness: A framework for data collection and analysis. *Sustainable mountain development, 52*, 20-23. Retrieved from http://www.disasterpreparedness.icimod.org/publications.php

Delery, J. E. (1998). Issues of fit in strategic human resource management: Implications for research. *Human Resource Management Review, 8*, 289–309.

Denison, D. R. (1996). What is the difference between organizational culture and organizational climate? A native's point of view on a decade of paradigm wars. *Academy of Management Review, 21*, 619-654.

Denning, P. J. (2006). Hastily formed networks. *Communications of the ACM, 49*(4), 15-20.

Denning, S. (2000). *The springboard: How storytelling ignites action in the knowledge-era organization*. Woburn, MA: Butterworth-Heinemann.

Dennis, A. (1996). Information exchange and use in group decision making: You can lead a group to information, but you can't make it think. *MIS Quarterly, 20*(4), 433-457.

Dennis, A., & Kinney, S. (1998). Testing media richness theory in the new media: The effects of cues, feedback and task equivocality. *Information Systems Research, 9*(3), 256-274.

DeSanctis, G., & Poole, M. S. (1994). Capturing the complexity in advanced technology use: Adaptive structuration theory. *Organization Science, 5*(2), 121-147.

Desouza, K. C. (2003). Knowledge management barriers: Why the technology imperative seldom works. *Business Horizons*, January-February, 25-29.

Desouza, K. C., & Awazu, Y. (2003). Constructing internal knowledge markets: Considerations from mini cases. *International Journal of Information Management, 23*, 345-353.

Deutsch, A. (1952). *The mentally ill in America* (2nd ed.). New York: Columbia University Press.

Dey, A. K., Salber, D.. & Abowd, G. D. (2001). A conceptual framework and a toolkit for supporting the rapid prototyping of context-aware applications. *Human-Computer Interaction (HCI) Journal, 16*(2-4), 97-166.

Dieng, R., & Hug, S. (1998). Comparison of personal ontologies represented through conceptual graphs. *Proceedings of the 13th European Conference on Artificial Intelligence*, 341-345.

DiMaggio, P. (1997). Culture and cognition. *Annual Review of Sociology, 23*, 263-287.

Ding, Y., & Foo, S. (2002). Ontology research and development. Part 1 - A review of Ontology Generation. *Journal of Information Science, Information Science, vol. 28, pp. 123-136, 2002.*

Dirks, T. K., & Ferrin, D. (2001). The role of trust in organizational settings. *Organization Science, 12*(4), 450-467.

Disterer, G. (2001). *Individual and social barriers to knowledge transfer*. Paper presented at the 34th Hawaii International Conference on System Sciences, Maui, Hawaii.

Dorfman, P. W., & Howell, J. P. (1988). Dimensions of national culture and effective leadership patterns: Hofstede revisited. *Advances in International Comparative Management, 3*, 127-50.

Dosi, G., Winter, S. G., & Teece, D. J. (1992). Towards a theory of corporate coherence. In G. Dosi, R. Giannetti, & P. A. Toninelli (Eds.), *Technology and enterprise in a historical perspective*. Oxford, UK: Clarendon Press

Dourish, P. (2001). Seeking a foundation for context-aware computing. *Human-Computer Interaction, 16*(2, 3, & 4), 229-241.

Dourish, P. (2003). Speech-gesture driven multimodal interfaces for crisis management. In *Proceedings of the IEEE 91* (pp. 1327-1354).

Dourish, P. (2004.) What we talk about when we talk about context. *Personal and Ubiquitous Computing, 8*(1), 19-30.

Doz, Y. L. (1988). Technology partnerships between larger and smaller firm: Some critical issues. In F. Contractor & P. Lorange (Eds), *Cooperative strategies in international business.* Lexington, MA.

Dragovic, B., & Crowcroft, J. (2004). Information exposure control through data manipulation for ubiquitous computing. In *Proceedings of the 2004 workshop on New security paradigms* (pp. 57-64).

Drucker, P. (1966). *The knowledge worker.* New York: Harper Collins.

Drucker, P. (1994). The age of social transformation. *The Atlantic Monthly, 274*(5), 53-80. Retrieved 02/03/2007, from http//www.providersedge.com/docs/leadership_articles/Age_of_Social_Transformation.pdf

Drucker, P. F. (1968). *The age of discontinuity guidelines to our changing society.* New York: Harper & Row.

Drucker, P. F. (1990). The emerging theory of manufacturing. *Harvard Business Review, 68*(3), 94-102.

Drucker, P. F. (1991). The new productivity challenge. *Harvard Business Review, 69*(November-December), 69-76.

Drucker, P. F. (1993). *Post-capitalist society.* New York: HarperBusiness.

Duan, Y., Xu, X., & Fu, Z. (2006). Understanding transnational knowledge transfer. In P. Feher (Ed.), *Proceedings of 7th European Conference of Knowledge Management (ECKM06)* (pp. 126-135), 4-5 Sept., Public Academic Conferences Ltd. Reading, UK.

Durfee, E. (1996). Planning in distributed artificial intelligence. In G. M. P. O'Hare & N. R. Jennings (Eds.), *Foundations of distributed artificial intelligence* (pp. 231–246). New York: Wiley.

Durfee, E. H., & Lesser, V. (1989). Negotiating task decomposition and allocation using partial global planning. In L. Gasser & M. Huhns M. (Eds.), *Distributed artificial*

intelligence, volume 2 (pp. 229–244). San Francisco, CA: Morgan Kaufmann.

Dushnitsky, G., & Lenox, M. (2005). When do incumbents learn from entrepreneurial ventures? Corporate venture capital and investing firm innovation rates. *Research Policy, 34*(5), 615-639.

Dutta, S. (2001). NCLIS policy recommendation on linking the information life cycle concept with digital libraries. *A comprehensive assessment of public information dissemination, 214.*

Dwight, S. S., Harris, M. A., Dolinski, K., Ball, C. A., Binkley, G., Christie, K. R., Fisk, D. G., Issel-Tarver, L., Schroeder, M., Sherlock, G., Sethuraman, A., Weng, S., Botstein, D., & Cherry, J. M. (2002). Saccharomyces Genome Database provides secondary gene annotation using the Gene Ontology. *Nucleic Acids Research 30(1),* 69-72.

Dyer, J. H., & Nobeoka, K. (2000). Creating and managing a high-performance knowledge-sharing network: The Toyota case. *Strategic Management Journal, 21,* 345-367

Dyer, J., & Singh, H. (1998). The relational view: cooperative strategy and sources of interorganizational competitive advantage. *Academy of Management Review, 23*(4), 660-79.

Earl, M. (2001). Knowledge management strategies: Toward a taxonomy. *Journal of Management Information Systems 18*(1), 215-233.

Easterby-Smith M., & Lyles M. A. (2003). Introduction watersheds of organizational learning and knowledge management. In M. Easterby-Smith, & M. A. Lyles (Eds.), *The blackwell handbook of organizational learning and knowledge management* (pp 1–15). Blackwell Publishing Ltd, Oxford.

Easterby-Smith, M, Snell, R., & Gherardi, S. (1998). Organizational learning: Diverging communities of practice? *Management Learning, 29*(3), 259-272.

Easterby-Smith, M., Burgoyne, J., & Araujo, L. (1999). *Organizational learning and the learning organization developments in theory and practice.* Gateshead: SAGE Publications Ltd.

Easton, G. (1992). Industrial networks. A review. In B. Axelsson & G. Easton, (Eds.), *Industrial networks, A new view of reality.* London: Routledge.

Eccles, J. S., & Wigfield, A. (2002). Motivational beliefs, values, and goals. *Annual Review of Psychology, 53*(1), 109-132.

Eccles, J. S., Adler, T. F., Futterman, R., Goff, S. B., Kaczala, C. M., Meece, J. L., et al. (1983). Expectancies, values, and academic behaviors. In J. T. Spence (Ed.), *Achievement and achievement motives* (pp.75-146). San Francisco, CA: W.H. Freeman.

Echeverri, M. (2006). *Factors affecting access to and use of scholarly scientific information: A model for health science graduate students in Colombia.* Unpublished doctoral dissertation, Tulane University, New Orleans, Louisiana

Economist. (2000). Inside the machine: A survey of e-management. *The Economist*, (November 11).

Edmondson, A. (2003). Speaking up in the operating room: How team leaders promote learning in interdisciplinary action teams. *Journal of Management Studies, 40*(6), 1419-1452.

Edvinsson, L. & Sullivan, P. (1996). Developing a model for managing intellectual capital. *European Management Journal, 14*(4), 356-364.

Edvinsson, L., & Malone, M. (1997). *Intellectual capital: Realizing your company's true value by finding its hidden brainpower.* New York: Harper Business.

Edvinsson, L., & Malone, M. S. (1997). *Intellectual capital: Realizing your company's true value by finding its hidden brainpower.* New York: Harper Business.

Eisenberg, M., & Johnson, D. (2002). Computer skills for information problem-solving: Learning and teaching technology in context. *Eric Digest* EDO-IR-2002-04. Retrieved September 10, 2007, from http://www.eric.ed.gov/ERICWebPortal/contentdelivery/servlet/ERICServlet?accno=ED465377

Eliot, T. S. (1934). *The rock.* MA: Harcourt, Braintree Book Rack.

Ellison, S., Simmerman, A. & Forelle, C. (2005). P&G's Gillette edge: The playbook honed at Wal-Mart. *Wall Street Journal*, (January 31), A1.

Elron, E., & Vigoda-Gadot. E. (2006). Influence and political processes in cyberspace: The case of global virtual teams. *International Journal of Cross Cultural Management, 6*(3), 295–317.

Empson, L. (2001). Fear of exploitation and fear of contamination: Impediments to knowledge transfer in mergers between professional service firms. *Human Relations, 54*(7), 839-862

Eovito, B. (2006). *The impact of synchronous text-based chat on military Command and Control.* Paper presented at the 11th International Command and Control Research and Technology Symposium, Cambridge, UK.

EPIC. (2001). *Online use & cost evaluation program: The use of electronic resources among undergraduate and graduate students.* Retrieved September 10, 2007, from http://www.epic.columbia.edu/eval/find03.html

Epple, D., Argote, L., & Devadas, R. (1991). Organizational learning curves: A method for investigating intraplant transfer of knowledge acquired through learning by doing. *Organization Science, 2*(1), 58-70.

Eppler, M., & Sukowski, O. (2000). Managing team knowledge: Core processes, tools and enabling factors. *European Management Journal, 18*(3), 334-341.

Eschenauer, L., & Gligor, V. (2002). A key-management scheme for distributed sensor networks. In *Proceedings of ACM Conference on Computer and Communication Security (CCS'02)*, Washington DC.

Fairclough, N. (1992). *Discourse and social change.* Cambridge: Polity Press.

Falkheimer, J., & Heide, M. (2006). Multicultural crisis communication: Towards a social constructionist perspective. *Journal of Contingencies and Crisis Management, 14*(4), 180-189.

Fang, T. (2003). A critique of Hofstede's Fifth National Culture Dimension. *International Journal of Cross Cultural Management, 3*(3), 347–368.

Faraj, S., & Johnson, S. L. (2005). Reciprocity or generalized exchange? Structuring of electronic knowledge networks. *Academy of Management Conference*, Honolulu, HI.

Faraj, S., & Xiao, Y. (2006). Coordination in fast-response organizations. *Management Science, 52*(8), 1155-1169.

Feigenbaum, E. A., & McCorduck, P. (1983). *The fifth generation: Artificial intelligence and Japan's computer challenge to the world.* MA: Addison-Wesley.

Feldman, M. S., & Pentland, B. T. (2003). Reconceptualizing organizational routines as a source of flexibility and change. *Administrative Science Quarterly, 48*(1), 94-113.

Fensel, D. (2001). *Ontologies: Silver bullet for knowledge management and electronic commerce.* Berlin: Springer-Verlag.

Fernie, S., Green, S. D., Weller, S. T., & Newcombe, R. (2003). Knowledge-sharing context confusion and controversy. *International Journal of Project Management, 21*, 177-187

Ferran-Urdaneta, C. (1999). Teams or communities? Organizational structures for knowledge management. In ACM SIGCPR (Ed.), *Conference on Computer Personnel Research* (pp. 128-134). New York, NY: ACM Press.

Fidel, R., & Green, M. (2004). The many faces of accessibility: Engineers' perception of information sources. *Information Processing and Management, 40*, 563-581.

Field, J. (2004). *Social capital.* London, UK; New York, NY: Routledge.

Filos, E. (2005). Virtuality and the future of organisations. In G. Putnik & M. M. Cunha (Eds.), *Virtual enterprise integration: Technological and organizational perspectives.* Hershey, PA: Idea Group Publishing.

FIRSTE. (2007). Retrieved January 18, 2007, from http://campus.umr.edu/firste/

Fishbein, M., & Ajzen, I. (1975). *Belief, attitude interaction and behavior: An introduction to theory and research.* Reading, MA: Addison-Wesley.

Flavian, C., & Guinaliu, M. (2005). The influence of virtual communities on distribution strategies in the Internet. *International Journal of Retail & Distribution Management, 33*(6), .405-425.

Fleisher, C. & Bensoussan, B. (2007). *Business and competitive analysis: Effective application of new and classic methods.* Upper Saddle River, NJ: FT Press.

Fletcher, S. (2001). *Competence-based assessment technique.* London: Kogan Page.

Flouris, G. (2006). *On belief change and ontology evolution.* PhD. Thesis. University of Crete.

Flouris, G., Plexousakis, D., & Antoniou, G. (2006). Evolving ontology evolution. In *Proceedings of the Current Trends in Theory and Practice of Computer Science Conference,* 14-29.

Foos, T., Schum, G., & Rothenberg, S. (2006). Tacit knowledge transfer and the knowledge disconnect. *Journal of Knowledge Management, 10*(1), 6-18.

Foray, D. (2004). *The economics of knowledge.* Boston: MIT Press.

Ford, D. P. (2003). Trust and knowledge management: The seeds of success. In C. W. Holsapple (Ed.), *Handbook on knowledge management* (Vol. 1, pp. 553-575). Berlin: Springer.

Foster, A. (2003). Scientists at the U. of California at San Francisco call for a boycott of 6 biology journals. *The Chronicle of Higher Education: Information Technology Section, 50*(10), Page A34. Retrieved September 10, 2007, from http://chronicle.com/weekly/v50/i10/10a03403.htm

Fox, G. (2004). *Virtual collaboration: Advantages and disadvantages in the planning and execution of operations in the information age,* Newport: Naval War College.

Franz, M., Freudenthaler, K., Kameny, M., & Schoen, S. (2002). The development of the Siemens Knowledge Community Support. In T. H. Davenport & G. J. B. Probst (Eds.), *Knowledge management case book* (pp. 147-159). Berlin: Wiley and Sons.

Fukuyama, F. (1995). *Trust. The social virtues and the creation of prosperity.* New York: The Free Press.

Fuld, L. (1995). *The new competitor intelligence.* New York: John Wiley & Sons.

Fulk, J., & DeSanctis, G. (1995). Electronic communication and changing organizational forms. *Organization Science, 6*(4), 337-349.

Fulk, J., Flanagin, A. J., et al. (1996). Connective and communal public goods in interactive communication systems. *Communication Theory, 6*(1), 60-87.

Gallaire, H., & Minker, J. (Eds) (1978). *Logic and databases.* New York: Plenum Press.

Garavelli, A. C., Gorgoglione, M., & Scozzi, B. (2002). Managing knowledge transfer by knowledge technologies. *Technovation, 22,* 269-279.

Gasser, L. (1991). Social conceptions of knowledge and action. *Artificial Intelligence, 47*(1–3), 107–138.

Gaved, M., & Mulholland, P. (2005). *Grassroots initiated networked communities: A study of hybrid physical/virtual communities.* Paper presented at the 38th Hawaii Conference on System Sciences, Big Island, Hawaii.

Georgiadou, E. (2001). *Software measurement for process and product improvement - controlled experiments and derivation of reengineering metrics.* School of Informatics and Multimedia Technology, Faculty of Science Computing and Engineering, University of North London, Transfer Report from Mphil to PhD.

Ghauri, P. N., & Prasad, B. (1995). A network approach to probing Asia's interfirm linkages. Advances, *International Comparative Management, 10,* 63-77.

Gherardi, S., Nicolini D., & Odella, F. (1998). Towards a social understanding of how people learn in the organization. *Management learning, 29*(3), 273-297.

Giddens, A. (1984). *The constitution of society.* Cambridge: Polity Press.

Giddens, A. (1984). *The constitution of society: Outline of the theory of structure.* Berkeley, CA: University of California Press.

Gilad, B. (1994). *Business blindspots.* Chicago: Probus Publishing.

Gillespie, D., & Colignon, R. (1993). Structural change in disaster preparedness networks. International *Journal of Mass Emergencies and Disasters, 11*(2), 143–62.

Gittell, J., & Weiss, L. (2004). Coordination networks within and across organizations: A multilevel framework. *Journal of Management Studies, 41*(1), 127-153.

Goh, S. C. (2002). Managing effective knowledge transfer: An integrative framework and some practice implications. *Journal of Knowledge Management, 6*(6), 23-30.

Gold, A. H., Malhotra A., & Segars A. H. (2001). Knowledge management: An organisational capabilities perspective. *Journal of Management Information Systems, 18*(1), 185-214.

Goldstein, E. (1985). *The use of technical information by engineers of the electrical sector in Mexico.* University of California, Los Angeles, UMI Doctoral Dissertation.

Goodenough, W. (1957). Componential analysis and the study of meaning. *Language, 32*, 195–216.

Gourlay, S. N. (2006). Towards conceptual clarity concerning "tacit knowledge": A review of empirical studies. *Knowledge Management Research and Practice, 4*(1), 60-69.

Graham, J. (2003). The search engine that could. *USA TODAY*, August 26, 2003.

Granovetter, M. S (1983).The strength of weak ties: A network theory revisited. *Sociological Theory,* (1), 201-233.

Granovetter, M. S. (1973). The strength of weak ties. *American Journal of Sociology, 78*(6), 1360-1380.

Grant, K. A. (2007). Tacit knowledge revisited – We can still learn from Polanyi. *The Electronic Journal of Knowledge Management, 5*(2), 173-180.

Grant, R. (1996). Prospering in dynamically competitive environments: Organizational capability as knowledge integration. *Organization Science, 7*(4), 375-387.

Grant, R. (1996). Toward a knowledge-based theory of the firm. *Strategic Management Journal, 17*(*Winter Special Issue*), 109-122.

Grant, R. M. (1991). The resource-based theory of competitive advantage. *California Management Review, 33*(3), 114–135.

Grant, R. M. (1996). Prospering in dynamically-competitive environments: Organizational capability as knowledge integration. *Organization Science, 7*(4), 375-387.

Grewal, R., Lilien, G. L., et al. (2006). Location, location, location: How network embeddedness affects project success in open source systems. *Management Science, 52*(7), 1043-1056.

Griesinger, D. (1990). The human side of economic organization. *Academy of Management Review, 15*(3), 478-499.

Griffith, D. A., & Harvey, M. G. (2001). Executive insights: An intercultural communication model for use in global interorganizational networks. *Journal of International Marketing, 9*(3), 87-103.

Grossman, M. (2006). An overview of knowledge management assessment approaches. *The Journal of American Academy of Business, 8*(2), 242-247.

Gruber, T. R. (1993). A translation approach to portable ontologies. *Knowledge Acquisition 5*(2), 199-220.

Gupta, A. K., & Govindarajan, V. (2000). Knowledge management social dimension lessons from Nucor steel. *Sloan Management Review,* 71-80.

Gupta, A., & Govindarajan, V. (2000). Knowledge flows within multinational corporations. *Strategic Management Journal, 21*(4), 473-496.

Gurteen, D. (1999). Creating a knowledge sharing culture. *Knowledge Management Magazine, 2*(5). Retrieved from http://www.gurteen.com/gurteen/gurteen.nsf/0/FD35AF9 606901C42802567C70068CBF5/

Gusfield, J. (1975). *The community: A critical response.* New York: Harper Colophon.

Haas, M., & Hansen, M. (2005). When using knowledge can hurt performance: The value of organizational capabilities in a management consulting company. *Strategic Management Journal, 26*(1), 1-24.

Haase, P., Ehrig, M., Hotho, A., & Schnizler, B. (2004). Personalized information access in a bibliographic peer-to-peer system. *Proceedings of the AAAI Workshop on Semantic Web Personalization,* 1-12.

Haase, P., Hotho, A., Schmidt-Thieme, L., & Sure, Y. (2005). Collaborative and usage-driven evolution of personal ontologies. *Proceedings of the European Semantic Web Conference*, 486-499.

Hackman, J. (1987). The design of work teams. In J. Lorsh (Ed.), *Handbook of organizational behavior* (pp. 315-342). Englewood Cliffs, NJ: Prentice Hall.

Hackman, R. (Ed.). (1990). *Groups that work and those that don't: Creating conditions for effective teamwork*. San Francisco: Jossey-Bass.

Haertwig, J., & Boehm, K. (2005). A process framework for an interoperable semantic enterprise environment. In *Proceedings of the 6th European Conference on Knowledge Management*, 227-236.

Hagel, J., & Armstrong, A. (1997). *Net gain: Expanding markets through virtual communities*. Boston, MA: Harvard Business School Press.

Häkanson, L. (2007). Creating knowledge: The power and logic of articulation. *Industrial and Corporate Change, 16*(1), 51-88.

Hakansson, H. (1989). *Corporate technological behaviour: Cooperation and networks.* London: Routledge.

Hall, H. (2001). *Social exchange for knowledge exchange.* Paper presented at Managing knowledge: Conversations and critiques, University of Leicester Management Center, 10-11 April 2001.

Halliday, M. A. K. (1994). *An introduction to functional grammar.* New York: Arnold.

Hambrick, D., Davison, S., Snell, S., & Snow, C. (1998). When groups consist of multiple nationalities: Toward a new understanding of implications. *Organisation Studies, 12*(2), 181-205.

Hambrick, D., Davison, S., Snell, S., & Snow, C. (1998). When groups consist of multiple nationalities: Towards a new understanding of implications. *Organization Studies, 19*(2), 181-205.

Hamilton, G., & Biggart, N. W. (1985). Why people obey: Theoretical observations of power and obedience in complex organizations. *Sociological Perspectives, 28*(1), 3-28.

Handy, C. (2000). Trust and the virtual organisation (HBR OnPoint Enhanced Edition). *HBR On Point*, June 2000

Handzic, M., & Lagumdzija, A. (2006). Motivational influences on knowledge sharing. In P. Feher (Ed.), Proceedings

of *7th European Conference of Knowledge Management (ECKM06)* (pp. 208 – 212), 4-5 Sept., Public Academic Conferences Ltd. Reading, UK.

Hansen, M. (1999). The search-transfer problem: The role of weak ties in sharing knowledge across organization subunits. *Administrative Science Quarterly, 44*(1), 82-111.

Hansen, M. (2002). Knowledge networks: Explaining effective knowledge sharing in multiunit companies, *Organization Science, 13*(3), 232-248.

Hansen, M. T., Nohria, N., & Tierney, T. (1999). What's your strategy for managing knowledge? *Harvard Business Review, 77*(2), 106-116.

Hansen, M., Mors, M., & Lovas, B. (2005). Knowledge sharing in organizations: Multiple networks, multiple phases. *Academy of Management Journal, 48*(5), 776-793.

Hansen, M., Nohria, N., & Tierney, T. (1999). What's your strategy for managing knowledge? *Harvard Business Review, 77*(2), 106-116.

Hansen, T. M. (2002). Knowledge networks: Explaining effective knowledge sharing in multiunit companies. *Organization Science, 13*(3). 232-248.

Hardin, R. (1996). Trustworthiness. *Ethics, 107(*1), 26-42.

Hardy, C., Philips, N., & Lawrence, T. (2003). Resources, knowledge and influence: The organizational effectiveness of interorganizational collaboration. *Journal of Management Studies, 40*(2), 321-347.

Harorimana, D. (2006), Knowledge networks: A mechanism of creation and transfer of knowledge in organisations? In P. Feher (Ed.), *European conference of knowledge management* (pp. 213-222). ACI.

Harorimana, D. (2006). Knowledge networks: A mechanism of creation and transfer of knowledge in organisations? In P. Feher (Ed.), *Proceedings of 7th European Conference of Knowledge Management (ECKM06)* (pp. 211-222), 4-5 Sept., Public Academic Conferences Ltd. Reading, UK.

Harris, P. R., & Morgan, R. T. (1991). *Managing cultural differences*, (3rd ed.). Houston, TX: Gulf Publishing Company.

Hatch, M. J. (1993). The dynamics of organisational culture. *Academy of Management Review, 18*(4), 657–693.

Hayes, P., & Menzel, C. (2001). A semantics for the knowledge interchange format. In *Proceedings of IJCAI 2001 Workshop on the IEEE Standard Upper Ontology.*

Hedlund, G., & Nonaka, I. (1993). Models of knowledge management in the West and Japan. In P. Lorange (Ed.), *Implementing strategic processes: Change, learning and cooperation.* Oxford: Basil Blackwell.

Hendriks, P. (1999). Why share knowledge? The influence of ICT on the motivation for knowledge sharing. *Knowledge and Process Management, 6*(2), 91-100.

Hendriks, P. H. J., & Vriens, D. J. (1999). Knowledge-based systems and knowledge management: Friends or foes? *Information & Management, 35*, 113-125.

Herbig, B., & Büssing, A.(2003). Comparison of the role of explicit and implicit knowledge in working. *Psychology Science, 45*(3), 165–188.

Herbig, B., Büssing, A., & Ewert, T. (2001). The role of tacit knowledge in the work context of nursing. *Journal of Advanced Nursing, 34*(5), 687–695.

Herder, P. M., Veeneman, W. W., Buitenhuis, M. D. J., & Schaller, A. (2003). Follow the rainbow: A knowledge management framework for new product introduction. *Journal of Knowledge Management, 7*(3), 105-115.

Herring, S. (1996). *Computer-mediated communication: Linguistic, social and cross-cultural perspectives.* Amsterdam, The Netherlands: Benjamins.

Herrmann, T., Jahnke, I., & Loser, K. U. (2004). The role concept as a basis for designing community systems. In F. Darses, R. Dieng, C. Simone, & M. Zackland (Eds.), *Cooperative systems design. Scenario-based design of collaborative systems* (pp. 163-178). Amsterdam: IOS Press.

Herschel, R. T., Nemati, H., & Steiger, D. (2001). Tacit to explicit knowledge conversion: Knowledge exchange protocols. *Journal of Knowledge Management, 5*(1), 107-116.

Herzberg, F. (1964). The Motivation-Hygiene Concept and the problems of manpower. *Personnel Administration, 27*, 3-7.

Herzog, A. J. (1981). The gatekeeper hypothesis and the international transfer of scientific knowledge .*The Journal of Technology Transfer, 6*(1).

Hesse, B., Sproull, L., et al. (1993). Returns to science: Computer networks in oceanography. *Communications of the ACM, 36*(8), 90-100.

Hewitt, C. (1986). Offices are open systems. *ACM Transactions of Office Automation Systems, 4*(3), 271–287.

Hildreth, P., & Kimble, C. (2004). *Knowledge networks innovation through communities of practice.* London, Hershey: Idea Group Inc.

Hiller, S. (2002). The impact of information technology and online library resources on research, teaching and library use at the University of Washington. *Performance Measurement and Metrics, 3(*2), 134-139.

Hindle, D. (1990). Noun classification from predicate-argument structures. *Meeting of the Association for Computational Linguistics,* 268-275.

Hislop, D. (2002). Mission impossible? Communicating and sharing knowledge via information technology. *Journal of Information Technology, 17,* 165-177.

Hof, R. D., & Browder, P. E. (1997). Internet communities-forget surfers. A new class of netizen is settling right. *Business Week,* 38–45.

Hofstede, G. (1994). *Cultures and organisations, intercultural cooperation and its importance for survival, software of the mind.* UK: McGraw-Hill.

Hofstede, G. (2001). *Culture's consequences: Comparing values, behaviours, institutions, and organisations.* Thousand Oaks, CA, London: Sage Publications.

Hofstede, G.. (2001). *Culture's consequences: Comparing values, behaviors, institutions and organizations across nations* (2nd ed.). Thousand Oaks, CA: Sage Publications.

Holden, N. (2001). Knowledge management: Raising the specter of the cross-cultural dimension. *Knowledge and Process Management, 8*(3), 155-63.

Holloway, W., & Jefferson, T. (2000). *Doing qualitative research differently free association, narrative and the interview method.* Wiltshire: Sage Publications Ltd.

Holsapple C. W., & Joshi K. D. (2004b). A formal knowledge management ontology: Conduct, activities, resources, and influences. *Journal of the American Society for Information Science and Technology, 55*(7), 593 – 612.

Holsapple, C. W. (2003a). Knowledge and its attributes. In C. W. Holsapple (Ed.), *Handbook of knowledge management* (pp. 165-188). Berlin: Springer-Verlag.

Holsapple, C. W. (2005). The inseparability of modern knowledge management and computer-based technology. *Journal of Knowledge Management, 9*(1), 42-52.

Holsapple, C. W. (Ed.). (2003). *Handbook of knowledge management.* Berlin: Springer-Verlag.

Holsapple, C. W., & Joshi, K. D. (2002). Knowledge management: A threefold framework. *The Information Society, 18,* 47-63.

Holsapple, C. W., & Joshi, K. D. (2006). Knowledge management ontology. In D. G. Schwartz (Ed.), *Encyclopedia of knowledge management* (pp. 397-402), Hershey, PA: Idea Group.

Holsapple, C. W., & Singh, M. (2001). The knowledge chain model: Activities for competitiveness. *Expert Systems with Applications, 20*(1), 77-98

Holsti, O. (1969). *Content analysis for the social sciences and humanities.* Reading, MA: Addison-Wesley.

Hong, J. I., & Landay, J. A. (2001). An infrastructure approach to context-aware computing. *Human-Computer Interaction, 16*(2, 3, & 4), 287-303.

Hong, J., Pöyhönen, A., & Kyläheiko, K. (2006). Cultural and communicative interaction and the development of dynamic capabilities. In P. Feher (Ed.), *European conference of knowledge management* (pp241-249). ACI.

Hooff, B., & de Ridder, J. A. (2004). Knowledge sharing in context: The influence of organizational commitment. Communication climate and CMC use on knowledge sharing. *Journal of Knowledge Management, 8*(6), 117-130.

Hoopes, D., & Postrel, S. (1999). Shared knowledge, "glitches," and product development performance. *Strategic Management Journal, 20*(9), 837-865.

Howells, J. L.(2002). Tacit knowledge, innovation and economic geography. *Urban Studies, 39*(56), 871-884.

Hsu, C. (2006). Privacy concerns, privacy practices and Web site categories: Toward a situational paradigm. *Online Information Review, 30*(5), 569-86.

Huber, G. P. (1991).Organizational learning: The contributing processes and the literature. *Organization Science, 2*(1), 88–115.

Huber, G., & Crisp, C. (2003). Organizations, information systems impact on. In. H. Bidgoli (Ed.), *Encyclopedia of information systems* (pp. 413-26). San Diego: Elsevier Science Publishers.

Hult, T., Ketchen, Jr. D., & Slater, S. (2004). Information processing, knowledge development, and strategic supply chain performance. *Academy of Management Journal, 47*(2), 241-253.

Hunt, J. W. (1981). Applying American behavioural science: Some cross-cultural problems. *Orgnisational Dynamics, 10*(1), 55-62.

Hutchings, K., & Michailova, S. (2004). Facilitating knowledge sharing in Russian and Chinese subsidiaries: The role of personal networks and group membership. *Journal of Knowledge Management, 8*(2), 84-94.

Hutchings, K., & Michailova, S. (2004). Facilitating knowledge sharing in Russian and Chinese subsidiaries: The role of personal networks and group membership. *Journal of Knowledge Management, 8*(2), 84-94.

Huysman, M., & de Wit, D. (2004). Practices of managing knowledge sharing: Towards a second wave of knowledge management. *Knowledge and Process Management, 11*(2), 81-92.

Huysman, M., & Wulf, V. (2006). IT to support the knowledge sharing in communities, towards a social capital analysis. *Journal of Information Technology, 21*, 40-51.

i2010 HLG. (2006). *The challenges of convergence.* Information Space Innovation & Investment in R&D Inclusion, i2010 High Level Group, 12.12.2006.

Iamnitchi, A., Ripeanu, M., & Foster, I. T. (2002). Locating data in (Small-World?) peer-to-peer scientific collaborations. In P. Druschel, M. F. Kaashoek, & A. I. Rowstron (Eds.), Revised Papers From the First international Workshop on Peer-To-Peer Systems. *Lecture Notes in Computer Science 2429* (pp. 232-241). London: Springer-Verlag.

IDA. (2000). *A proposed framework on building trust and confidence in electronic commerce: A consultation paper,* (September 2000). Retrieved 17/09/07, from http://unpan1.un.org/intradoc/groups/public/documents/APCITY/UN-PAN004853.pdf

Ilett, D. (2006). Out damned data—the lingering dangers of a hard disk's memory. *Wall Street Journal,* (October 4), 6.

Illeris, K. (1999). *Læring - aktuell læringsteori i spennings-feltet mellom Piaget, Freud og Marx (Learning – Current Learning Theory between Piaget, Freus and Marx).* Gylling: Roskilde Universitetsforlag.

Inkeles, A., & Levinson, D. (1969). National character: The study of module personality and sociocultural systems. In G. Lindsay & E. Aronson (Eds.), *The handbook of social psychology, vol. 4.* Addison-Wesley.

Inkpen, A., & Dinur, A. (1998). Knowledge management processes and international joint ventures. *Organization Science, 9*(4), 454-468.

Interview with Peter Suber, publisher of SPARC Open Access Newsletter. *Library Journal Academic Newswire,* The Publishing Report, July 24, 2003.

Ipe, M. (2003). Knowledge sharing in organizations: A conceptual framework. *Human Resource Development Review, 2*(4), 337-359.

Ivefors, G. M. (1995). Emergency information management and disaster preparedness on the Internet. *IDA Fifth Annual Conference on Computer and Information Science,* Lingköping, Sweden, November 1995. Retrieved January 10, 2007, from http://hb.se/bhs/ith/2-97/gi.htm

Jain, S., & McLean, C. (2003). A framework for modeling and simulation for emergency response. In *Proceedings of the 2003 Winter Simulation Conference* (pp. 1068-1076).

Järvenpää, S. L., & Leidner, D. E. (1999). Communication and trust in global virtual teams. *Organization Science, 10,* 791 – 815.

Jarvenpaa, S., & Staples, S. (2001). Exploring perceptions of organizational ownership of information and expertise. *Journal of Management Information Systems, 18*(1), 151-183.

Jary, D., & Jary, J. (Eds.). (1991). *The Harper Collins directory of sociology.* New York: Harper Collins.

Jasanoff, S. (1994). *Learning from disaster: Risk management after Bhopal.* Philadelphia: University of Pennsylvania Press.

Javidan, M., Stahl, G., Brodbeck, F., & Wilderom, C. (2005). Cross-border transfer of knowledge: Cultural lessons from project GLOBE. *Academy of Management Executive, 19*(2), 59-76.

Jensen, M. B., Johnson, B., Lorenz, E., & Lundvall, B.A. (2007). Forms of knowledge and modes of innovation. *Research Policy.*

Johannessen, J. A., & Olaisen, B. (2001). Mismanagement of tacit knowledge the importance of tacit knowledge, the danger of information technology, and what to do about it. *International Journal of Information Management, 21,* 3–20.

Johanson, B., Karlson, & Stough. (2004). The emerging digital economy entrepreneurship. In *Clusters and olicy.* Berlin: Springer-Verlag.

Johanson, J., & Vahlen, J. E. (1977). The internationalization process of the firm - A model of knowledge development and increasing foreign market commitments. *Journal of International Business Studies, 8*(1), 23–32.

Johnson, B., Lorenz, E., & Lundvall, B. A. (2002). Why all this fuss about codified and tacit knowledge? *Industrial and Corporate Change, 11*(2), 245-262.

Johnson, C. M. (2001). *A survey of current research on online communities of practice. The Internet and Higher Education, 4,* 45-60.

Joia, L. A. (2000). Measuring intangible corporate assets: Linking business strategy with intellectual capital. *Journal of Intellectual Capital, 1*(1), pp. 68-84.

Jones, K. (1996). Trust as an affective attitude. *Ethics 107*(1), 4-25.

Jones, Q., Ravid, G., et al. (2004). Information overload and the message dynamics of online interaction spaces: A theoretical model and empirical exploration. *Information Systems Research, 15*(2), 194-210.

Jordan, B. (2006). The Katrina response that worked. *Homeland Defense Journal, 4,* 8-12.

Jørgensen, M. W., & Phillips, L. (1999). *Diskurs analyse som teori og metode. (Discourse analysis as theory and method).* Gylling: Roskilde Universitetsforlag.

Kafentzis, K., Mentzas, G., Apostolou, D., & Georgolios, P. (2004). Knowledge marketplaces: Strategic issues and business models. *Journal of Knowledge Management, 8*(1), 130-146.

Kaluta, R. W. (2006). Organizing community-level emergency response with interoperable communications. *Homeland Defense Journal, 4,* 20-22.

Kankanhalli, A., & Tan, B. C. Y. (2004). A review of metrics for knowledge management systems and knowledge management initiatives. In *37ᵗʰ Hawaii International Conference on Systems Sciences (HICSS)* (pp.238-245). Computer Society Press.

Kankanhalli, A., Tan, B. C. Y., & Wei, K-K. (2006). Knowledge producers and consumers. In D. G. Schwartz (Ed.), *Encyclopedia of Knowledge Management* (pp. 459-466). Hershey, PA: Idea Group.

Kanter, R. M. (1982). Dilemmas of managing participation. *Organizational Dynamics, 11*(1), 5-27.

Kanter, V. D. (1999). Knowledge management, practically speaking. *Information Systems Management, Fall,* 7-15.

Katz, R. (1982). The effects of group longevity on project communication and performance. *Administrative Science Quarterly, 27*(1), 81-104.

Katzy, B. R., & Ma, X. (2002). Virtual professional communities – definitions and typology. In K. Pawar, F. Weber, & K. Thoben (Ed.), *Proceedings of the The 8th Interna-*

tional Conference on Concurrent Enterprising, Rome, Italy (pp.311-318). Nottingham: Nottingham University Press.

Kautz, K., & Mahnke, V. (2003). Value creation through IT-supported KM? The utilisation of a KM system in a global consulting company. *Informing Science*, (6), 75-88.

Ke, H.-R. et al. (2002). Exploring behavior of e-journal users in science and technology: Transaction log analysis of Elsevier's Science Direct Onsite in Taiwan. *Library & Information Science Research*, 24(3), 265-291.

Keane, B. T., & Mason, R. M. (2006). *On the nature of knowledge. Rethinking popular assumptions.* Paper presented at the 39th Hawaii International Conference on System Sciences, Maui, Hawaii.

Kelloway, E. K., & Barling, J. (2000). Knowledge work as organizational behavior. *International Journal of Management Review*, 2(3), 287-304.

Kennedy, L., Cole, C., & Carter, S. (1999). The false focus in online searching: The particular case of undergraduates seeking information for course assignments in the humanities and social sciences. *Reference & User Services Quarterly*, 38(3), 267-273.

Keong, L. C, & Al-Hawamdeh, S. (2002). Factors impacting knowledge sharing. *Journal of Information & Knowledge Management*, 1(1), 49-56.

Kim, A. J. (2000). *Community building on the Web. Secret strategies for successful online communities.* Berkeley: Peachpit.

Kim, S-K, & Trimi, S. (2007). IT for KM in the management consulting industry. *Journal of Knowledge Management*, 11(3), 145-155.

King, W. R. (2006). Knowledge transfer. In D. G. Schwatz (Ed.), *Encyclopedia of knowledge management*. Hershey, PA: Idea Group.

King, W. R. (2006). Knowledge sharing. In D. G. Schwartz (Ed.), *Encyclopedia of Knowledge Management* (pp. 493-498). Hershey, PA: Idea Group.

King, W. R. (2006). Knowledge transfer. In D. G. Schwartz (Ed.), *Encyclopedia of Knowledge Management* (pp. 538-543). Hershey, PA: Idea Group.

Kingston, J. (2008). Multiperspective ontologies: Resolving common ontology development problems. *Expert Systems With Applications* 34(1), 541-550.

Kitamoto, A. (2005). Digital Typhoon: Near real-time aggregation, recombination and delivery of typhoon-re-lated information. *Proceedings of the 4th International Symposium on Digital Earth*, pp. (CD-ROM), 2005-03. Available: http://agora.ex.nii.ac.jp/~kitamoto/research/publications/kisde05.pdf

Klein, M., & Fensel, D. (2001). Ontology versioning for the Semantic Web. *Proceedings of the 1st International Semantic Web Working Symposium*, 75-91.

Klein, M., & Noy, N. (2003). *A component-based framework for ontology evolution.* Technical Report IR-504, Vrije Universiteit Amsterdam.

Klein, S. (1989). A transaction cost explanation of vertical control in international markets. *Journal of the Academy of Marketing Science*, 17(3), 253-260.

Klein, S., Frazier, G. L., & Roth V. J. (1990). A transaction cost analysis model of channel integration in international markets. *Journal of Marketing Research*, 27(2), 196-208.

Kluckhohn, F. (1951). Values and value-orientation in the theory of action: An exploration in definition and classification. In T. Parsons & E A. Shils (Eds.), *Towards a general theory of action.* Cambridge MA: Harvard University Press.

Kluckhohn, F., & Strodtbeck, F. (1961). *Variations on value orientations.* Evanstone, IL: Row, Peterson & Company.

Koch, M. (2002). Interoperable community platforms and identity management in the university domain. *The International Journal on Media Management*, 1, 21-30.

Kock, N. (2005). Media richness or media naturalness? The evolution of our biological communication apparatus and its influence on our behaviour toward e-communication tools. *IEEE Transactions on Professional Communications*, 48(2), 117-130.

Kogut, B. & Zander, U. (1992). Knowledge of the firm, combinative capabilities, and the replication of technology. *Organization Science*, 3(3), 383-397.

Kogut, B., & Zander, U. (1993). Knowledge of the firm and the evolutionary theory of the multinational corporation. *Journal of International Business Studies*, 24(4), 62-645.

Kollock, P. (1999). The economies of online cooperation: Gifts, and public goods in cyberspace. In M. A. Smith and P. Kollock (Eds.), *Communities in cyberspace* (pp. 220-239). New York: Routledge.

Kollock, P., & Smith, M. A. (1996). Managing the virtual commons: Cooperation and conflict in computer communities. In S. Herring (Ed.), *Computer-mediated communica-*

tion: Linguistic, social and cross cultural perspectives (pp. 109-128). Amsterdam: John Benjamins.

Korzybski, A. (1993). Science and sanity - An introduction to non-aristotelean systems and general semantics. *Institute of General Semantics*, Lakeville, USA.

Kothandaraman P. & Wilson D. T. (2001). The future of competition: Value creating networks. *Industrial Marketing Management, 30(4)*, 379-389.

KPMG Consulting. (2000). *Knowledge Management Research Report*. KPMG.

KPMG. (2003). Insights from KPMG's European Knowledge Management Survey 2002/2003. *KPMG Knowledge Advisory Service Amsterdam*. Retrieved March 10, 2007, from http://ep2010.salzburgresearch.at/knowledge_base/kpmg_2003.pdf

Krackhardt, D. (1990). Assessing the political landscape: Structure, cognition and power in organizations. *Administrative Science Quarterly, 35*, 342-369.

Krakow, G. (2005). *Ham radio operators to the rescue after Katrina*. Retrieved December 10, 2006, from http://www.msnbc.msn.com/id/9228945/

Kramer, R. M. (1999). Trust and distrust in organizations: Emerging perspectives, enduring questions. *Annual Review of Psychology, 50*, 569-598

Kraut, R. E., & Streeter, L. A. (1995). Coordination in software development. *Communications of the ACM, 38*(3), 69-81.

Kreger, H., & IBM Software Group. (2001). *Web services conceptual architecture (WSCA 1.0)*. Retrieved November 1, 2006, from http://www-306.ibm.com/software/solutions/webservices/pdf/WSCA.pdf

Kreijns, K., Kirschner, P., & Jochems, W. (2003). Identifying the pitfalls for social interaction in computer-supported collaborative learning environments: A review of the research. *Computers in Human Behaviour, 19*, 335-353.

Kroeger, A., & Kluckhohn, F. (1952). *Culture: A critical review of concepts and definitions*. Cambridge: Harvard Business Review.

Kuhlthau, C. (1991). Inside the search process: Information seeking from the user's perspective. *Journal of the American Society for Information Science, 42*(5), 361-371.

Kuhlthau, C. (1993). *Seeking meaning: A process approach to library and information services*. Norwood, NJ: Ablex

Pub. Corp. Kyrillidou, *M., & Young, M. (2003)*. ARL Statistics 2001-02. *Association of Research Libraries –ARL, Washington, D.C.*

Kumar. K., & van Dissel, H. (1996). Sustainable collaboration: Managing conflict and cooperation in interorganizational systems. *MIS Quarterly, 22*(2), 199-226.

Kyrillidou, *M., & Young, M. (2004)*. ARL Statistics 2002-03. *Association of Research Libraries –ARL, Washington, D.C.*

Lakhani, K., & von Hippel, E. (2000, May). How open source software works: Free user-to-user assistance. *The 3rd Intangibles Conference*. Knowledge: Management, Measurement and Organization, Stern School of Business, NYU.

Lakhani, K., & von Hippel, E. (2003). How open source software works: Free user-to-user assistance. *Research Policy, 32*(6), 923-943.

Larsen, V. (1997). *Exploring user behavior utilizing statistical analysis of WWW HTTPD access logs:Aan enquiry employing Net-Frog*. Doctoral Dissertation, University of Virginia.

Lave, J., & Wenger, E. (1991). *Situated learning. Legitimate peripheral participation,* Cambridge: University of Cambridge Press.

Lawler, E. E. III (2000). *Rewarding excellence*. San Francisco, CA: Jossey-Bass.

Lawton, G. (2001). Knowledge management: ready for prime time? *IEEE Computer, 3*(2), 12-14.

LeBaron, J., Pulkkinen, J., & Scollin, P. (2000). Promoting cross-border communication in an international Web-based graduate course. *Electronic Journal of Computer Enhanced Learning, 2*(2). Retrieved February 6, 2001, from http://imej.wfu.edu/articles/2000/2/01/index.asp

Leckie, G. J., Pettigrew, K. E., & Sylvain, C., (1996). Modeling the information seeking of professionals: A general model derived from research on engineers, health care professionals, and lawyers. *Library Quarterly, 66*(2), 161–193.

Leimeister, J., Ebner, W., & Krcmar, H. (2005). Design, implementation and evaluation of trust supporting components in virtual communities for patients. *Journal of Management Information Systems, 21*(4), 101-135.

Leland, E. (2001). *Voice over IP: Is your telephone system outdated?* Retrieved January 12, 2007, from http://www.techsoup.org/learningcenter/internet/page5256.cfm

Lenat, D., & Guha, R. V. (1989). *Building large knowledge-Based systems: Representation and inference in the Cyc Project.* Addison-Wesley.

Leonard, D. & Sensiper, S. (1998). The role of tacit knowledge in group innovation. *California Management Review 40(3)*, 112-132.

Lesser, E., & Prusak, L. (1999). Communities of practice, social capital and organizational knowledge. In E. Lesser, M. Fontaine, & J. Slusher (Eds), *Knowledge and communities.* Woburn, MA: Butterworth-Heinemann.

Lesser, E., & Prusak, L. (1999). Communities of practice, Social capital and organizational knowledge. *Information Systems Review, 1*(1), 3-9.

Levin, D., & Cross, R. (2004). The strength of weak ties you can trust: The mediating role of trust in effective knowledge transfer. *Management Science, 50*(11), 1477-1490.

Levitz, J. (2006). Ameriprise, Massachusetts settle over company's loss of laptop. *Wall Street Journal,* (December 12), B2.

Leymann, F. (2001). Web services flow language (WSFL 1.0). *IBM Software Group.* Retrieved April 10, 2007, from http://xmlcoverpages.org/WSFL-Guide-200110.pdf

Li, M., Cabral, R., Doumeingts, G., & Popplewell K. (2006). *Enterprise interoperability – Research roadmap (Final Version).* Retrieved November 11, 2006, from http://cordis.europa.eu/ist/ict-ent-net/ei-roadmap_en.htm

Liang, T.-P., & Huang, J.-S. (1998). An empirical study on consumer acceptance of products in electronic markets: A transaction cost model. *Decision Support System, 24,* 29-43.

Lichtenthaler, U. (2005). External commercialization of knowledge: Review and research agenda. *International Journal of Management Reviews, 7*(4), 231-255.

Liebeskind, J. P. (1996). Knowledge, strategy, and the theory of the firm. *Strategic Management Journal, 17*(Winter), 93-107.

Liebowitz, J., & Suen, C. Y. (2000). Developing knowledge management metrics for measuring intellectual capital. *Journal of Intellectual Capital, 1*(1), 54-67.

Light, M., Bell, M., & Halpern, M. (2001). *What is collaboration? Virtual team success factors.* Gartner Research Note COM-14-4302. Gartner, Inc.

Lindkvist, L. (2005). Knowledge communities and knowledge collectivities: A typology of knowledge work in groups. *Journal of Management Studies, 42*(6), 1189-1210.

Lindquist, R., & Ortiz, D. (2001). 9/11/01: This is Not a Test. *QST, 11,* 28-34, 59.

Lindsey, K. L. (2006). Knowledge sharing barriers. In D. G. Schwartz (Ed.), *Encyclopedia of Knowledge Management* (pp. 499-506). Hershey, PA: Idea Group.

Lindvall, M., Rus, I., & Suman Sinha S. (2003). Software systems support for knowledge management. *Journal of Knowledge Management, 7*(5), 137-150.

Linton, (2003). OWL: A system for the automated sharing of expertise. In M. Ackerman., V. Pipek, & V. Wulf (Eds.), *Sharing expertise.* Cambridge MA: MIT-Press.

Lipnack, J., & Stamps, J. (1997). *Virtual teams: Reaching across space, time and organisations with technology.* New York: Wiley.

Lippman, S. A., & Rumelt, R. P. (1982). Uncertain imitability: An analysis of interfirm differences in efficiency under competition. *Bell Journal of Economics, 13*(2), 418-438.

Lissoni, F. (2001). Knowledge codification and the geography of innovation the case of Brescia mechanical cluster. *Research Policy, 30,* 1479-1500.

Litwin, G., & Stringer, R. (1968). *Motivation and organizational climate.* Boston: HUP

Loebecke, C., Van Fenema, P. C., & Powell, P. (1999). Coopetition and knowledge transfer. *The DATABASE for Advances in Information Systems, 30*(2), 14-25.

Lopez, F. (1999) Overview of methodologies for building ontologies. *Proceedings of the International Joint Conference on Artificial Intelligence workshop on Ontologies and Problem-Solving Methods.*

Lopez, S. P., Peon, J. M. M., & Ordas, C. J. V. (2004). Managing knowledge: The link between culture and organisational learning. *Journal of Knowledge Management, 8*(6), 93-104.

Lu, L. Leung, K., & Koch, P. (2006). Managerial knowledge sharing: The role of individual, interpersonal and organizational factors. *Management and Organization Review, 2*(1), 15-41.

Lundvall, B-Å., & Foray, D.(1996). *The knowledge-based economy from the economics of knowledge to the learning economy: OECD Employment and Growth in the Knowledge- Based Economy.* Paris: OECD.

Lundvall, B-A., & Johnson, B. (1994). The learning economy. *Journal of Industry Studies, 1*(2), 23-42.

Mack, T. et al. (2004). Designing for experts: How scholars approach an academic library Web site. *Information Technology and Libraries* (ITAL), *23*(1).

Mackinnon, L. (2006). *Questioning the level of correspondence between structure in economic theory and the structure in real world economic systems*. University of Queensland, Australia. Retrieved June 10th, 2007, from http://eprint.uq.edu.au/archive/00004559/01/Structure_in_economic_systems.pdf

Maedche, A., & Staab, S. (2000). Semiautomatic engineering of ontologies from text. In *Proceedings of the Twelfth International Conference on Software Engineering and Knowledge Engineering.*

Mahoney, T. A. (1996). Journal publishing and organization science: An analysis of intelligence application Nstitrte. *Organization Science, 7*(4), 443-455.

Maier, R. (2002). *Knowldege management systems. Information and communication technologies for knowledge management.* Berlin: Springer Verlag.

Maier, R. (2002). *Knowledge management aystems. Information and Communication Technologies for knowledge management.* Berlin: Springer.

Maier, R. (2002). State-of-practice of knowledge management systems: Results of an empirical study. *Upgrade, 3*(1). Retrieved October 10, 2006, from http://www.upgrade-cepis.org

Majchrzak, A., Rice, R., Malhotra, A., King, N., & Ba, S. (2000). Technology adaptation: The case of a computer-supported inter-organizational virtual team. *MIS Quarterly, 24*(4), 569-600

Malhotra, Y. (2000). Knowledge management for e-business performance: Advancing information strategy to "Internet time." *Information Strategy: The Executive's Journal, 16*(4), 5-16.

Malhotra, Y. (2005). Integrating knowledge management technologies in organizational business processes: Getting real time enterprises to deliver real business performance. *Journal of Knowledge Management, 9*(1), 7-28.

Malipiero, A., Munari, F., & Sobrero, M..(2005*). Focal firms as technological gatekeepers within industrial districts: Knowledge creation and dissemination in the Italian packaging machinery industry*. DRUID Working Paper N°05-05.

Malone, T., Yates, J., & Benjamin, R. (1987). Electronic markets and electronic hierarchies. *Communication ACM, 6*, 485-497.

Malperio, F. (2005). *Local firms and technological gatekeepers within industrial districts knowledge creation and dissemination in real-estate industry.* DRUID Research paper 15 (5)55

Mansour-Cole, D. (2001). Team identity formation in virtual teams. In S. Beyerlein, M. Beyerlein, & D. Johnson (Eds.), *Virtual teams, Advances in interdisciplinary studies of work teams, vol. 8.* Oxford: Elsevier Science.

March, J. G. (1991). Exploration and exploitation in organizational learning. *Organization Science, 2*(1), 71-87.

Marchant G., & Robinson J. 1999. Is knowing the tax code all it takes to be a tax expert? On the development of legal expertise. In Sternberg RJ & Horvath JA (Eds.) *Tacit Knowledge in Professional Practice,*(pp. 3–20). Mahwah, NJ: Lawrence Erlbaum Associates.

Marchington, M. (2001). Employee involvement at work. In J. Storey (Ed.), *Human resource management, a critical text (2nd. ed).* Cornwall: Thomson Learning.

Marcum, D., & Gerald, G. (2003). Who uses what? Report on a National Survey of Information Users in Colleges and Universities. *D-Lib Magazine, 9*(10). Retrieved September 10, 2007, from http://www.dlib.org/dlib/october03/george/10george.html

Marcy, J. (2005). Communicating after Katrina. *Homeland Defense Journal, 11*, 10-11.

Markus, M. L. (2001). Toward a theory of knowledge reuse: Types of knowledge reuse situations and factors in reuse success. *Journal of Management Information Systems, 18*(1), 27-93.

Markus, M. L., & Connolly, T. (1990). Why CSCW applications fail: Problems in the adoption of interdependent work tools. In *Proceedings of the ACM conference on Computer-supported cooperative work* (pp. 371-380). Los Angeles: ACM Press.

Marsden, P. V. (1983). Restricted access in networks and models of power. *American Journal of Sociology, 88*(4), 686-717

Marshall, L. (1997). Facilitating knowledge management and knowledge sharing: New opportunities for information processionals. *Online, 21*(5), 92-98.

Mårtensson, M. (2000). A critical review of knowledge management as a management tool. *Journal of Knowledge Management, 4*(3), 204-216.

Marwick, A. (2001). Knowledge management technology. *IBM Systems Journal, 40*(4), 814-830.

Marwick, A. D. (2001). Knowledge management technology. *IBM systems journal, 40*(4), 814-900.

Masrick, V. J. (1994). Trends in managerial reinvention: creating a learning map. *Managerial Learning, 25*(1), 11-34.

Matson, E., Patiath, P., & Shavers, T. (2003). Stimulating knowledge sharing: Strengthening your organization's internal knowledge market. *Organizational Dynamics, 32*(3), 275-287.

Matson, E., Patiath, P., & Shavers, T. (2003). Strengthening your organization's internal knowledge market. *Organizational Dynamics, 32*(3), 275-285.

Max Lock Centre. (2000). *Communication for development: Comments from peer review*. London: Max Lock Centre, University of Westminster.

May, A., & Carter, C. (2001). A case study of virtual team working in the European automotive industry. *International Journal of Industrial Ergonomics, 27,* 171-86.

McAdam, R., Mason, B., & McCroy, J. (2007). Exploring the dichotomies within the tacit knowledge literature: Toward a process of tacit knowing in organisation. *Journal of Knowledge Management, 11*(2), 43-59.

McCarthy, J. (1968). Programs with common sense. In M. Minsky (Ed.) *Semantic information processing* (pp. 75-91). Cambridge MA: MIT Press.

McCulloch, W. S., & Pitts, W. (1943). A logical calculus of the ideas immanent in nervous activity. *Bulletin of Mathematical Biophysics 5*, 115-133.

McDermott, R. (1999). Why information technology inspired but cannot deliver knowledge management. *California Management Review, 41*(4), 103-117.

McDermott, R. (2000). Knowing in community: 10 critical success factors in building communities of practice. *IHRIM Journal*. Retrieved May 25, 2007, from http://www.co-i-l.com/coil/iknowledge

McGee, D. R., Cohen, P. R., & Wu, L. (2000). Something from nothing: Augmenting a paper-based work practice via multimodal interaction. In *Proceedings of the ACM Designing Augmented Reality Environments (DARE)* (pp. 71-80). New York: ACM Press.

McGrath, J. (1990). Time matters in groups. In, J. Galegher, R. E. Kraut, & C. Egido

McGrath, J. E., & Argote, L. (2001). Group processes in organizational contexts. In M. A. Hogg & R. S. Tindale (Eds), *Blackwell handbook of social psychology, vol. 3* (pp. 603–627). Group Processes. Oxford, UK: Blackwell,.

McGregor, J. (2006). I can't believe they took the whole team. *Business Week*, (December 18), 120-122.

McGregor, P., Craighill, R., & Mosley, V. (2006). Government Emergency Telecommunications Service (GETS) and Wireless Priority Service (WPS) performance during Katrina. In M. H. Hamza (Ed.), *Communications, Internet, and Information Technology*, St. Thomas, U.S. Virgin Islands.

McGregor, R. (1990). *Loom users manual*. Working Paper ISI/WP 22, University of Southern California.

McKinnel Jacobson, C. (2006). Knowledge sharing between individuals. In D. G. Schwartz (Ed.), *Encyclopedia of Knowledge Management* (pp. 507-504). Hershey, PA: Idea Group.

McQueen, M. P. (2006). Laptop lockdown. *Wall Street Journal*, (June 28), D1.

McVeigh, M., & Pringle, J. (2005). Open access to the medical literature: How much content is available in published journals? *Serials, 18*(1), 45-50.

Meissner, A., Luckenbach, T., Risse, T., Kirste, T., & Kirchner, H. (2002). In *Design Challenges for an Integrated Disaster management Communication and Information System, First IEEE Workshop on Disaster Recovery Networks*, New York.

Menon, A., & Varadarajan, P. R. (1992). A model of marketing knowledge use within firms. *Journal of Marketing, 56*(4), 53 – 71.

Mentzas, G., Apostolou, D., Abecker, A., & Young, R. (2003). *Knowledge asset management – Beyond the process-centred and product-centred approaches*. London: Spinger-Verlag.

Mentzas, G., Apostolou, D., Kafentzis, K., & Georgolios, P. (2006). Interorganizational networks for knowledge sharing and trading. *Information Technology Management, 7*, 259-276.

Meyer, J. P., & Allen, N. J. (1997). *Commitment in the workplace: Theory, research, and application*. Thousand Oaks, CA: Sage Publications.

Mika, P., Iosif, V., Sure, Y., & Akkermans, H. (2003). Ontology-based content management in a virtual organization.

In S. Staab & R. Studer (Eds.), *Handbook on ontologies* (pp. 455-476). Heidelberg: Springer.

Miles, R., & Snow, C. (1986). Organizations: New concepts for new forms. *California Management Review, 28*(2), 68-73.

Milgram, S. (1967). The small world problem. *Psychology Today*, 60-67.

Millar, J., Demaid, A., & Quintas, P. (1997). Trans-organizational innovation: A framework for research. *Technology Analysis & Strategic Management, 9*(4), 399-418.

Minsky, M. (1975). A framework for representing knowledge. In P. Winston (Ed.), *The psychology vision*. Mc-Graw-Hill.

Mischel, W. (1977). The interaction of person and situation. In D. Maggusson, & N. S. Endler (Eds.), *Personality at the crossroads: Current issues in interactional psychology*. Hillsdale, NJ: Earlbaum.

Moffett, S., McAdam, R., & Parkinson, S. (2003). An empirical analysis of knowledge management applications. *Journal of Knowledge Management, 7*(3), 6-26.

Molm, L. D., Takahashi, N., & Peterson, G. (2000). Risk and trust in social exchange: An experimental test of a classical proposition. *American Journal of Sociology, 105*, 1396-1426.

Mooradian, N. (2005). Tacit knowledge:Pphilosophic roots and role in KM. *Journal of Knowledge Management, 9*(6), 104-113.

Moran, T. P. & Dourish, P. (2001). Introduction to special issue on context-aware computing. *Human-Computer Interaction, 16*(2, 3, & 4), 87-95.

Morrison, A. (2004). *Gatekeepers of knowledge within industrial districts: Who they are, how they interact*. Milan: Centro di Ricerca Sui Processi di Innovazione e Internazionalizzazione, CESPRI.

Morrison, E. W. (2002). Newcomers' relationships: The role of social network ties during socialization. *Academy of Management Journal, 45*(6), 1149-1160.

Moser, P. K., & Nat, A. V. (1987). *Human knowledge*. Oxford: Oxford University Press.

Mossberger, K., Tolbert, C., & Stansbury, M. (2003). Virtual inequality: Beyond the digital divide. Washington, DC: Georgetown University Press.

Mühlbauer, S., & Versteegen, G. (2000). *Wissensmanagement. Empirische Untersuchung, beste Praktiken und Evaluierung von Werkzeugen*. Höhenkirchen: IT Research.

Muller, E., & Zenker, A. (2001). Business services as actors of knowledge transformation: The role of KIBS in regional and national innovation systems. *Research Policy, 30*, 1501-1516.

Müller, H. M., Kenny, E. E., & Sternberg, P. W. (2004). Textpresso: An ontology-based information retrieval and extraction system for biological literature. *PLoS Biology 2*(11).

Musen, M. (1992). Dimensions of knowledge sharing and reuse. *Computer and Biomedical Research, 25*(5), 435-467.

Myers, B. A. (1990). Taxonomies of visual programming and program visualization. *Journal of Visual Languages and Computing 1*(1), 97-123.

Nagel, R., & Dove, R. (1993). *21st century manufacturing enterprise strategy*. Bethlehem, PA: Iacocca Institute, Lehigh University.

Nahapiet, J., & Ghoshal, S. (1998). Social capital, intellectual capital, and the organizational advantage. *Academy of Management Review, 23*(2), 242-266.

Nahapiet, J., & Goshal, S. (1998). Social capital, intellectual capital and the organizational advantage. *Academy of Management Review, 23*(2), 242-266.

National Research Council. (2002). *Making the nation safer: The role of science and technology in countering terrorism*. Washington DC: National Academies Press.

National Science Foundation –NSF. (2002). *Science and engineering: Indicators 2002*, volume 1. Arlington, VA: NSF.

Neches, R., Fikes, R., Finin, T., Gruber, T., Patil, P., Senator, T., & Swartout, W. (1991). Enabling technology for knowledge sharing. *AI Magazine, 12*(3), 37-56.

Nelson, D. (2001). The uptake of electronic journals by academics in the UK, Their attitudes towards them and their potential impact on scholarly communication. *Information Services & Use, 21*(3/4), 205-214.

Nelson, K., & Cooprider, J. (1996). The contribution of shared knowledge to IS group performance. *MIS Quarterly, 20*(4), 409-432.

Nelson, R. R., & Winter, S. G. (1982). *An evolutionary theory of economic change*. Cambridge, MA: Harvard University Press.

Nelson, R., & Winter, S. (1982). *An evolutionary theory of economic change.* Cambridge, MA: Belknap Press.

Neumann, R. (1999). *Die Organisation als Ordnung des Wissens.* Habilitation-Thesis, University of Klagenfurt.

Newell, S., Bresnen, M., Edelman, L., Scarbrough, H., & Swan, J. (2006). Sharing Knowledge Across Projects. *Limits to ICT-led Project Review Practice. Management Learning, 37*(2), 67-185.

Newell, S., Scarbrough, F., & Swan, J. (2000). Intranets and knowledge management: De-centred technologies and the limits of technological discourse. In C. Prichard, R. Hull, M. Chumer, & H. Willmott (Eds.), *Managing knowledge: Critical investigations of work and learning* (pp. 88-106). London, UK: Macmillan Business.

Newell, S., Scarbrough, H., Swan, J., & Hislop, D. (1999). Intranets and knowledge management: Complex processes and ironic outcomes. In IEEE Computer Society (Ed.), *32nd Annual Hawaii International Conference on System Sciences: Vol. 1. HICSS-32* (pp.10-27). Los Alamitos, CA: IEEE Computer Society.

Newman, B. (2003). Agents, artifacts, and transformations: The foundations of knowledge flows. In C.W . Holsapple (Ed.), *Handbook of knowledge management* (pp. 301-317). Berlin: Springer-Verlag.

Newman, M. E. J. (2003). The structure and function of complex networks. *SIAM Review 45*(2), 167-256.

Ngonga Ngomo, A.-C., & Schumacher, F. (2006). Implicit knowledge sharing. In *Proceedings of the 7th European Conference on Knowledge Management* (pp. 736-747).

Nickerson, J. A., & Zenger, T. R. (2004). A knowledge-based theory of the firm – The problem-solving perspective. *Organization Science, 15*(6), 617-632.

Nilakanta, S., & Scamell, R. (1990). The effect of information sources and communication channels on the diffusion of innovation in a data base development environment. *Management Science, 36*(1), 24-40.

NIST. (2007). *Dictionary of algorithms and data structures.* Retrieved August 29, 2007 from http://www.nist.gov/dads/

Noguera, E. (2003). Usability of e-journals and preference for the virtual periodicals room: A survey of mathematics faculty and graduate students. *Electronic Journal of Academic and Special Librarianship, 4*(2-3).

Nohria, N., & Ghoshal, S. (1997). *The differentiated network: Organizing multinational corporations for value creation.* San Francisco: Jossey-Bass.

Nomura, T. (2002). Design of "Ba" for successful knowledge management – how engterprises should design the places of interaction to gain competitive advantage. *Journal of Network and Computer Applications, 25,* 263-78.

Nonaka, I. (1991). The knowledge-creating company. *Harvard Business Review, 69*(6), 96-104.

Nonaka, I. (1994). A dynamic theory of organizational knowledge creation. *Organization Science, 5*(1), 14-34.

Nonaka, I. (2005). *Knowledge management critical perspectives on business and management.* Routledge.

Nonaka, I., & Konno, N. (1998). The concept of Ba: Building a foundation for knowledge creation. *California Management Review, 40*(3), 40-54.

Nonaka, I., & Takeuchi, H. (1994). A dynamic theory of organizational knowledge creation. *Organization Science, 5*(1), 14-37.

Nonaka, I., & Takeuchi, H. (1995). *The knowledge creating company: How Japanese companies create the dynamics of innovation?* New York: Oxford University Press.

N

Nonaka, I., & Takeuchi, H. (1995). *The knowledge-creating company.* Oxford: Oxford University Press.

Nonaka, I., & Takeuchi, H. (1995). *The knowledge-creating company.* New York: Oxford University Press.

Nonaka, I., & Takeuchi, K. (1995). *The knowledge creating company: How Japanese companies create the dynamics of innovation.* Oxford: Oxford University Press.

Nonaka, I., von Krogh, G., & Voelpel, S. (2006). Organizational knowledge creation theory: Evolutionary paths and future advances. *Organization Studies, 27*(8), 1179-1208.

Nonanka, I. (1994). A dynamic theory of organizational knowledge creation. *Organization Science, 5*(1), 14-37.

Novi Park Web pages. (2006). Retrieved January 15, 2006, from http://www.novi.dk

O'Dell, C., & Grayson, C. J. (1998). If only we knew what we know: Identification and transfer of internal best practices. *California Management Review, 40*(3), 154-174.

O'Grady v. Superior Court (2006). 139 Cal. App. 4Th 1423.

O'Hare, G., & Jennings, N. (1996). *Foundations of distributed artificial intelligence.* New York: Wiley.

O'Reilly, C. (1978). The intentional distortion of information in organizational communication: A laboratory and field investigation. *Human Relations, 31*,173-193.

O'Reilly, C. A., & Chatman, J. A. (1996). Culture as social control: Corporations, cults and commitment. *Research in Organizational Behavior, 18,* 157-200.

O'Reilly, T. (2005): *What Is Web 2.0? Design patterns and business models for the next generation of software.* Retrieved June, 25th, 2007, from http://tim.oreilly.com/

OECD (1996). *The knowledge-based economy.* OECD: Paris. Retrieved from http://www.oecd.org/dataoecd/51/8/1913021.pdf

OECD. (2001). *Understanding the digital divide.* Organisation for Economic Co-operation and Development. Retrieved February 15, 2004 from http://www.oecd.org/dataoecd/38/57/1888451.pdf

Ojukwu, D., & Georgiadou, E.(2007). *Towards improving inter-organisational trust amongst SMEs – A case study from developing countries.* Paper presented at the 9th IFIP International Conference on the Social Implications of Computers in Developing Countries, May 2007, Sao Paolo, Brazil. Retrieved from http://www.ifipwg94.org.br/fullpapers/R0096-1.pdf

Okhuysen, G., & Eisenhardt, K. (2002). Integrating knowledge in groups: How formal interventions enable flexibility. *Organization Science, 13*(4), 370-386.

Olivera, F. (2000). Memory systems in organizations: An empirical investigation of mechanisms for knowledge collection, storage and access. *Journal of Management Studies, 37*(6), 811-832.

Olsen, F. (2006). *FAA: Knowledge sharing shouldn't be forced. Agency's use of online collaboration space has expanded to solve workgroup problems.* Retrieved May 25, 2007, from http://www.fcw.com

Omelayenko, B. (2001). Learning of ontologies from the Web: The analysis of existing approaches. In *Proceedings of the International Workshop on Web Dynamics.*

Onwuegbuzie, J. (1997). Writing a research proposal: The role of library anxiety, statistics anxiety, and composition anxiety. *Library & Information Science Research, 19*(1), 5-33.

Open Access to Scientific Research Editorial. (2003). *New York Times,* August 7, 2003, p. A27. Published on February 10, 2007 by the Society of Scholarly Publishing (SSP). Retrieved August 31, 2007, from http://www.sspnet.org/custom/news/details.cfm?id=141

Organ, D. W. (1988). *Organizational citizenship behavior: The good soldier syndrome.* Lexington, MA: Lexington Books.

Orlikowski, W. (1992). The duality of technology: Rethinking the concept of technology in organizations. *Organization Science, 3*(3), 398-427.

Orlikowski, W. (2000). Using technology and constituting structures: A practice lens for studying technology in organizations. *Organization Science, 11*(4), 404-428.

Orlikowski, W. J. (1996). Learning from notes: Organizational issues in groupware implementation. In R. Kling (Ed.), *Computerization and controversy* (pp. 173-189). New York: Academic Press.

Orlikowski, W. J., Yates, J., et al. (1995). Shaping electronic communication: The metastructuring of technology in the context of use. *Organization Science, 6*(4), 423-444.

Orlikowski, W., & Robey, D. (1991). Information technology and the structuring of organizations. *Information Systems Research, 2*(2), 143-169.

Orr, J. (1996). *Talking about machines: An ethnography of a modern job.* Ithaca, NY: ILR Press.

Oshri, I. (2006). Knowledge reuse. In D. G. Schwartz (Ed.), *Encyclopedia of knowledge management* (pp. 487-492). Hershey, PA: Idea Group.

OST. (2007). Knowledge transfer. In *British Library's strategy (2005 – 2008) glossary.* Retrieved 20/07/2008, from http://www.bl.uk/about/strategic/glossary.html

Ostrom, E. (2003). Toward a behavioral theory linking trust, reciprocity and reputation. In E. Ostrom & J. Walker (Eds.), *Trust and reciprocity: Interdisciplinary lessons from experimental research* (pp. 19-79). New York: Sage.

Oviatt, S. L. (1996). Multimodal interfaces for dynamic interactive maps. In *Proceedings of the Conference on Human Factors in Computing Systems (CHI'96)* (pp. 95-102). New York: ACM Press.

Pajares, F. (1996). Self-efficacy beliefs in academic settings. *Review of Educational Research, 66,* 543-578.

Palmer, J. (1991). Scientists and information: I. Using cluster analysis to identify information style. *Journal of Documentation, 47*(2), 105-129.

Pan, C. C., Mitra, P., & Liu, P. (2006). Semantic access control for information interoperation. In *Proceedings of the eleventh ACM symposium on Access control models and technologies* (pp. 237-246).

Pan, S. L., & Scarbrough, H. (1999). Knowledge management in practice: An exploratory case study. *Technology Analysis & Strategic Management, 11*(3), 359 - 374.

Pan, S., & Scarbrough, H. (1998). A sociotechnical view of knowledge-sharing at Buckman laboratories. *Journal of Knowledge Management, 2*(1) 55-66.

Pantel, P., & Lin, D. (2002). Document clustering with committees. In *Proceedings of the 25th Annual international ACM SIGIR Conference on Research and Development in information Retrieval* (pp. 199-206).

Panteli, N. *(2002).* Richness, power cues and e-mail text. *Information and Management, 40*, 75-86.

Papoutsakis, H. (2007). Sharing knowledge in the organisation: A retrospective analysis and empirical studies. *The Electronic Journal of Knowledge Management, 5*(2), 231-244.

Park, A., & Burrows, P. (2001). Dell, the conqueror. *Business Week*, (September 24), 92-102.

Park, H., Ribiere, V., & Schulte, W. D. (2004). Critical attributes of organisational culture that promote knowledge management technology implementation success. *Journal of Knowledge Management, 8*(3), 106-117.

Patel, V., Arocha, J., & Kaufman, D. (1999). *Expertise and tacit knowledge in medicine*. In R. J. Sternbern & J. A. Horvath (Eds.), *Tacit knowledge in professional practice*. Mahwah, NJ: Lawrence Erlbaum Associates.

Patil, S. R, Fikes, R., Patel-Schneider, P., McKay, D. P., Finin,T., Gruber,T., & Neches R.(1992). *The DARPA knowledge sharing effort: Progress report*. Washington DC: United States Department of Defense.

Peña, I. (2002). Knowledge networks as parts of an integrated knowledge management approach. *Journal of Knowledge Management, 6*(5), 469-478.

Pentland, B. T. (1995). Grammatical models of organizational processes. *Organization Science, 6*(5), 541-556.

Persson, O. (1981). Critical comments on the gatekeeper concept: Science and technology. *R& D Management, 11*(1), 37-40.

Petrie, C., & Bussler, C. (2003). Service agents and virtual enterprises: A survey. *IEEE Internet Computing, July-August.*

Pfeffer, J., & Sutton, R. (2000). *The knowing doing gap: How smart companies turn knowledge into action.* Boston, MA: Harvard Business School Press.

Pickering, J. M., & King, J. L. (1995). Hardwiring weak ties: Interorganizational computer-mediated communication, occupational communities, and organizational change. *Organization Science, 6,* 479-486.

Pickering, J., & King, J. (1995). Hardwiring weak ties: Interorganizational computer-mediated communications, occupational communities, and organizational change. *Organization Science, 6*(4), 479-486.

Pinch, S., Henry, J. M., & Tallman, S. (2003). From industrial districts to knowledge clusters: A model of knowledge dissemination and competitive advantage in industrial agglomerations. *Journal of Economic Geography, 31*, 665-682.

Pinch, S..,& Henry, N. (1999). Discursive aspects of technology innovation from knowledge sharing perspective. *Environmental planning,* 373-388

Pinelli, T. (1991). NASA/DoD Report Number 6: The relationship between the use of U.S. Government Technical Reports by U.S. Aerospace Engineers and Scientists and selected institutional and sociometric variables. *Aerospace Knowledge Diffusion Project*. NASA Technical Memorandum 102774, Department of Defense, Indiana University.

Pipek, V., Hinrichs, J., & Wulf, V. (2002). Sharing expertise: Challenges for technical support. In M. Ackerman, V. Pipek, & V. Wulf (Eds), *Beyond knowledge management: Sharing expertise*, Cambridge MA: MIT-Press.

Play2Train. (2007). Retrieved January 18, 2007 from http://irhbt.typepad.com/play2train/

Polanyi, M. (1958). *Personal knowledge. Towards a post-critical philosophy.* Chicago: University of Chicago Press.

Polanyi, M. (1962). *Personal knowledge: Towards a post-critical philosophy.* New York: Harper & Row.

Polanyi, M. (1966). *The tacit dimension.* London, UK: Routledge & Kegan Ltd.

Polanyi, M. (1966). *The tacit dimension.* New York: Doubleday & Company Inc.

Polanyi, M. (1967). *The tacit dimension,* Garden City, NY: Doubleday Anchor.

Polanyi, M. (1967). *The tacit dimension.* New York: Anchor Day Books.

Polanyi, M. (1967). *The tacit dimension.* London: Routledge and Kegan Paul.

Polanyi, M. (1969). *Knowing and being.* London: Routledge and Kegan Paul.

Polanyi, M. (1983). *The tacit dimension.* USA: Peter Smith.

Polanyi, M. (1996). *The tacit dimension.* Garden City, NY: Doubleday.

Ponis, S., Tatsiopoulos, I. & Vagenas, G. (2006). Ontology support for virtual organisations: A proposed framework for knowledge management. *The International Journal of Knowledge, Culture and Change Management, 6*(8), 89-100.

Ponis, S., Tatsiopoulos, I. P., Vagenas, G., & Koronis, E. (in press). A process-based knowledge management framework supported by ARIS Enterprise Modelling architecture. *International Journal of Applied Systemic Studies.*

Porter, M. (1990). *The competitive advantage of nations.* New York: Free Press.

Powell, W. W., Koput, K., et al. (1996). Interorganizational collaboration and the locus of innovation: Networks of learning in biotechnology. *Administrative Science Quarterly, 41,* 116-145.

Powers, V. (2004). Virtual communities at Caterpillar foster knowledge sharing. *Training & Development, 58*(6), 40-45.

Prahalad, C. K. & Hamel, G. (1990). The core competence of the corporation. *Harvard Business Review, 68*(3) 79-92.

Preece, J. (2000). *Online communities. Designing usability, supporting sociability.* Chichester: Wiley & Sons, Ltd.

Preece, J., Abras, C., & Maloney-Krichmar, D. (2004). Designing and evaluating online communities: Research speaks to emerging practice. *International Journal Web based Communities, 1*(1), 2-18.

Preece, S. E. (1981). *A spreading activation network model for information retrieval.* PhD thesis, Universtiy of Illinois at Urbana-Champaign.

Preiss, K., Goldman, S. L., & Nagel, R. N. (1996). *Cooperate to compete. Building agile business relationships.* New York: Van Nostrand Reinhold.

Pritchard, C. (2000). Know, learn and share! The knowledge phenomena and the construction of a consumptive-communicative body. In C. Pritchard, R. Hull, M. Chumer, & H. Willmott (Eds.), *Managing knowledge: Critical investigations of work and learning.* London: MacMillan Press.

Probst, G., Raub, S., & Romhard, K. (1997). *Wissen Managen.* Wiesbaden: Gabler Verlag.

Pulido, J. R., Ruiz, M. A., Herrera, R., Cabello, E., Legrand, S., & Elliman, D. (2006). Ontology languages for the semantic Web: A never completely updated review. *Knowledge-Based Systems 19*(7), 489-497.

Putnam, L L., Phillips, N., & Chapman, P. (1996). Metaphors of communication and organization. In R. Stewart, C. H. Clegg, & W. R. Noord (Eds.), *Handbook of organization studies* (pp. 375-408). London: Sage Publications Ltd.

Putnam, R. D. (1995). Bowling alone: America's declining social capital. *Journal of Democracy, 6*(1), 65-78.

Quarantelli, E. L (1997). Problematical aspects of the information/communication revolution for disaster planning and research: ten non-technical issues and questions. *Disaster Prevention and Management, 6*(2), 94–106.

Quintas, P., Lefrere, P., & Jones, G. (1997). Knowledge management: A strategic agenda. *Long Range Planning, 30*(3), 385-391.

Raban, R., & Garner, B. (2001). *Ontological engineering for conceptual modelling.* Paper presented at the 9th Austrian Conference on Artificial Intelligence, Vienna, Austria.

Rahm, E., & Bernstein, P. (2001). A survey of approaches to automatic schema matching. *VLDB Journal 10*(4), 334–350.

RAIPON & UNEP. (2006). *Indigenous knowledge in disaster management.* Retrieved January 18, 2007, from http://www.raipon.org/ikdm/Default.aspx

Rasmussen G. J., Dahl, P. N., Mølbjerg Jørgensen, K., Laursen, E., & Rasmussen, P. (2001). *Perspektiver på organisatorisk læring* (VCL-serien nr. 28, ISSN 1399-7300). Aalborg, Denmark: Aalborg University, Center for Organisatorisk Læring Videncenter for Læreprocesser.

Rauschert, I., Agrawal, P., Sharma, R., Fuhrmann, S., Brewer, I., & MacEachren, A. (2002). Designing a human-centered, multimodal GIS interface to support emergency management. In *Proceedings of the 10th ACM International Symposium on Advances in Geographic Information Systems (GIS '02)* (pp. 8-9). New York: ACM Press.

Raynor, J. O. (1982). Future orientation, self-evaluation, and achievement motivation: Use of an expectancy-value theory of personality functioning and change. In N. T. Feather (Ed.), *Expectation and actions: Expectancy-value models in psychology* (pp. 97-124). Hillsdale, NJ: Lawrence Erlbaum Associations, Inc.

Read, W. H. (1962). Upward communication in industrial hierarchies. *Human Relations, 15*(1), 3-15

Redding, S. G. (1994). Comparative management theory: Jungle, zoo or fossil bed? *Organisation Studies, 15*(3), 323-359.

Reed, R., & DeFillippi, R. J. (1990). Causal ambiguity, barriers to imitation, and sustainable competitive advantage. *Academy of Management Review, 15*(1), 88-102.

Rheingold, H. (1993). *The virtual community: Homesteading on the electronic frontier*. Reading, MA: Addison Wesley.

Ridings, C. M., Gefen, D., et al. (2002). Some antecedents and effects of trust in virtual communities. *Journal of Strategic Information Systems, 11,* 271-295.

Riege, A. (2005). Three-dozen knowledge-sharing barriers managers must consider. *Journal of Knowledge Management, 9*(3), 18-35.

Riege, A. (2005). Three-dozen knowledge-sharing barriers managers must consider. *Journal of Knowledge Management, 9*(3), 18-35.

Riege, A. (2007). Actions to overcome knowledge transfer barriers in MNCs. *Journal of Knowledge Management, 11*(1), 48-67.

Riessman, K. C. (1993). *Narrative analysis*. CA: Sage Publications.

Ripley, B. D. (1996). *Pattern recognition and neural networks*. Cambridge: Cambridge University Press.

Robert, L., & Dennis, A. (2005). Paradox of richness: A cognitive model of media choice. *IEEE Transactions on Professional Communication, 48*(1), 10-21.

Roberts, J. (2000). From know how to show how: Questioning the role of information and communication technology in knowledge transfer. *Technology Analysis & Strategic Management, 12*(4), 429-443.

Roberts, J. (2000). From know-how to show-how? Questioning the role of information and communication technologies in knowledge transfer. *Technology Analysis and Strategic Management, 12*(4), 429-493.

Robins, M. (2006). New IP telephony solutions for the government enterprise. *Homeland Defense Journal, 1,* 22-27.

Rodrigues, C. A., & Blumberg, H. (2000). Do feminine cultures really behave more feminine than masculine cultures? A comparison of 48 countries' femininity-masculinity ranking to their human development rankings. *Cross-Cultural Management - An International Journal, 7*(3), 25-34.

Rodriguez, H., Trainor, J., & Quarantelli, E. L. (2006). Rising to the challenges of a catastrophe: the emergent and prosocial behavior following Hurricane Katrina. *The Annals of the American Academy of Political and Social Science, 604*(1), 82-101.

Roger, E. M. (1995). *Diffusion of innovations* (4th ed.). New York, NY: Free Press.

Rohwedder, C. (2006). No. 1 retailer in Britain uses "clubcard" to thwart Wal-Mart. *Wall Street Journal,* (June 6), A1.

Rokeach, M. (1973). *The nature of human values,* New York: Free Press.

Roos, J., Roos, G., Dragonetti, N., & Edvinsson, L. (1997). *Intellectual capital: Navigating in the new business landscape*. London: MacMillan Business.

Rosen, E. (2007). Real-time collaboration gets real. *Network World*. January 23, 2007. Retrieved May 25, 2007, from http://www.techworld.com

Rothberg, H. N, & Erickson, G. S. (2002). Competitive capital: A fourth pillar of intellectual capital? In N. Bontis (Ed.), *World Congress on Intellectual Capital Readings* (pp.94-103). Woburn, MA: Butterworth-Heinemann,

Rothberg, H. N., & Erickson, G. S. (2005). *From knowledge to intelligence: Creating competitive advantage in the next economy*. Woburn, MA: Elsevier Butterworth-Heinemann.

Ruggles, R. (1998). The state of notion: Knowledge management in practices. *California Management Review, 40*(3), 80-89.

Rulke, D., Zaheer, S., & Anderson, M. (2000). Sources of managers' knowledge of organizational capabilities. *Organizational Behavior and Human Decision Processes, 82*(1), 134-149.

Sackmann, S. A., & Phillips, M. E. (2004). One's many cultures: A multiple cultures perspective. In N. A. Boyacigiller (Ed.), *Crossing cultures: Insights from master teachers*.

Sagasti, A. (2001). The knowledge explosion and the digital divide. United Nations Development Programme (UNDP), *Human Development Reports*, background papers. Retrieved September 10, 2007, from http://hdr.undp.org/docs/publications/background_papers/sagasti.doc

Saks, A. M., & Ashforth, B. E. (1997). Organizational socialization: Making sense of the past and pre sent as a prologue for the future. *Journal of Vocation al Behavior, 51*, 234-279.

Salancik, G. R., & Pfeffer J. (1977). Who gets power and how they hold on to it: A strategic contingency model of power. *Organizational Dynamics, 5*, 3-21.

Sanchez, R., Heene, A., & Thomas, H. (1996). Toward the theory and practice of competence-based competition. In R. Sanchez, A. Heene, & H. Thomas(Eds.), *Dynamics of competence-based competition: Theory and practice in the new strategic management* (pp. 1-36). London: Elsevier Science.

Sandhu, R., Ranganathan, K., & Zhang, X. (2006). Secure information sharing enabled by Trusted Computing and PEI models. In *Proceedings of the 2006 ACM Symposium on Information, computer and communications security* (pp. 2-12).

Sarker, S. (2005). Knowledge transfer and collaboration in distributed US-Thai teams. *Journal of Computer-Mediated Communication, 10*(4). Article 15. Retrieved May 25, 2007, from http://jcmc.indiana.edu/vol10/issue4/sarker.html

Scarbough, H., Swan, J., & Preston, J. (1999). *Knowledge management: A literature review*. London: Institute of Personnel and Development.

Scarbrough, H. (1999). Knowledge as work: Conflicts in the management of knowledge workers. *Technology Analysis and Strategic Management, 11*(1), 5-16.

Scarso, E., Bolisani, E., & Di Biagi, M. (2006). Knowledge intermediation. In D. G. Schwartz (Ed.), *Encyclopedia of Knowledge Management* (pp. 360-367). Hershey, PA: Idea Group.

Scheer, A. W. (1999). *ARIS - Business process framework*. Berlin: Springer-Verlag.

Schein, E. H. (1985). How culture forms, develops and changes. In R. H. Kilmann, M. J. Saxton, & R. Serpa (Eds.), *Gaining control of the corporate culture*. San Francisco: Jossey Bass.

Schmaltz, R., Hagenhoff, S., & Kaspar, C. (2004). *Information technology support for knowledge management in cooperations*. Paper presented at The Fifth European Conference on Organizational Knowledge, Learning and Capabilities.

Schmidt, M. P. (2000). *Knowledge communities*. Munich, Germany: Addison-Wesley.

Schreiber, G., Akkermans, H., Anjewierden, A., de Hoog, R., Shadbold, N., van der Velde, W., & Wielinga, B. (1999). *Knowledge engineering and management, the common KADS methodology*. Cambridge: MIT Press.

Schuemie, M., Ver Der Straaten, P., Krijn, M., & Van Der Mast, C. (2001). Research on presence in virtual reality: A survey. *Cyberpsychology and Behavior, 4*(2), 183-201.

Schulz, M. (2001). The uncertain relevance of newness: Organizational learning and knowledge flows. *Academy of Management Journal, 44*, 661-681.

Schulz, M. (2003). Pathways of relevance: Exploring inflows of knowledge into subunits of multinational corporations. *Organization Science, 14*(4), 440-459.

Schwartz, D. G. (2006). Aristotelian view of knowledge management. In D. G. Schwartz (Ed.), *Encyclopedia of Knowledge Management* (pp. 10-16). Hershey, PA: Idea Group.

Scott, A., (2006). *Geography and economy: The Clerendon Lectures in Geography and Environmental Studies*. Oxford: Oxford University Press.

Scott, S., Cummings, M., Graeber, D., Nelson, W., & Bolia, R. (June). *Collaboration technology in military team operations: Lessons learned from the corporate domain*. Paper presented at the Command and Control Research and Technology Symposium, San Diego, CA.

Searing, D. D. (1991). Roles, rules and rationality in the new institutionalism. *The American Political Science Review, 85*(4), 1239-1260.

Segalla M. (2001). Overview: Understanding values and expectations of foreign employees creates a better company. *European Management Journal, 19*(1), 27-31.

Selznick, P. (1943). An approach to a theory of bureaucracy. *American Sociological Review, 8*, 47-54.

Senge, P. (1990). *The fifth discipline: The art and practice of the learning organization*. London, UK: Random House.

Senge, P. M (1990). *The fifth discipline: The art & practice of the learning Organization*. London: Century Business.

Seufert, A., von Krogh, G., & Bach, A. (1999). Towards knowledge networking. *Journal of Knowledge Management, 3*(3), 180-190.

Seymour, G., & Cowen, M. (2006). *A review of team collaboration tools for crisis response in the military and government.* Paper presented at the Command and Control Research and Technology Symposium, San Diego, CA.

Shackle, G. L. S. (1961). *Decision, order and time in human affairs.* Cambridge: Cambridge University Press.

Shanei, A., Sena, J., & Stebbins, M. (2000). Knowledge work teams and groupware technology: Learning from Seagate's experience. *Journal of Knowledge Management, 4*(2):111-124.

Shannon, C. E., & Weaver, W. (1949). *The mathematical theory of communication.* Chicago: University of Illinois Press.

Shannon, C., & Weaver, W. (1949). *The mathematical theory of communication.* Urbana, IL: University of Illinois Press.

Sharratt, M., & Usoro, A. (2003). Understanding knowledge sharing in online communities of practice. *Electronic Journal on Knowledge Management, 1*(2), 187-196.

Shenkar, O. (2001). Cultural distance revisited towards a more rigorous conceptualization and measurement of cultural differences. *Journal of International Business Studies, 32*(3), 519-535.

Sheth, A. P. (1998). Changing focus on interoperability in information systems: From system, syntax, structure to semantics. In M. F. Goodchild, M. J. Egenhofer, R. Fegeas, & C. A. Kottman (Eds.), *Interoperating geographic information systems.* Norwell, MA: Kluwer Academic Publishers.

Shibutani, T. (1962). Reference groups and social control. In *Human Behavior and Social Processes* (pp. 128-147). Boston, MA: Houghton Mifflin.

Shneiderman, B. (2000). Designing trust into online experiences. *Communication of ACM, 43*(12), 57-59.

Shneiderman, B., & Preece, J. (2007). 911.gov. *Science, 315*(5814), 944.

Siakas K. V., & Georgiadou E. (2003). Learning in a changing society and the importance of cultural awareness. In *IADIS 2003 (International Association for development of the Information Society)* (pp. 696-702), International Conference, Algarve, Portugal, 5-8 Nov. 2003, Vol. I.

Siakas K. V., Georgiadou E. (2003). Learning in a Changing Society and the Importance of Cultural Awareness, Paper presentet at *IADIS 2003 (International Association for development of the Information Society)* International Conference, Algarve, Portugal, 5-8 Nov. 2003, Vol. I, 696-702

Siakas K. V. & Hyvärinen J. (2006). On-line Assessment of the Fit between National and Organisational Culture; A new tool for Predicting Suitable Software Quality Management System. In R. Dawson, E. Georgiadou, P. Linecar, M. Ross., & G. Staples (eds), *Perspectives in Software Quality: Proceeding of the 14th Software Quality Management Conference (SQM 2006)*, April, Southampton, UK, The British Computer Society, pp. 197-204

Siakas K. V., & Hyvärinen J. (2006). On-line assessment of the fit between national and organisational culture; A new tool for predicting suitable software quality management system. In R. Dawson, E. Georgiadou, P. Linecar, M. Ross., & G. Staples (Eds), *Perspectives in software quality: Proceeding of the 14th Software Quality Management Conference (SQM 2006)* (pp. 197-204), April, Southampton, UK, The British Computer Society.

Siakas, K. V. (2002). *SQM-CODE: Software quality management – Cultural and organisational diversity evaluation.* PhD Thesis, London Metropolitan University, UK.

Siakas, K. V., & Balstrup, B. (2006). Software outsourcing quality achieved by global virtual collaboration, software process. *Improvement and Practice (SPIP) Journal, 11*(3), 319-328.

Siakas, K. V., & Georgiadou, E. (1999). Process improvement: The societal iceberg. In *European Software Process Improvement Conference, EuroSPI '99* (pp. 25-37), Pori, Finland, 25 - 27.10.

Siakas, K. V., & Georgiadou, E. (2006). Knowledge sharing: Cultural dynamics. In P. Feher (Ed.), *Proceedings of 7th European Conference of Knowledge Management (ECKM06)* (pp. 505-513), 4-5 Sept., Public Academic Conferences Ltd. Reading, UK.

Sieloff, C. G. (1999). If only HP knew what HP knows: The roots of knowledge management at Hewlett-Packard. *Journal of Knowledge Management, 3*(1), 47-53.

Silvio, J. (1998). The virtualization of higher education: Scope, possibilities and limitations. UNESCO, Regional Centre for Higher Education in Latin America and the Caribbean (CRESALC). *Rufis'98, International Congress.* Universidad Regiomontana. Monterrey N.L., México.

Simon, H. A. (1969). The architecture of complexity. In H. A. Simon (Ed.), *The Science of the artificial* (pp. 192-229). Cambridge, MA: MIT Press.

Simon, H. A. (1969). *The science of the artificial.* Cambridge, MA: MIT press.

Simon, H. A. (1979). *Models of thought.* New Haven, CT: Yale University Press.

Simon, H. A. (1982). *Models of bounded rationality: Behavioural economics and business organization, vol. 2.* Cambridge MA: MIT Press.

Simonin, B. (1997). The importance of developing collaborative know-how: An empirical test of the learning organization. *Academy of Management Journal, 40*(5), 1150–1174.

Simonin, B. (1999). Transfer of marketing know-how in international strategic alliances: An empirical investigation of the role and antecedents of knowledge ambiguity. *Journal of International Business Studies, 30*(3), 463-490.

Simonin, B. L. (1999a). Ambiguity and the process of knowledge transfer in strategic alliances. *Strategic Management Journal, 20*(7), 595-623.

Simonin, B. L. (1999b). Transfer of marketing know-how in international strategic alliances: An empirical investigation of the role and antecedents of knowledge ambiguity. *Journal of International Business Studies, 30*(3), 463-490.

Simpson, G. R., & Bridis, T. (2000). Oracle hired firm to probe Microsoft allies. *Wall Street Journal,* (June 28), A3.

Sindt, T. (2003). Formal operations for ontology evolution. In *Proceedings of the International Conference on Emerging Technologies.*

Singley, M. K., & Anderson, J. R. (1989). *The transfer of cognitive skill.* Cambridge, MA: Harvard Univ. Press.

Skaalvik, E. M., & Skaalvik, S. (2002). Internal and external frames of reference for academic self-concept. *Educational Psychologist, 37*(4), 233-244.

Smith, K. (2000). W*hat is the knowledge economy? Knowledge-intensive industries and distributed knowledge bases. The Learning Economy - Firms, Regions and Nation Specific Institutions.* DRUID Summer Conference. June 15-17.

Snowden, D. (2002). Complex acts of knowing; Paradox and descriptive self awareness. *Journal of Knowledge Management, 6*(2), 1-14.

Snyder, W. M. (1997). Communities of practice: Combining organizational learning and strategy insights to create a bridge to the 21st century. Presented at the 1997 *Academy of Management Conference,* p. 3.

Sole, D., & Wilson, D. (2002). *Storytelling in organizations: The power and the traps of using stories to share knowledge in organizations.* Learning Innovations Laboratory (LILA), Graduate School of Education, Harvard University. Retrieved January 18, 2007, from http://lila.pz.harvard.edu/_upload/lib/ACF14F3.pdf

Sondergaard, M. (1994). Research note: Hofstede's consequences: A study of reviews, citations and replications. *Organisation Studies, 15,* 447-456.

Song, S., Nerur, S., & Teng, J. T. (2007). An exploratory study on the roles of network structure and knowledge processing orientation in work unit knowledge management. *SIGMIS Database, 38*(2), 8-26.

Sonnenwald, D. H. (1995). Contested collaboration: A descriptive model of intergroup communication in information system design. *Information Processing and Management, 31*(6) 859-877.

Sonnenwald, D. H. (1996). Communication roles that support collaboration during the design process. *Design Studies, 17,* 277-301.

Sonnenwald, D. H., & Lievrouw, L. (1997). Collaboration during the design process: A case study of communication, information behavior, and project performance. In R. Savolainen, G. Taylor, & B. Dervin (Eds.), *Information seeking in context* (pp. 179-204).

Sonnenwald, D. H., & Pierce, L. (2000). Information behavior in dynamic group work contexts: Interwoven situational awareness, dense social networks and contested collaboration in command and control. *Information Processing and Management, 36*(3), 461-479.

Sowa, J. F. (2000). *KR: Logical, philosophical, and computational foundations.* Pacific Grove: Brooks Cole Publishing Co.

Sowa, J. F. (2003). *Ontology.* Retrieved January 10, 2007 from http://www.jfsowa.com/

Spender, J. C., & Grant, R. M.(1996). Knowledge and the firm: Overview. *Strategic Management Journal, 17*(Winter Special Issue), 5–9.

Spender, J.C. (1996). Making knowledge the basis of a dynamic theory of the firm. *Strategic Management Journal, Special Issue,* (17), 45-62.

Spender, J-C. (1996). Competitive advantage from tacit knowledge? Unpacking the concept and its strategic implication. In B. Moingeon & A. Edmondson (Eds.), *Organizational learning and competitive advantage.* London: Sage.

Spiegler, I. (2000). Knowledge management: A new idea or a recycled concept? *Communications of the Association for Information Systems (AIS),* June, *3*(14), 1-23.

Spiegler, I. (2000). Knowledge management: A new idea or a recycled concept. *Communications of the AIS, 3*(14), 1–24.

Spies, M., Clayton, A. J., & Noormohammadian, M. (2005). Knowledge management in a decentralized global financial services provider: A case study with Allianz Group. *Knowledge Management Research & Practice, 3*, 24-36.

Sproull, L., & Faraj, S. (1995). Atheism, sex and databases: The net as a social technology. In B. K. J. Keller (Ed.), *Public access to the Internet* (pp. 62-81). Cambridge, MA: MIT Press.

Stanford University Libraries. (2002). *Electronic journal user study: eJUST.* Retrieved September 10, 2007, from http://ejust.stanford.edu/index.html

Stanford. (2006). *The Protégé Ontology Editor and Knowledge Acquisition System.* Retrieved January 16, 2007 from http://protege.stanford.edu/

Stanton, T. K., Giles, D. E., & Cruz, N. I. (1999). *Service learning: a movement's pioneers: Reflections on its origins, practice, and future.* San Francisco: Jossey-Bass Publishers.

Stein, R. T. (1982). High status group members as exemplars: A summary of field research on the relationship of status to congruence conformity. *Small Group Behavior, 13*, 3-21.

Steiner, B., & Sands, R. (2000). Responding to a natural disaster with service learning. *Family Medicine, 32*(9), 645-649.

Steinmueller, W. E. (2002). Networked knowledge and knowledge-based economies. *International Journal of Social Science, 171*, 159-173.

Stevens, J. (1998). Integrating the supply chain. *International Journal of Physical Distribution and Materials Management, 13*(1), 37-56.

Stiglitz, J. (1999). Public policy for a knowledge economy. *OECD Report.* Retrieved September 18, 2007, from http://www.worldbank.org/html/extdr/extme/knowledge-economy.pdf

Stojanovic, L., Maedche, A., Stojanovic, N., & Studer, R. (2003). Ontology evolution as reconfiguration-design problem solving. In *Proceedings of the 2nd International Conference on Knowledge Capture* (pp. 162-171).

Stojanovic, L. (2004). *Methods and tools for ontology evolution.* PhD thesis, University of Karlsruhe.

Stone, D. N., & Warsono, S. (2003). Does accounting account for knowledge? In C. W. Holsapple (Ed.), *Handbook of knowledge management* (pp. 253-270). Berlin: Springer-Verlag.

Storey, J., & Barnett, E. (2000). Knowledge management initiatives: Learning from failure. *Journal of Knowledge Management, 4*(2), 145-156.

Strom, T. Q., & Miller, C. (2002). *Service learning. What works in preventing school violence: The safe and responsive fact sheet series.* Safe & Responsive Schools Project, Indiana Education Policy Center, Indiana University. Retrieved January 18, 2007, from http://www.indiana.edu/~safeschl/service_learning.pdf

Sullivan, D. (2004). Google Scholar offers access to academic information. *SearchEngineWatch* (Nov 18, 2004). Retrieved September 10, 2007, from http://searchenginewatch.com/searchday/article.php/3437471

Surowiecki, J. (2004). *The wisdom of crowds: Why the many are smarter than the few and how collective wisdom shapes business, economies, societies and nations.* Doubleday, Random House inc.

Sveiby, K. E. (1997). *The new organizational wealth.* San Francisco: Berret-Koehler.

Sverisson, (2001). Translation networks, knowledge brokers and novelty construction: Pragmatic environmentalism in Sweden. *Acta Sociologica, 44*(4), 313-327.

Swan, J., Newell, S., Scarbrough, H., & Hislop, D. (1999). Knowledge management and innovation: Networks and networking. *Journal of Knowledge Management, 17*(2), 109-122.

Swan, J., Newell, S., Scarbrough, H., & Hislop, D. (1999). Knowledge management and innovation: Networks and networking. *Journal of Knowledge Management, 3*(4), 262-275.

Swap, W., Leonard, D., Shields, M., & Abrams, L. (2001). Using mentoring and storytelling to transfer knowledge in the workplace. *Journal of Management Information Systems, 18*(1), 95-114.

Swidler A. (1986). Culture in action: Symbols and strategies. *American sociological Review, 51*, 273-286

Sycara, K. P. (1998). Multiagent systems. *AI magazine, 19*(2), 79-92.

Szulanski, G. (1996). Exploring internal stickiness: Impediments to the transfer of best practice. *Strategic Management Journal, 17*, 27-43.

Szulanski, G. (1996). Exploring internal stickiness: Impediments to the transfer of best practice within the firm. *Strategic Management Journal, 17*(Winter Special Issue), 27-43.

Szulanski, G. (1996). Exploring internal stickiness: Impediments to the transfer of best practice within the firm. *Strategic Management Journal, 17*, 27-43.

Szulanski, G. (2000). The process of knowledge transfer: A diachronic analysis of stickiness. *Organization Behavior and Human Decision Processes, 82* (1), 9-27.

Szulanski, G. (2003). *Sticky knowledge. Barriers to knowing in the firm*. London, UK: Sage Publications.

Tagiuri, R., & Litwin, G. (1968). *Organizational climate*. Boston: Division of Research, Harvard Graduate School of Business

Takeda, H., Iino, K., & Nishida T. (1995). Ontology-supported agent communication. In *Proceedings of the American Association for Artificial Intelligence Symposium*.

Takeishi, A. (2002). Knowledge partitioning in the interfirm division of labor: The case of automotive product development. *Organization Science, 13*(3), 321-338.

Tam, P. (2002). High-technology giant duels with nimble knock-off artists. *Wall Street Journal*, (September 25), A1.

Tanriverdi, H. (2005). Information technology relatedness, knowledge management capability and performance of multi-business firms. *MIS Quarterly, 29*(2 - June), 311-334.

Tarski, A. (1956). *Logic, semantics, and meta-mathematics*. Oxford: Oxford University Press.

Taylor, A., Skjei, S. M. (2002). A disaster-recovery plan for local municipalities using currently available communication satellite facilities and services, *National Conference on Digital Government, ACM International Conference Proceeding Series*, 1-11.

Teece, D. J. (1998). Capturing value from knowledge assets: The new economy, markets for know-how, and intangible assets. *California Management Review, 40*(3), 55-79.

Teece, D. J. (2003). Knowledge and competence as strategic assets. In C. W. Holsapple (Ed.), *Handbook of knowledge management* (pp. 129-152). Berlin: Springer-Verlag.

Teng, B-S., & Cummings, J. L. (2002). Trade-offs in managing resources and capabilities. *Academy of Management Executive, 16*(2), 81-91.

Tenopir, C. et al. (2003). *Use and users of electronic library resources: An overview and analysis of recent research studies*. Council on Library and Information Resources. Retrieved September 10, 2007, from http://www.clir.org/pubs/reports/pub120/contents.html

Tenopir, C., & King, D. (2000). *Towards electronic journals: Realities for scientists, librarians, pnd Publishers*. Washington, D.C.: Special Libraries Association.

Terhune, C. (2006). Coke legal battle with bottlers stalls on lawyer-conflict claim. *Wall Street Journal*, (August 10), A2.

Testa, J., & McVeigh, M. (2004). *The impact of open access journals: A citation study from Thomson ISI*. The Thomson Corporation. Retrieved September 10, 2007, from http://www.isinet.com/media/presentrep/acropdf/impact-oa-journals.pdf

Thoben, K. D., & Jagdev, H. (2001). Typological issues in enterprise networks, *Journal of Production Planning and Control, 12*(5), 421–436.

Thomes, K. (2000). *The economics and usage of digital library collections*. Bevier Engineering Library, University of Pittsburgh, The Association of Research Libraries (ARL)

Thurlow, C., Engel, L., & Tomic, A. (2004). *Computer-mediated communication: Social interaction and the Internet*. London, UK: Sage Publications.

Tichon, J., Hall, R. H., Hilgers, M. G., Leu, M. C., & Agarwal, A. (2003). Education and training in virtual environments for disaster management. In *Proceedings of the World Conference on Educational Multimedia, Hypermedia & Telecommunications* (EdMedia) (pp. 1191 – 1194).

Tiwana, A. (2000). *The knowledge management toolkit*. Upper Saddle River, NJ: Prentice Hall.

Tiwana, A., & Ramesh, B. (2001). Integrating knowledge on the Web. *IEEE Internet Computing, 5*(3), 32-39.

Tolsby, J. (2000). Taylorism given a new hand: How an IT system changed employees flexibility and personal involvement in their work. *Journal of Organizational Change Management, 13*(5), 482-492.

Torff, B. (1999). Tacit knowledge in teaching folk pedagogy and teacher education. In R. J. Sternberg & J. A. Horvath

(Eds.), *Tacit knowledge in professional practice*. Mahwah, NJ: Lawrence Erlbaum Associates.

Townsend, A. M., & Moss, M. M. (2005). Telecommunications infrastructures. In *Disasters: Preparing cities for crisis communications*. Retrieved January 18, 2007, from http://hurricane.wagner.nyu.edu/report1.pdf

Trolley, J. (1999). New wine and old vessels: The evaluation and integration of Web-based information in well established resources. *Asis '99 Proceedings of the 62nd Asis Annual Meeting: V36. Knowledge Creation, Organization and Use*, (pp. 628-632), Washington, DC

Tsai, W. (2001). Knowledge transfer in intraorganizational networks: Effects of network position and absorptive capacity on business unit innovation and performance. *Academy of Management Journal, 44*(5), 996-1004.

Tsatsou P. (2005). *Civil society in Greece: Shaping new digital divides? The digital divides as "cultural" divides*. Implications for closing divides, ESRC Seminar on "Bridging the Digital Divides," Oxford Internet Institute, UK, 4 March 2005. Retrieved from http://www.oii.ox.ac.uk/collaboration/seminars/20050304_Panayiota_Tsatsou_Paper.pdf

Tsoukas, C. & Chia, R. (2002). On organizational becoming: Rethinking organizational change. *Organization Science, 13*(5), 567-582.

Tsoukas, H. (2003). Do we really understand tacit knowledge? In M. Easterby-Smith & M. A. Lyles (Eds.), *Blackwell handbook of organizational learning and knowledge management*. Oxford: Blackwell Publishing Ltd.

Tsui, E. (2003). Tracking the role and evolution of commercial knowledge management software. In C. Holsapple (Ed.), *Handbook of Knowledge Management. Volume 2* (pp. 122-58). NY, NY: Springer-Verlap.

Tuomi, I. (2000). Data is more than knowledge: Implications of the reversed knowledge hierarchy for knowledge management and organizational memory. *Journal of Management Information Systems, 16*(3), 103-117.

Turoff, M., Chumer, M., Van de Walle, B., & Yao, X. (2004). The design of a dynamic emergency response management information system (DERMIS). *Journal of Information Technology Theory and Application (JITTA), 5*(4), 1-36.

Tushman, M. L., & Katz, R. (1980). External communication and project performance: An investigation into the role of gatekeepers. *Management Science, 26*, 1071-1085.

Tushman, M. L., & Romanelli, E. (1983). Uncertainty, social location and influence in decision making: A sociometric analysis. *Management Science, 29*(1), 12-23.

Tyler, R. T. (1997). The psychology of legitimacy: A relational perspective on voluntary deference to authorities. *Personality and Social Psychology Review, 1*(4), 323-345.

Tyre, M., & Von Hippel, E. (1997). The situative nature of adaptive learning in organizations. *Organization Science, 8*(1), 71-83.

Upkar Varshney, A. S., McGivern, M., & Howard, C. (2002). Voice over IP. *Communications of the ACM, January, 45*(1), 88-96.

Uzzi, B., & Gillespie, J. (2002). Knowledge spillover in corporate financing networks: Embeddedness and the firm's debt performance. *Strategic Management Journal, 23*(7), 595-618.

Vakkari, P. & Pennanen, M. (2001). Sources, relevance and contributory information of documents in writing a research proposal: A longitudinal case study. *The New Review of Information Behavior Research, 2*(November), 217 – 232

Vakkari, P. (2000). Relevance and contributing information types of searched documents in task performance. Proceedings of the 23rd annual international ACM SIGIR conference on Research and Development in Information Retrieval (pp. 2-9). Athens, Greece.

Van de Ven, A., & Ferry, D.L. (1980). *Measuring and assessing organizations*. New York: John Wiley.

Van den Hooff, B., Elving, W., Meeuwsen, J. M., & Dumoulin, C. (2003). Knowledge sharing in knowledge communities. In M. Huysman, E. Wenger, & V. Wulf (Eds.), *Communities and technologies* (pp. 119-141). Boston: Kluwer Academic Publishers.

Van Maanen, J., & Barley, S. R. (1984). Occupational communities: Culture and control in organizations. In B. M. Staw & L. L. Cummings (Eds.), *Research in organizational behavior* (pp. 287-365). Greenwich, CT: JAI Press.

Van Maanen, J., & Schein, E. H. (1979). Toward a theory of organizational socialization. *Research in Organizational Behavior, 1*, 209-264.

Van, Beveren J. (2002). A model of knowledge acquisition that refocuses knowledge management. *Journal of Knowledge Management, 6*(1), 18-22.

Vandenbosch, B., & Huff, S. (1997). Searching and scanning: How executives obtain information from executive information systems. *MIS Quarterly, 21*(1), 81-107.

Vandermerwe, S. (1999). The electronic "go-between service provider": A new "middle" role taking centre stage. *European Management Journal, 17*.

Vara, V. (2006). Offices co-opt consumer Web tools like "wikis" and social networking. *Wall Street Journal*, (September 12), B1.

Vara, V. (2007). Oracle's SAP suit casts light on technical support. *Wall Street Journal*, (March 23), B4.

Vesterager, J., Pedersen, J. D., & Tølle, M. (1999). *Virtual enterprise reference architecture and methodology*, a modified for publication extract of deliverable 1.3 "Final Report on Models" of IMS 95001/ESPRIT 26509 Globeman21 (Global Manufacturing in the 21st Century).

Vickery, S. K., Droge, C., Stank, T. P., Goldsby, T. J., & Markland, R. E. (2004). The performance implications of media richness in a business-to-business service environment: direct and indirect effects. *Management Science, 50*(8), 1106-1119.

Voelpel, S., Dous, M., & Davenport, T. (2005). Five steps to creating a global knowledge-sharing system: Siemens' ShareNet. *Academy of Management Executive, 19*(2), 9-23.

Von Hippel, E. (1994). "Sticky information" and the locus of problem solving: Implications for innovation. *Management Science, 40*(4), 429-439.

Von Hippel, E. (1994). Sticky information and the locus of problem solving: Implications for innovation. *Management Science, 40*, 429-440.

Von Hippel, E. (1994). Sticky information and the locus of problem solving: Implications for innovation. *Management Science, 40*(4).

Von Hippel, E. (2005). *Democratizing innovation*. MIT Press.

Voorbij, H. J. (1999). Searching scientific information on the Internet: A Dutch academic user survey. *Journal of American Society for Information Science, 50*(2), 598-615.

Vranica, S. (2001). Foote Cone loses two accounts from Coke in wake of Pepsi suit. *The Wall Street Journal*, (November 12), B3.

Vranica, S. (2005). Lowe's old gang flocks to new shop; string of former colleagues join still-unnamed agency; defections hurt Interpublic. *The Wall Street Journal*, (December 13), B11.

W3C. (2003). *Web Services Architecture, W3C Working Draft 8 August 2003*. Retrieved November 13, 2006, from http://www.w3.org/TR/2003/WD-ws-arch-20030808/

W3C. (2006). *Web Ontology Language (OWL)*. Retrieved January 11, 2007 from http://www.w3.org/2004/OWL/

Wagner, M., Eisenstadt, S., Hogan, W., & Pankaskie, M. (1998). Preferences of interns and residents for e-mail, paging, or traditional methods for the delivery of different types of clinical information. In *Proceedings of the AMIA 1998 Symposium*, Washington DC. Retrieved May 25, 2007, from http://www.amia.org

Wagner, R. K., & Sternberg R. J. (1985). Practical intelligence in real-world pursuits the role of tacit knowledge. *Journal of Personality and Social Psychology 49*(2) 436–458.

Wagner, R. K., & Sternberg R. J. (1986). Tacit knowledge and intelligence in the everyday world. In R. J. Sternberg, & R. K. Wagner (Eds.), *Practical Intelligence,* (pp. 51–83). Cambridge University Press, Cambridge.

Wagner, R. K., Sujan, J., Sujan, M., Rashotte, C. A., & Sternberg, R. J. (1999). Tacit knowledge in sales. In R. J. Sternberg & J. A. Horvath (Eds.), *Tacit knowledge in professional practice*. Mahwah, NJ: Lawrence Erlbaum Associates,.

Wainfain, L., & Davis, P. (2004). *Challenges in virtual collaboration: Videoconferencing, audioconferencing and computer-mediated communications*. Santa Monica, CA: Rand Corporation, National Defense Research Institute.

Wald, B. (1993). On the evolution of would and other modals in the English spoken in East Los Angeles. In N. Dittmar & A. Reich (Eds.), *Modality in language acquisition* (pp. 59-96). Berlin: Walter de Gruyter.

Wall Street Journal. (2007). Towers Perrin laptops, client data stolen. *Wall Street Journal*, (January 9), A17.

Walsh, J. P., & Ungson, G. R. (1991). Organizational memory. *Academy of Management Review, 16*, 57–91.

Walsham, G. (2001). Knowledge management: The benefits and limitations of computer systems. *European Management Journal, 19*(6), 599-608.

Walther, J. B. (1995). Relational aspects of computer-mediated communication: Experimental observations over time. *Organization Science, 6*(2), 186-203.

Warkentin, M., Sugumaran, V., & Bapna, R. (2001). E-knowledge networks for interorganisational collaborative e-business. *Logistics Information Management, 14*(1/2), 149-162.

Wasko, M. M., & Faraj, S. (2005). Why should I share? Examining knowledge contribution in electronic networks of practice. *MIS Quarterly, 29*(1), 1-23.

Wasko, M., & Faraj, S. (2000). It is what one does: Why people participate and help others in electronic communities of practice. *Journal of Strategic Information Systems, 9*(2-3), 155-173.

Webster, J., & Frederic, E. (1992). The changing role of marketing in the corporation, *Journal of Marketing, 56*(4), 17-37.

Weick, K. E. (1979) *The social psychology of organizing.* Reading, MA: Addison-Wesley.

Weick, K. E. (1995). *Sensemaking in organizations.* Thousand Oaks, CA: Sage Publications, Inc.

Weick, K. E., Sutcliffe, K. M., & Obstfeld, D. (2005). Organizing and the process of sensemaking. *Organization Science, 16*(4), 409-421.

Weiss, G. (Ed.) (2000). *Multiagent systems: A modern approach to distributed artificial intelligence.* London: MIT Press.

Weitzman, M. L. (1998). Recombinant growth. *The Quarterly Journal of Economics, 113*(2) 331-360.

Wellman, B., Hasse, A., Witte, J., & Hampton, K. (2001). Does the Internet increase, decrease or supplement social capital? Social networks, participation and community commitment. *American Behavioral Scientist, 3*(45), 437-456.

Wellman, B., Salaff, J., et al. (1996). Computer networks as social networks: Collaborative work, telework, and virtual community. *Annual Review of Sociology, 22,* 213-238.

Wenger, E. (1998). *Communities of practice learning, meaning, and identity.* Cambridge: Cambridge University Press.

Wenger, E. (1998). *Communities of practice.* Cambridge, UK, Cambridge: University Press.

Wenger, E. (1998). Communities of practice. Learning as a social system. *Systems Thinker, 9*(5- June).

Wenger, E. (1998). *Communities of practice. Learning, meaning and identity.* Cambridge: Cambridge University.

Wenger, E. (1998). *Communities of practice: Learning, meaning, and identity.* Cambridge, UK: Cambridge University Press.

Wenger, E. (1998). *Communities of practice: Learning, meaning, and identity.* New York: Cambridge University Press.

Wenger, E. (2000). Communities of practice and social learning systems. *Organization, 7*(2), 225-246

Wenger, E. (2001). *Supporting communities of practice: A survey of community-orientedtechnologies.* Shareware Report. Retrieved May 25, 2007, from http://www.ewenger.com/tech/

Wenger, E. C., McDermott, R., & Snyder, W. M. (2002). *Cultivating communities of practice.* Boston, MA: Harvard Business School Press.

Wenger, E., & Snyder, W. M. (2000). Communities of practice: The organizational frontier. *Harvard Business Review,* 139-145.

Wenger, E., & Snyder,B (2000). *Communities of practice: The organisational frontier.* Harvard Business Review, 78(1), 139–145.

Wenger, E., McDermott, R., & Snyder, W. M. (2002). Cultivating communities of practice. *A guide to managing knowledge.* Boston, MA: Harvard Business School Press.

White, J. (2002). *Retrospect of information technology's impact on society and warfare: revolution or dangerous hype?* Newport: Naval War College.

Wiener, Y. (1982). Commitment in organizations: A normative view. *Academy of Management Review, 7*(3), 418-428.

Wiesz, J. D., Erickson, T., & Kellog, W. A. (2006). Synchronous broadcast messaging: The use of ICT. In *Proceedings, Computer-Mediated Communication, CHI2006,* 22-27 April, 2006. Montreal, Canada. ACM.

Wigand, R. T. (1995). Electronic commerce and reduced transaction costs: Firms' migration into highly interconnected electronic markets. *Electronic markets, 16,* 1-5.

Wigfield, A. (1994). Expectancy-value theory of achievement motivation: A developmental perspective. *Educational Psychology Review, 6,* 49-78.

Wigfield, A., & Eccles, J. S. (2000). Expectancy-value theory of achievement. *Contemporary Educational Psychology, 25,* 68-81.

Wiig, K. M. (1997). Integrating intellectual capital and knowledge management. *Long RangePplanning, 30*(3), 399-405.

Wikipedia. (2007). *2004 Indian Ocean earthquake: Signs and warnings.* Retrieved January 18, 2007, from http://en.wikipedia.org/wiki/2004_Indian_Ocean_earthquake

Wildavsky, A. (1983). Information as an organizational problem. *Journal of Management Studies, 20*(1), 29-40.

Wildavsky, A. (1988). *Searching for safety.* New Brunswick, NJ: Transaction Press.

Williams, J. D., Han, S.-L., & Qualls, W. J. (1998). A conceptual model and study of cross-cultural business relationships. *Journal of Business Research, 42,* 135-143.

Williams, R. L., & Cothrel, J. (2000). Four smart ways to run online communities. *Sloan Management Review, Summer,* 81-91.

Williamson, O. E. (1981). The economics of organization: The transaction cost approach. *American Journal of Sociology 87*(3), 548–77.

Williamson, O. E. (1985). *The economic institutions of capitalism.* New York: Free Press.

Williamson, O. E. (1991). Comparative economic organization: The analysis of discrete structural alternatives. *Administrative Science Quarterly, 36,* 269-296.

Willinsky, J. (2006). *Altering the material conditions of access to the humanities. Tasks for the new humanities: Professing with Derrida* (pp. 118-136). London: Palgrave Macmillan. . Retrieved September 10, 2007, from http://pkp. sfu.ca/node/456

Willinsky, J. (2006a). Access to power: Research in international policymaking. *Harvard International Review,* summer 2006, 42-45. Retrieved September 10, 2007, from http://pkp.sfu.ca/node/432

Willinsky, J. (2006b). Why open access for research and scholarship? *Journal of Neuroscience, 26*(36), 9078-9079. Retrieved September 10, 2007, from http://www.jneurosci. org/cgi/reprint/26/36/9078

Wilson, C. (2005). *Network centric warfare: Background and oversight issues for Congress,* Washington, D.C.: Report for Congress, Congressional Research Service, The library of Congress.

Wimmer, B. S., Townsend, A. M., & Chezum, B. E. (2000). Information technologies and the middleman: The changing role of information intermediaries in an information - rich economy. *Journal of Labor Research, 21,* 407-416.

Wingfield, N. (2006). At Apple, secrecy complicates life but maintains buzz. *Wall Street Journal,* (June 28), A1.

Winograd, T. (1975). Frame representations and the declarative/procedural controversy. *Readings in Knowledge Representation,* 185-210.

Winograd, T., & Flores, F. (1986). *Understanding computers and cognition.* Reading, MA: Addison-Wesley.

Winter, S., (Ed.) (1987). *Knowledge and competence as strategic assets. The competitive challenge-Strategies for industrial innovation and renewal.* Cambridge, MA: Ballinger.

Witten, I. & Bainbridge, D. (2001). *How to build a digital library.* New Zealand Digital Library Project, University of Waikato, New Zealand, Morgan Kaufmann Publishers.

Witten, I. (2003). *Digital libraries and society: New perspectives on information dissemination.* Department of Computer Science, University of Waikato, New Zealand. Retrieved September 10, 2007, from http://www.cs.waikato. ac.nz/~ihw/DLs.and.society.pdf

World Bank. (2002). *Harnessing knowledge for development.* III World Knowledge Forum, World Bank Plenary, Seoul, October 18, 2002. Retrieved September 10, 2007, from http://lnweb18.worldbank.org/eap/eap.nsf/Attachments/speech/$File/WKF+Speech.pdf

World Bank. (2002b). *Information and communication technologies: A World Bank Group Strategy, Executive Summary.* The World Bank Group, Washington, D.C.

Xiao J., Zhang, Y., Jia, X., & Li, T. (2001). Measuring similarity of interests for clustering Web-users. In *Proceedings of the 12th Australasian Database Conference. ACM International Conference Proceeding Series,* 107-114.

Yarmosh, K. (2006). Why Web 2.0 matters to your business – knowledge sharing. Posted April 25, 2006 to *Tech and Productivity.* Retrieved May 25, 2007, from http://www. technosight.com/why-web-20-matters-to-your-business-knowledge-sharing/

Yih-Ton Sun, P., & Scott, J.L. (2005). An investigation of barriers to knowledge transfer. *Journal of Knowledge Management, 9*(2), 75-90.

Zack, M. (1998). An architecture for managing explicated knowledge. *Sloan Management Review, 39*(4), 45-58.

Zack, M. (1999). Managing codified knowledge. *Sloan Management Review, 40*(4), 45-58.

Zack, M. (2001). If managing knowledge is the solution, then what's the problem? In Y. Malhotra (Ed.), *Knowledge management and business model innovation* (pp. 16-36). Hershey, PA: Idea Group Publishing.

Zack, M. A. (1999). Managing codified knowledge. *Sloan Management Review*, (Summer), 45-58.

Zander, U., & Kogut B. (1995). Knowledge and the speed of the transfer and imitation of organizational capabilities: An empirical test. *Organization Science, 6*(1) 76–92.

Zeldin, T. (1998). *Conversations: How talk can change our lives*. London: Harville Press.

Zhang, Y. (1999). *Scholarly use of Internet-based electronic resources*. Doctoral Dissertation, University of Illinois at Urbana-Champaign. UMI Digital dissertation AAT 3013240.

Zhao, L., & Reisman, A. (1992). Toward metaresearch on technology transfer. *IEEE Transactions on Engineering Management, 39*(1), 13-21.

Zipf, G. (1949). Human behavior and the principle of least effort; An introduction to human ecology. Cambridge, MA: Addison-Wesley Press.

Zucker, L. G. (1977). The role of institutionalization in cultural persistence. *American Sociological Review, 42,* 726-743.

Zwegers, A., Wubben, H., & Hartel, I. (2002). Relationship management in enterprise networks. In V. Marik, L. M. Camarinha-Matos, & H. Afsarmanesh (Eds.), *Knowledge and technology integration in production and services – Balancing knowledge and technology in product and service life cycle* (pp. 157-164). Boston: Kluwer Academic Publishers.

About the Contributors

Ettore Bolisani has a degree in electronic engineering ("Laurea") and a PhD in innovation studies at the University of Padua (Italy). He is associate professor at the Faculty of Engineering at the University of Padua. Prior to this position, he was assistant professor at the University of Trieste (Italy) and, in 1997, research fellow at PREST (University of Manchester–UK), where he conducted a research project funded by the European Commission on the developments of electronic commerce. His research centres on technology assessment and technology management, with an emphasis on information and communication technologies. He has worked in several research projects funded by the European Union, by Italian public institutions, and private organisations as well. His current interest focuses on the economic implications of knowledge management and electronic commerce. On such topics, he has published various articles in international journals and chapters in books, and has been editor of *Special Issue*s.

* * *

Eileen G. Abels is Master's' Program director and associate professor in the College of Information Science and Technology at Drexel University. Prior to joining the faculty at Drexel in January 2007, Dr. Abels spent more than 15 years at the College of Information Studies at the University of Maryland. Dr. Abels received her PhD from UCLA. Her dissertation work explored the information behaviors of scientists and engineers in Mexico. Her current research focuses on access to information in electronic environments, remote reference services, and automated question answering services. She teaches courses related to information access and access in electronic environments.

Jaesoon An is a research scientist in the Pervasive Technology Labs at Indiana University. She formerly worked at Microsoft and Samsung Electronics as a member of research and development division. She completed her master's and doctoral programs in instructional technology at the University of Georgia and Indiana University-Bloomington, respectively.

Pierre Barbaroux is senior researcher at the Research Center of the French Air Force (CReA), in the Defense and Knowledge Management Department. He is also associate researcher at the GREDEG – UMR CNRS 6227, University of Nice – Sophia Antipolis, DEMOS laboratory. He holds a PhD degree in economics from the University of Nice – Sophia Antipolis. His privileged research fields are cognitive economics and complex adaptive systems theory. His current research interests focus on industrial organization, organization theory and innovation.

Jengchung V. Chen is assistant professor in telecommunications management at National Cheng Kung University, Tainan, Taiwan. He holds a PhD in communication and information sciences from the University of Hawaii. He has published articles dealing with privacy and trust issues in 20 refereed journals, including *Industrial Management and Data Systems, International Journal of Organizational Analysis, Information, Communication and Society, International Journal of Mobile Communications,* and *Labor Law Journal.*

Kimiz Dalkir is currently an assistant professor in the McGill School of Information Studies where she developed a specialization stream in knowledge management. Dr. Dalkir has published extensively on knowledge sharing and organizational memory challenges, including *Knowledge Management in Theory and Practice* (June 2005, Butterworth-Heineman). Dr. Dalkir pursues research on the effectiveness of knowledge processing in both profit and non-profit organizations, learning in peer networks, and measurement frameworks for assessing knowledge management success. Dr. Dalkir has developed and teaches courses on knowledge management, knowledge taxonomies, intellectual capital management, and communities of practice, and was awarded the Distinguished Teaching Award in 2007.

Margarita Echeverri is a research assistant professor at the School of Public Health and Tropical Medicine at Tulane University. Before this position, Dr Echeverri was the coordinator of the master in information management at the College of Information Studies at the University of Maryland and currently teaches as adjunct professor in the same program. Dr. Echeverri received her PhD in international development from Tulane University, and is a specialist in information technology and social management, with experience in national and international organizations in administration and organizational analysis, design, and implementation of information systems, electronic libraries, virtual classrooms, and WEB-based training. Her interests focus on the use of information technology to foster knowledge transfer, education, health, and research, as the main pillars for social development.

G. Scott Erickson is associate professor and chair of marketing/law in the School of Business, Ithaca College. He holds a PhD from Lehigh University. Research interests include knowledge management, intellectual property, and trade secrets. His book with Helen Rothberg, *From Knowledge to Intelligence: Creating Competitive Advantage in the Next Economy*, was published by Butterworth-Heinemann/Elsevier in 2005.

Samer Faraj is associate professor in the Desautels Faculty of Management, McGill University. He received his doctorate in MIS from Boston University's School of Management and an MS in technology and policy from MIT. Prior to getting his doctorate, he spent a decade working in a variety of consulting and IS positions. His research interests include the coordination of expertise in software development and health care, the development of online knowledge communities, and the organizational impact of IT. His work has appeared in journals, such as *Information Systems Research, Management Science, MIS Quarterly, Journal of Applied Psychology, IEEE Transactions on Engineering Management, Journal of Strategic Information Systems,* and *Information Technology & People.* He is senior editor at *Organization*

Science, an associate editor of *Information Systems Research* and on the editorial board of *Information and Organization*. In addition, he is currently coediting the special issue of *Organization Science* on IT and organizational form and function. He has received three NSF grants and a Fulbright award.

Elli Georgiadou is a principal lecturer in software engineering at the School of Computing, Middlesex University, London. Her teaching includes software quality, software measurement (metrics & estimation), methodologies, case, project & knowledge management, and software development. she is engaged in research in software measurement for product and process improvement, methodologies, knowledge management, metamodelling, cultural issues, and software quality management. She is a member of the university's Global Campus project (developing and offering ODL). She has extensive experience in academia and industry, and has been active in organising/chairing conferences and workshops under the auspices of the British Computer Society and the ACM British Chapter. She is her school's coordinator of european activities, projects and international exchanges.

Cécile Godé-Sanchez holds a PhD degree in economics from the University of Aix-Marseille III. She is currently senior researcher at the Research Center of the French Air Force (CReA), in the Defense and Knowledge Management Department. She is also associate researcher at the GREDEG – UMR CNRS 6227, university of Nice – Sophia Antipolis, DEMOS Department. Her privileged research fields are information systems management and technological change. Her current researches focus both on the cultural aspect of technological change and the coordination in network-centric organizations.

Deogratias Harorimana is a PhD student and part-time lecturer at Southampton Solent University (UK). Prior to that, Deogratias worked for some of the largest organisations in Africa and Europe. These include The American Rescue Committee and United Nations. Deogratias graduated in business information management. His doctorate's primary research focuses on the "Role of Gatekeepers in the Knowledge Creation and Transfer Process." He publishes in the area of knowledge gatekeepers, knowledge networks and communities of practice, identity formation, and impact of culture on knowledge transfer. Deogratias chairs the United Kingdom's Royal Geographical Society and the Institute of British Geographers Post Graduate Research Group, as well as a member of the Higher Education Research Group Committee of the Royal Geographical Society and the Institute of British Geographers. Harorimana is a member of the European Institute of Development Studies, a member of organising committee of the European Conference of Knowledge Management and a regular speaker and reviewer to the European Conference at Knowledge Management. Harorimana is the co author of the book "*Le Café et les Cafeiteurs du Rwanda, quels Sont les motivations*? Publibook, Paris (Forthcoming).

Anthony Ioannidis is an assistant professor of management at the Department of Business Administration, Athens University of Economics and Business, Greece. He has previously taught at the University of Patras, Greece, University of La Verne California, Athens Campus, and Baruch College, The City University of New York. He holds a BS from the University of Athens, Greece, and, an MBA, an MPhil, and a PhD from Baruch College, The City University of New York. He also possesses working experience as management consultant with leading consultancy firms in the United States and Greece, in the areas telecommunications, media, and technology. His current research interests include strategy formation, organizational design, knowledge management, reputation management and the role of CEO, and public-private partnerships.

Isa Jahnke, Dr. phil., studied social science in Germany. After this, she worked 3 years at a consultancy company. Later, from 2001 until 2004 she began her research in the field of socio-technical knowledge management and online communities at the University of Dortmund, Department Computer Science and Sociology. After her PhD, she moved as research assistant to the University of Bochum, Department of Information and Technology Management (IMTM). She works and researches about socio-technical systems, computer-supported cooperative work, as well as collaborative learning, and in particular knowledge management and cultivating Web-based communities. Further information: http://www.imtm-iaw.rub.de. Contact: isa.jahnke@rub.de

Shuhua (Monica) Liu is now a PhD Candidate in the Information School, University of Washington (Seattle, WA, USA). She graduated from Nankai University, China in 2002 with a master in management. She also got her bachelor in information sciences and bachelor in economics from Nankai University in 1999. Before coming to the University of Washington to pursue her research in knowledge management and employee knowledge sharing, Shuhua (Monica) worked as an assistant manager in Bridgestone China in Tianjin City and then a journalist in international news reporting in Xinhua News Agency, Beijing between 1999 and 2003. Shuhua (Monica) is now working on her doctoral dissertation on employee knowledge sharing and system integration. She will specifically investigate organizational factors influencing employees' decisions in sharing knowledge and organizational processes that challenge business process reengineering efforts facilitated by mobile information systems.

Sheetal Narayanan is a graduate student in the School of Informatics. After completing the requirements for the computer science master's degree, she is pursuing her second master's in human computer interaction. She is a research assistant for professor David Wild.

Axel-Cyrille Ngonga Ngomo was born in 1983. He received his diploma (MSc) in computer sciences from the University of Leipzig in 2004 with a thesis on the theoretical foundations of information spaces. He is currently completing his doctoral studies at the same university. His domains of interest include knowledge management, knowledge-free natural language processing, extraction techniques for terminological ontologies and their practical application in the domain of business information systems.

Stavros T. Ponis is a lecturer in the Section of Industrial Management and Operations Research of National Technical University Athens (NTUA), where he is teaching a number of courses in a graduate and post graduate level (supply chain management, e-commerce and management of information systems among others). Dr. Ponis is also an expert reviewer for the European Community, the general secretariat of research and development and the Greek Information Society S.A.. His current research interests and publications move around the areas of virtual enterprises, knowledge logistics for empowering supply chain effectiveness and performance, UML and agent modelling, e-commerce, and supply chain management systems.

Muhammad A. Razi is associate professor of computer information systems at Western Michigan University, Kalamazoo, Michigan. He has published papers in various topics. His research appeared in several academic journals, including *Journal of Small Business Strategy, International Journal of Industrial Engineering, Logistic Information Management, International Journal of Manufacturing Technology and Management* and others.

Helen Rothberg is associate professor of strategy in the School of Management, Marist College. She holds a PhD from City University Graduate Center. She is also the principal consultant for HNR Associates, a network of knowledge focusing on strategic change, competitive intelligence, and knowledge management challenges. Her research interests include competitive intelligence and knowledge management.

Enrico Scarso received a degree in electronic engineering and a PhD degree in industrial innovation from the University of Padua. He is associate professor of engineering management at the University of Padua. His current research interests include economics and management of technology, and knowledge management. He has published in several journals and has presented various papers at international conferences. He is a member of IAMOT (International Association for Management of Technology) and IEEE (Institute of Electrical and Electronics Engineers – Engineering Management Society).

Kalpana Shankar is an assistant professor of informatics at Indiana University School of informatics. She has a BS in molecular biology from Princeton University and a PhD in library and information science from the University of California, Los Angeles. She has worked in database design and management and government program evaluation. Her areas of expertise include data and knowledge management in research science, data sharing and research ethics, and the use of emerging technologies in establishing and maintaining communities of practice.

Sam S. Shoulders is a graduate student in the School of Informatics at Indiana University-Bloomington, completing his requirements in the master's degree program in human-computer interaction/design. His interests include context-aware computing, information security, and information searching in complex systems.

Evangelia Siachou is a PhD candidate at the Department of Business Administration, Athens University of Economics and Business, Greece. She holds a bachelor degree in international and european Studies from the Panteion University of Athens and an MSc in Industrial and personnel management from the London School of Economics. She possesses training experience in the DG Development of European Commission and work experience in the Strategic Planning Department of ATHOC 2004 (Athens Olympic Games). Her current research interests include knowledge transfer, business model innovation, and strategic human resources management.

Kerstin Siakas is an assistant professor at the Department of Informatics at the Alexander Technological Educational Institution of Thessaloniki, Greece since 1989. Her teaching includes management information systems (project & knowledge management), information society and software quality assurance. She is the project leader of the Entrepreneurship programme in the University and European coordinator of activities and exchange in the department. She has extensive experience in industry regarding development of large Information Systems projects in multicultural environments. She has a PhD in software quality management from London Metropolitan University. Her research spans a range of issues in information systems quality management, knowledge management and information society, in particular in human and cultural aspects, but also in pedagogic issues, such as technology based distance learning.

J. Michael Tarn is associate professor of computer information systems at Western Michigan University, Kalamazoo, Michigan. He holds a PhD and an MS in information systems from Virginia Commonwealth University, Richmond, Virginia. He taught at Chowan College, North Carolina for 3 years before he became a member of Broncos in Summer 1999. Dr. Tarn is the major adviser and coordinator for the new interdisciplinary and inter-collegial telecommunications & information management (TIM) program.

Ilias P. Tatsiopoulos is a professor in the School of Mechanical Engineering - National Technical University Athens (NTUA). He has been a member of the Senate of NTUA and he serves in the Editorial Board of the Production Planning & Control Journal. His research interests move around supply chain management and enterprise information systems.

June Tolsby works as a project manager, researcher and lecturer at Ostfold University College, Faculty of Engineering. June Tolsby holds a BSc in Computation from UMIST (University of Manchester Institute of Science and Technology, UK) and a MA within ESST (Education in Society Science and Technology) from Oslo University. She has worked as a programmer, consultant, and researcher for 18 years within various organizations in Norway. She affiliated with Aalborg University, Department of Business Studies in Denmark as a PhD student. Her research topics cover grounded theory, use of ICT, organizational learning and communication, learning theories, product development and design.

George Vagenas is a mechanical engineer of the National Technical University of Athens (NTUA), who specialized in industrial engineering. He is also a doctoral researcher in the Sector of Industrial Management and Operational Research of the NTUA's Mechanical Engineering School. His current research interests include the areas of supply chain management and knowledge management, with an emphasis on Web-based technological support.

Molly Wasko is an associate professor in the Department of Management Information Systems at Florida State University where she teaches primarily strategic information technologies, corporate information security, and research methods. She received her doctorate in MIS from the University of Maryland, College Park, and she holds an MBA from Averett University. Prior to getting her doctorate, she spent 8 years working in production and operations management. Her research interests include the intersection of digital and social networks, social network analysis, the development of online communities, and open source software projects. Her work has appeared in the *Journal of Strategic IS, Decision Sciences, MISQ, JAIS, JCMC* and *JITTA*, and has been presented at ICIS, ECIS, AOM, and AMCIS. She is a member of the Academy of Management, AIS and INFORMS.

David Wild is an assistant professor of informatics at Indiana University School of Informatics. After graduating with a BSc in Computing Science from Aston University, U.K., he completed a PhD and postdoctoral research in Information Studies at Sheffield University, U.K., specializing in chemical information handling. He worked for 6 years in the pharmaceutical industry, applying informatics techniques to science and drug design, before joining the School of Informatics in 2004.

Giuseppe Zollo is full professor of business and management at the Faculty of Engineering of the University of Naples Federico II, Italy and director of the Center for Communication and Organizational

Innovation at the University of Naples Federico II. During the years 1985-86 he was visiting research associate at the Dept. of Economics of Northeastern University, Boston (MA), USA. His research interests include Management of Technological Innovation, Small Innovative Enterprises, Information Technology Management, Competencies Management, soft computing for business and economics. He received several awards for his scientific activity such as: Entrepreneurship Award from the Universitat Autonoma de Barcelona (1992); RENT Award from the European Institute for Advanced Studies in Management, Brussels (1993, 1995, & 2000); Best Paper Award from FGF Universitat of Dortmund (1994); European Quality Award for research on T.Q.M from EFQM (1997), 2005 GITM conference Best paper award. He is Vice President of the International Association for Fuzzy Sets Economy and Management (SIGEF) and serves as editorial board member in the *Fuzzy Economic Review, the Journal of Information Technology: Cases and Application,* and the *Journal of Global Information Technology Management.* He is coauthor of the book *Organizational Cognition and Learning Building Systems for the Learning Organization* (ISP 2007).

Index

W